8079

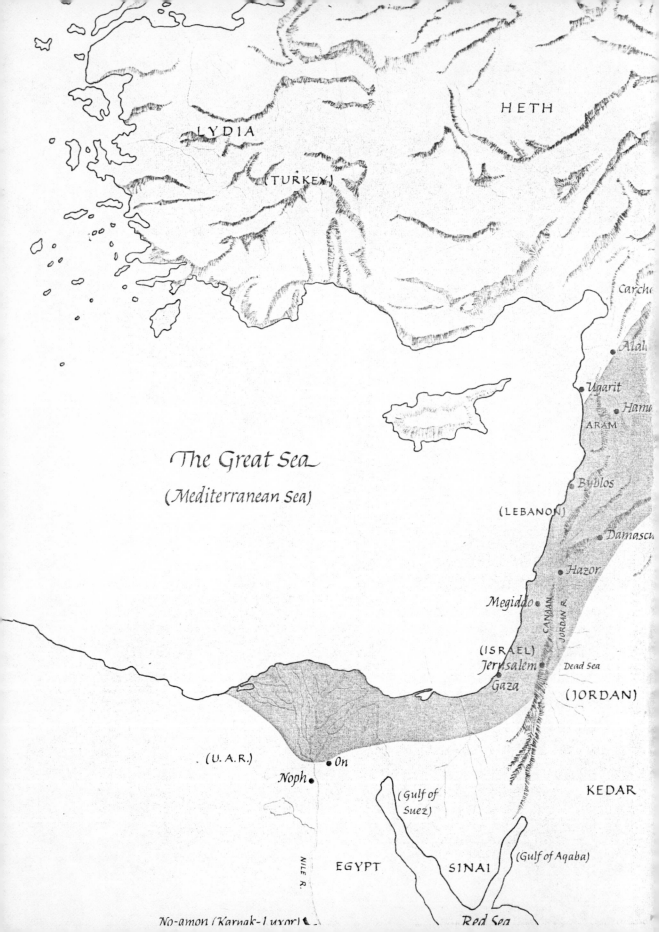

LYDIA

(TURKEY)

HETH

Carche

Alal

Ugarit

Hamu

ARAM

Byblos

(LEBANON)

Damascu

Hazor

The Great Sea

(Mediterranean Sea)

Megiddo

CANAAN

JORDAN R.

(ISRAEL)

Jerusalem

Dead Sea

Gaza

(JORDAN)

(U.A.R.)

On

Noph

(Gulf of
Suez)

KEDAR

EGYPT

SINAI

(Gulf of Aqaba)

NILE R.

No-amon (Karnak-Luxor)

Red Sea

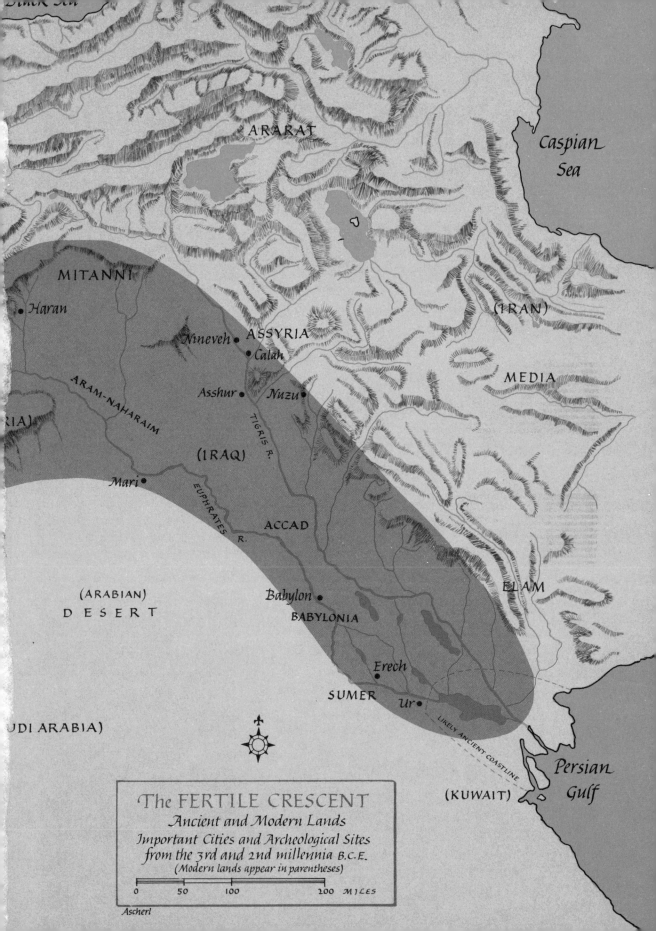

Black Sea

ARARAT

Caspian
Sea

MITANNI

Haran

(IRAN)

Nineveh •   ASSYRIA
            • Calah

Asshur •   Nuzu
                  •

MEDIA

RIA)

TIGRIS R.

ARAM-NAHARAIM

(IRAQ)

Mari •

EUPHRATES

R.

ACCAD

ELAM

(ARABIAN)
D E S E R T

Babylon •

BABYLONIA

Erech
•

SUMER   Ur •

UDI ARABIA)

LIKELY ANCIENT COASTLINE

Persian
Gulf

(KUWAIT)

The FERTILE CRESCENT
Ancient and Modern Lands
Important Cities and Archeological Sites
from the 3rd and 2nd millennia B.C.E.
(Modern lands appear in parentheses)

0   50   100   200   MILES

Ascherl

בראשית

GENESIS

בראשית

GENESIS

Commentary by

W. GUNTHER PLAUT

THE TORAH

*A
Modern
Commentary*

I

Union of American Hebrew Congregations

NEW YORK

LIBRARY OF CONGRESS CATALOGING IN PUBLICATION DATA

PLAUT, W. GUNTHER, 1912–

THE TORAH: *A Modern Commentary*

GENESIS.

    Includes Biblical text in Hebrew and English.
    1. Bible. O.T. Genesis—Commentaries.
    I. Bible. O.T. Genesis. Hebrew. 1974.
    II. Bible. O.T. Genesis. English. 1974.

BS1235.3.P55 1974   222'.11'07   73–16180

TO

The Emily R. *and* Kivie Kaplan Family

Everyone who honors the Torah is himself honored by mankind

PIRKE AVOT 4:8

PUBLICATION OF

The Torah: A Modern Commentary

HAS BEEN MADE POSSIBLE

BY THE GENEROSITY OF THE

Falk Foundation, Kivie Kaplan,

and Maurice Saltzman

Preface

THIS COMMENTARY on Genesis is the first part of a new commentary on the Torah and is the result of many years of planning and consultation. An advisory board responded to the first draft of my manuscript and a smaller board of consultants, consisting of Professors Stanley Gevirtz (then of the University of Chicago), William W. Hallo (of Yale University), Alexander Guttmann and Matitiahu Tsevat (both of Hebrew Union College - Jewish Institute of Religion), gave the subsequent drafts their detailed attention. Without this assistance and critique the book could not have taken its present form. I wish to express my deepest appreciation to all who were part of this labor and especially to my friend and colleague, Rabbi Robert I. Kahn (Houston), who chaired the advisory board.

The following scholars served as members of the board and by their comments afforded me many new insights: Rabbis Bernard J. Bamberger (New York), Sheldon H. Blank (Cincinnati), Solomon B. Freehof (Pittsburgh), Roland B. Gittelsohn (Boston), Samuel E. Karff (Chicago), Julius Kravetz, Leonard S. Kravitz, and Harry M. Orlinsky (all of New York). A particular word of thanks goes to Rabbi Mordecai M. Kaplan who not only gave freely of his time as a member of the advisory board but also made his own unpublished commentary on Genesis available to me. Professor Hallo contributed an introductory essay to this volume thereby greatly enriching its scope.

Despite the liberal assistance rendered by the consultants and advisors, the responsibility for all materials in the commentary, with the exception of statements bearing individual signatures, rests solely with the author.

The men and women associated with the publisher, the Union of American Hebrew Congregations, took a more than cursory interest in the progress of the work. A listing of their names gives but inadequate expression of my gratitude: Rabbis Maurice N. Eisendrath, Alexander M. Schindler, Jack D. Spiro, and Jack Bemporad. Messrs. Ralph Davis and Andor Braun saw to the complexities of production and Mesdames Josette Knight and Ruby S. Williams proofread the manuscript meticulously. Rabbi Amos Schauss of the library at Hebrew Union College - Jewish Institute of Religion in Cincinnati and his staff gave me ever-ready help; and for many a year Miss Margaret B. Davidson, my secretary, and Mrs. Kitty Cohen (both of Toronto) assisted me in preparing the manuscript. Mr. Arthur Grant (Toronto) helped to check the references as did my *eshet chayil*, Elizabeth, without whose constant encouragement and optimism the whole enterprise would not have succeeded.

I reserve the last acknowledgment and thanks for Miss Myrna Pollak (now of Tel Aviv), who served as my editor, whose keen perception and sensitive response to the needs of the reader had a great influence on the final form of the book; and to the members of my congregation, Holy Blossom Temple of Toronto, who have steadfastly believed that the pursuit of *talmud Torah* is a vital part of their rabbi's responsibility.

Lag Ba-Omer 5732
Spring 1972

תודה לאל עליון

CONTENTS

x

PART V   The Line of Jacob

Introducing Genesis

The Book

This commentary proceeds from the assumption that Genesis, as well as the other four books which constitute the Torah, is a human book composed by men.[1]

Many people deny this basic assumption. They believe that the Torah is "the word of God," given (by direct inspiration or in some other way) by God to Moses. Some agree that the text in being transmitted from generation to generation may have been marred by certain scribal errors. But the book as a whole, they insist, is the word of God and not of man. This orthodox or fundamentalist viewpoint maintains, therefore, that if the text says that "God created" then this is a fact, for the word of God is by definition truth itself. It maintains further that the Torah, being given by God, must carry meaning in every word and that not even one letter can be superfluous. One may not understand everything, but that is a human shortcoming. If modern scientific knowledge appears to contradict the biblical word, then either our present-day science will prove to be in error or we do not understand the Bible properly. This was and is the position of Orthodox Judaism, fundamentalist Christianity, and of most commentaries of the past.

[1] On how this took place, see below, p. xxi. Torah is the Hebrew term used for the Five Books of Moses or Pentateuch. Genesis is the first of these five books, and the Torah is the first part of the Bible. The term "Old Testament" is not used by Jews, since it implies a "new" testament. "Bible" as used in this book refers, therefore, to the Hebrew Bible and does not include the Christian Scripture.

The commentator who differs with this approach and proceeds on the premise of human rather than divine authorship faces two initial questions: Does God have anything to do with the Torah and how is the book different from any other significant literature of the past?

Does God have anything to do with the Torah?

While God is not the author of the Torah in the fundamentalist sense, the Torah is a book about man's understanding of and experience with God. This understanding has varied over the centuries as have man's experiences. Since the Torah tradition was at first repeated by word of mouth, and only after many generations set down in writing, the final text testifies to divergent ideas about God and man. These stand side by side in the book and tell us of our ancestors' changing and developing beliefs. In this sense, then, the book is not by God but by a people. While individual authors had a hand in its composition (see below, p. xxi), the People of the Book made the Torah their own and impressed their character upon it.

Some would leave it at that and go no further; they would approach the Torah primarily as an antique document and say: This is how the authors and their listeners saw the world. It is instructive to study their viewpoint and their faith.

This commentary goes further. We believe that it is possible to say: The Torah is ancient Israel's distinctive record of its search for God.

It attempts to record the meeting of the human and the Divine, the great moments of encounter. Therefore, the text is often touched by the ineffable Presence. The Torah tradition testifies to men of extraordinary spiritual sensitivity. God is not the author of the text, men are; but God's voice may be heard through theirs if we listen with open minds.

Is this true for every verse and story? Not in our view. But it is often hard to know whether the voice that speaks has the ring of permanence or resounds to the apprehensions and misapprehensions of a particular age. Our own insights are not so secure that we can judge past ages with any easy sense of superiority. In the face of the unique tradition before us, modesty and caution are a necessary rule.

This does not mean, however, that we abdicate all judgment, treat legend as fact, or gloss over those texts which represent God in anthropomorphic terms. This commentary is neither an apology for, nor an endorsement of, every passage. It will present the modern reader with tools for understanding and leave the option to him. It is also well to know in advance that despite the enormous and imaginative scholarship—archeological, linguistic, anthropological, and other—which has been lavished on the Torah we still must often conclude that we do not know how to interpret a word, or passage, or do not understand the original context.

How is the Torah different from any other significant literature of the past?

For those of us who see in the Torah a people's search for and meeting with God the answer is self-evident. The search and the meeting provide a record which by its very nature has something to say about the essentials of human existence.

But even for those who see in the book only the human quest, with all its strengths and weaknesses, there ought to be something special about it. For over two and one half millennia the Torah has been the keystone of Jewish life, the starting point of Christendom, and the background of Islam. As such it has played and continues to play a significant role in the world. Western man especially is what he is in part because of this book—because of what the Torah actually said or meant to say and because of what it was believed to have said and to have meant.

This distinction is important, for in reading the Torah one should keep in mind that what the authors said in their own time to their own contemporaries within their own intellectual framework is one thing and what later generations did with this text, what they contributed to it by commentary and homily is another. This long tradition of holding up the book like a prism, discovering through it and in it a vast spectrum of insights, makes the Torah unlike any other work. This is particularly true for the Jew. He cannot know his past or himself without this book, for in it he will discover the framework of his own existence.

The Torah is important for yet another reason. This commentary proceeds from the assumption that in addition to the original meaning and the interpretations offered over the centuries the Torah has relevance for our time. Of course, not everything that was relevant yesterday speaks to us today, and passages which held little or minor meaning in the past now speak to us suddenly with an urgent voice. For instance, the story of Babel was for many years seen as a tale of man's arrogance; today it speaks to us as a warning about the dehumanizing effects of urban life.

The relevance of this story, as well as many other portions of the Torah, may be found in questions rather than answers; in fact, one of the contemporary "attractions" of the

Torah is its open-endedness, which is to say, it raises issues without providing single answers that close the door to further inquiry. There is no doubt that tomorrow's generation will hear the words differently again and that the search for new answers will always continue. Our commentary attempts to reflect this open-ended quality of the Torah. It will often provide options, and it is our hope that many additional questions will be asked by the reader who will be motivated to search for his own answers.

But there are also a number of problems. Some of these arise needlessly, out of failure to read the text properly; others are due to the contrast between certain ancient and contemporary assumptions about our world and must be freely faced. The modern reader should clearly understand that biblical man thought and wrote in terms of his own time and not ours. For us, reading the Bible should be an attempt to understand it and not a cut-and-dried exercise in our own contemporary dogmatics. We must not come to the text with preconceptions but should try to let it speak to us in its own way. Only then will the door be open to meaningful reading.

Literalism

Contemporary man is often put off because he has been exposed to a method of biblical interpretation which understands the text in a literal way. Thus, if Genesis says that God created woman out of the rib of man, or tells of a serpent speaking, or of ancient man living several hundred years, the literalist interprets the story to mean precisely what the words convey. This literal application reaches down to individual words and phrases.

Quite aside from the indisputable fact that the Torah text we use today is merely one

available version (although the accepted one) and aside from the fact that most literalists not knowing the Hebrew original base their opinions on one particular translation (which is in itself a type of interpretation and therefore a secondary source),[2] the contemporary reader familiar with the history and nature of the text will have to remember that a literal understanding of the Torah may lead to grave misconceptions.

Even the ancient Jewish Sages, who believed that the Torah was a divinely authored book, did not take the text literally. They took it seriously, but they always looked behind the flat literal meaning. They realized that the Bible—in addition to everything else it was to them—abounded in subtle metaphors and allusions, that it used word plays and other literary devices, that it sometimes spoke satirically, and that its poetry could not be subjected to a simple approach. They agreed without embarrassment that one could disagree on what the Torah meant, and on this sound principle we ourselves should base our approach to the text.

Science in the Bible

Ancient man considered the earth the center of the universe and natural law not as unalterable but as subservient to the will of God. This view is the basic principle underlying many stories, especially the opening chapters of the Book of Genesis which have become a formidable obstacle to the reading of the Bible. Why—it is asked—should we concern ourselves at all with stories of the six days of creation, with Adam and Eve, and the Garden of Eden? All these are unscientific, antiquated myths, and therefore appear to be irrelevant.

In answer, many defenders of the Bible agree that while the book has indeed little to tell about the scientific origins of the world and its inhabitants it does have a great deal

[2] See below, p. XXII.

to tell about God's relationship to His world and about man and his destiny. Since the Bible's scientific comprehension, they say, is limited to the world view of the ancients, just as ours is to that of our own time, it would be futile to look to the Bible for references to evolution or to suggest that "one day" in creation may correspond to millennia in scientific reckoning.

This view, while it appears to rescue the Bible from the worst problems of an outmoded literalism, nonetheless does not do the book full justice, for it approaches it with a facile sense of modern superiority. To be sure, our knowledge of science is vastly greater than that of the ancients. But that does not necessarily make our world view, based on such scientific insights, any more advanced.

It would be better, therefore, to come to the biblical text with full respect for its intellectual convictions and to understand that these are often expressed in metaphors and always in the vocabulary and framework of antiquity. The contemporary reader thus should restrain his inclination to do battle with or look for modern comparisons to ancient notions of creation. He should read the Bible for what it suggests about the nature of human history, the meaning of existence, and the presence of God.

With Stanley Gevirtz, one may approach the book in much the same manner as one approaches poetry:

"To the question of the 'truth' of Genesis the sensitive response can only be: It is, indeed, true; not in the sense in which a statement of a physical law is true, but few things that really matter to the poet ever are. It is true in the way that great poetry is always true: to the imagination of the human heart and the orderliness of the human mind. This God-and-Israel centered account discriminates, as every good historical narrative must, in its choice of events and presents us

with history not, perhaps, as it was but as it ought to have been."[3]

Myth and Legend

The reader must further understand that the Torah contains a great variety of material: history, folk tales, songs, proverbial sayings, poetry, and, especially in the early parts of Genesis, myths and legends. By myth we understand a tale involving human beings and divine powers, a tale which was meant and understood as having happened and which by its existence expressed, explained, or validated important aspects of existence.[4] Thus the Eden myth explained the origin of death and validated, for Christian tradition, the concept of man's inherent sinfulness and need of salvation. Legends are sagas of the past amplified by folk memory, but they usually neither validate nor explain. Jacob's prowess at the well (Gen. 29:10) is of this category. As the Torah moves from the creation of the world toward the creation of the people of Israel, the mythic elements increasingly give way to legend and these in turn to history in the modern sense.[5]

In observing these distinctions the reader of the Bible should not, however, be misled into dismissing either myth or legend as "irrelevant" and accepting only history as "relevant." What usually passes for history is not an accurate scientific recording of events but an interpretation of such events—assuming even that one knows what the event "really" was. The best of modern historians is an interpreter, selective summarizer, com-

[3] Unpublished. By permission of the author.
[4] Angelo S. Rappoport—Raphael Patai, *Myth and Legend of Ancient Israel* (New York: Ktav, 1966), Vol. I, pp. xi f.
[5] One should also note that while there are myths in Genesis there is no mythology, i.e., there are no tales of the adventures of the gods (or God). The fragment in Gen. 6:1–4 is the only exception. Genesis is not concerned with the story of the divine realm but with the emergence of man; his drama is played

mentator, and often philosopher who brings a point of view to his material. This is precisely what the Book of Genesis does. While its material included myths and legends, these in time became incorporated into the consciousness of the people. For what people believe their past to mean assumes a dynamism of its own; the experience itself becomes creative. Thus, while Abraham's vision of a God who promised him the land of Canaan will not pass as historic "fact," its reality was accepted by generations of Abraham's descendants and, for them, validated their possession of the land.

One must not think that this kind of "mythicizing history" (as Buber called it[6]) is found only in ancient texts. Take for instance the selective way in which American tradition treats the lives of the old frontiersmen. They are presented primarily as enterprising pioneers, courageous people whose love of independence was indelibly stamped on the nation they helped to build. Such a picture is, of course, highly selective and slanted. It says little about the desire of the pioneers to get rich quickly or their need to move west after repeated failures in the east, and so on. But Americans have preferred to see their past in an idealized light, and their admiration of the value of personal independence and frontier virtues has itself shaped the psychology of the nation.

So it is with the Book of Genesis. It may be said to mirror the collective memory of our forefathers, and in the course of centuries this record became a source of truth for the children of Israel. The reader will therefore do well to keep in mind that Genesis (as well as the other books of the Bible) not only speaks of history but has made history by helping to shape the thought of man.

The origins of the Torah are one thing, its life through the centuries another, and its ability to speak to us today yet a third. This commentary is concerned with all three aspects separately and jointly.

Evolution

The Book of Genesis does not appear to tell of human growth and development in a way palatable to moderns, schooled in the principles of evolution. Indeed, Genesis as well as the succeeding books freely mix devolution (descent from primal eminence) with evolution (ascent from a lower to a higher stage). Religion and moral insight are not generally presented in the Bible as a process of slow and painful moral growth; quite the contrary, religious genius appears repeatedly without traceable antecedents— as, for instance, in the case of Abraham. This, however, should not cause us to dismiss such stories as "improbable," for moral history is not like physical history. Mutations in the realm of the spiritual seem to have occurred frequently in human experience, and the biblical record should in part be read as the record of such mutations. The very creation of the people of Israel, to which the Torah is devoted, bursts the rules of mechanical evolution.

God in Genesis

Beginning with the first sentence of Genesis, it is apparent that the existence of God is taken for granted. Nowhere is it doubted or argued; neither, however, is the existence of other gods ever questioned. In this respect Genesis is radically different from the other books of the Torah and from the

---

out not on a supernatural stage but on earth and has a theme of rebellion, sin, and potential redemption.

[6] Martin Buber, *Moses* (Oxford: Oxford University Press, 1947), p. 17. Buber considers the emotion with which an event was experienced an important aspect of history, one which is often played down in the usual annalistic or "factual" treatment. See also Gerhard von Rad, *Genesis: A Commentary* (Philadelphia: Westminster Press, 1961), pp. 3 ff.

Prophets. Abraham, Isaac, and Jacob were distinguished in that they worshiped the One God and served Him alone, but the exclusive monotheism of later days was not theirs. They may have even believed that other gods were real. But only One had made a covenant with them and to Him they committed their lives and the future of their offspring.[7]

This God appears in the pages of Genesis both as the Creator of the world and the Friend of the Patriarchs. In speaking of God, the book has no difficulty in moving from universal to personal proportions and concerns. Modern man is likely to experience some problems here, for his relationship to and concept of God is not usually as intimately personal and direct as that of biblical man. To the ancients, God was not an abstract force, principle, or process; rather, He was Father, Friend, King—all of which implied "person." Individuality was the highest expression of creation, and God the Creator could Himself be spoken of only in such terms. It would not have occurred to the ancients to speak of God in any way other than the way one spoke of man (because man was created in God's image), and it was therefore most natural to think of God as speaking, seeing, regretting, and occasionally as walking or descending. The divinity and majesty of God were thereby not diminished. For instance, the expression, "God said to Abraham," was the natural and even best method of recording a vital experience.[8] Only much later did these human ascriptions of God (called anthropomorphisms) begin to create the kind of serious problems which are being experienced by the modern Bible reader.

However one interprets the nature of God—as person or as process, as individual reality or generalized principle—there are three basic ideas which the contemporary reader can share with biblical man and which are implicit in Genesis:

THAT GOD, as Father or Creative Force, provides all creation with purpose and that therefore to understand God means to understand one's own potential;

THAT GOD, as Lawgiver, validates the principles of justice and righteousness which must govern the affairs of men;

THAT GOD, as Redeemer, guarantees the ultimate goals of existence and enables man to find meaning in his life.

Added to these is a pervasive theme which above all has made the Bible, from Genesis through Chronicles, a Jewish book—that through Abraham and his descendants the realization of God's plan for humanity will be hastened and, in fact, be made possible altogether.

[7] See Arnold B. Ehrlich, *Mikra Kifeshuto* (New York: Ktav, 1969), *ad* 12:3; Harry Orlinsky, *Ancient Israel* (Ithaca: Cornell University Press, 1954), pp. 27–29.

[8] "It was apparently easier in Old Testament faith to tolerate the danger of lessening God's greatness and 'absoluteness' by human description than to run the risk of giving up anything of God's personalness and His vital participation in everything earthly." (Von Rad, *op. cit.*, p. 114.) Umberto Cassuto adds another consideration:

"The Torah was not intended specifically for intellectuals but for the entire people, which is not concerned with philosophic or theological speculation. It uses ordinary language plainly and without sophistication and pays no heed to inferences that later readers who are accustomed to ways of thinking wholly alien to the Bible may draw from its works." (*From Adam to Noah*, Jerusalem: Magnes Press, 1961, p. 304.) Note also Herbert C. Brichto's important caution:

"Nor may we summarily rule out the possibility, nor even the likelihood, that an ancient author may have formulated a message in such a way as to be addressed simultaneously to the most naive and most sophisticated of his generation, to be comprehended by each according to his level. That *Gulliver's Travels* is read by children as naive fantasy leads no one to exclude a deeper, more serious intent on the author's part. It is not the reputation of the biblical authors but our own understanding of them that suffers when we arbitrarily accord them less of a hearing than we grant Jonathan Swift." (*Hebrew Union College Annual*, Vol. 39, p. 37.)

How the Torah Came to Be Written

Doubts that the Torah was a book set down by one author, Moses, developed some centuries ago, but it was not until the nineteenth century that extensive investigations made the critical study of the biblical text a highly specialized discipline. The early critics noted the differential use of the names of God in various parts of the Torah, the discrepancies of certain accounts and figures, and different literary styles (for examples, see below, pp. 57, 72). Later scholars further analyzed the text so that they could discern many authors and several editors, and they theorized about times and events when these sources and documents were created and finally combined into the Torah as we have it now.

The theory which commands the greatest scholarly adherence today is called the Documentary Hypothesis and is often referred to by two of its prominent expositors, Karl Graf and Julius Wellhausen. In substance it says that there were four major sources or documents (called J, E, P, and D), the combination of which during the fifth century B.C.E. resulted in the creation of a single book, the Torah, which was declared a sacred text by official canonization about the year 400. J is the name given by biblical critics to the author who uses the divine name יהוה (Jahweh or Yahveh) and is responsible for most of Genesis; E uses אלהים (Elohim) and authored the binding of Isaac (Gen. 22) and other passages of Genesis; P is the author of the first chapter of Genesis, the Book of Leviticus, and other sections characterized by interest in genealogies and priesthood; D is the author of Deuteronomy, which is said to be the book found by King Josiah in 621 B.C.E. (II Kings 22; some also assign Gen. 14 to D).

There are critics who find additional major sources—S (for Seir, believed to be an author of southern, possibly non-Israelite origin); K (originating with the tribe of the Kenites); and L (a lay writer). Others detect several subsources in J, E, P, and D; and then there is R (the redactor of the final text). There is no agreement on when these documents were composed, but most adherents of the critical schools would give 950 through 450 as the years during which this literary process took place, that is, from the days of the divided kingdoms of Israel and Judah to their destruction and the time of exile and return.

Since Moses lived in the thirteenth century B.C.E. he had, in this view, nothing to do with the writing of the Torah. His name was attached to it as author at the time of the book's canonization. This whole analysis is vigorously disputed by those who attempt to show that Moses was indeed the author. They view much or all higher literary criticism as erroneous and some of its foundations as infected by Christian bias.[9]

More recently, increasing numbers of critical scholars have denied the basic validity of the Graf-Wellhausen approach.[10] They say

---

[9] There are also those who, on the basis of critical studies, conclude that Moses' part in the creation of the Torah is commanding. For an advocacy of this view, see M. H. Segal, *The Pentateuch* (Jerusalem: Magnes Press, 1967); for a general critique, see Cassuto, *The Documentary Hypothesis* (Jerusalem: Magnes Press, 1961); for a specific critique, see Benno Jacob's massive commentaries on Genesis and Exodus.

"In general, it is probably true that much Jewish scholarship, even that which was not totally traditionalistic, was initially, and to a degree still remains, rather cool toward the standard results of German biblical scholarship, well aware of the subtle anti-Judaism, if not anti-Semitism, which by no means necessarily, but very often *de facto*, accompanies any depreciation of the Old Testament—and it is undeniable that such implications were often present in much of the classical 'critical' literature." (H. D. Hummel, *Encyclopaedia Judaica*, Vol. 4, col. 907.)

[10] Since, however, the Graf-Wellhausen school still commands wide support, our commentary indicates from time to time the differentiation of sources suggested by the school. A detailed example is provided in the analysis of the Flood story (see below, pp. 57, 72).

that the difference in the divine names in the text is not traceable to different sources but rather represents a largely intentional, stylistic alternation. They see the first four books of the Torah (Genesis to Numbers) to be one basic unified collection which came from a "traditionalist circle," which they are willing to call P (for the priestly school). These scholars assign the Book of Deuteronomy to a second collection (which reaches all the way to II Kings) which they ascribe to a "Deuteronomic circle." In this view the distinctions introduced by Wellhausen, who spoke of P, J, E, and similar sources, can no longer be maintained.[11]

There are still other scholars who, while they accept the existence of different sources, would see the contribution of these sources to the final text in a different light. In this view the various strands of tradition were very old—some of them older than Moses while others are assignable to him—and were transmitted for many centuries by word of mouth. As the centuries wore on, all of these strands coalesced in popular telling and in time, probably through the efforts of a literary genius of unknown name, became a single story with many facets. Variants of the same story and even contradictions were left untouched because one did not tamper with sacred memories and also because the ancient hearer did not demand an either-or but could say that together both sides of the account represented the truth. If in one place it says that Israel spent 400 years in Egypt and in another that it was 430, the modern reader is tempted to ask: How many years was it really? The ancient reader was satisfied that both 400 and 430 meant a long, long time.

In general, our commentary favors the position just outlined, namely, that Genesis (with which we are here concerned) is essentially the repository of centuries of traditions which became One Tradition and One Book. At what time it was set down as we have it

now will likely remain a matter of conjecture; what is important is to treat the book as an integral unit rather than a paste-up amalgam. With Franz Rosenzweig we might call the final editor R, not because the initial reminds us of redactor but of *rabbenu*, our teacher. The finished book represents the teaching tradition of Israel. We ask "What did the text mean originally?" and "What has it come to mean?" Our commentary disagrees with traditional interpreters over divine origin and Mosaic authorship (that is to say, it finds higher criticism admissible), but it does agree with them on treating the text as it is, a unified whole, for it was approached in this way by many generations and in this way it has made its impact on history. An antiquarian assessment will always be of historical interest and is reflected in this commentary, but to us the Bible is primarily the living textbook of the Jew and, with differing emphasis, of the Christian.

Text and Translation

Readers of the Bible are usually unaware that what they are reading is not "the" original version of the manuscript and that the translation they use is actually a kind of commentary on the Hebrew text which it means to render.

---

[11] One of the exponents of this theory is Ivan Engnell (see John T. Willis, ed., *A Rigid Scrutiny*, Nashville: Vanderbilt University Press, 1969). Engnell believes that the school he calls P stems from a Jerusalem—Hebron—Kadesh-Barnea background and is characterized by cultic and antiquarian interest, while the D-school stems from northern Israel and features a more abstract approach to religion and is concerned with a central sanctuary. In contrast, Graf-Wellhausen scholars of today suggest that the traditional J-source may reflect a pessimistic view of history directed to the overconfidence of David's "Golden Age" while the P-source reflects an optimistic antidote to the period of national depression following the destruction of the Temple in 586 B.C.E. (see R. J. Thompson, *Moses and the Law in a Century of Criticism since Graf*, Leiden: E. J. Brill, 1970).

There is no original manuscript available which was written by any of the authors of the Bible. The oldest extant parchment scroll of Genesis dates from about 600 C.E., which is perhaps as much as 1,500 years later than the likely time of its composition. Quite naturally, much happens to a text in the course of oral transmission and copying by hand, and one must not be astonished that a number of variants and versions arose. It is a great tribute to the care and devotion which were lavished on the text that the variants are relatively minor and the scribal corruptions rather few. Our commentary uses the Masoretic version. The Masoretes, so called because they transmitted the *Masorah* (מָסוֹרָה) or textual tradition, were scholars who over the centuries attempted to ascertain and preserve the best text. One of these versions, produced in Tiberias in the tenth century C.E., found general acceptance and is the standard Hebrew text in synagogue use today.

Because the knowledge of classical Hebrew diminished or disappeared among many Jews after they returned from the Babylonian exile, the need for translations arose. In the course of centuries there appeared translations in Aramaic (Targum) which was the popular language of post-exilic Jews, Greek (Septuagint), Latin (Vulgate), Syriac (Peshitta), Arabic, and in modern times into every written language of man. The im-portant ancient translations often give us significant clues about the original from which they were translated, for there are differences between them. What is even more important is to recognize that every translator interprets the original text, for he renders it as he understands (or misunderstands) it.

This becomes particularly apparent when one follows modern translations. For instance, there are great differences between the famous and beloved English King James Version (published in 1611, and often called "Authorized," i.e., for the Church of England) and later renditions such as the American version; or the German Luther Bible and the translation by Rosenzweig and Buber. Many of these differences are stylistic since the language of translation has itself undergone vast changes; others are due to new insights into the philology of ancient days and the political, social, and economic circumstances to which the text refers.

We used the revised translation of Genesis by the Jewish Publication Society (revised printing, 1967), with the kind permission of the publishers. This translation, in addition to its scholarly and linguistic merits, has been made particularly valuable by the publication of the translators' *Notes on the New Translation of the Torah* (1969, referred to as JPS *Notes*) which explain in detail why certain translations were chosen and others rejected.

On Reading This Commentary

Note first of all that text and commentary do not appear in the usual continuous fashion but are divided into a prologue and four major parts and into 40 separate sections. While this division has no precise warrant in prior practice,[12] it has been introduced for convenience of study and for those synagogues which do not read the entire traditional weekly portion. Our units and their commentaries are more or less of similar length, except in the early chapters of Genesis and in Chapter 22 because of the special importance of these sections. In attempting thus to divide the book both by reason of length and by subject matter, our arrangement frequently differs from the division into chapters which originated with medieval Christian scholarship.

In addition to the introductory essays, the Hebrew text and translation, this book is composed of the following parts:

1] THE TEXTUAL NOTES. These appear below and immediately following the text and are arranged by verse and number for easy reference to the text itself. The notes may be called "textual," i.e., they attempt to give the "plain meaning" (*peshat*) of words and sentences without going into deeper interpretations (which are reserved for the commentary proper). In the notes you will find explanations of terms, names, references to other biblical books, and notations on linguistic difficulties. It should be remembered that the notes comment not only on the English translation, and try to make it understandable, but also—and primarily—on the underlying Hebrew text. For instance, the Hebrew text uses word plays and assonances extensively, and these can rarely be translated into another language. The reader should also remember that the Torah tradition was originally transmitted by word of mouth so that many so-called etymological explanations of personal and place names may have served as popular memory devices. For instance, *Kayin* (Cain) is said to come from *kaniti* (I have gained) although linguistically there is no connection.

2] THE COMMENTARY. The brief essays which accompany each unit are largely interpretive: They attempt to explain the intent of the Torah, how Jewish tradition saw these meanings, and what relevancy modern man might find in them. The author has chosen and concentrated on a few themes in each section; he is aware that in so choosing he has omitted other themes which the reader might wish to have had included.

Just as the notes frequently offer alternative explanations, so does the commentary itself. Sometimes this is done because we really have at present no sure way of establishing one particular interpretation as *the* meaning; at other times the author feels that the Torah leaves us purposely with parallel or even contradictory ideas. If this seems unlikely to a modern reader who is used to a systematic and logical exposition of a subject, he must remember that the Torah is not a treatise, essay, or exposition, but poetry, prose, epic, and historic memory created in a pre-scientific age fundamentally different from ours. Where we are prone to say "either, or," the Bible may say "both" and let the unresolved tension between the two stand

---

[12] It resembles to some degree the divisions of the old triennial cycle of Torah readings.

without further comment. This sometimes lends the Torah a special quality of opaqueness which those who look for one and only one meaning are bound to miss.

3] THE GLEANINGS.   Appended to all sections are gleanings from world literature which have a bearing on the text. Here especially will be found selections from that vast compendium of ancient Jewish lore and homily called Midrash,[13] and also some writings from Christian and Moslem sources as well as contemporary observations not included in the commentary proper. (Where the source is not identified, the author himself is to be credited.) The gleanings are generally only brief excerpts; they are intended to suggest something of the vast range of response elicited by the Torah. It is hoped that the reader will be moved to explore these areas further by himself.

4] FOOTNOTES.   Occasionally the text of commentary and gleanings is expanded by brief additions. These are indicated by superior notes in the text—such as [5]—and are printed at the bottom of the page.

5] THE REFERENCES.   Notes, commentary, gleanings, and footnotes contain references only to the Bible (where no book is mentioned the reference is to Genesis). We follow the standard way of noting biblical passages;

[13] The total collection, spread over many sources, will be written Midrash (with a capital M), while an individual homily will be written midrash (plural: *midrashim*).

for instance, chapter 12, verse 3, is listed as 12:3.

All other sources may be found in the references, which for easier readability are grouped together at the end of the volume. These references—indicated by bracketed numbers such as [15]—are not meant primarily for scholars; hence they do not usually give alternative sources, divergent readings, and the like. They refer, wherever possible, to works which have appeared in English or English translation and to others only where no translation is available. (For abbreviations and principal bibliographical references, see pp. 503–509.)

6] HAFTAROT.   The synagogue, and subsequently the church, established a tradition which provides that on each Sabbath and holy day a special portion be read from the Bible. At Jewish services, a section from the Torah, called *sidrah* or *parashah*, and an additional selection from the Earlier and Later Prophets, called *haftarah* (originally signifying dismissal of the congregation), are always read. Tradition has divided Genesis into 12 *sidrot*, the cycle of which begins on the Sabbath after Simchat Torah and concludes two weeks after Chanukah.

The *haftarot* appear without commentary at the end of the book, together with alternate selections. These nontraditional additions are provided to give congregations a wider range of acquaintance with the Bible and therefore draw also on such books as Psalms, Proverbs, and Job which are not represented in the *haftarah* cycles of the traditional synagogue.

Transliterations

When comment is made on a Hebrew word or phrase, the latter is usually rendered in Hebrew characters. Transliterations are utilized only where they are deemed of special help to the reader who is unfamiliar with Hebrew.

This commentary has adopted the simplified transliteration proposed by Prof. Werner Weinberg of Hebrew Union College - Jewish Institute of Religion and brought it into consonance with the usage of the Union of American Hebrew Congregations. Based on the Sephardic pronunciation, it makes no distinction between ס and שׂ, between ח and כ, ט and ת, nor between כּ and ק. צ is represented by tz; בּ appears as v, and ח and כ as ch. It does not take note of א or ע except when two vowels inside a word should be separated in the pronunciation. In such cases a hyphen is introduced (as in רֹאִי, ro-i). The *dagesh* is omitted except where it is an aid to pronunciation (*shabbat* rather than *shabat*). Also omitted is the resting *sheva*; the moving *sheva* is shown as e when it represents a syllable (as in שְׁמַע, *shema*). Half vowels are transliterated as full vowels (as in אֱמֶת, *emet*). Other vowels are rendered as follows:

ָ and ַ		as a
ֶ and ֵ		as e
ִ and ִי		as i
וֹ and ֹ		as o
וּ and ֻ		as u

The letter י is represented as y, except in ִי and ֵי in which cases it is omitted.

There are a few Hebrew words which have become part of common usage, and therefore their usual spelling has been maintained. This is especially true for proper names, e.g., Ishmael rather than Yishmael. Also, the definite article *ha* (or *he*) has been separated from its noun by the introduction of a hyphen in order to facilitate the reading (*ha-yashar* rather than *hayashar*) except in some cases where by virtue of common usage the hyphen has been omitted.

Genesis as a Book

NAME. The name Genesis ("origin") goes back to the Greek translation, the Septuagint, while the usual Hebrew name is the same as the initial word in the book, בְּרֵאשִׁית (*bereshit*).

CONTENTS. Genesis tells a story which reaches from the creation of the world to the death of Joseph in Egypt. The first eleven chapters deal with universal history, the rest with the lives of Abraham, Isaac, Jacob and their families. The total time elapsed from the beginning adds up to 1,946 (or 1,948) years.

A SEPARATE BOOK. It is likely that the first eleven chapters once constituted a separate tradition which at some later date was integrated with the patriarchal tales and the other parts of the Torah. Some scholars believe that all of Genesis was originally a book apart because it contains settings, customs, and practices greatly at variance with other Torah accounts and legislation. (For instance, Abraham plants a sacred tree and Jacob sets up a stone pillar—worship acts forbidden in later Torah passages; Genesis knows of no war on idolatry as do the later books.)

DIVISIONS. Genesis in its final form may be seen as a book of five parts. Part I is Prologue, and thereafter each part is introduced by the phrase "These are the lines" (*toledot*): the lines or genealogies of heaven, earth, and primeval man (Part II); of Terah, Abraham's father (Part III); of Isaac and of Jacob (Parts IV and V). (See p. 19.)

THEMES. The overriding theme of the book is God's role in human affairs. He created the world and fashioned man to perfect it. But mankind disappointed Him again and again, and in time God decided to make a new start by calling Abraham to be the father of a special people who would carry out His will. Among the subthemes interwoven into this major story are the basic unity of all mankind, man's propensity for evil, human rebellion, and the covenant between God and Abraham's people. In a larger sense, Genesis is the introduction to the Torah and the rest of the Bible.

Genesis
and Ancient Near Eastern Literature

WILLIAM W. HALLO

The recovery of ancient Near Eastern literature has basically revolutionized our understanding of the Bible and of no book more so than Genesis. A glance at the authoritative volume, *Ancient Near Eastern Texts Relating to the Old Testament*,[1] will confirm this. Only Psalms and Proverbs outnumber Genesis in the parallels suggested by the various translators.[2] But the parallels to Proverbs all come from the well-nigh universal tradition of preceptual epigrams, most of them Egyptian. And when it is remembered that the five books of Psalms contain over 2,500 verses, compared to the 1,500 in Genesis, it will be seen that, proportionately, the first book of the Bible is most widely and most significantly paralleled in the literature of the ancient Near East.

The reasons behind these statistics are not difficult to find. Alone among the books of the Hebrew Bible, Genesis has the whole ancient Near East for its stage. Its first eleven chapters are set entirely in Babylonia, its last twelve in Egypt. The intervening 27 chapters occupy the geographical terrain between these two countries. They tell of repeated semi-nomadic movements back and forth throughout the entire broad stretch of Syria-Palestine including both sides of the Euphrates and Jordan rivers. The presence of ancient Near Eastern literary motifs in the tales of Genesis is thus no more startling than that of classical ones in Shakespeare's Greek and Roman dramas. Many of them are identified in this commentary, together with the similarities and differences between the biblical and other ancient Near Eastern treatments of common themes. It is not the purpose of this overview to anticipate them here one by one. Rather, we wish to sum up the evidence by analyzing the nature of the knowledge gained through the confrontation of Genesis and its ancient literary cognates.

To "prove" the accuracy or validity of one literary text by another is, of course, at once the most difficult and the most heatedly debated task of the critics. Many have wanted to employ the discoveries of archeology for this very purpose, many more for the opposite reason, and still others have despaired of resolving the issue. Unanimity is indeed impossible to achieve here, but at least we can hope to agree on what kind of questions we wish to prove. Put this way, it quickly becomes clear that we cannot gain greater

[1] Edited by James B. Pritchard (Princeton: Princeton University Press, 2nd ed. 1955). [Hereafter the work is referred to as Pritchard, *ANET.*]
[2] See the Index of Biblical References, *ibid.*, pp. 504–507

confidence in the biblical version of the end of immortality simply because similar accounts have been found in the cuneiform sources (cf. chapters 2 and 3 below). Nor, on the contrary, are the rather variant Egyptian and Sumerian versions of creation needed to "disprove" that of Genesis. Whether Genesis accurately reports on these events is not the proper question. Rather we must ask: Does the text of Genesis, as we have it, accurately report what the ancient Israelites believed or asserted to have happened?

It is today generally assumed that an extended period of oral transmission introduced distortions into the traditions, that these distortions were aggravated by successive generations of scribes when the oral traditions were reduced to writing, and that their final canonization involved picking and choosing among the conflicting textual traditions on grounds other than that of their presumed antiquity or reliability.

On this premise, much modern criticism of Genesis has devoted itself to textual emendations and other attempts to recover a presumed original text. Such an "original text" is, however, unlikely ever to be found by the spade of the Palestinian archeologist, and all efforts to reconstruct it must therefore remain speculations not subject to scientific verification. Now the history of other ancient Near Eastern literatures has shown that, at least in a literate environment, textual transmission was indeed subject to occasional periods of substantial change and adaptation. To illustrate this point, we may cite the Mesopotamian versions of the story of the Flood. As a historical event and a chronological turning point, the concept of a great flood was an early and familiar fixture in cuneiform literature. The Sumerian King List[3] teaches that kingship came down (respectively, came back) from heaven after the Flood and the idiom "before the Flood" (*lam abubi*) signified pristine time. The earliest

literary treatments of the theme are in Sumerian;[4] their hero is Ziusudra, ruler (or "son") of Shuruppak and last of the antediluvian dynasts. The first Akkadian flood story is associated with Atar-chasis whose epic is preserved in copies of the second and early first millennia B.C.E.[5] Finally, the flood story was incorporated into the eleventh tablet of the Akkadian Gilgamesh Epic, where its hero is Uta-napishtim, who is variously equated with both Ziusudra and Atar-chasis.[6] The Gilgamesh Epic in its final form cannot, as of now, be traced further back than circa 1100 B.C.E., and the extent to which it departed from its older Sumerian and Akkadian prototypes can be gauged even in translation. Certainly no Assyriologist would have ventured to reconstruct either of them from the late canonical version. Such an example inspires similar caution in current attempts to recover the original version or documents from which the canonical biblical text is presumed to have developed.

But, more than this, the recovery of the separate stages of many ancient Near Eastern compositions has revealed, by the side of a certain amount of editorial revision, a tenacious faithfulness to many received texts which is little short of astounding. Over widely scattered areas of cuneiform or hieroglyphic writing, and in periods separated by many centuries, certain canonical texts were copied verbatim and with an attention to textual detail not matched until the Alexandrian Greeks, or the Koranic specialists of the Good Caliphs, or the Tiberian Masoretes who codified the Bible, counting, vocalizing, and accentuating its every letter. To cite just one

[3] See the translation by A. L. Oppenheim, *ibid.*, pp. 265–266.
[4] See the translations by S. N. Kramer, *ibid.*, pp. 42–44 and in *Expedition*, 9, 4 (1967), pp. 12–18.
[5] Partial translation by E. A. Speiser in Pritchard, *ANET*, pp. 104–106.
[6] See the translation by Speiser, *ibid.*, pp. 93–97.

example: The Sumerian myth of the warrior-god Ninurta probably was composed before the end of the third millennium; its first actual manuscripts date back to circa 1800 B.C.E., and it is known also in neo-Assyrian and neo-Babylonian copies beginning a thousand years later in which the Sumerian text is accompanied by an interlinear translation into Akkadian. Yet for all the time interval, the differences between the earlier and later Sumerian versions are little more than orthographic and dialectal. Such fidelity to a received text tradition has taught most biblical critics a new respect for the possibility of an equally reliable textual tradition underlying the Hebrew canon. It is little enough that we know of the technical details of textual creation and transmission in Israel before the time of the Dead Sea Scrolls.[7] Now we must at least reckon with the possibility that the process rated as much care as in the surrounding Near East before we venture to "improve" on the received text.

Thus ancient Near Eastern literary texts are seen to have met with different fates in the course of their millennial transmission; in some cases adaptation and reediting on a scale which defies prediction, in others extreme fidelity to the received text. Yet for all their differences, both examples impose the same conclusion for the biblical text: We cannot hope to achieve certainty in recovering a more authentic text than that codified by the Masoretes after the Arab conquest. Even with the discoveries at Qumran and elsewhere, we still have far fewer pre-Masoretic manuscripts than the Masoretes disposed of, and like them we lack a conclusive meth-odology for choosing between conflicting readings.[8]

But the history of ancient Near Eastern literature is relevant not only to the text of the Hebrew Bible but to its meaning. To return to the case of the Ninurta Epic, the Akkadian translations, added to the late versions, are, generally speaking, quite literal, but despite the best efforts of the late Assyrian and Babylonian scholars they are frequently faulty. They commit errors which modern philologists, with better knowledge of the original Sumerian, can often recognize as errors and sometimes correct. In other instances, they deliberately understand the Sumerian text in a new way not intended in the original. In still other cases, they obviously despaired of making any sense of the original and simply created de novo a meaning for the passage. All three of these tendencies can likewise be detected, albeit less clearly, in the absence of translations, i.e., in texts handed down from first to last in one and the same language. The conclusion to be drawn from all this is important for biblical criticism: The integrity of a textual tradition is no guarantee for the preservation, intact, of a continuous tradition of interpretation. On the contrary, the meaning assigned to a passage may change from age to age in part *in order to preserve* the integrity of the text. Here, then, we may use ancient Near Eastern literature to confirm a cardinal tenet of biblical criticism: Given the traditional text of a certain passage, we may hope to come closer to its original meaning than the traditional interpretations have done. In this attempt, specific ancient Near Eastern parallels are frequently of crucial help. Our examples here are taken from two levels.

On the level of exegesis, or exposition of the text, the comparative approach may serve to illumine a word, form, or phrase which has proved a philological crux to all other approaches. Thus, for example, when Joseph

[7] Cf. J. Philip Hyatt, "The Writing of an Old Testament Book," *Biblical Archaeologist Reader*, 1 (1961), pp. 22–31; reprinted from *Biblical Archaeologist*, 6 (1943), pp. 71–80.
[8] See F. M. Cross, Jr., "The Contribution of the Qumran Discoveries to the Study of the Biblical Text," *Israel Exploration Journal*, 16 (1966), pp. 81–95.

is introduced to the Egyptians as Pharaoh's vizier, it is to the accompaniment of a shout "Abrek" (41:43) which has puzzled commentators ever since. Modern scholars have tended to see in it an Egyptian word meaning "Attention!" or a Coptic word meaning "incline." But the Greek translation prepared in Egypt by Jews who might have been expected to recognize such forms left the word untranslated. Other ancient versions came up with Hebrew or even Latin etymologies which defy both literary and linguistic considerations. Such counsels of desperation led to discord among the tannaitic rabbis, as Rashi reports *ad loc*. But it is now known that Akkadian *abarakku* means "chief steward of a private or royal household" and that this title was widely attested wherever and whenever cuneiform was used; this almost certainly solves our textual problem. It also raises new questions.

Though now open to rational explanation without resort to emendations, popular etymology, or midrashic exegesis, the single word does not stand alone but in a context. Thus we move on to the level of hermeneutics, the interpretation and evaluation of the biblical context.

The presence of an Assyrian title (if this is conceded) in the midst of the Joseph stories raises significant questions about their date of composition and their source or sources of inspiration. Again we must avoid extreme positions. These stories are not to be rejected because they are not verbatim transcripts of eyewitness accounts, neither are they to be elevated above all criticism on the grounds of poetic (or theological) license. A sober appraisal must acknowledge the existence of different and even conflicting evidence within the stories themselves that bear on their possible place and date of origin. That they contain Egyptian elements is undeniable. There are proper names such as Potiphar with reasonable Egyptian etymologies; loan-

words generally conceded to be Egyptian such as those for reed, magician, linen, and two different ones for signet ring; whole motifs paralleled in Egyptian literature such as the "Story of Two Brothers"[9] or the late tradition of seven lean years followed by years of plenty.[10]

But these elements bear some closer scrutiny. That an Israelite author should have some knowledge of Egyptian geographical and personal names is of no particular literary significance, given the near proximity and repeated contacts of the two cultures. As for the loanwords, they must be viewed in the perspective of biblical Hebrew as a whole. On the most conservative estimate, some forty Egyptian loanwords are attested with greater or lesser frequency in the Hebrew Bible.[11] Of these, only five occur in the Joseph stories. None of them is unique to these stories, and one cannot, therefore, describe them as inordinately full of authentic local diction. Finally, the thematic similarities cited are not of a kind to suggest that the Joseph stories are directly dependent on the Egyptian parallels or both on a common source. In sum, these stories are simply embellished with Egyptian names, words, and literary motifs, all of which may have enjoyed a fairly wide currency. The presence of an intrusive Assyrianism in the story may or may not be a hint that the cycle of stories originated in an Assyrian setting, or in Egypt, or even in Israel, when these were under Assyrian rule. More important is the general conclusion to be derived from this example: Given sufficient familiarity with the literature, language, and proper names of an ancient Near Eastern culture such as Egypt,

[9] See chs. 39–40, Gleanings, and the translation by J. A. Wilson, Pritchard, *ANET*, pp. 23–25.
[10] *Ibid.*, pp. 31–32.
[11] See T. O. Lambdin, *Journal of the American Oriental Society*, 73 (1953), pp. 145–155. [Hereafter this journal is referred to as *JAOS*.]

we can better evaluate the amount of influence it has exercised on a specific biblical composition. If in the case cited this amount is relatively negligible, that does not make the conclusion negative. Rather, it frees us to look for other sources, including native ones, of the biblical treatment.

So far we have dealt, broadly speaking, with the text of Genesis and its context and with the considerable contribution of ancient Near Eastern literature to our evaluation of the one and interpretation of the other. But we need not confine our search to the biblical text or to the immediate parallels (and contrasts) from the cognate literatures. Rather, we may hope to gain a greater understanding of biblical people, places, and events than the text of Genesis explicitly vouchsafes us. True, we cannot expect to know more than the author or authors of Genesis knew, but we can sometimes hope to know more than he, or they, told. Here too ancient Near Eastern literature comes to our aid, though the examples will be chosen from the Syro-Palestinian area which, lying between the high civilizations of Babylonia and Egypt, did not match either of them in general literacy or specifically literary productivity. But we may take a broader view of written evidence and include in it not only strictly literary (so-called "canonical") writings but also historical (or "monumental") and economic ("archival") texts. Then this area too comes alive with a considerable corpus of inscriptions to fill in the interstices of Genesis.

Again we must put a reasonable limit on our expectations. The patriarchal narratives are no longer pure legend, like the tales of the antediluvians, and not yet the polished artifice of the "romance of Joseph." But neither are they to be understood as straightforward history. Therefore it is fruitless to look in the cuneiform or hieroglyphic inscriptions for references to the Patriarchs or in Gen. 12–38 for the names of ancient Near Eastern kings. Much effort has gone into both attempts, but even Gen. 14, potentially the most promising source in this regard, has resisted all such efforts. And small wonder, when it is remembered that the first identifiable foreign royal names reported as such in the Bible are Hiram of Tyre and Pharaoh Sheshonk of the Twenty-second Egyptian Dynasty, both dating to the tenth century B.C.E., while the first allusion to a Mesopotamian king[12] is the unnamed deliverer, probably Adad-nirari III of Assyria, who was a contemporary of Jehoahaz of Israel in the ninth century (II Kings 13:15). And, conversely, his predecessor "Jehu son of Omri" is the first Israelite king whose name (and portrait!) has turned up in the extra-biblical sources. No such individual connections can yet be provided for the second millennium, not even for its latter centuries. We should not therefore expect them for the patriarchal period.

What we do find, instead, are more general connections with the geography, history, and institutions of the second millennium as these are revealed one after the other in the monuments and archives of the area. One example must suffice. The palace of the ancient city of Mari has yielded an archive of over twenty thousand tablets which, as it is published, throws the history of the Middle Euphrates area into a wholly new and sharp relief for the first half of the second millennium. The Mari tablets are particularly valuable for illuminating tribal structure, terminology, and genealogies. In the last connection, even the seemingly tedious family trees of Genesis assume a new significance. Some tribes and clans, for example, are linked to the Patriarchs by concubinage with an eponymous ancestress; as A. Malamat has shown, these

---

[12] An earlier ninth-century Assyrian king, Shalmaneser III, is recalled as Shalman in Hosea 10:14 according to M. C. Astour, *JAOS*, 91 (1971), pp. 383–9.

represent the splitting off of tribal segments and their migration, freely or otherwise, to the margins of the tribal terrain. This is in effect stated, if obliquely, in the case of Abraham's "sons" by Hagar and Keturah (Gen. 25:6). But it is also implied where not actually stated, e.g., for the origin of Amalek (Gen. 36:12) on the strength of ample evidence for the process of tribal subdivision at Mari. The genealogies of Genesis, and their complements in Chronicles and elsewhere, have long been regarded, at best, as an artificial framework imposed on the text; at worst, they have been ignored altogether. But in the light of the cuneiform sources they may yet turn out to yield up, for those who can read between the lines, the most authentic remnants of early Israelite history.

It may be noted in passing that the reverse is also true, i.e., that ancient Near Eastern documents frequently defy understanding without help from the Bible. To return to Mari, its scribes wrote in Akkadian, the language of the settled East Semitic population of Babylonia. For tribal terminology, however, they had to turn to the West Semitic vocabulary of the nomadic and semi-nomadic Amorites. This language was much closer to biblical Hebrew, which therefore contributes fundamentally to the understanding of its tribal terminology. Many more examples could be cited to show that the comparative method thus works in both directions, but this is not the place to do so. Suffice it to say that, within its limitations, the method deserves an honored place in the canons of biblical criticism. The limitations of the comparative method have been well-defined by W. A. Irwin thus: "The Bible itself is our first and altogether best source for the study of the Bible . . . the Bible itself with whatever we can make of it by all best known procedures is alone to tell us what the Bible is and what it means."[13] But surely the comparative method is one of the very best procedures for telling us what the Bible is and means, and what we make of Genesis today inevitably depends, in some measure, on the proper utilization of the literature of all of the ancient Near East.

[13] Presidential address to the Society of Biblical Literature, 1958; cf. *Journal of Biblical Literature*, 78 (1959), p. 3. [Hereafter, this journal is referred to as *JBL*.]

PART I

Prologue

Creation

The Book of Genesis is a book of beginnings. Chapter 1 and the first three verses of chapter 2 serve as the poetic prologue, setting the stage for the universal drama that is about to commence. Once the scene is set, once order has been brought out of chaos, once heaven and earth, plants and animals have been created, the epic story of man himself can begin.

The prologue is cast in the form of a prose poem. It is written in terse, controlled phrases with rhythmic repetitions, the slow ascent of the cosmic drama culminating in the creation of man and the serene postscript describing the sanctification of the seventh day. In sparse, austere language it speaks of God, the world, and man in relationship to each other and reveals the basic and unalterable dependence of the world on the presence of God. The prologue tells, with the assurance of faith, of life's foundations, and it is in the light of this faith that it must be read and understood. (On the relationship of biblical insights to scientific knowledge, see p. xvii; and on the relationship of the Bible to ancient Near Eastern literature, see p. xxix).

Genesis 1

1–7

בְּרֵאשִׁ֖ית בָּרָ֣א אֱלֹהִ֑ים אֵ֥ת הַשָּׁמַ֖יִם וְאֵ֥ת הָאָֽרֶץ׃ א

וְהָאָ֗רֶץ הָיְתָ֥ה תֹ֨הוּ֙ וָבֹ֔הוּ וְחֹ֖שֶׁךְ עַל־פְּנֵ֣י תְה֑וֹם וְר֣וּחַ ב

אֱלֹהִ֔ים מְרַחֶ֖פֶת עַל־פְּנֵ֥י הַמָּֽיִם׃ וַיֹּ֥אמֶר אֱלֹהִ֖ים יְהִ֣י ג

א֑וֹר וַֽיְהִי־אֽוֹר׃ וַיַּ֧רְא אֱלֹהִ֛ים אֶת־הָא֖וֹר כִּי־ט֑וֹב ד

וַיַּבְדֵּ֣ל אֱלֹהִ֔ים בֵּ֥ין הָא֖וֹר וּבֵ֥ין הַחֹֽשֶׁךְ׃ וַיִּקְרָ֨א ה

אֱלֹהִ֤ים ׀ לָאוֹר֙ י֔וֹם וְלַחֹ֖שֶׁךְ קָ֣רָא לָ֑יְלָה וַֽיְהִי־עֶ֥רֶב

וַֽיְהִי־בֹ֖קֶר י֥וֹם אֶחָֽד׃ פ

וַיֹּ֣אמֶר אֱלֹהִ֔ים יְהִ֥י רָקִ֖יעַ בְּת֣וֹךְ הַמָּ֑יִם וִיהִ֣י מַבְדִּ֔יל ו

בֵּ֥ין מַ֖יִם לָמָֽיִם׃ וַיַּ֣עַשׂ אֱלֹהִים֮ אֶת־הָֽרָקִיעַ֒ וַיַּבְדֵּ֗ל ז

* א ב׳ רבתי.

1] When God began to create the heaven and the earth— 2] the earth being un-formed and void, with darkness over the surface of the deep and a wind from God sweeping over the water— 3] God said, "Let there be light"; and there was light. 4] God saw how good the light was, and God separated the light from the darkness. 5] God called the light Day, and the darkness He called Night. And there was evening and there was morning, a first day.

6] God said, "Let there be an expanse in the midst of the water, that it may separate water from water." 7] God made the expanse, and it separated the water

1:1–2] *When God began to create . . . the earth being unformed and void.* Other translations render this, "In the beginning God created." Both translations are possible, but we cannot be sure that this difference is more than stylistic. / Our translation follows Rashi, who said that the text would have been written בְּרִאשׁוֹנָה if its *primary* purpose had been to teach the order in which creation took place. Later scholars used the translation "In the beginning" as proof that God created out of nothing (*ex nihilo*), but it is not likely that the biblical author was concerned with this problem [1]. /

2] *The deep.* The Hebrew, תְּהוֹם (*tehom*), echoes the Mesopotamian creation story where it is told that heaven and earth were formed from the carcass of the sea dragon, Tiamat.

A wind from God. רוּחַ (*ruach*) can mean both "wind" and "spirit" [2]. Wind, however, provides a closer parallel to Babylonian texts than the traditional translation, "spirit of God" [3].

The water. Here, as in other ancient traditions, it is given priority of existence.

3] *God said.* As though He were addressing the universe.

6] *An expanse.* רָקִיעַ (*rakia*) suggests a firm vault or dome over the earth. According to ancient belief, this vault, which held the stars, provided the boundary beyond which the Divine dwelt.

בֵּין הַמַּיִם אֲשֶׁר מִתַּחַת לָרָקִיעַ וּבֵין הַמַּיִם אֲשֶׁר

מֵעַל לָרָקִיעַ וַיְהִי־כֵן: וַיִּקְרָא אֱלֹהִים לָרָקִיעַ שָׁמָיִם

וַיְהִי־עֶרֶב וַיְהִי־בֹקֶר יוֹם שֵׁנִי: פ

וַיֹּאמֶר אֱלֹהִים יִקָּווּ הַמַּיִם מִתַּחַת הַשָּׁמַיִם אֶל־מָקוֹם

אֶחָד וְתֵרָאֶה הַיַּבָּשָׁה וַיְהִי־כֵן: וַיִּקְרָא אֱלֹהִים לַיַּבָּשָׁה

אֶרֶץ וּלְמִקְוֵה הַמַּיִם קָרָא יַמִּים וַיַּרְא אֱלֹהִים

כִּי־טוֹב: וַיֹּאמֶר אֱלֹהִים תַּדְשֵׁא הָאָרֶץ דֶּשֶׁא עֵשֶׂב

מַזְרִיעַ זֶרַע עֵץ פְּרִי עֹשֶׂה פְּרִי לְמִינוֹ אֲשֶׁר זַרְעוֹ־בוֹ

עַל־הָאָרֶץ וַיְהִי־כֵן: וַתּוֹצֵא הָאָרֶץ דֶּשֶׁא עֵשֶׂב

מַזְרִיעַ זֶרַע לְמִינֵהוּ וְעֵץ עֹשֶׂה־פְּרִי אֲשֶׁר זַרְעוֹ־בוֹ

לְמִינֵהוּ וַיַּרְא אֱלֹהִים כִּי־טוֹב: וַיְהִי־עֶרֶב וַיְהִי־בֹקֶר

יוֹם שְׁלִישִׁי: פ

וַיֹּאמֶר אֱלֹהִים יְהִי מְאֹרֹת בִּרְקִיעַ הַשָּׁמַיִם לְהַבְדִּיל

Genesis 1

8–14

which was below the expanse from the water which was above the expanse. And it was so.   **8]** God called the expanse Sky. And there was evening and there was morning, a second day.

9] God said, "Let the water below the sky be gathered into one area, that the dry land may appear." And it was so.   **10]** God called the dry land Earth, and the gathering of waters He called Seas. And God saw how good this was.   **11]** And God said, "Let the earth sprout vegetation: seed-bearing plants, fruit trees of every kind on earth that bear fruit with the seed in it." And it was so.   **12]** The earth brought forth vegetation: seed-bearing plants of every kind, and trees of every kind bearing fruit with the seed in it. And God saw how good this was.   **13]** And there was evening and there was morning, a third day.

14] God said, "Let there be lights in the expanse of the sky to separate day from

6

בֵּין הַיּוֹם וּבֵין הַלַּיְלָה וְהָיוּ לְאֹתֹת וּלְמוֹעֲדִים

טו וּלְיָמִים וְשָׁנִים: וְהָיוּ לִמְאוֹרֹת בִּרְקִיעַ הַשָּׁמַיִם לְהָאִיר

טז עַל־הָאָרֶץ וַיְהִי־כֵן: וַיַּעַשׂ אֱלֹהִים אֶת־שְׁנֵי הַמְּאֹרֹת

הַגְּדֹלִים אֶת־הַמָּאוֹר הַגָּדֹל לְמֶמְשֶׁלֶת הַיּוֹם וְאֶת־

הַמָּאוֹר הַקָּטֹן לְמֶמְשֶׁלֶת הַלַּיְלָה וְאֵת הַכּוֹכָבִים:

יז וַיִּתֵּן אֹתָם אֱלֹהִים בִּרְקִיעַ הַשָּׁמָיִם לְהָאִיר עַל־

יח הָאָרֶץ: וְלִמְשֹׁל בַּיּוֹם וּבַלַּיְלָה וּלְהַבְדִּיל בֵּין הָאוֹר

יט וּבֵין הַחֹשֶׁךְ וַיַּרְא אֱלֹהִים כִּי־טוֹב: וַיְהִי־עֶרֶב וַיְהִי־

בֹקֶר יוֹם רְבִיעִי: פ

כ וַיֹּאמֶר אֱלֹהִים יִשְׁרְצוּ הַמַּיִם שֶׁרֶץ נֶפֶשׁ חַיָּה וְעוֹף

כא יְעוֹפֵף עַל־הָאָרֶץ עַל־פְּנֵי רְקִיעַ הַשָּׁמָיִם: וַיִּבְרָא

אֱלֹהִים אֶת־הַתַּנִּינִם הַגְּדֹלִים וְאֵת כָּל־נֶפֶשׁ הַחַיָּה

Genesis 1

15–21

night; they shall serve as signs for the set times—the days and the years;   15] and they shall serve as lights in the expanse of the sky to shine upon the earth." And it was so.   16] God made the two great lights, the greater light to dominate the day and the lesser light to dominate the night, and the stars.   17] And God set them in the expanse of the sky to shine upon the earth,   18] to dominate the day and the night, and to separate light from darkness. And God saw how good this was. 19] And there was evening and there was morning, a fourth day.

20] God said, "Let the waters bring forth swarms of living creatures, and birds that fly above the earth across the expanse of the sky."   21] God created the great sea monsters, and all the living creatures of every kind that creep, which the waters

16] *Two great lights.* The sun and the moon are mentioned as part of creation but have none of the divine or semidivine status attributed to them in other ancient mythologies.

21] *The great sea monsters.* Elsewhere the Bible reflects popular legends about certain forces of the deep that battled with God. Here they are simply listed with the other animals.

/ The monsters are variously called Nahar, Yam, Leviathan, and Rahab. The latter especially recalls an ancient poetic tradition of a "lord of the sea" [4]./

הָרֹמֶשֶׂת אֲשֶׁר שָׁרְצוּ הַמַּיִם לְמִינֵהֶם וְאֵת כָּל־עוֹף

כב כָּנָף לְמִינֵהוּ וַיַּרְא אֱלֹהִים כִּי־טוֹב: וַיְבָרֶךְ אֹתָם

אֱלֹהִים לֵאמֹר פְּרוּ וּרְבוּ וּמִלְאוּ אֶת־הַמַּיִם בַּיַּמִּים

כג וְהָעוֹף יִרֶב בָּאָרֶץ: וַיְהִי־עֶרֶב וַיְהִי־בֹקֶר יוֹם

חֲמִישִׁי: פ

כד וַיֹּאמֶר אֱלֹהִים תּוֹצֵא הָאָרֶץ נֶפֶשׁ חַיָּה לְמִינָהּ בְּהֵמָה

כה וָרֶמֶשׂ וְחַיְתוֹ־אֶרֶץ לְמִינָהּ וַיְהִי־כֵן: וַיַּעַשׂ אֱלֹהִים

אֶת־חַיַּת הָאָרֶץ לְמִינָהּ וְאֶת־הַבְּהֵמָה לְמִינָהּ וְאֵת

כָּל־רֶמֶשׂ הָאֲדָמָה לְמִינֵהוּ וַיַּרְא אֱלֹהִים כִּי־טוֹב:

כו וַיֹּאמֶר אֱלֹהִים נַעֲשֶׂה אָדָם בְּצַלְמֵנוּ כִּדְמוּתֵנוּ וְיִרְדּוּ

בִדְגַת הַיָּם וּבְעוֹף הַשָּׁמַיִם וּבַבְּהֵמָה וּבְכָל־הָאָרֶץ

כז וּבְכָל־הָרֶמֶשׂ הָרֹמֵשׂ עַל־הָאָרֶץ: וַיִּבְרָא אֱלֹהִים אֶת־

Genesis 1

22–27

brought forth in swarms; and all the winged birds of every kind. And God saw how good this was. **22]** God blessed them, saying, "Be fertile and increase, fill the waters in the seas, and let the birds increase on the earth." **23]** And there was evening and there was morning, a fifth day.

24] God said, "Let the earth bring forth every kind of living creature: cattle, creeping things, and wild beasts of every kind." And it was so. **25]** God made wild beasts of every kind and cattle of every kind, and all kinds of creeping things of the earth. And God saw how good this was. **26]** And God said, "I will make man in My image, after My likeness. They shall rule the fish of the sea, the birds of the sky, the cattle, the whole earth, and all the creeping things that creep on earth." **27]** And

---

26] *Let us make man.* Either a majestic plural / Christian theology generally takes the phrase to
or spoken to an angelic court [5]. indicate the triune nature of God./

8

הָאָדָם בְּצַלְמוֹ בְּצֶלֶם אֱלֹהִים בָּרָא אֹתוֹ זָכָר וּנְקֵבָה

כח בָּרָא אֹתָם: וַיְבָרֶךְ אֹתָם אֱלֹהִים וַיֹּאמֶר לָהֶם אֱלֹהִים

פְּרוּ וּרְבוּ וּמִלְאוּ אֶת־הָאָרֶץ וְכִבְשֻׁהָ וּרְדוּ בִּדְגַת

הַיָּם וּבְעוֹף הַשָּׁמַיִם וּבְכָל־חַיָּה הָרֹמֶשֶׂת עַל־הָאָרֶץ:

כט וַיֹּאמֶר אֱלֹהִים הִנֵּה נָתַתִּי לָכֶם אֶת־כָּל־עֵשֶׂב זֹרֵעַ

זֶרַע אֲשֶׁר עַל־פְּנֵי כָל־הָאָרֶץ וְאֶת־כָּל־הָעֵץ אֲשֶׁר־

ל בּוֹ פְרִי־עֵץ זֹרֵעַ זָרַע לָכֶם יִהְיֶה לְאָכְלָה: וּלְכָל־

חַיַּת הָאָרֶץ וּלְכָל־עוֹף הַשָּׁמַיִם וּלְכֹל רוֹמֵשׂ עַל־

הָאָרֶץ אֲשֶׁר־בּוֹ נֶפֶשׁ חַיָּה אֶת־כָּל־יֶרֶק עֵשֶׂב לְאָכְלָה

לא וַיְהִי־כֵן: וַיַּרְא אֱלֹהִים אֶת־כָּל־אֲשֶׁר עָשָׂה וְהִנֵּה־

טוֹב מְאֹד וַיְהִי־עֶרֶב וַיְהִי־בֹקֶר יוֹם הַשִּׁשִּׁי: פ

Genesis 1
28–31

God created man in His image, in the image of God He created him; male and female He created them. **28]** God blessed them and God said to them, "Be fertile and increase, fill the earth and master it; and rule the fish of the sea, the birds of the sky, and all the living things that creep on earth."

29] God said, "See, I give you every seed-bearing plant that is upon all the earth, and every tree that has seed-bearing fruit; they shall be yours for food. **30]** And to all the animals on land, to all the birds of the sky, and to everything that creeps on earth, in which there is the breath of life, [I give] all the green plants for food." And it was so. **31]** And God saw all that He had made, and found it very good. And there was evening and there was morning, the sixth day.

28] *Be fertile and increase.* A blessing. Jewish tradition considers this to be the first of the Torah's 613 commandments.
/ The halachah derived therefrom establishes man's duty to marry and have children [6]. Extensive passages in the Talmud and the codes deal with the question whether this duty devolves only upon the man or also upon the woman. Preponderant opinion favored the male's sole responsibility (incurred at age eighteen, while all other commandments are obligatory at age thirteen)./

30] *Green plants for food.* According to the biblical

אַ וַיְכֻלּוּ הַשָּׁמַיִם וְהָאָרֶץ וְכָל־צְבָאָם: וַיְכַל אֱלֹהִים
בַּיּוֹם הַשְּׁבִיעִי מְלַאכְתּוֹ אֲשֶׁר עָשָׂה וַיִּשְׁבֹּת בַּיּוֹם
ג הַשְּׁבִיעִי מִכָּל־מְלַאכְתּוֹ אֲשֶׁר עָשָׂה: וַיְבָרֶךְ אֱלֹהִים
אֶת־יוֹם הַשְּׁבִיעִי וַיְקַדֵּשׁ אֹתוֹ כִּי בוֹ שָׁבַת מִכָּל־
מְלַאכְתּוֹ אֲשֶׁר־בָּרָא אֱלֹהִים לַעֲשׂוֹת: פ

1] The heaven and the earth were finished, and all their array. 2] And on the seventh day God finished the work which He had been doing, and He ceased on the seventh day from all the work which He had done. 3] And God blessed the seventh day and declared it holy, because on it God ceased from all the work of creation which He had done.

scheme, men and beasts became carnivorous only after the Flood (Gen. 9:3). At first they had been vegetarians. According to Isaiah, in the messianic age man and beast will return to this original state of harmony: beasts will become vegetarians once more; "the lion will eat straw like the ox" (11:7).

2:1] *Finished*. Heaven and earth "were finished," and God too "finished" His work. Both in Hebrew and in English, the word can have dual meanings. The same ambiguity is also echoed in the "Gilgamesh" epic.

2] *He ceased*. Or rested. שָׁבַת (*shavat*) is related to שַׁבָּת (Sabbath).

/ If creation ceased "on" the seventh day, was this not, at least in part, another day of creating? This question was much argued by the ancients [7]./

The Creation of Man

The Rabbis said that God, the Master Architect, worked with a master plan of creation before Him. This plan was the Torah, which provided that His world would exist not merely for the sake of existing but for a moral purpose bound up with the creation of man [8].

Man is placed on the stage of creation after all else has been formed; he is represented as the crown of God's labors. In anticipation, the text shifts into a slower gear; the words "God said" are not, as previously, directly followed by a creative act but by a further resolve, almost contemplative in nature: "Let us make man" [9].

The creature called man is formed in the image of God, in His likeness. These words reflect the Torah's abiding wonder over man's special stature in creation, over his unique intellectual capacity, which bears the imprint of the Creator. Marveling at man's powers, the Bible finds him to be "but little lower than the angels" (Ps. 8:6).[1]

This likeness also describes man's moral potential. Man's *nature* is radically different from God's, but man is capable of approaching God's *actions*: His love, His mercy, His justice [11]. Man becomes truly human as he attempts to do godly deeds.[2]

Man's likeness to the Divine has a third and most important meaning: It stresses the essential holiness and, by implication, the dignity of all men, without any distinctions.

"Above all demarcations of races and nations, castes and classes, oppressors and servants, givers and recipients, above all delineations even of gifts and talents stands one certainty: Man. Whoever bears this image is created and called to be a revelation of human dignity" [13].

Six times the Bible says that God found His creation "good"; after man was created He found it "very good": Being is better than nothingness, order superior to chaos, and man's existence—with all its difficulties—a blessing. But creation is never called perfect; it will in fact be man's task to assist the Creator in perfecting His creation, to become His co-worker.

The Seventh Day

The Bible mentions the number seven more than 500 times. Some trace the concern with this number to the prominence of the sun, moon, and the five planets observed in antiquity; others to the fact that the lunar month falls roughly into four quarters of seven days each. Whatever the reason, it is the most prominent number in the Bible. In addition to the weekly cycle, the Pesach festival is governed by seven; so are the seven weeks' period between Pesach and Shavuot and the sabbatical year. There are some scholars who suggest that the entire Book of Genesis and even the Torah itself are elaborately and ingeniously constructed around this sacred number [14].

When and how the seventh day became the holy day of Israel has never been ascertained. A Babylonian division of the lunar month into four seven-day periods and the designation of the day of the full moon as *shapattu* are possible links. Whatever the origins, in Genesis the day becomes the divine seal of creation. And while it is not yet called the Sabbath, its significance is unmistakable: It is built into the very structure of the universe;

---

[1] In a midrash the angels at first mistook man for a divine person and sang hymns to him [10]. The word for "image" (*tzelem*) is related to the Akkadian *salmu*, which had the double meaning of image and statue and which applied specifically to divine statues in human guise. The biblical use is, of course, different.

[2] The Rabbis said: "As God is merciful, so be thou merciful; as He is just, so be thou just" [12].

it is God's holy time; and Israel in ages to come will be called upon to make it the center of its existence, the mark of its covenant with God, "a memorial of the work of creation."[3]

Thus, in the biblical view, creation and history belong together. Creation is the foundation of a covenantal relationship between God and world and, in a specific and important sense, between God and Israel.[4]

[3] So in the Sabbath Kiddush. In the major Christian tradition, the seventh-day Sabbath was supplanted by a first-day Sabbath—"Lord's Day"—in memory of the Resurrection [15].

[4] Isaiah describes God's creation of Israel in the same terms that Genesis uses in describing the creation of the world (Isa. 43:1, 7, 15, 21; 44:2, 21, 24; 45:11).

GLEANINGS

Very Good

It says that God found His creation to be "very good," which implies a comparison. From this, it may be inferred that God had created and destroyed previous worlds.   MIDRASH [16]

God would not have created the world if among all possible creations it had not been the best.

GOTTFRIED VON LEIBNITZ [17]

Of Every Kind

Of beasts it says that they were created "of every kind." Not so of man; there is only one human species.   BENNO JACOB [18]

Let Us Make Man

As long as God is still creating, He does not in fact say "I," He says "We," an absolute, all-inclusive term which does not refer to an I outside the self but is the plural of all-encompassing majesty. It is an impersonal I, an I that does not face another Thou, that does not reveal anything but lives, like the metaphysical God of pre-creation, only in itself.   FRANZ ROSENZWEIG [19]

In the Image

Beloved is man for he was created in the image of God. Still greater was God's love in that He gave to man the knowledge of his having been so created.   ETHICS OF THE FATHERS [20]

Like None Other

A king of flesh and blood stamps his image on a coin, hence all coins look and are alike; but the King of Kings put the stamp of the first man on humanity, yet no man is like any other.

MISHNAH [21]

Created Single

Man was created single for the sake of peace among men, so that no one might say to his fellow: "My father was greater than yours."

MISHNAH [22]

Created Unique

Every man should know that since creation no other man ever was like him. Had there been such another, there would be no need for him to be. Each is called on to perfect his unique qualities. And it is his failure to heed this call which delays the Messiah.   BAAL SHEM TOV [23]

Another Creation Story

[From an Akkadian epic dating probably to the early second millennium B.C.E.]

Then the lord [Marduk] paused to view her
  [Tiamat's] dead body,
That he might divide the monster and do
  artful works.
He split her like a shellfish into two parts:
Half of her he set up and ceiled it as a sky,
Pulled down the bar and posted guards.
He bade them to allow not her waters to
  escape,
He crossed the heavens and surveyed its
  regions. . . .
He constructed nations for the great gods,
Fixing their astral likenesses as constella-
  tions. . . .
In her [Tiamat's] belly he established the
  zenith.
The moon he caused to shine, the night to
  him entrusting.
[Marduk reveals his plan to create man]
Blood I will mass and cause bones to be.
I will establish a savage, "man" shall be his
  name.
Verily, savage man I will create.
He shall be charged with the service of the
  gods that they might be at ease!

FROM "ENUMA ELISH" [24]

Ancient Cosmology and Biblical Creation

Although the Bible takes for granted the con-tours of ancient cosmology, it has demythologized the ancient understanding of existence. The Hebrew Bible contains no theogony, no myth which traces the creation to a primordial battle between divine powers, no ritual which enabled men to repeat the mythological drama and thereby ensure the supremacy of the national god. Mythological allusions have been torn out of their ancient context of polytheism and nature religion and have acquired a completely new meaning within the historical syntax of Israel's faith. The pagan language survives only as poetic speech for the adoration of the Lord of History.

BERNHARD W. ANDERSON [25]

The Sabbath and God's Freedom

[The first feature of God revealed by His rest on the seventh day is His freedom.]

A world-principle without this limit to its creative activity would not be free like God but would be tied to the infinite motion of its own development and evolution. In its unlimited creative activity it would not really belong to itself. It would not really be active but entangled in a process imposed upon it and subjected to its higher necessity. A being is free only when it can determine and limit its activity. God's creative activity has its limit in the rest from His works determined by Himself, i.e., the rest of the seventh day. His freedom revealed in this rest is a first criterion of the true deity of the Creator in the biblical saga.

KARL BARTH [26]

Dream of Perfection

The Sabbath is the dream of perfection, but it is only a dream. Only in its being both does it become the cornerstone of life, only as the festival of perfection does it become the constant renewal of creation.   FRANZ ROSENZWEIG [27]

Uncompleted

The Lord created the world in a state of beginning. The universe is always in an uncompleted state, in the form of its beginning. It is not like a vessel at which the master works to finish it; it requires continuous labor and renewal by creative forces. Should these cease for only a second, the universe would return to primeval chaos.

SIMCHAH BUNAM OF PRZYSUCHA [28]

Fill the Earth and Master It (Gen. 1:28)

To claim that [this verse] provides "justification" for the exploitation of the environment, leading to the poisoning of the atmosphere, the pollution of our water, and the spoliation of natural resources is...a complete distortion of the truth. On the contrary, the Hebrew Bible and the Jewish interpreters *prohibit* such exploitation. Judaism goes much further and insists that man has an obligation not only to conserve the world of nature but to enhance it because man is the "co-partner of God in the work of creation." ... All animal life and all growing and life-giving things have rights in the cosmos that man must consider, even as he strives to ensure his own survival. The war against the spoliation of nature and the pollution of the environment is therefore the command of the hour and the call of the ages.

ROBERT GORDIS [29]

Truth at Creation

A midrash begins as follows: Rabbi Shimon said: "In the hour when God was about to create Adam, the angels of service were divided. Some said, 'Let him not be created,' others, 'Let him be created, for he will do loving deeds.' But Truth said, 'Let him not be created, for he will be all falsity.' Righteousness said, 'Let him be created, for he will do righteous deeds.' Peace said, 'Let him not be created, for he will be full of strife.' What then did God do? He seized hold of Truth and cast her to the earth, as it is said [Dan. 8:12], 'Thou didst cast Truth to the ground.'"

That Truth alone is singled out for this treatment suggests the ominous possibility that all that might be said in favor of the creation of man is nothing but pious illusion; that Truth is so horrendous as to destroy everything for us unless we shun it, avoid it, evade it; that only after having cast Truth to the ground can God create man at all.

The midrash ends as follows: Then the angels of service said to God, "Lord of the universe, how canst Thou despise Thy seal? Let Truth arise from the earth, as it is said [Ps. 85:12], 'Truth springs from the earth.'"

Somehow it is possible for man to face Truth and yet to be. But do we know how?

EMIL L. FACKENHEIM [30]

PART II

Beginnings

THE LINES OF HEAVEN, EARTH,

AND PRIMEVAL MAN

Man in Eden

Chapter 2, verse 4, begins the tale of "earth and heaven" and particularly the epic of man. Language and tone change markedly: spare rhythms mark chapter 1; a familiar, personal, and frankly human manner when speaking of God marks what follows. He is referred to as Lord God, while before He was merely called God. The order of creation is changed, too: in chapter 1 the animals precede man, in chapter 2 the order is reversed; in chapter 1 humanity begins with male and female, in chapter 2 with male only. Where before man appeared in generic form, he now becomes concretely human: he speaks and feels. Because of these differences the two creation stories have been seen as stemming from two different traditions. The former is usually assigned to the P-source, the latter to the J-source (see p. xxi), though this division is disputed by other scholars.

ד אֵלֶּה תוֹלְדוֹת הַשָּׁמַיִם וְהָאָרֶץ בְּהִבָּֽרְאָם* בְּיוֹם עֲשׂוֹת

ה יְהוָה אֱלֹהִים אֶרֶץ וְשָׁמָיִם: וְכֹל שִׂיחַ הַשָּׂדֶה טֶרֶם

יִהְיֶה בָאָרֶץ וְכָל־עֵשֶׂב הַשָּׂדֶה טֶרֶם יִצְמָח כִּי לֹא

הִמְטִיר יְהוָה אֱלֹהִים עַל־הָאָרֶץ וְאָדָם אַיִן לַעֲבֹד

ו אֶת־הָֽאֲדָמָה: וְאֵד יַעֲלֶה מִן־הָאָרֶץ וְהִשְׁקָה אֶת־כָּל־

ז פְּנֵי הָֽאֲדָמָה: וַיִּיצֶר יְהוָה אֱלֹהִים אֶת־הָֽאָדָם עָפָר

מִן־הָאֲדָמָה וַיִּפַּח בְּאַפָּיו נִשְׁמַת חַיִּים וַיְהִי הָֽאָדָם

ח לְנֶפֶשׁ חַיָּה: וַיִּטַּע יְהוָה אֱלֹהִים גַּן־בְּעֵדֶן מִקֶּדֶם

Genesis 2

4–8

*ד ה' זעירא.

4] Such is the story of heaven and earth as they were created.

When the LORD God made earth and heaven— 5] no shrub of the field being yet in the earth and no grains having yet sprouted, because the LORD God had not sent rain upon the earth and there was no man to till the soil, 6] but a flow would well up from the ground and water the whole surface of the earth— 7] the LORD God formed man from the dust of the earth, and He blew into his nostrils the breath of life; and man became a living being.

8] The LORD God planted a garden in Eden, in the east, and placed there the man

---

2:4] *Such is the story.* אֵלֶּה תוֹלְדוֹת is elsewhere in Genesis rendered as "These are the lines of . . ." (i.e., the genealogy), making descent a keystone of biblical history. אֵלֶּה תוֹלְדוֹת serves as a heading for the major divisions of Genesis (see p. xxvii) and, therefore, here too we should translate: "These are the lines of heaven and earth." In later chapters we hear of the lines of Adam, Noah, and the sons of Noah (of Shem in particular); and further, of Terah (Abraham's father), Isaac, and Jacob.

The Lord God. יְהוָה אֱלֹהִים is pronounced Adonai Elohim (see p. 23).

7] *Man.* אָדָם (*adam*) is formed from the earth (אֲדָמָה, *adamah*). In modern terms, this is an assonance rather than correct etymology. Like-sounding words were thought to hint at a special association of concepts. An English equivalent might be: God fashioned an earthling from the earth.

Living being. A better translation than the older "living soul" [1].

8] *Eden.* A word derived ultimately from the Sumerian, where it referred originally to a specific locale noted at first for its fertility but which subsequently became barren. The word then came to have the meaning of the uncultivated steppe or hinterland generally. In the Greek translation, Paradise, an Iranian word meaning park, was used for Eden. In Jewish tradition, גַּן עֵדֶן (the Garden of Eden) came to stand for the after-death abode

ט וַיָּשֶׂם שָׁם אֶת־הָאָדָם אֲשֶׁר יָצָר: וַיַּצְמַח יְהוָֹה אֱלֹהִים
מִן־הָאֲדָמָה כָּל־עֵץ נֶחְמָד לְמַרְאֶה וְטוֹב לְמַאֲכָל
י וְעֵץ הַחַיִּים בְּתוֹךְ הַגָּן וְעֵץ הַדַּעַת טוֹב וָרָע: וְנָהָר
יֹצֵא מֵעֵדֶן לְהַשְׁקוֹת אֶת־הַגָּן וּמִשָּׁם יִפָּרֵד וְהָיָה
יא לְאַרְבָּעָה רָאשִׁים: שֵׁם הָאֶחָד פִּישׁוֹן הוּא הַסֹּבֵב
יב אֵת כָּל־אֶרֶץ הַחֲוִילָה אֲשֶׁר־שָׁם הַזָּהָב: וּזֲהַב הָאָרֶץ
יג הַהִוא טוֹב שָׁם הַבְּדֹלַח וְאֶבֶן הַשֹּׁהַם: וְשֵׁם־הַנָּהָר
יד הַשֵּׁנִי גִּיחוֹן הוּא הַסּוֹבֵב אֵת כָּל־אֶרֶץ כּוּשׁ: וְשֵׁם־
הַנָּהָר הַשְּׁלִישִׁי חִדֶּקֶל הוּא הַהֹלֵךְ קִדְמַת אַשּׁוּר
טו וְהַנָּהָר הָרְבִיעִי הוּא פְרָת: וַיִּקַּח יְהוָֹה אֱלֹהִים אֶת־

Genesis 2
9–15

whom He had formed.   9] And from the ground the LORD God caused to grow every tree that was pleasing to the sight and good for food, with the tree of life in the middle of the garden, and the tree of knowledge of good and bad.

10] A river issues from Eden to water the garden, and from there it divides and becomes four branches.   11] The name of the first is Pishon, the one that winds through the whole land of Havilah, where the gold is.   12] The gold of that land is good; bdellium is there, and lapis lazuli.   13] The name of the second river is Gihon, the one that winds through the whole land of Cush.   14] The name of the third river is Tigris, the one that flows east of Asshur; and the fourth river is the Euphrates.

15] The LORD God took the man and placed him in the garden of Eden, to till

of the righteous; it was no longer thought of as a geographic location on earth.

10] *A river . . . four branches.* This concept occurs also in other cultures, notably in India and China [2].

12] *Lapis lazuli.* Others translate as "onyx"; the meaning of the Hebrew is uncertain.

13] *Cush.* Usually refers to Ethiopia or Midian, but here it is most probably the land of the Kassites, in Babylonia.

טז הָאָדָם וַיַּנִּחֵהוּ בְגַן־עֵדֶן לְעָבְדָהּ וּלְשָׁמְרָהּ: וַיְצַו
יְהֹוָה אֱלֹהִים עַל־הָאָדָם לֵאמֹר מִכֹּל עֵץ־הַגָּן אָכֹל
יז תֹּאכֵל: וּמֵעֵץ הַדַּעַת טוֹב וָרָע לֹא תֹאכַל מִמֶּנּוּ כִּי
יח בְּיוֹם אֲכָלְךָ מִמֶּנּוּ מוֹת תָּמוּת: וַיֹּאמֶר יְהֹוָה אֱלֹהִים
לֹא־טוֹב הֱיוֹת הָאָדָם לְבַדּוֹ אֶעֱשֶׂה־לּוֹ עֵזֶר כְּנֶגְדּוֹ:
יט וַיִּצֶר יְהֹוָה אֱלֹהִים מִן־הָאֲדָמָה כָּל־חַיַּת הַשָּׂדֶה וְאֵת
כָּל־עוֹף הַשָּׁמַיִם וַיָּבֵא אֶל־הָאָדָם לִרְאוֹת מַה־יִּקְרָא־
לוֹ וְכֹל אֲשֶׁר יִקְרָא־לוֹ הָאָדָם נֶפֶשׁ חַיָּה הוּא שְׁמוֹ:
כ וַיִּקְרָא הָאָדָם שֵׁמוֹת לְכָל־הַבְּהֵמָה וּלְעוֹף הַשָּׁמַיִם
וּלְכֹל חַיַּת הַשָּׂדֶה וּלְאָדָם לֹא־מָצָא עֵזֶר כְּנֶגְדּוֹ:
כא וַיַּפֵּל יְהֹוָה אֱלֹהִים תַּרְדֵּמָה עַל־הָאָדָם וַיִּישָׁן וַיִּקַּח

Genesis 2

16–21

it and tend it.   **16]** And the LORD God commanded the man, saying, "Of every tree of the garden you are free to eat;   **17]** but as for the tree of knowledge of good and bad, you must not eat of it; for as soon as you eat of it, you shall be doomed to die."

18] The LORD God said, "It is not good for man to be alone; I will make a fitting helper for him."   **19]** And the LORD God formed out of the earth all the wild beasts and all the birds of the sky, and brought them to the man to see what he would call them; and whatever the man called each living creature, that would be its name.   **20]** And the man gave names to all the cattle and to the birds of the sky and to all the wild beasts; but for Adam no fitting helper was found.   **21]** So the LORD God cast a deep sleep upon the man and he slept; and He took one of his ribs

17]   *Knowledge of good and bad.* Others translate as "of good and evil."

As soon as you eat of it, you shall die. You shall become mortal.

21]   *One of his ribs.* Some scholars suggest that this relates to a Sumerian story that knew of Nin-ti, meaning either "Lady of the Rib" or "Lady of Life" (hence the name Eve, Gen. 3:20) [3].

21

כב אַחַת מִצַּלְעֹתָיו וַיִּסְגֹּר בָּשָׂר תַּחְתֶּנָּה: וַיִּבֶן יְהוָה
אֱלֹהִים אֶת־הַצֵּלָע אֲשֶׁר־לָקַח מִן־הָאָדָם לְאִשָּׁה
כג וַיְבִאֶהָ אֶל־הָאָדָם: וַיֹּאמֶר הָאָדָם זֹאת הַפַּעַם עֶצֶם
מֵעֲצָמַי וּבָשָׂר מִבְּשָׂרִי לְזֹאת יִקָּרֵא אִשָּׁה כִּי מֵאִישׁ
כד לֻקֳחָה־זֹּאת: עַל־כֵּן יַעֲזָב־אִישׁ אֶת־אָבִיו וְאֶת־אִמּוֹ
וְדָבַק בְּאִשְׁתּוֹ וְהָיוּ לְבָשָׂר אֶחָד:

Genesis 2

22–24

and closed up the flesh at that spot.   **22]** And the LORD God fashioned into a woman the rib that He had taken from the man, and He brought her to the man.   **23]** Then the man said, "This one at last / Is bone of my bones / And flesh of my flesh. / This one shall be called Woman, / For from man was she taken."   **24]** Hence a man leaves his father and mother and clings to his wife, so that they become one flesh.

23] *Woman.* אִשָּׁה is here derived from אִישׁ (man). **24]** *Clings to his wife.* This may be more than simply a statement of personal relationship; it may echo the custom of having the man become part of his wife's family and household (see note to Gen. 31:43).

Man and Woman

Biblical man was undoubtedly aware of the pervasive bisexual pattern of nature and knew that in this regard humanity was not different from the rest of creation. But the Torah gives this fact a special dimension by recognizing that man enters a fundamentally new state of life when he ceases to be alone. The words, "It is not good for man to be alone," speak about man's greatest need. The creation of woman becomes in effect the beginning of man's social history; man is able to fulfil his destiny completely only as a social being. Aloneness, in turn, is man's primary helplessness. Woman is more than man's female counterpart; like his rib, she is part of him, part of his structure, and without her he is essentially incomplete. The Talmud says: "He is called man only if he has a wife" [4].

However, the Bible does not see man and woman as equals. The Torah tradition is frankly male-oriented.

The Names of God

In the opening chapter of Genesis, the Creator is called "God" (Elohim), and now He is referred to as "Lord God" (Adonai Elohim). This difference has been noted since ancient days and has been the starting point for midrashic comment, as well as for modern biblical criticism, which has seen in the uses of different divine names important clues to the authorship of such passages (see p. xxi).

Elohim (אֱלֹהִים, God or gods) is the generic term for divinity most frequently found in the Bible. It is used as a plural noun for gods of other nations and as a singular noun when applied to Israel's God. Elohim appears as an amplification of Eloah (אֱלֹהַ), a poetic form that does not occur in Genesis, and of El (אֵל), which in Genesis occurs only in conjunction with other terms such as El Elyon (God Most High), El Bethel (God of Bethel), El Shaddai (usually rendered God Almighty), and as a part of proper names such as Israel.

Adonai (יְהֹוָה, Lord) is the unique, personal name of God and the name most frequently used in the Bible. The Torah gives the meaning of יהוה in Exod. 3:14, but that explanation is not clear. The original pronunciation was most likely Yahveh (יַהְוֶה), but since Jewish tradition permitted the name to be voiced only by the High Priest, it became customary, after the destruction of the Second Temple, to substitute the word Adonai (meaning "my Lord") when reading יהוה.[1] The Masoretes who vocalized the Hebrew text (see p. xxiii) therefore took the vowels from the word Adonai (אֲדֹנָי) and put them with יהוה to remind the reader not to read Yahveh but Adonai. Hence, all vocalized texts of the Bible now read יְהֹוָה.[2] A Christian writer of the sixteenth century who was unaware of this substitution transcribed יְהֹוָה as he saw it, namely, as Jehovah, and this has since entered many Christian Bible translations.

Jewish tradition interprets the names Elohim and Adonai as explanations of the two sides of the nature of God, the former representing the quality of justice, the latter reflecting the quality of mercy. The Midrash says that the world was originally created by God as Elohim (Gen. 1), but that afterward He is called Adonai Elohim (Gen. 2) because He saw that without the added quality of mercy creation could not have endured.

---

[1] Orthodox Jews now go even further and use the substitutional "Adonai" only in prayer or actual Torah reading. Otherwise they substitute "Adoshem" for it and, in similar circumstances, say "Elokim" when speaking of God. They carry this respect for the sacredness of the divine name into translation as well and write "G-d" and "L-rd."

[2] However, when the combination אדני יהוה occurs, as in 15:2, the reading is Adonai Elohim and the vocalization is יְהֹוִה.

GLEANINGS

Another Beginning

When on high [*enuma elish*] the heavens had
   not been named,
Firm ground below had not been called by
   name,
Nought but primordial Apsu, their begetter,
And Mummu-Tiamat, she who bore them all,
Their waters commingling as a single body;
No reed but had been matted, no marsh land
   had appeared,
When no gods whatever had been brought into
   being,
Uncalled by name, their destinies undetermined,
Then it was that the gods were formed within
   them.   FROM "ENUMA ELISH" [5]

The Sumerian Paradise

[The Sumerian epic, "Enki and Ninhursag,"
is considerably older than "Enuma Elish." Note
also the images of lion, wolf, lamb, and kid living
peacefully in Dilmun. Well over a millennium
later, Isaiah used these images in his prophecy of
the end of time (11:6).]

The land Dilmun is clean, the land Dilmun is
   most bright.
In Dilmun the raven utters no cries,
The ittidu-bird utters not the cry of the
   ittidu-bird,
The lion kills not,
The wolf snatches not the lamb,
Unknown is the kid-devouring wild dog,
Unknown is the grain-devouring . . .,
The dove droops not the head,
The sick-eyed says not "I am sick-eyed,"
The sick-headed says not "I am sick-headed,"
Its old man says not "I am an old man."
                FROM "ENKI AND NINHURSAG" [6]

From the Dust

God took dust from the four corners of the

earth so that man might be at home everywhere.
                                    RASHI [7]
[According to Islamic legend, the dust was red,
white, and black—hence the skin colors of mankind. "At home" is represented by the possibility
of finding a suitable *permanent* home, i.e., a grave.
Every man can rest peacefully anywhere on earth.]

Solitude

In the process of naming the animals, Adam
realizes that he needs a helpmate (Gen. 2:20). How
are the two related? Man discovers his solitude
when he begins to give names, i.e., to use words,
and cannot say "man" to any other creature.

The Creation of Woman

God created woman while Adam slept so as
to prevent him from observing the divine power.
The deepest mysteries of divine creativity are
withheld from human gaze.   BENNO JACOB [8]

Undivided

Man and woman were originally undivided,
i.e., Adam was at first created bisexual, a herma-
phrodite.   MIDRASH [9]

The Original Adam

From our biblical text grew a considerable
body of ancient stories about the "Original Adam,"
Adam Harishon or *Adam Kadmon* (or *Kadmoni*) as
he was called. He was thought to have preceded
the biblical Adam and to have been a perfect man
who would return to the world at the time of
redemption. [10]

The Two Adams

The Adam of Genesis 1 was the idea of man,
and hence this ideal man never appeared on earth;
it was the Adam of Genesis 2, fashioned out of
material dust and immaterial spirit, who was the

24

ancestor of the race. Fashioned as he was of antithetical materials, he lived as all men live, under the tension in which the material aspect of him tugged in one direction, the immaterial aspect in the opposite. PHILO [11][3]

Mercy and Justice

The quality of mercy is not strain'd,
It droppeth as the gentle rain from heaven
Upon the place beneath: it is twice bless'd;
It blesseth him that gives and him that takes:
'Tis mightiest in the mightiest; it becomes
The throned monarch better than his crown;
His sceptre shows the force of temporal power,
The attribute to awe and majesty,
Wherein doth sit the dread and fear of kings;
But mercy is above this sceptred sway,
It is enthroned in the hearts of kings,
It is an attribute to God himself,
And earthly power doth then show likest God's
When mercy seasons justice.
WILLIAM SHAKESPEARE [12]

Blessing and Curse

At the end of the first creation story stands a double blessing—of the first man and the first Shabbat; at the end of the second creation story stands a double curse—on the first man and the earth. Between both stands Sin. Natural man is established by a blessing; historical man by a curse. Both together form the dual nature and the dual fate of man. MARTIN BUBER [13]

Man and Woman

Sexuality was an aspect of beings created by YHVH and did not precede the existence of the earth or man. The animals were formed from earth as man had been, but the man rejected the animals as companions. In contrast to Enkidu in the Gilgamesh Epic, the lone man in Genesis rejected the animals, the animals did not reject the man. No woman came to seduce Adam from his wild beasts. Indeed, woman was created after the man rejected the animals and still yearned for a friend. Enkidu enjoyed the harlot, learned from her, but not even considered her as a companion. Rejected by the animals, Enkidu yearned for a friend, a man like himself. In startling contrast, Adam immediately and enthusiastically recognized the woman as his companion.
ADRIEN J. BLEDSTEIN [14]

Man has no part in making woman. He exercises no control over her existence: He is neither participant nor spectator nor consultant at her birth. Like man, woman owes her life solely to God. To claim that the rib means inferiority or subordination is to assign the man qualities over the woman which are not in the narrative itself. Superiority, strength, aggressiveness, dominance, and power do not characterize man in Genesis 2. By contrast he is formed from dirt; his life hangs by a breath which he does not control; and he himself remains silent and passive while the Deity plans and interprets his existence. PHYLLIS TRIBLE [15]

[3] According to Philo (in Sandmel's words), "the original Adam (of Gen. 1:27) was a heavenly creation and unmixed with material things. He is the rational, preexistent soul. This soul becomes mixed with clay from the earth when God "fashions" the earthy Adam of Gen. 2:7. There is joined to him Eve, sense-perception; but the serpent, pleasure, intrudes to divert man from lofty obligations into harmful ones. Man (mind) thereupon is quite different in his individual earthy state from what pure, generic mind was before it became mixed with body (in birth), and the mind intent on salvation must therefore free itself of the encumbrance of the body so as to regain its pristine immaterial purity."

The Expulsion from Eden

The first two chapters of Genesis spoke of the origins of the world in its ideal condition. Now, it turns to growth, to man's actual condition, and to the problems he encounters in his humanness.

Here, once again, the underlying Near Eastern traditions that helped to shape the Eden story have been radically recast to express the specific biblical view of God and man: the transcendent Creator of all who forms man that he might freely do His will. In the Babylonian epic of "Gilgamesh" the hero loses his immortality not only through weakness but also through accident, for the serpent steals the life-giving plant. In another Near Eastern tradition, the tale of "Adapa," immortality is lost by deliberate misrepresentation. In the Bible, the loss of Eden is ultimately traceable to man's own volition and action. If man fails to live up to his potential, it is his and no one else's doing.

כה וַיִּהְיוּ שְׁנֵיהֶם עֲרוּמִּים הָאָדָם וְאִשְׁתּוֹ וְלֹא יִתְבֹּשָׁשׁוּ:

א וְהַנָּחָשׁ הָיָה עָרוּם מִכֹּל חַיַּת הַשָּׂדֶה אֲשֶׁר עָשָׂה יְהוָה אֱלֹהִים וַיֹּאמֶר אֶל־הָאִשָּׁה אַף כִּי־אָמַר אֱלֹהִים

ב לֹא תֹאכְלוּ מִכֹּל עֵץ הַגָּן: וַתֹּאמֶר הָאִשָּׁה אֶל־הַנָּחָשׁ

ג מִפְּרִי עֵץ־הַגָּן נֹאכֵל: וּמִפְּרִי הָעֵץ אֲשֶׁר בְּתוֹךְ־הַגָּן אָמַר אֱלֹהִים לֹא תֹאכְלוּ מִמֶּנּוּ וְלֹא תִגְּעוּ בּוֹ פֶּן

ד תְּמֻתוּן: וַיֹּאמֶר הַנָּחָשׁ אֶל־הָאִשָּׁה לֹא־מוֹת תְּמֻתוּן:

ה כִּי יֹדֵעַ אֱלֹהִים כִּי בְּיוֹם אֲכָלְכֶם מִמֶּנּוּ וְנִפְקְחוּ

ו עֵינֵיכֶם וִהְיִיתֶם כֵּאלֹהִים יֹדְעֵי טוֹב וָרָע: וַתֵּרֶא

Genesis 2; 3

25; 1–6

25] The two of them were naked, the man and his wife, yet they felt no shame.

1] Now the serpent was the shrewdest of all the wild beasts that the LORD God had made. He said to the woman, "Did God really say: You shall not eat of any tree of the garden?"   **2]** And the woman said to the serpent, "We may eat of the fruit of the other trees of the garden.   **3]** It is only about fruit of the tree in the middle of the garden that God said: You shall not eat of it or touch it, lest you die."   **4]** And the serpent said to the woman, "You are not going to die. **5]** God knows that, as soon as you eat of it, your eyes will be opened and you will be like God, who knows good and bad."   **6]** When the woman saw that the tree was

---

2:25] *Naked.* עֲרוּמִּים, word play on עָרוּם (shrewd), in Gen. 3:1. The above printings of the text group verse 25 with chapter 3 because the sentence appears to introduce the subsequent story. The verse should, however, be considered a bridge, connecting one story to the other.

3:1] *The serpent.* The association of serpents with guile is an old one. In Mesopotamian, Hurrian, and Ugaritic myths serpents oppose the will of the gods; "snake" was already a derogatory term in an old Hittite document. A post-biblical book identifies the serpent of Eden with Satan and says: "Through Satan's envy death entered

the world" [1].   Serpents play an important part in two incidents in Israel's history: Rods are turned into serpents by Moses and the Egyptian magicians (Exod. 4:3; 7:9–15), and serpents are agents of a plague in the wilderness (Num. 21:6–9; cf. II Kings 18:4).

5] *Like divine beings.* אֱלֹהִים (*elohim*) usually means "God or gods" but at times also refers to celestial beings (as in Gen. 6:4) or to human judges and rulers (i.e., those who are "powerful") [2]. Another translation: "You will be like God in telling good from bad."

6] *Fruit.* Jewish tradition suggests wheat, grape,

הָאִשָּׁה כִּי טוֹב הָעֵץ לְמַאֲכָל וְכִי תַאֲוָה־הוּא לָעֵינַיִם

וְנֶחְמָד הָעֵץ לְהַשְׂכִּיל וַתִּקַּח מִפִּרְיוֹ וַתֹּאכַל וַתִּתֵּן

ז גַּם־לְאִישָׁהּ עִמָּהּ וַיֹּאכַל: וַתִּפָּקַחְנָה עֵינֵי שְׁנֵיהֶם וַיֵּדְעוּ

כִּי עֵירֻמִּם הֵם וַיִּתְפְּרוּ עֲלֵה תְאֵנָה וַיַּעֲשׂוּ לָהֶם

ח חֲגֹרֹת: וַיִּשְׁמְעוּ אֶת־קוֹל יְהוָה אֱלֹהִים מִתְהַלֵּךְ בַּגָּן

לְרוּחַ הַיּוֹם וַיִּתְחַבֵּא הָאָדָם וְאִשְׁתּוֹ מִפְּנֵי יְהוָה

ט אֱלֹהִים בְּתוֹךְ עֵץ הַגָּן: וַיִּקְרָא יְהוָה אֱלֹהִים אֶל־

י הָאָדָם וַיֹּאמֶר לוֹ אַיֶּכָּה: וַיֹּאמֶר אֶת־קֹלְךָ שָׁמַעְתִּי

יא בַגָּן וָאִירָא כִּי־עֵירֹם אָנֹכִי וָאֵחָבֵא: וַיֹּאמֶר מִי הִגִּיד

לְךָ כִּי עֵירֹם אָתָּה הֲמִן־הָעֵץ אֲשֶׁר צִוִּיתִיךָ לְבִלְתִּי

יב אֲכָל־מִמֶּנּוּ אָכָלְתָּ: וַיֹּאמֶר הָאָדָם הָאִשָּׁה אֲשֶׁר נָתַתָּה

good for eating and a delight to the eyes, and that the tree was desirable as a source of wisdom, she took of its fruit and ate; and she gave some to her husband also, and he ate.   **7]** Then the eyes of both of them were opened and they perceived that they were naked; and they sewed together fig leaves and made themselves loincloths.

8] They heard the sound of the LORD God moving about in the garden at the breezy time of day; and the man and his wife hid from the LORD God among the trees of the garden.   **9]** The LORD God called out to the man and said to him, "Where are you?"   **10]** He replied, "I heard the sound of You in the garden, and I was afraid because I was naked, so I hid."   **11]** Then He said, "Who told you that you were naked? Did you eat of the tree from which I had forbidden you to eat?" **12]** The man said, "The woman You put at my side—she gave me of the tree, and

fig, or citron, all prominent Near Eastern products [3]. In Christian tradition, the fruit is generally thought to be an apple, both because it was a popular fruit in Europe and because the

Latin translation of רַע (bad) is *malum* which also means apple.

 8] *Moving about.* God is pictured in human terms as inspecting His creation.

יג עִמָּדִי הִוא נָתְנָה־לִּי מִן־הָעֵץ וָאֹכֵל: וַיֹּאמֶר יְהוָה
אֱלֹהִים לָאִשָּׁה מַה־זֹּאת עָשִׂית וַתֹּאמֶר הָאִשָּׁה הַנָּחָשׁ
הִשִּׁיאַנִי וָאֹכֵל: יד וַיֹּאמֶר יְהוָה אֱלֹהִים אֶל־הַנָּחָשׁ כִּי
עָשִׂיתָ זֹּאת אָרוּר אַתָּה מִכָּל־הַבְּהֵמָה וּמִכֹּל חַיַּת
הַשָּׂדֶה עַל־גְּחֹנְךָ תֵלֵךְ וְעָפָר תֹּאכַל כָּל־יְמֵי חַיֶּיךָ:
טו וְאֵיבָה אָשִׁית בֵּינְךָ וּבֵין הָאִשָּׁה וּבֵין זַרְעֲךָ וּבֵין
זַרְעָהּ הוּא יְשׁוּפְךָ רֹאשׁ וְאַתָּה תְּשׁוּפֶנּוּ עָקֵב: ס
טז אֶל־הָאִשָּׁה אָמַר הַרְבָּה אַרְבֶּה עִצְּבוֹנֵךְ וְהֵרֹנֵךְ בְּעֶצֶב
תֵּלְדִי בָנִים וְאֶל־אִישֵׁךְ תְּשׁוּקָתֵךְ וְהוּא יִמְשָׁל־בָּךְ: ס
יז וּלְאָדָם אָמַר כִּי שָׁמַעְתָּ לְקוֹל אִשְׁתֶּךָ וַתֹּאכַל מִן־

Genesis 3

13–17

I ate."   **13]** And the LORD God said to the woman, "What is this you have done!" The woman replied "The serpent duped me, and I ate."   **14]** And the LORD God said to the serpent, "Because you did this, / Banned shall you be from all cattle / And all wild beasts; / On your belly shall you crawl / And dirt shall you eat / All the days of your life. /   **15]** I will put enmity / Between you and the woman, / And between your offspring and hers; / They shall strike at your head, / And you shall strike at their heel."   **16]** And to the woman He said, "I will make most severe / Your pangs in childbearing; / In pain shall you bear children. / Yet your urge shall be for your husband, / And he shall rule over you."

17] To Adam He said, "Because you heeded your wife and ate of the tree about

---

14] *More cursed . . . than all cattle.* Lower than cattle, which at least have legs to walk on.

16] *In pain shall you bear.* An explanation of birth pangs. Note also the expression "woman's curse" for menstruation.

17] *Cursed be the ground.* The earth was thought to share in man's guilt. "When man corrupts his way the land is corrupted" [4].

By toil shall you eat. Man's need to work appears to be part of God's curse. The Rabbis, however, interpreted God's dictum as a concession: By work man is able to fend for and feed himself.

/ The Rabbis further interpreted that the task of providing human sustenance is God's greatest problem [5]. /

הָעֵץ אֲשֶׁר צִוִּיתִיךָ לֵאמֹר לֹא תֹאכַל מִמֶּנּוּ אֲרוּרָה
הָאֲדָמָה בַּעֲבוּרֶךָ בְּעִצָּבוֹן תֹּאכֲלֶנָּה כֹּל יְמֵי חַיֶּיךָ:
יח וְקוֹץ וְדַרְדַּר תַּצְמִיחַ לָךְ וְאָכַלְתָּ אֶת־עֵשֶׂב הַשָּׂדֶה:
יט בְּזֵעַת אַפֶּיךָ תֹּאכַל לֶחֶם עַד שׁוּבְךָ אֶל־הָאֲדָמָה כִּי
מִמֶּנָּה לֻקָּחְתָּ כִּי־עָפָר אַתָּה וְאֶל־עָפָר תָּשׁוּב:
כ וַיִּקְרָא הָאָדָם שֵׁם אִשְׁתּוֹ חַוָּה כִּי הִוא הָיְתָה אֵם
כא כָּל־חָי: וַיַּעַשׂ יְהוָה אֱלֹהִים לְאָדָם וּלְאִשְׁתּוֹ כָּתְנוֹת
עוֹר וַיַּלְבִּשֵׁם:　פ
כב וַיֹּאמֶר יְהוָה אֱלֹהִים הֵן הָאָדָם הָיָה כְּאַחַד מִמֶּנּוּ
לָדַעַת טוֹב וָרָע וְעַתָּה פֶּן־יִשְׁלַח יָדוֹ וְלָקַח גַּם מֵעֵץ
כג הַחַיִּים וְאָכַל וָחַי לְעֹלָם: וַיְשַׁלְּחֵהוּ יְהוָה אֱלֹהִים

which I commanded you, saying, 'You shall not eat of it,' Cursed be the ground because of you; / In anguish shall you eat of it / All the days of your life. / **18]** Thorns and thistles / Shall it bring forth for you, / And you shall feed on the grains of the field. / **19]** By the sweat of your brow / Shall you get bread to eat, / Until you return to the ground, / For from it you were taken: / For dust you are, / And to dust you shall return."

20] The man named his wife Eve, because she was the mother of all the living. **21]** And the LORD God made for Adam and his wife garments of skins, and He clothed them.

22] And the LORD God said, "Now that the man has become like one of us, knowing good and bad, what if he should stretch out his hand and take also from the tree of life and eat, and live forever!" **23]** So the LORD God banished him from the

---

20] *Eve.* חַוָּה (*chavah*); the text explains the name by connecting it with "living" (חַי, *chai*), but the true etymology of the name is obscure. This is probably a case of assonance. "Mother of all the living" may be an honorific title, like "Mother of all gods" in the "Atrahasis" epic.

32

מִגַּן־עֵדֶן לַעֲבֹד אֶת־הָאֲדָמָה אֲשֶׁר לֻקַּח מִשָּׁם׃
כד וַיְגָרֶשׁ אֶת־הָאָדָם וַיַּשְׁכֵּן מִקֶּדֶם לְגַן־עֵדֶן אֶת־הַכְּרֻבִים
וְאֵת לַהַט הַחֶרֶב הַמִּתְהַפֶּכֶת לִשְׁמֹר אֶת־דֶּרֶךְ עֵץ־
הַחַיִּים׃ ס

Genesis 3

24

garden of Eden, to till the soil from which he was taken.   24] He drove the man out, and stationed east of the garden of Eden the cherubim and the fiery ever-turning sword, to guard the way to the tree of life.

24] *Cherubim.* Legendary winged beings who protect sacred places. The flaming sword may represent bolts of lightning.

The Tree of Knowledge

Adam and Eve are depicted as living in an environment of ease, free from pain and worry. Man's only task is to till and tend the garden, as a steward of his Creator.[1] The tale of expulsion, of "Paradise Lost," which relates how man came to forfeit this condition, has been the subject of much theological speculation, which in turn has had a profound effect on the religious and psychological orientations of Western society.

At the center of the story, as in the middle of the garden, stands the Tree of Knowledge. The tree is unique to biblical tradition, and three major interpretations have been offered to explain it.

Ethical Interpretation. Eating from the Tree of Knowledge of good and bad (or "good and evil" as most older translations render it) provided man with moral discrimination and thereby made him capable of committing sin. Yielding to the serpent's temptation and eating the fruit were two parts of the same act; once it was done, the relationship of man to God was essentially changed. Man's expulsion from Eden meant that he could never return to his former state of ethical indifference; he had become a "choosing" creature. Two radically different theologies developed from this interpretation:

Christianity, building on certain, largely sectarian Jewish teachings,[2] taught that after Adam's transgression all men were inherently evil. In this interpretation the event has come to be known as "the fall of man," an expression absent from the Bible itself and from Jewish literature. "By one man, sin entered the world," says Paul in the Christian Scripture and again: "by the offense of one, judgment came upon all men to condemnation" [8]. An old New England primer put it simply: "In Adam's fall we sinned all." This was man's original sin, a fatal flaw, from which he could be redeemed only after Jesus came into the world as the Christ. Without faith in him as the redemptive savior men would live and die in their original sin. In the course of centuries the doctrine of man's inherent sinfulness led to a thoroughly pessimistic view of man and a heavy emphasis on the right kind of faith.[3]

The mainstream of Judaism refused to make the tale of Eden an important part of its world view and maintained that the only road to salvation was through godly deeds (*mitzvot*), rather than through belief in a savior, and that, while man tended to corruption (Gen. 6:5; 8:21), he was not basically a corrupt creature. Though he was constantly exposed to the evil impulse (יֵצֶר הָרַע), by carrying out God's commandments he could overcome or at least control it and thereby could develop his impulse for good (יֵצֶר טוֹב). The more closely he attended to *mitzvot*, the greater would be his protection from sin.

Intellectual Interpretation. In the Bible, the expression "good and bad" (טוֹב וָרָע) sometimes means "everything" (Deut. 1:39; II Sam.

[1] In Babylonian mythology, the task of raising food for the gods was the main reason for the creation of man [6].

[2] Especially, "O thou Adam, what hast thou done! For though it was thou that sinned, the fall was not thine alone, but ours also who are descendants" [7].

[3] God's judgment on Adam ("For dust you are and to dust you shall return") is spoken by the Catholic priest as he puts ashes on the worshiper's head on Ash Wednesday. The Mormons, however, say: "We believe that men will be punished for their own sins and not for Adam's transgressions" (Second Article of Faith). Original sin was also denied by the Pelagians (fifth century C.E.), who held that it was transmitted by bad example.

[4] Ethical interpretation: If Adam and Eve had no understanding of right and wrong, how could they be punished for their ignorance?

Intellectual interpretation: Man, having eaten of

19:35), as when we say, "I know its good and its bad features," meaning that I know everything about it that can be known [9]. The tale may therefore be understood to say that primal man ate of the Tree of Omniscience. Having tasted of it, man forever after will attempt to know everything; he will, in other words, play the part of God.

This intellectual overreaching is what the Greeks called *hubris*, self-exaltation. Man strives to be godlike, but God will not permit him to become "like one of us." When man persists in deifying his own powers, God will call him to account and exact a terrible punishment. Like Adam, man will have to leave his Eden, his desire for divine power turned back by the flaming sword at the gate of attainment [10].

Sexual Interpretation. The Eden story may also be read as the discovery not of man's ethical or intellectual knowledge but of his sexuality. This is suggested by the Hebrew word for "knowledge" (דַּעַת), which has the meaning of experience, especially of sexual

the Tree of Knowledge is said to have become like God. However, man does not in fact attain omniscience. Note also the question put to Maimonides, "It is a thing to be wondered at that man's punishment for his disobedience should consist in his being granted a perfection that he did not possess before, namely, the intellect." Maimonides' answer: "There is a difference between 'necessary' and 'apparent' truths. Before his sin Adam knew the former, afterwards the latter" [11].

Sexual interpretation: In Gen. 3:22, after the eating of the fruit, God says that man has now "become like one of us, knowing good and bad." If "knowing" here refers to sexuality, it would be in contrast to the biblical concept of a God who otherwise never bears a tinge of sexuality. For this reason the ancients suggested that Adam and Eve had marital relations *before* they ate of the fruit [12]. The biblical Eve can also be compared to the harlot in "Gilgamesh" as an agent of civilization [13].

experience. Note that the story of the expulsion from Eden begins with a discovery of nakedness and sexual shame (Gen. 3:7). (Other ancient sources also stress the sexual theme, see p. 37.)

Reading the Eden tale in this light we see a link between the Tree of (Sexual) Knowledge and the Tree of Life. The latter, whose fruit would have bestowed earthly immortality, is no longer accessible. Man must now perpetuate his species through procreation, in the same way as other creatures do. But being man, his sexuality has a special dimension; his process of passing from childhood to adulthood, from innocence to maturity, is shot through with love and pain. Each man repeats in his person the journey from Eden into the world. As a child he lives in a garden of innocence; when he discovers his sexual impulse and grows up, he must leave the garden forever.

Summary. All three interpretations do justice to the story, although there is some textual objection in each case.[4] Whatever intent went into the earliest strands of the story, the three major themes outlined above have been thoroughly interwoven so that the fabric of the text exhibits not one theme but all and each is discernible, depending on the light in which the text is viewed.

This becomes particularly evident when we ask the questions: How did the storyteller view the intention of God? What did he believe God wanted man to be? Thoroughly obedient or potentially defiant? A moral automaton or a free spirit? Did God want man to stay in Eden? And what was the punishment? Man was, in the end, "condemned" to be human.

These questions arise not only from the biblical text but also, in a wider sense, from the very creation of man. Man eats the tantalizing fruit, only to meet with disappointment and frustration. His is an act of disobedience and defiance, yet at the same time of growth and liberation. God appears to provide man with the possibility of remaining in Eden, but the very temptation of knowledge makes this impossible. God tempts man to be like Him, but, when man yields, God rejects the attempt decisively.

Thus the emergence of that contradictory creature called man is in itself a process of contradictions. Adam is free to defy God, at a price, and the theme of man's defiance runs through much of the Bible. For while man's freedom may be limited in all other respects, he must believe that toward God his freedom is without limits [14].

The Tree of Life

Questions of immortality were of central concern to many ancient peoples, and it was widely believed that eating or drinking a sacred substance might bestow eternal life. Egyptian mythology spoke of a sycamore from which the gods obtained their immortality, the Greeks told of ambrosia, and the Indians of soma. Gilgamesh was promised access to a life-giving sea plant, and the "Adapa" tale spoke of magical bread and water. Some Christian sacraments, though they have long been spiritualized, still reflect their origins in the tree-of-life motif. The Bible, however, while retaining the symbolism of a life-endowing tree, gives it a minor role (which explains why no prohibition is issued to Adam in this respect) and shifts its main attention to the Tree of Knowledge. The latter, whatever meaning assigned to its "knowledge," in effect became a Tree of Death, for eating of its fruit caused expulsion from Eden and the permanent inaccessibility of any magical fruit from the Tree of Life. By choosing "knowledge," man attained death. Immortality and knowledge are pictured as incompatible in the human sphere; man desires both but cannot have both.[5] Since man chose knowledge, mortality is now built into the very structure of human life, distinguishing creature from Creator.[6] By procreating, man can in part overcome death, but, like the rest of the creatures, he cannot "be like God."

[5] "Only ignorance holds life and human knowledge, death" [15]. The "Adapa" tale also deals with man being offered life but choosing death, a theme recurring in the Bible, which may be viewed as a guide to those who want to mitigate the effects of the choice [16].

[6] Midrash Tanchuma speculates that God created the Angel of Death before He created man, thus relating man's mortality not to human sin so much as to Providence itself and that, in fact, "death is good" [17]. The Talmud records a rabbinical debate which concludes that there is "death without sin" [18].

GLEANINGS

The Civilization of Savage Man

[Gilgamesh suggests that Enkidu, the savage man who dwells with beasts, be seduced by a woman and thereby be enticed away from his savage companions. Thus he would be civilized. Compare this passage to the sexual interpretation of the biblical Eden story.]

> She treated him, the savage, to a woman's task,
> As his love was drawn unto her.
> For six days and seven nights Enkidu comes forth, mating with the lass.
> After he had his fill of her charms,
> He set his face toward his wild beasts.
>
> On seeing him, Enkidu, the gazelles ran off,
> The wild beasts of the steppe drew away from his body.
> Enkidu had to slacken his pace—it was not as before;
> But he now had wisdom, broader understanding . . .
> The harlot says to him, to Enkidu:
> "Thou art wise, Enkidu, art become like a god."
>
> FROM "GILGAMESH" [19]

The Serpent Speaking

The serpent is the symbol of pleasure. It is said to have uttered a human voice, because pleasure employs innumerable champions and defenders who take care to advocate its interests and who dare to assert that it should exercise power over everything.   PHILO [20]

Or Touch It (Gen. 3:3)

Eve said to the serpent that she was not even allowed to touch the fruit, although this was not part of the original prohibition. The Rabbis consider this (and any) embroidery of the truth to be the opening wedge of sin. [21]

They Perceived That They Were Naked (Gen. 3:7)

Man is the being who shudders at his own naturalness.

CARL FRIEDRICH VON WEIZSÄCKER [22]

Where Are You? (Gen. 3:9)

Did God not know where Adam was? He asked in order to open the way to repentance.

MIDRASH [23]

I Was Afraid Because I Was Naked (Gen. 3:10)

Not physical, but religious nakedness is meant. Adam was afraid because by his transgression he was stripped of the one commandment he had received. Man without a *mitzvah* is truly naked.

MIDRASH [24]

Paradise Lost

> Of Man's First Disobedience, and the Fruit
> Of that Forbidden Tree, whose mortal taste
> Brought Death into the World, and all our woe,
> With loss of *Eden* . . .
> Sing, Heav'nly Muse . . .   JOHN MILTON [25]

[To Milton, as to much of the Christian tradition, the serpent was Satan incarnate.]

Freedom

Man has freedom, he can choose God or reject God, he can lead the world to perdition and to redemption. The creation of this being Man with such power of freedom means that God has made room for a co-determining power alongside of Himself. Man is the crossroad of the world.

HENRY SLONIMSKY [26]

The Eden of the World-to-Come

In Jewish and Christian traditions, Paradise or *Gan-Eden* also becomes a projection of the future. In the messianic era men will return to the harmony of Eden (see p. 19). This expectation is also

37

applied to the afterlife of the righteous who will join the angels in singing the praises of God and in studying the holy books.

The traditional prayer book (*siddur*), in the memorial prayer (*El male rachamim*), asks God to accept the departed in Eden; the Reform prayer book has omitted the phrase.

A Controversy

For two years and a half the House of Shammai and the House of Hillel were arguing. The former said: "It would have been better if man had not been created." The latter said: "Better that he was created than that he had not been created." They concluded that it would have been better if man had not been created but, now that he has been created, let him examine his past deeds. Some say: "Let him consider his future actions."

TALMUD [27]

The Cherubim

According to tradition, they were angels of destruction, while those hovering over the ark [Exod. 25:22] were guardian angels. All had the faces of children. From this we may learn that if a child is trained properly he resembles the cherubim of the ark; if not, those of Eden.

MOSHE MORDECAI EPSTEIN [28]

Not against God

We can, objectively considered, speak of a "fall" of the soul of the primeval light man, only by overemphasizing the moral factor. The soul, certainly, has sinned against itself, frivolously sacrificing its original blissful and peaceful state—but not against God in the sense of offending any prohibition of His in its passional enterprise, for such a prohibition, at least according to the doctrine we have received, was not issued. True, pious tradition has handed down to us the command of God to the first man, not to eat of the tree of the "knowledge of good and evil"; but we must remember that we are here dealing with a secondary and already earthly event and with human beings who had with God's own creative aid been generated out of the knowledge of matter by the soul; if God really set them this test, He undoubtedly knew beforehand how it would turn out, and the only obscurity lies in the question, why He did not refrain from issuing a prohibition which, being disobeyed, would simply add to the malicious joy of His angelic host, whose attitude towards man was already most unfavourable. But the expression "good and evil" is a recognized and admitted gloss upon the text, and what we are really dealing with is knowledge, which has as its consequence not the ability to distinguish between good and evil but rather death itself; so that we need scarcely doubt that the "prohibition" too is a well-meant but not very pertinent addition of the same kind.

THOMAS MANN [29]

Cain and Abel

Man's eviction from Eden and his consequent mortality imply a transfer of important powers from God to man. Both the creation and termination of life now rest with man—the former "with the help of the Lord" (Gen. 4:1), the latter in defiance of God (the killing of Abel). In the story of Cain and Abel, man's relationship to God is explored in a social setting. It is in the context of human relationships that choices between good and evil will henceforth have to be made. And it is in this context that the interplay between human and divine responsibility must be viewed.

The story of the brothers also introduces a secondary theme that will recur often in the Bible: the struggle between siblings. Time after time our sympathies are directed toward the younger one, and, even when like Abel he dies, it is a still younger sibling, Seth, who provides the link with the future.*

---

* Note the struggle between Jacob and Esau and between Joseph and his brothers. The first-born is often passed over: Ishmael, Reuben, Aaron, etc. This pattern may reflect a protest against the institution of primogeniture (see p. 250). The theme persists in later folklore.

א וְהָאָדָם יָדַע אֶת־חַוָּה אִשְׁתּוֹ וַתַּהַר וַתֵּלֶד אֶת־קַיִן

ב וַתֹּאמֶר קָנִיתִי אִישׁ אֶת־יְהוָה: וַתֹּסֶף לָלֶדֶת אֶת־

אָחִיו אֶת־הָבֶל וַיְהִי־הֶבֶל רֹעֵה צֹאן וְקַיִן הָיָה עֹבֵד

ג אֲדָמָה: וַיְהִי מִקֵּץ יָמִים וַיָּבֵא קַיִן מִפְּרִי הָאֲדָמָה

ד מִנְחָה לַיהוָה: וְהֶבֶל הֵבִיא גַם־הוּא מִבְּכֹרוֹת צֹאנוֹ

וּמֵחֶלְבֵהֶן וַיִּשַׁע יְהוָה אֶל־הֶבֶל וְאֶל־מִנְחָתוֹ: וְאֶל־

ה קַיִן וְאֶל־מִנְחָתוֹ לֹא שָׁעָה וַיִּחַר לְקַיִן מְאֹד וַיִּפְּלוּ

ו פָנָיו: וַיֹּאמֶר יְהוָה אֶל־קָיִן לָמָּה חָרָה לָךְ וְלָמָּה

ז נָפְלוּ פָנֶיךָ: הֲלוֹא אִם־תֵּיטִיב שְׂאֵת וְאִם לֹא תֵיטִיב

1] Now the man knew his wife Eve, and she conceived and bore Cain, saying, "I have gained a male child with the help of the LORD." 2] She then bore his brother Abel. Abel became a keeper of sheep, and Cain became a tiller of the soil. 3] In the course of time, Cain brought an offering to the LORD from the fruit of the soil; 4] and Abel, for his part, brought the choicest of the firstlings of his flock. The LORD paid heed to Abel and his offering, 5] but to Cain and his offering He paid no heed. Cain was much distressed and his face fell. 6] And the LORD said to Cain, "Why are you distressed, / And why is your face fallen? / 7] Surely, if you do right, /

4:1] *Knew.* On the use of יָדַע (yada) in the sense of sexual experience, see p. 35.

Cain. The name is explained in the text by a word play (קַיִן־קָנִיתִי, kayin–kaniti)—"I have gained [or made] a male child with the help of the Lord."
/Others: "I have bought a male offspring from the Lord," reflecting the idea that the first-born belongs to God and must be bought from Him (see Num. 3:46–47 and note the surviving ceremony of *pidyon ha-ben*, redemption of the first-born son). Some commentators see in Cain the ancestor of the Kenites, nomadic tribesmen in the Negev who earned their living as itinerant tinkers and smiths (*kenaya* in

Aramaic, *kaynum* in Arabic). Thus the lowly status of the Kenites in later days would be explained by the curse put upon their progenitor [1]./

2] *Abel.* The name is not explained in the text. /The Hebrew הֶבֶל usually means "breath" or "puff" or "vanity" as in Ps. 144:4: "Man is like a breath, his days are as a passing shadow," or as in Job 7:16: "My days are as a breath."/

4] *Choicest.* An idiomatic rendering of the Hebrew, literally, "the fat of" [2].

7] *There is uplift.* From the descent into evil. The

לְפֶתַח חַטָּאת רֹבֵץ וְאֵלֶיךָ תְּשׁוּקָתוֹ וְאַתָּה תִּמְשָׁל־

ח בּוֹ: וַיֹּאמֶר קַיִן אֶל־הֶבֶל אָחִיו וַיְהִי בִּהְיוֹתָם בַּשָּׂדֶה

ט וַיָּקָם קַיִן אֶל־הֶבֶל אָחִיו וַיַּהַרְגֵהוּ: וַיֹּאמֶר יְהוָה אֶל־

קַיִן אֵי הֶבֶל אָחִיךָ וַיֹּאמֶר לֹא יָדַעְתִּי הֲשֹׁמֵר אָחִי

י אָנֹכִי: וַיֹּאמֶר מֶה עָשִׂיתָ קוֹל דְּמֵי אָחִיךָ צֹעֲקִים

יא אֵלַי מִן־הָאֲדָמָה: וְעַתָּה אָרוּר אָתָּה מִן־הָאֲדָמָה

אֲשֶׁר פָּצְתָה אֶת־פִּיהָ לָקַחַת אֶת־דְּמֵי אָחִיךָ מִיָּדֶךָ:

יב כִּי תַעֲבֹד אֶת־הָאֲדָמָה לֹא־תֹסֵף תֵּת־כֹּחָהּ לָךְ נָע

There is uplift. / But if you do not do right / Sin is the demon at the door, / Whose urge is toward you, / Yet you can be his master."

8] And Cain said to his brother Abel . . . and when they were in the field, Cain set upon his brother Abel and killed him. **9]** The LORD said to Cain, "Where is your brother Abel?" And he said, "I do not know. Am I my brother's keeper?" **10]** Then He said, "What have you done? Hark, your brother's blood cries out to Me from the ground! **11]** Therefore, you shall be banned from the soil, which opened its mouth wide to receive your brother's blood from your hand. **12]** If you till the soil, it shall no longer yield its strength to you. You shall become a ceaseless wanderer on earth."

meaning of the Hebrew is not clear, and any translation is merely an educated guess.

Sin couches at the door. Others translate as "sin is the demon at the door."
/The suggestion is that רבץ is connected with the Akkadian word for demon [3]./

8] *Cain said to his brother Abel.* The text does not quote what was said. The Septuagint and Targum supply these words: "Come, let us go out into the field" [4].
/However, the omission of what Cain said may be a purposeful ellipsis [5].

12] *A ceaseless wanderer.* The banished Cain did settle, but in the land of Nod, the land of "restlessness" (Gen. 4:16), for nowhere could he be at rest.

יג וְנָ֥ד תִּֽהְיֶ֖ה בָּאָ֑רֶץ וַיֹּ֥אמֶר קַ֖יִן אֶל־יְהֹוָ֑ה גָּד֥וֹל עֲוֺנִ֖י
יד מִנְּשֹֽׂא׃ הֵן֩ גֵּרַ֨שְׁתָּ אֹתִ֜י הַיּ֗וֹם מֵעַל֙ פְּנֵ֣י הָֽאֲדָמָ֔ה
וּמִפָּנֶ֖יךָ אֶסָּתֵ֑ר וְהָיִ֜יתִי נָ֤ע וָנָד֙ בָּאָ֔רֶץ וְהָיָ֥ה כׇל־מֹצְאִ֖י
טו יַֽהַרְגֵֽנִי׃ וַיֹּ֧אמֶר ל֣וֹ יְהֹוָ֗ה לָכֵן֙ כׇּל־הֹרֵ֣ג קַ֔יִן שִׁבְעָתַ֖יִם
יֻקָּ֑ם וַיָּ֨שֶׂם יְהֹוָ֤ה לְקַ֙יִן֙ א֔וֹת לְבִלְתִּ֥י הַכּוֹת־אֹת֖וֹ כׇּל־
טז מֹצְאֽוֹ׃ וַיֵּ֥צֵא קַ֖יִן מִלִּפְנֵ֣י יְהֹוָ֑ה וַיֵּ֥שֶׁב בְּאֶֽרֶץ־נ֖וֹד
יז קִדְמַת־עֵֽדֶן׃ וַיֵּ֤דַע קַ֙יִן֙ אֶת־אִשְׁתּ֔וֹ וַתַּ֖הַר וַתֵּ֣לֶד אֶת־
חֲנ֑וֹךְ וַֽיְהִי֙ בֹּ֣נֶה עִ֔יר וַיִּקְרָא֙ שֵׁ֣ם הָעִ֔יר כְּשֵׁ֖ם בְּנ֥וֹ חֲנֽוֹךְ׃
יח וַיִּוָּלֵ֤ד לַֽחֲנוֹךְ֙ אֶת־עִירָ֔ד וְעִירָ֕ד יָלַ֖ד אֶת־מְחֽוּיָאֵ֑ל
וּמְחִיָּיאֵ֗ל יָלַד֙ אֶת־מְת֣וּשָׁאֵ֔ל וּמְתוּשָׁאֵ֖ל יָלַ֥ד אֶת־לָֽמֶךְ׃

Genesis 4

13–18

13] Cain said to the LORD, "My punishment is too great to bear! 14] Since You have banished me this day from the soil, and I must avoid Your presence and become a restless wanderer on earth—anyone who meets me may kill me!" 15] The LORD said to him, "Therefore, if anyone kills Cain, sevenfold vengeance shall be taken on him." And the LORD put a mark on Cain, lest anyone who met him should kill him. 16] And Cain left the presence of the LORD and settled in the land of Nod, east of Eden.

17] Cain knew his wife, and she conceived and bore Enoch. And he then founded a city, and named the city after his son Enoch. 18] To Enoch was born Irad, and Irad begot Mehujael, and Mehujael begot Methusael, and Methusael begot Lamech.

14] *You have banished me this day from the soil.* Which had sustained him as a farmer. Cain is punished by being exiled from his accustomed environment, from his occupation, and also from access to God. Human life, according to the Bible, is sacred; its wanton destruction is seen as a crime against God himself [6].

15] *I promise.* When God says לָכֵן (*lachen,* assuredly), it is a promise [7].

Sevenfold. Here meaning "many times."

A mark. Not a brand of rejection but a sign of protection against blood revenge.

לְקַיִן אֹת/ is read by some scholars as: "And the Lord put Cain as a mark," i.e., Cain himself was the sign

יט וַיִּקַּח־לוֹ לֶמֶךְ שְׁתֵּי נָשִׁים שֵׁם הָאַחַת עָדָה וְשֵׁם

כ הַשֵּׁנִית צִלָּה: וַתֵּלֶד עָדָה אֶת־יָבָל הוּא הָיָה אֲבִי

כא יֹשֵׁב אֹהֶל וּמִקְנֶה: וְשֵׁם אָחִיו יוּבָל הוּא הָיָה אֲבִי כָּל־

כב תֹּפֵשׂ כִּנּוֹר וְעוּגָב: וְצִלָּה גַם־הִוא יָלְדָה אֶת־תּוּבַל
קַיִן לֹטֵשׁ כָּל־חֹרֵשׁ נְחֹשֶׁת וּבַרְזֶל וַאֲחוֹת תּוּבַל־קַיִן

כג נַעֲמָה: וַיֹּאמֶר לֶמֶךְ לְנָשָׁיו עָדָה וְצִלָּה שְׁמַעַן קוֹלִי
נְשֵׁי לֶמֶךְ הַאֲזֵנָּה אִמְרָתִי כִּי אִישׁ הָרַגְתִּי לְפִצְעִי וְיֶלֶד

כד לְחַבֻּרָתִי: כִּי שִׁבְעָתַיִם יֻקַּם־קָיִן וְלֶמֶךְ שִׁבְעִים

כה וְשִׁבְעָה: וַיֵּדַע אָדָם עוֹד אֶת־אִשְׁתּוֹ וַתֵּלֶד בֵּן וַתִּקְרָא

19] Lamech took to himself two wives: the name of the one was Adah, and the name of the other was Zillah.   20] And Adah bore Jabal; he was the ancestor of those who dwell in tents and amidst herds.   21] The name of his brother was Jubal; he was the ancestor of all who play the lyre and the pipe.   22] As for Zillah, she bore Tubal-cain, who forged all implements of copper and iron. And the sister of Tubal-cain was Naamah.

23] And Lamech said to his wives, "Adah and Zillah, hear my voice; / O wives of Lamech, give ear to my speech. / I have slain a man for wounding me, / And a lad for bruising me. /   24] If Cain is avenged sevenfold, / Then Lamech seventy-sevenfold."

25] Adam knew his wife again, and she bore a son and named him Seth, mean-

---

that warned men against murder. Medieval Christianity justified the Jewish badge as a "mark of Cain." /

23–24] It is not clear why the Bible recorded this fragment. Lamech's song is possibly meant to relate his invention of weapons to his vengefulness

or brutal arrogance. His life span of 777 years (Gen. 5:31) is a sequence of the 7 and 77 of Gen. 4:24.

25] *God has provided.* A word play, שֵׁת–שָׁת (Seth-provided).

אֶת־שְׁמוֹ שֵׁת כִּי שָׁת־לִי אֱלֹהִים זֶרַע אַחֵר תַּחַת הֶבֶל

כ׳ כִּי הֲרָגוֹ קָיִן: וּלְשֵׁת גַּם־הוּא יֻלַּד־בֵּן וַיִּקְרָא אֶת־שְׁמוֹ

אֱנוֹשׁ אָז הוּחַל לִקְרֹא בְּשֵׁם יְהֹוָה: ס

ing, "God has provided me with another offspring in place of Abel," for Cain had killed him.   **26]** And to Seth, in turn, a son was born, and he named him Enosh. It was then that men began to invoke the LORD by name.

26]   *Enosh.* A poetic term for "man."
Began to invoke the Lord. Antediluvian man is pictured as being close to God and knowing Him by name [8].

Farmer and Shepherd

Much of Israel's early history is connected with shepherds, the nomadic life, and experiences encountered in traveling through desert lands. The Patriarchs were nomads or semi-nomads, and both Moses and David were shepherds. The nomad looked upon all settlers, urban as well as rural, with contempt: They were slaves to possession and therefore prone to corruption and idolatry.

Cain is a farmer, a settler, and Abel is a shepherd. One reading of the story suggests that the brothers represent man's two original cultures in tension.[1] It is interesting to note, however, that Cain is *condemned* to be a nomad. If the nomadic way of life is, indeed, superior, why this choice of punishment? Most probably, the farmer–shepherd theme contributed to the original story but was blurred in later generations. From time to time, the Bible returns to this theme, and especially when the city is portrayed as an object of distrust (see p. 106).

The Rejected Sacrifice

Both Cain and Abel bring sacrifices to God, but only Abel's is accepted, and the biblical writer offers no explanation for God's choice.

Some commentators maintain that the key to God's preference may be found in the intent of the two worshipers. While Cain brings merely "an offering," Abel brings "the choicest" of his flock. One performs outward motions, the other offers the service of his heart [9].

A better interpretation, however, is that God's rejection of Cain's offering is inexplicable in human terms. God acts in accordance with His own wisdom: "I will be gracious to whom I will be gracious" (Exod. 33:19). His reasons are unknown to man. The inexplicability of divine preferment marks Cain as an essentially tragic character; he reacts with blind violence to a rejection he cannot comprehend. "We are accustomed to think of him with revulsion: but the text of Genesis aims rather at evoking our sympathy for a man who atoned for his crime with homelessness and fear—a fate worse than death" [10].

Am I My Brother's Keeper?

Few phrases have been quoted more often than this bold counter-question that Cain flings back at God. But the meaning is far from clear. The following explanations have been suggested:

The question implies the answer, for by asking the question of God Cain acknowledges a higher moral authority. There is someone to whom man must answer for his deeds.

The theme is human responsibility. God, by the punishment He metes out, asserts that Cain was indeed his brother's keeper.

Cain's question is essentially defiant: "How would I know—or care?" Cain, the first product of the post-Eden world, is a man who defies God himself. "The idea of man's rebelliousness, by which Genesis explains the origins of the human condition, is a fundamental idea of biblical literature and of Israelite religion in general. One might call the Bible a chronicle of human rebellion" [11].

According to Rabbi Shimon bar Yochai, when God asked Cain "Where is your brother Abel?" Cain answered "Am *I* my brother's keeper? *You* are God. You have created man. It is Your task to watch him, not mine. If I ought not to have done what I did, You could have prevented me from doing it." Thus, Cain makes God responsible or at least co-responsible for his own actions.

Note that God does not reply. The question, "Am *I* my brother's keeper?" remains unanswered and has remained so despite the

---

[1] It also appears in Sumerian literature, but as a more friendly rivalry.

46

questions of succeeding generations. Why is God silent when men kill each other? Where does His power begin and where does it end? God asks man to account for his deeds. Man in turn asks God to account for His. Am I alone my brother's keeper? Are You not as well? If my brother's blood cries out against me, does it not cry out against You, too?[2]

This interpretation is appealing not only because it asks questions of great urgency today but also because it allows for a direct continuation of the Eden story. There, man's choice was essentially between life and death; now, in the post-Eden world, God offers man a new choice, the choice between good and evil. Cain chooses murder, the ultimate evil. And having granted man moral freedom, God, in a sense, shares in man's transgressions. But though man may ask where God was in the hour of violence, God's failure to answer does not reduce man's responsibility.

---

[2] Rabbi Shimon emphasizes this by pointing out that a slight shift in Gen. 4:10 (עלי instead of אלי) would make God, who now accuses Cain by stating, "Your brother's blood cries out *to* Me," say sorrowfully, "Your brother's blood cries out *against* Me." Rabbi Shimon, aware of the implications of his comment, says: "It is difficult to say such a thing [i.e., to read the text as it ought to be read] and the mouth cannot utter it [as it would imply the blaming of God]." He compared the God–Cain–Abel triangle to two gladiators fighting before a king. The ruler could stop the contest any minute, but he lets it proceed to the bitter, deadly end. Is he not, by his silence, involved in the killing [12]? Also note the talmudic saying: "Man does not lift a finger unless it is decreed from above" [13].

GLEANINGS

Cain Was Tested

The text says of sin that "its urge is toward you" [Gen. 4:7]. This implies that sin wants to be conquered by man; but if man fails to conquer it, sin returns to God and accuses man.

SAMSON RAPHAEL HIRSCH

[This interpretation suggests that Cain was tested by God and that the temptation was instituted for Cain's benefit. Such a theme is explicit in the stories of Abraham and Job.]

The Quarrel

Abel said: "My sacrifice was accepted because my good deeds exceeded yours." Cain answered: "There is no justice and there is no judge, there is no world-to-come and no reward or punishment for the righteous and wicked." About this the brothers quarreled. Cain set upon his brother Abel and killed him with a stone.

JONATHAN BEN UZZIEL [14]

Cain's Freedom

Say not: "God has led me astray," for He does not desire sin. No one is bidden to be godless, and to no one did He give permission to sin.

BEN SIRA [15]

Who is strong? He who masters his urge.

ETHICS OF THE FATHERS [16]

It is true that a man's temperament may make it easier to act in a certain way, but he is never thereby forced to do or not to do.

MAIMONIDES [17]

Your Brother's Blood

The Hebrew דְּמֵי [Gen. 4:10] appears to read "bloods," as if it were collective: Abel's unborn descendants also cried out to God.   MISHNAH [18]

From this we also learn that one man's life is equal to all of creation.   MIDRASH [19]

Cain Built a City

To the ancient way of thinking, nothing seemed more natural than to represent a murderer and outlaw as the first builder of cities. The ancients did not think of a city as arising out of the exigencies of barter and trade. The complexity, the turmoil, and the degeneration which marked human life in the larger centers of population were to them proof that the city had sinister origins. Towns and cities were to them abnormal and the product of unnatural circumstances. The fact that nearly every town harbored refugees from justice or vengeance gave color to the belief that the corrupt character of town populations was due to the degenerate character of the founders.

MORDECAI M. KAPLAN [20]

To Conquer Death

One more war. The last. They always say that. Let us fight so as to fight no more. Let us kill so as to conquer death. Who knows, perhaps Cain himself aspired to be not just the first murderer in history but the last as well.

ELIE WIESEL [21]

The Rise of Civilization

The pessimistic interpretation of 4:17–22 [seeing the rise of civilization essentially as a turning from God] became prominent in the Occidental Christian tradition. It is, in fact, closer to the tale of Prometheus and the spirit of Greek mythology than to the Bible itself, which quite undramatically relates the acquisition of technical skills and intimates that it was God who enabled His creatures to accomplish such feats.

CLAUS WESTERMANN [22]

Primeval Man

In this section the Bible presents the second of its genealogical lines. The first was that of heaven and earth (Gen. 2:4), the second is the line of human progeny. The careful listing of names (which occurs twice) and the detailed accounts of legendary long lives find their parallels in other ancient Near Eastern traditions. These annotated genealogies bridge the gap between Adam and Noah, show the rise of civilization, and try to explain the present-day limitations of man's life expectancy.

א   זֶה סֵפֶר תּוֹלְדֹת אָדָם בְּיוֹם בְּרֹא אֱלֹהִים אָדָם

ב   בִּדְמוּת אֱלֹהִים עָשָׂה אֹתוֹ: זָכָר וּנְקֵבָה בְּרָאָם

וַיְבָרֶךְ אֹתָם וַיִּקְרָא אֶת־שְׁמָם אָדָם בְּיוֹם הִבָּרְאָם:

ג   וַיְחִי אָדָם שְׁלֹשִׁים וּמְאַת שָׁנָה וַיּוֹלֶד בִּדְמוּתוֹ כְּצַלְמוֹ

ד   וַיִּקְרָא אֶת־שְׁמוֹ שֵׁת: וַיִּהְיוּ יְמֵי־אָדָם אַחֲרֵי הוֹלִידוֹ

אֶת־שֵׁת שְׁמֹנֶה מֵאֹת שָׁנָה וַיּוֹלֶד בָּנִים וּבָנוֹת: וַיִּהְיוּ

ה   כָּל־יְמֵי אָדָם אֲשֶׁר־חַי תְּשַׁע מֵאוֹת שָׁנָה וּשְׁלֹשִׁים שָׁנָה

ו   וַיָּמֹת: ס וַיְחִי־שֵׁת חָמֵשׁ שָׁנִים וּמְאַת שָׁנָה וַיּוֹלֶד

ז   אֶת־אֱנוֹשׁ: וַיְחִי־שֵׁת אַחֲרֵי הוֹלִידוֹ אֶת־אֱנוֹשׁ שֶׁבַע

ח   שָׁנִים וּשְׁמֹנֶה מֵאוֹת שָׁנָה וַיּוֹלֶד בָּנִים וּבָנוֹת: וַיִּהְיוּ

כָּל־יְמֵי־שֵׁת שְׁתֵּים עֶשְׂרֵה שָׁנָה וּתְשַׁע מֵאוֹת שָׁנָה

וַיָּמֹת: ס

Genesis 5

1–8

1] This is the record of Adam's line.—When God created man, He made him in the likeness of God;   2] male and female He created them. And when they were created, He blessed them and called them Man.— 3] When Adam had lived 130 years, he begot a son in his likeness after his image, and he named him Seth.   4] After the birth of Seth, Adam lived 800 years and begot sons and daughters.   5] All the days that Adam lived came to 930 years; then he died.

6] When Seth had lived 105 years, he begot Enosh.   7] After the birth of Enosh, Seth lived 807 years and begot sons and daughters.   8] All the days of Seth came to 912 years; then he died.

5:5] *Adam lived ... 930 years.* We do not know whether these figures had any symbolic meaning or followed some particular scheme. In the Masoretic text the years of the antediluvians add up to 1656, in the Samaritan version to 1307, in the Septuagint to 2422.

ט וַיְחִי אֱנוֹשׁ תִּשְׁעִים שָׁנָה וַיּוֹלֶד אֶת־קֵינָן: וַיְחִי

י אֱנוֹשׁ אַחֲרֵי הוֹלִידוֹ אֶת־קֵינָן חֲמֵשׁ עֶשְׂרֵה שָׁנָה

יא וּשְׁמֹנֶה מֵאוֹת שָׁנָה וַיּוֹלֶד בָּנִים וּבָנוֹת: וַיִּהְיוּ כָּל־יְמֵי

יב אֱנוֹשׁ חָמֵשׁ שָׁנִים וּתְשַׁע מֵאוֹת שָׁנָה וַיָּמֹת: ס וַיְחִי

יג קֵינָן שִׁבְעִים שָׁנָה וַיּוֹלֶד אֶת־מַהֲלַלְאֵל: וַיְחִי קֵינָן

אַחֲרֵי הוֹלִידוֹ אֶת־מַהֲלַלְאֵל אַרְבָּעִים שָׁנָה וּשְׁמֹנֶה

יד מֵאוֹת שָׁנָה וַיּוֹלֶד בָּנִים וּבָנוֹת: וַיִּהְיוּ כָּל־יְמֵי קֵינָן עֶשֶׂר

טו שָׁנִים וּתְשַׁע מֵאוֹת שָׁנָה וַיָּמֹת: ס וַיְחִי מַהֲלַלְאֵל

טז חָמֵשׁ שָׁנִים וְשִׁשִּׁים שָׁנָה וַיּוֹלֶד אֶת־יָרֶד: וַיְחִי

מַהֲלַלְאֵל אַחֲרֵי הוֹלִידוֹ אֶת־יֶרֶד שְׁלֹשִׁים שָׁנָה וּשְׁמֹנֶה

יז מֵאוֹת שָׁנָה וַיּוֹלֶד בָּנִים וּבָנוֹת: וַיִּהְיוּ כָּל־יְמֵי מַהֲלַלְאֵל

חָמֵשׁ וְתִשְׁעִים שָׁנָה וּשְׁמֹנֶה מֵאוֹת שָׁנָה וַיָּמֹת: ס

יח וַיְחִי־יֶרֶד שְׁתַּיִם וְשִׁשִּׁים שָׁנָה וּמְאַת שָׁנָה וַיּוֹלֶד אֶת־

יט חֲנוֹךְ: וַיְחִי־יֶרֶד אַחֲרֵי הוֹלִידוֹ אֶת־חֲנוֹךְ שְׁמֹנֶה מֵאוֹת

Genesis 5

9–19

9] When Enosh had lived 90 years, he begot Kenan.   10] After the birth of Kenan, Enosh lived 815 years and begot sons and daughters.   11] All the days of Enosh came to 905 years; then he died.

12] When Kenan had lived 70 years, he begot Mahalalel.   13] After the birth of Mahalalel, Kenan lived 840 years and begot sons and daughters.   14] All the days of Kenan came to 910 years; then he died.

15] When Mahalalel had lived 65 years, he begot Jared.   16] After the birth of Jared, Mahalalel lived 830 years and begot sons and daughters.   17] All the days of Mahalalel came to 895 years; then he died.

18] When Jared had lived 162 years, he begot Enoch.   19] After the birth of

52

כ שָׁנָה וַיּוֹלֶד בָּנִים וּבָנוֹת: וַיִּהְיוּ כָּל־יְמֵי־יֶרֶד שְׁתַּיִם

כא וְשִׁשִּׁים שָׁנָה וּתְשַׁע מֵאוֹת שָׁנָה וַיָּמֹת: ס וַיְחִי חֲנוֹךְ

כב חָמֵשׁ וְשִׁשִּׁים שָׁנָה וַיּוֹלֶד אֶת־מְתוּשָׁלַח: וַיִּתְהַלֵּךְ חֲנוֹךְ

אֶת־הָאֱלֹהִים אַחֲרֵי הוֹלִידוֹ אֶת־מְתוּשֶׁלַח שְׁלֹשׁ מֵאוֹת

כג שָׁנָה וַיּוֹלֶד בָּנִים וּבָנוֹת: וַיְהִי כָּל־יְמֵי חֲנוֹךְ חָמֵשׁ

כד וְשִׁשִּׁים שָׁנָה וּשְׁלֹשׁ מֵאוֹת שָׁנָה: וַיִּתְהַלֵּךְ חֲנוֹךְ אֶת־

כה הָאֱלֹהִים וְאֵינֶנּוּ כִּי־לָקַח אֹתוֹ אֱלֹהִים: ס וַיְחִי

מְתוּשֶׁלַח שֶׁבַע וּשְׁמֹנִים שָׁנָה וּמְאַת שָׁנָה וַיּוֹלֶד אֶת־

כו לָמֶךְ: וַיְחִי מְתוּשֶׁלַח אַחֲרֵי הוֹלִידוֹ אֶת־לֶמֶךְ שְׁתַּיִם

וּשְׁמוֹנִים שָׁנָה וּשְׁבַע מֵאוֹת שָׁנָה וַיּוֹלֶד בָּנִים וּבָנוֹת:

כז וַיִּהְיוּ כָּל־יְמֵי מְתוּשֶׁלַח תֵּשַׁע וְשִׁשִּׁים שָׁנָה וּתְשַׁע

מֵאוֹת שָׁנָה וַיָּמֹת: ס

Genesis 5

20–27

Enoch, Jared lived 800 years and begot sons and daughters. 20] All the days of Jared came to 962 years; then he died.

21] When Enoch had lived 65 years, he begot Methuselah. 22] After the birth of Methuselah, Enoch walked with God 300 years; and he begot sons and daughters. 23] All the days of Enoch came to 365 years. 24] Enoch walked with God; then he was no more, for God took him.

25] When Methuselah had lived 187 years, he begot Lamech. 26] After the birth of Lamech, Methuselah lived 782 years and begot sons and daughters. 27] All the days of Methuselah came to 969 years; then he died.

24] *Enoch walked with God.* Like Noah later on (Gen. 6:9), he was a righteous man.

God took him. Like Moses and Elijah, he died in a way befitting one of God's intimates. Many legends grew around Enoch, and the Book of Enoch (probably written in the first century c.e.) relates how he was shown the mysteries of heaven and the ushering in of the messianic era. Islamic legend identifies him with Idris ("the expounder of books") in the Koran.

כח וַיְחִי־לֶמֶךְ שְׁתַּיִם וּשְׁמֹנִים שָׁנָה וּמְאַת שָׁנָה וַיּוֹלֶד

כט בֵּן: וַיִּקְרָא אֶת־שְׁמוֹ נֹחַ לֵאמֹר זֶה יְנַחֲמֵנוּ מִמַּעֲשֵׂנוּ

וּמֵעִצְּבוֹן יָדֵינוּ מִן־הָאֲדָמָה אֲשֶׁר אֵרְרָהּ יְהֹוָה:

ל וַיְחִי־לֶמֶךְ אַחֲרֵי הוֹלִידוֹ אֶת־נֹחַ חָמֵשׁ וְתִשְׁעִים

לא שָׁנָה וַחֲמֵשׁ מֵאֹת שָׁנָה וַיּוֹלֶד בָּנִים וּבָנוֹת: וַיְהִי

כָּל־יְמֵי־לֶמֶךְ שֶׁבַע וְשִׁבְעִים שָׁנָה וּשְׁבַע מֵאוֹת שָׁנָה

לב וַיָּמֹת: ס וַיְהִי־נֹחַ בֶּן־חֲמֵשׁ מֵאוֹת שָׁנָה וַיּוֹלֶד נֹחַ

אֶת־שֵׁם אֶת־חָם וְאֶת־יָפֶת:

א וַיְהִי כִּי־הֵחֵל הָאָדָם לָרֹב עַל־פְּנֵי הָאֲדָמָה וּבָנוֹת

ב יֻלְּדוּ לָהֶם: וַיִּרְאוּ בְנֵי־הָאֱלֹהִים אֶת־בְּנוֹת הָאָדָם כִּי

Genesis 5; 6

28–32; 1–2

28] When Lamech had lived 182 years, he begot a son. **29]** And he named him Noah, saying, "This one will provide us relief from our work and from the toil of our hands, out of the very soil which the LORD placed under a curse." **30]** After the birth of Noah, Lamech lived 595 years and begot sons and daughters. **31]** All the days of Lamech came to 777 years; then he died.

32] When Noah had lived 500 years, Noah begot Shem, Ham, and Japheth.

1] When men began to increase on earth and daughters were born to them, **2]** the

---

/According to legend, Moses died by a kiss of God [1] and Elijah was taken to heaven on a fiery chariot (II Kings 2:11)./

29] *He named him Noah.* A word play on נֹחַ יְנַחֲמֵנוּ (Noah shall provide relief).

6:2] *Divine beings.* בְּנֵי הָאֱלֹהִים. Others translate as "the sons of God" [2]. Hurrian, Phoenician, and Greek myths told of Titans, supermen of great stature and strength, who were supposedly the offspring of unions between gods and men.

/One old understanding was that these were angels, perhaps fallen ones [3]. Another view is that the text in Gen. 6:2 records an angelic sin and that Ps. 82:1, 6, 7 are references to this incident [4]. Cassuto (*ad loc.*) denies this as does the view that "It is not so much survival of mythology as a reply to it. It is not a fragment: the biblical author disposes of a distasteful subject as quickly as he can" [5].

Still another interpretation takes "divine beings" to refer to the descendants of Seth and takes "human daughters" to refer to the descendants of Cain [6]. The phrase has also been taken as recording inter-

טבת הֵנָּה וַיִּקְחוּ לָהֶם נָשִׁים מִכֹּל אֲשֶׁר בָּחָרוּ:

ג וַיֹּאמֶר יְהוָה לֹא־יָדוֹן רוּחִי בָאָדָם לְעֹלָם בְּשַׁגַּם הוּא

ד בָשָׂר וְהָיוּ יָמָיו מֵאָה וְעֶשְׂרִים שָׁנָה: הַנְּפִלִים הָיוּ

בָאָרֶץ בַּיָּמִים הָהֵם וְגַם אַחֲרֵי־כֵן אֲשֶׁר יָבֹאוּ בְּנֵי

הָאֱלֹהִים אֶל־בְּנוֹת הָאָדָם וְיָלְדוּ לָהֶם הֵמָּה הַגִּבֹּרִים

אֲשֶׁר מֵעוֹלָם אַנְשֵׁי הַשֵּׁם: פ

ה וַיַּרְא יְהוָה כִּי רַבָּה רָעַת הָאָדָם בָּאָרֶץ וְכָל־יֵצֶר

ו מַחְשְׁבֹת לִבּוֹ רַק רַע כָּל־הַיּוֹם: וַיִּנָּחֶם יְהוָה כִּי־עָשָׂה

Genesis 6

3–6

divine beings saw how beautiful the daughters of man were, and they took as wives any they liked. **3]** Then the LORD said, "My spirit shall not shield man forever, since he is but flesh; let the days allowed him be one hundred and twenty years." **4]** It was in those days, and later, that the Nephilim appeared on earth—after the divine beings had consorted with the daughters of man, who bore them sons. They were the heroes of old, the men of renown.

5] The LORD saw how great was man's wickedness on earth, and how every plan devised by his mind was nothing but evil all the time. **6]** And the LORD regretted

class marital unions: sons of the aristocracy married daughters of the common folk [7]./

3] *Shield.* The Hebrew meaning is uncertain.

One hundred and twenty years. Becomes the *ideal* life span (Moses will live 120 years), while the *expected* age of man is reduced to 70. "The days of our years are threescore years and ten" (Ps. 90:10). One hundred twenty is the multiple of 1 × 2 × 3 × 4 × 5 and reflects the biblical predilection for number symbolism [8] (see p. 11).
/According to some, one hundred twenty years represents a probationary period [9]./

4] *Nephilim.* A borrowed term or an archaism. Rashi, like most older sources, relates Nephilim

to the word נָפַל (*nafal*, fall): They are "the fallen ones." The Septuagint translation is "giants."
/When the spies whom Moses had sent returned, they reported that they had seen Nephilim in Canaan: "and we looked like grasshoppers to ourselves, and so we must have looked to them" (Num. 13:33). In another view, the "heroes of old," not the Nephilim, were the result of the superhuman marriages [10]./

5] *Plan devised by his mind.* This translation of לִבּוֹ (literally, "his heart") is idiomatic, since the heart was believed to be the seat of thought. The word יֵצֶר has been translated as "temperament" rather than "plan" [11].

6] *The Lord regretted.* The Hebrew root נחם can

אֶת־הָאָדָם בָּאָרֶץ וַיִּתְעַצֵּב אֶל־לִבּֽוֹ׃ וַיֹּאמֶר יְהוָֹה

אֶמְחֶה אֶת־הָאָדָם אֲשֶׁר־בָּרָאתִי מֵעַל פְּנֵי הָאֲדָמָה

מֵאָדָם עַד־בְּהֵמָה עַד־רֶמֶשׂ וְעַד־עוֹף הַשָּׁמָיִם כִּי

נִחַמְתִּי כִּי עֲשִׂיתִֽם׃ וְנֹחַ מָצָא חֵן בְּעֵינֵי יְהוָֹה׃

פ פ פ

Haftarah Bereshit, p. 513

that He had **made** man on earth, and His heart was saddened.   7] The LORD said,
"I will blot out from the earth the men whom I created—men together with beasts,
creeping things, and birds of the sky; for I regret that I made them."   8] But Noah
found favor with the LORD.

mean both "to change one's mind" and also
"comfort," a word play referring to Gen. 5:29.

7] *Together with beasts.* Animals are included in

the impending destruction because, according to
the biblical view, they existed for the sake of man.
According to Rashi, what use would there be for
animals if man ceased to exist?

The Early Generations

The reader will look in vain for an explanation of how the world suddenly became filled with people, the men and women of whom Cain was apparently afraid and who would build cities. The ancients tried to solve this difficulty by suggesting that twin sisters were born to Cain, Abel, and later Seth, and that in this fashion the earth was populated.

There is, however, no need for the modern student of the Bible to follow this line of speculation. If the text is silent on the matter, it is probably because it is not the purpose of this chapter to present mankind's ongoing story as much as it is to present an explanation of man's spiritual state. Thus, the Bible should here be understood as speaking of prototypes, not of actual people.

A comparison between the names of Cain's and Seth's descendants reveals a startling similarity and some duplication:

Adam	1	Enosh
Cain	2	Kenan
Enoch	3	Mahalalel
Irad	4	Jared
Mehujael	5	Enoch
Methusael	6	Methuselah
Lamech	7	Lamech
Naamah	8	Noah

Adam and Enosh both mean "man." Other names in the two lists are like-sounding, and by exchanging the places of Enoch and Mehujael we arrive at a single basic list, which in the biblical tradition is presented in two variants. Mankind has one ancestor (Adam or Enosh) and one line of descent.[1] Noah appears when the seven generations of prehistoric man have run their course.

There are strong parallels between these biblical genealogies and the Babylonian lists of antediluvian kings and their counselors. In both cases they name "culture-heroes" responsible for basic contributions to civilization, including the first cities. In both cases they end with the protagonist of the Deluge story. The genealogical interest was characteristic of the Western Semites [13]. "To dedicated guardians of sacred traditions, unbroken lineage meant a secure link with the remotest past and hence also a firm basis from which to face the future. These were vital statistics in more ways than one" [14].

While the parallels between the biblical and Babylonian traditions are clearly visible, there are also significant differences. The Babylonians attached these traditions only to their king lists, but the Bible treats the antediluvians as ancestors of one another and ultimately of all mankind. The Bible eschews all mythological allusions in these lists; that is, it deals with men and not with semidivine kings. Even the longevity attributed to Seth's line must be compared with that of the Babylonians, who were reputed to live for thousands of years. In the Bible, a thousand years is regarded as a day of God (Ps. 90:4), and no one of the ancients in the biblical account reaches the millennial age.

The longevity of the antediluvians should, therefore, be seen in the context of such ancient traditions. To say that Methuselah's 969 years were meant as shorter units, such as months, merely subjects the Torah to artificial interpretation. The Bible presents the list of the primevals and their long lives as an intermediate stage in man's development. Adam possessed potential immortality; his immediate descendants had, by our standards, very long life spans; the Patriarchs,

---

[1] The inclusion of Seth and the change from Cain to Kenan was probably due to the understandable disinclination to have all men appear to be descended from a murderer. It may also be that for this reason the term תּוֹלְדוֹת (*toledot*) is denied the Cain line. Note the midrash that suggests Naamah was Noah's wife [12].

Joseph, Moses, and Joshua, all lived past the century mark; thereafter, however, men have only the "normal" life span. In the biblical view, man's longevity is limited severely at some stage between prehistory and history, and only in the messianic days will man again reach the high ages of old (Isa. 65:20).

The Divine Beings

The notation about the legendary "divine beings" and their giant offspring may be regarded as the one mythological fragment retained in Genesis (see p. xviii). Why was it not excised? Possibly because it served as an introduction to the Flood story and as such appeared to say: Men became giants, achieved renown in their time, and were heroes by their own values. When God evaluated human development, He looked neither at man's size nor at his reputation but at his heart, and He found its devices evil. Hence, God resolved to make a new start with Noah.

GLEANINGS

Lamech

Marital problems, occasioned by the taking of two women, brought him mental distress, which explains the violent song attributed to him.

SAMUEL DAVID LUZZATTO [15]

Lamech's descendants were worthy of him: They developed great wealth and other doubtful accouterments of civilization; they refined the art of war and altogether encouraged man's belief in his own self-sufficiency. Lamech, the father of all of them, is thus represented as the very embodiment of human presumption.

MORDECAI M. KAPLAN [16]

The Most Important Verse in the Torah

Two second-century scholars, Rabbi Akiba and Ben Azzai, debated which was the most important principle in the Torah. Rabbi Akiba said: "Love your neighbor as yourself" [Lev. 19:18] is the greatest [for what is hateful to you do not do unto your neighbor]. Ben Azzai said: The greatest principle is Genesis 5:1: "This is the record of Adam's line. When God created man, He made him in the likeness of God." TALMUD [17]

Ben Azzai laid down a fundamental teaching of Judaism. For in the verse quoted, the scholar saw the basic declaration of human brotherhood: By tracing back the whole of the human race to one single ancestor, created by one God, the Bible taught that all men have *one* Creator—the heavenly Father—and *one* ancestor—the human father.

MENAHEM M. KASHER [18]

One Man

The same word, תּוֹלְדוֹת [lines], is used to describe the creation of the whole world [Gen. 2:4] and the creation of one man [Gen. 5:1]. This teaches that the life of one man is as dear in God's eyes as the whole universe. MIDRASH [19]

Men of Renown

Human corruption began at that time, and it began with the heroes of old, the men of renown (Gen. 6:4). Ever since, the debasement of society has started with "men of renown," that is, with those entrusted with responsibility and leadership. [20]

The Flood

Many diverse cultures tell stories about a great flood. It has been suggested that these recall an earth-wide catastrophe brought on either by a terrestrial eruption or by a celestial collision, which may have resulted in a rise in sea level sufficient to cover all continents. Recent scientific investigations have shown that, at some time near the transition between prehistory and history, flood waters from the Persian gulf may have covered the southern section of the Mesopotamian valley.

But the biblical account is far more than prehistoric memory or a variant of ancient folk legends; it is above all a story with a moral. Its themes are sin, righteousness, and man's second opportunity to live in accordance with, rather than opposed to, the will of God.

There is agreement between the biblical and other Near Eastern flood stories on many details—the ark, the raven, the dove—but there are fundamental differences in approach. In the Bible, it is human sin that causes the Flood; in the Babylonian-Akkadian epic of "Atrahasis," human boisterousness and noise disturb the sleep of the gods and cause them to react. In the Bible, Noah is saved so that he might begin the human voyage over again; in "Gilgamesh," the flood hero is elevated to immortal status and thereby is removed from human history.

ט אֵלֶּה תּוֹלְדֹת נֹחַ נֹחַ אִישׁ צַדִּיק תָּמִים הָיָה בְּדֹרֹתָיו
י אֶת־הָאֱלֹהִים הִתְהַלֶּךְ־נֹחַ: וַיּוֹלֶד נֹחַ שְׁלֹשָׁה בָנִים
יא אֶת־שֵׁם אֶת־חָם וְאֶת־יָפֶת: וַתִּשָּׁחֵת הָאָרֶץ לִפְנֵי
יב הָאֱלֹהִים וַתִּמָּלֵא הָאָרֶץ חָמָס: וַיַּרְא אֱלֹהִים אֶת־
הָאָרֶץ וְהִנֵּה נִשְׁחָתָה כִּי־הִשְׁחִית כָּל־בָּשָׂר אֶת־דַּרְכּוֹ
יג עַל־הָאָרֶץ: ס וַיֹּאמֶר אֱלֹהִים לְנֹחַ קֵץ כָּל־בָּשָׂר
בָּא לְפָנַי כִּי־מָלְאָה הָאָרֶץ חָמָס מִפְּנֵיהֶם וְהִנְנִי
יד מַשְׁחִיתָם אֶת־הָאָרֶץ: עֲשֵׂה לְךָ תֵּבַת עֲצֵי־גֹפֶר קִנִּים
תַּעֲשֶׂה אֶת־הַתֵּבָה וְכָפַרְתָּ אֹתָהּ מִבַּיִת וּמִחוּץ בַּכֹּפֶר:
טו וְזֶה אֲשֶׁר תַּעֲשֶׂה אֹתָהּ שְׁלֹשׁ מֵאוֹת אַמָּה אֹרֶךְ
הַתֵּבָה חֲמִשִּׁים אַמָּה רָחְבָּהּ וּשְׁלֹשִׁים אַמָּה קוֹמָתָהּ:

9] This is the line of Noah.—Noah was a righteous man; he was blameless in his age; Noah walked with God.— 10] Noah had three sons: Shem, Ham, and Japheth.

11] The earth became corrupt before God; the earth was filled with injustice. 12] When God saw how corrupt the earth was, for all flesh had corrupted its ways on earth, 13] God said to Noah, "I have decided to put an end to all flesh, for the earth is filled with lawlessness because of them: I am about to destroy them with the earth. 14] Make yourself an ark of gopher wood; make it an ark with compartments, and cover it inside and out with pitch. 15] This is how you shall make it: the length of the ark shall be three hundred cubits, its width fifty cubits, and its

---

6:11] *Lawlessness.* חָמָס. Others translate as "violence."

13] *Destroy them with the earth.* Others translate as "*from the earth*" [1].

14] *Gopher wood.* A species still unidentified.

15] *Cubit.* Figuring a cubit to be about eighteen inches, the ark's tonnage was over 40,000 tons, or as large as a good-sized modern passenger ship. To ancient man, such dimensions must have evoked a sense of great awe.

צֹהַר תַּעֲשֶׂה לַתֵּבָה וְאֶל־אַמָּה תְּכַלֶּנָּה מִלְמַעְלָה וּפֶתַח
הַתֵּבָה בְּצִדָּהּ תָּשִׂים תַּחְתִּיִּם שְׁנִיִּם וּשְׁלִשִׁים תַּעֲשֶׂהָ:

וַאֲנִי הִנְנִי מֵבִיא אֶת־הַמַּבּוּל מַיִם עַל־הָאָרֶץ לְשַׁחֵת
כָּל־בָּשָׂר אֲשֶׁר־בּוֹ רוּחַ חַיִּים מִתַּחַת הַשָּׁמָיִם כֹּל

אֲשֶׁר־בָּאָרֶץ יִגְוָע: וַהֲקִמֹתִי אֶת־בְּרִיתִי אִתָּךְ וּבָאתָ
אֶל־הַתֵּבָה אַתָּה וּבָנֶיךָ וְאִשְׁתְּךָ וּנְשֵׁי־בָנֶיךָ אִתָּךְ:

וּמִכָּל־הָחַי מִכָּל־בָּשָׂר שְׁנַיִם מִכֹּל תָּבִיא אֶל־הַתֵּבָה

לְהַחֲיֹת אִתָּךְ זָכָר וּנְקֵבָה יִהְיוּ: מֵהָעוֹף לְמִינֵהוּ וּמִן־
הַבְּהֵמָה לְמִינָהּ מִכֹּל רֶמֶשׂ הָאֲדָמָה לְמִינֵהוּ שְׁנַיִם

מִכֹּל יָבֹאוּ אֵלֶיךָ לְהַחֲיוֹת: וְאַתָּה קַח־לְךָ מִכָּל־
מַאֲכָל אֲשֶׁר יֵאָכֵל וְאָסַפְתָּ אֵלֶיךָ וְהָיָה לְךָ וְלָהֶם

לְאָכְלָה: וַיַּעַשׂ נֹחַ כְּכֹל אֲשֶׁר צִוָּה אֹתוֹ אֱלֹהִים כֵּן
עָשָׂה:

Genesis 6

16—22

height thirty cubits.   16] Make an opening for daylight in the ark, and terminate it within a cubit of the top. Put the entrance to the ark in its side; make it with bottom, second, and third decks.

17] "For My part, I am about to bring the Flood—waters upon the earth—to destroy all flesh under the sky in which there is breath of life; everything on earth shall perish.   18] But I will establish My covenant with you, and you shall enter the ark—you, your sons, your wife, and your sons' wives.   19] And of all that lives, of all flesh, you shall take two of each into the ark to keep alive with you; they shall be male and female.   20] From birds of every kind, cattle of every kind, every kind of creeping thing on earth, two of each shall come to you to stay alive.   21] For your part, take of everything that is eaten and store it away, to serve as food for you and for them."   22] Noah did so; just as God commanded him, so he did.

וַיֹּ֤אמֶר יְהוָה֙ לְנֹ֔חַ בֹּֽא־אַתָּ֥ה וְכָל־בֵּיתְךָ֖ אֶל־הַתֵּבָ֑ה א
כִּֽי־אֹתְךָ֥ רָאִ֛יתִי צַדִּ֥יק לְפָנַ֖י בַּדּ֣וֹר הַזֶּֽה: מִכֹּ֣ל ב
הַבְּהֵמָ֣ה הַטְּהוֹרָ֗ה תִּֽקַּֽח־לְךָ֛ שִׁבְעָ֥ה שִׁבְעָ֖ה אִ֣ישׁ
וְאִשְׁתּ֑וֹ וּמִן־הַבְּהֵמָ֡ה אֲ֠שֶׁר לֹ֣א טְהֹרָ֥ה הִ֛וא שְׁנַ֥יִם אִ֖ישׁ
וְאִשְׁתּֽוֹ: גַּ֣ם מֵע֧וֹף הַשָּׁמַ֛יִם שִׁבְעָ֥ה שִׁבְעָ֖ה זָכָ֣ר וּנְקֵבָ֑ה ג
לְחַיּ֥וֹת זֶ֖רַע עַל־פְּנֵ֥י כָל־הָאָֽרֶץ: כִּי֩ לְיָמִ֨ים ע֜וֹד ד
שִׁבְעָ֗ה אָֽנֹכִי֙ מַמְטִ֣יר עַל־הָאָ֔רֶץ אַרְבָּעִ֣ים י֔וֹם
וְאַרְבָּעִ֖ים לָ֑יְלָה וּמָחִ֗יתִי אֶֽת־כָּל־הַיְקוּם֙ אֲשֶׁ֣ר עָשִׂ֔יתִי
מֵעַ֖ל פְּנֵ֥י הָֽאֲדָמָֽה: וַיַּ֖עַשׂ נֹ֑חַ כְּכֹ֥ל אֲשֶׁר־צִוָּ֖הוּ יְהוָֽה: ה
וְנֹ֕חַ בֶּן־שֵׁ֥שׁ מֵא֖וֹת שָׁנָ֑ה וְהַמַּבּ֣וּל הָיָ֔ה מַ֖יִם עַל־הָאָֽרֶץ: ו
וַיָּ֣בֹא נֹ֗חַ וּ֠בָנָיו וְאִשְׁתּ֧וֹ וּנְשֵֽׁי־בָנָ֛יו אִתּ֖וֹ אֶל־הַתֵּבָ֑ה ז
מִפְּנֵ֖י מֵ֣י הַמַּבּֽוּל: מִן־הַבְּהֵמָה֙ הַטְּהוֹרָ֔ה וּמִן־הַ֨בְּהֵמָ֔ה ח

1] Then the LORD said to Noah, "Go into the ark, you and all your household, for you alone have I found righteous before Me in this generation. 2] Of every clean animal you shall take seven pairs, males and their mates, and of every animal which is not clean, two, a male and its mate; 3] of the birds of the sky also, seven pairs, male and female, to keep seed alive upon all the earth. 4] For in seven days' time I will make it rain upon the earth, forty days and forty nights, and I will blot out from the earth all existence that I created." 5] And Noah did just as the LORD commanded him.

6] Noah was six hundred years old when the Flood came, waters upon the earth. 7] Noah, with his sons, his wife, and his sons' wives, went into the ark because of the waters of the Flood. 8] Of the clean animals, of the animals that are not clean,

7:2] *Clean animal*. Fit, according to the laws of the Torah, for sacrifice.
Rashi and others: "Clean" according to dietary laws; fit for eating.

אֲשֶׁר אֵינֶנָּה טְהֹרָה וּמִן־הָעוֹף וְכֹל אֲשֶׁר־רֹמֵשׂ עַל־

ט הָאֲדָמָה: שְׁנַיִם שְׁנַיִם בָּאוּ אֶל־נֹחַ אֶל־הַתֵּבָה זָכָר

י וּנְקֵבָה כַּאֲשֶׁר צִוָּה אֱלֹהִים אֶת־נֹחַ: וַיְהִי לְשִׁבְעַת

יא הַיָּמִים וּמֵי הַמַּבּוּל הָיוּ עַל־הָאָרֶץ: בִּשְׁנַת שֵׁשׁ־מֵאוֹת

שָׁנָה לְחַיֵּי־נֹחַ בַּחֹדֶשׁ הַשֵּׁנִי בְּשִׁבְעָה־עָשָׂר יוֹם לַחֹדֶשׁ

בַּיּוֹם הַזֶּה נִבְקְעוּ כָּל־מַעְיְנוֹת תְּהוֹם רַבָּה וַאֲרֻבֹּת

יב הַשָּׁמַיִם נִפְתָּחוּ: וַיְהִי הַגֶּשֶׁם עַל־הָאָרֶץ אַרְבָּעִים יוֹם

יג וְאַרְבָּעִים לָיְלָה: בְּעֶצֶם הַיּוֹם הַזֶּה בָּא נֹחַ וְשֵׁם־וְחָם

וָיֶפֶת בְּנֵי־נֹחַ וְאֵשֶׁת נֹחַ וּשְׁלֹשֶׁת נְשֵׁי־בָנָיו אִתָּם אֶל־

יד הַתֵּבָה: הֵמָּה וְכָל־הַחַיָּה לְמִינָהּ וְכָל־הַבְּהֵמָה לְמִינָהּ

וְכָל־הָרֶמֶשׂ הָרֹמֵשׂ עַל־הָאָרֶץ לְמִינֵהוּ וְכָל־הָעוֹף

טו לְמִינֵהוּ כָּל־צִפּוֹר כָּל־כָּנָף: וַיָּבֹאוּ אֶל־נֹחַ אֶל־הַתֵּבָה

Genesis 7

9–15

of the birds, and of everything that creeps on the ground,   9] two of each, male
and female, came to Noah into the ark, as God had commanded Noah.   10] And
on the seventh day the waters of the Flood came upon the earth.

11] In the six hundredth year of Noah's life, in the second month, on the seventeenth day of the month, on that day

All the fountains of the great deep burst apart,

And the flood-gates of the sky broke open.

12] The rain fell on the earth forty days and forty nights.   13] That same day Noah
and Noah's sons, Shem, Ham, and Japheth, went into the ark, with Noah's wife and
the three wives of his sons— 14] they and all beasts of every kind, all cattle of every
kind, all creatures of every kind that creep on the earth, and all birds of every kind,
every bird, every winged thing.   15] They came to Noah into the ark, two each of

---

11] *In the second month.* Probably of the fall, when the rainy season begins in the Near East.

טז שְׁנַיִם שְׁנַיִם מִכָּל־הַבָּשָׂר אֲשֶׁר־בּוֹ רוּחַ חַיִּים: וְהַבָּאִים זָכָר וּנְקֵבָה מִכָּל־בָּשָׂר בָּאוּ כַּאֲשֶׁר צִוָּה אֹתוֹ אֱלֹהִים

יז וַיִּסְגֹּר יְהוָה בַּעֲדוֹ: וַיְהִי הַמַּבּוּל אַרְבָּעִים יוֹם עַל־הָאָרֶץ וַיִּרְבּוּ הַמַּיִם וַיִּשְׂאוּ אֶת־הַתֵּבָה וַתָּרָם מֵעַל הָאָרֶץ:

יח וַיִּגְבְּרוּ הַמַּיִם וַיִּרְבּוּ מְאֹד עַל־הָאָרֶץ וַתֵּלֶךְ הַתֵּבָה עַל־פְּנֵי הַמָּיִם: וְהַמַּיִם גָּבְרוּ מְאֹד מְאֹד עַל־

יט הָאָרֶץ וַיְכֻסּוּ כָּל־הֶהָרִים הַגְּבֹהִים אֲשֶׁר־תַּחַת כָּל־הַשָּׁמָיִם: חֲמֵשׁ עֶשְׂרֵה אַמָּה מִלְמַעְלָה גָּבְרוּ הַמָּיִם

כ וַיְכֻסּוּ הֶהָרִים: וַיִּגְוַע כָּל־בָּשָׂר הָרֹמֵשׂ עַל־הָאָרֶץ

כא בָּעוֹף וּבַבְּהֵמָה וּבַחַיָּה וּבְכָל־הַשֶּׁרֶץ הַשֹּׁרֵץ עַל־הָאָרֶץ וְכֹל הָאָדָם: כֹּל אֲשֶׁר נִשְׁמַת־רוּחַ חַיִּים

כב בְּאַפָּיו מִכֹּל אֲשֶׁר בֶּחָרָבָה מֵתוּ: וַיִּמַח אֶת־כָּל־

כג הַיְקוּם אֲשֶׁר עַל־פְּנֵי הָאֲדָמָה מֵאָדָם עַד־בְּהֵמָה

Genesis 7

16—23

all flesh in which there was breath of life.   16] Thus they that entered comprised male and female of all flesh, as God had commanded him. And the LORD shut him in.

17] The Flood continued forty days on the earth, and the waters increased and raised the ark so that it rose above the earth.   18] The waters swelled and increased greatly upon the earth, and the ark drifted upon the waters.   19] When the waters had swelled much more upon the earth, all the highest mountains everywhere under the sky were covered.   20] Fifteen cubits higher did the waters swell, as the mountains were covered.   21] And all flesh that stirred on earth perished— birds, cattle, beasts, and all the things that swarmed upon the earth, and all mankind. 22] All in whose nostrils was the merest breath of life, all that was on dry land, died.   23] All existence on earth was blotted out—man, cattle, creeping things,

עַד־רֶמֶשׂ וְעַד־עוֹף הַשָּׁמַיִם וַיִּמָּחוּ מִן־הָאָרֶץ וַיִּשָּׁאֶר

כד אַךְ־נֹחַ וַאֲשֶׁר אִתּוֹ בַּתֵּבָה: וַיִּגְבְּרוּ הַמַּיִם עַל־הָאָרֶץ

חֲמִשִּׁים וּמְאַת יוֹם:

א וַיִּזְכֹּר אֱלֹהִים אֶת־נֹחַ וְאֵת כָּל־הַחַיָּה וְאֶת־כָּל־

הַבְּהֵמָה אֲשֶׁר אִתּוֹ בַּתֵּבָה וַיַּעֲבֵר אֱלֹהִים רוּחַ עַל־

ב הָאָרֶץ וַיָּשֹׁכּוּ הַמָּיִם: וַיִּסָּכְרוּ מַעְיְנֹת תְּהוֹם וַאֲרֻבֹּת

הַשָּׁמָיִם וַיִּכָּלֵא הַגֶּשֶׁם מִן־הַשָּׁמָיִם: וַיָּשֻׁבוּ הַמַּיִם מֵעַל

ג הָאָרֶץ הָלוֹךְ וָשׁוֹב וַיַּחְסְרוּ הַמַּיִם מִקְצֵה חֲמִשִּׁים

ד וּמְאַת יוֹם: וַתָּנַח הַתֵּבָה בַּחֹדֶשׁ הַשְּׁבִיעִי בְּשִׁבְעָה־

ה עָשָׂר יוֹם לַחֹדֶשׁ עַל הָרֵי אֲרָרָט: וְהַמַּיִם הָיוּ הָלוֹךְ

וְחָסוֹר עַד הַחֹדֶשׁ הָעֲשִׂירִי בָּעֲשִׂירִי בְּאֶחָד לַחֹדֶשׁ

Genesis 7; 8

24; 1–5

and birds of the sky; they were blotted out from the earth. Only Noah was left, and those with him in the ark.

24] And when the waters had swelled on the earth one hundred and fifty days,

1] God remembered Noah and all the beasts and all the cattle that were with him in the ark, and God caused a wind to blow across the earth, and the waters subsided.   2] The fountains of the deep and the flood-gates of the sky were stopped up, and the rain from the sky was held back;   3] the waters then receded steadily from the earth. At the end of one hundred and fifty days the waters diminished, 4] so that in the seventh month, on the seventeenth day of the month, the ark came to rest on the mountains of Ararat.   5] The waters went on diminishing until the tenth month; in the tenth month, on the first of the month, the tops of the mountains became visible.

8:4] *Ararat*. A district in Armenia, known in ancient history as Urartu.

/ Later traditions point to the Zagros mountains, east of the middle Tigris, as the resting place of Noah's and Utnapishtim's arks./

י נִרְאוּ רָאשֵׁי הֶהָרִים: וַיְהִי מִקֵּץ אַרְבָּעִים יוֹם וַיִּפְתַּח

ז נֹחַ אֶת־חַלּוֹן הַתֵּבָה אֲשֶׁר עָשָׂה: וַיְשַׁלַּח אֶת־הָעֹרֵב

וַיֵּצֵא יָצוֹא וָשׁוֹב עַד־יְבֹשֶׁת הַמַּיִם מֵעַל הָאָרֶץ:

ח וַיְשַׁלַּח אֶת־הַיּוֹנָה מֵאִתּוֹ לִרְאוֹת הֲקַלּוּ הַמַּיִם מֵעַל

ט פְּנֵי הָאֲדָמָה: וְלֹא־מָצְאָה הַיּוֹנָה מָנוֹחַ לְכַף־רַגְלָהּ

וַתָּשָׁב אֵלָיו אֶל־הַתֵּבָה כִּי מַיִם עַל־פְּנֵי כָל־הָאָרֶץ

י וַיִּשְׁלַח יָדוֹ וַיִּקָּחֶהָ וַיָּבֵא אֹתָהּ אֵלָיו אֶל־הַתֵּבָה: וַיָּחֶל

עוֹד שִׁבְעַת יָמִים אֲחֵרִים וַיֹּסֶף שַׁלַּח אֶת־הַיּוֹנָה מִן־

יא הַתֵּבָה: וַתָּבֹא אֵלָיו הַיּוֹנָה לְעֵת עֶרֶב וְהִנֵּה עֲלֵה־זַיִת

טָרָף בְּפִיהָ וַיֵּדַע נֹחַ כִּי־קַלּוּ הַמַּיִם מֵעַל הָאָרֶץ:

יב וַיִּיָּחֶל עוֹד שִׁבְעַת יָמִים אֲחֵרִים וַיְשַׁלַּח אֶת־הַיּוֹנָה

וְלֹא־יָסְפָה שׁוּב־אֵלָיו עוֹד:

Genesis 8

6–12

6] At the end of forty days, Noah opened the window of the ark that he had made 7] and sent out the raven; it went to and fro until the waters had dried up from the earth.   8] Then he sent out the dove to see whether the waters had decreased from the surface of the ground.   9] But the dove could not find a resting place for its foot, and returned to him to the ark, for there was water over all the earth. So putting out his hand, he took it into the ark with him.   10] He waited another seven days, and again sent out the dove from the ark.   11] The dove came back to him toward evening, and there in its bill was a plucked-off olive leaf! Then Noah knew that the waters had decreased on the earth.   12] He waited still another seven days and sent the dove forth; and it did not return to him any more.

7] *The raven.* Birds were often used by ancient mariners as compasses. The Akkadian flood story also features a raven.

יג וַיְהִי בְּאַחַת וְשֵׁשׁ־מֵאוֹת שָׁנָה בָּרִאשׁוֹן בְּאֶחָד לַחֹדֶשׁ חָרְבוּ הַמַּיִם מֵעַל הָאָרֶץ וַיָּסַר נֹחַ אֶת־מִכְסֵה הַתֵּבָה וַיַּרְא וְהִנֵּה חָרְבוּ פְּנֵי הָאֲדָמָה: יד וּבַחֹדֶשׁ הַשֵּׁנִי בְּשִׁבְעָה וְעֶשְׂרִים יוֹם לַחֹדֶשׁ יָבְשָׁה הָאָרֶץ: ס

13] In the six hundred and first year, in the first month, on the first of the month, the waters began to dry from the earth; and when Noah removed the covering of the ark, he saw that the surface of the ground was drying.   14] And in the second month, on the twenty-seventh day of the month, the earth was dry.

The Generation of the Flood

According to the Bible, Methuselah died just before the Flood,[1] and except for Noah the period of the antediluvians had run its course. Thus, the Flood closes the first era in man's post-Eden story. The Torah pictures this era as marked by devolution: The moral fibre of man deteriorated beyond hope of regeneration.

What was the monstrous evil that brought on God's judgment? The Bible does not specify it beyond calling it חָמָס (chamas, lawlessness). But lawlessness (or violence, as some render it) is the manifestation of a social disease and not its cause. The Midrash speculates that it was unbounded affluence that caused men to become depraved, that wealth afforded them the leisure to discover new thrills and to commit sexual aberrations. Hand in hand with material prosperity went an overbearing attitude toward God [3], whom people judged to be incapable of hearing prayer and of enforcing moral standards.[2]

In the Christian tradition, Noah and his generation prefigure the end of time: Only those who take refuge in faith will escape judgment [5]. Similarly, the water of baptism represents salvation brought through water to Noah and his family [6].

The Man Noah

The Bible says that God chose to save Noah and his family from the Flood because he was "blameless in his age." A discussion of this phrase is recorded in the Talmud:

Rabbi Jochanan said: "Noah was blameless only in *his* age, but in other ages he would not have been considered righteous." Resh Lakish said: "He was righteous *even* in his age; how much more so would he have been righteous in other ages." In Rabbi Jochanan's view, Noah stood out only because so much evil surrounded him, so that "in his age" is a dubious compliment; in Resh Lakish's opinion, Noah is rendered special homage, for nothing is more difficult than to be honest, peaceful, and loving when deceit, violence, and hatred are the accepted patterns of society [7].

It is not possible to say which reading was intended by the biblical author. But Resh Lakish's interpretation of Noah as a nonconformist who opposed the value system of his own time appears to speak more clearly across the centuries.[3]

Two Questions about God

How can natural events be understood as judgments of God? Biblical man saw the hand of God in the Flood, just as he saw it working in other natural phenomena. Thus, the Flood is said to have lasted 364 days, to indicate that the very cycle of nature was interrupted until heaven and earth returned to their spheres a year later. While there are those whose faith still permits them to see a warning in every bolt of lightning and a retribution of the Divine in every natural disaster, most modern men do not believe in a God who arranges natural forces for the sake of man. In their view, the relevance of the Noah story is confined to its emphasis on God's moral judgment.

---

[1] Traditional sources insist that it is no coincidence that God held off the Flood until the mourning period for Methuselah had passed [2].

[2] There was also a tradition that the chief sin of the generation of the Flood lay in their refusal to beget children. Even Noah originally refused to marry and have children—note that his first child was not born until he was 500 years old. For he too said: "Why should I bring offspring into a world which will likely be destroyed?" [4].

[3] Resh Lakish may have based his view on Ezek. 14:14, where Noah, Daniel, and Job are considered truly righteous.

In considering the story as a homily on the consequences of man's corruption, lawlessness, and violence, we can affirm that they do bring on the judgment of God. We may experience it in man's social and moral conditions, or in nature's physical realm (as in our pollution of the atmosphere and water, or our disturbance of the ecological balance) [8]. God guarantees life and its laws. An offense against these is an offense against Him and may occasion dire and unforeseen consequences.[4]

How are we to understand the phrase, "God remembered" (Gen. 8:1)? The expression וַיִּזְכֹּר (*va-yizkor*), referring to God, occurs frequently in the Bible and consistently reflects a belief in moral continuity. What happened yesterday is not forgotten. It is stored up in divine memory and has a bearing on God's judgment in the future. The remembering God thus makes justice possible, even as among men there can be no ethical presence without ethical memories.

Many prayers in Jewish and Christian traditions ask God to remember. The Jewish memorial prayer begins with the words יִזְכֹּר אֱלֹהִים (*yizkor Elohim*, may God remember).

The Two Biblical Sources of the Flood Story

The Flood story presents a particularly striking example of the confluence of two traditions in the Torah. Occasionally—as in the first two chapters of Genesis and in the relation of the lines of Cain and Seth—the variant sources are fairly apparent. At other times, as here, the two traditions are so closely interwoven that at first glance they present a single strand. (See pp. xxi–xxii for a discussion of these sources and the reasons for maintaining them side by side, despite their contradictions.)

The following excerpts will show how the two sources (generally assigned to the J and P traditions) may have told the basic story. The condensed J-version is seen in chapters 6:5–6; 7:1–4, 10, 12; 8:8–12; 8:20–22; the P-version in chapters 6:12–13; 6:14, 20; 7:11, 24; 8:3, 7; 8:13, 18–19; 9:1–17. Note, for instance, how J speaks of God's feelings while P merely reports the decree. Bible scholars disagree over details; for instance, the tale of the raven is often ascribed to J. There are also those who deny altogether that the text can be dissected in this way.

---

[4] The Sages paid special attention to the relationship of human sin to the destruction of the animals [9].

J

The Lord saw man's wickedness and He regretted that He had made him. The Lord's heart was saddened.

Then He said to Noah: "Go into the ark for you alone have I found righteous . . . take with you seven pairs of clean and one pair of unclean animals, and seven pairs of birds. I will send forty days and nights of rain."

After seven days the Flood came. Rain fell for forty days and nights. Noah sent out a dove, but the dove found no place to

P

God saw how corrupt man was and He said to Noah: "I have decided to put an end to all flesh.

Make yourself an ark. Take with you two of everything that lives, male and female, of birds, cattle, and creeping things."

In the six-hundredth year of Noah's life, in the second month, on the seventeenth day the rain began. The

J

rest; he waited seven days, and the dove came back with an olive leaf. After another seven days the dove went out but did not return.

Noah left the ark. He built an altar and sacrificed of every clean animal and clean bird. The Lord in turn promised never to bring another flood.

P

waters swelled for one hundred and fifty days. At the end of that time the waters diminished. Noah sent out a raven. It went to and fro until the waters had dried up.

In Noah's six hundred and first year, on the twenty-seventh day of the second month, he and his family left the ark. God then made a covenant with Noah and set His rainbow in the sky as a sign that He would not bring another flood.

GLEANINGS

Two Flood Story Parallels from the Ancient Near East

The land became wide, the people became
    numerous,
The land bellowed like wild oxen.
The god was disturbed by their uproar.
[Enlil] heard their clamor
[and] said to the great gods:
"Oppressive has become the clamor of mankind.
By their uproar they prevent sleep."
FROM "ATRAHASIS" [10]

When the seventh day arrived
I sent forth and set free a dove.
The dove went forth but came back;
There was no resting place for it and she turned
    round.
Then I sent forth and set free a swallow.
The swallow went forth but came back;
There was no resting place for it and she turned
    round.
Then I sent forth and set free a raven.
The raven went forth and seeing the waters had
    diminished
He eats, circles, caws, but turns not round.
It ate, but returned not again.
FROM "GILGAMESH" [11]

Three Parallels to Noah

[The theme of the Flood hero's relationship to
his contemporaries appears in the following three
separate sources, which were written over a period
spanning more than 2,000 years. The "Gilgamesh"
passage may also echo an older tradition of conflict between Enlil and Ea (Enki). The Koran
clearly follows the midrashic tradition.]

Man of Shuruppak, son of Ubartutu,
Tear down this house, build a ship!
Give up possessions, seek thou life.
Despise property and keep the soul alive!

Aboard the ship take thou the seed of all living
    things.
The ship that thou shalt build,
Her dimensions shall be to measure.
Equal shall be her width and her length.
Like the Apsu thou shalt ceil her.

I understood, and I said to Ea, my lord:
"Behold, my lord, what thou hast thus ordered,
I shall be honored to carry out.
But what shall I answer the city, the people and
    elders?"
Ea opened his mouth to speak,
Saying to me, his servant:
"Thou shalt then thus speak unto them:
'I have learned that Enlil is hostile to me,
So that I cannot reside in your city,
Nor set my foot in Enlil's territory.
To the Deep I will therefore go down,
To dwell with my lord Ea.' "
FROM "GILGAMESH" [12]

Why did the Holy One, praised be He, command
Noah to make an ark? So that his fellow men might
see him at his labor and be moved to repent. Thus
thought God, but they paid no attention to Noah's
urgings.
MIDRASH [13]

We sent Noah to his people.
He said: "O my people,
Worship God! ye have
No other god but Him.
I fear for you the punishment
Of a dreadful day!"
The leaders of his people

Said: "Ah! we see thee
Evidently wandering (in mind)."
He said: "O my people!
No wandering is there

74

In my (mind): on the contrary
I am an apostle from
The Lord and cherisher
Of the worlds!

Do ye wonder that
There hath come to you
A message from your Lord,
Through a man of your own
People, to warn you,
So that ye may fear God
And haply receive His mercy?"

But they rejected him,
And We delivered him,
And those with him,
In the ark:
But We overwhelmed
In the Flood those
Who rejected Our signs.
They were indeed
A blind people!   KORAN [14]

Noah Lacked Compassion

Nowhere did Noah show a feeling of sadness
and pathos that an entire generation was to be
lost, and the world destroyed; that men had lost
their way of life and surrendered to their own
primeval drives and dark passions. At no time did
a word of concern, of solicitude escape Noah's lips.
It was as though he stood apart from the rest of
the world. Nowhere was there an expression of
tenderness, of regret that even though these men
were wicked they would be lost—they, their wives,
and their children. He did not leap forward with
a request to God to spare those who, perhaps with
the extension of greater mercy, might have been
spared.

Noah was a righteous man; Noah deserves to be
in the circle of the great. But there was a fatal
flaw in Noah, and so he did not become the father
of a new religion, a new faith, and a new community. He lacked compassion and, because he
lacked compassion, he forfeited the far greater
place in history that might have been accorded
him.   MORRIS ADLER [15]

Noah and Abraham

Noah's fate is bound to "his generation," but
Abraham's goes beyond his time, toward history.
Abraham's faithfulness is God's hope—not because of what Abraham *is* "in his generation" but
what he will *become*.   MARTIN BUBER [16]

After the Flood

With the Flood over, man begins once more to face the problems of existence. He is reassured that God will not again "destroy every living being" (Gen. 8:21) and that there is an immutable order that God himself will not abrogate. The rainbow is seen as God's signature to His promise, and the sons of Noah set out to people the world.

טו וַיְדַבֵּר אֱלֹהִים אֶל־נֹחַ לֵאמֹר:

טז צֵא מִן־הַתֵּבָה אַתָּה וְאִשְׁתְּךָ וּבָנֶיךָ וּנְשֵׁי־בָנֶיךָ אִתָּךְ:

יז כָּל־הַחַיָּה אֲשֶׁר־אִתְּךָ מִכָּל־בָּשָׂר בָּעוֹף וּבַבְּהֵמָה וּבְכָל־הָרֶמֶשׂ הָרֹמֵשׂ עַל־הָאָרֶץ הוֹצֵא* אִתָּךְ וְשָׁרְצוּ בָאָרֶץ וּפָרוּ וְרָבוּ עַל־הָאָרֶץ:

יח וַיֵּצֵא־נֹחַ וּבָנָיו וְאִשְׁתּוֹ וּנְשֵׁי־בָנָיו אִתּוֹ:

יט כָּל־הַחַיָּה כָּל־הָרֶמֶשׂ וְכָל־הָעוֹף כֹּל רוֹמֵשׂ עַל־הָאָרֶץ לְמִשְׁפְּחֹתֵיהֶם יָצְאוּ מִן־הַתֵּבָה:

כ וַיִּבֶן נֹחַ מִזְבֵּחַ לַיהוָה וַיִּקַּח מִכֹּל הַבְּהֵמָה הַטְּהֹרָה וּמִכֹּל הָעוֹף הַטָּהוֹר וַיַּעַל עֹלֹת בַּמִּזְבֵּחַ:

כא וַיָּרַח יְהוָה אֶת־רֵיחַ הַנִּיחֹחַ וַיֹּאמֶר יְהוָה אֶל־לִבּוֹ לֹא אֹסִף לְקַלֵּל

Genesis 8

15–21

* יז הוצא קרי.

15] God spoke to Noah, saying, 16] "Come out of the ark together with your wife, your sons, and your sons' wives. 17] Bring out with you every living thing of all flesh that is with you: birds, animals, and everything that creeps on earth; and let them swarm on the earth and be fertile and increase on earth." 18] So Noah came out, together with his sons, his wife, and his sons' wives. 19] Every animal, every creeping thing, and every bird, everything that stirs on earth came out of the ark by families.

20] Then Noah built an altar to the Lord and, taking of every clean animal and of every clean bird, he offered burnt offerings on the altar. 21] The Lord smelled the pleasing odor, and the Lord said to Himself: "Never again will I doom the world

8:21] *Smelled.* The Torah speaks of God in human terms. In its language, "smelling the pleasing odor" is equivalent to "accepting favorably" [1]. Compare this with a parallel incident in "Gilga- mesh": "The gods smelled the savor, / The gods smelled the goodly savor, / The gods gathered like flies over the sacrificer" [2].

Evil from his youth. The Flood has not changed the nature of man.

עוֹד אֶת־הָאֲדָמָה בַּעֲבוּר הָאָדָם כִּי יֵצֶר לֵב הָאָדָם

רַע מִנְּעֻרָיו וְלֹא־אֹסִף עוֹד לְהַכּוֹת אֶת־כָּל־חַי כַּאֲשֶׁר

כב עָשִׂיתִי: עֹד כָּל־יְמֵי הָאָרֶץ זֶרַע וְקָצִיר וְקֹר וָחֹם

וְקַיִץ וָחֹרֶף וְיוֹם וָלַיְלָה לֹא יִשְׁבֹּתוּ:

א וַיְבָרֶךְ אֱלֹהִים אֶת־נֹחַ וְאֶת־בָּנָיו וַיֹּאמֶר לָהֶם פְּרוּ

ב וּרְבוּ וּמִלְאוּ אֶת־הָאָרֶץ: וּמוֹרַאֲכֶם וְחִתְּכֶם יִהְיֶה עַל

כָּל־חַיַּת הָאָרֶץ וְעַל כָּל־עוֹף הַשָּׁמָיִם בְּכֹל אֲשֶׁר

ג תִּרְמֹשׂ הָאֲדָמָה וּבְכָל־דְּגֵי הַיָּם בְּיֶדְכֶם נִתָּנוּ: כָּל־

רֶמֶשׂ אֲשֶׁר הוּא־חַי לָכֶם יִהְיֶה לְאָכְלָה כְּיֶרֶק עֵשֶׂב

ד נָתַתִּי לָכֶם אֶת־כֹּל: אַךְ־בָּשָׂר בְּנַפְשׁוֹ דָמוֹ לֹא תֹאכֵלוּ:

ה וְאַךְ אֶת־דִּמְכֶם לְנַפְשֹׁתֵיכֶם אֶדְרֹשׁ מִיַּד כָּל־חַיָּה

Genesis 8; 9
22; 1–5

because of man, since the devisings of man's mind are evil from his youth; nor will I ever again destroy every living being, as I have done. **22]** So long as the earth endures, / Seedtime and harvest, / Cold and heat, / Summer and winter, / Day and night, / Shall not cease."

1] God blessed Noah and his sons, and said to them, "Be fertile and increase, and fill the earth. **2]** The fear and the dread of you shall be upon all the beasts of the earth and upon all the birds of the sky—everything with which the earth is astir—and upon all the fish of the sea; they are given into your hand. **3]** Every creature that lives shall be yours to eat; as with the green grasses, I give you all these. **4]** You must not, however, eat flesh with its life-blood in it. **5]** For your life-blood, too, I will require a reckoning: of every beast will I require it; of man, too, will I require

9:3] *Yours to eat.* Adam was restricted to a vegetarian diet (Gen. 1:29); Noah and his descendants are permitted the flesh of animals.

4] *Life-blood in it.* The prohibition reflects the conviction that blood has a sacral character.

5] *I will require it of every beast.* Animals, too, are held responsible for acts of violence against man: "When an ox gores a man or a woman to death, the ox shall be stoned" (Exod. 21:28) [3].

אֶדְרְשֶׁנּוּ וּמִיַּד הָאָדָם מִיַּד אִישׁ אָחִיו אֶדְרֹשׁ אֶת־נֶפֶשׁ

ו הָאָדָם: שֹׁפֵךְ דַּם הָאָדָם בָּאָדָם דָּמוֹ יִשָּׁפֵךְ כִּי

ז בְּצֶלֶם אֱלֹהִים עָשָׂה אֶת־הָאָדָם: וְאַתֶּם פְּרוּ וּרְבוּ

ח שִׁרְצוּ בָאָרֶץ וּרְבוּ־בָהּ: ס וַיֹּאמֶר אֱלֹהִים אֶל־נֹחַ

ט וְאֶל־בָּנָיו אִתּוֹ לֵאמֹר: וַאֲנִי הִנְנִי מֵקִים אֶת־בְּרִיתִי

י אִתְּכֶם וְאֶת־זַרְעֲכֶם אַחֲרֵיכֶם: וְאֵת כָּל־נֶפֶשׁ הַחַיָּה

אֲשֶׁר אִתְּכֶם בָּעוֹף בַּבְּהֵמָה וּבְכָל־חַיַּת הָאָרֶץ אִתְּכֶם

יא מִכֹּל יֹצְאֵי הַתֵּבָה לְכֹל חַיַּת הָאָרֶץ: וַהֲקִמֹתִי אֶת־

בְּרִיתִי אִתְּכֶם וְלֹא־יִכָּרֵת כָּל־בָּשָׂר עוֹד מִמֵּי הַמַּבּוּל

יב וְלֹא־יִהְיֶה עוֹד מַבּוּל לְשַׁחֵת הָאָרֶץ: וַיֹּאמֶר אֱלֹהִים

זֹאת אוֹת־הַבְּרִית אֲשֶׁר־אֲנִי נֹתֵן בֵּינִי וּבֵינֵיכֶם וּבֵין

Genesis 9

6–12

---

a reckoning for human life, of every man for that of his fellow man!   **6]** Whoever sheds the blood of man, / By man shall his blood be shed; / For in the image of God / Was man created.   **7]** Be fertile, then, and increase; abound on the earth and increase on it."

8] And God said to Noah and to his sons with him,   **9]** "I now establish My covenant with you and your offspring to come,   **10]** and with every living thing that is with you—birds, cattle, and every wild beast as well—all that have come out of the ark, every living thing on earth.   **11]** I will maintain My covenant with you: never again shall all flesh be cut off by the waters of a flood, and never again shall there be a flood to destroy the earth."

12] God further said, "This is the sign of the covenant that I set between Me and

---

9] *My covenant.* This is the first time the word בְּרִית (berit) is mentioned in the Bible. The term is often used with the verb כָּרַת (cut). "To cut a berit" is idiomatic for "to conclude a covenant." (See Gen. 15:10.)

81

כָּל־נֶפֶשׁ חַיָּה אֲשֶׁר אִתְּכֶם לְדֹרֹת עוֹלָם: אֶת־קַשְׁתִּי
נָתַתִּי בֶּעָנָן וְהָיְתָה לְאוֹת בְּרִית בֵּינִי וּבֵין הָאָרֶץ:

וְהָיָה בְּעַנְנִי עָנָן עַל־הָאָרֶץ וְנִרְאֲתָה הַקֶּשֶׁת בֶּעָנָן:

וְזָכַרְתִּי אֶת־בְּרִיתִי אֲשֶׁר בֵּינִי וּבֵינֵיכֶם וּבֵין כָּל־נֶפֶשׁ
חַיָּה בְּכָל־בָּשָׂר וְלֹא־יִהְיֶה עוֹד הַמַּיִם לְמַבּוּל לְשַׁחֵת
כָּל־בָּשָׂר: וְהָיְתָה הַקֶּשֶׁת בֶּעָנָן וּרְאִיתִיהָ לִזְכֹּר בְּרִית
עוֹלָם בֵּין אֱלֹהִים וּבֵין כָּל־נֶפֶשׁ חַיָּה בְּכָל־בָּשָׂר אֲשֶׁר
עַל־הָאָרֶץ: וַיֹּאמֶר אֱלֹהִים אֶל־נֹחַ זֹאת אוֹת־הַבְּרִית
אֲשֶׁר הֲקִמֹתִי בֵּינִי וּבֵין כָּל־בָּשָׂר אֲשֶׁר עַל־הָאָרֶץ: פ

וַיִּהְיוּ בְנֵי־נֹחַ הַיֹּצְאִים מִן־הַתֵּבָה שֵׁם וְחָם וָיָפֶת וְחָם
הוּא אֲבִי כְנָעַן: שְׁלֹשָׁה אֵלֶּה בְּנֵי־נֹחַ וּמֵאֵלֶּה נָפְצָה

Genesis 9

13–19

you, and every living creature with you, for all ages to come.   13] I have set My bow in the clouds, and it shall serve as a sign of the covenant between Me and the earth.   14] When I bring clouds over the earth, and the bow appears in the clouds, 15] I will remember My covenant between Me and you and every living creature among all flesh, so that the waters shall never again become a flood to destroy all flesh.   16] When the bow is in the clouds, I will see it and remember the everlasting covenant between God and all living creatures, all flesh that is on earth. 17] That," God said to Noah, "shall be the sign of the covenant that I have established between Me and all flesh that is on earth."

18] The sons of Noah who came out of the ark were Shem, Ham, and Japheth— Ham being the father of Canaan.   19] These three were the sons of Noah, and from these the whole world branched out.

18] *Shem.* Ancestor of all Semites.
Ham being the father of Canaan. As far as the

Torah is concerned, this is Ham's primary importance.

כא כָּל־הָאָרֶץ: וַיָּחֶל נֹחַ אִישׁ הָאֲדָמָה וַיִּטַּע כָּרֶם: וַיֵּשְׁתְּ
כב מִן־הַיַּיִן וַיִּשְׁכָּר וַיִּתְגַּל בְּתוֹךְ אָהֳלֹה: וַיַּרְא חָם אֲבִי
כג כְנַעַן אֵת עֶרְוַת אָבִיו וַיַּגֵּד לִשְׁנֵי־אֶחָיו בַּחוּץ: וַיִּקַּח
שֵׁם וָיֶפֶת אֶת־הַשִּׂמְלָה וַיָּשִׂימוּ עַל־שְׁכֶם שְׁנֵיהֶם וַיֵּלְכוּ
אֲחֹרַנִּית וַיְכַסּוּ אֵת עֶרְוַת אֲבִיהֶם וּפְנֵיהֶם אֲחֹרַנִּית
כד וְעֶרְוַת אֲבִיהֶם לֹא רָאוּ: וַיִּיקֶץ נֹחַ מִיֵּינוֹ וַיֵּדַע אֵת
כה אֲשֶׁר־עָשָׂה לוֹ בְּנוֹ הַקָּטָן: וַיֹּאמֶר אָרוּר כְּנָעַן עֶבֶד
כו עֲבָדִים יִהְיֶה לְאֶחָיו: וַיֹּאמֶר בָּרוּךְ יְהֹוָה אֱלֹהֵי שֵׁם
כז וִיהִי כְנַעַן עֶבֶד לָמוֹ: יַפְתְּ אֱלֹהִים לְיֶפֶת וְיִשְׁכֹּן

Genesis 9

20–27

20] Noah, the tiller of the soil, was the first to plant a vineyard. 21] He drank of the wine and became drunk, and he uncovered himself within his tent. 22] Ham, the father of Canaan, saw his father's nakedness and told his two brothers outside. 23] But Shem and Japheth took a cloth, placed it against both their backs and, walking backwards, they covered their father's nakedness; their faces were turned the other way, so that they did not see their father's nakedness. 24] When Noah woke up from his wine and learned what his youngest son had done to him, 25] he said, "Cursed be Canaan; / The lowest of slaves / Shall he be to his brothers." 26] And he said, "Blessed be the LORD, / The God of Shem; / Let Canaan be a slave to them. / 27] May God enlarge

20] *To plant a vineyard.* Wine growing is represented as an ancient practice.
/Compare the Greek stories of Deucalion and Dionysus and of "Gilgamesh" which tells of Utnapishtim giving wine to his ark-building workmen./
24] *His youngest son.* Ham is here called the youngest; elsewhere (Gen. 9:18; 10:1) he is listed as the middle brother. Critics see two separate traditions here. Older commentators took "youngest" to mean "unworthy," as in Gen. 32:11.
25] *The lowest of slaves.* The Hebrew idiom is

"slave of slaves."
26] *Blessed be the Lord.* Noah blesses not Shem but Shem's God, for blessing a person's divine protector represented or reinforced the blessing of the person himself (cf. I Sam. 25:32).
Canaan be a slave. Advocates of the black man's slavery used to base their beliefs on this text, but this passage deals with political subjection and has nothing whatsoever to do with race.
27] *May God enlarge Japheth.* A word play on יַפְתְּ–יֶפֶת. Japheth here most likely refers to the

כח בְּאָהֳלֵי־שֵׁם וִיהִי כְנַעַן עֶבֶד לָמוֹ: וַיְחִי־נֹחַ אַחַר

כט הַמַּבּוּל שְׁלֹשׁ מֵאוֹת שָׁנָה וַחֲמִשִּׁים שָׁנָה: וַיִּהְיוּ כָּל־

יְמֵי־נֹחַ תְּשַׁע מֵאוֹת שָׁנָה וַחֲמִשִּׁים שָׁנָה וַיָּמֹת: פ

Japheth, / And let him dwell in the tents of Shem; / And let Canaan be a slave to them."

28] Noah lived after the Flood 350 years.   29] And all the days of Noah came to 950 years; then he died.

Philistines, while Shem refers to the Israelites. Genesis (unlike Judges and Samuel) envisions the Philistines and Israelites as living in harmony. The verse, therefore, probably means: "May God make room for the Philistines that they might dwell peacefully with Israel" [4].

The Rainbow

In ancient mythologies a rainbow represented instruments used by gods in battle. The bows would be hung in the sky as symbols of victory. In Babylonian tradition, for example, the god Marduk suspended his bow in the heavens after he had defeated Tiamat, the goddess of the deep waters. The Bible has retained aspects of such myths. The Hebrew word קֶשֶׁת (keshet) means both "bow of war" and "rainbow," but as usual the Torah has assimilated the material to convey a deeper meaning.

It believes that God is the proximate cause of all natural events and that manifestations of the natural order are invested with divine portent.[1] Thunder, earthquakes, and floods fall under this rubric as does the rainbow (see p. 71). The text sees the bow both as a sign of God's rulership over the natural order and as God's permanent signature to His promise. The rainbow is thought to remind God of this promise and to remind man of the grace and forbearance of his Creator.

The Crime of Ham

The punishment meted out to Ham seems harsh in the extreme, and this harshness suggests that the Bible was referring to a transgression far more serious than seeing one's father naked and in a drunken stupor. Uncovering a relative's nakedness was a biblical euphemism for sexual relations (see Lev. 18). The story of Ham and Noah should be read, therefore, as one of sexual perversion.

The brevity of the biblical story may be due to the expurgation of a more detailed version, but even in the condensed form the ancient Israelites doubtlessly understood its implication.[2] In the context of Genesis, the tale was a subtle assertion that the Hamites (Egyptians) and the Canaanites were the descendants of sexual deviates. The crime of Ham, therefore, belongs to the genre of polemics employed against Israel's nearest neighbors and dearest enemies.

It is worth noting that the Bible assigned a prominent place to the theme of sexuality in the stories of both the first antediluvians (Adam and Eve) and the first postdiluvians (Noah and his offspring). Further, the motif of sexual aberration linked to drunkenness occurs again in the story of Lot and his daughters—a story that ends by asserting that Moab and Ammon also were nations of indecent sexual background (Gen. 19:32–38).

The Noahide Laws

Even before the revelation at Sinai there were certain laws, according to the Rabbis, that were binding on all men. This view holds that while Jews are subject to the extensive provisions of the Torah all non-Jews must observe at least a number of fundamental precepts deemed essential for the maintenance of a decent society. These laws are called "Noahide"; they were believed to have been incumbent on the sons of Noah and therefore to have become obligatory for man-

---

[1] A number of commentators follow Saadia who interprets Gen. 9:13 to mean that while God had previously created the rainbow as part of the natural order He now invested it with meaning [5]. Ibn Ezra rejects this view.

[2] The Talmud records an argument on this matter between Rav and Samuel. One of them believed that Noah had been castrated, the other that he had been abused sexually [6]. The argument may appear far-fetched unless viewed in conjunction with an old Canaanite myth that told how the god El-Kronos had emasculated his father and with the Hurrian legend that told how Kumarbis severed the genitals of his father, the god Anu. In the Midrash [7] Ham is portrayed as laughing at his father, and so is Kumarbis who like Ham is cursed for his deed. Evidently these old mythic traditions were current millennia after they were first told, and we may assume that they were familiar to the biblical author.

kind, since from Noah's sons "the whole world branched out" (Gen. 9:19) [8].

In interpreting chapter 2, verse 16,[3] the Rabbis established six such basic laws: Man may not worship idols; he may not blaspheme God; he must establish courts of justice; he may not kill; he may not commit adultery; and he may not rob. A seventh law—that man may not eat flesh cut from a living animal—was added after the Flood (Gen. 9:4). Rabbinic lists vary [10], but the basic concept remains the same: every man can arrive at and must come to observe a minimum of religious and legal precepts.[4]

Consequently, Jewish tradition distinguished between three types of Gentiles: the *Nochri* (*Akkum*), who does not observe the Noahide laws; the *Ben Noah*, who does; and the *Ger Toshav*, who officially declares before a court that he will observe the seven precepts. The latter was then given the privilege of becoming a resident alien in the Holy Land. "Unlike Christianity, Judaism does not deny salvation to those outside of its fold, for, according to Jewish law, all non-Jews who observe the Noahide laws will participate in salvation and in the rewards of the world to come" [12].

But if most of these laws were already known to Adam, why were they named for Noah and not Adam? "The answer is that all law must be rooted in a covenant, and before Noah there was no covenant. There is a legal relationship implied in the fulfilment of ethical commandments" [13]. God's covenant with Noah established the framework in which it became possible to speak of law.

A Source of Jewish Law

Several biblical passages in this section became the reference points or proof texts for certain regulations of later Jewish law.

The prohibition against consuming blood was based on "You must not, however, eat flesh with its life-blood in it" (Gen. 9:4). While this was taken to refer primarily to a limb from a living animal (אֵבֶר מִן הַחַי), it also became a foundation for many Jewish dietary and slaughtering regulations [14].

The prohibition against self-injury and suicide was based on "for your own life-blood I will require a reckoning" (Gen. 9:5) [15]. Note that in biblical times suicide was rare (except under stress of battle; see I Sam. 31:4; I Kings 16:18). The only other incident recorded is the death of Ahithophel (II Sam. 17:23).

The limits of self-defense were discussed in reference to chapter 9, verse 6, which forbids bloodshed because God made man in His image. Since one man's blood is not redder (i.e., better) than another's, no man may take an innocent life even if this is the only way to save his own [16].

The prohibition against abortion was based on the same verse, but reading it in a different way: "Whoever sheds the blood of *man in man*" [17].

The duty to have children was derived from "Be fertile and increase" (Gen. 9:1, 7). When God first said that man should be fertile (Gen. 1:28), it was a blessing: here it is issued as a command, and several children must be fathered in order to fulfil it [18].

---

[3] The command (in Gen. 2:16) to Adam (i.e., to all men) is taken to imply that all men can have a concept of God and are therefore forbidden to blaspheme Him or to practice idolatry. "Commanded" is taken to presuppose law hence meaning that every society is bound to establish courts of law. In this homiletic fashion three other basic prohibitions are derived [9].

[4] The rabbinic tradition is reflected in Paul's teaching about Noahides. He requires of Gentiles that they abstain from the pollutions of idols, from eating blood and the meat of strange animals, and from fornication [11].

GLEANINGS

Carnivorous Man

God, surveying the survivors of the Flood, judges man to have remained what he always was, namely, "evil from his youth" (Gen. 8:21). Antediluvian man had been rapacious and violent, and postdiluvian man still is. The permission to eat flesh appears therefore as God's resigned adjustment to the human reality.

Noah's Drunkenness

God said to Noah: "You should have been warned by the example of Adam whose perdition came about through eating the fruit of the vine." It is taught that the tree from which the original Adam ate was the vine, for there is nothing which brings man as much misery as wine.

TALMUD [19]

The story of Noah's drunkenness expresses the healthy recoil of primitive Semitic morality from the licentious habits engendered by a civilization the salient feature of which was the enjoyment and abuse of wine.

JOHN SKINNER [20]

The Waters of Noah

For this is as the waters of Noah unto Me;
For as I have sworn that the waters of Noah
Should no more go over the earth,
So have I sworn that I would not be wroth with
  you,
Nor rebuke you.

For the mountains may depart,
And the hills be removed;
But My kindness shall not depart from you,
Neither shall My covenant of peace be removed,
Says the Lord that has compassion on you.

ISAIAH 54:9–10

[Read as the prophetic portion (*Haftarah*) when the Noah story is the assigned weekly Torah reading (*sidrah*).]

The Nations

Chapter 10 is an overview of the nations known to biblical tradition. It belongs to the last segment of the book in which the canvas is universal; thereafter, its focus contracts toward its major theme: the emergence of one family and the people who will descend from it. The table of nations is therefore more than a catalog of names; it is the background for the stories to follow.

בראשית י
א–ז

א וְאֵלֶּה תּוֹלְדֹת בְּנֵי־נֹחַ שֵׁם חָם וָיָפֶת וַיִּוָּלְדוּ לָהֶם
ב בָּנִים אַחַר הַמַּבּוּל: בְּנֵי יֶפֶת גֹּמֶר וּמָגוֹג וּמָדַי וְיָוָן
ג וְתֻבָל וּמֶשֶׁךְ וְתִירָס: וּבְנֵי גֹּמֶר אַשְׁכְּנַז וְרִיפַת וְתֹגַרְמָה:
ד וּבְנֵי יָוָן אֱלִישָׁה וְתַרְשִׁישׁ כִּתִּים וְדֹדָנִים: מֵאֵלֶּה
ה נִפְרְדוּ אִיֵּי הַגּוֹיִם בְּאַרְצֹתָם אִישׁ לִלְשֹׁנוֹ לְמִשְׁפְּחֹתָם
ו בְּגוֹיֵהֶם: וּבְנֵי חָם כּוּשׁ וּמִצְרַיִם וּפוּט וּכְנָעַן: וּבְנֵי

Genesis 10

1–7

1] These are the lines of Shem, Ham, and Japheth, the sons of Noah: sons were born to them after the Flood.

2] The descendants of Japheth: Gomer, Magog, Madai, Javan, Tubal, Meshech, and Tiras. 3] The descendants of Gomer: Ashkenaz, Riphath, and Togarmah. 4] The descendants of Javan: Elishah and Tarshish, the Kittim, and the Dodanim. 5] From these the maritime nations branched out. [These are the sons of Japheth] by their lands—each with its language—their clans and their nations.

6] The descendants of Ham: Cush, Mizraim, Put, and Canaan. 7] The descend-

10:2] *Gomer.* Probably the Cimmerians (from which today's Welsh derive their name Cymry).

Magog. The land of Gog (Ezek. 38:2; 39:6), in Armenia.

3] *Ashkenaz.* Probably the Scythians. In Medieval Hebrew this name was given to Germany, and Jews from Central and Eastern Europe were called Ashkenazim, in contrast to the Spanish and Oriental Jews, called Sephardim.

4] *Tarshish.* Best known as the place to which Jonah tried to flee. It is usually identified as Tartessos in Spain.

/However, since Spain seems to lie outside the geographic range mentioned in Gen. 10, this may refer to another place by the same name, perhaps Tarsus in Cilicia, Asia Minor. It is also possible that Tarshish was originally a generic word meaning refinery./

Dodanim. In I Chron. 1:7 and the Septuagint, the name given is *Rodanim,* possibly referring to people from Rhodes.

/Others have *Dordanim,* which would refer to Dardania, near Troy [1]./

5] *Descendants of Japheth.* The bracketed portion of the sentence was probably omitted through scribal error.

6] *Cush.* Either Ethiopia or Midian (north of the Gulf of Aqaba).

/In other contexts the name may refer to the Kassites, a people who ruled Babylonia from the sixteenth to the twelfth centuries B.C.E. and then retreated to the highlands east of the Tigris. That Cush may refer to Midian is evidenced by Exod. 2:16, 21 ff. and Num. 12:1 [2] as well as by Egyptian execration texts which place Cush south of the Dead Sea./

Mizraim. Egypt.

Canaan. His listing as a descendant of Ham

כוּשׁ סְבָא וַחֲוִילָה וְסַבְתָּה וְרַעְמָה וְסַבְתְּכָא וּבְנֵי

ח רַעְמָה שְׁבָא וּדְדָן: וְכוּשׁ יָלַד אֶת־נִמְרֹד הוּא הֵחֵל

ט לִהְיוֹת גִּבֹּר בָּאָרֶץ: הוּא־הָיָה גִבֹּר־צַיִד לִפְנֵי יְהֹוָה

י עַל־כֵּן יֵאָמַר כְּנִמְרֹד גִּבּוֹר צַיִד לִפְנֵי יְהֹוָה: וַתְּהִי

רֵאשִׁית מַמְלַכְתּוֹ בָּבֶל וְאֶרֶךְ וְאַכַּד וְכַלְנֵה בְּאֶרֶץ

יא שִׁנְעָר: מִן־הָאָרֶץ הַהִוא יָצָא אַשּׁוּר וַיִּבֶן אֶת־נִינְוֵה

יב וְאֶת־רְחֹבֹת עִיר וְאֶת־כָּלַח: וְאֶת־רֶסֶן בֵּין נִינְוֵה וּבֵין

ants of Cush: Seba, Havilah, Sabtah, Raamah, and Sabteca. The descendants of Raamah: Sheba and Dedan.

8] Cush also begot Nimrod, who was the first man of power on earth.   9] He was a mighty hunter by the grace of the LORD; hence the saying, "Like Nimrod a mighty hunter by the grace of the LORD."   10] The mainstays of his kingdom were Babylon, Erech, Accad, and Calneh in the land of Shinar.   11] From that land Asshur went forth and built Nineveh, Rehoboth-ir, Calah,   12] and Resen between Nineveh and Calah, that is the great city.

suggests an age in which Egypt's rule extended into Asia, Canaan, and beyond, before the invasions of the sea peoples (the Japhethites in the latter part of the second millennium B.C.E.) put an effective end to Egypt's Asiatic empire.

8] *Nimrod.* The brief reference to Nimrod is probably a fragment from a large epic, well known in its time, which likely dealt with Tukulti-Ninurta I, who ruled Assyria *ca.* 1244–1208 B.C.E. and who controlled both Babylonia and Assyria (as verse 10 suggests) [3].

9] *Hunter.* Hunting was practiced in ancient Israel (see Lev. 17:13) but apparently played only a small role in its largely agrarian and urban society.

/In later centuries Jews considered the hunt a cruel and therefore uncivilized sport. "He who hunts game

with dogs as Gentiles do will not enjoy the life to come" [4]./

10] *And Calneh.* Probably a case of faulty vocalization of the text. The original Hebrew manuscript was written without vowels, which were added more than a thousand years later. By changing כַּלְנֵה (*kalneh*) to כֻּלָּנָה (*kulanah*, all of these), the sentence reads: "The mainstays of his kingdom were Babylon, Erech, Accad, all of these [being] in the land of Shinar" (see Gen. 42:36, where כֻּלָּנָה occurs).

Shinar. Biblical name for the area of Babylonia, and especially for Sumer.

12] *Calah.* A Mesopotamian city founded by Shalmaneser I (*ca.* 1274–1245 B.C.E.), which has been thoroughly explored by archeologists. It was a "great city" in its day.

יג כָּלַח הוא הָעִיר הַגְּדֹלָה: וּמִצְרַיִם יָלַד אֶת־לוּדִים

יד וְאֶת־עֲנָמִים וְאֶת־לְהָבִים וְאֶת־נַפְתֻּחִים: וְאֶת־פַּתְרֻסִים

וְאֶת־כַּסְלֻחִים אֲשֶׁר יָצְאוּ מִשָּׁם פְּלִשְׁתִּים וְאֶת־

טו כַּפְתֹּרִים: ס וּכְנַעַן יָלַד אֶת־צִידֹן בְּכֹרוֹ וְאֶת־חֵת:

טז וְאֶת־הַיְבוּסִי וְאֶת־הָאֱמֹרִי וְאֵת הַגִּרְגָּשִׁי: וְאֶת־הַחִוִּי

יח וְאֶת־הָעַרְקִי וְאֶת־הַסִּינִי: וְאֶת־הָאַרְוָדִי וְאֶת־הַצְּמָרִי

יט וְאֶת־הַחֲמָתִי וְאַחַר נָפֹצוּ מִשְׁפְּחוֹת הַכְּנַעֲנִי: וַיְהִי

גְּבוּל הַכְּנַעֲנִי מִצִּידֹן בֹּאֲכָה גְרָרָה עַד־עַזָּה

בֹּאֲכָה סְדֹמָה וַעֲמֹרָה וְאַדְמָה וּצְבֹיִם* עַד־לָשַׁע:

Genesis 10

13–19

* יט וצבוים קרי.

13] And Mizraim begot the Ludim, the Anamim, the Lehabim, the Naphtuhim,
14] the Pathrusim, the Casluhim, and the Caphtorim, whence the Philistines came
forth.

15] Canaan begot Sidon his first-born, and Heth;   16] and the Jebusites, the
Amorites, the Girgashites,   17] the Hivites, the Arkites, the Sinites,   18] the
Arvadites, the Zemarites, and the Hamathites. Afterward the clans of the Canaanites
branched out,   19] so that the Canaanite border extended from Sidon as far as Gerar,
near Gaza, and as far as Sodom, Gomorrah, Admah, and Zeboiim, near Lasha.

/It served as one of the great capital cities of the
neo-Assyrian kings from 880–615 B.C.E. Today it is
known as Nimrud./

13] *Begot.* To be understood as "was the ancestor
of." Similarly, the expressions "father" and "son"
often mean ancestor and descendant.

14] *And the Caphtorim.* In the Hebrew text these
words come at the end of the sentence. The transposition in this translation is made because the
Philistines came from Caphtor (see Amos 9:7).

The Caphtorim are usually identified as Cretans.
However, no archeological evidence has been found
to make the identification certain.

15] *Sidon.* North of Acre.
    Heth. A reference to the Hittites, who played
a significant role in Near Eastern history in the
latter half of the second millennium B.C.E.
/Others: They were the Hittite successor states
established in northern Syria after the overthrow
of the Hittite empire in Anatolia, about 1200
B.C.E./

כ אֵ֣לֶּה בְנֵי־חָ֧ם לְמִשְׁפְּחֹתָ֛ם לִלְשֹׁנֹתָ֖ם בְּאַרְצֹתָ֑ם בְּגֹויֵהֶֽם: ס

כא וּלְשֵׁ֥ם יֻלַּ֖ד גַּם־ה֑וּא אֲבִי֙ כָּל־בְּנֵי־עֵ֔בֶר אֲחִ֖י יֶ֥פֶת

כב הַגָּדֽוֹל: בְּנֵ֣י שֵׁ֔ם עֵילָ֣ם וְאַשּׁ֑וּר וְאַרְפַּכְשַׁ֖ד וְל֥וּד

כג וַאֲרָֽם: וּבְנֵ֖י אֲרָ֑ם ע֥וּץ וְח֖וּל וְגֶ֥תֶר וָמַֽשׁ: וְאַרְפַּכְשַׁ֖ד

כה יָלַ֣ד אֶת־שָׁ֑לַח וְשֶׁ֖לַח יָלַ֣ד אֶת־עֵֽבֶר: וּלְעֵ֥בֶר יֻלַּ֖ד
שְׁנֵ֣י בָנִ֑ים שֵׁ֣ם הָֽאֶחָ֞ד פֶּ֗לֶג כִּ֤י בְיָמָיו֙ נִפְלְגָ֣ה הָאָ֔רֶץ

כו וְשֵׁ֥ם אָחִ֖יו יָקְטָֽן: וְיָקְטָ֣ן יָלַ֔ד אֶת־אַלְמוֹדָ֖ד וְאֶת־

כז שָׁ֑לֶף וְאֶת־חֲצַרְמָ֖וֶת וְאֶת־יָֽרַח: וְאֶת־הֲדוֹרָ֥ם וְאֶת־אוּזָ֖ל

כח וְאֶת־דִּקְלָֽה: וְאֶת־עוֹבָ֥ל וְאֶת־אֲבִימָאֵ֖ל וְאֶת־שְׁבָֽא:

Genesis 10
20–28

20] These are the descendants of Ham, according to their clans and languages, by their lands and nations.

21] Sons were also born to Shem, ancestor of all the descendants of Eber and older brother of Japheth.   **22]** The descendants of Shem: Elam, Asshur, Arpachshad, Lud, and Aram.   **23]** The descendants of Aram: Uz, Hul, Gether, and Mash. **24]** Arpachshad begot Shelah, and Shelah begot Eber.   **25]** Two sons were born to Eber: the name of the first was Peleg, for in his days the earth was divided; and the name of his brother was Joktan.   **26]** Joktan begot Almodad, Sheleph, Hazarmaveth, Jerah,   **27]** Hadoram, Uzal, Diklah,   **28]** Obal, Abimael, Sheba,

21] *Eber.* See Gen. 11:16 and p. 140.

22] *Elam.* A country mentioned frequently in the literature of antiquity. Its capital city was Susa (Shushan, cf. Esther 1:2), located southeast of modern Luristan, in Iran.
/The Christian Scripture notes that Elamites along with Parthians and Medes were found in Jerusalem on Shavuot (Pentecost) [5]./
Arpachshad. Identified by some scholars as Ur-Casdim, the place of Abraham's origin.

Aram. Ancestor of the Arameans whose script and language (Aramaic) began to spread in the Near East before 1,000 B.C.E. By the sixth century B.C.E., Aramaic was widely used in the area and after the Babylonian exile displaced Hebrew as the popular language in Palestine. Portions of the Books of Daniel and Ezra are in Aramaic, which is also the dominant language of the Talmud.

25] *In his days the earth was divided.* נִפְלְגָה is a

כט וְאֶת־אוֹפִר וְאֶת־חֲוִילָה וְאֶת־יוֹבָב כָּל־אֵלֶּה בְּנֵי יָקְטָן:

ל וַיְהִי מוֹשָׁבָם מִמֵּשָׁא בֹּאֲכָה סְפָרָה הַר הַקֶּדֶם:

לא אֵלֶּה בְנֵי־שֵׁם לְמִשְׁפְּחֹתָם לִלְשֹׁנֹתָם בְּאַרְצֹתָם לְגוֹיֵהֶם:

לב אֵלֶּה מִשְׁפְּחֹת בְּנֵי־נֹחַ לְתוֹלְדֹתָם בְּגוֹיֵהֶם וּמֵאֵלֶּה
נִפְרְדוּ הַגּוֹיִם בָּאָרֶץ אַחַר הַמַּבּוּל: פ

Genesis 10

29—32

29] Ophir, Havilah, and Jobab; all these were the descendants of Joktan.
30] Their settlements extended from Mesha as far as Sephar, the hill country
to the east.   31] These are the descendants of Shem according to their clans and
languages, by their lands, according to their nations.

32] These are the groupings of Noah's descendants, according to their origins,
by their nations; and from these the nations branched out on the earth after the Flood.

word play on פֶּלֶג. The phrase means that during
Peleg's lifetime the event described in Gen. 9:19
took place, i.e., the whole world branched out and
became settled.

The Table of Nations

The geographic area covered by the biblical table reaches from the Caucasus mountains in the north to Ethiopia in the south, from the Aegean Sea in the west to the highlands of Iran in the east. Broadly speaking, Japheth refers to the peoples at the northern and western periphery of the Fertile Crescent, including the Medes, the Cypriots, the Scythians, and the Ionians. The offspring of Ham dwell about the Red Sea and include Ethiopians, Egyptians, and Canaanites. The descendants of Shem live in the heart of the Crescent itself and include Arabs, Arameans, and Assyrians.

This chapter represents the combination of two separate traditions. The older one (Gen. 10:8–19, 21, 22–30) is concerned primarily with tribes and clans; the more recent one stresses the term גוֹי (goy, nation) and is mainly a catalog of states and languages (as, for instance, in verses 5, 20, 31, 32). The table of nations is remarkable for its wide scope and may be considered a pioneering effort among the ethnographic inquiries of antiquity [6]. It is presented in a nonmythological way, unlike a comparable Babylonian list, which states that "when kingship came down from heaven the kingdom was in Eridu."

It is, however, important to see the biblical list as more than ethnographic information. It is an integral part of the story of God's promise to Noah; it portrays the peoples of the earth, related through this promise, as one common humanity. The implicit theme of the text is the unity of man within the framework of apparent diversity.

No reference to "race" or skin color can be detected in this list. This is not to say that the Bible is without prejudices or preferences (see p. 85). Occasionally it reflects certain political animosities, and repeatedly it condemns various nations because of their immoral or idolatrous practices, but it is totally devoid of any notion of racial superiority. The dispassionate character of this chapter is indicative of the Bible's overall approach to the structure of humanity.

Israel is not listed in the catalog. In fact, the text underplays the origins of the people to whom, after all, the Bible is devoted. Israel's origins are (like the stories of Eden and Noah) located outside Israelite territory, and just as in its territory there was no original distinction so there was none in its early ancestry. Its origins were seen as no different from those of any other nation. Only through its covenantal relationship with God would Israel pursue a special destiny.

Although Shem was the oldest of Noah's sons, he is listed last in the table of nations. Most probably this was done because his genealogy commands the Bible's eventual focus and, after the brief interruption occasioned by the Tower of Babel story, the text turns (Gen. 11:10) to a detailed description of Shem's line, i.e., of Abraham's antecedents.

GLEANINGS

Nimrod

The name means "one who stirred up rebellion" (הִמְרִיד) so that people no longer trusted God but their own power. "Nimrod knew his Master but decided to rebel against Him."

TALMUD [7]

Nimrod was responsible for the building of the Tower of Babel; he wanted it to be his throne so that divine honors would be accorded him. He was king when the boy Abraham was brought before him. Nimrod worshiped fire while Abraham tried to convince him of the supremacy of God. Nimrod cast the boy into the fire but God saved him, thus demonstrating the supremacy of His power.

MIDRASH [8]

"He was a mighty hunter" means that he hunted men's souls; he ensnared them and incited them against God. The building of the Tower of Babel was the culmination of his activities.

RASHI [9]

Why is Nimrod's name linked to that of God in Gen. 10:9? Because he oppressed people in God's name.

He was the prototype of all tyrants who piously pretend that their crown is "by God's grace," and thus their power politics and hypocrisy are characterized by the expression, "like Nimrod, who pretends to hunt in God's name."

SAMSON RAPHAEL HIRSCH

But another tradition admired Nimrod for being "the first man of might on earth." As late as the Middle Ages Jewish fathers when blessing their sons would wish them "to be like Nimrod."

The Table of Nations

Israel cannot pass by the existence of nations without discovering a profound moral intent therein, for Israel is the poet of the spiritual life of mankind as other peoples are the poets of nature.

MORDECAI M. KAPLAN [10]

The differences among men emerge naturally, that is, as a consequence of the sinfulness of men, amply attested in the generations after the Flood by their decreasing longevity. Looking out at the triumphant, unbridled paganism which surrounded them simply verified the biblical judgment for the rabbis: nationhood is natural, but a natural expression of man's will to do evil.

EUGENE B. BOROWITZ [11]

Babel and after:

THE END OF PREHISTORY

The Tower of Babel story, interrupting the catalog of nations begun in chapter 10 and continued in chapter 11, verse 10, stands between the universal tableau of humanity and that specific list of families from which Terah, Abraham, and their line will spring.

The story attempts to answer two questions: Where did the variety of languages come from? How did man disperse and populate the world? These questions were not considered in chapter 10. By setting out to answer them, the Bible brings us a special tradition, one which must have existed independently from the table of nations. For the Babel story presents all mankind living undivided in one small area. This unity of language and living space ends because man's rebellious action once again brings down the judgment of God.

While there is a Sumerian story of the confounding of tongues, no parallel account has so far been found in Near Eastern records that would afford us the kind of comparison and contrast through which the biblical purpose of the Flood tale is seen in high relief.

Biblical scholars generally believe that the opening section of Genesis which concludes here was originally separate from the patriarchal cycles which follow. The joining of prehistory and history (in its wider sense) affords the biblical editors the opportunity to show the rise of Abraham and his descendants in the full context of God's plans for mankind.

אַ וַיְהִי כָל־הָאָרֶץ שָׂפָה אֶחָת וּדְבָרִים אֲחָדִים: וַיְהִי
בְּנָסְעָם מִקֶּדֶם וַיִּמְצְאוּ בִקְעָה בְּאֶרֶץ שִׁנְעָר וַיֵּשְׁבוּ
ג שָׁם: וַיֹּאמְרוּ אִישׁ אֶל־רֵעֵהוּ הָבָה נִלְבְּנָה לְבֵנִים
וְנִשְׂרְפָה לִשְׂרֵפָה וַתְּהִי לָהֶם הַלְּבֵנָה לְאָבֶן וְהַחֵמָר
ד הָיָה לָהֶם לַחֹמֶר: וַיֹּאמְרוּ הָבָה נִבְנֶה־לָּנוּ עִיר
וּמִגְדָּל וְרֹאשׁוֹ בַשָּׁמַיִם וְנַעֲשֶׂה־לָּנוּ שֵׁם פֶּן־נָפוּץ עַל־
ה פְּנֵי כָל־הָאָרֶץ: וַיֵּרֶד יְהֹוָה לִרְאֹת אֶת־הָעִיר וְאֶת־
י הַמִּגְדָּל אֲשֶׁר בָּנוּ בְּנֵי הָאָדָם: וַיֹּאמֶר יְהֹוָה הֵן עַם

Genesis 11

1–6

1] All the earth had the same language and the same words.   2] And as men migrated from the east, they came upon a valley in the land of Shinar and settled there.   3] They said to one another, "Come, let us make bricks and burn them hard."—Brick served them as stone, and bitumen served them as mortar.—4] And they said, "Come, let us build us a city, and a tower with its top in the sky, to make a name for ourselves; else we shall be scattered all over the world."   5] The LORD came down to look at the city and tower which man had built,   6] and the LORD

11:1] *The same words.* The expression parallels "the same language." (Chapter 10 speaks of לָשׁוֹן [tongue]; the author of the Babel story calls language שָׂפָה [lip].) Historically, the principal languages of Mesopotamia in the third millennium were Sumerian and Akkadian. The latter is a Semitic language related to Hebrew, though not as closely as are Amorite, Canaanite, and Aramaic. Today, the Semitic language most widely spoken in the area is Arabic.

2] *Men migrated from the east.* Where they had settled after the Flood.

Shinar. See note to Gen. 10:10.

3] *Bricks . . . stone, bitumen . . . mortar.* The Bible means to explain that in Babylon brick and bitumen were used instead of stone and mortar

as in Israel. The entire story abounds in assonances and alliterations: לְבֵנָה־לְאָבֶן, חֵמָר־חֹמֶר.
/In "Enuma Elish" we find this description of the building of a shrine to Marduk: "The first year they molded bricks. When the second year arrived they raised high the head of Esagila, the counterpart of Apsu" (Apsu was a poetic term for the abyss) [1]. Herodotus describes the construction of a Mesopotamian moat as follows: "As fast as they dug the moat, the soil which they got from the cutting was made into bricks, and when a sufficient number were completed they baked the brick in kilns. Then they set to building, using hot bitumen throughout for their cement" [2]./

5] *The Lord came down.* In order to judge man. The expression is also used in telling the story of Sodom and Gomorrah (Gen. 18:21).

אֶחָד וְשָׂפָה אַחַת לְכֻלָּם וְזֶה הַחִלָּם לַעֲשׂוֹת וְעַתָּה

ז–יא לֹא־יִבָּצֵר מֵהֶם כֹּל אֲשֶׁר יָזְמוּ לַעֲשׂוֹת: הָבָה נֵרְדָה

וְנָבְלָה שָׁם שְׂפָתָם אֲשֶׁר לֹא יִשְׁמְעוּ אִישׁ שְׂפַת רֵעֵהוּ:

ח וַיָּפֶץ יְהֹוָה אֹתָם מִשָּׁם עַל־פְּנֵי כָל־הָאָרֶץ וַיַּחְדְּלוּ

ט לִבְנֹת הָעִיר: עַל־כֵּן קָרָא שְׁמָהּ בָּבֶל כִּי־שָׁם בָּלַל

יְהֹוָה שְׂפַת כָּל־הָאָרֶץ וּמִשָּׁם הֱפִיצָם יְהֹוָה עַל־פְּנֵי

כָּל־הָאָרֶץ: פ

י אֵלֶּה תּוֹלְדֹת שֵׁם שֵׁם בֶּן־מְאַת שָׁנָה וַיּוֹלֶד אֶת־

יא אַרְפַּכְשָׁד שְׁנָתַיִם אַחַר הַמַּבּוּל: וַיְחִי־שֵׁם אַחֲרֵי

הוֹלִידוֹ אֶת־אַרְפַּכְשָׁד חֲמֵשׁ מֵאוֹת שָׁנָה וַיּוֹלֶד בָּנִים

said, "If, as one people with one language for all, this is how they have begun to act, then nothing that they may propose to do will be out of their reach.   7] Let Me, then, go down and confound their speech there, so that they shall not understand one another's speech."   8] Thus the LORD scattered them from there over the face of the whole earth; and they stopped building the city.   9] That is why it was called Babel, because there the Lord confounded the speech of the whole earth; and from there the LORD scattered them over the face of the whole earth.

10] This is the line of Shem. Shem was 100 years old when he begot Arpachshad, two years after the Flood.   11] After the birth of Arpachshad, Shem lived 500 years and begot sons and daughters.

7] *Let us.* See note to Gen. 1:26.

8] *They stopped building the city.* And, of course, the tower that was in it.

9] *Babel.* While Babylonian tradition explained the name as "Gate of God," the biblical author substituted a satirical play on words: Babylon is only confusion. An English parallel might be Babel-babble.

10–26] With the exception of Shem, all ancestral names down to Terah appear to reflect the names of cities in upper Mesopotamia, a district later called Aram-Naharaim and Paddan-Aram [3]. Hence, the Israelites considered themselves to be Arameans in origin (Deut. 26:5).

Most of the pre-Patriarchs father their children at thirty years of age. Further, note the round numbers 100 and 500 and that 403, like 30, occurs twice. Whether the system is based on

בראשית יא

יב–יט

יב וּבָנוֹת: ס וְאַרְפַּכְשַׁד חַי חָמֵשׁ וּשְׁלֹשִׁים שָׁנָה וַיּוֹלֶד

יג אֶת־שָׁלַח: וַיְחִי אַרְפַּכְשַׁד אַחֲרֵי הוֹלִידוֹ אֶת־שֶׁלַח

שָׁלֹשׁ שָׁנִים וְאַרְבַּע מֵאוֹת שָׁנָה וַיּוֹלֶד בָּנִים וּבָנוֹת: ס

יד וְשֶׁלַח חַי שְׁלֹשִׁים שָׁנָה וַיּוֹלֶד אֶת־עֵבֶר: וַיְחִי־שֶׁלַח

טו אַחֲרֵי הוֹלִידוֹ אֶת־עֵבֶר שָׁלֹשׁ שָׁנִים וְאַרְבַּע מֵאוֹת

טז שָׁנָה וַיּוֹלֶד בָּנִים וּבָנוֹת: ס וַיְחִי־עֵבֶר אַרְבַּע וּשְׁלֹשִׁים

שָׁנָה וַיּוֹלֶד אֶת־פָּלֶג: וַיְחִי־עֵבֶר אַחֲרֵי הוֹלִידוֹ אֶת־

יז פֶּלֶג שְׁלֹשִׁים שָׁנָה וְאַרְבַּע מֵאוֹת שָׁנָה וַיּוֹלֶד בָּנִים

יח וּבָנוֹת: ס וַיְחִי־פֶלֶג שְׁלֹשִׁים שָׁנָה וַיּוֹלֶד אֶת־רְעוּ:

יט וַיְחִי־פֶלֶג אַחֲרֵי הוֹלִידוֹ אֶת־רְעוּ תֵּשַׁע שָׁנִים וּמָאתַיִם

שָׁנָה וַיּוֹלֶד בָּנִים וּבָנוֹת: ס

Genesis 11

12–19

12] When Arpachshad had lived 35 years, he begot Shelah.   13] After the birth of Shelah, Arpachshad lived 403 years and begot sons and daughters.

14] When Shelah had lived 30 years, he begot Eber.   15] After the birth of Eber, Shelah lived 403 years and begot sons and daughters.

16] When Eber had lived 34 years, he begot Peleg.   17] After the birth of Peleg, Eber lived 430 years and begot sons and daughters.

18] When Peleg had lived 30 years, he begot Reu.   19] After the birth of Reu, Peleg lived 209 years and begot sons and daughters.

multiples of six and seven, or of seven, ten, twelve, and forty, is in doubt, but that an underlying scheme exists appears certain despite the fact that the ancient versions differ somewhat in their figures. The symbolism must once have been comprehensible but became less so as time went on.

/The numbers were later used to this end by the Seder Olam Rabba to arrive at 3760 B.C.E. as the year of creation and by Bishop Ussher to arrive similarly at 4004. These figures are not far from the archeologically suggested age for the emergence of civilization in Mesopotamia./

11] *After the birth of.* Literally, "after he begot."

16] *Eber.* Ancestors of the Hebrews (see p. 140).

כ וַיְחִי רְעוּ שְׁתַּיִם וּשְׁלֹשִׁים שָׁנָה וַיּוֹלֶד אֶת־שְׂרוּג:

כא וַיְחִי רְעוּ אַחֲרֵי הוֹלִידוֹ אֶת־שְׂרוּג שֶׁבַע שָׁנִים וּמָאתַיִם שָׁנָה וַיּוֹלֶד בָּנִים וּבָנוֹת: ס

כב וַיְחִי שְׂרוּג שְׁלֹשִׁים שָׁנָה וַיּוֹלֶד אֶת־נָחוֹר: וַיְחִי שְׂרוּג אַחֲרֵי הוֹלִידוֹ אֶת־נָחוֹר מָאתַיִם שָׁנָה וַיּוֹלֶד בָּנִים

כד וּבָנוֹת: ס וַיְחִי נָחוֹר תֵּשַׁע וְעֶשְׂרִים שָׁנָה וַיּוֹלֶד אֶת־

כה תָּרַח: וַיְחִי נָחוֹר אַחֲרֵי הוֹלִידוֹ אֶת־תֶּרַח תְּשַׁע־

כו עֶשְׂרֵה שָׁנָה וּמְאַת שָׁנָה וַיּוֹלֶד בָּנִים וּבָנוֹת: ס וַיְחִי־ תֶּרַח שִׁבְעִים שָׁנָה וַיּוֹלֶד אֶת־אַבְרָם אֶת־נָחוֹר וְאֶת־ הָרָן:

20] When Reu had lived 32 years, he begot Serug.   21] After the birth of Serug, Reu lived 207 years and begot sons and daughters.

22] When Serug had lived 30 years, he begot Nahor.   23] After the birth of Nahor, Serug lived 200 years and begot sons and daughters.

24] When Nahor had lived 29 years, he begot Terah.   25] After the birth of Terah, Nahor lived 119 years and begot sons and daughters.

26] When Terah had lived seventy years, he begot Abram, Nahor, and Haran.

Conclusion of the Prologue

This chapter is a transition from universal prehistory to a story of more limited scope—that of Abraham and his people. The Bible sees humanity's early history as a series of rebellions against the will of God. The rebellion of the people of Babel prompts God to look for a new channel to man. To Abraham and his descendants He now entrusts the task of bringing blessings to all the nations of the earth (Gen. 12:3). The remainder of the Torah is devoted to the story of this particular people and to the road they must follow in order to fulfil their universal responsibility. The Babel tale of divine displeasure and the subsequent genealogical list thus constitute both the conclusion of the prologue and the introduction to the first act of the main biblical drama.

Historic Background

A tower-like structure called *zikurat*—literally, "that which has been raised high"—was a distinctive feature of all Babylonian temple complexes and may have served as the humanly constructed equivalent of the mythical holy mountain in Babylonian mythology. The *zikurat* called Etemenanki ("house of the foundation of heaven and earth") was reported to have consisted of seven stories receding in pyramid-like fashion toward a flat top and reaching a height of nearly 300 feet. Archeologists have uncovered the foundation of this *zikurat*, and its extent would seem to coincide with the reputed size of the Tower of Babel [4]. Scholars have also confirmed the special use of hardened brick for such an enterprise.

The biblical writer's contempt for the paganism of Babylon determined not only his interpretation of the catastrophe that befell the city and its tower but also the style of the story, with its obvious overtones of sarcasm, its repeated word plays, and its explanation of Babel as a place of confusion.

Interpretations

While we are told that God's judgment consisted of scattering the people of Babel and confounding their speech, their actual transgression is not specified. A city was built and in it a tower, and the builders hoped that its summit would reach high into the heavens. In viewing this activity, God said: "This is how they have begun to act" (Gen. 11:6). What the word "this" refers to is not explained. A number of interpretations have been offered:

Self-Aggrandizement. According to the great majority of commentators, the tower represents man's tendency to reach too high, his attempt to equal if not displace God. Just as Adam desired to be like God and in consequence was driven from Eden, so in Babel, too, men exhibited excessive arrogance. They prided themselves on their accomplishments —they invented brick, knew how to use bitumen, and proceeded to build a large city with a skyscraping tower. Like the generation of the Flood, they were given to self-exaltation. Having a common dwelling place and a unified language encouraged their designs. Once these elements were removed, their pretentious enterprise collapsed.

Rebellion. The sin of the generation of Babel consisted of their refusal to "fill the earth." They had been commanded to do so but still tried to defy the divine will. God's action, therefore, was not so much a punishment as a carrying out of His plan. Confounding the human language was merely an assurance that the Babel incident would not be repeated. Man proposed, but God disposed [5].

A certain pathos adheres to this interpretation of the story. It senses in the generation of Babel not arrogance but anxiety, not a desire to reach the heavens so much as the need to press together on earth. According to Benno Jacob, the tale is "a condemnation of extreme centralization, the last consequence of which is one huge universal megalopolis which sees its final goal in bringing all men under One Tower" [6].

The City. Related to the previous interpretation is one that sees the city as the center of the account and all else as secondary [7]. The tower is merely the embodiment of the city, and when the story closes it speaks only of the city. A brief notation reveals the whole purpose of the Babel story: "and they stopped building the city" (Gen. 11:8).

This understanding reflects most clearly a pervasive biblical motif. The city is the ultimate expression of man's presumption. Babel was *the* city, and, to the anti-urban tradition of the Bible, its downfall appeared as a proper divine judgment. Babel referred of course to Babylon, but it also symbolized all empire building, corruption, arrogance, craving to erect monuments, desire for fame; it meant a turning away from what were considered the primary occupations of man— agriculture and the tending of flocks. Farmers and nomads "fill the earth," i.e., they live close to it and its creatures; city-dwellers flee from the earth. Babel was an alienation of man from the simple life, and it is no accident that the Bible next turns to Abraham, a semi-nomad, as the source of all future blessings.

GLEANINGS

Babel—A Problem in Communication

Men spoke one language and "the same words." The Hebrew could also be interpreted as "few words," which is to say that man had a small vocabulary. Since both the learned and the unlearned spoke "the same words," there was no philosophic or technical "jargon" to separate people from each other.　　IBN EZRA, MALBIM

Language promotes communication and understanding within the group, but it also accentuates the differences in traditions and beliefs between groups; it erects barriers between tribes, nations, regions, social classes. The Tower of Babel is an archetypal symbol of the process which turns the blessing into a curse and prevents man from reaching into heaven. According to Margaret Mead, among the two million aborigines in New Guinea, 750 different languages are spoken in 750 villages which are at permanent war with one another.　　ARTHUR KOESTLER [8]

Ancient Affluence

The Torah says that the people "settled" in Shinar. This expression implies a social criticism. The problem of the people of Babel was their mindless affluence. For whenever the Torah uses the term יָשַׁב [settled] it means that people are overly at ease. Rabbi Helbo said: "Wherever you find contented satisfaction, Satan is active."

MIDRASH [9]

The Lord Came Down

If God himself did this, how much more so is this incumbent on a human judge who must personally examine the accused and gain the fullest comprehension of all details.　　MIDRASH [10]

God must draw near, not because He is nearsighted, but because He dwells at such tremendous heights and man's work is so small. God's movement must, therefore, be understood as a remarkable satirical contrast to man's behavior.

OTTO PROCKSCH [11]

The Tower and Human Values

As the tower grew in height it took one year to get bricks from the base to the upper stories. Thus, bricks became more precious than human life. When a brick slipped and fell the people wept, but when a man fell and died no one paid attention.　　MIDRASH [12]

They drove forth multitudes of both men and women to make bricks; among whom, a woman making bricks was not allowed to be released in the hour of childbirth, but brought forth while she was making bricks, and carried her child in her apron, and continued to make bricks.

BARUCH [13]

Why was the generation of the Flood destroyed while that of Babel was merely dispersed? The Babylonians said to one another: Come, let *us* build [Gen. 11:4]. They worked together, in peace and harmony. This distinguished them from the people of the Flood who committed violence against one another and were, therefore, destroyed. The generation of the Tower defied God openly, yet, because they practiced brotherhood toward each other, they were merely scattered.

MIDRASH [14]

The City

With the city as its critical object the Babel story has a particularly contemporary ring. Western urbanized man also struggles with his estrangement from God. He, too, reaches for and appears to achieve powers formerly ascribed to God. One may, therefore, find in the Babel tale a suggestion that ever greater urbanization, coupled with a concentration on technology and a reaching toward outer space as a step toward further conquests, leads man not to unity but to division. To put it in other terms: Will modern man drive God into deeper hiding and further dramatize His eclipse, or will his actions call forth, as they did in ancient days, a God who will "come down and look" and then confound man again?

The Blessing of Diversity

The real crime of the builders was that they tried to impose one religion on mankind. God prevented this and, by dispersing the peoples, kept alive a variety of idolatries. But He knew that out of this diversity would eventually come a recognition of the Supreme Ruler. SFORNO

Not Sin But Exuberance

From that day to this, whenever men have become skilful architects at all, there has been a tendency in them to build high; not in any religious feeling but in mere exuberance of spirit and power—as they dance or sin—with a certain mingling of vanity—like the feeling in which a child builds a tower of cards. JOHN RUSKIN [15]

Science

Babel is here, and now. Who speaks my language? —no one.
Science is so tall that no man sees its face:
This tower will not touch God.

The trick is this,—and it is a good trick worthy a divine
Chicanery: in our impious determination
To build this bean-stalk, Science; climb it; peep
On the ultimate Mystery; spy on God; learn all;
No man can both climb and see.
EDNA ST. VINCENT MILLAY [16]

One Language, Many Tongues

It is possible that the report of all the earth having one language [11:1] has a historic foundation. The co-existence of one lingua franca and many national tongues is attested at various stages of history. Greek, Latin, French, and English have at certain times served as the "one language" for many peoples, and such co-existence is reported also for the pre-Columbian Central America. The loss of a means of international communication must at all times be the prelude to international strife. CYRUS H. GORDON [17]

PART III

The Line of Terah

ABRAHAM

The Book of Genesis now enters a new phase by moving from myth toward history. Abraham (although the Patriarch's name is Abram and that of his wife is Sarai until Gen. 15:5, 7, the later and more familiar names of Abraham and Sarah are used throughout this commentary) has been called the first major historical figure in the book; unlike Adam, Shem, or Noah, who were the symbols or legendary standard-bearers of primeval memories and traditions, he appears as an identifiable person at a certain time. We reach this conclusion because of the nature of his biography and because many details and references are corroborated by other sources—even though so far none has been found to mention Abraham by name. This is not surprising, for in his day he was not the great and commanding figure that he was to become in the light of later history. This absence of extra-biblical references makes it difficult to date Abraham precisely, a difficulty we encounter with biblical figures until Moses. Various elements in the patriarchal narratives seem to correspond to different periods; from the old Babylonian (nineteenth century B.C.E.) to the Hurrian (fifteenth century B.C.E.) to the Amarna age (fourteenth century B.C.E.). While this commentary leans toward accepting the earliest period, our data are not precise enough for a definite decision in favor of any one school of thought [1].

We have a good deal of information about the political, social, and religious life of the Mesopotamian lands where the Abraham cycle had its beginnings. Documents and archeological evidence tell us that the culture of this area flowered during the second millennium B.C.E. Science, law, and social institutions were highly developed. We do not know the particular circumstances that caused Abraham's father, Terah, to leave Ur and to settle in Haran, nor do we know his occupation. Of Abraham we do know that he was a semi-nomad with cattle, and we may assume that this was his ancestors' way of life as well, since in ancient days the sons usually followed in the footsteps of their fathers. They were not Bedouin on camels, like the Midianites, but rather nomads with small cattle whose movements between the steppe and tilled areas were determined by the needs of their animals and by their relationships with the permanent population.

"A degree of settledness is not at all incompatible with their nomadic existence. Cities do attract them, but not to settle in them by force, which would at once compel them to give up their nomadic life as shepherds;

but they attract them rather because of their character as cultural centers—primarily therefore for reasons of commerce and connubium" [2].

Calling Abraham "historical" does not mean that everything the Book of Genesis says about him is history in the accepted sense of the word. Our text was written down many centuries after Abraham lived, and the intervening ages developed different traditions about him. There is a good deal of what may be called legendary embellishment, which, along with interpretive material, was added to the basic tradition in the course of time. Together these elements came to assume the form that we now have before us.

But it is not so important to fix Abraham's era or to determine which of the stories about Abraham are history and which are legendary. What is important is his role as the father of the nation.* While the authors of the Bible were concerned with history as the recounting of facts, it was the meaning of history that was their primary focus, the account of a spiritual message born of the continuing encounter between God and Abraham's descendants. The Torah does not purpose to teach antiquities as such but to give religious instruction.

* The Torah does not depict him as the founder of a new religion. On the contrary, as Yehezkel Kaufmann has shown, in Genesis primeval mankind from Adam on appears to have been monotheistic. Abraham was "a prince of God" who kept the faith in the one God pure and bequeathed it to his descendants, setting them aside from a world which became idolatrous. According to Kaufmann, this biblical view contrasts, however, with what we know of the history of religion. Monotheism in the narrower sense has its origins not with Abraham but with Moses. The latter is a fighter for יהוה, the former a man of unusual piety and moral principles (see also below, p. 121) [3]. A different view is held by Theophile J. Meek. He calls Abraham and Moses "monolatrous" and argues that not until the Hebrew prophets did monotheism arise [4].

The Call of Abraham

The opening passages of the Abraham story relate the genealogy of the Patriarch and then tell of the family's migration to Haran. This city—the name means "highway" or "crossroads"—was located in north-western Mesopotamia and played a large part in the patriarchal story. It was the crossing point of important highways and a center of the cult devoted to the moon-god Sin. A large collection of Hurrian records found in the town of Nuzi tells much about the area's life and law.

The Bible says that God spoke to Abraham at the "crossroads" of his life. This address of the Divine to one human being, the message and its portent form the starting point of Israel's history. For while Abraham's story must be read as the biography of an individual, he (and this applies to the other Patriarchs as well) is more than an individual. The Bible sees the Patriarch as the archetype who represents his descendants and their fate. He is the forefather, whose life hints at the later history of the people of Israel. This prefiguration begins when Abraham becomes a wanderer. Time and again his descendants will wander across the earth, along the highways of history.*

* כָּל מָה שֶׁאִירַע לוֹ אִירַע לְבָנָיו [1]. A variety of other classical sayings expresses the thought that the stories of the forefathers are signposts pointing to the history of their descendants [2]. There is disagreement over whether Abraham's knowledge of God may be considered the beginning of monotheism.

כז וְאֵ֣לֶּה תּוֹלְדֹ֣ת תֶּ֔רַח תֶּ֚רַח הוֹלִ֣יד אֶת־אַבְרָ֔ם אֶת־
כח נָח֖וֹר וְאֶת־הָרָ֑ן וְהָרָ֖ן הוֹלִ֥יד אֶת־ל֑וֹט: וַיָּ֣מָת הָרָ֗ן עַל־
כט פְּנֵ֛י תֶּ֥רַח אָבִ֖יו בְּאֶ֣רֶץ מוֹלַדְתּ֑וֹ בְּא֖וּר כַּשְׂדִּֽים: וַיִּקַּ֨ח
אַבְרָ֧ם וְנָח֛וֹר לָהֶ֖ם נָשִׁ֑ים שֵׁ֣ם אֵֽשֶׁת־אַבְרָם֙ שָׂרַ֔י וְשֵׁ֤ם
אֵֽשֶׁת־נָחוֹר֙ מִלְכָּ֔ה בַּת־הָרָ֛ן אֲבִי־מִלְכָּ֖ה וַֽאֲבִ֥י יִסְכָּֽה:
ל וַתְּהִ֥י שָׂרַ֖י עֲקָרָ֑ה אֵ֥ין לָ֖הּ וָלָֽד: וַיִּקַּ֨ח תֶּ֜רַח אֶת־
לא אַבְרָ֣ם בְּנ֗וֹ וְאֶת־ל֞וֹט בֶּן־הָרָן֙ בֶּן־בְּנ֔וֹ וְאֵת֙ שָׂרַ֣י כַּלָּת֔וֹ
אֵ֖שֶׁת אַבְרָ֣ם בְּנ֑וֹ וַיֵּֽצְא֨וּ אִתָּ֜ם מֵא֣וּר כַּשְׂדִּ֗ים לָלֶ֨כֶת֙
לב אַ֣רְצָה כְּנַ֔עַן וַיָּבֹ֥אוּ עַד־חָרָ֖ן וַיֵּ֥שְׁבוּ שָֽׁם: וַיִּֽהְי֣וּ
יְמֵי־תֶ֗רַח חָמֵ֥שׁ שָׁנִ֛ים וּמָאתַ֥יִם שָׁנָ֖ה וַיָּ֥מָת תֶּ֖רַח
בְּחָרָֽן:

Genesis 11

27–32

Haftarah Noach, p. 518

27] Now this is the line of Terah: Terah begot Abram, Nahor, and Haran; and Haran begot Lot.   28] Haran died in the lifetime of his father Terah, in his native land, Ur of the Chaldeans.   29] Abram and Nahor took to themselves wives, the name of Abram's wife being Sarai and that of Nahor's wife Milcah, the daughter of Haran, the father of Milcah and Iscah.   30] Now Sarai was barren, she had no child.

31] Terah took his son Abram, his grandson Lot the son of Haran, and his daughter-in-law Sarai, the wife of his son Abram, and they set out together from Ur of the Chaldeans for the land of Canaan; but when they had come as far as Haran, they settled there.   32] The days of Terah came to 205 years; and Terah died in Haran.

11:28] *Ur.* In southeastern Mesopotamia, near the mouth of the Euphrates at the Persian Gulf.   / Or Ura in northern Syria, which is much closer to Haran [3]. /

בְּרֵאשִׁית יב
א–ה

Genesis 12
1–5

א וַיֹּאמֶר יְהוָֹה אֶל־אַבְרָם לֶךְ־לְךָ מֵאַרְצְךָ וּמִמּוֹלַדְתְּךָ

ב וּמִבֵּית אָבִיךָ אֶל־הָאָרֶץ אֲשֶׁר אַרְאֶךָּ: וְאֶעֶשְׂךָ לְגוֹי

ג גָּדוֹל וַאֲבָרֶכְךָ וַאֲגַדְּלָה שְׁמֶךָ וֶהְיֵה בְּרָכָה: וַאֲבָרְכָה

מְבָרְכֶיךָ וּמְקַלֶּלְךָ אָאֹר וְנִבְרְכוּ בְךָ כֹּל מִשְׁפְּחֹת

ד הָאֲדָמָה: וַיֵּלֶךְ אַבְרָם כַּאֲשֶׁר דִּבֶּר אֵלָיו יְהוָֹה וַיֵּלֶךְ

אִתּוֹ לוֹט וְאַבְרָם בֶּן־חָמֵשׁ שָׁנִים וְשִׁבְעִים שָׁנָה בְּצֵאתוֹ

ה מֵחָרָן: וַיִּקַּח אַבְרָם אֶת־שָׂרַי אִשְׁתּוֹ וְאֶת־לוֹט בֶּן־

אָחִיו וְאֶת־כָּל־רְכוּשָׁם אֲשֶׁר רָכָשׁוּ וְאֶת־הַנֶּפֶשׁ אֲשֶׁר־

עָשׂוּ בְחָרָן וַיֵּצְאוּ לָלֶכֶת אַרְצָה כְּנַעַן וַיָּבֹאוּ אַרְצָה

1] The LORD said to Abram, "Go forth from your native land and from your father's house to the land that I will show you.   2] I will make of you a great nation, / And I will bless you; / I will make your name great, / And you shall be a blessing: / 3] I will bless those who bless you, / And curse him that curses you; / All the families of the earth / Shall bless themselves by you."   4] Abram went forth as the LORD had spoken to him, and Lot went with him. Abram was seventy-five years old when he left Haran.   5] Abram took his wife Sarai and his brother's son Lot, and all the wealth that they had amassed, and the persons that they had acquired in Haran; and they set out for the land of Canaan. When they arrived in the land of

12:1] *Your native land.* However, Ur, not Haran, was Abraham's native place (Gen. 11:26–28). This verse would better be rendered "land of your kindred."

2] *A great nation.* גּוֹי (*goy*, nation); used in the Bible to refer to the descendants of Abraham as well as to other peoples.

3] *Shall bless themselves.* When they utter a blessing they will invoke Abraham as a model [4] (cf. Gen. 48:20). Others interpret this: "In you all the families of the earth shall be blessed," i.e., "you will be the cause of their blessings."

כְּנָֽעַן: וַיַּעֲבֹ֤ר אַבְרָם֙ בָּאָ֔רֶץ עַ֚ד מְק֣וֹם שְׁכֶ֔ם עַ֖ד אֵל֣וֹן מוֹרֶ֑ה וְהַֽכְּנַעֲנִ֖י אָ֥ז בָּאָֽרֶץ: וַיֵּרָ֤א יְהוָֹה֙ אֶל־אַבְרָ֔ם וַיֹּ֕אמֶר לְזַ֨רְעֲךָ֔ אֶתֵּ֖ן אֶת־הָאָ֣רֶץ הַזֹּ֑את וַיִּ֤בֶן שָׁם֙ מִזְבֵּ֔חַ לַֽיהוָֹ֖ה הַנִּרְאֶ֥ה אֵלָֽיו: וַיַּעְתֵּ֨ק מִשָּׁ֜ם הָהָ֗רָה מִקֶּ֛דֶם לְבֵֽית־אֵ֖ל וַיֵּ֣ט אָֽהֳלֹ֑ה בֵּֽית־אֵ֤ל מִיָּם֙ וְהָעַ֣י מִקֶּ֔דֶם וַיִּֽבֶן־שָׁ֤ם מִזְבֵּ֨חַ֙ לַֽיהוָֹ֔ה וַיִּקְרָ֖א בְּשֵׁ֥ם יְהוָֹֽה: וַיִּסַּ֣ע אַבְרָ֔ם הָל֥וֹךְ וְנָס֖וֹעַ הַנֶּֽגְבָּה: פ

Canaan,   6] Abram passed through the land as far as the site of Shechem, at the terebinth of Moreh. The Canaanites were then in the land.

7] The LORD appeared to Abram and said, "I will give this land to your offspring." And he built an altar there to the LORD who had appeared to him.   8] From there he moved on to the hill country east of Bethel and pitched his tent, with Bethel on the west and Ai on the east; and he built there an altar to the LORD and invoked the LORD by name.   9] Then Abram journeyed by stages toward the Negeb.

6] *Shechem.* Near Nablus, north of Jerusalem.

The terebinth of Moreh. מוֹרֶה (*moreh*, teaching, informing), a large tree famed as a site of oracles. Trees played an important role in ancient religions (see Deut. 12:2; Isa. 1:29).

/Hence some render *elon moreh* as "oracle tree" [5]. The Septuagint mentions its height [6]. Note also the "terebinths of Mamre" in Gen. 18:1./

The Canaanites were then in the land. This passage has been a problem to those who believe that the Torah was written by Moses. For in his age the Canaanites were indeed living in the land while the expression "then" (but not now) appears to deny it.

/Rashi substitutes "already" for "then" (אָז); Ibn Ezra hints that tradition here faces an insurmountable difficulty; and Spinoza pursues this further [7]./

7] *I will give this land.* This promise is to be repeated again and again to Abraham and his descendants.

8] *Bethel . . . Ai.* Located north of Jerusalem, about a third of the way to Shechem.

9] *Negeb.* Or Negev, the south land.

The Call

Did God in fact speak to Abraham and make the promise reported in this chapter? To biblical man and to believers today the matter was and is clear: God did speak, and His relationship to Abraham's children and to the land of Canaan was secured by His promise. Many interpreters, however, would understand God's challenge as something Abraham *believed* he had heard and that consequently he acted in accordance with this belief.

The issue here is, of course, not subject to objective verification. Those who cannot accept the possibility of God communicating directly with man will not be convinced by the biblical or any other report. But they will be able to agree that Abraham was indeed impelled by a voice he identified as the voice of God. We stand here face to face with "internal" history. Abraham acted on his comprehension of the Divine, and his descendants appropriated his experience and made it their own.

The Choice

Abraham is an old man when he is called by God. Why did God choose a man so advanced in age, and why him at all? The text is silent on this matter, but two divergent interpretations have been suggested.

The first maintains that God's reason is not humanly discernible. He arbitrarily cast His favor on Abraham, hence the Bible says nothing about Abraham's righteousness though it commented on Noah's. Abraham, through no merit of his own, is the vessel, the recipient of God's grace. This reasoning has been favored by Christian interpreters of the Bible, although it has had some Jewish supporters as well.[1]

The second interpretation says that Abraham, like Noah before him, deserved to be chosen. Just as Noah stood out as a uniquely righteous and moral man in his time, Abraham possessed and demonstrated qualities that caused God to single him out also. This approach, which has generally been favored by Jewish tradition, pictures Abraham from his earliest youth in search of God. To put it differently: Abraham found God because of an original intuition [9]. Thus, when God addressed the adult Abraham, He was in fact responding to Abraham's earlier dedication and searching; God reacted to the man's merits.

The Bible at times seems to support the former and at times the latter view. But both approaches together appear to offer the best answer: Man needs to be addressed by God, and God needs men who are capable of responding. It is a mutual relationship. The text begins with the divine urging, "Go forth!" It is couched as a demand but, like all divine demands, it implies a question: "Are you ready to do My will?" Abraham's "Yes" is therefore his human choice, as God's address to him is the divine choice. Both find each other ready; Abraham is open to God's desire and God opens the future to Abraham.

The Challenge

God's challenge to Abraham has a progressive sequence: "Go forth from your native land and from your father's house." This is more poetry than geographic information. It emphasizes the difficulties of the challenge Abraham is about to accept. It is difficult to leave one's land and to be an unprotected wanderer abroad; it is even more difficult to abjure all that is most dear in one's accus-

---

[1] "Scripture does not begin by reciting Abraham's merit in order to indicate that the choice was a divine mystery and by His will alone—a choice that would never be dissolved or denied. Israel will always remain the 'holy seed,' for though he sins Israel remains what he is" [8].

tomed house; it is most difficult of all to reject one's father's values and standards. The passage makes it clear that God's demand represents a severe trial of faith for Abraham, the first of several fundamental choices he will have to make in his life [10].

Blessing and Curse

Few biblical dicta have been more clearly reflected in history than the statement that those who bless Israel will be blessed and those who curse it will be cursed, or that those who are blessed bless Israel and those who are cursed curse Israel. The decline of a nation can often be clearly related to the way it has treated the Jew, and its prosperity stands in direct proportion to its sense of equity and human dignity. For if the Jew rests indeed at the fulcrum of spiritual history, his condition must be essential to the welfare of his environment. Enough historical evidence can be advanced—from the appearance of the Prophets to the events of the holocaust—to make a persuasive case for the archetypal significance of Jewish existence in the world, a significance that Jews themselves have considered central ever since patriarchal days.

To be sure, the world has but rarely given credence to this view. It has not usually seen the Jews as a "great nation," typifying man's highest and noblest aspirations. Christians and Moslems have exalted Abraham as their spiritual father and at the same time have denied validity to the religious quest of the Jews. The latter, however, have stoutly maintained, through ancient, medieval, and modern persecutions, that the blessing issued to Abraham has not been abrogated and that it is more important for the children of Abraham to be worthy of it than that others accord them recognition.

GLEANINGS

The Fathers

Not sole was I born, but entire genesis:
For to the fathers that begat me, this
Body is residence. Corpuscular,
They dwell in my veins, they eavesdrop at my
  ear,
They circle, as with Torahs, round my skull,
In exit and in entrance all day pull
The latches of my heart, descend, and rise—
And there look generations through my eyes.

ABRAHAM M. KLEIN [11]

Young Abraham

Young Abraham was an assistant to his father, a dealer in idols. After Abraham became convinced that there was only one true God, he tried to convince his father's customers of the folly of idolatry. Once a man came to buy and Abraham asked his age. On being told that he was fifty years old, the boy exclaimed: "Woe to him who at fifty would worship a one-day idol." The customer then departed in shame. Another story pictures Abraham as smashing the idols and facing the wrath of his father. "Who smashed the gods?" demanded Terah. "The chief god there," said Abraham. "You know perfectly well that clay idols don't move," said the father. "Why then do you adore them?" rejoined the boy. MIDRASH [12]

A Comparison

In what way did God's choice of Abraham differ from the earlier choices of Adam and Noah? The blessing of Adam and the blessing of Noah were natural, bestowing natural gifts, promising fertility alone, whereas this third blessing [to Abraham] is dialogic, promising and demanding at the same time; promising the formation of a people and imposing the obligations of a people, addressing the people in the person of its father and demanding in his person from it to "become a blessing," a blessing for the world of nations.

MARTIN BUBER [13]

A Gift

Man, until aware of God as a condition of his
  spiritual environment,
Would know no need of prayer.
Man, then, has not invented God, he has
  developed Faith,
To meet a God already there...
The Divine Gift, which empowers a man to
  believe,
Is marvellous and simple, like a gift of light...
Not to the sightless, but to men with eyes, who
  wander groping in the night.

EDNA ST. VINCENT MILLAY [14]

Go Forth—לֶךְ־לְךָ

Perhaps the Hebrew implies "Go by yourself." This is one journey which must be made alone. One must become a stranger in the world to view it clearly, a wanderer to find its resting point. Abraham is God's possession, not the world's. The aloneness of Abraham foreshadows that of all religious seekers and, above all, that of the people of Israel in their historic solitude.

BASED ON SAMSON RAPHAEL HIRSCH

Or the expression may be interpreted to mean, "Go to yourself," i.e., go to your roots, to find your potential. CHASIDIC [15]

[Strictly speaking the Hebrew may not be translated this way. Nachmanides interprets it as "Get on with you" (similarly Hizkuni).]

Why did Abraham have to go forth to the world?

At home he was like a flask of myrrh with a tight-fitting lid. Only when it is open can the fragrance be scattered to the winds.   MIDRASH [16]

An Allegorical Interpretation of "Go Forth"

Depart out of the earthly matter that encompasses you: escape, man, from the foul prison-house, your body, with all your might and main, and from the pleasures and lusts that act as its jailers.   PHILO [17]

Abraham's Monotheism

The Bible itself attests indirectly to the fact that Israel's monotheism is postpatriarchal. Historical monotheism is associated always with certain phenomena which serve as its organic framework: apostolic prophecy, the battle with idolatry, and the name of YHWH. Patriarchal times know none of these. Genesis records divine manifestations and prophecies, but there is no trace of apostolic prophecy. No patriarch is charged with a prophetic mission; the first apostolic prophet is Moses. Nowhere in Genesis is there reference to a battle with idolatry. The divine covenants with the patriarchs promise personal protection and future material blessings. But they never involve a fight with idolatry, nor do the patriarchs ever appear as reproaching their contemporaries for idolatry. Indeed, there is no religious contrast between the patriarchs and their surroundings.
YEHEZKEL KAUFMANN [18]

A Blessing?

It is unlikely that the word gives the true meaning of that which happened to him in his vision and which corresponded to his temperament and to his experience of himself. For the word "blessing" carries with it an idea which but ill describes men of his sort: men, that is, of roving spirit and discomfortable mind, whose novel conception of the deity is destined to make its mark upon the future. The life of men with whom new histories begin can seldom or never be a sheer unclouded blessing; not this it is which their consciousness of self whispers in their ears. "And thou shalt be a destiny": such is the purer and more precise meaning of the promise, in whatever language it may have been spoken.   THOMAS MANN [19]

Wanderings

Abraham emerges more clearly as a person. We meet him as a husband, as an uncle, and as a man who attempts to meet personal danger in what appears to be an ambiguous manner. This is an unadorned tale of the ancestor of a thoroughly human people who, like him, must respond to the claim of God, the claim of kin, and finally (as in the Sodom story) to the claim of all men. The land is promised again, this time in an extended fashion, which raises the question for the contemporary reader of how Abraham's descendants relate to the land.

וַיְהִי רָעָב בָּאָרֶץ וַיֵּרֶד אַבְרָם מִצְרַיְמָה לָגוּר שָׁם י

כִּי־כָבֵד הָרָעָב בָּאָרֶץ: וַיְהִי כַּאֲשֶׁר הִקְרִיב לָבוֹא יא

מִצְרַיְמָה וַיֹּאמֶר אֶל־שָׂרַי אִשְׁתּוֹ הִנֵּה־נָא יָדַעְתִּי כִּי

אִשָּׁה יְפַת־מַרְאֶה אָתְּ: וְהָיָה כִּי־יִרְאוּ אֹתָךְ הַמִּצְרִים יב

וְאָמְרוּ אִשְׁתּוֹ זֹאת וְהָרְגוּ אֹתִי וְאֹתָךְ יְחַיּוּ: אִמְרִי־נָא יג

אֲחֹתִי אָתְּ לְמַעַן יִיטַב־לִי בַעֲבוּרֵךְ וְחָיְתָה נַפְשִׁי

בִּגְלָלֵךְ: וַיְהִי כְּבוֹא אַבְרָם מִצְרַיְמָה וַיִּרְאוּ הַמִּצְרִים יד

אֶת־הָאִשָּׁה כִּי־יָפָה הִוא מְאֹד: וַיִּרְאוּ אֹתָהּ שָׂרֵי טו

פַרְעֹה וַיְהַלְלוּ אֹתָהּ אֶל־פַּרְעֹה וַתֻּקַּח הָאִשָּׁה בֵּית

פַּרְעֹה: וּלְאַבְרָם הֵיטִיב בַּעֲבוּרָהּ וַיְהִי־לוֹ צֹאן טז

וּבָקָר וַחֲמֹרִים וַעֲבָדִים וּשְׁפָחֹת וַאֲתֹנֹת וּגְמַלִּים:

וַיְנַגַּע יְהוָֹה אֶת־פַּרְעֹה נְגָעִים גְּדֹלִים וְאֶת־בֵּיתוֹ עַל־ יז

Genesis 12

10–17

10] There was a famine in the land, and Abram went down to Egypt to sojourn there, for the famine was severe in the land.   11] As he was about to enter Egypt, he said to his wife Sarai, "I am well aware that you are a beautiful woman.   12] When the Egyptians see you, they will say, 'She is his wife,' and they will kill me, but let you live.   13] Say then that you are my sister, that it may go well with me because of you, and that I may remain alive thanks to you."

14] When Abram entered Egypt, the Egyptians saw how very beautiful the woman was.   15] Pharaoh's courtiers saw her and praised her to Pharaoh, and the woman was taken into Pharaoh's palace.   16] And because of her, it went well with Abram; he acquired sheep, oxen, asses, male and female slaves, she-asses, and camels.

17] But the LORD afflicted Pharaoh and his household with mighty plagues on

12:10] *There was a famine in the land.* Canaan depended on rainfall, which was often insufficient, while Egypt, with its Nile waters, at times served as the bread basket of the area.

11] *A beautiful woman.* This story is told again with slight variations in chapter 20 and then a third time in chapter 26, where Isaac and Rebekah play the main roles. The tale here sees Sarah as young

יח דְּבַר שָׂרַי אֵשֶׁת אַבְרָם: וַיִּקְרָא פַרְעֹה לְאַבְרָם וַיֹּאמֶר
מַה־זֹּאת עָשִׂיתָ לִּי לָמָּה לֹא־הִגַּדְתָּ לִּי כִּי אִשְׁתְּךָ הִוא:

יט לָמָה אָמַרְתָּ אֲחֹתִי הִוא וָאֶקַּח אֹתָהּ לִי לְאִשָּׁה וְעַתָּה

כ הִנֵּה אִשְׁתְּךָ קַח וָלֵךְ: וַיְצַו עָלָיו פַּרְעֹה אֲנָשִׁים
וַיְשַׁלְּחוּ אֹתוֹ וְאֶת־אִשְׁתּוֹ וְאֶת־כָּל־אֲשֶׁר־לוֹ:

א וַיַּעַל אַבְרָם מִמִּצְרַיִם הוּא וְאִשְׁתּוֹ וְכָל־אֲשֶׁר־לוֹ וְלוֹט

ב עִמּוֹ הַנֶּגְבָּה: וְאַבְרָם כָּבֵד מְאֹד בַּמִּקְנֶה בַּכֶּסֶף

ג וּבַזָּהָב: וַיֵּלֶךְ לְמַסָּעָיו מִנֶּגֶב וְעַד־בֵּית־אֵל עַד־הַמָּקוֹם
אֲשֶׁר־הָיָה שָׁם אָהֳלֹה בַּתְּחִלָּה בֵּין בֵּית־אֵל וּבֵין הָעָי:

ד אֶל־מְקוֹם הַמִּזְבֵּחַ אֲשֶׁר־עָשָׂה שָׁם בָּרִאשֹׁנָה וַיִּקְרָא

ה שָׁם אַבְרָם בְּשֵׁם יְהֹוָה: וְגַם־לְלוֹט הַהֹלֵךְ אֶת־אַבְרָם

ו הָיָה צֹאן־וּבָקָר וְאֹהָלִים: וְלֹא־נָשָׂא אֹתָם הָאָרֶץ

Genesis 12; 13
18–20; 1–6

account of Sarai, the wife of Abram.   18] Pharaoh sent for Abram and said, "What is this you have done to me! Why did you not tell me that she was your wife? 19] Why did you say, 'She is my sister,' so that I took her as my wife? Now, here is your wife; take her and be gone!"   20] And Pharaoh put men in charge of him, and they sent him away with his wife and all that he possessed.

1] From Egypt, Abram went up into the Negeb, with his wife and all that he possessed, together with Lot.   2] Now Abram was very rich in cattle, silver, and gold.   3] And he proceeded by stages from the Negeb as far as Bethel, to the place where his tent had been formerly, between Bethel and Ai,   4] the site of the altar which he had built there at first; and there Abram invoked the LORD by name.

5] Lot, who went with Abram, also had flocks and herds and tents,   6] so that

enough to attract the Egyptians, whereas in Gen. 12:4 we are told that Abraham was seventy-five years old, which would make Sarah (who was ten years younger, according to Gen. 17:17) sixty-five.

לָשֶׁבֶת יַחְדָּו כִּי־הָיָה רְכוּשָׁם רָב וְלֹא־יָכְלוּ לָשֶׁבֶת

יַחְדָּו: וַיְהִי־רִיב בֵּין רֹעֵי מִקְנֵה־אַבְרָם וּבֵין רֹעֵי

מִקְנֵה־לוֹט וְהַכְּנַעֲנִי וְהַפְּרִזִּי אָז יֹשֵׁב בָּאָרֶץ: וַיֹּאמֶר

אַבְרָם אֶל־לוֹט אַל־נָא תְהִי מְרִיבָה בֵּינִי וּבֵינֶךָ וּבֵין

רֹעַי וּבֵין רֹעֶיךָ כִּי־אֲנָשִׁים אַחִים אֲנָחְנוּ: הֲלֹא כָל־

הָאָרֶץ לְפָנֶיךָ הִפָּרֶד נָא מֵעָלָי אִם־הַשְּׂמֹאל וְאֵימִנָה

וְאִם־הַיָּמִין וְאַשְׂמְאִילָה: וַיִּשָּׂא־לוֹט אֶת־עֵינָיו וַיַּרְא

אֶת־כָּל־כִּכַּר הַיַּרְדֵּן כִּי כֻלָּהּ מַשְׁקֶה לִפְנֵי שַׁחֵת

יְהוָה אֶת־סְדֹם וְאֶת־עֲמֹרָה כְּגַן־יְהוָה כְּאֶרֶץ מִצְרַיִם

בֹּאֲכָה צֹעַר: וַיִּבְחַר־לוֹ לוֹט אֵת כָּל־כִּכַּר הַיַּרְדֵּן

וַיִּסַּע לוֹט מִקֶּדֶם וַיִּפָּרְדוּ אִישׁ מֵעַל אָחִיו: אַבְרָם

Genesis 13

7–12

the land could not support them staying together; for their possessions were so great that they could not remain together.   **7]** And there was quarreling between the herdsmen of Abram's cattle and those of Lot's cattle.—The Canaanites and Perizzites were then dwelling in the land.— **8]** Abram said to Lot, "Let there be no strife between you and me, between my herdsmen and yours, for we are kinsmen. **9]** Is not the whole land before you? Let us separate: if you go north, I will go south; and if you go south, I will go north."   **10]** Lot looked about him and saw how well watered was the whole plain of the Jordan, all of it—this was before the LORD had destroyed Sodom and Gomorrah—all the way to Zoar, like the garden of the LORD, like the land of Egypt.   **11]** So Lot chose for himself the whole plain of the Jordan, and Lot journeyed eastward. Thus they parted from each other;   **12]** Abram

13:10] *Plain of the Jordan.* Recent explorations have shown that the area was once densely inhabited. It was probably one of the first settled sections of the country as well as one of its richest parts. "It remains today potentially what it was then indubitably, a garden of God" [1].

11] *Thus they parted.* Abraham stays in Canaan proper while Lot abandons it. One purpose of the story is to underscore that Moab and Ammon, Lot's descendants, have no right to the land which, in the passage immediately following, is once more promised to Abraham.

יָשַׁב בְּאֶרֶץ־כְּנָעַן וְלוֹט יָשַׁב בְּעָרֵי הַכִּכָּר וַיֶּאֱהַל

יג עַד־סְדֹם: וְאַנְשֵׁי סְדֹם רָעִים וְחַטָּאִים לַיהוָה מְאֹד:

יד וַיהוָה אָמַר אֶל־אַבְרָם אַחֲרֵי הִפָּרֶד־לוֹט מֵעִמּוֹ שָׂא

נָא עֵינֶיךָ וּרְאֵה מִן־הַמָּקוֹם אֲשֶׁר־אַתָּה שָׁם צָפֹנָה

טו וָנֶגְבָּה וָקֵדְמָה וָיָמָּה: כִּי אֶת־כָּל־הָאָרֶץ אֲשֶׁר־אַתָּה

טז רֹאֶה לְךָ אֶתְּנֶנָּה וּלְזַרְעֲךָ עַד־עוֹלָם: וְשַׂמְתִּי אֶת־

זַרְעֲךָ כַּעֲפַר הָאָרֶץ אֲשֶׁר אִם־יוּכַל אִישׁ לִמְנוֹת

יז אֶת־עֲפַר הָאָרֶץ גַּם־זַרְעֲךָ יִמָּנֶה: קוּם הִתְהַלֵּךְ

יח בָּאָרֶץ לְאָרְכָּהּ וּלְרָחְבָּהּ כִּי לְךָ אֶתְּנֶנָּה: וַיֶּאֱהַל

אַבְרָם וַיָּבֹא וַיֵּשֶׁב בְּאֵלֹנֵי מַמְרֵא אֲשֶׁר בְּחֶבְרוֹן וַיִּבֶן

שָׁם מִזְבֵּחַ לַיהוָה: פ

Genesis 13

13–18

remained in the land of Canaan, while Lot settled in the cities of the Plain, pitching his tents near Sodom.   13] Now the inhabitants of Sodom were very wicked sinners against the LORD.

14] And the LORD said to Abram, after Lot had parted from him, "Raise your eyes and look out from where you are, to the north and south, to the east and west, 15] for I give all the land that you see to you and your offspring forever.   16] I will make your offspring as the dust of the earth, so that if one can count the dust of the earth, then your offspring too can be counted.   17] Up, walk about the land, through its length and its breadth, for I give it to you."   18] And Abram moved his tent, and came to dwell at the terebinths of Mamre which are in Hebron; and he built an altar there to the LORD.

14] *Look out from where you are.* That is, from Bethel, from which there is a good view of the southern Jordan Valley.

18] *Hebron.* South of Jerusalem. Elsewhere Hebron is called Kiriath-arba (Gen. 23:2; 35:27). It became the Patriarchs' primary home in Canaan, as well as their burial place.

You Are My Sister

Abraham instructed his wife to tell the Egyptians that she was his sister. She was to say nothing of their marriage. This raises a number of historical as well as moral questions.

There is evidence that Sarah was indeed Abraham's sister. In the second version of the story we learn that although the two had different mothers they shared the same father (Gen. 20:12). It is possible that this latter notation reflects a stage of civilization in which descent was traced through the mother and marriages between offspring of the same father (but not the same mother) were permissible.[1] Hence, according to this assumption, when Abraham instructed Sarah to say she was his sister, he based his request on a real relationship.

Another explanation is based on the assumption that Abraham lived about 1500 B.C.E., when the word "sister" could have an additional, special meaning [3]. In American English today, "sister" can mean "nun." In English, French, German, and Hebrew, it can mean "nurse." In Abraham's time, "sister" was also a Hurrian legal term. Abraham and Sarah came from a Hurrian cultural background and it would have been natural for them to use Hurrian terminology. As documents from Nuzi show, a Hurrian could adopt his wife as his sister, thereby giving her special status, for she would be treated as a blood relative of her husband's family. It may be assumed that such adoptions took place in the upper stratum of society where inheritance and family bonds were important. Thus, in this interpretation Abraham instructed his wife to mention her privileged "sister" status, in order to provide assurance that both of them would be treated with respect. The Egyptians apparently understood Hurrian terminology and no harm befell the couple. It was in this fashion that the story was first told. Later on, however, as knowledge of Hurrian custom faded, Abraham's request seemed incomprehensible except as a lie and the story became transformed into one of deceit and divine intervention.

Whatever the early context, the biblical text shows us how Abraham's action caused Pharaoh, who did not know that Sarah was married, to take her into his house. Some commentators excuse Abraham's behavior by saying that his ruse was meant to bid for time, until the famine in Canaan would be ended and he could take his wife and leave Egypt [4]. Others frankly disapprove [5] and note that Abraham could not make reply to Pharaoh's reprimand since the latter's generosity had left the Patriarch in the rather embarrassing situation of having lied and having been rewarded for it.[2]

Abraham's behavior raises still another question. A man can be judged guilty when he has a choice—but what choices are open to a man who, like Abraham, believes he is faced with mortal danger? What could Abraham have done, given the knowledge

---

[1] This system of family relations is called metronymic, in contrast to patronymic which considers children born of the same father as members of the family. Traces of a metronymic society appear in various parts of the Bible, e.g., it is usually the mothers who name the children; descent is at times traced through mothers rather than fathers; a marriage between Amnon and Tamar is permissible even though they have the same father (II Sam. 13:13) [2].

[2] One view: The gifts were for teaching the Egyptians astronomy and mathematics [6]. Another view: "The narrator gloats over Abraham's astoundingly successful lie, which made a virtue out of necessity. He identifies himself joyfully with his forebears' sharp practice" [7]. And: "That is why they are so proudly conscious of the fact that their women are more beautiful than those living in the city . . . In moral considerations, too, they consider themselves superior: The city dwellers are weak and susceptible to feminine charm" [8].

of the prospects available to him? The text, as it does so often, merely states the problem, leaving it to the reader to ponder it further.

Jewish teaching has generally held that, even under duress, no man may intentionally kill or commit a sexual crime on an innocent person.[3] The application of this principle often poses agonizing questions that can be decided only within a given context. (The trials for war crimes after World War II essentially attempted to define the limits of a man's right to say, "I had no choice.") Since both Sarah and Pharaoh were put in jeopardy by Abraham, the proper judgment would seem to support Nachmanides' comment: "It was a sin."

The Promised Land

We can hardly overemphasize the importance of those biblical passages which, like Gen. 13:15, state that God gave Canaan to Abraham and his offspring forever. From these traditions and memories, amplified by centuries of sacred sentiment, grew a unique relationship between a people and a land. Some commentators deny the Abrahamic antiquity of the tradition and claim that it arose in later ages to give the military conquest of the land by Joshua an *ex post facto* religious legitimation. Even if this were so, it would emphasize that for Abraham's descendants military acquisition and physical possession—sufficient for all other nations' claims—were not the core of their relationship to the land. For them Canaan, Palestine, Zion, Israel, by whatever name it was known, was linked to the will and promise of God, and hence it was a Holy and Promised Land, as it was later to be called.

To someone who believes that God did indeed will the land to Abraham's people, the Jews' subsequent claim to it is beyond dispute. The claim has total force, encompassing legal and moral rights. But the matter should be left open as a question of faith, taking into account that for millennia Jews have *believed* that their relationship to the land had the sanction of God. Thus their claim obtained a spiritual basis nurtured in thousands of years of possession and loss, presence and absence, reality and memory. To be sure, the people survived without the land and the land without the people—but somehow God and Torah entered into this relationship and gave it a special stamp.

To the Jew, therefore, Zion has been more than a place of pilgrimage or a collection of ancestral sites. It has been both sacred dream and holy potential, the place where God's kingdom on earth would first emerge. The Jew has steadfastly believed that it is God's will that he possess the land and that he possess it in justice—for God casts out of this land those who defile it. The Amorites lost possession because of their sinfulness, and Israel itself was warned always to be heedful of this possibility (Gen. 15:16; Lev. 18:24; Deut. 9:5). Only a community of righteousness would match the dreams and prayers centered on this small strip of earth: "Zion shall be redeemed by justice, and those who return to her, by righteousness" (Isa. 1:27).

In the course of centuries, and especially in modern times, many Jews came to feel that God's role no longer needed to be considered in their relationship to the land. They were satisfied that history had forged an indissoluble bond between land and people and that as homeland and as the cultural and political center of Jewry it remained the focus of the age-old dreams. Thus, religion and history became intertwined for Zion's children: Believers and nonbelievers alike took the land to heart in their own way and made it the object of their hopes.

[3] A man came to Rabba and told him: "The governor of my town told me to kill a certain man, else I would be killed." Rabba said: "You must suffer death rather than commit murder. Who knows whether your blood is redder [i.e., more valuable] than his: perhaps the blood of the intended victim is redder than yours!" [9].

GLEANINGS

Sarah's Beauty
> Of all the virgins and brides
> That walk beneath the canopy,
> None can compare with Sarah.

GENESIS APOCRYPHON [10]

> When Abraham went with Sarah into Egypt,
> The land was all illumined with her beauty.

HENRY WADSWORTH LONGFELLOW [11]

The Possibility of Adultery

Did not Abraham by his deception expose Sarah to adultery? Yes, but there was a possibility it might not occur, and in such a case his plan, executed under duress, was justified. Had adultery occurred, Abraham would have been held guilty.

MIDRASH [12]

The Scheme Which Failed

On this journey from Canaan to Egypt, Abraham first observed the beauty of Sarah. Chaste as he was, he had never before looked at her, but now, when they were wading through a stream, he saw the reflection of her beauty in the water like the brilliance of the sun. Wherefore he spoke to her thus, "The Egyptians are very sensual, and I will put thee in a casket that no harm befall me on account of thee." At the Egyptian boundary, the tax collectors asked him about the contents of the casket, and Abraham told them he had barley in it. "No," they said, "it contains wheat." "Very well," replied Abraham, "I am prepared to pay the tax on wheat." The officers then hazarded the guess, "It contains pepper!" Abraham agreed to pay the tax on pepper, and, when they charged him with concealing gold in the casket, he did not refuse to pay the tax on gold, and finally on precious stones. Seeing that he demurred to no charge, however high, the tax collectors, made thoroughly suspicious, insisted upon his unfastening the casket and letting them examine the contents. When it was forced open, the whole of Egypt was resplendent with the beauty of Sarah. MIDRASH [13]

In Arabic Literature

Sarah, the wife of Abraham, was, according to some accounts, the sister of Lot and the daughter of Aran, Abraham's paternal uncle. According to others, she was the daughter of the king of Haran, and her mother was daughter of Kutba, king of Babylon. Sarah was the most beautiful woman of her time and possessed a perfect figure. She resembled Eve, to whom God gave two-thirds of all beauty; indeed, she was so beautiful that Abraham transported her in a chest. When, on entering Egypt, Abraham was obliged to give a tithe of all his goods, he at first refused to open the chest in which Sarah was, and when he was finally forced to do so the official ran and told the king. Questioned by the latter regarding Sarah, Abraham replied that she was his sister, having instructed her to say the same. When, on that supposition, the king wished to marry her and reached out to take her, Sarah prayed God to wither his hand; and when the king promised not to touch her, she prayed God to restore it. Forgetful of his promise, the king reached toward her once more and his hand was again withered. This was repeated three times. Abraham was a witness of this interview, God causing the walls of the house to become transparent for the purpose. Finally the king restored Sarah to Abraham and loaded her with presents. He insisted on her choosing for herself one of his slave girls, and she selected Hagar for whom she had conceived a liking.

JEWISH ENCYCLOPEDIA [14]

The War of the Four against the Five

The war of the four against the five appears as an intrusion in an otherwise smoothly flowing narrative. It is likely that this chapter comes from an Abrahamic tradition not otherwise represented in the Torah. Despite enormous research, both source and purpose of this story have remained an enigma [1]. Are we here face-to-face with a historic incident? Does the event have some special significance? We do not have enough knowledge to answer these questions.

We are told of certain kings who were bound for El-paran (near today's Eilat, in the Negev), possibly for the copper mines located there. The invaders had come from Mesopotamia, and after accomplishing their objective in the south they returned home, carrying Lot with them as a prisoner. Subsequently we meet Abraham in the unfamiliar role of warrior.

יא וַיְהִי בִּימֵי אַמְרָפֶל מֶלֶךְ־שִׁנְעָר אַרְיוֹךְ מֶלֶךְ אֶלָּסָר

ב כְּדָרְלָעֹמֶר מֶלֶךְ עֵילָם וְתִדְעָל מֶלֶךְ גּוֹיִם: עָשׂוּ
מִלְחָמָה אֶת־בֶּרַע מֶלֶךְ סְדֹם וְאֶת־בִּרְשַׁע מֶלֶךְ עֲמֹרָה
שִׁנְאָב מֶלֶךְ אַדְמָה וְשֶׁמְאֵבֶר מֶלֶךְ צְבֹיִים* וּמֶלֶךְ

ג בֶּלַע הִיא־צֹעַר: כָּל־אֵלֶּה חָבְרוּ אֶל־עֵמֶק הַשִּׂדִּים

ד הוּא יָם הַמֶּלַח: שְׁתֵּים עֶשְׂרֵה שָׁנָה עָבְדוּ אֶת־

ה כְּדָרְלָעֹמֶר וּשְׁלֹשׁ־עֶשְׂרֵה שָׁנָה מָרָדוּ: וּבְאַרְבַּע עֶשְׂרֵה
שָׁנָה בָּא כְדָרְלָעֹמֶר וְהַמְּלָכִים אֲשֶׁר אִתּוֹ וַיַּכּוּ אֶת־
רְפָאִים בְּעַשְׁתְּרֹת קַרְנַיִם וְאֶת־הַזּוּזִים בְּהֶם וְאֵת

Genesis 14
1–5

* ב צבוים קרי.

1] Now, when Amraphel king of Shinar, Arioch king of Ellasar, Chedorlaomer king of Elam, and Tidal king of Goiim   2] made war on Bera king of Sodom, Birsha king of Gomorrah, Shinab king of Admah, Shemeber king of Zeboiim, and the king of Bela, which is Zoar,   3] all the latter joined forces at the Valley of Siddim, now the Dead Sea.   4] Twelve years they had served Chedorlaomer, and in the thirteenth year they rebelled.   5] In the fourteenth year Chedorlaomer and the kings who were with him came and defeated the Rephaim in Ashteroth-karnaim, the Zuzim

14:1] *Shinar.* A name for Babylonia (Gen. 10: 10).
/Some scholars suggest that Shinar must here refer to a location closer to Canaan [2]./
   Arioch. This name is found in cuneiform sources, but Ellasar is not.
   Elam. An eastern rival of Mesopotamia.
   Tidal. A Hittite name.
   Goiim. Literally, "nations," possibly used here to mean "foreigners," a term, like the Greek "barbarians," that came to have contemptuous overtones.

2] *Bera . . . Birsha.* Probably two unhistorical names that refer to the depravity of Sodom and Gomorrah (Gen. 18:16ff.). Bera could mean "with evil," and the consonants of Birsha, "with wickedness."

3] *Valley of Siddim, now the Dead Sea.* In Hebrew the "Salt Sea." The text recalls the time before the waters of the Dead Sea had submerged the valley at its southern end.

5] *Rephaim.* A mythical nation of giants.

הָאֵימִים בְּשָׁוֵה קִרְיָתָיִם: וְאֶת־הַחֹרִי בְּהַרְרָם שֵׂעִיר

עַד אֵיל פָּארָן אֲשֶׁר עַל־הַמִּדְבָּר: וַיָּשֻׁבוּ וַיָּבֹאוּ אֶל־

עֵין מִשְׁפָּט הִוא קָדֵשׁ וַיַּכּוּ אֶת־כָּל־שְׂדֵה הָעֲמָלֵקִי

וְגַם אֶת־הָאֱמֹרִי הַיֹּשֵׁב בְּחַצְצֹן תָּמָר: וַיֵּצֵא מֶלֶךְ־

סְדֹם וּמֶלֶךְ עֲמֹרָה וּמֶלֶךְ אַדְמָה וּמֶלֶךְ צְבֹיִּם* וּמֶלֶךְ

בֶּלַע הִוא־צֹעַר וַיַּעַרְכוּ אִתָּם מִלְחָמָה בְּעֵמֶק הַשִּׂדִּים:

אֵת כְּדָרְלָעֹמֶר מֶלֶךְ עֵילָם וְתִדְעָל מֶלֶךְ גּוֹיִם

וְאַמְרָפֶל מֶלֶךְ שִׁנְעָר וְאַרְיוֹךְ מֶלֶךְ אֶלָּסָר אַרְבָּעָה

מְלָכִים אֶת־הַחֲמִשָּׁה: וְעֵמֶק הַשִּׂדִּים בֶּאֱרֹת בֶּאֱרֹת

חֵמָר וַיָּנֻסוּ מֶלֶךְ־סְדֹם וַעֲמֹרָה וַיִּפְּלוּ־שָׁמָּה וְהַנִּשְׁאָרִים

הֶרָה נָּסוּ: וַיִּקְחוּ אֶת־כָּל־רְכֻשׁ סְדֹם וַעֲמֹרָה וְאֶת־

Genesis 14

6–11

* ח צבוים קרי.

in Ham, the Emim in Shaveh-kiriathaim,   6] and the Horites in their hill country
of Seir as far as El-paran, which is by the wilderness.   7] On their way back they
came to En-mishpat, which is Kadesh, and subdued all the territory of the Amalek-
ites, and also the Amorites who dwelt in Hazazon-tamar.   8] Then the king of
Sodom, the king of Gomorrah, the king of Admah, the king of Zeboiim, and the king
of Bela, which is Zoar, went forth and engaged them in battle in the Valley of Siddim:
9] Chedorlaomer king of Elam, Tidal king of Goiim, Amraphel king of Shinar, and
Arioch king of Ellasar—four kings against five.

10] Now the Valley of Siddim was dotted with bitumen pits; and the kings of
Sodom and Gomorrah, in their flight, threw themselves into them, while the rest
escaped to the hill country.   11] [The invaders] seized all the wealth of Sodom and

7] *Hazazon-tamar.* Possibly another name for En-Gedi
(see II Chron. 20:2) [3].

יג כָּל־אָכְלָם וַיֵּלֵכוּ: וַיִּקְחוּ אֶת־לוֹט וְאֶת־רְכֻשׁוֹ בֶּן־אֲחִי

אַבְרָם וַיֵּלֵכוּ וְהוּא יֹשֵׁב בִּסְדֹם: וַיָּבֹא הַפָּלִיט וַיַּגֵּד

לְאַבְרָם הָעִבְרִי וְהוּא שֹׁכֵן בְּאֵלֹנֵי מַמְרֵא הָאֱמֹרִי

אֲחִי אֶשְׁכֹּל וַאֲחִי עָנֵר וְהֵם בַּעֲלֵי בְרִית־אַבְרָם:

יד וַיִּשְׁמַע אַבְרָם כִּי נִשְׁבָּה אָחִיו וַיָּרֶק אֶת־חֲנִיכָיו יְלִידֵי

טו בֵיתוֹ שְׁמֹנָה עָשָׂר וּשְׁלֹשׁ מֵאוֹת וַיִּרְדֹּף עַד־דָּן: וַיֵּחָלֵק

עֲלֵיהֶם לַיְלָה הוּא וַעֲבָדָיו וַיַּכֵּם וַיִּרְדְּפֵם עַד־חוֹבָה

טז אֲשֶׁר מִשְּׂמֹאל לְדַמָּשֶׂק: וַיָּשֶׁב אֵת כָּל־הָרְכֻשׁ וְגַם

אֶת־לוֹט אָחִיו וּרְכֻשׁוֹ הֵשִׁיב וְגַם אֶת־הַנָּשִׁים וְאֶת־

יז הָעָם: וַיֵּצֵא מֶלֶךְ־סְדֹם לִקְרָאתוֹ אַחֲרֵי שׁוּבוֹ מֵהַכּוֹת

Genesis 14

12–17

Gomorrah and all their provisions, and went their way.   12] They also took Lot, the son of Abram's brother, and his possessions, and departed; for he had settled in Sodom.

13] A fugitive brought the news to Abram the Hebrew, who was dwelling at the terebinths of Mamre the Amorite, kinsman of Eshkol and Aner, these being Abram's allies.   14] When Abram heard that his kinsman had been taken captive, he mustered his retainers, born into his household, numbering three hundred and eighteen, and went in pursuit as far as Dan.   15] At night, he and his servants deployed against them and defeated them; and he pursued them as far as Hobah, which is north of Damascus.   16] He brought back all the possessions; he also brought back his kinsman Lot and his possessions, and the women and the rest of the people.

17] When he returned from defeating Chedorlaomer and the kings with him,

14] *Retainers.* Meaning of חֲנִיכָיו is uncertain.

Three hundred and eighteen. Probably either a conventional number used for groups or a number that is part of the symbolism built around the

number seven in the Book of Genesis. The prime numbers between 7 and 49 (7 × 7), when added together, total 318.

/The number 318 is also found in a description of the

אֶת־כְּדָרְלָעֹמֶר וְאֶת־הַמְּלָכִים אֲשֶׁר אִתּוֹ אֶל־עֵמֶק

יח שָׁוֵה הוּא עֵמֶק הַמֶּלֶךְ: וּמַלְכִּי־צֶדֶק מֶלֶךְ שָׁלֵם

יט הוֹצִיא לֶחֶם וָיָיִן וְהוּא כֹהֵן לְאֵל עֶלְיוֹן: וַיְבָרְכֵהוּ

וַיֹּאמַר בָּרוּךְ אַבְרָם לְאֵל עֶלְיוֹן קֹנֵה שָׁמַיִם וָאָרֶץ:

כ וּבָרוּךְ אֵל עֶלְיוֹן אֲשֶׁר־מִגֵּן צָרֶיךָ בְּיָדֶךָ וַיִּתֶּן־לוֹ

כא מַעֲשֵׂר מִכֹּל: וַיֹּאמֶר מֶלֶךְ־סְדֹם אֶל־אַבְרָם תֶּן־לִי

כב הַנֶּפֶשׁ וְהָרְכֻשׁ קַח־לָךְ: וַיֹּאמֶר אַבְרָם אֶל־מֶלֶךְ סְדֹם

הֲרִמֹתִי יָדִי אֶל־יְהוָֹה אֵל עֶלְיוֹן קֹנֵה שָׁמַיִם וָאָרֶץ:

כג אִם־מִחוּט וְעַד שְׂרוֹךְ־נַעַל וְאִם־אֶקַּח מִכָּל־אֲשֶׁר־לָךְ

Genesis 14

18–23

the king of Sodom came out to meet him in the Valley of Shaveh, which is the Valley of the King. **18]** And Melchizedek, king of Salem, brought out bread and wine; he was a priest of God Most High. **19]** He blessed him, saying, "Blessed be Abram of God Most High, / Creator of heaven and earth. / **20]** And blessed be God Most High, / Who has delivered your foes into your hand." And [Abram] gave him a tenth of everything.

21] Then the king of Sodom said to Abram, "Give me the persons, and take the possessions for yourself." **22]** But Abram said to the king of Sodom, "I swear to the LORD, God Most High, Creator of heaven and earth, **23]** that I will not take so much as a thread or a sandal strap, or anything that is yours, lest you say, 'It is

retinue of a Mitanni princess [4]. It has also been noted that in the *Iliad* the number of men killed is 318. Another opinion is that the figure 318 is actual ancient memory: "To this very day there are old men in the tents of Arabia who can recite the history of their ancestors for forty generations, and, if in their recital they stray but a jot from the facts, others within hearing will immediately correct them, or supply forgotten details" [5]./

20] *A tenth of everything.* The tithe customarily given to the priests (see Num. 18:21).

22] *I swear.* Literally, "lift up my hand."

23] *Will not take.* Abraham, true to nomadic tradition, does not wish to be beholden to anyone. Besides, as a trader, he need not rely on plunder as a source of income [6]. It is also possible that his bruskness signifies some contempt for the king of Sodom.

כד וְלֹא תֹאמַר אֲנִי הֶעֱשַׁרְתִּי אֶת־אַבְרָם: בִּלְעָדַי רַק

אֲשֶׁר אָכְלוּ הַנְּעָרִים וְחֵלֶק הָאֲנָשִׁים אֲשֶׁר הָלְכוּ אִתִּי

עָנֵר אֶשְׁכֹּל וּמַמְרֵא הֵם יִקְחוּ חֶלְקָם: ס

I who made Abram rich.'   **24]** For me, nothing but what my servants have used up; as for the share of the men who went with me—Aner, Eshkol, and Mamre—let them take their share."

Abraham the Hebrew

For the first time since his introduction into the biblical text, Abraham is referred to—without preparation or explanation—as an *Ivri*, a Hebrew. The term is difficult to trace, but many scholars agree that it is in some way connected with the word "Habiru."

During the nineteenth to fourteenth centuries B.C.E. a class of people known as Habiru lived in the Fertile Crescent. They may originally have come from Arabia [7] and may have been related by family ties; they became prominent in Mesopotamia and later spread out all the way to Egypt. The Habiru were a group with distinct occupations and appear to have specialized as mercenaries and administrators. Although at first they were nomads or semi-nomads, they later settled in the countries of their choice. They were, however, usually considered foreigners, which means that they succeeded in maintaining their group identity. Their status was often akin to that of modern civil servants, and when they were sufficiently numerous they would on occasion, by shifting their allegiance, influence a country's political fortunes. They were sometimes feared, and their cognomen was "wanderers who are also known as robbers." Thus, Habiru was not so much a gentilic term referring to a particular ethnic or linguistic group but rather a term of social or political significance [8].

What is the relationship between the Hebrews and these Habiru? Linguistically the words Habiru and *Ivri* appear to share a common root [9]. It is likely that in Egypt and elsewhere members of the Israelite tribes occupied positions similar to, or because of familial ties were identified with, the Habiru. The repeated application of this term by non-Israelites in time caused the Israelites themselves to use the cognomen Habiru,

which they pronounced *Ivri* (עִבְרִי; plural *Ivrim*, עִבְרִים). After the Habiru themselves had disappeared as an identifiable group, the name *Ivrim* was traced to the antediluvian Eber (עֵבֶר, *Ever*), who was installed in the catalog of descent as the legendary ancestor or eponym (Gen. 11:16). Later folk etymology understood *Ever* to mean "the other side of"—presumably the Euphrates—thus linking the Israelites with Abraham who had come from Ur.

It is possible that for some time the term *Ivrim* was used only when the members of the Israelite tribes spoke of themselves to outsiders and when outsiders referred to them. Thus, Abraham is called *Ivri* vis-à-vis an outsider (Gen. 14:13) [10]; and Jonah says, "I am an *Ivri*," when asked his identity by gentile sailors (Jonah 1:9). Otherwise the people referred to themselves by their tribes (e.g., Judah, Ephraim) or by their more immediate common ancestor, Israel.

Melchizedek

The king of Salem, whose name may mean "The King Is Justice"[1] was the priest of *El Elyon* (Gen. 14:18), a deity mentioned in Phoenician records. *Elyon* later came to mean "Most High," and the expression *El Elyon* (God Most High) was also applied to the God of Abraham.

This identification led later tradition to classify Melchizedek with those righteous Gentiles who, like Job and Jethro, acknowledged the Lord of Abraham as their God. The Jews of Alexandria, who were interested in proselytizing the Gentiles, considered Melchizedek a monotheist whom Abraham admired and whose example other Gentiles followed. Thus, Melchizedek became a subject of speculation in Jewish and Christian traditions. Already in Psalms he is called the

---

[1] Or "King of Justice," or "The King Is Tzedek" (Tzedek being a divine name) [11].

prototype of the ideal king who will spring from the line of David:

The Lord has sworn and will not repent:
You are a priest forever,
After the manner of Melchizedek (Ps. 110:4).

The Christian Scripture developed this tradition further and called Jesus the "high priest after the order of Melchizedek" [12]; the ancient king was also said to have resembled the Son of God [13] and to have been superior to Abraham. Melchizedek's merit is recalled in the daily Mass, and the entire communion tradition of bread and wine is traced back to this story.

The original importance accorded Melchizedek most likely arose from the fact that he was king of Salem and that Salem was identified with Jerusalem (Ps. 76:3) [14]. In this way tradition established a link between Abraham and the Holy City, for Abraham was thought to prefigure his people who in the centuries to come would pay their tithes to the Temple in the very spot where Abraham made his first covenant [15].

GLEANINGS

Three Hundred Eighteen Retainers

Abraham's victory over the kings was not due to the assistance of 318 men but of one single helper. For 318 is the numerical equivalent of the letters in Eliezer, the servant of Abraham. Having established that 318 means Eliezer, we further note that the word Eliezer itself means "God is my help" —which is to say that Abraham's helper was God, and that he defeated the kings with faith rather than force.   MIDRASH [16]

[The equivalency refers to an old method of biblical interpretation called *gematria*. Each letter of the Hebrew alphabet has a numerical value (א=1, ב=2, etc.); words of equal numerical value were compared and conclusions drawn on that basis. Thus the letters in Eliezer add up to 318: א=1, ל=30, י=10, ע=70, ז=7, ר=200.]

Abraham the Ivri

The word עִבְרִי [*Ivri*] is said to be derived from עֵבֶר [*ever*], on the other side of, or beyond. According to Rabbi Judah, the words "Abraham the *Ivri*" meant that the whole world stood on one side and he on the other, i.e., Abraham's faith ran counter to what all other men believed.   MIDRASH [17]

War

Why did Abraham get involved in the wars of those kings? Because his kinsman Lot was taken captive. Is there ever a war when Abraham does not hear the message, "Your brother is in trouble"?   MOSES AVIGDOR AMIEL [18]

The Language of Prayer

Melchizedek and Abraham use the same term, *El Elyon*, but they attach different meanings to it. Each refers to his own God—the pagan king to his pagan deity and Abraham to "God Most High." They worship together, each respecting the faith of the other. Thus, they set an example of ancient "interfaith worship": They use formulations, wholly acceptable to each other, and thereby make common prayer possible.

Abraham's God

There were no stories about God. That was indeed perhaps the most remarkable thing: the courage with which Abram represented and expressed God's essence from the first, without more ado, simply in that he said "God."

   THOMAS MANN [19]

The Covenant between the Pieces;
the Birth of Ishmael

For a second time Abraham hears the divine promise that he will be the father of a great nation. The promise is made to him in a special and most solemn form—with darkness, smoking oven, and flaming torch.

A *berit*, or covenant, is made. Thereafter, God's promise seems to move toward its first stage of fulfilment: Abraham will at last have an offspring. But again there is a delay; the Patriarch finally fathers a son, yet not with Sarah. Chapter 16 heightens the dramatic tension by introducing Hagar and Ishmael as counterfoils to the main personages.

אַחַר הַדְּבָרִים הָאֵלֶּה הָיָה דְבַר־יְהֹוָה אֶל־אַבְרָם
בַּמַּחֲזֶה לֵאמֹר אַל־תִּירָא אַבְרָם אָנֹכִי מָגֵן לָךְ
שְׂכָרְךָ הַרְבֵּה מְאֹד: וַיֹּאמֶר אַבְרָם אֲדֹנָי יֶהֹוִה מַה־
תִּתֶּן־לִי וְאָנֹכִי הוֹלֵךְ עֲרִירִי וּבֶן־מֶשֶׁק בֵּיתִי הוּא
דַּמֶּשֶׂק אֱלִיעֶזֶר: וַיֹּאמֶר אַבְרָם הֵן לִי לֹא נָתַתָּה
זָרַע וְהִנֵּה בֶן־בֵּיתִי יוֹרֵשׁ אֹתִי: וְהִנֵּה דְבַר־יְהֹוָה
אֵלָיו לֵאמֹר לֹא יִירָשְׁךָ זֶה כִּי־אִם אֲשֶׁר יֵצֵא מִמֵּעֶיךָ
הוּא יִירָשֶׁךָ: וַיּוֹצֵא אֹתוֹ הַחוּצָה וַיֹּאמֶר הַבֶּט־נָא
הַשָּׁמַיְמָה וּסְפֹר הַכּוֹכָבִים אִם־תּוּכַל לִסְפֹּר אֹתָם

Genesis 15

1–5

1] Some time later, the word of the LORD came to Abram in a vision, saying, "Fear not, Abram, / I am a shield to you; / Your reward shall be very great."   **2]** But Abram said, "O Lord GOD, what can You give me, seeing that I continue childless, and the one in charge of my household is Dammesek Eliezer!"   **3]** Abram said further, "Since You have granted me no offspring, one of my household will be my heir."   **4]** The word of the LORD came to him in reply, "That one shall not be your heir; none but your very own issue shall be your heir."   **5]** He took him outside and said, "Look toward heaven and count the stars, if you are able to count

15:1] *The word of the Lord came to.* The phrase is used frequently in Jeremiah and Ezekiel to introduce a prophetic vision. It occurs here, but nowhere else in the Torah.

I am a shield to you. Hence in Jewish tradition God is often referred to as "Shield of Abraham" (e.g., in the first of the eighteen benedictions in the prayer book).

2] *Dammesek Eliezer.* Most likely Abraham's servant, "the Damascan." Abraham may have adopted him as a son and, if Hurrian practice was applicable, he would be Abraham's beneficiary.

/ This was not so in later Jewish (rabbinic) law, in which technical adoption comparable to the Roman *adrogatio* did not exist, though it has a place in modern Israeli law. Albright believes that Abraham adopted Eliezer so that he would be able to obtain credit. The native-born Eliezer could own property, thus extending Abraham's credit base [1]./

י וַיֹּאמֶר לוֹ כֹּה יִהְיֶה זַרְעֶךָ: וְהֶאֱמִן בַּיהוָה וַיַּחְשְׁבֶהָ

ז לּוֹ צְדָקָה: וַיֹּאמֶר אֵלָיו אֲנִי יְהוָה אֲשֶׁר הוֹצֵאתִיךָ

מֵאוּר כַּשְׂדִּים לָתֶת לְךָ אֶת־הָאָרֶץ הַזֹּאת לְרִשְׁתָּהּ:

ח וַיֹּאמַר אֲדֹנָי יֱהוִֹה בַּמָּה אֵדַע כִּי אִירָשֶׁנָּה: וַיֹּאמֶר

ט אֵלָיו קְחָה לִי עֶגְלָה מְשֻׁלֶּשֶׁת וְעֵז מְשֻׁלֶּשֶׁת וְאַיִל

מְשֻׁלָּשׁ וְתֹר וְגוֹזָל: וַיִּקַּח־לוֹ אֶת־כָּל־אֵלֶּה וַיְבַתֵּר אֹתָם

י בַּתָּוֶךְ וַיִּתֵּן אִישׁ־בִּתְרוֹ לִקְרַאת רֵעֵהוּ וְאֶת־הַצִּפֹּר

יא לֹא בָתָר: וַיֵּרֶד הָעַיִט עַל־הַפְּגָרִים וַיַּשֵּׁב אֹתָם

יב אַבְרָם: וַיְהִי הַשֶּׁמֶשׁ לָבוֹא וְתַרְדֵּמָה נָפְלָה עַל־

אַבְרָם וְהִנֵּה אֵימָה חֲשֵׁכָה גְדֹלָה נֹפֶלֶת עָלָיו:

them." And He added, "So shall your offspring be." **6]** And because he put his trust in the LORD, He reckoned it to his merit.

7] Then He said to him, "I am the LORD who brought you out from Ur of the Chaldeans to give you this land as a possession." **8]** And he said, "O Lord GOD, how shall I know that I am to possess it?" **9]** He answered, "Bring Me a three-year-old heifer, a three-year-old she-goat, a three-year-old ram, a turtledove, and a young bird." **10]** He brought Him all these and cut them in two, placing each half opposite the other; but he did not cut up the birds. **11]** Birds of prey came down upon the carcasses, and Abram drove them away. **12]** As the sun was about to set, a trance fell upon Abram, and a deep dark dread descended upon him.

6] *He reckoned it to his merit.* God rewards the faithful (repeated in Ps. 106:31). Paul, in the Christian Scripture, uses this verse to prove that merit depends on faith rather than law [2]; but James draws the opposite conclusion: Man is justified by works and not by faith only [3].

10] *And cut them.* The *berit* is concluded through a process of cutting, hence the Hebrew phrase, "to cut a covenant." Smoke and flame are a frequent accompaniment of the divine presence (see also note to Gen. 9:9).

11] *Birds of prey.* Most likely forces that try to prevent the covenant from being concluded.

יג וַיֹּאמֶר לְאַבְרָם יָדֹעַ תֵּדַע כִּי־גֵר יִהְיֶה זַרְעֲךָ בְּאֶרֶץ
יד לֹא לָהֶם וַעֲבָדוּם וְעִנּוּ אֹתָם אַרְבַּע מֵאוֹת שָׁנָה: וְגַם
אֶת־הַגּוֹי אֲשֶׁר יַעֲבֹדוּ דָּן אָנֹכִי וְאַחֲרֵי־כֵן יֵצְאוּ
טו בִּרְכֻשׁ גָּדוֹל: וְאַתָּה תָּבוֹא אֶל־אֲבֹתֶיךָ בְּשָׁלוֹם תִּקָּבֵר
טז בְּשֵׂיבָה טוֹבָה: וְדוֹר רְבִיעִי יָשׁוּבוּ הֵנָּה כִּי לֹא־שָׁלֵם
יז עֲוֹן הָאֱמֹרִי עַד־הֵנָּה: וַיְהִי הַשֶּׁמֶשׁ בָּאָה וַעֲלָטָה
הָיָה וְהִנֵּה תַנּוּר עָשָׁן וְלַפִּיד אֵשׁ אֲשֶׁר עָבַר בֵּין
יח הַגְּזָרִים הָאֵלֶּה: בַּיּוֹם הַהוּא כָּרַת יְהוָה אֶת־אַבְרָם
בְּרִית לֵאמֹר לְזַרְעֲךָ נָתַתִּי אֶת־הָאָרֶץ הַזֹּאת מִנְּהַר

Genesis 15

13–18

13] And He said to Abram, "Know well that your offspring shall be strangers in a land not theirs, and they shall be enslaved and oppressed four hundred years; 14] but I will pass judgment on the nation they shall serve, and in the end they shall go free with great wealth.   15] As for you, You shall go to your fathers in peace; / You shall be buried at a ripe old age.   16] And they shall return here in the fourth generation, for the iniquity of the Amorites will not be fulfilled until then."

17] When the sun set and it was very dark, there appeared a smoking oven, and a flaming torch which passed between those pieces.   18] On that day the LORD made a covenant with Abram, saying, "To your offspring I give this land, from the

13] *Four hundred years.* In Exod. 12:40 the figure is 430. We have here an example of history presented in prophetic form: The sojourn in Egypt is envisioned as having been ordained in the time of Abraham.

16] *Fourth generation.* A round figure, meaning "much later."

The iniquity of the Amorites. Once it reaches its full measure, it will cause them to lose the land. This relationship of morality and possession is part of the Holy Land's special nature, which was to have a profound effect on the children of Israel (see p. 130).

18] *From the river of Egypt.* The boundaries of the Promised Land vary throughout the Torah (cf. Num. 34:1-12 and Deut. 1:7-8). Certainly, in these ancient conceptions, the borders were far greater than those of the State of Israel in 1948, or even after the Six Day War in 1967 [4].

מִצְרַיִם עַד־הַנָּהָר הַגָּדֹל נְהַר־פְּרָת: אֶת־הַקֵּינִי וְאֶת־   בראשית טו; טז

הַקְּנִזִּי וְאֵת הַקַּדְמֹנִי: וְאֶת־הַחִתִּי וְאֶת־הַפְּרִזִּי וְאֶת־   יט-כא; א-ג

הָרְפָאִים: וְאֶת־הָאֱמֹרִי וְאֶת־הַכְּנַעֲנִי וְאֶת־הַגִּרְגָּשִׁי

וְאֶת־הַיְבוּסִי: ס

וְשָׂרַי אֵשֶׁת אַבְרָם לֹא יָלְדָה לוֹ וְלָהּ שִׁפְחָה מִצְרִית

וּשְׁמָהּ הָגָר: וַתֹּאמֶר שָׂרַי אֶל־אַבְרָם הִנֵּה־נָא עֲצָרַנִי יְהוָה מִלֶּדֶת בֹּא־נָא אֶל־שִׁפְחָתִי אוּלַי אִבָּנֶה מִמֶּנָּה

וַיִּשְׁמַע אַבְרָם לְקוֹל שָׂרָי: וַתִּקַּח שָׂרַי אֵשֶׁת־אַבְרָם אֶת־הָגָר הַמִּצְרִית שִׁפְחָתָהּ מִקֵּץ עֶשֶׂר שָׁנִים לְשֶׁבֶת

Genesis 15; 16
19–21; 1–3

river of Egypt to the great river, the river Euphrates: **19]** the Kenizzites, the Kenizzites, the Kadmonites, **20]** the Hittites, the Perizzites, the Rephaim, **21]** the Amorites, the Canaanites, the Girgashites, and the Jebusites."

1] Sarai, Abram's wife, had borne him no children. She had an Egyptian maidservant whose name was Hagar. **2]** And Sarai said to Abram, "See, the LORD has kept me from bearing. Consort with my maid; perhaps I shall have a son through her." And Abram heeded Sarai's request. **3]** So Sarai, Abram's wife, took her maid, Hagar the Egyptian—after Abram had dwelt in the land of Canaan ten years—and

19] *The Kenites.* Kenites and Kenizzites lived in the Negev; Kadmonites means "easterners" or "ancients." On Perizzites, see Gen. 13:7; on Rephaim, Gen. 14:5; Hittites, Amorites, Canaanites, Girgashites, and Jebusites are mentioned in chapter 10.

16:2] *The Lord has kept me from bearing.* Childlessness is considered a mark of divine disfavor. The Bible relates several instances of barrenness, induced and then eliminated by God's will (e.g., Rachel, Hannah). This theme makes the late appearance of a first child (always a son) especially important.

/Compare the proverb: "One without a child is as dead and razed to the ground" [5]. See also Gen. 30:1./

Have a son. Literally, "be built up," a word play on בֵּן (*ben*, son) and בָּנָה (*banah*, build up).

3] *Concubine.* The Hebrew word אִשָּׁה (*ishah*) is also the term used for wife. Hagar becomes Abraham's אִשָּׁה, but she remains Sarah's servant. The Code of Hammurabi warns expressly that a slave girl elevated by her mistress should not and could not claim equality [6]. A Nuzi contract

אַבְרָם בְּאֶרֶץ כְּנַעַן וַתִּתֵּן אֹתָהּ לְאַבְרָם אִישָׁהּ לוֹ

ד לְאִשָּׁה: וַיָּבֹא אֶל־הָגָר וַתַּהַר וַתֵּרֶא כִּי הָרָתָה וַתֵּקַל

ה גְּבִרְתָּהּ בְּעֵינֶיהָ: וַתֹּאמֶר שָׂרַי אֶל־אַבְרָם חֲמָסִי עָלֶיךָ

אָנֹכִי נָתַתִּי שִׁפְחָתִי בְּחֵיקֶךָ וַתֵּרֶא כִּי הָרָתָה וָאֵקַל

ו בְּעֵינֶיהָ יִשְׁפֹּט יְהֹוָה בֵּינִי וּבֵינֶיךָ*: וַיֹּאמֶר אַבְרָם אֶל־

שָׂרַי הִנֵּה שִׁפְחָתֵךְ בְּיָדֵךְ עֲשִׂי־לָהּ הַטּוֹב בְּעֵינָיִךְ

ז וַתְּעַנֶּהָ שָׂרַי וַתִּבְרַח מִפָּנֶיהָ: וַיִּמְצָאָהּ מַלְאַךְ יְהֹוָה

ח עַל־עֵין הַמַּיִם בַּמִּדְבָּר עַל־הָעַיִן בְּדֶרֶךְ שׁוּר: וַיֹּאמַר

הָגָר שִׁפְחַת שָׂרַי אֵי־מִזֶּה בָאת וְאָנָה תֵלֵכִי וַתֹּאמֶר

Genesis 16

4–8

* ה נקוד על י' בתרא.

---

gave her to her husband Abram as concubine.   4] And he cohabited with Hagar
and she conceived; and when she saw that she had conceived, her mistress was
lowered in her esteem.   5] And Sarai said to Abram, "The wrong done me is your
fault! I myself gave my maid into your bosom; now that she sees that she is pregnant,
I am lowered in her esteem. The LORD decide between you and me!"   6] Abram
said to Sarai, "Your maid is in your hands. Deal with her as you think right." Then
Sarai treated her harshly, and she ran away from her.

7] The angel of the LORD found her by a spring of water in the wilderness, the
spring on the road to Shur,   8] and said, "Hagar, slave of Sarai, where have you
come from, and where are you going?" And she said, "I am running away from my
mistress Sarai."

---

provided: "If Gillimninu bears children, Shennima
shall not take another wife. But if Gillimninu fails
to bear children, she shall get for him a slave girl
as concubine. In that case, Gillimninu herself shall
have authority over the offspring" [7].

6] *Sarai treated her harshly.* Since in her position
Hagar could no longer be sold or expelled [8],
Sarah abuses her maid, thereby causing her to
leave of her own accord (cf. Deut. 21:14).

7] *Angel.* See p. 170.

מִפְּנֵי שָׂרַי גְּבִרְתִּי אָנֹכִי בֹּרַחַת: וַיֹּאמֶר לָהּ מַלְאַךְ ט

יְהוָה שׁוּבִי אֶל־גְּבִרְתֵּךְ וְהִתְעַנִּי תַּחַת יָדֶיהָ: וַיֹּאמֶר י

לָהּ מַלְאַךְ יְהוָה הַרְבָּה אַרְבֶּה אֶת־זַרְעֵךְ וְלֹא

יִסָּפֵר מֵרֹב: וַיֹּאמֶר לָהּ מַלְאַךְ יְהוָה הִנָּךְ הָרָה יא

וְיֹלַדְתְּ בֵּן וְקָרָאת שְׁמוֹ יִשְׁמָעֵאל כִּי־שָׁמַע יְהוָה אֶל־

עָנְיֵךְ: וְהוּא יִהְיֶה פֶּרֶא אָדָם יָדוֹ בַכֹּל וְיַד כֹּל בּוֹ יב

וְעַל־פְּנֵי כָל־אֶחָיו יִשְׁכֹּן: וַתִּקְרָא שֵׁם־יְהוָה הַדֹּבֵר יג

אֵלֶיהָ אַתָּה אֵל רֳאִי כִּי אָמְרָה הֲגַם הֲלֹם רָאִיתִי

אַחֲרֵי רֹאִי: עַל־כֵּן קָרָא לַבְּאֵר בְּאֵר לַחַי רֹאִי הִנֵּה יד

בֵּין־קָדֵשׁ וּבֵין בָּרֶד: וַתֵּלֶד הָגָר לְאַבְרָם בֵּן וַיִּקְרָא טו

Genesis 16

9–15

9] And the angel of the LORD said to her, "Go back to your mistress, and submit to her harsh treatment." **10]** And the angel of the LORD said to her, "I will greatly increase your offspring, / And they shall be too many to count." **11]** The angel of the LORD said to her further, "Behold, you are with child / And shall bear a son; / You shall call him Ishmael, / For the LORD has paid heed to your suffering. / **12]** He shall be a wild ass of a man; / His hand against everyone, / And everyone's hand against him; / And in defiance of all his kinsmen he shall camp." **13]** And she called the LORD who spoke to her, "You Are El-roi," by which she meant, "Have I not gone on seeing after He saw me!" **14]** Therefore the well was called Beer-lahai-roi; t is between Kadesh and Bered. **15]** And Hagar bore a son to Abram,

11] *Ishmael.* יִשְׁמָעֵאל means God heeds.

12] *A wild ass of a man.* A reference to the character of the Bedouin, who, like the wild ass of the desert, lives in highly mobile groups. On Ishmael as the ancestor of the Arabs, see p. 200.

13] *El-roi.* Apparently, "God of my vision"; the remainder of the Hebrew is obscure. / Various emendations have been offered to produce the sense: "I have lived after seeing God" [9]. /

14] *Beer-lahai-roi.* Meaning is uncertain, perhaps "the well of the Living One who sees me."

Between Kadesh and Bered. In the Negev.

טז אַבְרָם שֶׁם־בְּנוֹ אֲשֶׁר־יָלְדָה הָגָר יִשְׁמָעֵאל: וְאַבְרָם
בֶּן־שְׁמֹנִים שָׁנָה וָשֵׁשׁ שָׁנִים בְּלֶדֶת־הָגָר אֶת־יִשְׁמָעֵאל
לְאַבְרָם:
ס

and Abram gave the son that Hagar bore him the name Ishmael.   **16]** Abram was eighty-six years old when Hagar bore Ishmael to Abram.

The Reality of the Covenant

Did God really speak to Abraham and enter into a covenant or *berit* (בְּרִית) built on the verbal commitment reported by the text?

If we take the literal view (and Jewish as well as Christian tradition took it unequivocally), the nature of the compact cannot be in doubt. If, on the other hand, we read the story as the spiritual experience of one man who understood his God to address him in this unique fashion, the emphasis is shifted to a recounting of Abraham's internal vision. It is through him that God's promise is made known to us; it is through his eyes that the reality of the covenant must be viewed.

However we view the story, we are face to face with a remarkable human being who saw more in his environment than earth and sky, mountains and valleys: the story of a man who looked at the world as the proving ground for human opportunities, seeing all this in the context of mutual trust and obligation expressed in the concept of *berit*.

The *berit* thus adds a new dimension to human existence, a deepening of the call that he first heard in Haran, "Go forth!" These experiences of Abraham were the foundations on which his descendants built their house of faith and contributed their commitment to a covenant first envisioned in the dark of ancient Negev nights.

The Nature of the Covenant

"In a society in which the capriciousness[1] of the gods was taken for granted," writes Nahum Sarna, " 'the covenant between the pieces,' like the covenant with Noah, set religion on a bold, new, independent course" [10].

Both covenants have one outstanding feature in common: They obligate God but demand nothing of man. In contradistinction to many later references to *berit*—in which God's covenant with Israel is made dependent on the latter's continued faithfulness—the Bible here makes God's commitment unconditional. Not only has He created a physical universe with immutable laws, He has established conditions for an unchanging spiritual world as well. He is a faithful God—faithful in His natural as well as transnatural manifestations. And unlike the pagan deities whose universes were unpredictable and erratic, God shows himself, in the covenant between the pieces, to be an אֵל נֶאֱמָן (*El Ne-eman*)—a God who is both dependable and trustworthy. No such religious covenant is known outside of Israel.

The Ritual

What is the meaning of the ritual itself, which persisted into the time of Jeremiah (34:18)? It may have been a vestige of ancient blood magic that by Abraham's time had assumed legal importance amongst various nations. Thus, the Amorites finalized a pact by slaying an ass and cutting it into pieces [11]. It has been suggested that the current custom of cutting a ribbon to symbolize the opening of a bridge or a highway is a remnant of such ancient sentiments. The cutting ritual may have symbolized that the contracting parties were now the guarantors of wholeness. Abraham sees God himself passing through the pieces, thereby emphasizing that the divine promise is secure.

---

[1] The gods were capricious to the extent that they behaved like human beings, and it was human beings who by prayer, penance, and sacrifice could check this capriciousness.

GLEANINGS

The Friend of God

Who has a better religion than he who submits his whole self to God, who does what is good, and follows the way of Abraham, the true in faith? For God did take Abraham for a friend.

KORAN [12]

[Islamic tradition derives the very word Moslem from the Abraham story: "This is the religion of your father Abraham. He called you *muslimin*" (those who dedicate themselves to God).]

Abraham Was Free to Disbelieve

[Gen. 15:6 says that after God had appeared to Abraham the latter evinced his trust in God, whereupon "He reckoned it to his merit."]

Scripture finds it necessary to make explicit what one should have thought to be obvious, that a divine revelation engendered faith in the first of the Patriarchs; and indeed deems it important to underscore this faith as being particularly meritorious!

Scripture is drawing our attention to the phenomena of revelation and faith and to the relation between them: Every revelation is a human experience; whatever its manner or form, its degree or content, it is a discrete event; it takes place in time—it has a beginning and an end. And after the event man is free—to remember or to forget, to formulate in words the impact of the event or the message—if any, to accept it or—yes—to question its reality. Was it a dream, a figment, a chimera, an illusion, a delusion, a hallucination?

HERBERT C. BRICHTO [13]

The Word of the Lord Came to Abram (Gen. 15:1)

Of course you can't imagine such a thing as that the word of God should ever come to you? Is that because you are worse, or better, than Abraham?—because you are a more, or less, civilized person than he? I leave you to answer that question for yourself;—only as I have told you often before, but cannot repeat too often, find out first what the word *is*.   JOHN RUSKIN [14]

The Covenant

In the language of the Bible the word *berit* became a characteristically religious word, one of those words in which the idea of great interrelatedness, the great unity of all, of mystery and ordered certainty seeks to express itself. The God-given order was to find expression in this term.... The Old Aramaic translation of the Bible translated *berit* as *kayama* [that which is established], indicating that which is above all change, above all that comes and goes.   LEO BAECK [15]

Barren Marriage in Jewish Law

In theory, when a man had lived with his wife for ten years and they had no children, even though it could not definitely be proven that she was barren, the court could force the man to divorce her. But this law fell into disuse.

Isserles, in the sixteenth century, wrote that in his day it was no longer customary for a court to force the divorce of a barren woman, even when her husband had not fulfilled the *mitzvah* of procreation. [16]

The Covenant of Circumcision

Heretofore God made no demands on Abraham in return for His promise. But a fundamental change in this one-sided obligation is about to take place. Henceforth Abraham—his name changed from Abram —and his descendants will bear the mark of the covenant on their flesh. Circumcision, so important to Jews and sometimes controversial in their history, makes Abraham and his descendants partners in the obligations of the covenant.

The Government of Curiosity

א וַיְהִי אַבְרָם בֶּן־תִּשְׁעִים שָׁנָה וְתֵשַׁע שָׁנִים וַיֵּרָא יְהֹוָה אֶל־אַבְרָם וַיֹּאמֶר אֵלָיו אֲנִי־אֵל שַׁדַּי הִתְהַלֵּךְ לְפָנַי

ב וֶהְיֵה תָמִים: וְאֶתְּנָה בְרִיתִי בֵּינִי וּבֵינֶךָ וְאַרְבֶּה אוֹתְךָ

ג בִּמְאֹד מְאֹד: וַיִּפֹּל אַבְרָם עַל־פָּנָיו וַיְדַבֵּר אִתּוֹ

ד אֱלֹהִים לֵאמֹר: אֲנִי הִנֵּה בְרִיתִי אִתָּךְ וְהָיִיתָ לְאַב

ה הֲמוֹן גּוֹיִם: וְלֹא־יִקָּרֵא עוֹד אֶת־שִׁמְךָ אַבְרָם וְהָיָה

ו שִׁמְךָ אַבְרָהָם כִּי אַב־הֲמוֹן גּוֹיִם נְתַתִּיךָ: וְהִפְרֵתִי

ז אֹתְךָ בִּמְאֹד מְאֹד וּנְתַתִּיךָ לְגוֹיִם וּמְלָכִים מִמְּךָ יֵצֵאוּ:

ז וַהֲקִמֹתִי אֶת־בְּרִיתִי בֵּינִי וּבֵינֶךָ וּבֵין זַרְעֲךָ אַחֲרֶיךָ

Genesis 17

1–7

1] When Abram was ninety-nine years old, the LORD appeared to Abram and said to him, "I am El Shaddai. Walk in My ways and be blameless. **2]** I will establish My covenant between Me and you, and I will make you exceedingly numerous."

3] Abram threw himself on his face, as God continued speaking to him, **4]** "As for Me, this is My covenant with you: You shall be the father of a multitude of nations. **5]** And you shall no longer be called Abram, but your name shall be Abraham, for I make you the father of a multitude of nations. **6]** I will make you exceedingly fertile, and make nations of you; and kings shall come forth from you. **7]** I will maintain My covenant between Me and you, and your offspring to come, as an ever-

---

17:1] *I am El Shaddai.* The meaning of "Shaddai" is in doubt. "God Almighty" is the most frequent translation.
/Some scholars derive the word *Shaddai* from the Akkadian for "mountain" or from the root "to send rain." Rashi explained the name homiletically: "I am He whose divinity is sufficient (שַׁדַּי) to all creation."/
    Be blameless. Like Noah, for whom the same phrase was used (Gen. 6:9).

3] *Abram threw himself on his face.* The common form of showing submission to gods, kings, and other important personages (cf. I Kings 18:7; Ruth 2:10).

5] *Abram.* This name is probably a contraction of *Abi-ram,* "my father is exalted." The additional syllable (*ha*) added by God to Abram's name is most likely an extension or enlargement of the original name [1], so that the biblical explana-

לְדֹרֹתָם לִבְרִית עוֹלָם לִהְיוֹת לְךָ לֵאלֹהִים וּלְזַרְעֲךָ

ח אַחֲרֶיךָ: וְנָתַתִּי לְךָ וּלְזַרְעֲךָ אַחֲרֶיךָ אֵת אֶרֶץ מְגֻרֶיךָ

אֵת כָּל־אֶרֶץ כְּנַעַן לַאֲחֻזַּת עוֹלָם וְהָיִיתִי לָהֶם

ט לֵאלֹהִים: וַיֹּאמֶר אֱלֹהִים אֶל־אַבְרָהָם וְאַתָּה אֶת־

י בְּרִיתִי תִשְׁמֹר אַתָּה וְזַרְעֲךָ אַחֲרֶיךָ לְדֹרֹתָם: זֹאת

בְּרִיתִי אֲשֶׁר תִּשְׁמְרוּ בֵּינִי וּבֵינֵיכֶם וּבֵין זַרְעֲךָ אַחֲרֶיךָ

יא הִמּוֹל לָכֶם כָּל־זָכָר: וּנְמַלְתֶּם אֵת בְּשַׂר עָרְלַתְכֶם

יב וְהָיָה לְאוֹת בְּרִית בֵּינִי וּבֵינֵיכֶם: וּבֶן־שְׁמֹנַת יָמִים

יִמּוֹל לָכֶם כָּל־זָכָר לְדֹרֹתֵיכֶם יְלִיד בָּיִת וּמִקְנַת־

יג כֶּסֶף מִכֹּל בֶּן־נֵכָר אֲשֶׁר לֹא מִזַּרְעֲךָ הוּא: הִמּוֹל

יִמּוֹל יְלִיד בֵּיתְךָ וּמִקְנַת כַּסְפֶּךָ וְהָיְתָה בְרִיתִי

Genesis 17

8–13

lasting covenant throughout the ages, to be God to you and to your offspring to come. **8]** I give the land you sojourn in to you and your offspring to come, all the land of Canaan, as an everlasting possession. I will be their God."

9] God further said to Abraham, "As for you, you shall keep My covenant, you and your offspring to come, throughout the ages. **10]** Such shall be the covenant, which you shall keep, between Me and you and your offspring to follow: every male among you shall be circumcised. **11]** You shall circumcise the flesh of your foreskin, and that shall be the sign of the covenant between Me and you. **12]** At the age of eight days, every male among you throughout the generations shall be circumcised, even the homeborn slave and the one bought from an outsider who is not of your seed.— **13]** The slave that is born in your household or bought with your money

tion of Abraham ("father of a multitude") is an assonance rather than correct etymology.

10] *Circumcised*. By removal of the foreskin of the penis (see p. 164). Later in the Bible the term is applied figuratively to removing obstacles to understanding (Deut. 10:16; 30:6). Jer. 4:4 speaks of the "foreskin of the heart."

יד בְּבְשַׂרְכֶם לִבְרִית עוֹלָם: וְעָרֵל זָכָר אֲשֶׁר לֹא־יִמּוֹל אֶת־בְּשַׂר עָרְלָתוֹ וְנִכְרְתָה הַנֶּפֶשׁ הַהִוא מֵעַמֶּיהָ אֶת־

טו בְּרִיתִי הֵפַר: ס וַיֹּאמֶר אֱלֹהִים אֶל־אַבְרָהָם שָׂרַי אִשְׁתְּךָ לֹא־תִקְרָא אֶת־שְׁמָהּ שָׂרָי כִּי שָׂרָה שְׁמָהּ:

טז וּבֵרַכְתִּי אֹתָהּ וְגַם נָתַתִּי מִמֶּנָּה לְךָ בֵּן וּבֵרַכְתִּיהָ וְהָיְתָה לְגוֹיִם מַלְכֵי עַמִּים מִמֶּנָּה יִהְיוּ: וַיִּפֹּל אַבְרָהָם

יז עַל־פָּנָיו וַיִּצְחָק וַיֹּאמֶר בְּלִבּוֹ הַלְּבֶן מֵאָה־שָׁנָה יִוָּלֵד וְאִם־שָׂרָה הֲבַת־תִּשְׁעִים שָׁנָה תֵּלֵד: וַיֹּאמֶר אַבְרָהָם

יח אֶל־הָאֱלֹהִים לוּ יִשְׁמָעֵאל יִחְיֶה לְפָנֶיךָ: וַיֹּאמֶר

יט אֱלֹהִים אֲבָל שָׂרָה אִשְׁתְּךָ יֹלֶדֶת לְךָ בֵּן וְקָרָאתָ אֶת־שְׁמוֹ יִצְחָק וַהֲקִמֹתִי אֶת־בְּרִיתִי אִתּוֹ לִבְרִית

Genesis 17

14–19

must be circumcised!—Thus shall My covenant be marked in your flesh as an ever-lasting pact.   14] An uncircumcised male who does not circumcise the flesh of his foreskin—such a person shall be cut off from his kin; he has broken My covenant."

15] And God said to Abraham, "As for your wife Sarai, you shall not call her Sarai, but her name shall be Sarah.   16] I will bless her; indeed, I will give you a son by her. I will bless her so that she shall give rise to nations; rulers of peoples shall issue from her."   17] Abraham threw himself on his face and laughed, as he said to himself, "Can a child be born to a man a hundred years old, or can Sarah bear a child at ninety?"   18] And Abraham said to God, "Oh that Ishmael might live by Your favor!"   19] God said, "Nevertheless, Sarah your wife shall bear you a son, and you shall name him Isaac; and I will maintain My covenant with him as an everlasting

15]   *Sarai.* This is probably an older linguistic form for Sarah, i.e., "princess."
/The Talmud records the opinion that Sarai's name change symbolized the end of her barrenness [2]./

18]   *Oh that Ishmael might live by Your favor!* A rejoinder either of humility [3]   or of anxiety [4].

19]   *Isaac.* From צחק (to laugh).

עוֹלָם לְזַרְעוֹ אַחֲרָיו: וּלְיִשְׁמָעֵאל שְׁמַעְתִּיךָ הִנֵּה
בֵּרַכְתִּי אֹתוֹ וְהִפְרֵיתִי אֹתוֹ וְהִרְבֵּיתִי אֹתוֹ בִּמְאֹד
מְאֹד שְׁנֵים־עָשָׂר נְשִׂיאִם יוֹלִיד וּנְתַתִּיו לְגוֹי גָּדוֹל:
וְאֶת־בְּרִיתִי אָקִים אֶת־יִצְחָק אֲשֶׁר תֵּלֵד לְךָ שָׂרָה
לַמּוֹעֵד הַזֶּה בַּשָּׁנָה הָאַחֶרֶת: וַיְכַל לְדַבֵּר אִתּוֹ וַיַּעַל
אֱלֹהִים מֵעַל אַבְרָהָם: וַיִּקַּח אַבְרָהָם אֶת־יִשְׁמָעֵאל
בְּנוֹ וְאֵת כָּל־יְלִידֵי בֵיתוֹ וְאֵת כָּל־מִקְנַת כַּסְפּוֹ כָּל־
זָכָר בְּאַנְשֵׁי בֵּית אַבְרָהָם וַיָּמָל אֶת־בְּשַׂר עָרְלָתָם
בְּעֶצֶם הַיּוֹם הַזֶּה כַּאֲשֶׁר דִּבֶּר אִתּוֹ אֱלֹהִים: וְאַבְרָהָם
בֶּן־תִּשְׁעִים וָתֵשַׁע שָׁנָה בְּהִמֹּלוֹ בְּשַׂר עָרְלָתוֹ:
וְיִשְׁמָעֵאל בְּנוֹ בֶּן־שְׁלֹשׁ עֶשְׂרֵה שָׁנָה בְּהִמֹּלוֹ אֵת בְּשַׂר

covenant for his offspring to come.   20] As for Ishmael, I have heeded you. I hereby bless him. I will make him fertile and exceedingly numerous. He shall be the father of twelve chieftains, and I will make of him a great nation.   21] But My covenant I will maintain with Isaac, whom Sarah shall bear to you at this season next year."   22] And when He was done speaking with him, God was gone from Abraham.

23] Then Abraham took his son Ishmael, and all his homeborn slaves and all those he had bought, every male among Abraham's retainers, and he circumcised the flesh of their foreskins on that very day, as God had spoken to him.   24] Abraham was ninety-nine years old when he circumcised the flesh of his foreskin   25] and his son Ishmael was thirteen years old when he was circumcised in the flesh of his

20] *I have heeded you.* שְׁמַעְתִּיךָ, a word play on יִשְׁמָעֵאל (Ishmael—God will heed).

כו   עָרְלָתוֹ: בְּעֶצֶם הַיּוֹם הַזֶּה נִמּוֹל אַבְרָהָם וְיִשְׁמָעֵאל

כז   בְּנוֹ: וְכָל־אַנְשֵׁי בֵיתוֹ יְלִיד בָּיִת וּמִקְנַת־כֶּסֶף מֵאֵת

בֶּן־נֵכָר נִמֹּלוּ אִתּוֹ:

Genesis 17

26—27

Haftarah Lech Lecha, p. 522

foreskin.   26] Thus Abraham and his son Ishmael were circumcised on that very

day;   27] and all his retainers, his homeborn slaves and those that had been bought

from outsiders, were circumcised with him.

Circumcision

Few, if any, Jewish practices are more significant than *berit milah*, the covenant of circumcision. While it does not make a child born to Jewish parents into a Jew, it confirms his special relationship to the God and the traditions of Israel. The Zohar considered the safeguarding of circumcision important to all mankind: "As long as Israel observes the custom of circumcision, heaven and earth will go on their appointed courses, but if Israel neglects the covenant, heaven and earth are disturbed" [5]. Neglecting to circumcise a child was, therefore, more than merely neglect of a rite; it was a rejection of God's sign and was subject to divine punishment, to being "cut off from the people," i.e., from the covenant. Indeed, throughout history, the continued observance of circumcision has been a mark of the Jewish will to survive, while its discontinuance has been a signal of assimilation.

Thus, during the reign of Antiochus IV (165 B.C.E), circumcision was prohibited by royal decree, but Jews observed the rite even at the risk of death. Some one hundred years later, political conditions had changed drastically and many upper-class Jews desirous of assimilation to the dominant Greco-Roman way of life began to neglect *berit milah*.[1] Two hundred years later, during the Hadrianic persecution (*ca.* 135 C.E.), the practice of this rite—as well as the teaching of Torah in general—was forbidden once again. Yet many Jews defied the edict and suffered death. During the Nazi reign of terror, circumcision was often the means by which the persecutors determined the Jewishness of their male victims; still the vast majority of Jewish parents continued to enter their children into the covenant. In present-day Soviet lands, on the other hand, the discouragement of all religious practices has caused the virtual disappearance of circumcision and, with it, widespread assimilation of the Jews.

In North America today, circumcision is encouraged by the medical profession as a hygienic measure and is accepted by most Gentiles. This generalized practice has made it essential that Jews should re-emphasize the religious aspects of the rite. Surgical circumcision alone is by no means the equivalent of *berit milah*. The act obtains its value not from the physical operation and its presumed medical benefits but from the idea and the history that underlie it, from the prayers that accompany it, and from the father's affirmation that his child will be brought up in the religion of his fathers. (In Christian tradition, baptism has taken the place of circumcision.)

An Ancient Practice

The antiquity of the rite of circumcision is attested by the biblical record itself. In the days of Moses and Joshua, when the Bronze Age was coming to an end, it was still a custom to use flint knives for the rite, that is to say, tools going back to the Stone Age (cf. Exod. 4:25; Josh. 5:2).

Circumcision has been practiced by many peoples besides the Jews. Jeremiah indicates that the Egyptians, Moabites, and Ammonites all underwent circumcision (9:24); among the nations bordering on Israel, only the Philistines did not practice it. In Mohammed's time (seventh century C.E.) it was apparently so generally observed by the peoples of the Middle East that the Koran no longer found it necessary to command it specifically [6].

Why was it so widespread? Although Herodotus ascribed it to hygienic reasons and Maimonides claimed that it reduced sexual activity to a manageable level [7],

---

[1] Often, in public athletic events, participants who were expected to compete in the nude submitted to an operation so that the sign of their Jewishness would be obliterated.

[2] In Arabic, too, the same term (*chatana*) means "to circumcise."

[3] "The commands were given to Israel to purify themselves" [9].

[4] Why was Adam not born circumcised? Because

its ubiquity was doubtlessly due to the persistent popularity of ancient fertility rites. Originally, circumcision served as an initiation into puberty or into manhood prior to marriage. This is still reflected in the language of the Talmud [8], where the word חָתָן (*chatan*) means both a bridegroom and an infant fit for circumcision.[2]

The command to Abraham shifts the practice away from young adulthood to the eighth day after birth and thereby from sexual to spiritual significance.[3] Its purpose is now to be a "sign of the covenant." (Women received no such sign, because biblical tradition was male-oriented.) The rite of cutting, which is elsewhere associated with the *berit* (see Gen. 15:10), is here accorded special sanctity. Abraham circumcised is now a man fundamentally changed, in name and identity as well as in body. He is, as the Midrash puts it, a more nearly perfect human being.[4]

Identity and Name

Abram's name is changed to Abraham, and Sarai's to Sarah. Similar changes occur several times in the Bible: For instance, Jacob's name is changed to Israel, Hoshea's to Joshua, Mattaniah's to Zedekiah. In each case, the change of name symbolizes a change in the personality or status of the bearer. Thus, kings as well as popes take on new names when they accede to the throne, and so do some nuns on entering orders. A woman assumes the family name of her husband upon marriage. In the United States, some blacks have signified their strengthened sense of identity by the adoption of new names.[5]

everything God created needed perfecting [10] (see p. 11).

[5] Related to this was the widespread Jewish custom of giving a desperately sick person a new name. It was believed that the heavenly decree of death was issued against the person as he was, his name being an integral part of his personality. With a new name he was therefore thought to have a better chance of recovery [11].

Names express the predilections and traditions of a family and often say much about a civilization. For example, the medieval combination of Hebrew names with the Arabic word for son (*Ibn* Ezra, *Ibn* Chayim) expressed the joining of two cultural strands. The biblical names given to Christians in Puritan times expressed that age's commitment to religious tradition. The recent neglect of such names as Abraham and Sarah and the substitution of fashionable names among Jews suggest a lessening adherence to traditional values and an advance of assimilation.

In Europe, where familial traditions are still strong, a change of name (especially of a family name) is discouraged and made difficult. In North America, name changing is easy and widely practiced. Thus, names are increasingly losing their significance, especially in modern metropolitan societies. Many people already bear the same name; naming a Jewish child after a deceased relative is often done only in symbolic form by having the child's name start with the same initial. Some people change their first as well as their family names and become even less distinguishable in an environment that tends toward anonymity for the individual.

Naming a child at circumcision or in the synagogue can, therefore, be an important counteragent to the community's lack of tradition and the individual's sense of rootlessness. The giving of a Hebrew name, which may honor a member of the family or simply be a recognition of the child's membership in the covenant, can add a religious element to the important process of name-giving, which is nowadays primarily a matter of taste.

In Genesis, God is the supreme name-giver. The bestowal is, and must remain, a sacred act so that one's name may speak of identity, tradition, commitment, and membership in the Eternal People. "To honor a name" is not only to be true to one's self but also to that tradition for which the name stands.

GLEANINGS

Laws of Circumcision

[Over the centuries, a great body of laws and customs about circumcision developed. A few excerpts follow.]

If the father knows how to perform the circumcision he should do it himself. Usually, however, the rite is performed by someone familiar with all required procedures and prayers, a professional circumciser (*mohel*).

Among liberal Jews, and in many smaller communities, a doctor often takes the place of the *mohel*, and the rabbi reads the accompanying prayers. [12]

Since the fulfilment of all precepts must be postponed in deference to human life, extreme care should be taken not to circumcise a sick infant. In such cases, circumcision may be performed at a later date than that prescribed by law, because the life of a human being, once sacrificed, can never be restored. ✳

If a woman has lost two sons from the effects of circumcision (it having been proven that circumcision weakened their physical condition), her third son must not be circumcised until he is grown up and has a stronger constitution.

Circumcision is to be performed on the eighth day after birth and may take place on the Sabbath and festivals. If at all possible, it should be performed on the eighth day, not earlier and not later. [13]

After the circumcision the father of the child says this benediction: "Praised be Thou, O Lord, our God, King of the universe, who hast sanctified us with Thy commandments and hast bidden us to enter him into the covenant of Abraham, our father." Those present respond: "As he has been entered into the covenant, may he be introduced to the study of Torah, to the nuptial canopy, and to good deeds."

The custom of naming a child at the circumcision is of medieval origin, although traditional sentiment traces it back to Abraham who received a new name at the time of his circumcision. [14]

It is customary to make a feast on the day of the circumcision. [15]

Creation Uncompleted

A pagan sage asked Rabbi Judah: "If circumcision is so beloved of God, why was the mark of circumcision not given to Adam at his creation?" The rabbi replied: "Almost everything that was created during the six days of creation needs finishing—even man needs finishing."

MIDRASH [16]

The Messengers

A brief interlude tells how God once again assures Abraham and this time Sarah, too, of an offspring. The announcement is made by three "men," mysterious messengers of the Deity. The account sets forth an additional characteristic of Abraham—his hospitality.

בְּרֵאשִׁית יח
א–ה

Genesis 18
1–5

א וַיֵּרָא אֵלָיו יְהוָֹה בְּאֵלֹנֵי מַמְרֵא וְהוּא יֹשֵׁב פֶּתַח־
ב הָאֹהֶל כְּחֹם הַיּוֹם: וַיִּשָּׂא עֵינָיו וַיַּרְא וְהִנֵּה שְׁלֹשָׁה
אֲנָשִׁים נִצָּבִים עָלָיו וַיַּרְא וַיָּרָץ לִקְרָאתָם מִפֶּתַח
ג הָאֹהֶל וַיִּשְׁתַּחוּ אָרְצָה: וַיֹּאמַר אֲדֹנָי אִם־נָא מָצָאתִי
ד חֵן בְּעֵינֶיךָ אַל־נָא תַעֲבֹר מֵעַל עַבְדֶּךָ: יֻקַּח־נָא
ה מְעַט־מַיִם וְרַחֲצוּ רַגְלֵיכֶם וְהִשָּׁעֲנוּ תַּחַת הָעֵץ: וְאֶקְחָה
פַת־לֶחֶם וְסַעֲדוּ לִבְּכֶם אַחַר תַּעֲבֹרוּ כִּי־עַל־כֵּן
עֲבַרְתֶּם עַל־עַבְדְּכֶם וַיֹּאמְרוּ כֵּן תַּעֲשֶׂה כַּאֲשֶׁר

1] The LORD appeared to him by the terebinths of Mamre; he was sitting at the entrance of the tent as the day grew hot.   2] Looking up, he saw three men standing near him. As soon as he saw them, he ran from the entrance of the tent to greet them and, bowing to the ground,   3] he said, "My lords, if it please you, do not go on past your servant.   4] Let a little water be brought; bathe your feet and recline under the tree.   5] And let me fetch a morsel of bread that you may refresh your-selves; then go on—seeing that you have come your servant's way." They replied, "do as you have said."

18:1] *The Lord appeared.* The aim of this introduction is to make it clear that the visitors in the following story are an apparition of the Divine.

Terebinths of Mamre. Near Hebron, where Abraham had built an altar (Gen. 13:18).

2] *Three men standing near him.* Abraham did not see them coming and seems startled by their sudden appearance.

3] *My lords.* אֲדֹנָי (or, my Lord). The Hebrew

sentences are couched alternately in the singular and plural, suggesting the fusion of two literary traditions. Maimonides understood the entire episode to have been a vision [1].

/Harmonizers suggest that the syntactical variance is due to Abraham's uncertainty over whether the messengers were mere men or represented God. In any case, tradition prescribes that אֲדֹנָי here be read as a sacred word./

5] *A morsel of bread.* The modest understate-

דִּבַּרְתָּ׃ וַיְמַהֵר אַבְרָהָם הָאֹהֱלָה אֶל־שָׂרָה וַיֹּאמֶר

מַהֲרִי שְׁלֹשׁ סְאִים קֶמַח סֹלֶת לוּשִׁי וַעֲשִׂי עֻגוֹת׃

וְאֶל־הַבָּקָר רָץ אַבְרָהָם וַיִּקַּח בֶּן־בָּקָר רַךְ וָטוֹב

וַיִּתֵּן אֶל־הַנַּעַר וַיְמַהֵר לַעֲשׂוֹת אֹתוֹ׃ וַיִּקַּח חֶמְאָה

וְחָלָב וּבֶן־הַבָּקָר אֲשֶׁר עָשָׂה וַיִּתֵּן לִפְנֵיהֶם וְהוּא־

עֹמֵד עֲלֵיהֶם תַּחַת הָעֵץ וַיֹּאכֵלוּ׃ וַיֹּאמְרוּ אֵלָיו אַיֵּה

שָׂרָה אִשְׁתֶּךָ וַיֹּאמֶר הִנֵּה בָאֹהֶל׃ וַיֹּאמֶר שׁוֹב אָשׁוּב

אֵלֶיךָ כָּעֵת חַיָּה וְהִנֵּה־בֵן לְשָׂרָה אִשְׁתֶּךָ וְשָׂרָה

שֹׁמַעַת פֶּתַח הָאֹהֶל וְהוּא אַחֲרָיו׃ וְאַבְרָהָם וְשָׂרָה

* ט נקוד על איו.

6] Abraham hastened into the tent to Sarah, and said, "Quick, three measures of choice flour! Knead and make cakes!"   7] Then Abraham ran to the herd, took a calf, tender and choice, and gave it to a servant-boy, who hastened to prepare it. 8] He took curds and milk and the calf that had been prepared, and set these before them; and he waited on them under the tree as they ate.

9] They said to him, "Where is your wife Sarah?" And he replied, "There, in the tent."   10] Then one said, "I will return to you when life is due, and your wife Sarah shall have a son!" Sarah was listening at the entrance of the tent, which was behind him.   11] Now Abraham and Sarah were old, advanced in years; Sarah

ment of a gracious host who expects to serve much more.

6] *Three measures.* סְאִים (singular, סְאָה), probably about twenty-eight cups, an overgenerous amount for three guests. However, it may have been customary on such occasions to include the important members of the household [2] or to supply provisions for the way [3].

8] *They ate.* Traditional interpreters experience great difficulties here. If the three are divine messengers, why do they eat? According to the Midrash, they merely appeared to eat [4]. According to Rashi, they pretended out of courtesy. And why does Abraham serve milk and meat at the same meal in contravention of the laws of *kashrut*? According to Hertz, the milk was consumed a sufficient time before the meat [5].

10] *When life is due.* After nine months (see II Kings 4:16–17, where Elisha uses the same expression [כָּעֵת] when promising a child to the Shunammite woman).

זְקֵנִים בָּאִים בַּיָּמִים חָדַל לִהְיוֹת לְשָׂרָה אֹרַח כַּנָּשִׁים:

יב וַתִּצְחַק שָׂרָה בְּקִרְבָּהּ לֵאמֹר אַחֲרֵי בְלֹתִי הָיְתָה־לִּי

עֶדְנָה וַאדֹנִי זָקֵן: וַיֹּאמֶר יְהֹוָה אֶל־אַבְרָהָם לָמָּה זֶּה יג

צָחֲקָה שָׂרָה לֵאמֹר הַאַף אֻמְנָם אֵלֵד וַאֲנִי זָקַנְתִּי:

הֲיִפָּלֵא מֵיְהֹוָה דָּבָר לַמּוֹעֵד אָשׁוּב אֵלֶיךָ כָּעֵת יד

חַיָּה וּלְשָׂרָה בֵן: וַתְּכַחֵשׁ שָׂרָה לֵאמֹר לֹא צָחַקְתִּי טו

כִּי יָרֵאָה וַיֹּאמֶר לֹא כִּי צָחָקְתְּ:

Genesis 18

12–15

had stopped having the periods of women.   12] And Sarah laughed to herself, saying, "Now that I am withered, am I to have enjoyment—with my husband so old?"   13] Then the LORD said to Abraham, "Why did Sarah laugh, saying, 'Shall I in truth bear a child, old as I am?'   14] Is anything too wondrous for the LORD? I will return to you at the time that life is due, and Sarah shall have a son."   15] Sarah dissembled, saying, "I did not laugh," for she was frightened. He replied, "But you did laugh."

12] *Sarah laughed.* וַתִּצְחַק (*va-titzchak*). Sarah's behavior explains the name Isaac, יִצְחָק (*yitzchak*) (see Gen. 21:6).

/ The Septuagint has: "Sarah laughed openly" (instead of "to herself")./

15] *She lied.* To Abraham when he confronted her.

Angels

The three "men" of whom the story speaks belong, according to the biblical setting, to a category of superior beings with special powers. They appear in a variety of forms, sometimes as men and sometimes in other shapes (such as cherubim). They can speak, stand, sit, walk, be clothed; they can have weapons, ride horses, descend from heaven on a ladder. Their function may be to worship God, to do His bidding (such as observing the activities of men, see Job 1:6–8), or, most frequently, to carry a divine message. Because of this latter function the name מַלְאָךְ (messenger) is often given to these beings. Its Greek translation is *angelos*, hence our English "angel."

As a group, angels were considered by tradition as a kind of nobility at God's court, singing His praises and acting at His counsel. As individuals, they were go-betweens. In this capacity they were thought to bring instruction, transmit revelation to prophets, announce the coming of events (here, Isaac's birth; in Genesis 19 the destruction of Sodom), and guard places (such as Eden or Bethel) or individuals (such as Hagar and Ishmael, Isaac and Jacob). However, they were not distinguished by name except for Gabriel and Michael (Dan. 9:21; 10:21). Angels were believed to have existed before the creation of the world (hinted at in Gen. 1:26) and to be generally benevolent to men.

Belief in angels was widespread in the ancient Near East. Mesopotamian and Hittite deities had their subordinate ministers, and Egyptian sources tell how the gods communicated with each other through couriers. In addition, the motif of hospitality to a divine being in disguise was well-known in ancient legend.[1] These ancient concepts formed the background out of which the biblical stories emerged. In post-biblical Judaism, as well as in Christianity and Islam, these concepts were developed into an elaborate structure of "angelology" [7].

In the biblical story, the "annunciation" by the angels is no more than an announcement of Isaac's forthcoming birth. There is no further hint of superhuman paternity as in similar myths of the Greeks. The announcement is supernatural, but not the conception. Isaac will not have the dual paternity of the Homeric heroes, who assume the office of their human fathers and derive their power from their divine fathers. Far from becoming a superman, Isaac will, in fact, be a rather undistinguished link in the patriarchal chain.[2]

---

[1] Note, e.g., the Greek story of Hyrieus and Tamagra who entertain three men not knowing that these men are gods. The couple is also recompensed by the gift of a son [6]. It has been noted that the biblical P-source does not speak of angels at all.

[2] However, it has been suggested that something of a much larger original "Isaac cycle" existed in which conception through divine agency played a much clearer role. The Bible reduced this and perhaps other aspects of some earlier Isaac saga; and normative Judaism divested itself of the consequences of the annunciation, which came to reecho in Christianity: "Jesus derives his human-office of Messianic King from Joseph, but his divine quality from his Divine Father. Moreover, the Church tradition that connects the sacrifice of Isaac with the sacrifice of Christ apparently rests on sound exegesis, for the sacrifice of Isaac would have meant not only the sacrifice of Abraham's son but of God's" [8].

GLEANINGS

The Mitzvah of Visiting the Sick

Why is the story of Abraham's circumcision [Gen. 17:10–14] followed by the visitation of God? He came to visit while Abraham was recuperating, to make clear the importance of the *mitzvah* of visiting the sick. TALMUD [9]

The Mitzvah of Hospitality

Why was Abraham sitting in the door of his tent? To watch for passing strangers whom he might invite into his abode. He who receives his fellow man kindly is regarded as though he had received the *Shechinah*. MIDRASH [10]

Abraham had his servant assist him in order to instruct him in the *mitzvah* of hospitality. The נַעַר [servant, literally, "lad"] was none other than his son Ishmael. MIDRASH [11]

Such instruction in the duty of hospitality to strangers may appear superfluous in the eyes of some parents and teachers today. They are in error. JOSEPH H. HERTZ

Once, however, Abraham's love of strangers clashed with his zeal for God. He invited a wayfarer to his home and, finding him praying to his idol, chased him away. God reprimanded Abraham severely: "I have borne with him these many years although he rebelled against Me, and you cannot bear with him one night?" Abraham realized his sin and did not rest until he had brought the stranger back. [12]

[Benjamin Franklin composed his "Parable against Persecution" on this theme.]

Three Men

The story opens by saying that *God* appeared to Abraham [Gen. 18:1], but when Abraham applies the vision to his own world he suddenly sees *three men* standing before him [Gen. 18:2]. Abraham is the religious man par excellence for he sees God in the human situation.

FRANZ ROSENZWEIG [13]

For the Sake of Peace

Sarah laughed skeptically and said: "Am I to have enjoyment—with *my husband* so old?" [Gen. 18:12]; but God, repeating this to Abraham, reported her as saying: "...old as *I* am." He did this to safeguard Abraham's feelings and to preserve domestic peace. TALMUD [14]

Sodom and Gomorrah

No parallels in extra-biblical literature exist to the story of Sodom and Gomorrah. Yet the destruction of the cities is referred to so frequently in the Bible that only a historic cataclysm of startling proportions could have impressed itself so deeply on popular memory. The cities most likely stood near the south end of the present Dead Sea (where today's Sodom is situated). The district is filled with bitumen and salt formations (Gen. 14:10; 19:26; Deut. 29:22) and is part of a deep rift that reaches from Armenia to Central Africa and that runs north/south through the Aravah Valley. The rift is presumed to be the result of a catastrophic earthquake, which might have raised the level of the Dead Sea sufficiently to flood what was formerly the Valley of Siddim (Gen. 14:3) and to submerge the cities.★

The purpose of the biblical tale is not, however, to report natural events as such but to present these events in the light of religious insight. God destroyed the cities because the people were evil. The story therefore intertwines the natural and the supernatural, employing symbols and folklore, in order to teach the effects of moral depravity.

A remarkable confrontation introduces the drama. Apprised of the impending destruction of Sodom and Gomorrah, Abraham rises to argue God's justice and questions Him to His face. Abraham's pleading fails not

---

★ The destruction encompassed apparently all the "cities of the Plain" (Gen. 13:12; 19:25), i.e., the cities mentioned in Gen. 14. Only Zoar was spared.

because his moral stance is faulty but because his premise is wrong: There are no righteous men in the cities.

With this story it becomes clear that Abraham's religion is more than a set of cultic practices. It deals with human beings and their problems and with Abraham's faith in a God of righteousness.

וַיָּקֻמוּ מִשָּׁם הָאֲנָשִׁים

וַיַּשְׁקִפוּ עַל־פְּנֵי סְדֹם וְאַבְרָהָם הֹלֵךְ עִמָּם לְשַׁלְּחָם:

יז וַיהֹוָה אָמָר הַמְכַסֶּה אֲנִי מֵאַבְרָהָם אֲשֶׁר אֲנִי עֹשֶׂה:

יח וְאַבְרָהָם הָיוֹ יִהְיֶה לְגוֹי גָּדוֹל וְעָצוּם וְנִבְרְכוּ־בוֹ כֹּל

יט גּוֹיֵי הָאָרֶץ: כִּי יְדַעְתִּיו לְמַעַן אֲשֶׁר יְצַוֶּה אֶת־בָּנָיו

וְאֶת־בֵּיתוֹ אַחֲרָיו וְשָׁמְרוּ דֶּרֶךְ יְהֹוָה לַעֲשׂוֹת צְדָקָה

וּמִשְׁפָּט לְמַעַן הָבִיא יְהֹוָה עַל־אַבְרָהָם אֵת אֲשֶׁר־

כ דִּבֶּר עָלָיו: וַיֹּאמֶר יְהֹוָה זַעֲקַת סְדֹם וַעֲמֹרָה כִּי־

כא רָבָּה וְחַטָּאתָם כִּי כָבְדָה מְאֹד: אֵרֲדָה־נָּא וְאֶרְאֶה

הַכְּצַעֲקָתָהּ הַבָּאָה אֵלַי עָשׂוּ כָּלָה וְאִם־לֹא אֵדָעָה:

Genesis 18
16–21

16] The men set out from there and looked down toward Sodom, Abraham walking with them to see them off. 17] Now the LORD had said, "Shall I hide from Abraham what I am about to do, 18] since Abraham is to become a great and populous nation and all the nations of the earth are to bless themselves by him? 19] For I have singled him out, that he may instruct his children and his posterity to keep the way of the LORD by doing what is just and right, in order that the LORD may bring about for Abraham what He has promised him." 20] Then the LORD said, "The outrage of Sodom and Gomorrah is so great, and their sin so grave! 21] I will go down to see whether they have acted altogether according to the outcry that has come to Me; if not, I will know."

18:17] *Shall I hide from Abraham what I am about to do?* God muses whether to share His thoughts with His chosen one. Perhaps He *wants* Abraham to argue the justice of the divine plan. Rashi writes: God has appointed Abraham as the "father of a multitude of nations" (Gen. 17:5), and hence the people of Sodom are his children, too. Should the people of Sodom are his children, too. Should

God not tell a father the fate of his children? /Rashi's argument reflects the mishnaic discussion about Hebrew prayers to be recited by converts. The proof text in the argument is in Gen. 17:5, because there Abraham is called the "father of a multitude of nations," and hence all converts to Judaism are called sons of Abraham [1]./

כב וַיִּפְנוּ מִשָּׁם הָאֲנָשִׁים וַיֵּלְכוּ סְדֹמָה וְאַבְרָהָם עוֹדֶנּוּ

כג עֹמֵד לִפְנֵי יְהֹוָה: וַיִּגַּשׁ אַבְרָהָם וַיֹּאמַר הַאַף תִּסְפֶּה

כד צַדִּיק עִם־רָשָׁע: אוּלַי יֵשׁ חֲמִשִּׁים צַדִּיקִם בְּתוֹךְ

הָעִיר הַאַף תִּסְפֶּה וְלֹא־תִשָּׂא לַמָּקוֹם לְמַעַן חֲמִשִּׁים

כה הַצַּדִּיקִם אֲשֶׁר בְּקִרְבָּהּ: חָלִלָה לְּךָ מֵעֲשֹׂת כַּדָּבָר

הַזֶּה לְהָמִית צַדִּיק עִם־רָשָׁע וְהָיָה כַצַּדִּיק כָּרָשָׁע

חָלִלָה לָּךְ הֲשֹׁפֵט כָּל־הָאָרֶץ לֹא יַעֲשֶׂה מִשְׁפָּט:

כו וַיֹּאמֶר יְהֹוָה אִם־אֶמְצָא בִסְדֹם חֲמִשִּׁים צַדִּיקִם בְּתוֹךְ

הָעִיר וְנָשָׂאתִי לְכָל־הַמָּקוֹם בַּעֲבוּרָם: וַיַּעַן אַבְרָהָם

כז וַיֹּאמַר הִנֵּה־נָא הוֹאַלְתִּי לְדַבֵּר אֶל־אֲדֹנָי וְאָנֹכִי עָפָר

כח וָאֵפֶר: אוּלַי יַחְסְרוּן חֲמִשִּׁים הַצַּדִּיקִם חֲמִשָּׁה

הֲתַשְׁחִית בַּחֲמִשָּׁה אֶת־כָּל־הָעִיר וַיֹּאמֶר לֹא אַשְׁחִית

22] The men went on from there to Sodom, while Abraham remained standing before the LORD. **23]** Abraham came forward and said, "Will You sweep away the innocent along with the guilty? **24]** What if there should be fifty innocent within the city; will You then wipe out the place and not forgive it for the sake of the innocent fifty who are in it? **25]** Far be it from You to do such a thing, to bring death upon the innocent as well as the guilty, so that innocent and guilty fare alike. Far be it from You! Shall not the Judge of all the earth deal justly?" **26]** And the LORD answered, "If I find within the city of Sodom fifty innocent ones, I will forgive the whole place for their sake." **27]** Abraham spoke up, saying "Here I venture to speak to the LORD, I who am but dust and ashes: **28]** What if the fifty innocent should lack five? Will You destroy the whole city for want of the five?" And He

22] *Abraham remained standing before the Lord.* In this verse "the men" are clearly distinguished Abraham begins the dialogue but God finishes it.   from God.

כט אִם־אֶמְצָא שָׁם אַרְבָּעִים וַחֲמִשָּׁה: וַיֹּסֶף עוֹד לְדַבֵּר
אֵלָיו וַיֹּאמַר אוּלַי יִמָּצְאוּן שָׁם אַרְבָּעִים וַיֹּאמֶר לֹא
ל אֶעֱשֶׂה בַּעֲבוּר הָאַרְבָּעִים: וַיֹּאמֶר אַל־נָא יִחַר לַאדֹנָי
וַאֲדַבֵּרָה אוּלַי יִמָּצְאוּן שָׁם שְׁלֹשִׁים וַיֹּאמֶר לֹא אֶעֱשֶׂה
לא אִם־אֶמְצָא שָׁם שְׁלֹשִׁים: וַיֹּאמֶר הִנֵּה־נָא הוֹאַלְתִּי
לְדַבֵּר אֶל־אֲדֹנָי אוּלַי יִמָּצְאוּן שָׁם עֶשְׂרִים וַיֹּאמֶר לֹא
לב אַשְׁחִית בַּעֲבוּר הָעֶשְׂרִים: וַיֹּאמֶר אַל־נָא יִחַר לַאדֹנָי
וַאֲדַבְּרָה אַךְ־הַפַּעַם אוּלַי יִמָּצְאוּן שָׁם עֲשָׂרָה וַיֹּאמֶר
לג לֹא אַשְׁחִית בַּעֲבוּר הָעֲשָׂרָה: וַיֵּלֶךְ יְהוָֹה כַּאֲשֶׁר
כִּלָּה לְדַבֵּר אֶל־אַבְרָהָם וְאַבְרָהָם שָׁב לִמְקֹמוֹ:
א וַיָּבֹאוּ שְׁנֵי הַמַּלְאָכִים סְדֹמָה בָּעֶרֶב וְלוֹט יֹשֵׁב

Genesis 18; 19
29–33; 1

answered, "I will not destroy if I find forty-five there." **29]** But he spoke to Him again, and said, "What if forty should be found there?" And He answered, "I will not do it, for the sake of the forty." **30]** And he said, "Let not the LORD be angry if I go on: What if thirty should be found there?" And He answered, "I will not do it if I find thirty there." **31]** And he said, "I venture again to speak to the LORD: What if twenty should be found there?" And He answered, "I will not destroy, for the sake of the twenty." **32]** And he said, "Let not the LORD be angry if I speak but this last time: What if ten should be found there?" And He answered, "I will not destroy, for the sake of the ten."

33] When the LORD had finished speaking to Abraham, He departed; and Abraham returned to his place.

1] The two angels arrived in Sodom in the evening, as Lot was sitting in the gate

---

19:1] *The two angels.* Earlier, the Bible speaks of three men (Gen. 18:2), suggesting that there were two different sources for the story. / Traditional explanation: The third messenger represented God himself who had spoken with Abraham. /

בְּשַׁעַר־סְדֹם וַיַּרְא־לוֹט וַיָּקׇם לִקְרָאתָם וַיִּשְׁתַּחוּ אַפַּיִם

ב] אָרְצָה: וַיֹּאמֶר הִנֶּה־נָּא אֲדֹנַי סוּרוּ נָא אֶל־בֵּית

עַבְדְּכֶם וְלִינוּ וְרַחֲצוּ רַגְלֵיכֶם וְהִשְׁכַּמְתֶּם וַהֲלַכְתֶּם

ג] לְדַרְכְּכֶם וַיֹּאמְרוּ לֹא כִּי בָרְחוֹב נָלִין: וַיִּפְצַר־בָּם

מְאֹד וַיָּסֻרוּ אֵלָיו וַיָּבֹאוּ אֶל־בֵּיתוֹ וַיַּעַשׂ לָהֶם מִשְׁתֶּה

ד] וּמַצּוֹת אָפָה וַיֹּאכֵלוּ: טֶרֶם יִשְׁכָּבוּ וְאַנְשֵׁי הָעִיר

אַנְשֵׁי סְדֹם נָסַבּוּ עַל־הַבַּיִת מִנַּעַר וְעַד־זָקֵן כָּל־הָעָם

ה] מִקָּצֶה: וַיִּקְרְאוּ אֶל־לוֹט וַיֹּאמְרוּ לוֹ אַיֵּה הָאֲנָשִׁים

אֲשֶׁר־בָּאוּ אֵלֶיךָ הַלָּיְלָה הוֹצִיאֵם אֵלֵינוּ וְנֵדְעָה אֹתָם:

ו] וַיֵּצֵא אֲלֵהֶם לוֹט הַפֶּתְחָה וְהַדֶּלֶת סָגַר אַחֲרָיו:

of Sodom. When Lot saw them, he rose to greet them and, bowing low with his face to the ground, **2]** he said, "Please, my lords, turn aside to your servant's house to spend the night, and bathe your feet; then you may be on your way early." But they said, "No, we will spend the night in the square." **3]** But he urged them strongly, so they turned his way and entered his house. He prepared a feast for them and baked unleavened bread, and they ate.

4] They had not yet lain down, when the townspeople, the men of Sodom, young and old—all the people to the last man—surrounded the house. **5]** And they shouted to Lot and said to him, "Where are the men who came to you tonight? Bring them out to us, that we may be intimate with them." **6]** So Lot went out

Arrived in Sodom in the evening. The distance from Hebron and Mamre to Sodom could not be covered in an afternoon's journey. However, since the messengers are thought of as supernatural beings, this presents no problem to narrator or listener.

3] *Unleavened bread.* Which can be quickly baked.

4] *To the last man.* It is clear now that not a single righteous man dwelled in Sodom. (Lot was a sojourner, not a citizen.)

5] *That we may be intimate with them.* The Sodomites wanted the men for homosexual or other deviate practices (hence the term sodomy for unnatural sexual behavior).

ח וַיֹּאמַר אַל־נָא אַחַי תָּרֵעוּ: הִנֵּה־נָא לִי שְׁתֵּי בָנוֹת אֲשֶׁר לֹא־יָדְעוּ אִישׁ אוֹצִיאָה־נָּא אֶתְהֶן אֲלֵיכֶם וַעֲשׂוּ לָהֶן כַּטּוֹב בְּעֵינֵיכֶם רַק לָאֲנָשִׁים הָאֵל אַל־תַּעֲשׂוּ דָבָר כִּי־עַל־כֵּן בָּאוּ בְּצֵל קֹרָתִי: ט וַיֹּאמְרוּ גֶּשׁ־הָלְאָה וַיֹּאמְרוּ הָאֶחָד בָּא־לָגוּר וַיִּשְׁפֹּט שָׁפוֹט עַתָּה נָרַע לְךָ מֵהֶם וַיִּפְצְרוּ בָאִישׁ בְּלוֹט מְאֹד וַיִּגְּשׁוּ לִשְׁבֹּר הַדָּלֶת: י וַיִּשְׁלְחוּ הָאֲנָשִׁים אֶת־יָדָם וַיָּבִיאוּ אֶת־לוֹט אֲלֵיהֶם הַבָּיְתָה וְאֶת־הַדֶּלֶת סָגָרוּ: וְאֶת־הָאֲנָשִׁים אֲשֶׁר־ יא פֶּתַח הַבַּיִת הִכּוּ בַּסַּנְוֵרִים מִקָּטֹן וְעַד־גָּדוֹל וַיִּלְאוּ לִמְצֹא הַפָּתַח: יב וַיֹּאמְרוּ הָאֲנָשִׁים אֶל־לוֹט עֹד מִי־לְךָ

Genesis 19
7–12

to them to the entrance, shut the door behind him,   7] and said, "I beg you, my friends, do not commit such a wrong.   8] See, I have two daughters who have not known a man. Let me bring them out to you, and you may do to them as you please; but do not do anything to these men, since they have come under the shelter of my roof."   9] But they said, "Stand back! The fellow," they said, "came here as an alien, and already he acts the ruler! Now we will deal worse with you than with them." And they pressed hard against the person of Lot, and moved forward to break the door.   10] But the men stretched out their hands and pulled Lot into the house with them, and shut the door.   11] And the people who were at the entrance of the house, young and old, they struck with blinding light, so that they were helpless to find the entrance.

12] Then the men said to Lot, "Whom else have you here? Sons-in-law, your

---

8] *I have two daughters.* Lot's offer of his daughters to protect his guests may seem fantastically disproportionate. The implication in the text, however, is that Lot is a model host who will go to extreme lengths to honor the hospitality code.

9] *An alien, and already he acts the ruler!* The reaction of the native-born to the immigrant.

פֹּה חָתָן וּבָנֶיךָ וּבְנֹתֶיךָ וְכֹל אֲשֶׁר־לְךָ בָּעִיר הוֹצֵא

יג מִן־הַמָּקוֹם: כִּי־מַשְׁחִתִים אֲנַחְנוּ אֶת־הַמָּקוֹם הַזֶּה כִּי־

גָדְלָה צַעֲקָתָם אֶת־פְּנֵי יְהֹוָה וַיְשַׁלְּחֵנוּ יְהֹוָה לְשַׁחֲתָהּ:

יד וַיֵּצֵא לוֹט וַיְדַבֵּר אֶל־חֲתָנָיו לֹקְחֵי בְנֹתָיו וַיֹּאמֶר

קוּמוּ צְּאוּ מִן־הַמָּקוֹם הַזֶּה כִּי־מַשְׁחִית יְהֹוָה אֶת־

טו הָעִיר וַיְהִי כִמְצַחֵק בְּעֵינֵי חֲתָנָיו: וּכְמוֹ הַשַּׁחַר

עָלָה וַיָּאִיצוּ הַמַּלְאָכִים בְּלוֹט לֵאמֹר קוּם קַח אֶת־

אִשְׁתְּךָ וְאֶת־שְׁתֵּי בְנֹתֶיךָ הַנִּמְצָאֹת פֶּן־תִּסָּפֶה בַּעֲוֹן

טז הָעִיר: וַיִּתְמַהְמָהּ וַיַּחֲזִיקוּ הָאֲנָשִׁים בְּיָדוֹ וּבְיַד־אִשְׁתּוֹ

וּבְיַד שְׁתֵּי בְנֹתָיו בְּחֶמְלַת יְהֹוָה עָלָיו וַיֹּצִאֻהוּ וַיַּנִּחֻהוּ

יז מִחוּץ לָעִיר: וַיְהִי כְהוֹצִיאָם אֹתָם הַחוּצָה וַיֹּאמֶר

sons and daughters, or anyone else that you have in the city—bring them out of the place.   13] For we are about to destroy this place; because the outcry against them before the LORD has become so great that the LORD has sent us to destroy it."   14] So Lot went out and spoke to his sons-in-law, who had married his daughters, and said, "Up, get out of this place, for the LORD is about to destroy the city." But he seemed to his sons-in-law as one who jests.

15] As dawn broke, the angels urged Lot on, saying, "Up, take your wife and your two remaining daughters, lest you be swept away because of the iniquity of the city."   16] Still he delayed. So the men seized his hand, and the hands of his wife and his two daughters—in the LORD's mercy on him—and brought him out and left him outside the city.   17] When they had brought them outside, one said,

---

15] *Two remaining daughters.* The married daughters apparently chose to stay with their Sodomite husbands.

17] *Do not look behind you.* Meaning either, "Do not waste a precious second," or "Do not look back in regret."

הִמָּלֵט עַל־נַפְשֶׁךָ אַל־תַּבִּיט אַחֲרֶיךָ וְאַל־תַּעֲמֹד בְּכָל־

הַכִּכָּר הָהָרָה הִמָּלֵט פֶּן־תִּסָּפֶה: וַיֹּאמֶר לוֹט אֲלֵהֶם

יט אַל־נָא אֲדֹנָי: הִנֵּה־נָא מָצָא עַבְדְּךָ חֵן בְּעֵינֶיךָ וַתַּגְדֵּל

חַסְדְּךָ אֲשֶׁר עָשִׂיתָ עִמָּדִי לְהַחֲיוֹת אֶת־נַפְשִׁי וְאָנֹכִי

לֹא אוּכַל לְהִמָּלֵט הָהָרָה פֶּן־תִּדְבָּקַנִי הָרָעָה וָמַתִּי:

כ הִנֵּה־נָא הָעִיר הַזֹּאת קְרֹבָה לָנוּס שָׁמָּה וְהִוא מִצְעָר

אִמָּלְטָה נָּא שָׁמָּה הֲלֹא מִצְעָר הִוא וּתְחִי נַפְשִׁי:

כא וַיֹּאמֶר אֵלָיו הִנֵּה נָשָׂאתִי פָנֶיךָ גַּם לַדָּבָר הַזֶּה לְבִלְתִּי

כב הָפְכִּי אֶת־הָעִיר אֲשֶׁר דִּבַּרְתָּ: מַהֵר הִמָּלֵט שָׁמָּה כִּי

לֹא אוּכַל לַעֲשׂוֹת דָּבָר עַד־בֹּאֲךָ שָׁמָּה עַל־כֵּן קָרָא

כג שֵׁם־הָעִיר צוֹעַר: הַשֶּׁמֶשׁ יָצָא עַל־הָאָרֶץ וְלוֹט בָּא

כד צֹעֲרָה: וַיהֹוָה הִמְטִיר עַל־סְדֹם וְעַל־עֲמֹרָה גָּפְרִית

Genesis 19
18–24

"Flee for your life! Do not look behind you, nor stop anywhere in the Plain; flee to the hills, lest you be swept away." **18]** But Lot said to them, "Oh no, my Lord! **19]** Please, if you favor your servant, having already shown me so much kindness by saving my life—I cannot flee to the hills, lest disaster overtake me and I die. **20]** See, that town there is near enough to flee to; it is such a little place! Let me flee there—it is such a little place—and let my life be saved." **21]** He replied, "Very well, I will grant you this favor too, and I will not annihilate the town of which you have spoken. **22]** Hurry, flee there, for I cannot do anything until you arrive there." Hence the town came to be called Zoar.

23] As the sun rose upon the earth and Lot entered Zoar, **24]** the LORD rained

---

22] *Zoar.* Lot does not state why he prefers Zoar's safety and why, as soon as he reaches it, he finds it even more unbearable than a cave. The name

Zoar is connected with the word מִצְעָר (*mitzar*, a little, insignificant thing) in Gen. 19:20.

24] *The Lord.* The repetition of the divine name

כה וָאֵשׁ מֵאֵת יְהֹוָה מִן־הַשָּׁמָיִם: וַיַּהֲפֹךְ אֶת־הֶעָרִים הָאֵל
וְאֵת כָּל־הַכִּכָּר וְאֵת כָּל־יֹשְׁבֵי הֶעָרִים וְצֶמַח הָאֲדָמָה:

כו וַתַּבֵּט אִשְׁתּוֹ מֵאַחֲרָיו וַתְּהִי נְצִיב מֶלַח: וַיַּשְׁכֵּם
אַבְרָהָם בַּבֹּקֶר אֶל־הַמָּקוֹם אֲשֶׁר־עָמַד שָׁם אֶת־

כח פְּנֵי יְהֹוָה: וַיַּשְׁקֵף עַל־פְּנֵי סְדֹם וַעֲמֹרָה וְעַל כָּל־פְּנֵי
אֶרֶץ הַכִּכָּר וַיַּרְא וְהִנֵּה עָלָה קִיטֹר הָאָרֶץ כְּקִיטֹר

כט הַכִּבְשָׁן: וַיְהִי בְּשַׁחֵת אֱלֹהִים אֶת־עָרֵי הַכִּכָּר וַיִּזְכֹּר
אֱלֹהִים אֶת־אַבְרָהָם וַיְשַׁלַּח אֶת־לוֹט מִתּוֹךְ הַהֲפֵכָה

ל בַּהֲפֹךְ אֶת־הֶעָרִים אֲשֶׁר־יָשַׁב בָּהֵן לוֹט: וַיַּעַל לוֹט
מִצּוֹעַר וַיֵּשֶׁב בָּהָר וּשְׁתֵּי בְנֹתָיו עִמּוֹ כִּי יָרֵא לָשֶׁבֶת

Genesis 19
25–30

upon Sodom and Gomorrah sulfurous fire from the LORD out of heaven.   25] He annihilated those cities and the entire Plain, and all the inhabitants of the cities and the vegetation of the ground.   26] Lot's wife, behind him, looked back, and she thereupon turned into a pillar of salt.

27] Next morning, Abraham hurried to the place where he had stood before the LORD,   28] and, looking down toward Sodom and Gomorrah and all the land of the Plain, he saw the smoke of the land rising like the smoke of a kiln.   29] Thus it was that, when God destroyed the cities of the Plain and annihilated the cities where Lot dwelt, God was mindful of Abraham and removed Lot from the midst of the upheaval.

30] Lot went up from Zoar and settled in the hill country with his two daughters,

---

in this sentence means to emphasize the supernatural origin of the catastrophe.

Sulfurous fire. Older translations: "Brimstone and fire," from which the proverbial "fire and brimstone."

26] *Pillar of salt.* To this day, salt-encrusted rock formations in the area suggest all manner of shapes. The legend has parallels in various mythologies, e.g., the Greek story of Orpheus and Eurydice.

/ Ancient tradition thought it could fully identify the encrusted remains of Lot's wife [2]./

בְּצוֹעַר וַיֵּשֶׁב בַּמְּעָרָה הוּא וּשְׁתֵּי בְנֹתָיו: וַתֹּאמֶר לא

הַבְּכִירָה אֶל־הַצְּעִירָה אָבִינוּ זָקֵן וְאִישׁ אֵין בָּאָרֶץ

לָבוֹא עָלֵינוּ כְּדֶרֶךְ כָּל־הָאָרֶץ: לְכָה נַשְׁקֶה אֶת־ לב

אָבִינוּ יַיִן וְנִשְׁכְּבָה עִמּוֹ וּנְחַיֶּה מֵאָבִינוּ זָרַע: וַתַּשְׁקֶיןָ לג

אֶת־אֲבִיהֶן יַיִן בַּלַּיְלָה הוּא וַתָּבֹא הַבְּכִירָה וַתִּשְׁכַּב

אֶת־אָבִיהָ וְלֹא־יָדַע בְּשִׁכְבָהּ וּבְקוּמָהּ: וַיְהִי מִמָּחֳרָת לד

וַתֹּאמֶר הַבְּכִירָה אֶל־הַצְּעִירָה הֵן־שָׁכַבְתִּי אֶמֶשׁ אֶת־

אָבִי נַשְׁקֶנּוּ יַיִן גַּם־הַלַּיְלָה וּבֹאִי שִׁכְבִי עִמּוֹ וּנְחַיֶּה

מֵאָבִינוּ זָרַע: וַתַּשְׁקֶיןָ גַּם בַּלַּיְלָה הַהוּא אֶת־אֲבִיהֶן לה

יַיִן וַתָּקָם הַצְּעִירָה וַתִּשְׁכַּב עִמּוֹ וְלֹא־יָדַע בְּשִׁכְבָהּ

וּבְקֻמָהּ: וַתַּהֲרֶיןָ שְׁתֵּי בְנוֹת־לוֹט מֵאֲבִיהֶן: וַתֵּלֶד לו
לז

Genesis 19
31–37

for he was afraid to dwell in Zoar; and he and his two daughters lived in a cave. **31]** And the older one said to the younger, "Our father is old, and there is not a man on earth to consort with us in the way of all the world. **32]** Come, let us make our father drink wine, and let us lie with him, that we may maintain life through our father." **33]** That night they made their father drink wine, and the older one went in and lay with her father; he did not know when she lay down or when she rose. **34]** The next day the older one said to the younger, "See, I lay with Father last night; let us make him drink wine tonight also, and you go and lie with him, that we may maintain life through our father." **35]** That night also they made their father drink wine, and the younger one went and lay with him; he did not know when she lay down or when she rose.

36] Thus the two daughters of Lot came to be with child by their father. **37]** The

37] *Moab.* A word play on מֵאָב (*me-av,* from [my] father).

הַבְּכִירָה בֵּן וַתִּקְרָא שְׁמוֹ מוֹאָב הוּא אֲבִי־מוֹאָב
עַד־הַיּוֹם: וְהַצְּעִירָה גַם־הִוא יָלְדָה בֵּן וַתִּקְרָא שְׁמוֹ
בֶּן־עַמִּי הוּא אֲבִי בְנֵי־עַמּוֹן עַד־הַיּוֹם: ס

older one bore a son and named him Moab; he is the father of the Moabites of today.
38] And the younger also bore a son, and she called him Ben-ammi; he is the father
of the Ammonites of today.

38] *Ben-ammi.* "Son of my [paternal] kindred." It is possible that this tale
of sexual aberration arose to explain the names of Moab and Ammon.

Abraham's Argument with God

The dramatic confrontation between Abraham and God is told with the utmost simplicity; the cadences of repetitions vary as subtly as the repetitions of a symphonic theme.

Abraham does not doubt the existence of God's justice, he only asks its extent and limitations. The important thing is that he asks altogether and that God does not reject his question out of hand. The Bible thereby makes clear that man may, with impunity, question the behavior of God. Like Abraham, man need not surrender his own sense of justice; he remains free to accept or reject the divine judgment—although he will have to submit to it in the end. Man is not reduced to a moral automaton, his spiritual freedom is preserved.

It has been suggested that Abraham bargains with God, but in fact he does no more than plead. His pleas may be seen as attempts to penetrate the division separating the earthly and heavenly realms. In the end, Abraham has greater knowledge of the divine intention, but neither he nor the reader is given an intimation whether Abraham succeeded in changing God's mind, or whether—more likely—he merely learned what had been God's plan from the beginning. God's ways are ultimately "past finding out" (Job 9:10), but this does not prevent man from trying to bring them as much as possible within his own horizon of understanding.

And this horizon is not, in Abraham's case, limited by tribal considerations. His is a universal concept of justice. He is not concerned merely with Lot or his family but with people outside his tribe. He is a man for all men.

The Merit of the Few

Abraham does not plead merely for the innocent but for the sinners as well, through the merit of the few righteous. The story thereby introduces the concept of merit

(זְכוּת), important in biblical and especially in post-biblical religion [3]. The concept stipulates that a handful of concerned, decent, and "righteous" men could have averted Sodom's calamity by their merit.

Yet the story also suggests that there are limits to the influence of even the best men. Unless they find a minimum of like-minded associates, they will be ineffective. Eventually, if they persist in living in such a society, they will perish with it. Thus, Abraham does not, in his pursuit of divine equity, go below the number ten. The Rabbis advised that if one could not find ten religiously minded people in a city one should move away. They also set ten as the minimal number (*minyan*) required for communal worship [4]. There comes a time when God, with all His mercy and justice, is "finished speaking" with man (Gen. 18:33) and when the punishment for unchecked evil will take its inevitable course and engulf all of society.

The Sins of Sodom and Gomorrah

The terms "outrage," "outcry," "destroy," are reminiscent of the story of the Flood, where we were told that the world was "filled with lawlessness." While here such a general definition is lacking, the similarity of expressions suggests that comparable moral conditions existed in both instances. We can infer from the story itself that Sodomites were inhospitable and that they were accustomed to some form or forms of sexual deviation. But while deviate sexual practice is strongly condemned in the Torah (Lev. 18), Jewish tradition stresses social rather than sexual aberrations as the reason for the cities' destruction.

Ezekiel, for instance, describes the sins of Sodom in social terms: "pride, fulness of bread, and careless ease was in her and in her daughters; neither did she strengthen the hand of the poor and needy. And they were haughty" (16:49–50). The tradition of Sodom's moral insensitivity, based on the way the

185

Sodomites treated strangers, highlighted, to biblical man, the community's essential depravity. To the ancients, hospitality included vastly more than good manners; it meant the treatment and acceptance of strangers and was a vital aspect of religion (Deut. 10:19). If Sodom had been a poor city, the sin of inhospitality might have been understandable and forgivable. But the city was rich, "like the garden of the Lord" (Gen. 13:10). The Midrash tells of the tradition that the streets were paved with gold and that the Sodomites flooded the approaches to their town so that strangers would be kept away and immigration effectively restricted [5].

Social evil, then, caused Sodom to perish. The Bible thus takes the old story of the physical destruction of the plain and turns it into a moral tale that carries its warning to all ages: Affluence without social concern is self-destructive; it hardens the conscience against repentance; it engenders cruelty and excess. The treatment accorded newcomers and strangers was then and may always be considered a touchstone of the community's moral condition.

Lot

Lot is in many ways the average man. He has streaks of greatness, moments of courage, but he is all too often subject to the attractions of comfort and pleasure. These in the end cause his downfall.

He appears in the text for the first time when he decides to leave the security of Haran to follow Abraham into an insecure future. Apparently he is a man of some conviction and initiative. But later, probably attracted by Sodom's affluence, he chooses that city as his home, despite its debased condition. Whatever other customs and habits of Sodom he adopts, he preserves his sense of hospitality and decency toward strangers. He risks his own and his family's safety in order to protect the men who are under his roof. This courage redeems much of his indecisiveness, faint-heartedness, and anxiety, which the remainder of the story reveals.

GLEANINGS

I Will Go Down to See (Gen. 18:21)

God wanted to give the cities time to repent. This, like the story of Babel, teaches that a judge must scrupulously examine a case before pronouncing judgment; and further, that just as God "went down" to see, so must man not judge his fellow man until he has come to see things from the other's viewpoint. MIDRASH [6]

[This interpretation is also offered to counter the question: Did God not know whether Sodom was wicked?]

The Promethean

Abraham ranks among the biblical personages whose persuasive powers God had to acknowledge. Abraham would have surely snatched Sodom from destruction if only those few—ten, even—had been worthy of his prayer. SHELDON H. BLANK [7]

The Sin

The sin of Sodom consisted not only in what its people did but in what they failed to do. Thus, no one raised his voice in protest when the crowd molested Lot's guests. Failure to protest is to participate in the sin of a community. [8]

Of Sodom it is written that it was well-watered everywhere [Gen. 13:10]; it possessed all the luxuries of the world, and its inhabitants were unwilling to share them with others. They punished anyone who offered food to a stranger; they even polled their fig trees lest birds would eat of them. R. Hiya said: "They deserved punishment both for their immorality and their uncharitableness. For whoever grudges assistance to the poor does not deserve to exist in this world, and he also forfeits the life of the world-to-come. Contrariwise, whoever is generous towards the poor deserves to exist in the world, and it is for his sake that the world exists, and the fulness of life is reserved for him in the world-to-come." MIDRASH, ZOHAR [9]

Because They Passed Wisdom By

Wisdom rescued a righteous man when the ungodly were perishing;
he escaped the fire that descended on the Five Cities.
Evidence of their wickedness still remains:
a continually smoking wasteland,
plants bearing fruit that does not ripen,
and a pillar of salt standing as a monument to an unbelieving soul.
For because they passed wisdom by,
they not only were hindered from recognizing the good,
but also left for mankind a reminder of their folly,
so that their failures could never go unnoticed.
WISDOM OF SOLOMON [10]

The Site

From ancient times right down to the present day, popular imagination has been fascinated by the figure of Lot's thoughtless and inquisitive wife who, for disregarding God's command, was turned into a pillar of salt. As early as the time of the Second Temple, the pillar of salt was thought to be in the region of Mount Sodom. Thus Josephus writes: "I saw the pillar of salt on my travels, for it exists to this day."

Mount Sodom, at the southwestern corner of the Dead Sea, is remarkable for its sharp pinnacles, the lower parts of which consist of salt layers and the upper of salt and marl columns. One or another of these pinnacles which look like a human shape is regarded by popular tradition as the wife of Lot. However, as a result of climatic and geological factors the "pillars" are in a constant state of formation and disintegration. This has given rise to various legends about the transformation of Lot's wife. VIEWS OF THE BIBLICAL WORLD [11]

Crises

After a repetition of the "sister" incident, the Bible finally tells of the long-awaited birth of Sarah's son. Two brief, almost anticlimactic verses tell us that the divine promise is now fulfilled and the spiritual continuity of Abraham guaranteed. But no sooner is the first stage reached than difficulties arise between the sons of Abraham. The text relates the harsh manner in which the rivalry is resolved.

Then follows a brief interlude dealing with another relationship, that of Abraham and Abimelech. This too finds its adjustment, leaving the reader with the impression that all is well in the household of the Patriarch. But the respite is short. This section may therefore be viewed as the introduction to the story of the Akedah, which follows.

א וַיִּסַּע מִשָּׁם אַבְרָהָם אַרְצָה הַנֶּגֶב וַיֵּשֶׁב בֵּין־קָדֵשׁ וּבֵין
ב שׁוּר וַיָּגָר בִּגְרָר: וַיֹּאמֶר אַבְרָהָם אֶל־שָׂרָה אִשְׁתּוֹ
אֲחֹתִי הִוא וַיִּשְׁלַח אֲבִימֶלֶךְ מֶלֶךְ גְּרָר וַיִּקַּח אֶת־
ג שָׂרָה: וַיָּבֹא אֱלֹהִים אֶל־אֲבִימֶלֶךְ בַּחֲלוֹם הַלָּיְלָה
וַיֹּאמֶר לוֹ הִנְּךָ מֵת עַל־הָאִשָּׁה אֲשֶׁר־לָקַחְתָּ וְהִוא
ד בְּעֻלַת בָּעַל: וַאֲבִימֶלֶךְ לֹא קָרַב אֵלֶיהָ וַיֹּאמַר
ה אֲדֹנָי הֲגוֹי גַּם־צַדִּיק תַּהֲרֹג: הֲלֹא הוּא אָמַר־לִי
אֲחֹתִי הִוא וְהִיא־גַם־הִוא אָמְרָה אָחִי הוּא בְּתָם־לְבָבִי
ו וּבְנִקְיֹן כַּפַּי עָשִׂיתִי זֹאת: וַיֹּאמֶר אֵלָיו הָאֱלֹהִים
בַּחֲלֹם גַּם אָנֹכִי יָדַעְתִּי כִּי בְתָם־לְבָבְךָ עָשִׂיתָ זֹּאת
וָאֶחְשֹׂךְ גַּם־אָנֹכִי אוֹתְךָ מֵחֲטוֹ־לִי עַל־כֵּן לֹא־נְתַתִּיךָ

Genesis 20
1–6

1] Abraham journeyed from there to the region of the Negeb and settled between Kadesh and Shur. While he was sojourning in Gerar,   2] Abraham said of Sarah his wife, "She is my sister." So Abimelech king of Gerar had Sarah brought to him. 3] But God came to Abimelech in a dream by night and said to him, "You are to die because of the woman that you have taken, for she is a married woman." 4] Now Abimelech had not approached her. He said, "O Lord, will You slay people even though innocent? 5] He himself said to me, 'She is my sister!' Moreover, she said, 'He is my brother.' When I did this, my heart was blameless and my hands were clean." 6] And God said to him in the dream, "I knew that you did this with a blameless heart, and so I kept you from sinning against Me. That was why I did

20:1] *Gerar*. Between Gaza and Beer-sheba. There are two other versions of the story (see chapters 12 and 26). Scholars assign authorship of this version to the E-school and authorship of the others to the J-school. Among the differences: Chapter 12 offers no excuse for Abraham's behavior; the excuse in this section is elaborate. J does not say what happened to Sarah in Pharaoh's court; E tells us she remained untouched. E is apologetic about Abraham and Sarah; J is not (for background, see Gen. 12:10–20).

ז לִנְגֹּעַ אֵלֶיהָ: וְעַתָּה הָשֵׁב אֵשֶׁת־הָאִישׁ כִּי־נָבִיא הוּא
וְיִתְפַּלֵּל בַּעַדְךָ וֶחְיֵה וְאִם־אֵינְךָ מֵשִׁיב דַּע כִּי־מוֹת

ח תָּמוּת אַתָּה וְכָל־אֲשֶׁר־לָךְ: וַיַּשְׁכֵּם אֲבִימֶלֶךְ בַּבֹּקֶר
וַיִּקְרָא לְכָל־עֲבָדָיו וַיְדַבֵּר אֶת־כָּל־הַדְּבָרִים הָאֵלֶּה

ט בְּאָזְנֵיהֶם וַיִּירְאוּ הָאֲנָשִׁים מְאֹד: וַיִּקְרָא אֲבִימֶלֶךְ
לְאַבְרָהָם וַיֹּאמֶר לוֹ מֶה־עָשִׂיתָ לָּנוּ וּמֶה־חָטָאתִי לָךְ
כִּי־הֵבֵאתָ עָלַי וְעַל־מַמְלַכְתִּי חֲטָאָה גְדֹלָה מַעֲשִׂים

י אֲשֶׁר לֹא־יֵעָשׂוּ עָשִׂיתָ עִמָּדִי: וַיֹּאמֶר אֲבִימֶלֶךְ אֶל־

יא אַבְרָהָם מָה רָאִיתָ כִּי עָשִׂיתָ אֶת־הַדָּבָר הַזֶּה: וַיֹּאמֶר
אַבְרָהָם כִּי אָמַרְתִּי רַק אֵין־יִרְאַת אֱלֹהִים בַּמָּקוֹם

יב הַזֶּה וַהֲרָגוּנִי עַל־דְּבַר אִשְׁתִּי: וְגַם־אָמְנָה אֲחֹתִי בַת־

not let you touch her.   7] But you must restore the man's wife—since he is a prophet, he will intercede for you—to save your life. If you fail to restore her, know that you shall surely die, you and all that are yours."

8] Early next morning, Abimelech called all his servants and told them all that had happened; and the men were greatly frightened.   9] Then Abimelech summoned Abraham and said to him, "What have you done to us? What wrong have I done you that you should bring so great a guilt upon me and my kingdom? You have done to me things that ought not to be done.   10] What, then," Abimelech demanded of Abraham, "was your purpose in doing this thing?"   11] "I thought," said Abraham, "surely there is no fear of God in this place, and they will kill me because of my wife.   12] And besides, she is in truth my sister, my father's daughter

---

7] *He is a prophet.* נָבִיא (navi), one who speaks up or announces God's will.

He will intercede for you. Objectively, you have wronged Abraham and Sarah, but Abraham will not press his claim and, on the contrary, will speak in your behalf.

12] *She is in truth my sister.* On the position and meaning of "sister" (see p. 129).

אָבִי הוּא אַךְ לֹא בַת־אִמִּי וַתְּהִי־לִי לְאִשָּׁה: וַיְהִי יג
כַּאֲשֶׁר הִתְעוּ אֹתִי אֱלֹהִים מִבֵּית אָבִי וָאֹמַר לָהּ זֶה
חַסְדֵּךְ אֲשֶׁר תַּעֲשִׂי עִמָּדִי אֶל כָּל־הַמָּקוֹם אֲשֶׁר נָבוֹא
שָׁמָּה אִמְרִי־לִי אָחִי הוּא: וַיִּקַּח אֲבִימֶלֶךְ צֹאן וּבָקָר יד
וַעֲבָדִים וּשְׁפָחֹת וַיִּתֵּן לְאַבְרָהָם וַיָּשֶׁב לוֹ אֵת שָׂרָה
אִשְׁתּוֹ: וַיֹּאמֶר אֲבִימֶלֶךְ הִנֵּה אַרְצִי לְפָנֶיךָ בַּטּוֹב טו
בְּעֵינֶיךָ שֵׁב: וּלְשָׂרָה אָמַר הִנֵּה נָתַתִּי אֶלֶף כֶּסֶף טז
לְאָחִיךְ הִנֵּה הוּא־לָךְ כְּסוּת עֵינַיִם לְכֹל אֲשֶׁר אִתָּךְ
וְאֵת כֹּל וְנֹכָחַת: וַיִּתְפַּלֵּל אַבְרָהָם אֶל־הָאֱלֹהִים יז
וַיִּרְפָּא אֱלֹהִים אֶת־אֲבִימֶלֶךְ וְאֶת־אִשְׁתּוֹ וְאַמְהֹתָיו

Genesis 20
13–17

though not my mother's; and she became my wife. **13]** So when God made me wander from my father's house, I said to her, 'Let this be the kindness that you shall do me: whatever place we come to, say there of me: He is my brother.' "

14] Abimelech took sheep and oxen, and male and female slaves, and gave them to Abraham; and he restored his wife Sarah to him. **15]** And Abimelech said, "Here, my land is before you; settle wherever you please." **16]** And to Sarah he said, "I herewith give your brother a thousand pieces of silver; this will serve you as vindication before all who are with you, and you are cleared before everyone."

17] Abraham then prayed to God, and God healed Abimelech, his wife and his slave

---

13] *God.* The verb form attached to אֱלֹהִים (*elohim*) is here used in a rare plural construction. According to the Talmud [1], this is the only passage in the Abraham story where אֱלֹהִים is not holy, i.e., where it does not mean "God" (see p. 23).

16] *As vindication.* Literally, "a covering of the eyes." The meaning of this is obscure but most probably it implies: In this fashion people cannot say I cast you out because I was tired of you [2].

17] *Abraham then prayed.* While he probably prayed previously, this is the first mention of prayer in the Torah. In early cuneiform sources, too, individual prayer is rarely mentioned and seems to have evolved rather slowly. Note that Abraham's prayer for fertility is effective for others, but not as yet for his own wife. Abraham's power derives solely from God.

/The development of personal prayer in Mesopotamia has been traced from the early letters to the deity to a fixed poetic form much like the individual laments of the biblical Psalter [3]./

יח וַיֵּלֵדוּ: כִּי־עָצֹר עָצַר יְהֹוָה בְּעַד כָּל־רֶחֶם לְבֵית

אֲבִימֶלֶךְ עַל־דְּבַר שָׂרָה אֵשֶׁת אַבְרָהָם: ס

א וַיהֹוָה פָּקַד אֶת־שָׂרָה כַּאֲשֶׁר אָמָר וַיַּעַשׂ יְהֹוָה לְשָׂרָה

ב כַּאֲשֶׁר דִּבֵּר: וַתַּהַר וַתֵּלֶד שָׂרָה לְאַבְרָהָם בֵּן לִזְקֻנָיו

ג לַמּוֹעֵד אֲשֶׁר־דִּבֶּר אֹתוֹ אֱלֹהִים: וַיִּקְרָא אַבְרָהָם אֶת־

ד שֶׁם־בְּנוֹ הַנּוֹלַד־לוֹ אֲשֶׁר־יָלְדָה־לּוֹ שָׂרָה יִצְחָק: וַיָּמָל

אַבְרָהָם אֶת־יִצְחָק בְּנוֹ בֶּן־שְׁמֹנַת יָמִים כַּאֲשֶׁר צִוָּה

ה אֹתוֹ אֱלֹהִים: וְאַבְרָהָם בֶּן־מְאַת שָׁנָה בְּהִוָּלֶד לוֹ אֵת

ו יִצְחָק בְּנוֹ: וַתֹּאמֶר שָׂרָה צְחֹק עָשָׂה לִי אֱלֹהִים כָּל־

ז הַשֹּׁמֵעַ יִצְחַק־לִי: וַתֹּאמֶר מִי מִלֵּל לְאַבְרָהָם הֵינִיקָה

ח בָנִים שָׂרָה כִּי־יָלַדְתִּי בֵן לִזְקֻנָיו: וַיִּגְדַּל הַיֶּלֶד וַיִּגָּמַל

וַיַּעַשׂ אַבְרָהָם מִשְׁתֶּה גָדוֹל בְּיוֹם הִגָּמֵל אֶת־יִצְחָק:

girls, so that they bore children;   18] for the LORD had closed fast every womb of the household of Abimelech because of Sarah, the wife of Abraham.

1] The LORD took note of Sarah as He had promised, and the LORD did for Sarah as He had spoken.   2] Sarah conceived and bore a son to Abraham in his old age, at the set time of which God had spoken.   3] Abraham gave his new-born son, whom Sarah had borne him, the name of Isaac.   4] And when his son Isaac was eight days old, Abraham circumcised him, as God had commanded him.   5] Now Abraham was a hundred years old when his son Isaac was born to him.   6] Sarah said, "God has brought me laughter; everyone who hears will laugh with me."   7] And she added, / "Who would have said to Abraham / That Sarah would suckle children! / Yet I have borne a son in his old age."   8] The child grew up and was weaned, and Abraham held a great feast on the day that Isaac was weaned.

21:8] *A great feast.* Probably in connection with a weaning ceremony. According to the Talmud, children were weaned between eighteen and twenty-four months; the Book of Maccabees puts

בְּרֵאשִׁית כא
ט–יד

ט וַתֵּרֶא שָׂרָה אֶת־בֶּן־הָגָר הַמִּצְרִית אֲשֶׁר־יָלְדָה
י לְאַבְרָהָם מְצַחֵק: וַתֹּאמֶר לְאַבְרָהָם גָּרֵשׁ הָאָמָה
הַזֹּאת וְאֶת־בְּנָהּ כִּי לֹא יִירַשׁ בֶּן־הָאָמָה הַזֹּאת עִם־
יא בְּנִי עִם־יִצְחָק: וַיֵּרַע הַדָּבָר מְאֹד בְּעֵינֵי אַבְרָהָם עַל
יב אוֹדֹת בְּנוֹ: וַיֹּאמֶר אֱלֹהִים אֶל־אַבְרָהָם אַל־יֵרַע
בְּעֵינֶיךָ עַל־הַנַּעַר וְעַל־אֲמָתֶךָ כֹּל אֲשֶׁר תֹּאמַר אֵלֶיךָ
יג שָׂרָה שְׁמַע בְּקֹלָהּ כִּי בְיִצְחָק יִקָּרֵא לְךָ זָרַע: וְגַם
יד אֶת־בֶּן־הָאָמָה לְגוֹי אֲשִׂימֶנּוּ כִּי זַרְעֲךָ הוּא: וַיַּשְׁכֵּם
אַבְרָהָם בַּבֹּקֶר וַיִּקַּח־לֶחֶם וְחֵמַת מַיִם וַיִּתֵּן אֶל־הָגָר

Genesis 21
9–14

9] Sarah saw the son, whom Hagar the Egyptian had borne to Abraham, playing.
10] She said to Abraham, "Cast out that slavewoman and her son, for the son of that slave shall not share in the inheritance with my son Isaac." **11]** The matter distressed Abraham greatly, for it concerned a son of his. **12]** But God said to Abraham, "Do not be distressed over the boy or your slave; whatever Sarah tells you, do as she says, for it is through Isaac that offspring shall be continued for you. **13]** As for the son of the slave-woman, I will make a nation of him, too, for he is your seed."

14] Early next morning Abraham took some bread and a skin of water, and gave

the age at three years; in some parts of the Orient weaning is delayed even further [4].

9] *Playing.* Some commentators have suggested that it was sexual play that brought forth Sarah's strong reaction [5]. There is nothing, however, to substantiate this. The use of מְצַחֵק (*metzachek*) is an allusion to יִצְחָק (*yitzchak*, i.e., Isaac). The word play seems to indicate that Sarah, seeing the children together, suddenly realizes their close affinity. It is then that she resolves to end the relationship by freeing Hagar and sending her away.
/ According to the laws of Lipit-Ishtar (25), which antedate Hammurabi by 150 years, the slave-girl and

her son may become free but are not then entitled to an inheritance [6]./

12] *Shall be continued.* Literally, "called."

13] *A nation.* Some versions have "a great nation." Ishmael, too, will reflect Abraham's greatness. In both Jewish and Islamic traditions, many Arabs are considered Ishmael's descendants.

14] *Together with the child.* The Hebrew text is not clear. The Septuagint portrays Ishmael as a small child whom Hagar carries on her shoulder, even though according to Gen. 16:16 he is fourteen years older than Isaac.
Beer-sheba. See Gen. 21:31.

שָׁם עַל־שִׁכְמָהּ וְאֶת־הַיֶּלֶד וַיְשַׁלְּחֶהָ וַתֵּלֶךְ וַתֵּתַע
בְּמִדְבַּר בְּאֵר שָׁבַע: וַיִּכְלוּ הַמַּיִם מִן־הַחֵמֶת וַתַּשְׁלֵךְ
אֶת־הַיֶּלֶד תַּחַת אַחַד הַשִּׂיחִם: וַתֵּלֶךְ וַתֵּשֶׁב לָהּ מִנֶּגֶד
הַרְחֵק כִּמְטַחֲוֵי קֶשֶׁת כִּי אָמְרָה אַל־אֶרְאֶה בְּמוֹת
הַיָּלֶד וַתֵּשֶׁב מִנֶּגֶד וַתִּשָּׂא אֶת־קֹלָהּ וַתֵּבְךְּ: וַיִּשְׁמַע
אֱלֹהִים אֶת־קוֹל הַנַּעַר וַיִּקְרָא מַלְאַךְ אֱלֹהִים אֶל־
הָגָר מִן־הַשָּׁמַיִם וַיֹּאמֶר לָהּ מַה־לָּךְ הָגָר אַל־תִּירְאִי
כִּי־שָׁמַע אֱלֹהִים אֶל־קוֹל הַנַּעַר בַּאֲשֶׁר הוּא־שָׁם:
קוּמִי שְׂאִי אֶת־הַנַּעַר וְהַחֲזִיקִי אֶת־יָדֵךְ בּוֹ כִּי־לְגוֹי
גָּדוֹל אֲשִׂימֶנּוּ: וַיִּפְקַח אֱלֹהִים אֶת־עֵינֶיהָ וַתֵּרֶא בְּאֵר
מָיִם וַתֵּלֶךְ וַתְּמַלֵּא אֶת־הַחֵמֶת מַיִם וַתַּשְׁקְ אֶת־הַנָּעַר:
וַיְהִי אֱלֹהִים אֶת־הַנַּעַר וַיִּגְדָּל וַיֵּשֶׁב בַּמִּדְבָּר וַיְהִי

Genesis 21
15–20

them to Hagar. He placed them on her shoulder, together with the child, and sent her away. And she wandered about in the wildnerness of Beer-sheba. 15] When the water was gone from the skin, she left the child under one of the bushes, 16] and went and sat down at a distance, a bowshot away; for she thought, "Let me not look on as the child dies." And sitting thus afar, she burst into tears.

17] God heard the cry of the boy, and an angel of God called to Hagar from heaven and said to her, "What troubles you, Hagar? Fear not, for God has heeded the cry of the boy where he is. 18] Come, lift up the boy and hold him by the hand, for I will make a great nation of him." 19] Then God opened her eyes and she saw a well of water. She went and filled the skin with water, and let the boy drink. 20] God was with the boy and he grew up; he dwelt in the wilderness and

---

16] *A bowshot away.* Alluding to Ishmael's later profession as a bowman (Gen. 21:20).

19] *Opened her eyes.* To see what she did not notice

before. The Torah uses this expression in the figurative sense [7].

כא רבָה קַשָּׁת: וַיֵּשֶׁב בְּמִדְבַּר פָּארָן וַתִּקַּח־לוֹ אִמּוֹ אִשָּׁה
מֵאֶרֶץ מִצְרָיִם: פ

כב וַיְהִי בָּעֵת הַהִוא וַיֹּאמֶר אֲבִימֶלֶךְ וּפִיכֹל שַׂר־צְבָאוֹ
אֶל־אַבְרָהָם לֵאמֹר אֱלֹהִים עִמְּךָ בְּכֹל אֲשֶׁר־אַתָּה

כג עֹשֶׂה: וְעַתָּה הִשָּׁבְעָה לִּי בֵאלֹהִים הֵנָּה אִם־תִּשְׁקֹר לִי
וּלְנִינִי וּלְנֶכְדִּי כַּחֶסֶד אֲשֶׁר עָשִׂיתִי עִמְּךָ תַּעֲשֶׂה

כד עִמָּדִי וְעִם־הָאָרֶץ אֲשֶׁר־גַּרְתָּה בָּהּ: וַיֹּאמֶר אַבְרָהָם

כה אָנֹכִי אִשָּׁבֵעַ: וְהוֹכִחַ אַבְרָהָם אֶת־אֲבִימֶלֶךְ עַל־

כו אֹדוֹת בְּאֵר הַמַּיִם אֲשֶׁר גָּזְלוּ עַבְדֵי אֲבִימֶלֶךְ: וַיֹּאמֶר
אֲבִימֶלֶךְ לֹא יָדַעְתִּי מִי עָשָׂה אֶת־הַדָּבָר הַזֶּה וְגַם־
אַתָּה לֹא־הִגַּדְתָּ לִּי וְגַם אָנֹכִי לֹא שָׁמַעְתִּי בִּלְתִּי

כז הַיּוֹם: וַיִּקַּח אַבְרָהָם צֹאן וּבָקָר וַיִּתֵּן לַאֲבִימֶלֶךְ

Genesis 21
21–27

became a bowman.   21] He lived in the wilderness of Paran; and his mother got a
wife for him from the land of Egypt.

22] At that time Abimelech and Phicol, chief of his troops, said to Abraham,
"God is with you in everything that you do.   23] Therefore swear to me here by
God that you will not deal falsely with me or with my kith and kin, but will deal
with me and with the land in which you have sojourned as loyally as I have dealt
with you."   24] And Abraham said, "I swear it."

25] Then Abraham reproached Abimelech for the well of water which the servants of Abimelech had seized.   26] But Abimelech said, "I do not know who did
this; you did not tell me, nor have I heard of it until today."   27] Abraham took
sheep and oxen and gave them to Abimelech, and the two of them made a pact.

21] *His mother got a wife for him.* As was the custom.   feast for Isaac.
Egypt. Hagar's homeland.
22] *At that time.* Most probably at the weaning
25] *The well of water.* The incident has not been
mentioned previously.

כח וַיִּכְרְתוּ שְׁנֵיהֶם בְּרִית: וַיַּצֵּב אַבְרָהָם אֶת־שֶׁבַע כִּבְשֹׂת

כט הַצֹּאן לְבַדְּהֶן: וַיֹּאמֶר אֲבִימֶלֶךְ אֶל־אַבְרָהָם מָה

הֵנָּה שֶׁבַע כְּבָשֹׂת הָאֵלֶּה אֲשֶׁר הִצַּבְתָּ לְבַדָּנָה:

ל וַיֹּאמֶר כִּי אֶת־שֶׁבַע כְּבָשֹׂת תִּקַּח מִיָּדִי בַּעֲבוּר תִּהְיֶה־

לא לִּי לְעֵדָה כִּי חָפַרְתִּי אֶת־הַבְּאֵר הַזֹּאת: עַל־כֵּן

קָרָא לַמָּקוֹם הַהוּא בְּאֵר שָׁבַע כִּי שָׁם נִשְׁבְּעוּ שְׁנֵיהֶם:

לב וַיִּכְרְתוּ בְרִית בִּבְאֵר שָׁבַע וַיָּקָם אֲבִימֶלֶךְ וּפִיכֹל

לג שַׂר־צְבָאוֹ וַיָּשֻׁבוּ אֶל־אֶרֶץ פְּלִשְׁתִּים: וַיִּטַּע אֶשֶׁל

לד בִּבְאֵר שָׁבַע וַיִּקְרָא־שָׁם בְּשֵׁם יְהוָה אֵל עוֹלָם: וַיָּגָר

אַבְרָהָם בְּאֶרֶץ פְּלִשְׁתִּים יָמִים רַבִּים: פ

28] Abraham then set seven ewes of the flock by themselves,   29] and Abimelech said to Abraham, "What mean these seven ewes which you have set apart?"   30] He replied, "You are to accept these seven ewes from me as proof that I dug this well." 31] Hence that place was called Beer-sheba, for there the two of them swore an oath. 32] When they had concluded the pact at Beer-sheba, Abimelech and Phicol, chief of his troops, departed and returned to Philistine country.   33] [Abraham] planted a tamarisk at Beer-sheba, and invoked there the name of the LORD, the Everlasting God.   34] And Abraham resided in the land of the Philistines a long time.

31] *Beer-sheba*. Well of seven, or well of oath. Abraham and Abimelech conclude a mutual non-aggression pact [8].

33] *Planted a tamarisk*. Similar tree-planting ceremonies survive in later Jewish tradition. Later they are called "a planting of joy." At Betar they planted a cedar at the birth of a boy, a cypress when a girl was born. Later, the trees were used for the marriage canopy [9].

Everlasting God. אֵל עוֹלָם (El Olam), an unusual name, occurring in only one other verse in the Bible where God is called אֱלֹהֵי עוֹלָם (Isa. 40:28).

34] *A long time*. This appears inconsistent with the immediately preceding passage wherein Abraham dwells at Beer-sheba. Therefore, the verse should not be read as an end to the passage but should be detached and taken as a general postscript to the preceding chapters and as an introduction to what follows. In other words, during this time of his life, Abraham lived in the area later known as Philistia.

Human Feelings and Divine Purpose

Underlying this episode is the essential affinity between the Israelites and Ishmaelites; there can be no question over the writer's sympathy for his tribal cousin.

As in chapter 16, this sympathy is elicited for Hagar and her child, and again Abraham and Sarah are depicted as human and fallible. The aged Matriarch prevails upon her husband to relieve her of the presence of her maid. The Bible attempts no justification of Abraham or Sarah, nor certainly of God. In the story, His ultimate designs prevail; He directs the actions of men in His own mysterious way. What on a human plane appears as Sarah's harsh and overprotective behavior is on the divine level part of God's plan. Sarah's desires coincide with the idea of destiny; hence her actions find God's approval while Abraham's do not.

Here may be seen the deeper meaning of the story. Abraham's natural feelings of compassion for Hagar and Ishmael must yield to the divine scheme in which Isaac and his descendants will have a special place. The Bible portrays the human sentiments of the Patriarch in tension with the inexplicable divine choice, a tension between human love and divine will [10].

This is also the theme of the Akedah, of Isaac's sacrifice, which follows at once. There, too, Abraham's human love is pitted against the stern demands of God. Thus, the stories complement each other: Both deal with the mysterious purposes of the One who encompasses the whole world and is at the same time the Guiding Force of the people of Abraham and Isaac.

The Sages arranged that both stories be read on Rosh Hashanah. This remains the custom in Orthodox and Conservative synagogues, which assign chapter 21 to the first and chapter 22 to the second day. Reform synagogues, observing a single day of Rosh Hashanah, read only chapter 22.[1]

---

[1] Various reasons have been advanced for the choice of these Torah readings on Rosh Hashanah, e.g., that the opening sentence of Gen. 21, "The Lord took note...," fits with the holy day theme of remembrance (*zichronot*) and that Gen. 22 was chosen because a ram figures in the story, connecting it thereby with the practice of blowing the shofar on Rosh Hashanah.

GLEANINGS

Elohim (Gen. 20:13)

Since the word is in the plural construction it cannot mean "God," but must mean "rulers." Abraham must therefore be understood to say: "Rulers made me go into exile because I was a God-seeker."   HAKETAV VE-HAKABBALAH

Abraham Prayed to God

R. Hama ben Hanina said: "This expression [prayed] occurs here for the first time in the Book of Genesis. When Abraham prayed, a knot was untied, i.e., the tangled relationship between man and God was straightened out and from now on men could pray."   MIDRASH [11]

Why was Abraham's prayer necessary? To emphasize that Abraham and his wife were totally vindicated.

The duty to pray was a punishment for Abraham, for he had to humble himself before God.
                    BENNO JACOB

Christian Scripture

Christian tradition utilizes the Ishmael–Isaac story as an allegory: As Ishmael is born in bondage but Isaac in freedom, so the first-born religion (Judaism) is in the bondage of law and the later (Christianity) free from it. [12]

Islam

In Moslem tradition, Hagar (Hadjar) went to Arabia after her quarrel with Sarah, and Abraham (Ibrahim), guided by God, followed her there. Ishmael (Ismail) and Abraham became founders of the Kaaba in Mecca, and both were buried in that city. Ismail is considered the ancestor of one of the three major Arabic groups. [13]

Also mention in the Book
The story of Ismail:
He was strictly true
To what he promised,
And he was an apostle
And a prophet.   KORAN [14]

Where He Is (Gen. 21:17)

God hears Ishmael's cry "where he is." God always hears and judges man on his present circumstances, not for where he was or will be.
                    MIDRASH [15]

Sarah's Laughter

The entire beginning of the Jewish people is laughable, its history, its expectations, its hopes. God waited with the foundation of this people until its forefather had reached a "ridiculous" high age; therefore He began the realization of His promise only after all human hopes had come to an end. For a people was about to be created which was to stand with its whole existence in contrast to all historical experience. Therefore, until today, to those who in their shortsightedness deny God, this people must appear as the most ridiculous joke of all. The derisive laughter which has followed the Jew through history is the surest proof of the divine nature of its path. The Jew is not touched by this ridicule because from the beginning he has been prepared for it.

                    SAMSON RAPHAEL HIRSCH

Abraham Planted a Tamarisk (Gen. 21:33)

The Hebrew for tamarisk is אֶשֶׁל [eshel] and its three letters signify the essentials of Abraham's hospitality: א for אֲכִילָה [food], שׁ for שְׁתִיָּה [drink], and ל for לְוָיָה [escort].   MIDRASH [16]

Beer-sheba stands at the edge of the desert. The

verse is the first notice of the transformation of the life of Abraham from that of the wandering nomad with his flocks to a settled agriculturist. Is it not possible that he planted those tamarisks for the same purpose as they are being planted today, as a windbreak against the sandstorms which blew in from the desert?   LOUIS I. RABINOWITZ [17]

[The comment implies Abraham planted an orchard which, unlike the low-growing grain of the Negev, needed a windbreak.]

Ishmael

Abraham, modest and unassuming as he was, was ready to do justice to Sarah and he conferred full power upon her to dispose of Hagar according to her pleasure. He added but one caution, "Having once made her a mistress, we cannot again reduce her to the state of a bondwoman." Unmindful of this warning, Sarah exacted the services of a slave from Hagar. Not alone this, she tormented her, and finally she cast an evil eye upon her, so that the unborn child dropped from her, and she ran away. On her flight she was met by several angels, and they bade her return, at the same time making known to her that she would bear a son who should be called Ishmael—one of the six men who have been given a name by God before their birth, the others being Isaac, Moses, Solomon, Josiah, and the Messiah.

Thirteen years after the birth of Ishmael the command was issued to Abraham that he put the sign of the covenant upon his body and upon the bodies of the male members of his household. Abraham was reluctant at first to do the bidding of God, for he feared that the circumcision of his flesh would raise a barrier between himself and the rest of mankind. But God said unto him, "Let it suffice thee that I am thy God and thy Lord, as it sufficeth the world that I am its God and its Lord."   MIDRASH [18]

The Akedah

Few narrative sections of the Torah have been subjected to as much comment and study as the עֲקֵדָה (*akedah*, binding [of Isaac]). Jewish, Christian, and Moslem theologies have tried to fathom its intention. In his introduction to this chapter, Abarbanel called the story "worthier of study and investigation than any other section." Its subject matter ranges from the God who tests to the man who is tested, from the nature of faith to the demands it makes, and it considers many other questions as well. Says Von Rad: "One should renounce any attempt to discover one basic idea as *the* meaning of the whole. There are many levels of meaning."

The literary pattern of the section is reminiscent of the first passage of the Abraham story: A divine command is issued asking Abraham to set out toward an as yet unannounced place. The same unusual reflexive phrasing (see Gen. 12:1) contains the directive לֶךְ־לְךָ (*lech-lecha*, go forth). It is almost as though the external elements of the tale, while clear enough, hide deeper problems under the cover of simple words.

A small postscript follows the Akedah: a genealogical notation on the lines of Nahor. This serves as a bridge to the subsequent stories of Isaac and Rebekah.

אַ וַיְהִי אַחַר הַדְּבָרִים הָאֵלֶּה וְהָאֱלֹהִים נִסָּה אֶת־

בַ אַבְרָהָם וַיֹּאמֶר אֵלָיו אַבְרָהָם וַיֹּאמֶר הִנֵּנִי: וַיֹּאמֶר

קַח־נָא אֶת־בִּנְךָ אֶת־יְחִידְךָ אֲשֶׁר־אָהַבְתָּ אֶת־יִצְחָק

וְלֶךְ־לְךָ אֶל־אֶרֶץ הַמֹּרִיָּה וְהַעֲלֵהוּ שָׁם לְעֹלָה עַל

גַ אַחַד הֶהָרִים אֲשֶׁר אֹמַר אֵלֶיךָ: וַיַּשְׁכֵּם אַבְרָהָם

בַּבֹּקֶר וַיַּחֲבֹשׁ אֶת־חֲמֹרוֹ וַיִּקַּח אֶת־שְׁנֵי נְעָרָיו אִתּוֹ

וְאֵת יִצְחָק בְּנוֹ וַיְבַקַּע עֲצֵי עֹלָה וַיָּקָם וַיֵּלֶךְ אֶל־

דַ הַמָּקוֹם אֲשֶׁר־אָמַר־לוֹ הָאֱלֹהִים: בַּיּוֹם הַשְּׁלִישִׁי וַיִּשָּׂא

הַ אַבְרָהָם אֶת־עֵינָיו וַיַּרְא אֶת־הַמָּקוֹם מֵרָחֹק: וַיֹּאמֶר

אַבְרָהָם אֶל־נְעָרָיו שְׁבוּ־לָכֶם פֹּה עִם־הַחֲמוֹר וַאֲנִי

Genesis 22
1–5

1] Some time afterward, God put Abraham to the test. He said to him, "Abraham," and he answered, "Here I am." 2] And He said, "Take your son, your favored one, Isaac, whom you love, and go to the land of Moriah, and offer him there as a burnt offering on one of the heights which I will point out to you." 3] So early next morning, Abraham saddled his ass and took with him two of his servants and his son Isaac. He split the wood for the burnt offering, and he set out for the place of which God had told him. 4] On the third day Abraham looked up and saw the place from afar. 5] Then Abraham said to his servants, "You stay here with the

22:1] *Some time afterward.* According to the Rabbis, Isaac was thirty-seven years old. However, the story should be read not in chronological order but rather as an unrelated unit; here Isaac is a mere boy.

/ The Rabbis took the death of Sarah (Gen. 23:1) to be immediately related to the Akedah (see p. 224); therefore, with Sarah dying at 127 years of age, Isaac would be 37, having been born when his mother was 90 [1]./

2] *Moriah.* The original name is obscure and the actual location unknown. Subsequent biblical tradition, however, has suggested that it refers to the Temple mount in Jerusalem (II Chron. 3:1) [2]. It is believed that the city's famed Dome of the Rock is built over the rock on which Abraham bound his son.

/The Vulgate relates Moriah to מַרְאֶה (vision); the Septuagint to "high" or "lofty"—two word plays rather than etymologies./

וְהַנַּעַר נֵלְכָה עַד־כֹּה וְנִשְׁתַּחֲוֶה וְנָשׁוּבָה אֲלֵיכֶם:

ו וַיִּקַּח אַבְרָהָם אֶת־עֲצֵי הָעֹלָה וַיָּשֶׂם עַל־יִצְחָק בְּנוֹ וַיִּקַּח בְּיָדוֹ אֶת־הָאֵשׁ וְאֶת־הַמַּאֲכֶלֶת וַיֵּלְכוּ שְׁנֵיהֶם

ז יַחְדָּו: וַיֹּאמֶר יִצְחָק אֶל־אַבְרָהָם אָבִיו וַיֹּאמֶר אָבִי וַיֹּאמֶר הִנֶּנִּי בְנִי וַיֹּאמֶר הִנֵּה הָאֵשׁ וְהָעֵצִים וְאַיֵּה הַשֶּׂה

ח לְעֹלָה: וַיֹּאמֶר אַבְרָהָם אֱלֹהִים יִרְאֶה־לּוֹ הַשֶּׂה לְעֹלָה

ט בְּנִי וַיֵּלְכוּ שְׁנֵיהֶם יַחְדָּו: וַיָּבֹאוּ אֶל־הַמָּקוֹם אֲשֶׁר אָמַר־לוֹ הָאֱלֹהִים וַיִּבֶן שָׁם אַבְרָהָם אֶת־הַמִּזְבֵּחַ וַיַּעֲרֹךְ אֶת־הָעֵצִים וַיַּעֲקֹד אֶת־יִצְחָק בְּנוֹ וַיָּשֶׂם אֹתוֹ

י עַל־הַמִּזְבֵּחַ מִמַּעַל לָעֵצִים: וַיִּשְׁלַח אַבְרָהָם אֶת־

יא יָדוֹ וַיִּקַּח אֶת־הַמַּאֲכֶלֶת לִשְׁחֹט אֶת־בְּנוֹ: וַיִּקְרָא אֵלָיו

ass. The boy and I will go up there; we will worship and we will return to you."

6] Abraham took the wood for the burnt offering and put it on his son Isaac. He himself took the firestone and the knife; and the two walked off together.   7] Then Isaac said to his father Abraham, "Father!" And he answered, "Yes, my son." And he said, "Here is the firestone and the wood; but where is the sheep for the burnt offering?"   8] And Abraham said, "God will see to the sheep for His burnt offering, my son." And the two of them walked on together.

9] They arrived at the place of which God had told him. Abraham built an altar there; he laid out the wood; he bound his son Isaac; he laid him on the altar, on top of the wood.   10] And Abraham picked up the knife to slay his son.   11] Then an

9] Note the staccato phrases that heighten the tension. Abraham seems to move "like a sleep-walker" [3].

מַלְאַ֤ךְ יְהוָה֙ מִן־הַשָּׁמַ֔יִם וַיֹּ֖אמֶר אַבְרָהָ֣ם ׀ אַבְרָהָ֑ם

יב וַיֹּ֖אמֶר הִנֵּֽנִי: וַיֹּ֗אמֶר אַל־תִּשְׁלַ֤ח יָֽדְךָ֙ אֶל־הַנַּ֔עַר וְאַל־
תַּ֥עַשׂ ל֖וֹ מְא֑וּמָה כִּ֣י ׀ עַתָּ֣ה יָדַ֗עְתִּי כִּֽי־יְרֵ֤א אֱלֹהִים֙

יג אַ֔תָּה וְלֹ֥א חָשַׂ֛כְתָּ אֶת־בִּנְךָ֥ אֶת־יְחִֽידְךָ֖ מִמֶּֽנִּי: וַיִּשָּׂ֨א
אַבְרָהָ֜ם אֶת־עֵינָ֗יו וַיַּרְא֙ וְהִנֵּה־אַ֔יִל אַחַ֕ר נֶאֱחַ֥ז בַּסְּבַ֖ךְ
בְּקַרְנָ֑יו וַיֵּ֣לֶךְ אַבְרָהָ֗ם וַיִּקַּ֤ח אֶת־הָאַ֙יִל֙ וַיַּעֲלֵ֣הוּ לְעֹלָ֔ה

יד תַּ֥חַת בְּנֽוֹ: וַיִּקְרָ֧א אַבְרָהָ֛ם שֵֽׁם־הַמָּק֥וֹם הַה֖וּא יְהוָ֣ה ׀

טו יִרְאֶ֑ה אֲשֶׁר֙ יֵֽאָמֵ֣ר הַיּ֔וֹם בְּהַ֥ר יְהוָ֖ה יֵרָאֶֽה: וַיִּקְרָ֛א

טז מַלְאַ֥ךְ יְהוָ֖ה אֶל־אַבְרָהָ֑ם שֵׁנִ֖ית מִן־הַשָּׁמָֽיִם: וַיֹּ֕אמֶר
בִּ֣י נִשְׁבַּ֖עְתִּי נְאֻם־יְהוָ֑ה כִּ֗י יַ֚עַן אֲשֶׁ֤ר עָשִׂ֙יתָ֙ אֶת־הַדָּבָ֣ר

Genesis 22

12–16

angel of the LORD called to him from heaven: "Abraham! Abraham!" And he answered, "Here I am." **12]** And he said, "Do not raise your hand against the boy, or do anything to him. For now I know that you fear God, since you have not withheld your son, your favored one, from Me." **13]** When Abraham looked up, his eye fell upon a ram, caught in the thicket by its horns. So Abraham went and took the ram and offered it up as a burnt offering in place of his son. **14]** And Abraham named that site Adonai-yireh, whence the present saying, "On the mount of the LORD there is vision."

15] The angel of the LORD called to Abraham a second time from heaven, **16]** and said, "By Myself I swear, the LORD declares: because you have done this

13] *Ram.* The ram occupied an important place in ancient Israel's sacrificial cult (e.g., Lev. 5-15, 18; 19:21; Num. 5:8; 6:17). The image of a ram caught in the thicket was known in Ur of the Chaldees, where archeologists have found two Sumerian statues depicting the animal tied to a bush [4]. A similar substitutional offering is portrayed in Greek mythology [5].

The above translation is based, following ancient versions, on the reading אַיִל אֶחָד (a ram), while the Masoretic text has אַחַר (after or afterward).

14] *Adonai-yireh.* The Lord will see, an allusion to verse 8.

There is vision. Another assonance: *Adonai yera-eh.*

יז הָיָה וְלֹא חָשַׂכְתָּ אֶת־בִּנְךָ אֶת־יְחִידְךָ: כִּי־בָרֵךְ
אֲבָרֶכְךָ וְהַרְבָּה אַרְבֶּה אֶת־זַרְעֲךָ כְּכוֹכְבֵי הַשָּׁמַיִם
וְכַחוֹל אֲשֶׁר עַל־שְׂפַת הַיָּם וְיִרַשׁ זַרְעֲךָ אֵת שַׁעַר
יח אֹיְבָיו: וְהִתְבָּרְכוּ בְזַרְעֲךָ כֹּל גּוֹיֵי הָאָרֶץ עֵקֶב
יט אֲשֶׁר שָׁמַעְתָּ בְּקֹלִי: וַיָּשָׁב אַבְרָהָם אֶל־נְעָרָיו וַיָּקֻמוּ
וַיֵּלְכוּ יַחְדָּו אֶל־בְּאֵר שָׁבַע וַיֵּשֶׁב אַבְרָהָם בִּבְאֵר
שָׁבַע: פ

כ וַיְהִי אַחֲרֵי הַדְּבָרִים הָאֵלֶּה וַיֻּגַּד לְאַבְרָהָם לֵאמֹר
כא הִנֵּה יָלְדָה מִלְכָּה גַם־הִוא בָּנִים לְנָחוֹר אָחִיךָ: אֶת־
עוּץ בְּכֹרוֹ וְאֶת־בּוּז אָחִיו וְאֶת־קְמוּאֵל אֲבִי אֲרָם:

Genesis 22

17–21

and have not withheld your son, your favored one,   **17]** I will bestow My blessing upon you and make your descendants as numerous as the stars of heaven and the sands on the seashore; and your descendants shall capture the gates of their enemies.   **18]** All the nations of the earth shall bless themselves by your descendants, because you have obeyed My command."   **19]** Abraham then returned to his servants, and they departed together for Beer-sheba; and Abraham stayed in Beer-sheba.

20] Some time later, Abraham was told, "Milcah too has borne children to your brother Nahor: **21]** Uz the first-born, and Buz his brother, and Kemuel

17]   *Seize the gates of their foes.* Whereby they will possess the city.

20]   *Milcah too.* Like Sarah. The names listed represent twelve tribes or princes. They parallel the twelve tribes of Israel and illustrate a duodecimal principle of tribal organization found also in extra-biblical sources.

/Others have suggested that these tribes were all Arameans [6]./

21]   *Uz.* The name occurs several times in Genesis (10:23; 36:28). Job comes from "the land of Uz" (Job 1:1).

/Hence the talmudic tradition that Job lived in the days of Abraham [7]./

כב וְאֶת־כֶּשֶׂד וְאֶת־חֲזוֹ וְאֶת־פִּלְדָּשׁ וְאֶת־יִדְלָף וְאֵת
כג בְּתוּאֵל: וּבְתוּאֵל יָלַד אֶת־רִבְקָה שְׁמֹנָה אֵלֶּה יָלְדָה
כד מִלְכָּה לְנָחוֹר אֲחִי אַבְרָהָם: וּפִילַגְשׁוֹ וּשְׁמָהּ רְאוּמָה
וַתֵּלֶד גַּם־הִוא אֶת־טֶבַח וְאֶת־גַּחַם וְאֶת־תַּחַשׁ וְאֶת־
מַעֲכָה:

Genesis 22

22–24

Haftarah Vayera, p. 528

the father of Aram;   22] and Chesed, Hazo, Pildash, Jidlaph and Bethuel"—
23] Bethuel being the father of Rebekah. These eight Milcah bore to Nahor,
Abraham's brother.   24] And his concubine, whose name was Reumah, also bore
children: Tebah, Gaham, Tahash, and Maacah.

22]   *Chesed*. Probably related to *Casdim*, Chaldeans.
24]   *Concubine*. The institution of multiple marriage, with first-rank and second-rank wives, was
widespread in the Fertile Crescent.

The Sacrifice

The practice of human sacrifice, which was well-known to the ancients and central to the cults of Israel's neighbors, stands as a backdrop to chapter 22.[1] In the framework of his time and experience, Abraham could have considered the command to sacrifice his son entirely legitimate. Otherwise he might have protested God's command with the kind of insistence he exhibited at Sodom and Gomorrah. God's demand must have struck Abraham as harsh and bitter but not as ungodly. It is therefore important to notice that in the beginning of the test the command is issued by Elohim—the generic term for God or gods—and the command is one that other elohim could and did make. But when the sacrifice is about to be performed it is Abraham's God, Adonai, who stays his hand. Elohim might ask him to proceed, but Adonai says "No." He, too, will ask extreme devotion, but it will never again take this form.

Abraham's religion not only rejects the sacrifice of a son by a father but rejects, as well, its use as a theological theme. This is in stark contrast to Eastern religions and to Christianity [9], in which a father's sacrificial gift of his son plays an important role.[2]

The Test

The text sets forth the main theme by saying that God puts Abraham to the test, but it does not state precisely what He is testing him for. Is it to test Abraham's faith that God will not go back on His promise, that somehow His design can be trusted? Or is it to test Abraham's unquestioning obedience, his faithfulness rather than his faith, his total submission to a mysterious divine will? Most likely both, for faith and faithfulness are dual aspects of biblical man's relation to God. Together they may be said to represent the quality of אֱמוּנָה (emunah, adherence without faltering, obedience with

complete trust), which is as authentic a reflection of God's qualities as is humanly possible. For even God is obedient, not to man, to be sure, but to His own law and promise. Hence it is possible for the Bible to call God אֵל אֱמוּנָה (El emunah, a faithful God, in Deuteronomy 32:4). And in this sense we can speak of Abraham as אִישׁ אֱמוּנָה (ish emunah, a faithful man).

Abraham's act is represented as the ultimate sanctification of God in this world, the offering up of that which is dearest to him.[3] Such devotion is also shown by Hannah in Maccabean times ("She was in her spirit and courage equal to Abraham") [13] and by scores of generations to follow.

Yet the test, like Abraham's hand, remains suspended in air; like life, the test remains open-ended. When it is over, Abraham has proved himself for the moment. God sees what Abraham *is*, but what he *will be* remains hidden even from God himself. There will be new trials and challenges awaiting him in the future. In pursuing this thought, the Midrash reads the whole story of Abraham as a succession of ten severe tests [14].

Questions about the God of the Akedah

Why must God test man? Does He not know all things?

Maimonides answers that God tested (נִסָּה) Abraham precisely because he knew that he would pass the test. Abraham's faith would shine like a beacon and be a sign (נֵס) to

---

[1] Compare II Kings 3:27 where it is related that the king of Moab sacrificed his first-born. Sacrificing a child or passing him through fire belonged to the great abominations (see, e.g., Lev. 18:21; 20:2; Deut. 18:10), and the prophets inveighed against it (e.g., Mic. 6:7). There is some question whether Jephthah's daughter was indeed sacrificed (Judg. 11:29–40) and whether the custom ever did prevail in ancient Israel or what fire rites were involved [8].

[2] Note, however, the Greek tale of Phrixus in which

the nations. The emphasis is therefore not on Abraham's ordeal but on his strength [15].

A radically different explanation is offered by Franz Rosenzweig, who sees in the test a *temptation* by God. According to this view, God purposely conceals His true purpose; in fact, He must occasionally mislead man. If everything were clear, men would be automatons and those least free, most timid and fearful, would be the most "pious." But evidently God wants only the free to be His. He must make it difficult, nay impossible to understand His actions, so as to give man the opportunity truly to believe, that is, to ground his faith in trust and freedom. And so there remains nothing for God but to tempt man, even to deceive him [16].

Many will find it difficult to believe in a "misleading God," but if we believe at all in God we must believe in a deity who is free, just as we believe that man is free, free even to defy God's will or foreknowledge. There remains an unresolved contradiction between these freedoms, a contradiction inherent in God's relationship to man ever since the days of Eden.

What kind of a God is He? How can the compassionate God of the Bible be portrayed as asking for the sacrifice of a child?

One answer is that the test came at a time when human sacrifice was still an acceptable practice and that, therefore, in terms of its own age it was merely *the* extreme test (and after all, God did not exact the final price). God thus may require of man in every age to give up that which he loves most. God often asks not the expected but the awesomely unexpected. Perhaps the final proof of faith and obedience rests indeed in attempting the impossible for the sake of God.

Another explanation re-interprets the text to say that it only *appeared* to Abraham that God asked him to sacrifice his child; such a request could not possibly square with the fundamental laws of morality. A midrash, therefore, suggests that Abraham misunderstood God altogether. It has God saying: "Did I tell you 'Slaughter him'? Did I not rather tell you 'Bring him up'? [A word play in Hebrew.] You brought him up on the altar, now take him down again!" [17]. In this view of the story the test both succeeds and fails. It succeeds in that it proves Abraham to be a man of faith and obedience, but it fails in that Abraham's understanding of God's nature remains deficient.

Father and Son

Even as God is the dominant Father and Abraham a trusting and obedient son, so in the purely human realm Abraham appears as the dominant father and Isaac as the archetype of the submissive son. Only once does Isaac speak and ask the fateful question; thereafter he is a mere object of the drama. Abraham, the prince and Patriarch, the honored and aged friend of God, overawes his timid son, whose will to independence may well have been crippled by doting and protective parents. He has no personality apart from his father. As one they walk together to the sacrifice (Gen. 22:8), and silently Isaac submits to the dreadful act.[4]

The story may thus be read as a paradigm of a father-and-son relationship. In a way every parent seeks to dominate his child and is in danger of seeking to sacrifice him to his

human sacrifice is averted at the last moment because "Zeus, King of Heaven, loathes human sacrifices" [10].

[3] Compare the Christian Scripture's appraisal of Abraham's faith and the theme of justification by faith [11]. The Zohar emphasizes the quality of obedience that overcame Abraham's sense of compassion [12].

[4] One version suggests that, in fact, Isaac encouraged Abraham to proceed with the sacrifice [18].

parental plans or hopes. In the biblical story, God is present and can therefore stay the father's hand.[5] In all too many repetitions of the scene God is absent and the knife falls. Thus is the Akedah repeated forever, with its test and its terror.

[5] There was, however, a remarkable tradition that insisted that Abraham completed the sacrifice and that afterward Isaac was miraculously revived. In part this arises out of the discussion on the question: "Why do people place ashes on their heads on the occasion of a public fast?" The answer is related to the "ashes of Isaac." According to this haggadah, Abraham slew his son, burnt his victim, and the ashes remain as a stored-up merit and atonement for Israel in all generations. For this reason Isaac's sacrifice is invoked in prayer, and Rabbi Ephraim ben Jacob of Bonn (twelfth century C.E.) composed a poem on the subject. This interpretation of the Akedah was given bitter relevance in medieval times when many Jewish parents killed their own children and then committed suicide to avoid forcible conversion, captivity, and torture [19].

GLEANINGS

Abraham Misunderstood

A God who asks man what the text appears to ask is not the true God but one whom man fashions in his own image. Man often believes that God wants him to sacrifice his children to an imagined demand. But then it is not God who is cruel but man; it is man who all too frequently is prepared to immolate his offspring to satisfy his own concept of duty and who will restrain his compassion before his own sense of righteousness. The history of humanity is replete with misdeeds committed in the name of religion.

AFTER A MIDRASH [20]

Go to the Land of Moriah

Two mountains were chosen by God: Mount Sinai upon which the Torah was given to Israel and Mount Moriah upon which Abraham bound his son Isaac and upon which the Temple was built. Now the matter makes one wonder: Why, indeed, was the Temple not built upon Mount Sinai which had been sanctified by the giving of the law? The answer is: The place on which a Jew bares his neck is sanctified by God more than any other place. Upon it the *Shechinah* appears and there, so to speak, the Torah is given again.

RABBI CHAIM OF TSANS [21]

Isaac Liberated

The text says that Abraham returned from Moriah but omits a mention of Isaac. Is it possible that Isaac did not come back with his father, that the trauma of near-death tore the taut strings that bound the son to the father? That Isaac now became a man who for the first time could let his father go and who would return later, at his own choosing and time? Isaac's nature is not radically changed in the Akedah, nor can his early childhood be denied its formative influence, but in the binding Isaac becomes an individual in his own right. If Abraham was tested and purified in agony, Isaac was liberated by it.

The Shofar

The shofar (usually made from a ram's horn) is nowadays blown on Rosh Hashanah and at the conclusion of Yom Kippur. It is also blown at morning services during the month preceding the new year; and it has been sounded on special occasions, such as the recapture of the Western or Wailing Wall by Israeli troops in 1967.

Said Rabbi Abbahu: "Why do we sound the horn of a ram? Because the Holy One, blessed be He, said: 'Blow Me a ram's horn that I may remember unto you the binding of Isaac the son of Abraham, and I shall account it unto you for a binding of yourselves before Me.'" TALMUD [22]

The shofar should be bent so that the children of Israel may bend their hearts toward their Father in Heaven. It is also best to blow the horn of a ram so that He may remember unto us the binding of Isaac. SHULCHAN ARUCH SHEL HA-RAV [23]

There are ten reasons for blowing the shofar.... The sixth is to remind us of the binding of Isaac who offered himself to Heaven. So ought we be ready at all times to offer our lives for the sanctification of His name. SAADIA [24]

Take Your Son

The Hebrew does not say merely קַח [take]. It says קַח־נָא [literally, "please take"]. This indicates that Abraham acted freely, and not from compulsion. It is also important to remember that the journey to Moriah took three days—time enough to arrive at a free decision. ALBO [25]

Note further that God says not merely "your son" but follows it by saying "your favored one," and then "Isaac." He issued the command gently, step by step, to a reluctant Abraham.　　RASHI

A Prayer

Remember unto us, O Lord our God, the covenant and the lovingkindness and the oath which Thou didst swear on Mt. Moriah, and may the binding with which our father Abraham bound his son Isaac on the altar appear before Thee: how he overcame his compassion in order to perform Thy will with all his heart.

MACHZOR FOR ROSH HASHANAH [26]

The Service of Heaven

[In the Sephardic Rosh Hashanah ritual, between *Maftir* and shofar, a special hymn is sung that stresses the readiness of both Abraham and Isaac to do God's will. It also speculates about what Abraham said to Sarah before they left.]

Said he to Sarah: "Your darling Isaac is growing up,
But to serve the Heavens has he not yet learned.
I will go and teach him that he has a demanding God."
Said she: "Go, master, but go not far!"
Said he: "Rest your heart in God and trust in Him."　　JUDAH SAMUEL ABBAS

Christian Interpretation

The Church Fathers saw in Akedah a prefiguration of the sacrifice of Jesus. This was based on the parallel drawn by Paul: As Abraham "did not withhold his son Isaac, so God did not withhold His own son [Jesus] but gave him up for us all."　　ROMANS 8:32

The Moslem Story

And when he became a full-grown youth,
His father said to him, "My son, I have seen in a dream that I should sacrifice thee; therefore, consider what thou seest right."
He said, "My father, do what thou art bidden; of the patient, if God please, shalt thou find me."
And when they had surrendered them to the will of God, he laid him down upon his forehead.

We cried unto him, "O Abraham!
Now hast thou satisfied the vision." See how we recompense the righteous.
This was indeed a decisive test.
And we ransomed his son with a costly victim,
And we left this (salutation) for him among posterity, "Peace be on Abraham!"

KORAN [27]

A Second Time

"The angel of the Lord called to Abraham a second time" [Gen. 22:15]. Why this repetition? The reason is found in the concluding words, "because you have done this." These words place the Abrahamic promise in a totally different light. For, while hitherto the promise given to Abraham is mainly an expression of divine favor, it now comes for the first time as an acknowledgment of Abraham's worth. This is the point where divine effort meets with full response in the human being. It is toward this goal, first in Israel and then in all of mankind, that all divine efforts from the viewpoint of the Torah tend.

MORDECAI M. KAPLAN [28]

The Test

The sacrifice, though commanded, was not exacted. Abraham's hand was stayed before the fatal act was completed. This showed, once and for all, clearly and unmistakably, that, in contrast to what was imagined of the heathen deities worshiped by Israel's neighbors, the God of Israel did not demand human sacrifices of his worshipers. He demanded in reality only the surrender of Abraham's will. Abraham, by his obedience, demonstrated his readiness to part with what was dearest to him, and with something on which all his hopes for the future depended: Thus his character was "proved," the sincerity of his religion was established, and his devotion to God confirmed and strengthened. It was the supreme trial of his faith; and it triumphed. And so the narrative teaches two great lessons. On the one hand, it teaches the value set by God upon the surrender of self and obedience; on the other, it demonstrates, by a signal example, the moral superiority of Jehovah's religion above the religions of Israel's neighbors.　　SAMUEL R. DRIVER [29]

Three Days

A journey is made, because God has designated the place where the sacrifice is to be performed; but we are told nothing about the journey except that it took three days, and even that we are told in a mysterious way: Abraham and his followers rose "early in the morning" and "went unto" the place of which God had told him; on the third day he lifted up his eyes and saw the place from afar. That gesture is the only gesture, is indeed the only occurrence during the whole journey, of which we are told; and though its motivation lies in the fact that the place is elevated, its uniqueness still heightens the impression that the journey took place through a vacuum; it is as if, while he traveled on, Abraham had looked neither to the right nor to the left, had suppressed any sign of life in his followers and himself save only their footfalls.

Thus the journey is like a silent progress through the indeterminate and the contingent, a holding of the breath, a process which has no present, which is inserted, like a blank duration, between what has passed and what lies ahead, and which yet is measured: three days! Three such days positively demand the symbolic interpretation which they later received.

ERICH AUERBACH [30]

Abraham Appals Me

Why then did Abraham do it? For God's sake and [in complete identity with this] for his own sake. He did it for God's sake because God required this proof of his faith; for his own sake he did it in order that he might furnish the proof. The unity of these two points of view is perfectly expressed by the word which has always been used to characterize this situation: It is a trial, a temptation. A temptation—but what does that mean? What ordinarily tempts a man is that which would keep him from doing his duty, but in this case the temptation is itself the ethical . . . which would keep him from doing God's will.

Therefore, though Abraham arouses my admiration, he at the same time appals me. . . . He who has explained this riddle has explained my life.

SÖREN KIERKEGAARD [31]

I Revere Abraham

I revere Abraham who lived the human paradox to the extreme and yet had faith that it was not fatal . . . Abraham waits for us, as the potential father of every Jew aspiring to be a good Jew: for he teaches us to live courageously the ethical under the moral law, in an existence which requires divine love superseding the ethical if it is to be healed of its tragic tensions. Hence we can confess with Kierkegaard: "No one is so great as Abraham! Who is capable of understanding him?"

EMIL L. FACKENHEIM [32]

A Psychological Interpretation

The Akedah motif is the biblical aspect of the psychology of family relationships. It is the biblical extension of the Oedipus Complex.

According to our interpretation of the Akedah motif the image of man's divine calling is introjected, in addition to the images of the parents. The introjected call of God contains an altruistic aim, and therefore love for this ego-ideal decreases narcissistic love and increases object-love. . . . The torturing inner struggle is overcome by the choice to follow the altruistic call. This is the turning point in the Akedah experience. It is accompanied by a modification of instincts. The life instinct and desire for action are promoted, and the death instinct and contentment with meditation only are relegated. Object-love is amplified to embrace all human beings and future generations. It becomes messianic love.

ERIC WELLISCH [33]

The Death of Sarah

The recounting of the death of Sarah gives us an occasion for an assessment of the life and personality of the first Matriarch. The chapter itself is taken up with Abraham's acquisition of the cave of Machpelah for his wife's burial. The transaction is told in considerable detail because it is more than an act of deep sentiment on the part of a grieving husband.

בראשית כג

א־ז

א   וַיִּהְיוּ חַיֵּי שָׂרָה מֵאָה שָׁנָה וְעֶשְׂרִים שָׁנָה וְשֶׁבַע שָׁנִים

ב   שְׁנֵי חַיֵּי שָׂרָה: וַתָּמָת שָׂרָה בְּקִרְיַת אַרְבַּע הִוא

חֶבְרוֹן בְּאֶרֶץ כְּנָעַן וַיָּבֹא אַבְרָהָם לִסְפֹּד לְשָׂרָה

ג   וְלִבְכֹּתָהּ: וַיָּקָם אַבְרָהָם מֵעַל פְּנֵי מֵתוֹ וַיְדַבֵּר אֶל־

ד   בְּנֵי־חֵת לֵאמֹר: גֵּר־וְתוֹשָׁב אָנֹכִי עִמָּכֶם תְּנוּ לִי אֲחֻזַּת־

ה   קֶבֶר עִמָּכֶם וְאֶקְבְּרָה מֵתִי מִלְּפָנָי: וַיַּעֲנוּ בְנֵי־חֵת

ו   אֶת־אַבְרָהָם לֵאמֹר לוֹ: שְׁמָעֵנוּ אֲדֹנִי נְשִׂיא אֱלֹהִים

אַתָּה בְּתוֹכֵנוּ בְּמִבְחַר קְבָרֵינוּ קְבֹר אֶת־מֵתֶךָ אִישׁ

ז   מִמֶּנּוּ אֶת־קִבְרוֹ לֹא־יִכְלֶה מִמְּךָ מִקְּבֹר מֵתֶךָ: וַיָּקָם

* ב כ׳ זעירא.

Genesis 23

1–7

1] Sarah's lifetime—the span of Sarah's life—came to one hundred and twenty-seven years.   2] Sarah died in Kiriath-arba—now Hebron—in the land of Canaan; and Abraham proceeded to mourn for Sarah and to bewail her.   3] Then Abraham rose from beside his dead, and spoke to the children of Heth, saying,   4] "I am a resident alien among you; sell me a burial site among you, that I may remove my dead for burial."   5] And the children of Heth replied to Abraham, saying to him,   6] "Hear us, my lord: you are the elect of God among us. Bury your dead in the choicest of our burial places; none of us will withhold his burial place from you for burying your dead."   7] Thereupon Abraham bowed low to the people

23:2] *Kiriath-arba—now Hebron.* See note at Gen. 13:18.
/Kiriath-arba may mean "City of Arba" (a non-Semitic name) or "City of Four" (the alternate "Hebron" might mean "group city")./
   Mourn . . . bewail. A description both of sentiment and of a set ritual.

3] *The Hittites.* Probably not of the well-known

northern nation but a non-Semitic group of original inhabitants. Aborigines according to one commentator [1].

4] *A resident alien.* Who lacks certain privileges that citizens have, in this case, the right to own land. The community must rule on any exceptions.

6] *Elect of God.* Or "mighty prince."

אַבְרָהָם וַיִּשְׁתַּחוּ לְעַם־הָאָרֶץ לִבְנֵי־חֵת: וַיְדַבֵּר אִתָּם
לֵאמֹר אִם־יֵשׁ אֶת־נַפְשְׁכֶם לִקְבֹּר אֶת־מֵתִי מִלְּפָנַי
ט שְׁמָעוּנִי וּפִגְעוּ־לִי בְּעֶפְרוֹן בֶּן־צֹחַר: וְיִתֶּן־לִי אֶת־
מְעָרַת הַמַּכְפֵּלָה אֲשֶׁר־לוֹ אֲשֶׁר בִּקְצֵה שָׂדֵהוּ בְּכֶסֶף
י מָלֵא יִתְּנֶנָּה לִּי בְּתוֹכְכֶם לַאֲחֻזַּת־קָבֶר: וְעֶפְרוֹן יֹשֵׁב
בְּתוֹךְ בְּנֵי־חֵת וַיַּעַן עֶפְרוֹן הַחִתִּי אֶת־אַבְרָהָם בְּאָזְנֵי
יא בְנֵי־חֵת לְכֹל בָּאֵי שַׁעַר־עִירוֹ לֵאמֹר: לֹא־אֲדֹנִי שְׁמָעֵנִי
הַשָּׂדֶה נָתַתִּי לָךְ וְהַמְּעָרָה אֲשֶׁר־בּוֹ לְךָ נְתַתִּיהָ לְעֵינֵי
יב בְנֵי־עַמִּי נְתַתִּיהָ לָּךְ קְבֹר מֵתֶךָ: וַיִּשְׁתַּחוּ אַבְרָהָם

יג לִפְנֵי עַם־הָאָרֶץ: וַיְדַבֵּר אֶל־עֶפְרוֹן בְּאָזְנֵי עַם־הָאָרֶץ
לֵאמֹר אַךְ אִם־אַתָּה לוּ שְׁמָעֵנִי נָתַתִּי כֶּסֶף הַשָּׂדֶה

of the land, the children of Heth,   8] and he said to them, "If it is your wish that I remove my dead for burial, you must agree to intercede for me with Ephron, the son of Zohar.   9] Let him sell me the cave of Machpelah which he owns, which is at the edge of his land. Let him sell it to me in your presence, at the full price, for a burial site."

10] Ephron was present among the children of Heth; so Ephron the Hittite answered Abraham in the hearing of the children of Heth, all who sat on the council of his town, saying,   11] "No, my lord, hear me: I give you the field and I give you the cave that is in it; I give it to you in the presence of my people. Bury your dead."   12] Then Abraham bowed low before the people of the land,   13] and spoke to Ephron in the hearing of the people of the land, saying, "If only you would hear me out! Let me pay the price of the land; accept it from me, that I may bury

10]   *All who entered the gate.* All his fellow townsmen.

יד קַח מִמֶּנִּי וְאֶקְבְּרָה אֶת־מֵתִי שָׁמָּה: וַיַּעַן עֶפְרוֹן אֶת־
טו אַבְרָהָם לֵאמֹר לוֹ: אֲדֹנִי שְׁמָעֵנִי אֶרֶץ אַרְבַּע מֵאֹת
שֶׁקֶל־כֶּסֶף בֵּינִי וּבֵינְךָ מַה־הִוא וְאֶת־מֵתְךָ קְבֹר:
טז וַיִּשְׁמַע אַבְרָהָם אֶל־עֶפְרוֹן וַיִּשְׁקֹל אַבְרָהָם לְעֶפְרֹן
אֶת־הַכֶּסֶף אֲשֶׁר דִּבֶּר בְּאָזְנֵי בְנֵי־חֵת אַרְבַּע מֵאוֹת
יז שֶׁקֶל כֶּסֶף עֹבֵר לַסֹּחֵר: וַיָּקָם שְׂדֵה עֶפְרוֹן אֲשֶׁר
בַּמַּכְפֵּלָה אֲשֶׁר לִפְנֵי מַמְרֵא הַשָּׂדֶה וְהַמְּעָרָה אֲשֶׁר־
בּוֹ וְכָל־הָעֵץ אֲשֶׁר בַּשָּׂדֶה אֲשֶׁר בְּכָל־גְּבֻלוֹ סָבִיב:
יח לְאַבְרָהָם לְמִקְנָה לְעֵינֵי בְנֵי־חֵת בְּכֹל בָּאֵי שַׁעַר־

Genesis 23
14–18

my dead there." **14]** And Ephron replied to Abraham, saying to him, **15]** "My lord, do hear me! A piece of land worth four hundred shekels of silver—what is that between you and me? Go and bury your dead." **16]** Abraham accepted Ephron's terms. Abraham paid out to Ephron the money that he had named in the hearing of the children of Heth—four hundred shekels of silver at the going merchants' rate.

17] So Ephron's land in Machpelah, facing Mamre—the field with its cave and all the trees anywhere within the confines of that field— **18]** passed to Abraham as his possession, in the presence of the children of Heth, of all who sat on the council

---

15] *Four hundred shekels.* A description not of generosities exchanged but of a typical business procedure that follows a pattern of introductory offers and refusals. Abraham wants no gift, he needs a purchase title like any citizen. Ephron takes full advantage of the situation and exacts what appears to be a very high price. While differences in time and monetary value make comparisons difficult, it might be noted that Omri (ninth century B.C.E.) paid 6,000 shekels (two talents) for the land on which Samaria was built

(I Kings 16:24) and that a small plot like Machpelah could be had for 17 shekels *ca.* 600 B.C.E. (Jer. 32:9).
/ The contractual arrangements between Abraham and Ephron follow a definite legal pattern known in the ancient Near East. Recent studies have suggested a relationship of Gen. 23 to the so-called "Dialogue Document" of neo-Babylonian times, attested first for the eighth century B.C.E. [2]./

16] *Merchants' rate.* For silver. There being no

יט עִירוֹ: וְאַחֲרֵי־כֵן קָבַר אַבְרָהָם אֶת־שָׂרָה אִשְׁתּוֹ אֶל־
מְעָרַת שְׂדֵה הַמַּכְפֵּלָה עַל־פְּנֵי מַמְרֵא הוּא חֶבְרוֹן
כ בְּאֶרֶץ כְּנָעַן: וַיָּקׇם הַשָּׂדֶה וְהַמְּעָרָה אֲשֶׁר־בּוֹ
לְאַבְרָהָם לַאֲחֻזַּת־קָבֶר מֵאֵת בְּנֵי־חֵת: ס

of his town.   **19]** And then Abraham buried his wife Sarah in the cave of the field of Machpelah, facing Mamre—now Hebron—in the land of Canaan.   **20]** Thus the field with its cave passed from the children of Heth to Abraham, as a burial site.

coinage, the silver was weighed. Shekel was a weight, hence there was a "shekel of silver" as well as a "shekel of gold."

19] *Machpelah*. Pilgrims of all three faiths visit the cave in Hebron as a holy site. The sarcophagi shown there, however, belong to a later age and may or may not stand over actual burial grounds [3].

There is a Moslem tradition that Joseph too was buried here and a Jewish tradition that Joseph's brothers found their resting place in Machpelah (see *EJ*, Vol. 11, col. 673). According to Genesis all the Patriarchs and Matriarchs except for Rachel were buried here (Gen. 49:29–32; 50:13). No reference to Machpelah occurs in any other book of the Bible outside of Genesis.

Sarah

A midrash says that we hear of Sarah's death in connection with her lifetime (Gen. 23:1) because her years were truly filled with life and that this is one of the reasons why the Hebrew text expresses her life span of 127 years in an unusually extended fashion as 100 years and 20 years and 7 years [4].

The biblical text gives us relatively few facts about her life: She accompanied her husband to Haran and then on his fateful journey to Canaan; she was childless till her old age and then could not believe the prophecy of the divine messenger; she herself gave Hagar as a concubine to Abraham, only to expel her thereafter; and twice—in Egypt and Gerar—Sarah found that her beauty endangered Abraham and, therefore, agreed to dissemble their relationship. In the process, she incurred the grave peril of possibly becoming another man's mistress to save her husband's life.

What kind of woman was she? Above all, she was the wife of a pioneer. She left the ease of the city for the dangers of a semi-nomadic existence; she left her family to become, with her husband, a stranger in a strange land. She was a beautiful woman, jealous of her husband's love and zealous for her own position; she was a mother who, craving the best for her child, was cruel for his sake. Despite this, later generations considered her a paragon of beauty and piety (see Gen. 12:10–20 and p. 131). Her name means princess, and, though the information about her is scanty, we may conclude that the name properly describes the helpmate of the great Patriarch.

Machpelah

Why is the Bible so concerned with the acquisition of a grave site?

A close reading of the text reveals a profound anxiety behind Abraham's measured phrases. After all, he has no assurance that the Hittites will agree to his request. He might have to bury his wife somewhere by the roadside, in no man's land, just as Jacob was later forced to do. At this moment of his life, after the fearful trial at Moriah and bereaved of his beloved wife, Abraham seeks desperately for something physical, some place—even a grave site—to call his own. Yet again his hope is tried and he must ask others, strangers, to do what he cannot do for himself and what God can only promise— to obtain a mere piece of earth. The few moments of bargaining represent, therefore, another trial of the Patriarch. In the glimpse of this man bowing low before the Hittites, we see the friend of God torn once more between agony and hope.

Further, the burial place is a token. God promised Abraham and his descendants the land; Machpelah, then, is a visible sign of the future. A burial place for the dead is the only piece of land that Abraham, a nonresident, can hope to acquire. It represents a token title to the Promised Land and a symbol of possession when the people are far from the land— whether in Egyptian slavery or European exile.[1]

But why did Abraham, the faithful one, need Machpelah as a token? Simply because he was human; by his very humanity he represents the possibilities as well as the limits of faith. Men will live and die for ideals that they know will not be realized in their lifetime, yet they strive to see at least a portion, however small, accomplished. And just as Abraham represents the religious man, so does the Holy Land represent the possibilities and potentials of Jewish hope. Often a part has stood for the whole; often the acquisition of a single dunam of ground has been the promise of larger settlement in the future. Judaism has always been more than mere hope, or fulfilment postponed, and has always looked to some this-worldly expression of progress toward its long-range hopes.

[1] A midrash says: "Let no one claim that the land was stolen" [5]. The Talmud records a series of arguments over conflicting claims of the children of Isaac and of Ishmael [6].

GLEANINGS

Why Sarah Died

Abraham returned alone from Moriah, and Sarah, believing Isaac to have been sacrificed, died of grief. MIDRASH [7]

Woman of Valor

Twenty-two biblical women are worthy of the term "woman of valor" [Prov. 31:10]. Among them, Sarah was the greatest, and therefore she is the only woman whose age is given in Scripture. MIDRASH [8]

Abraham Mourned and Bewailed

One weeps for three days, mourns for seven, and, in some ways, for thirty. TALMUD [9]

Humility

He who possesses these three traits is one of the disciples of our father Abraham: a generous eye, a meek spirit, and a humble soul. How do we know that Abraham possessed a meek spirit? While the children of Heth call him a prince, he refers to himself by saying: "I am a resident alien among you" [Gen. 23:4]. MIDRASH [10]

It further says: "Abraham bowed low before the people of the land" [Gen. 23:12]. The Hebrew literally says "before the עַם הָאָרֶץ" [am ha-aretz], which later came to mean "the common people." To do what Abraham did is the sign of the great man. CHASIDIC [11]

By Purchase

Today, when Israel is again settled in its own land, Machpelah is of minor significance except, of course, for the sentiments of religious and historical respect it elicits. In ancient times, Machpelah represented title by purchase. Similarly in modern times, land in Israel was acquired by purchase only, until the wars of 1948 and 1967 unexpectedly altered the process.

Machpelah Today

The site of the cave is today generally identified with Kharam el Khalil in Hebron. A huge wall surrounds the area. Inside the compound, the Byzantines built a Christian church which was later converted into a mosque by the Moslems who gained possession of the city and the site. In time, both Jews and Christians were prohibited from praying inside the area, but Jews could approach it by ascending the first five (later, seven) steps. After 1967, when Israel conquered the city, all faiths were once more permitted to visit the tombs.

The actual cave which is below the site is presently inaccessible. Two small openings lead to it from inside the mosque. It is surmised that there are two or possibly three caverns below; their actual shape is not known.

ENCYCLOPAEDIA JUDAICA [12]

Rebekah at the Well

The story of Rebekah's betrothal is set in a society that was becoming increasingly patriarchal and that was also polygamous. However, the beginnings of monogamous alliances can already be found in Genesis. The phrase "Man leaves his father and mother and clings to his wife" (Gen. 2:24) strongly indicates this trend. Note that Isaac, unlike Abraham and Jacob, is monogamous [1].

A bride was obtained for a price (מֹהַר, *mohar*); although, as in Jacob's case, a bridegroom could on occasion substitute personal services for money. The marriage ceremony itself was minimal: The bride was veiled and brought to the bridegroom's tent.

With the idyllic narrative of Isaac's marriage to Rebekah, the Abraham cycle comes to a close. The focus shifts from the Patriarch to Rebekah, Matriarch-to-be of the next generation. Again, the reader is made aware of the ever-present theme of Genesis—behind all human arrangements stands God.

א וְאַבְרָהָם זָקֵן בָּא בַּיָּמִים וַיהוָה בֵּרַךְ אֶת־אַבְרָהָם

ב בַּכֹּל: וַיֹּאמֶר אַבְרָהָם אֶל־עַבְדּוֹ זְקַן בֵּיתוֹ הַמֹּשֵׁל

ג בְּכָל־אֲשֶׁר־לוֹ שִׂים־נָא יָדְךָ תַּחַת יְרֵכִי: וְאַשְׁבִּיעֲךָ

בַּיהוָה אֱלֹהֵי הַשָּׁמַיִם וֵאלֹהֵי הָאָרֶץ אֲשֶׁר לֹא־תִקַּח

אִשָּׁה לִבְנִי מִבְּנוֹת הַכְּנַעֲנִי אֲשֶׁר אָנֹכִי יוֹשֵׁב בְּקִרְבּוֹ:

ד כִּי אֶל־אַרְצִי וְאֶל־מוֹלַדְתִּי תֵּלֵךְ וְלָקַחְתָּ אִשָּׁה לִבְנִי

ה לְיִצְחָק: וַיֹּאמֶר אֵלָיו הָעֶבֶד אוּלַי לֹא־תֹאבֶה הָאִשָּׁה

לָלֶכֶת אַחֲרַי אֶל־הָאָרֶץ הַזֹּאת הֶהָשֵׁב אָשִׁיב אֶת־

Genesis 24

1–5

1] Abraham was now old, advanced in years, and the LORD had blessed Abraham in all things.   2] And Abraham said to the senior servant of his household, who had charge of all that he owned, "Put your hand under my thigh   3] and I will make you swear by the LORD, the God of heaven and the God of the earth, that you will not take a wife for my son from the daughters of the Canaanites among whom I dwell,   4] but will go to the land of my birth and get a wife for my son Isaac."   5] And the servant said to him, "What if the woman does not consent to follow me to this land, shall I then take your son back to the land from which you

24:2] *The senior servant.* Possibly (though not definitely) the Eliezer of Gen. 15:2.

Under my thigh. See Gen. 47:29. The symbolic gesture may have implied a curse of sterility on the offender. (Sons are said to issue "from the thigh." See the Hebrew text of Exod. 1:5). Some suggest that this act involved touching the testicles [2].   Assyrians placed the hand on the breast; Greeks, on the knee; Arabs, under the armpit or on the belt. The custom of swearing while placing one's hand on some object persists in our time; in Jewish tradition certain oaths were made while holding *tefilin* or a scroll of the Torah. The servant is probably the executor of Abraham's will; hence

he and not Isaac swears [3].
/Rashi compares the servant's procedure with oaths which require the holding of an object (חֵפֶץ שֶׁל מִצְוָה). Ibn Ezra considers the act to be a symbol of submission; similarly Abarbanel who compares it to the servant holding the stirrup./

3] *Daughters of the Canaanites.* Abraham wants his son to remain a stranger in Canaan, hence he commands marriage within his own group. Here are the beginning strands of Judaism's strong feelings about mixed marriages—although the term cannot yet, of course, be applied for many centuries. What is at stake is religion and family tradition, not ethnic or racial "purity."

בְּנֶךְ אֶל־הָאָרֶץ אֲשֶׁר־יָצָאתָ מִשָּׁם: וַיֹּאמֶר אֵלָיו

אַבְרָהָם הִשָּׁמֶר לְךָ פֶּן־תָּשִׁיב אֶת־בְּנִי שָׁמָּה: יְהוָה

אֱלֹהֵי הַשָּׁמַיִם אֲשֶׁר לְקָחַנִי מִבֵּית אָבִי וּמֵאֶרֶץ

מוֹלַדְתִּי וַאֲשֶׁר דִּבֶּר־לִי וַאֲשֶׁר נִשְׁבַּע־לִי לֵאמֹר

לְזַרְעֲךָ אֶתֵּן אֶת־הָאָרֶץ הַזֹּאת הוּא יִשְׁלַח מַלְאָכוֹ

לְפָנֶיךָ וְלָקַחְתָּ אִשָּׁה לִבְנִי מִשָּׁם: וְאִם־לֹא תֹאבֶה

הָאִשָּׁה לָלֶכֶת אַחֲרֶיךָ וְנִקִּיתָ מִשְּׁבֻעָתִי זֹאת רַק אֶת־

בְּנִי לֹא תָשֵׁב שָׁמָּה: וַיָּשֶׂם הָעֶבֶד אֶת־יָדוֹ תַּחַת יֶרֶךְ

אַבְרָהָם אֲדֹנָיו וַיִּשָּׁבַע לוֹ עַל־הַדָּבָר הַזֶּה: וַיִּקַּח

הָעֶבֶד עֲשָׂרָה גְמַלִּים מִגְּמַלֵּי אֲדֹנָיו וַיֵּלֶךְ וְכָל־טוּב

אֲדֹנָיו בְּיָדוֹ וַיָּקָם וַיֵּלֶךְ אֶל־אֲרַם נַהֲרַיִם אֶל־עִיר

Genesis 24

6–10

came?"   6] Abraham answered him, "On no account must you take my son back
there!   7] The LORD, the God of heaven, who took me from my father's house
and from the land of my birth, who promised me under oath, saying, 'I will give
this land to your offspring'—He will send His angel before you, and you will get a
wife for my son from there.   8] And if the woman does not consent to follow
you, you shall then be clear of this my oath; but do not take my son back there."
9] So the servant put his hand under the thigh of Abraham his master and swore
to him as bidden.

10] Then the servant took ten of his master's camels and set out, taking with
him all the bounty of his master; and he made his way to Aram-naharaim, to the

7] *My native land.* Or "land of my kindred"   9] *As bidden.* Literally, "about this matter."
(see Gen. 12:1).

God . . . promised me on oath. That is, solemnly.   10] *Aram-naharaim.* Literally, "Aram-of-the-two-
Abraham's last words are about land and posterity.   rivers." On Haran, see p. 113.

יא נָחוֹר: וַיַּבְרֵךְ הַגְּמַלִּים מִחוּץ לָעִיר אֶל־בְּאֵר הַמָּיִם

יב לְעֵת עֶרֶב לְעֵת צֵאת הַשֹּׁאֲבֹת: וַיֹּאמַר יְהוָה אֱלֹהֵי
אֲדֹנִי אַבְרָהָם הַקְרֵה־נָא לְפָנַי הַיּוֹם וַעֲשֵׂה־חֶסֶד עִם

יג אֲדֹנִי אַבְרָהָם: הִנֵּה אָנֹכִי נִצָּב עַל־עֵין הַמָּיִם וּבְנוֹת

יד אַנְשֵׁי הָעִיר יֹצְאֹת לִשְׁאֹב מָיִם: וְהָיָה הַנַּעֲרָ* אֲשֶׁר
אֹמַר אֵלֶיהָ הַטִּי־נָא כַדֵּךְ וְאֶשְׁתֶּה וְאָמְרָה שְׁתֵה וְגַם־
גְּמַלֶּיךָ אַשְׁקֶה אֹתָהּ הֹכַחְתָּ לְעַבְדְּךָ לְיִצְחָק וּבָהּ

טו אֵדַע כִּי־עָשִׂיתָ חֶסֶד עִם־אֲדֹנִי: וַיְהִי־הוּא טֶרֶם כִּלָּה
לְדַבֵּר וְהִנֵּה רִבְקָה יֹצֵאת אֲשֶׁר יֻלְּדָה לִבְתוּאֵל
בֶּן־מִלְכָּה אֵשֶׁת נָחוֹר אֲחִי אַבְרָהָם וְכַדָּהּ עַל־שִׁכְמָהּ:

טז וְהַנַּעֲרָ* טֹבַת מַרְאֶה מְאֹד בְּתוּלָה וְאִישׁ לֹא יְדָעָהּ

* יד הנערה קרי.   טז והנערה קרי.

Genesis 24

11–16

city of Nahor.   **11]** He made the camels kneel down by the well outside the city, at evening time, the time when women come out to draw water.   **12]** And he said, "O LORD, God of my master Abraham, grant me good fortune this day, and deal graciously with my master Abraham: **13]** As I stand here by the spring and the daughters of the townsmen come out to draw water,   **14]** let the maiden to whom I say, 'Please, lower your jar that I may drink,' and who replies, 'Drink, and I will also water your camels'—let her be the one whom You have decreed for Your servant Isaac. Thereby shall I know that You have dealt graciously with my master."

15] He had scarcely finished speaking, when Rebekah, who was born to Bethuel, the son of Milcah the wife of Abraham's brother Nahor, came out with her jar on her shoulder.   **16]** The maiden was very beautiful, a virgin whom no man had

11]   *By the well.* Jacob and Moses also wooed at a well (Gen. 29:9–11; Exod. 2:15–21).

12]   The vocalizers of the Hebrew text put the musical sign *shalshelet* (chain) over וַיֹּאמַר. The *shalshelet* indicates a pause and occurs relatively seldom. Possibly its placement here was to indicate the hesitation of the servant.

יז וַתֵּרֶד הָעַיְנָה וַתְּמַלֵּא כַדָּהּ וַתָּעַל: וַיָּרָץ הָעֶבֶד לִקְרָאתָהּ וַיֹּאמֶר הַגְמִיאִינִי נָא מְעַט־מַיִם מִכַּדֵּךְ:

יח וַתֹּאמֶר שְׁתֵה אֲדֹנִי וַתְּמַהֵר וַתֹּרֶד כַּדָּהּ עַל־יָדָהּ

יט וַתַּשְׁקֵהוּ: וַתְּכַל לְהַשְׁקֹתוֹ וַתֹּאמֶר גַּם לִגְמַלֶּיךָ אֶשְׁאָב

כ עַד אִם־כִּלּוּ לִשְׁתֹּת: וַתְּמַהֵר וַתְּעַר כַּדָּהּ אֶל־הַשֹּׁקֶת וַתָּרָץ עוֹד אֶל־הַבְּאֵר לִשְׁאֹב וַתִּשְׁאַב לְכָל־גְּמַלָּיו:

כא וְהָאִישׁ מִשְׁתָּאֵה לָהּ מַחֲרִישׁ לָדַעַת הַהִצְלִיחַ יְהוָה

כב דַּרְכּוֹ אִם־לֹא: וַיְהִי כַּאֲשֶׁר כִּלּוּ הַגְּמַלִּים לִשְׁתּוֹת וַיִּקַּח הָאִישׁ נֶזֶם זָהָב בֶּקַע מִשְׁקָלוֹ וּשְׁנֵי צְמִידִים עַל־

כג יָדֶיהָ עֲשָׂרָה זָהָב מִשְׁקָלָם: וַיֹּאמֶר בַּת־מִי אַתְּ הַגִּידִי

כד נָא לִי הֲיֵשׁ בֵּית־אָבִיךְ מָקוֹם לָנוּ לָלִין: וַתֹּאמֶר אֵלָיו

Genesis 24

17–24

known. She went down to the spring, filled her jar, and came up.   17] The servant ran toward her and said, "Please, let me sip a little water from your jar."   18] "Drink, my lord," she said, and she quickly lowered her jar upon her hand and let him drink.   19] When she had let him drink his fill, she said, "I will also draw for your camels, until they finish drinking."   20] Quickly emptying her jar into the trough, she ran back to the well to draw, and she drew for all his camels.

21] The man, meanwhile, stood gazing at her in silence, to learn whether the Lord had made his errand successful or not.   22] When the camels had finished drinking, the man took a gold nose-ring weighing a half-shekel, and two gold bands for her arms, ten shekels in weight.   23] "Pray tell me," he said, "whose daughter are you? Is there room in your father's house for us to spend the night?"   24] She

22] *Nose-ring.* A gift of special prominence that everyone would see (cf. the simile of God giving a nose-ring to Israel; Ezek. 16:12).

Weighing a half-shekel. בֶּקַע (*beka*), about 1/5 ounce (see Exod. 38:26).

בַּת־בְּתוּאֵל אָנֹכִי בֶּן־מִלְכָּה אֲשֶׁר יָלְדָה לְנָחוֹר:

כה וַתֹּאמֶר אֵלָיו גַּם־תֶּבֶן גַּם־מִסְפּוֹא רַב עִמָּנוּ גַּם־מָקוֹם

כו לָלוּן: וַיִּקֹּד הָאִישׁ וַיִּשְׁתַּחוּ לַיהֹוָה: וַיֹּאמֶר בָּרוּךְ

יְהֹוָה אֱלֹהֵי אֲדֹנִי אַבְרָהָם אֲשֶׁר לֹא־עָזַב חַסְדּוֹ

וַאֲמִתּוֹ מֵעִם אֲדֹנִי אָנֹכִי בַּדֶּרֶךְ נָחַנִי יְהֹוָה בֵּית אֲחֵי

כח אֲדֹנִי: וַתָּרָץ הַנַּעֲרָ* וַתַּגֵּד לְבֵית אִמָּהּ כַּדְּבָרִים

כט הָאֵלֶּה: וּלְרִבְקָה אָח וּשְׁמוֹ לָבָן וַיָּרָץ לָבָן אֶל־הָאִישׁ

ל הַחוּצָה אֶל־הָעָיִן: וַיְהִי כִּרְאֹת אֶת־הַנֶּזֶם וְאֶת־הַצְּמִדִים

עַל־יְדֵי אֲחֹתוֹ וּכְשָׁמְעוֹ אֶת־דִּבְרֵי רִבְקָה אֲחֹתוֹ לֵאמֹר

כֹּה־דִבֶּר אֵלַי הָאִישׁ וַיָּבֹא אֶל־הָאִישׁ וְהִנֵּה עֹמֵד עַל־

לא הַגְּמַלִּים עַל־הָעָיִן: וַיֹּאמֶר בּוֹא בְּרוּךְ יְהֹוָה לָמָּה

תַעֲמֹד בַּחוּץ וְאָנֹכִי פִּנִּיתִי הַבַּיִת וּמָקוֹם לַגְּמַלִּים:

Genesis 24
25–31

* כח הנערה קרי.

replied, "I am the daughter of Bethuel the son of Milcah whom she bore to Nahor."
25] And she went on, "There is plenty of straw and feed at home, and also room to spend the night."   26] The man bowed low in homage to the LORD   27] and said, "Blessed be the LORD, the God of my master Abraham, who has not withheld His steadfast kindness from my master. For I am on the road on which the LORD has guided me—to the house of my master's kinsmen."

28] The maiden ran and told all this to her mother's household.   29] Now Rebekah had a brother whose name was Laban. Laban ran out to the man at the spring   30] when he saw the nose-ring and the bands on his sister's arms, and when he heard his sister Rebekah say, "Thus the man spoke to me." He went up to the man, who was still standing beside the camels by the spring.   31] "Come in, O blessed of the LORD," he said, "why do you remain outside, when I have made

25] *Straw.* תֶּבֶן (shredded straw), which in the East is mixed with feed (cf. verse 32).

לב וַיָּבֹא הָאִישׁ הַבַּיְתָה וַיְפַתַּח הַגְּמַלִּים וַיִּתֵּן תֶּבֶן וּמִסְפּוֹא לַגְּמַלִּים וּמַיִם לִרְחֹץ רַגְלָיו וְרַגְלֵי הָאֲנָשִׁים אֲשֶׁר

לג אִתּוֹ: וַיּישֶׂם* לְפָנָיו לֶאֱכֹל וַיֹּאמֶר לֹא אֹכַל עַד אִם־

לד דִּבַּרְתִּי דְּבָרָי וַיֹּאמֶר דַּבֵּר: וַיֹּאמַר עֶבֶד אַבְרָהָם

לה אָנֹכִי: וַיהוָה בֵּרַךְ אֶת־אֲדֹנִי מְאֹד וַיִּגְדָּל וַיִּתֶּן־לוֹ צֹאן וּבָקָר וְכֶסֶף וְזָהָב וַעֲבָדִם וּשְׁפָחֹת וּגְמַלִּים וַחֲמֹרִים:

לו וַתֵּלֶד שָׂרָה אֵשֶׁת אֲדֹנִי בֵן לַאדֹנִי אַחֲרֵי זִקְנָתָהּ

לז וַיִּתֶּן־לוֹ אֶת־כָּל־אֲשֶׁר־לוֹ: וַיַּשְׁבִּעֵנִי אֲדֹנִי לֵאמֹר לֹא־ תִקַּח אִשָּׁה לִבְנִי מִבְּנוֹת הַכְּנַעֲנִי אֲשֶׁר אָנֹכִי יֹשֵׁב

לח בְּאַרְצוֹ: אִם־לֹא אֶל־בֵּית־אָבִי תֵּלֵךְ וְאֶל־מִשְׁפַּחְתִּי

לט וְלָקַחְתָּ אִשָּׁה לִבְנִי: וָאֹמַר אֶל־אֲדֹנִי אֻלַי לֹא־תֵלֵךְ

Genesis 24
32–39

* לג וישם קרי.

ready the house and a place for the camels?" **32]** So the man entered the house. The camels were unloaded and given straw and feed, and water was brought to bathe his feet and the feet of the men with him. **33]** But when food was set before him, he said, "I will not eat until I have told my tale." He said, "Speak, then."

34] "I am Abraham's servant," he began. **35]** "The LORD has greatly blessed my master, and he has become rich: He has given him sheep and cattle, silver and gold, male and female slaves, camels and asses. **36]** And Sarah, my master's wife, bore my master a son in her old age, and he has given him everything he owns. **37]** Now my master made me swear, saying, 'You shall not get a wife for my son from the daughters of the Canaanites in whose land I dwell; **38]** but you shall go to my father's house, to my kindred, and get a wife for my son.' **39]** And I

34-41] Amidst the elaborate repetition (a device found also in other Near Eastern literature), we can observe subtle and finely worked out differences; for instance, Abraham's instructions are tactfully omitted here.

מ הָאִשָּׁה אַחֲרָי: וַיֹּאמֶר אֵלַי יְהֹוָה אֲשֶׁר־הִתְהַלַּכְתִּי
לְפָנָיו יִשְׁלַח מַלְאָכוֹ אִתָּךְ וְהִצְלִיחַ דַּרְכֶּךָ וְלָקַחְתָּ

מא אִשָּׁה לִבְנִי מִמִּשְׁפַּחְתִּי וּמִבֵּית אָבִי: אָז תִּנָּקֶה מֵאָלָתִי
כִּי תָבוֹא אֶל־מִשְׁפַּחְתִּי וְאִם־לֹא יִתְּנוּ לָךְ וְהָיִיתָ נָקִי

מב מֵאָלָתִי: וָאָבֹא הַיּוֹם אֶל־הָעָיִן וָאֹמַר יְהֹוָה אֱלֹהֵי
אֲדֹנִי אַבְרָהָם אִם־יֶשְׁךָ־נָּא מַצְלִיחַ דַּרְכִּי אֲשֶׁר אָנֹכִי

מג הֹלֵךְ עָלֶיהָ: הִנֵּה אָנֹכִי נִצָּב עַל־עֵין הַמָּיִם וְהָיָה
הָעַלְמָה הַיֹּצֵאת לִשְׁאֹב וְאָמַרְתִּי אֵלֶיהָ הַשְׁקִינִי־נָא

מד מְעַט־מַיִם מִכַּדֵּךְ: וְאָמְרָה אֵלַי גַּם־אַתָּה שְׁתֵה וְגַם
לִגְמַלֶּיךָ אֶשְׁאָב הִוא הָאִשָּׁה אֲשֶׁר־הֹכִיחַ יְהֹוָה לְבֶן

מה אֲדֹנִי: אֲנִי טֶרֶם אֲכַלֶּה לְדַבֵּר אֶל־לִבִּי וְהִנֵּה רִבְקָה
יֹצֵאת וְכַדָּהּ עַל־שִׁכְמָהּ וַתֵּרֶד הָעַיְנָה וַתִּשְׁאָב וָאֹמַר

Genesis 24
40–45

said to my master, 'What if the woman does not follow me?'   40] He replied to me, 'The LORD, whose ways I follow, will send His angel with you and make your errand successful; and you will get a wife for my son from my kindred, from my father's house.   41] Thus only shall you be freed from my adjuration: if, when you come to my kindred, they refuse you—only then shall you be freed from my adjuration.'

42] "I came today to the spring, and I said: O LORD, God of my master Abraham, if You would indeed grant success to the errand on which I am engaged!   43] As I stand by the spring of water, let the young woman who comes out to draw and to whom I say, 'Please, let me drink a little water from your jar,'   44] and who answers, 'You may drink, and I will also draw for your camels'—let her be the wife whom the LORD has decreed for my master's son.'   45] I had scarcely finished praying in my heart, when Rebekah came out with her jar on her shoulder, and went down to the spring and drew. And I said to her, 'Please give me a drink.'

מו אֵלֶיהָ הַשְׁקִינִי נָא: וַתְּמַהֵר וַתֹּרֶד כַּדָּהּ מֵעָלֶיהָ
וַתֹּאמֶר שְׁתֵה וְגַם־גְּמַלֶּיךָ אַשְׁקֶה וָאֵשְׁתְּ וְגַם הַגְּמַלִּים

מז הִשְׁקָתָה: וָאֶשְׁאַל אֹתָהּ וָאֹמַר בַּת־מִי אַתְּ וַתֹּאמֶר
בַּת־בְּתוּאֵל בֶּן־נָחוֹר אֲשֶׁר יָלְדָה־לּוֹ מִלְכָּה וָאָשִׂם

מח הַנֶּזֶם עַל־אַפָּהּ וְהַצְּמִידִים עַל־יָדֶיהָ: וָאֶקֹּד וָאֶשְׁתַּחֲוֶה
לַיהֹוָה וָאֲבָרֵךְ אֶת־יְהֹוָה אֱלֹהֵי אֲדֹנִי אַבְרָהָם אֲשֶׁר
הִנְחַנִי בְּדֶרֶךְ אֱמֶת לָקַחַת אֶת־בַּת־אֲחִי אֲדֹנִי לִבְנוֹ:

מט וְעַתָּה אִם־יֶשְׁכֶם עֹשִׂים חֶסֶד וֶאֱמֶת אֶת־אֲדֹנִי הַגִּידוּ
לִי וְאִם־לֹא הַגִּידוּ לִי וְאֶפְנֶה עַל־יָמִין אוֹ עַל־שְׂמֹאל:

נ וַיַּעַן לָבָן וּבְתוּאֵל וַיֹּאמְרוּ מֵיהֹוָה יָצָא הַדָּבָר לֹא

נא נוּכַל דַּבֵּר אֵלֶיךָ רַע אוֹ־טוֹב: הִנֵּה־רִבְקָה לְפָנֶיךָ

Genesis 24

46–51

46] She quickly lowered her jar and said, 'Drink, and I will also water your camels.' So I drank, and she also watered the camels. 47] I inquired of her, 'Whose daughter are you?' And she said, 'The daughter of Bethuel son of Nahor, whom Milcah bore to him.' And I put the ring on her nose and the bands on her arms. 48] Then I bowed low in homage to the LORD and blessed the LORD, the God of my master Abraham, who led me on the right way to get the daughter of my master's brother for his son. 49] And now, if you mean to treat my master with true kindness, tell me; and if not, tell me also, that I may turn right or left."

50] Then Laban and Bethuel answered, "The matter stems from the LORD; we cannot speak to you bad or good. 51] Here is Rebekah before you; take her and

50] *Bethuel*. Some believe that the name was added later and that the story reads more easily if we assume that Laban acted as head of the family because Bethuel had already died. It is more likely, however, that this is a trace of an earlier societal pattern in which the "mother's household" (verse 28) played a sizable role (see p. 129, note 1).

קַח וָלֵךְ וּתְהִי אִשָּׁה לְבֶן־אֲדֹנֶיךָ כַּאֲשֶׁר דִּבֶּר יְהוָה:

נב וַיְהִי כַּאֲשֶׁר שָׁמַע עֶבֶד אַבְרָהָם אֶת־דִּבְרֵיהֶם וַיִּשְׁתַּחוּ

נג אַרְצָה לַיהוָה: וַיּוֹצֵא הָעֶבֶד כְּלֵי־כֶסֶף וּכְלֵי זָהָב

וּבְגָדִים וַיִּתֵּן לְרִבְקָה וּמִגְדָּנֹת נָתַן לְאָחִיהָ וּלְאִמָּהּ:

נד וַיֹּאכְלוּ וַיִּשְׁתּוּ הוּא וְהָאֲנָשִׁים אֲשֶׁר־עִמּוֹ וַיָּלִינוּ וַיָּקוּמוּ

נה בַבֹּקֶר וַיֹּאמֶר שַׁלְּחֻנִי לַאדֹנִי: וַיֹּאמֶר אָחִיהָ וְאִמָּהּ

נו תֵּשֵׁב הַנַּעֲרָ* אִתָּנוּ יָמִים אוֹ עָשׂוֹר אַחַר תֵּלֵךְ: וַיֹּאמֶר

אֲלֵהֶם אַל־תְּאַחֲרוּ אֹתִי וַיהוָה הִצְלִיחַ דַּרְכִּי שַׁלְּחוּנִי

נז וְאֵלְכָה לַאדֹנִי: וַיֹּאמְרוּ נִקְרָא לַנַּעֲרָ* וְנִשְׁאֲלָה אֶת־

נח פִּיהָ: וַיִּקְרְאוּ לְרִבְקָה וַיֹּאמְרוּ אֵלֶיהָ הֲתֵלְכִי עִם־

Genesis 24

52–58

* נה הנערה קרי.   נז לנערה קרי.

go, and let her be a wife to your master's son, as the LORD has spoken." **52]** When Abraham's servant heard their words, he bowed low to the ground before the LORD. **53]** The servant brought out objects of silver and gold, and garments, and gave them to Rebekah; and he gave presents to her brother and her mother. **54]** Then he and the men with him ate and drank, and they spent the night. When they arose next morning, he said, "Give me leave to go to my master." **55]** But her brother and her mother said, "Let the maiden remain with us some ten days; then you may go." **56]** He said to them "Do not delay me, now that the LORD has made my errand successful. Give me leave that I may go to my master." **57]** And they said, "Let us call the girl and ask for her reply." **58]** They called Rebekah and

---

53] *Presents.* Representing also the purchase price of the bride.

55] *Some ten days.* Literally, "days or ten." According to Rashi, the phrase means "a year or ten months" (the expression "days" is used in this way in Lev. 25:29). The Mishnah records: "An

engaged virgin is to be granted twelve months to prepare herself" [4]. The servant would not have refused a delay of a mere ten days.

57] *Let us call the girl.* Note that Rebekah is asked to consent to the marriage, as was customary also in Nuzi.

נט הָאִישׁ הַזֶּה וַתֹּאמֶר אֵלֵךְ: וַיְשַׁלְּחוּ אֶת־רִבְקָה אֲחֹתָם

ס וְאֶת־מֵנִקְתָּהּ וְאֶת־עֶבֶד אַבְרָהָם וְאֶת־אֲנָשָׁיו: וַיְבָרֲכוּ
אֶת־רִבְקָה וַיֹּאמְרוּ לָהּ אֲחֹתֵנוּ אַתְּ הֲיִי לְאַלְפֵי רְבָבָה

סא וְיִירַשׁ זַרְעֵךְ אֵת שַׁעַר שֹׂנְאָיו: וַתָּקָם רִבְקָה וְנַעֲרֹתֶיהָ
וַתִּרְכַּבְנָה עַל־הַגְּמַלִּים וַתֵּלַכְנָה אַחֲרֵי הָאִישׁ וַיִּקַּח

סב הָעֶבֶד אֶת־רִבְקָה וַיֵּלַךְ: וְיִצְחָק בָּא מִבּוֹא בְּאֵר

סג לַחַי רֹאִי וְהוּא יוֹשֵׁב בְּאֶרֶץ הַנֶּגֶב: וַיֵּצֵא יִצְחָק
לָשׂוּחַ בַּשָּׂדֶה לִפְנוֹת עָרֶב וַיִּשָּׂא עֵינָיו וַיַּרְא וְהִנֵּה

סד גְּמַלִּים בָּאִים: וַתִּשָּׂא רִבְקָה אֶת־עֵינֶיהָ וַתֵּרֶא אֶת־

סה יִצְחָק וַתִּפֹּל מֵעַל הַגָּמָל: וַתֹּאמֶר אֶל־הָעֶבֶד מִי־
הָאִישׁ הַלָּזֶה הַהֹלֵךְ בַּשָּׂדֶה לִקְרָאתֵנוּ וַיֹּאמֶר הָעֶבֶד

Genesis 24

59–65

said to her, "Will you go with this man?" And she said, "I will."   59] So they sent off their sister Rebekah and her nurse along with Abraham's servant and his men. 60] And they blessed Rebekah and said to her, "O sister! / May you grow into / Thousands of myriads; / May your offspring seize / The gates of their foes." 61] Then Rebekah and her maids arose, mounted the camels, and followed the man. So the servant took Rebekah and went his way.

62] Isaac had just come back from the vicinity of Beer-lahai-roi, for he was settled in the region of the Negeb.   63] And Isaac went out walking in the field toward evening, and looking up, he saw camels approaching.   64] Raising her eyes, Rebekah saw Isaac. She alighted from the camel   65] and said to the servant, "Who is that man walking in the field toward us?" And the servant said, "That is

---

63] *Walking.* Or perhaps "meditating," which better fits the characterization of Isaac (see p. 261).

65] *She took her veil.* Veiling the bride was required of free women in Middle Assyrian law.

A traditional Jewish marriage is even now preceded by the *bedecken* ceremony—the covering of the bride with a veil, while the groom utters the words from Gen. 24:60: "May you grow into/Thousands of myriads."

סו הוּא אֲדֹנִי וַתִּקַּח הַצָּעִיף וַתִּתְכָּס: וַיְסַפֵּר הָעֶבֶד

סז לְיִצְחָק אֵת כָּל-הַדְּבָרִים אֲשֶׁר עָשָׂה: וַיְבִאֶהָ יִצְחָק

הָאֹהֱלָה שָׂרָה אִמּוֹ וַיִּקַּח אֶת-רִבְקָה וַתְּהִי-לוֹ לְאִשָּׁה

וַיֶּאֱהָבֶהָ וַיִּנָּחֵם יִצְחָק אַחֲרֵי אִמּוֹ: פ

א וַיֹּסֶף אַבְרָהָם וַיִּקַּח אִשָּׁה וּשְׁמָהּ קְטוּרָה: וַתֵּלֶד לוֹ

ב אֶת-זִמְרָן וְאֶת-יָקְשָׁן וְאֶת-מְדָן וְאֶת-מִדְיָן וְאֶת-יִשְׁבָּק

ג וְאֶת-שׁוּחַ: וְיָקְשָׁן יָלַד אֶת-שְׁבָא וְאֶת-דְּדָן וּבְנֵי דְדָן

ד הָיוּ אַשּׁוּרִם וּלְטוּשִׁם וּלְאֻמִּים: וּבְנֵי מִדְיָן עֵיפָה

וָעֵפֶר וַחֲנֹךְ וַאֲבִידָע וְאֶלְדָּעָה כָּל-אֵלֶּה בְּנֵי קְטוּרָה:

ה וַיִּתֵּן אַבְרָהָם אֶת-כָּל-אֲשֶׁר-לוֹ לְיִצְחָק: וְלִבְנֵי

ו הַפִּילַגְשִׁים אֲשֶׁר לְאַבְרָהָם נָתַן אַבְרָהָם מַתָּנֹת

Genesis 24; 25
66–67; 1–6

my master." So she took her veil and covered herself.   66] The servant told Isaac
all the things that he had done.   67] Isaac then brought her into the tent of his
mother Sarah, and he took Rebekah as his wife. Isaac loved her, and thus found
comfort after his mother's death.

1] Abraham took another wife, whose name was Keturah.   2] She bore him
Zimran, Jokshan, Medan, Midian, Ishbak, and Shuah.   3] Jokshan begot Sheba
and Dedan. The descendants of Dedan were the Asshurim, the Letushim, and the
Leummim.   4] The descendants of Midian were Ephah, Epher, Enoch, Abida,
and Eldaah. All these were descendants of Keturah.   5] Abraham willed all that
he owned to Isaac;   6] but to Abraham's sons by concubines Abraham gave gifts

67] *Comfort after his mother's death.* A clue to
Isaac's personality (see p. 261).
25:1–8] Clearly a postscript. Some commentators
took this section to refer not to the time after
Sarah's death but to an earlier phase in Abraham's
life and identified Keturah with Hagar [5].   There
is no textual evidence for this interpretation.
    Medanites and Shebaites (Sabeans) were mer-
chants in the Red Sea area as were the Midianites
who dwelled farther to the north. Asshurim are
not Assyrians but an Arab tribe. Others, like
Hanoch (Enoch), are difficult to identify.
5–6] The notation about Abraham's will and the

וַיְשַׁלְּחֵם מֵעַל יִצְחָק בְּנוֹ בְּעוֹדֶנּוּ חַי קֵדְמָה אֶל־

ז אֶרֶץ קֶדֶם: וְאֵלֶּה יְמֵי שְׁנֵי־חַיֵּי אַבְרָהָם אֲשֶׁר־חָי

ח מְאַת שָׁנָה וְשִׁבְעִים שָׁנָה וְחָמֵשׁ שָׁנִים: וַיִּגְוַע וַיָּמָת

אַבְרָהָם בְּשֵׂיבָה טוֹבָה זָקֵן וְשָׂבֵעַ וַיֵּאָסֶף אֶל־עַמָּיו:

ט וַיִּקְבְּרוּ אֹתוֹ יִצְחָק וְיִשְׁמָעֵאל בָּנָיו אֶל־מְעָרַת

הַמַּכְפֵּלָה אֶל־שְׂדֵה עֶפְרֹן בֶּן־צֹחַר הַחִתִּי אֲשֶׁר עַל־

י פְּנֵי מַמְרֵא: הַשָּׂדֶה אֲשֶׁר־קָנָה אַבְרָהָם מֵאֵת בְּנֵי־חֵת

יא שָׁמָּה קֻבַּר אַבְרָהָם וְשָׂרָה אִשְׁתּוֹ: וַיְהִי אַחֲרֵי מוֹת

אַבְרָהָם וַיְבָרֶךְ אֱלֹהִים אֶת־יִצְחָק בְּנוֹ וַיֵּשֶׁב יִצְחָק

עִם־בְּאֵר לַחַי רֹאִי: פ

יב וְאֵלֶּה תֹּלְדֹת יִשְׁמָעֵאל בֶּן־אַבְרָהָם אֲשֶׁר יָלְדָה הָגָר

Genesis 25

7–12

while he was still living; and he sent them away from his son Isaac eastward, to the land of the East.

7] This was the total span of Abraham's life: one hundred and seventy-five years. **8]** And Abraham breathed his last, dying at a good ripe age, old and contented; and he was gathered to his kin. **9]** His sons Isaac and Ishmael buried him in the cave of Machpelah, in the field of Ephron the son of Zohar the Hittite, facing Mamre, **10]** the field that Abraham had bought from the children of Heth; there Abraham was buried, and Sarah his wife. **11]** After the death of Abraham, God blessed his son Isaac. And Isaac settled near Beer-lahai-roi.

12] This is the line of Ishmael, Abraham's son, whom Hagar the Egyptian, Sarah's

gifts to the other children serve to insure Isaac's title to the inheritance.

8] *Gathered to his kin.* An idiomatic expression for "he died."

9] *Isaac and Ishmael.* After Abraham's death, or

possibly after Sarah's, the two brothers seem to live in harmony.

12–16] The list is a formal one, also featuring twelve tribes (see note to Gen. 22:20). Best known is Kedar, mentioned in prophetic writings (cf. Isa. 21:16; Jer. 2:10).

הַמִּצְרִית שִׁפְחַת שָׂרָה לְאַבְרָהָם: וְאֵלֶּה שְׁמוֹת בְּנֵי יג

יִשְׁמָעֵאל בִּשְׁמֹתָם לְתוֹלְדֹתָם בְּכֹר יִשְׁמָעֵאל נְבָיֹת

וְקֵדָר וְאַדְבְּאֵל וּמִבְשָׂם: וּמִשְׁמָע וְדוּמָה וּמַשָּׂא: חֲדַד יד

וְתֵימָא יְטוּר נָפִישׁ וָקֵדְמָה: אֵלֶּה הֵם בְּנֵי יִשְׁמָעֵאל טז

וְאֵלֶּה שְׁמֹתָם בְּחַצְרֵיהֶם וּבְטִירֹתָם שְׁנֵים־עָשָׂר נְשִׂיאִם

לְאֻמֹּתָם: וְאֵלֶּה שְׁנֵי חַיֵּי יִשְׁמָעֵאל מְאַת שָׁנָה וּשְׁלֹשִׁים יז

שָׁנָה וְשֶׁבַע שָׁנִים וַיִּגְוַע וַיָּמָת וַיֵּאָסֶף אֶל־עַמָּיו: וַיִּשְׁכְּנוּ יח

מֵחֲוִילָה עַד־שׁוּר אֲשֶׁר עַל־פְּנֵי מִצְרַיִם בֹּאֲכָה אַשּׁוּרָה

עַל־פְּנֵי כָל־אֶחָיו נָפָל:

Genesis 25
13–18

Haftarah Chaye Sarah, p. 533

slave, bore to Abraham.   13] These are the names of the sons of **Ishmael**, by their names, in the order of their birth: Nebaioth, the first-born of Ishmael, Kedar, Adbeel, Mibsam,   14] Mishma, Dumah, Massa,   15] Hadad, Tema, Jetur, Naphish, and Kedmah.   16] These are the sons of Ishmael and these are their names by their villages and by their encampments: twelve chieftains of as many tribes.— 17] These were the years of the life of Ishmael: one hundred and thirty-seven years; then he breathed his last and died, and was gathered to his kin.— 18] They ranged from Havilah, by Shur, which is close to Egypt, all the way to Asshur; they made raids against all their kinsmen.

On Marriage

The story of Rebekah's betrothal reveals the biblical attitude toward the nature and content of marriage. The union between man and woman must be grounded in the finest qualities, and Rebekah exhibits them to perfection. Her behavior shows modesty and hospitality; she is kind to animals and respectful of her own family. It is for such attributes that the servant prays; a woman who possesses them is indeed "very beautiful."

The marriage was arranged although the two principals had not as yet met. Modern man who thinks of marriage primarily as the fulfilment of a romantic relationship will find it difficult to see significant values in arranged marriages. But, for biblical man, the ideal was not "first love, then marriage," as it is today, but the reverse, "first marriage, then love."

The older system rested on the assumption that two persons will have a proper foundation for marriage if their backgrounds are generally compatible and if they set themselves to establish a home in which each partner plays his expected role. The two will come to know each other through marriage, and it is hoped that in time love will follow. Such love grows from shared experience, from mutual respect, and from affection for offspring. This arrangement raised fewer expectations and, therefore, was less subject to breakdown. At its best, it was no less productive of deep and abiding love than modern marriages that are expected to begin with it and maintain it forever.

The acceptability of marital arrangements was strengthened by an ancient belief that marriages were literally "made in heaven." According to one midrash, arranging marriages has been one of God's important occupations since creation [6]. This midrash is not only a wry comment on the complexity of the problem but also implies that God is the ultimate guarantor of the union.[1] The relationship of man and wife is more than cohabitation and convenience, it is קִדּוּשִׁין (kiddushin, holiness), a sacred partnership. God directed the servant's way to Rebekah, whose qualities would match the great task to which Isaac was committed: to carry forward the divine promise to generations yet unborn. Thus, the story of Abraham, the friend of God, comes to its end with a vision of the future.

The Servant's Prayer

In chapter 24, verse 12, Abraham's servant prays for "good fortune" (הַקְרֵה, literally, bring something [good] to pass). This is the first prayer for divine guidance recorded in the Bible, and it comes from the heart and mouth of a nameless individual.

He asks for a sign, not a miracle; he uses neither magic nor divination and does not attempt to force the hand of God. To the storyteller, the fact that the ideal conditions stipulated in the servant's prayer were met precisely signifies that God guided not only the destiny of Isaac and Rebekah but also the prayer of the servant [8]. There is, in the framework of this story, no dividing line between the natural and the supernatural. Biblical man had a deep conviction about God's role in human affairs. God was thought to be approachable, as near as prayer itself, a guide and guardian who like a father looked after his children or like a master looked after his servants.

Abraham's messenger did what most modern men who pray still do: He looked for external manifestations of the Divine. Men who believe in God may differ on what prayer should be or how it is answered; they will disagree on whether the servant had a "right" to ask for a sign; but they themselves will frequently pray as did the servant and say simply, directly, and with hope: "Grant me good fortune."

[1] Another saying: "A heavenly voice goes forth and proclaims: so and so shall marry so and so" [7].

GLEANINGS

The Way of the Bible

The patriarchal stories, like the previous Genesis tales, frequently use numbers as symbols. Abraham lived for 175 years, Isaac 180, Jacob 147. These numbers form a series: 7×5^2 (175), 5×6^2 (180), 3×7^2 (147).

The use of numerical symmetry is Scripture's way of conveying the conviction that the formative age in Israel's history was not a series of haphazard incidents but the fulfilment of God's grand design. . . . The patriarchal chronologies constitute paradigmatic rather than pragmatic history.

NAHUM SARNA [9]

Abraham Was Old

Until Abraham's time old people did not look their age; but Abraham asked God to match his looks to his age.

R. Aha said: "One may have the dignity of old age without its years, or length of days without the dignity of old age." Here, however, the dignity of old age was matched by length of days, and a long life was matched by the dignity of age.

MIDRASH [10]

Rebekah's Decision

She said "I will" (Gen. 24:58), meaning she would go of her own will even without her parents' consent. From this a halachah is derived that even if parents object to a child's moving to the land of Israel (as Rebekah was prepared to do) one need not listen to them. [11]

The Death of Abraham

While sitting under the oak of Mamre, Abraham perceived a flashing of light and a smell of sweet odor, and turning around he saw Death coming toward him in great glory and beauty. And Death said unto Abraham: "Think not, Abraham, that this beauty is mine or that I come thus to every man. Nay, but, if any one is righteous like thee, I thus take a crown and come to him; but, if he is a sinner, I come in great corruption and out of their sins I make a crown for my head, and I shake them with great fear so that they are dismayed." Abraham said to him, "And art thou, indeed, he that is called Death?" He answered and said, "I am the bitter name." But Abraham answered, "I will not go with thee." And Abraham said to Death, "Show us thy corruption." And Death revealed his corruption, showing two heads, the one had the face of a serpent, the other head was like a sword. All the servants of Abraham, looking at the fierce mien of Death, died, but Abraham prayed to the Lord, and He raised them up. As the looks of Death were not able to cause Abraham's soul to depart from him, God removed the soul of Abraham as in a dream, and the archangel Michael took it up into heaven. After great praise and glory had been given to the Lord by the angels who brought Abraham's soul, and after Abraham bowed down to worship, then came the voice of God, saying thus: "Take My friend Abraham into Paradise, where are the tabernacles of My righteous ones and the abodes of My saints Isaac and Jacob in his bosom, where there is no trouble, nor grief, nor sighing, but peace and rejoicing and life unending."

MIDRASH [12]

PART IV

The Line of Isaac

The Twins

With Abraham's death we might expect the Bible's attention to focus on Isaac. But it shifts immediately from him to his children, for Isaac serves primarily as the link between Abraham and Jacob.

The main theme continues: God watches over His chosen ones as they grow in understanding of the divine element in their lives.

ס   ס   ס

יט וְאֵ֗לֶּה תּוֹלְדֹ֛ת יִצְחָ֥ק בֶּן־אַבְרָהָ֖ם אַבְרָהָ֥ם הוֹלִ֖יד

כ אֶת־יִצְחָֽק׃ וַיְהִ֤י יִצְחָק֙ בֶּן־אַרְבָּעִ֣ים שָׁנָ֔ה בְּקַחְתּ֣וֹ אֶת־

רִבְקָ֗ה בַּת־בְּתוּאֵל֙ הָֽאֲרַמִּ֔י מִפַּדַּ֖ן אֲרָ֑ם אֲח֥וֹת לָבָ֛ן

כא הָאֲרַמִּ֖י ל֥וֹ לְאִשָּֽׁה׃ וַיֶּעְתַּ֨ר יִצְחָ֤ק לַֽיהוָה֙ לְנֹ֣כַח אִשְׁתּ֔וֹ

כִּ֥י עֲקָרָ֖ה הִ֑וא וַיֵּעָ֤תֶר לוֹ֙ יְהוָ֔ה וַתַּ֖הַר רִבְקָ֥ה אִשְׁתּֽוֹ׃

כב וַיִּתְרֹֽצֲצ֤וּ הַבָּנִים֙ בְּקִרְבָּ֔הּ וַתֹּ֣אמֶר אִם־כֵּ֔ן לָ֥מָּה זֶּ֖ה

כג אָנֹ֑כִי וַתֵּ֖לֶךְ לִדְרֹ֥שׁ אֶת־יְהוָֽה׃ וַיֹּ֨אמֶר יְהוָ֜ה לָ֗הּ שְׁנֵ֤י

*גֹיִים֙ בְּבִטְנֵ֔ךְ וּשְׁנֵ֣י לְאֻמִּ֔ים מִמֵּעַ֖יִךְ יִפָּרֵ֑דוּ וּלְאֹם֙

* כג גוים קרי.

Genesis 25

19–23

19] This is the story of Isaac, son of Abraham. Abraham begot Isaac.   20] Isaac was forty years old when he took to wife Rebekah, daughter of Bethuel the Aramean of Paddan-aram, sister of Laban the Aramean.   21] Isaac pleaded with the LORD on behalf of his wife, because she was barren; and the LORD responded to his plea, and his wife Rebekah conceived.   22] But the children struggled in her womb, and she said, "If so, why do I exist?" She went to inquire of the LORD, 23] and the LORD answered her, "Two nations are in your womb, / Two peoples apart while still in your body; / One people shall be mightier than the other, /

25:19] *The story.* Or "the line."

20] *Paddan-aram.* The area where Haran was located. The name came into use after the Arameans displaced the Hurrians.

21] *Barren.* For twenty years. Isaac was forty years old when he married and sixty when his children were born (Gen. 25:26). On the theme of barrenness, see Gen. 16:2. The Bible considers Rebekah's condition to be God's will.

22] *If so, why do I exist?* The intent of the Hebrew text is uncertain. Rebekah is probably asking, "What good is life if I have to suffer like this?"

She went to inquire. Rebekah consulted an oracle. The answer she is given explains her pain: She will give birth to twins who are at strife within her womb and who will be at odds with each other in years to come.

/ Rashi, like the Midrash: "She inquired at the teaching house of Shem."/

כד מִלְאֹם יֶאֱמָץ וְרַב יַעֲבֹד צָעִיר: וַיִּמְלְאוּ יָמֶיהָ לָלֶדֶת

כה וְהִנֵּה תוֹמִ֗ם בְּבִטְנָהּ: וַיֵּצֵא הָרִאשׁוֹן אַדְמוֹנִי כֻּלּוֹ

כו כְּאַדֶּרֶת שֵׂעָר וַיִּקְרְאוּ שְׁמוֹ עֵשָׂו: וְאַחֲרֵי־כֵן יָצָא אָחִיו וְיָדוֹ אֹחֶזֶת בַּעֲקֵב עֵשָׂו וַיִּקְרָא שְׁמוֹ יַעֲקֹב

כז וְיִצְחָק בֶּן־שִׁשִּׁים שָׁנָה בְּלֶדֶת אֹתָם: וַיִּגְדְּלוּ הַנְּעָרִים וַיְהִי עֵשָׂו אִישׁ יֹדֵעַ צַיִד אִישׁ שָׂדֶה וְיַעֲקֹב אִישׁ תָּם

כח יֹשֵׁב אֹהָלִים: וַיֶּאֱהַב יִצְחָק אֶת־עֵשָׂו כִּי־צַיִד בְּפִיו:

* כד חסר.

And the older shall serve the younger." 24] When her time to give birth was at hand, there were twins in her womb. 25] The first one emerged red, like a hairy mantle all over; so they named him Esau. 26] Then his brother emerged, holding on to the heel of Esau; so they named him Jacob. Isaac was sixty years old when they were born.

27] When the boys grew up, Esau became a skillful hunter, a man of the outdoors; but Jacob was a mild man, who stayed in camp. 28] Isaac favored Esau

25] *Esau.* Possibly related to the Arabic *a'tha* (thick-haired); synonym of שֵׂעִיר (*se-ir*), a word play on שֵׂעָר (*se-ar*, hair). Esau resembles the uncivilized man of "Gilgamesh," Enkidu, who has shaggy hair and lives in open spaces [1].

Esau is later also known as Edom (Gen. 25:30). Esau, Seir, and Edom were probably geographical names originally, which in their application to the son of Isaac became largely interchangeable in the Bible.

26] *Jacob.* יַעֲקֹב, a word play on עֵקֶב (*akev*, heel). The verb means to overreach (Jer. 9:3): Jacob tried to overreach his brother. Other names from the root are Akiba and Ukba. Modern scholars compare the name Jacob with Yakub-el (May El protect), a name found in numerous Syrian and Mesopotamian documents of the early second millennium B.C.E. [2].

/Note also A. Jeremias, who finds the ancient circle motif in Jacob's holding onto Esau's heel and compares it to the Eve-and-snake circle. Jacob in turn fears that Esau will try to crush him [3]./

27] *A mild man.* תָּם (*tam*) can also mean "simple" as in the Passover Haggadah in reference to the third son. Jacob, the mild indoor man, rather than Esau, the outdoor man and hunter, emerges as God's favorite.

/Compare also the stories of Parsifal and others that cast the physically inferior (or even the "perfect fool") in the role of hero. In Oriental tales the huntsman belongs to the lower (i.e., undesirable) world [4]./

28] *He had a taste for game.* Literally, "game was in his mouth." The literal reading may reflect the ancient custom of relatives pre-chewing food for children and old parents [5].

כט וְרִבְקָה אֹהֶבֶת אֶת־יַעֲקֹב: וַיָּזֶד יַעֲקֹב נָזִיד וַיָּבֹא
ל עֵשָׂו מִן־הַשָּׂדֶה וְהוּא עָיֵף: וַיֹּאמֶר עֵשָׂו אֶל־יַעֲקֹב
הַלְעִיטֵנִי נָא מִן־הָאָדֹם הָאָדֹם הַזֶּה כִּי עָיֵף אָנֹכִי
לא עַל־כֵּן קָרָא־שְׁמוֹ אֱדוֹם: וַיֹּאמֶר יַעֲקֹב מִכְרָה כַיּוֹם
לב אֶת־בְּכֹרָתְךָ לִי: וַיֹּאמֶר עֵשָׂו הִנֵּה אָנֹכִי הוֹלֵךְ לָמוּת
לג וְלָמָּה־זֶּה לִי בְּכֹרָה: וַיֹּאמֶר יַעֲקֹב הִשָּׁבְעָה לִּי כַּיּוֹם
לד וַיִּשָּׁבַע לוֹ וַיִּמְכֹּר אֶת־בְּכֹרָתוֹ לְיַעֲקֹב: וְיַעֲקֹב נָתַן
לְעֵשָׂו לֶחֶם וּנְזִיד עֲדָשִׁים וַיֹּאכַל וַיֵּשְׁתְּ וַיָּקָם וַיֵּלַךְ
וַיִּבֶז עֵשָׂו אֶת־הַבְּכֹרָה: פ

Genesis 25
29–34

because he had a taste for game; but Rebekah loved Jacob.   29] Once when Jacob was cooking a stew, Esau came in from the open, famished.   30] And Esau said to Jacob, "Give me some of that red stuff to gulp down, for I am famished"—which is why he was named Edom.   31] Jacob said, "First sell me your birthright."   32] And Esau said, "I am at the point of death, so of what use is my birthright to me?"   33] But Jacob said, "Swear to me first." So he swore to him, and sold his birthright to Jacob.   34] Jacob then gave Esau bread and lentil stew; and he ate, drank, rose, and went his way. Thus did Esau spurn the birthright.

29] *Was cooking.* Among nomads and semi-nomads the males often prepared the food.
30] *Edom.* אֱדוֹם, word play on אָדֹם (*adom*, red); others relate the word to *idam*, an Arabic dish [6]. Esau wants to "gulp down" the food and this depicts him as the uncouth, outdoor man.

The Birthright

In many cultures the first-born son has had preferred inheritance and status, succeeding his father as head of the family. In Canaan as in various Near Eastern countries, he received a double portion of inheritance and was given a seat of honor amongst his brothers (Gen. 43:33). In Judaism he had a special relation not only to his parents and siblings but also to God. He was considered quasi-holy, set aside as a possession of God (like the first fruit of herd and field), and this relationship was recognized in ceremonial ways (as in Exod. 13:12-15; 34:20; Num. 18:15; and the custom of *pidyon ha-ben*, redeeming the first-born on the thirtieth day of his life, which still survives in traditional Jewish practice). The people of Israel were called God's first-born (Exod. 4:22), which meant that they had a particular position in the divine scheme.

First-born status came through natural birth, although in early biblical days the right could be lost because of a misdeed as in Reuben's case (Gen. 49:3-4; I Chron. 5:1), cancelled through blessings as in Ephraim's case (Gen. 48:13-20), or sold as in Esau's case.[1] In later biblical times, depriving the first-born of his rights was expressly forbidden (Deut. 21:15-17).

While the natural order of birth was believed to have divine approval, God was not bound by it in an automatic relationship. He remains free to change His mind and to choose whom He needs in critical moments of history. This is the meaning of the recurrent theme of preferring the younger brother to the older. Many of Israel's great men came to their prominence because God took them out of their inferior natural position: Joseph, Ephraim, Moses, and David all were second- or late-born. While the sibling motif is not unique to biblical tradition—the Greeks have the story of Akrisios and Proitos, the Romans of Romulus and Remus—it is an important and even essential way of showing how divine guidance continually governs the history of Israel. For, though Jacob's acquisition of the birthright is given a legal basis,[2] the story is primarily one of spiritual blessings rather than legal advantages.

The Moral Problem

Buying and selling, indeed any change of birthright was no ordinary matter, yet here this important right is bartered away in what appears to be a shoddy manner. How could divine privilege come to a man such as Jacob who emerges from the story as somewhat less than admirable?

Some interpreters stress the folksy nature of the tale, saying that it is intended to make the listener or reader laugh at the way the stupid Esau stumbled into the trap laid by the clever Jacob. In those days, they say, Jacob's action was not subject to disapproval, so that the tale was one of gamesmanship without moral overtones [10].

Other commentators deny any presence of humor and, instead, see Jacob desperately striving to become the one who carries on the religious heritage of his fathers. Jewish tradition interpreted the fact that he "stayed in camp" to mean that he gave himself to learning and study and that through meditation came to a knowledge of God [11]. He believed himself to be more suited for the great task than Esau and, therefore, would not let this boorish and obviously indifferent brother stand in his way [12].

This latter theme is also pursued by others

---

[1] Nuzi records also deal with these relationships, and a document from northwest Syria permits the prenatal selection of the first-born [7].

[2] This was hermeneutically derived from כַּיּוֹם in Gen. 25:33 [8]. The lentil stew was considered a token of the sale, not the true price [9].

who try to exculpate Jacob.[3] Esau was a hunter, they say, whose chief pleasure in life was killing and eating. "Esau's belly was his god; Esau's want lay in his fleshly appetite" [15]. He despised the birthright that he should have held sacred; to satisfy his appetite, he was willing to sacrifice eternity.

In this way the story is seen as a paradigm, i.e., as presenting a truth applicable to other men and other times. Esau stands for the run-of-the-mill man, Jacob for the exception. As Roger Williams wrote 300 years ago:

"What are all the contentions and wars of this world about, generally, but for greater dishes and bowls of porridge, of which, if we believe God's Spirit in Scripture, Esau and Jacob were types? Esau will part with the heavenly birthright for his supping, after his hunting, for god belly; and Jacob will part with porridge for an eternal inheritance" [16].

But although such explanations establish that Jacob was in fact more capable than his brother to carry the divine responsibility, they do not answer the question: Are the means Jacob employs to gain his ends morally justifiable? The answer must be no. On closer examination the Bible itself makes this judgment on Jacob. But the judgment is implicit, not explicit; it must be seen in the full context of Jacob's life, which develops into a tragedy.[4]

Where Abraham's life was struggle and triumph and Isaac's essentially one of quiescence and persistence, Jacob's is a long succession of trials and tragedies. What he touches often turns to ashes; from the moment he grasps his brother's heel at birth he desperately tries to fashion his fortune. Yet even as he succeeds, he fails. The doubtful exchange of food for birthright brings him a brother's enmity and still does not insure him his father's blessing. He deceives his father and will be deceived in turn by Laban; he will lose his beloved wife and his favorite son; and he will end his days in a strange land, a pensioner of his child. It is no wonder he will say in restrospect that his years were "few and evil" (Gen. 47:9) [18].

There is then a judgment; it lies in the tragic biography of a God-seeker who comprehends neither how to seek nor how to find. Much will happen before he becomes Israel. His failures and successes, his sufferings and joys, as well as his moral debilities and strengths, will foreshadow what will happen to the people who bear his name.

---

[3] A favorite explanation: Esau was wicked from the moment he was born and even before [13]. But one tradition at least suggests that, since the birthright was obtained by cunning, Jacob's descendants were destined to serve the descendants of Esau [14].

[4] See notes at Gen. 29:25, 26. Sarna, however, finds the Bible's disapproval to be quite explicit and remarkable as a moral stance at a time when what Jacob did was perfectly acceptable [17].

GLEANINGS

Heel and Hand

In allegorical language the present corrupt age is presented as Esau, the glorious age which is to follow at once is represented as Jacob: Jacob's hand held Esau's heel from the beginning. The "heel" of the first age is Esau; the "hand" of the second is Jacob. "The beginning of a man is his hand, and the end of a man is his heel. Between heel and hand seek for nothing else, Ezra!"

ESDRAS [19]

The Fateful Day

Esau sold his birthright on the day of Abraham's death; had the latter lived to see Esau despise his birthright, he could not have been said to have died in ripe old age. Jacob had prepared a mourner's meal. Why lentils? Because they are round, and mourning rolls from one person to another. Further, as lentils have no opening, so should one while mourning speak of no extraneous matters. From this also derives the custom of serving eggs at the beginning of a mourner's meal, for they roll and have no opening.   RASHI

Esau's Failing

Esau was huntsman, nothing but huntsman, delivered up, heart and soul, body and spirit, to the ferocious pursuit of food when that stage of human subjection to nature had been left behind. He was a throwback, a case of arrested development. He despised his birthright as a civilized man, and how much more his birthright as the son of Isaac and the grandson of Abraham!

MAURICE SAMUEL [20]

A Psychological Interpretation

The submissive father encouraged in his son, Esau, what was repressed in him during his own childhood—the freedom of the hunter. The aggressive mother liked Jacob more, because she could not dominate the freer Esau as she dominated her husband and the younger twin. Each of the twins was only half-loved. Insufficiently loved by his feminine father, Jacob was filled with fear. Insufficiently loved by his masculine mother, Esau was filled with hate. It took the therapy of life's hardships before the twins matured enough to respect each other and be reconciled. The records of the families of the Bible are as up-to-date as modern texts in child rearing and much more fascinating because they are better written.

HENRY E. KAGAN [21]

The Life of Isaac

This one brief chapter relates the adult years of Isaac. The only other references to him concern his youth and his old age.

The episode in Gerar is an almost exact duplicate of Abraham's experience in the same city (Gen. 20). In both cases the Patriarch, in order to protect himself, states that his female companion is his "sister." Bible critics suggest that the duplication of these stories may be traced to two literary variants of one basic tradition, the first authored by E (in chapter 20), the second by J (in chapter 26). The basic differences in the tales are that in the J-version there is no divine intervention and no gifts are offered.

א וַיְהִי רָעָב בָּאָרֶץ מִלְּבַד הָרָעָב הָרִאשׁוֹן אֲשֶׁר הָיָה
בִּימֵי אַבְרָהָם וַיֵּלֶךְ יִצְחָק אֶל־אֲבִימֶלֶךְ מֶלֶךְ־
ב פְּלִשְׁתִּים גְּרָרָה: וַיֵּרָא אֵלָיו יְהֹוָה וַיֹּאמֶר אַל־תֵּרֵד
ג מִצְרַיְמָה שְׁכֹן בָּאָרֶץ אֲשֶׁר אֹמַר אֵלֶיךָ: גּוּר בָּאָרֶץ
הַזֹּאת וְאֶהְיֶה עִמְּךָ וַאֲבָרֲכֶךָּ כִּי־לְךָ וּלְזַרְעֲךָ אֶתֵּן
אֶת־כָּל־הָאֲרָצֹת הָאֵל וַהֲקִמֹתִי אֶת־הַשְּׁבֻעָה אֲשֶׁר
ד נִשְׁבַּעְתִּי לְאַבְרָהָם אָבִיךָ: וְהִרְבֵּיתִי אֶת־זַרְעֲךָ
כְּכוֹכְבֵי הַשָּׁמַיִם וְנָתַתִּי לְזַרְעֲךָ אֵת כָּל־הָאֲרָצֹת
ה הָאֵל וְהִתְבָּרֲכוּ בְזַרְעֲךָ כֹּל גּוֹיֵי הָאָרֶץ: עֵקֶב אֲשֶׁר־
שָׁמַע אַבְרָהָם בְּקֹלִי וַיִּשְׁמֹר מִשְׁמַרְתִּי מִצְוֺתַי חֻקּוֹתַי
ו וְתוֹרֹתָי: וַיֵּשֶׁב יִצְחָק בִּגְרָר: וַיִּשְׁאֲלוּ אַנְשֵׁי הַמָּקוֹם

Genesis 26
1–7

1] There was a famine in the land—aside from the previous famine that had occurred in the days of Abraham—and Isaac went to Abimelech, king of the Philistines, in Gerar.   2] The LORD had appeared to him and said, "Do not go down to Egypt; stay in the land which I point out to you.   3] Reside in this land, and I will be with you and bless you; I will give all these lands to you and to your offspring, fulfilling the oath that I swore to your father Abraham.   4] I will make your descendants as numerous as the stars of heaven, and give to your descendants all these lands, so that all the nations of the earth shall bless themselves by your offspring— 5] inasmuch as Abraham obeyed Me and followed My mandate: My commandments, My laws, and My teachings."

6] So Isaac stayed in Gerar.   7] When the men of the place asked him about

26:1] *Abimelech.* Apparently the same king who figured in the similar incident in the Abraham story (chapter 20). In both cases the king's chief officer is called Phicol.

King of the Philistines. An anachronism. Most scholars believe that the Philistines came to Canaan ca. 1200 B.C.E., much after Isaac's day, suggesting that the story comes from a later time when Philistines were prominent in the land and appeared to have been there for many centuries.

Gerar. See note at Gen. 20:1.

לְאִשְׁתּוֹ וַיֹּאמֶר אֲחֹתִי הִוא כִּי יָרֵא לֵאמֹר אִשְׁתִּי פֶּן־
יַהַרְגֻנִי אַנְשֵׁי הַמָּקוֹם עַל־רִבְקָה כִּי־טוֹבַת מַרְאֶה
הִוא: וַיְהִי כִּי אָרְכוּ־לוֹ שָׁם הַיָּמִים וַיַּשְׁקֵף אֲבִימֶלֶךְ
מֶלֶךְ פְּלִשְׁתִּים בְּעַד הַחַלוֹן וַיַּרְא וְהִנֵּה יִצְחָק מְצַחֵק
אֵת רִבְקָה אִשְׁתּוֹ: וַיִּקְרָא אֲבִימֶלֶךְ לְיִצְחָק וַיֹּאמֶר
אַךְ הִנֵּה אִשְׁתְּךָ הִוא וְאֵיךְ אָמַרְתָּ אֲחֹתִי הִוא וַיֹּאמֶר
אֵלָיו יִצְחָק כִּי אָמַרְתִּי פֶּן־אָמוּת עָלֶיהָ: וַיֹּאמֶר
אֲבִימֶלֶךְ מַה־זֹּאת עָשִׂיתָ לָּנוּ כִּמְעַט שָׁכַב אַחַד הָעָם
אֶת־אִשְׁתֶּךָ וְהֵבֵאתָ עָלֵינוּ אָשָׁם: וַיְצַו אֲבִימֶלֶךְ אֶת־
כָּל־הָעָם לֵאמֹר הַנֹּגֵעַ בָּאִישׁ הַזֶּה וּבְאִשְׁתּוֹ מוֹת יוּמָת:
וַיִּזְרַע יִצְחָק בָּאָרֶץ הַהִוא וַיִּמְצָא בַּשָּׁנָה הַהִוא מֵאָה

Genesis 26
8–12

his wife, he said, "She is my sister," for he was afraid to say "my wife," thinking,
"The men of the place might kill me on account of Rebekah, for she is beautiful."
8] When some time had passed, Abimelech king of the Philistines, looking out of
the window, saw Isaac fondling his wife Rebekah.   **9]** Abimelech sent for Isaac
and said, "So she is your wife! Why then did you say: She is my sister?" Isaac said
to him, "Because I thought I might lose my life on account of her."   **10]** Abimelech
said, "See what you have done to us! One of the people might have lain with your
wife, and you would have brought guilt upon us."   **11]** Abimelech then charged
all the people, saying, "Anyone who molests this man or his wife shall be put to
death."

12] Isaac sowed in that land and reaped a hundredfold the same year. The LORD

8] *Isaac fondling.* יִצְחָק מְצַחֵק, a word play similar to Gen. 21:9.

12] *A hundredfold.* Many times. Isaac does occasional
farming and comes close to settling permanently.

שְׁעָרִים וַיְבָרֲכֵהוּ יְהֹוָה: וַיִּגְדַּל הָאִישׁ וַיֵּלֶךְ הָלוֹךְ

וְגָדֵל עַד כִּי־גָדַל מְאֹד: וַיְהִי־לוֹ מִקְנֵה־צֹאן וּמִקְנֵה

בָקָר וַעֲבֻדָּה רַבָּה וַיְקַנְאוּ אֹתוֹ פְּלִשְׁתִּים: וְכָל־

הַבְּאֵרֹת אֲשֶׁר חָפְרוּ עַבְדֵי אָבִיו בִּימֵי אַבְרָהָם אָבִיו

סִתְּמוּם פְּלִשְׁתִּים וַיְמַלְאוּם עָפָר: וַיֹּאמֶר אֲבִימֶלֶךְ

אֶל־יִצְחָק לֵךְ מֵעִמָּנוּ כִּי־עָצַמְתָּ מִמֶּנּוּ מְאֹד: וַיֵּלֶךְ

מִשָּׁם יִצְחָק וַיִּחַן בְּנַחַל־גְּרָר וַיֵּשֶׁב שָׁם: וַיָּשָׁב יִצְחָק

וַיַּחְפֹּר אֶת־בְּאֵרֹת הַמַּיִם אֲשֶׁר חָפְרוּ בִּימֵי אַבְרָהָם

אָבִיו וַיְסַתְּמוּם פְּלִשְׁתִּים אַחֲרֵי מוֹת אַבְרָהָם וַיִּקְרָא

לָהֶן שֵׁמוֹת כַּשֵּׁמֹת אֲשֶׁר־קָרָא לָהֶן אָבִיו: וַיַּחְפְּרוּ

עַבְדֵי־יִצְחָק בַּנָּחַל וַיִּמְצְאוּ־שָׁם בְּאֵר מַיִם חַיִּים:

Genesis 26
13–19

blessed him,   13] and the man grew richer and richer until he was very wealthy:
14] he had acquired flocks and herds, and a large household, so that the Philistines
envied him.   15] And the Philistines stopped up all the wells which his father's
servants had dug in the days of his father Abraham, filling them with earth.
16] And Abimelech said to Isaac, "Go away from us, for you have become far too
big for us."

17] Isaac departed from there; he encamped in the valley of Gerar and settled
there.   18] Isaac dug anew the water wells which had been dug in the days of his
father Abraham and which the Philistines had stopped up after Abraham's death;
and he gave them the same names that his father had given them.   19] But
when Isaac's servants, digging in the valley, found there a well of spring water,

15] *Wells.* They belonged to the person who dug
them. Stopping them up was a most serious in-
vasion of property rights in an area where water
was precious.

18] *The same names.* Meaning, "these wells have
belonged to my family."

19] *Spring water.* Literally, "living water." This
was later given a figurative meaning.

כ וַיָּרִיבוּ רֹעֵי גְרָר עִם־רֹעֵי יִצְחָק לֵאמֹר לָנוּ הַמָּיִם

כא וַיִּקְרָא שֵׁם־הַבְּאֵר עֵשֶׂק כִּי הִתְעַשְּׂקוּ עִמּוֹ: וַיַּחְפְּרוּ

בְּאֵר אַחֶרֶת וַיָּרִיבוּ גַּם־עָלֶיהָ וַיִּקְרָא שְׁמָהּ שִׂטְנָה:

כב וַיַּעְתֵּק מִשָּׁם וַיַּחְפֹּר בְּאֵר אַחֶרֶת וְלֹא רָבוּ עָלֶיהָ

וַיִּקְרָא שְׁמָהּ רְחֹבוֹת וַיֹּאמֶר כִּי־עַתָּה הִרְחִיב יְהוָה

כג לָנוּ וּפָרִינוּ בָאָרֶץ: וַיַּעַל מִשָּׁם בְּאֵר שָׁבַע: וַיֵּרָא

כד אֵלָיו יְהוָה בַּלַּיְלָה הַהוּא וַיֹּאמֶר אָנֹכִי אֱלֹהֵי אַבְרָהָם

אָבִיךָ אַל־תִּירָא כִּי־אִתְּךָ אָנֹכִי וּבֵרַכְתִּיךָ וְהִרְבֵּיתִי

כה אֶת־זַרְעֲךָ בַּעֲבוּר אַבְרָהָם עַבְדִּי: וַיִּבֶן שָׁם מִזְבֵּחַ

וַיִּקְרָא בְּשֵׁם יְהוָה וַיֶּט־שָׁם אָהֳלוֹ וַיִּכְרוּ־שָׁם עַבְדֵי־

כו יִצְחָק בְּאֵר: וַאֲבִימֶלֶךְ הָלַךְ אֵלָיו מִגְּרָר וַאֲחֻזַּת

Genesis 26
20–26

20] the herdsmen of Gerar quarreled with Isaac's herdsmen, saying, "The water is ours." He named that well Esek, because they contended with him.   21] And when they dug another well, they disputed over that one also; so he named it Sitnah. 22] He moved from there and dug yet another well, and they did not quarrel over it; so he called it Rehoboth, saying, "Now at last the LORD has granted us ample space to increase in the land."

23] From there he went up to Beer-sheba.   24] That night the LORD appeared to him and said, "I am the God of your father Abraham. Fear not, for I am with you, and I will bless you and increase your offspring for the sake of Abraham My servant."   25] There he built an altar and invoked the LORD by name; there too he pitched his tent and Isaac's servants started digging a well.   26] And Abimelech

---

20] *Esek*. Contention.

21] *Sitnah*. Harassment.

22] *Rehoboth*. רְחֹבוֹת connected with רָחָב (ample, broad space). The location was some short distance southwest of Beer-sheba, not where today's Rehovot is found.

24] *For the sake of My servant Abraham*. On the principle of the merit of one's forebears, see p. 185.

כז מֵרֵעֵהוּ וּפִיכֹל שַׂר־צְבָאוֹ: וַיֹּאמֶר אֲלֵהֶם יִצְחָק מַדּוּעַ בָּאתֶם אֵלָי וְאַתֶּם שְׂנֵאתֶם אֹתִי וַתְּשַׁלְּחוּנִי מֵאִתְּכֶם:

כח וַיֹּאמְרוּ רָאוֹ רָאִינוּ כִּי־הָיָה יְהֹוָה עִמָּךְ וַנֹּאמֶר תְּהִי נָא אָלָה בֵּינוֹתֵינוּ בֵּינֵינוּ וּבֵינֶךָ וְנִכְרְתָה בְרִית עִמָּךְ:

כט אִם־תַּעֲשֵׂה עִמָּנוּ רָעָה כַּאֲשֶׁר לֹא נְגַעֲנוּךָ וְכַאֲשֶׁר עָשִׂינוּ עִמְּךָ רַק־טוֹב וַנְּשַׁלֵּחֲךָ בְּשָׁלוֹם אַתָּה עַתָּה בְּרוּךְ יְהֹוָה: ל וַיַּעַשׂ לָהֶם מִשְׁתֶּה וַיֹּאכְלוּ וַיִּשְׁתּוּ:

לא וַיַּשְׁכִּימוּ בַבֹּקֶר וַיִּשָּׁבְעוּ אִישׁ לְאָחִיו וַיְשַׁלְּחֵם יִצְחָק

לב וַיֵּלְכוּ מֵאִתּוֹ בְּשָׁלוֹם: וַיְהִי בַּיּוֹם הַהוּא וַיָּבֹאוּ עַבְדֵי יִצְחָק וַיַּגִּדוּ לוֹ עַל־אֹדוֹת הַבְּאֵר אֲשֶׁר חָפָרוּ וַיֹּאמְרוּ

לג לוֹ מָצָאנוּ מָיִם: וַיִּקְרָא אֹתָהּ שִׁבְעָה עַל־כֵּן שֵׁם־

Genesis 26

27–33

came to him from Gerar, with Ahuzzath his councilor and Phicol chief of his troops. **27]** Isaac said to them, "Why have you come to me, seeing that you have been hostile to me and have driven me away from you?" **28]** And they said, "We now see plainly that the Lord has been with you, and we thought: Let there be a sworn treaty between our two parties, between you and us. Let us make a pact with you **29]** that you will not do us harm, just as we have not molested you but have always dealt kindly with you and sent you away in peace. From now on, be you blessed of the Lord!" **30]** Then he made them a feast, and they ate and drank.

31] Early in the morning, they exchanged oaths. Isaac then bade them farewell, and they departed from him in peace. **32]** That same day Isaac's servants came and told him about the well they had dug, and said to him, "We have found water!" **33]** He named it Shibah; therefore the name of the city is Beer-sheba to this day.

29] *Be you blessed of the Lord.* By this solemn invocation Abimelech cancels the previous decree of expulsion [1].

33] *Shibah.* Beer-sheba is here connected with "oath," and elsewhere with the number seven.

לד הָעִיר בְּאֵר שֶׁבַע עַד הַיּוֹם הַזֶּה: ס וַיְהִי עֵשָׂו בֶּן־
אַרְבָּעִים שָׁנָה וַיִּקַּח אִשָּׁה אֶת־יְהוּדִית בַּת־בְּאֵרִי
לה הַחִתִּי וְאֶת־בָּשְׂמַת בַּת־אֵילֹן הַחִתִּי: וַתִּהְיֶיןָ מֹרַת
רוּחַ לְיִצְחָק וּלְרִבְקָה: ס

34] When Esau was forty years old, he took to wife Judith daughter of Beeri the Hittite, and Basemath daughter of Elon the Hittite;   35] and they were a source of bitterness to Isaac and Rebekah.

34] *When Esau was forty years old.* The same age at which his father Isaac married. The number forty occurs so frequently in the Bible that it may have been a round number: e.g., the Flood lasted forty days (Gen. 7:17); Moses spent forty days and nights on Mount Sinai (Exod. 34:28); Israel spent forty years in the desert (Josh. 5:6); and Elijah fasted forty days (I Kings 19:8).

Judith. This popular Jewish name of our day belonged originally to a Hittite woman. It appears nowhere else in the Bible but does recur in the Apocrypha, where it is the name of a book.

Isaac's Personality

Of the three Patriarchs, Isaac's personality is the least clearly defined. Much in his life is a repetition of Abraham's experience, and some critics have even suggested that Isaac never existed at all, that he was the creation of later legendary amplifications of the Abraham cycle. But it is rather unlikely for any people to invent a tradition with an ancestor of such obvious weaknesses. The biblical record makes Isaac a very real product of realistic circumstances.

He was the child of his parents' old age and was probably overprotected in his youth. Sarah was a woman of strong will, Abraham a man of deep conviction and great status who must have appeared as a towering giant to his son. It is not surprising that when Isaac was being offered as a sacrifice at Moriah he could not even raise his voice in protest. By coincidence (or, as the text seems to suggest, by divine design), the wife who was obtained for him turned out to be aggressive and resourceful, a "manager" [2]. The text is at pains to point out that Rebekah brought Isaac "comfort after his mother's death" (Gen. 24:67), which in contemporary terms may be said to indicate that he saw in Rebekah a mother substitute. Further, he repeated his father's experience with Abimelech, and the wells he dug were the old wells of Abraham.

Bad experiences seem to have followed him. He was nearly sacrificed by his father; he was caught in the crossfire of Sarah's and Hagar's jealousies; his children did not get along with each other; and in old age, when he was stricken with blindness, his wife and son conspired to deceive him, so that the one thing he truly owned, his paternal blessing, was bestowed equivocally on the son he did not prefer.

Still, Isaac had real strengths. He endured Mount Moriah, and the faith of Abraham became a vibrant force in his life. He remained in Palestine, even in times of hardship. He tried his hand at agriculture—a venture his father had not attempted—and became enormously successful at it. He was evidently a man of peace, and he gained the respect of a king who covenanted with him. We know little about his feelings, but we may assume that precisely because of suffering and difficulties, and because he was surrounded by strong and active people, Isaac became a reflective, perhaps even an introverted person (hinted at in Gen. 24:63).

Isaac thus represents an important stage in the patriarchal drama. After the revolutionary and often stormy experiences of his father, the son's life becomes the necessary halting place where new religious insights are absorbed and incorporated into patterns of thought and deed. Isaac is the bridge between Abraham and Jacob, the essential link in the chain of greatness.

GLEANINGS

Old Names

It is suggested that Abraham had named the wells with names which recalled religious experiences, like Adonai-yireh. Stopping these wells up was equivalent to eradicating evidences of Abraham's religion. That is why Isaac gave the wells the old names.　　　　HAKETAV VE-HAKABBALAH

Too Big

Note what Abimelech says to Isaac: "You have become too big for us" (מִמֶּנּוּ). One should translate "through us," meaning: "You have become wealthy at our expense"—an old accusation against the Jew.　　　　NEHAMA LEIBOWITZ [3]

Assimilation

Why did Isaac move away just when conditions were favorable for staying, i.e., after he concluded a covenant with Abimelech [Gen. 26:31]? When Isaac was being harassed, he was in no danger of adopting Philistinian ways, but when peace came he said to himself: "Who knows whether I can preserve my spiritual identity."　　　　MORDECAI HACOHEN [4]

Isaac's Contribution

Nothing spectacular happened to Isaac. He made no particular contribution, no addition to the tradition he received from Abraham; he injected no idea, no startling insight. The tradition arising out of a great intellectual ferment seems, in the life of Isaac, to have reached a plateau.

What, then, did Isaac do? He preserved a tradition; he held on to it; he received it and he was loyal to it. In a world of constant change, in a world where new fashions are sought and new habits constantly arise, in a world that never stops for a moment in its fluctuations, Isaac is not simply a negative character. He is the son of Abraham and the father of Jacob. He kept the chain that was handed to him, and the tradition did not break with him. He remained loyal, and in all of his actions a tradition was preserved.

　　　　MORRIS ADLER [5]

Isaac Was Sacrificed

Was he not so in truth?
What there the child's eyes—wide with fear—
For once have seen, think you they can forget?
The hand—the father's hand—that shyly tender
Used to caress his fever-stricken face—
That arm which once embraced, clung so tightly
As though such nearness were not near enough—
That eye—whose look was longing, care and
　　blessing—
And that whole countenance, that earliest
　　childhood's home,
Whereto old age, long, weary and disheartened,
Still as to some enchanted island flies . . .
And now all this—hand, arm, eye,
　　countenance—
Transformed into a madness filled with God,
Blind, deaf—forgetting his very self.
A single outcry only: "Kill!"
Whose faith was thus—in childhood—crushed
　　by God—
In whom shall he then trust, where feel secure?

　　　　RICHARD BEER-HOFMANN [6]

Isaac Blesses His Sons

The Isaac story combines tragedy and play-acting as it reaches its climax in the tale of parental blessing. Such a blessing was accorded special significance, especially when it was given at life's end. The parent appeared to be in God's stead, and while he had no power to bind the Divinity he invoked his words were believed to reflect prophetic vision. In blessing his sons, Isaac assists God in revealing and confirming the future (see p. 463).

As the story unfolds, observe the strong note of sympathy for Esau and, once again, the absence of explicit moral judgment, which is characteristic of many Genesis-narratives. It is in this section that Rebekah is clearly depicted as wife and mother.

א וַיְהִי כִּי־זָקֵן יִצְחָק וַתִּכְהֶיןָ עֵינָיו מֵרְאֹת וַיִּקְרָא אֶת־
עֵשָׂו בְּנוֹ הַגָּדֹל וַיֹּאמֶר אֵלָיו בְּנִי וַיֹּאמֶר אֵלָיו הִנֵּנִי:
ב וַיֹּאמֶר הִנֵּה־נָא זָקַנְתִּי לֹא יָדַעְתִּי יוֹם מוֹתִי: וְעַתָּה
שָׂא־נָא כֵלֶיךָ תֶּלְיְךָ וְקַשְׁתֶּךָ וְצֵא הַשָּׂדֶה וְצוּדָה לִּי
צֵידָה*: וַעֲשֵׂה־לִי מַטְעַמִּים כַּאֲשֶׁר אָהַבְתִּי וְהָבִיאָה
לִּי וְאֹכֵלָה בַּעֲבוּר תְּבָרֶכְךָ נַפְשִׁי בְּטֶרֶם אָמוּת:
ה וְרִבְקָה שֹׁמַעַת בְּדַבֵּר יִצְחָק אֶל־עֵשָׂו בְּנוֹ וַיֵּלֶךְ עֵשָׂו
הַשָּׂדֶה לָצוּד צַיִד לְהָבִיא: וְרִבְקָה אָמְרָה אֶל־
יַעֲקֹב בְּנָהּ לֵאמֹר הִנֵּה שָׁמַעְתִּי אֶת־אָבִיךְ מְדַבֵּר
אֶל־עֵשָׂו אָחִיךָ לֵאמֹר: הָבִיאָה לִּי צַיִד וַעֲשֵׂה־לִי

* ג ה' יתירה.

1] When Isaac was old and his eyes were too dim to see, he called his older son Esau and said to him, "My son." He answered, "Here I am."   2] And he said, "I am, you see, so old that I do not know how soon I may die.   3] Take, then, your gear, your quiver and bow, and go out into the country and hunt me some game. 4] Then make me a tasty dish such as I like, and bring it to me to eat, so that I may give you my innermost blessing before I die."

5] Rebekah had been listening as Isaac spoke to his son Esau. When Esau had gone out to the country to hunt game to bring home,   6] Rebekah said to her son Jacob, "I overheard your father speaking to your brother Esau, saying,   7] 'Bring

27:2] *I am old now.* Nuzi records indicate that these words were a legal formula introducing a death-bed declaration and last will.

4] *My innermost blessing.* Indicating a blessing of special importance. Eating a meal was probably part of the ritual.

7] *With the Lord's approval.* Rebekah adds this to what Isaac has said in order to convince Jacob that the blessing will have divine sanction, thereby implying that once given it cannot be revoked [1] (see verse 33).

/According to some, Rebekah expected the blessing to have prophetic power [2]./

מַטְעַמִּים וְאֹכֵלָה וַאֲבָרֶכְכָה לִפְנֵי יְהוָה לִפְנֵי מוֹתִי:

ח] וְעַתָּה בְנִי שְׁמַע בְּקֹלִי לַאֲשֶׁר אֲנִי מְצַוָּה אֹתָךְ: לֶךְ־
נָא אֶל־הַצֹּאן וְקַח־לִי מִשָּׁם שְׁנֵי גְּדָיֵי עִזִּים טֹבִים

י] וְאֶעֱשֶׂה אֹתָם מַטְעַמִּים לְאָבִיךָ כַּאֲשֶׁר אָהֵב: וְהֵבֵאתָ
לְאָבִיךָ וְאָכָל בַּעֲבֻר אֲשֶׁר יְבָרֶכְךָ לִפְנֵי מוֹתוֹ:

יא] וַיֹּאמֶר יַעֲקֹב אֶל־רִבְקָה אִמּוֹ הֵן עֵשָׂו אָחִי אִישׁ שָׂעִר

יב] וְאָנֹכִי אִישׁ חָלָק: אוּלַי יְמֻשֵּׁנִי אָבִי וְהָיִיתִי בְעֵינָיו

יג] כִּמְתַעְתֵּעַ וְהֵבֵאתִי עָלַי קְלָלָה וְלֹא בְרָכָה: וַתֹּאמֶר
לוֹ אִמּוֹ עָלַי קִלְלָתְךָ בְּנִי אַךְ שְׁמַע בְּקֹלִי וְלֵךְ קַח־

יד] לִי: וַיֵּלֶךְ וַיִּקַּח וַיָּבֵא לְאִמּוֹ וַתַּעַשׂ אִמּוֹ מַטְעַמִּים

טו] כַּאֲשֶׁר אָהֵב אָבִיו: וַתִּקַּח רִבְקָה אֶת־בִּגְדֵי עֵשָׂו בְּנָהּ
הַגָּדֹל הַחֲמֻדֹת אֲשֶׁר אִתָּהּ בַּבָּיִת וַתַּלְבֵּשׁ אֶת־יַעֲקֹב

טז] בְּנָהּ הַקָּטָן: וְאֵת עֹרֹת גְּדָיֵי הָעִזִּים הִלְבִּישָׁה עַל־

Genesis 27
8–16

me some game and make me a tasty dish to eat that I may bless you, with the LORD's approval, before I die.' 8] Now, my son, listen carefully as I instruct you. 9] Go to the flock and fetch me two choice kids, and I will make of them a tasty dish for your father, such as he likes. 10] Then take it to your father to eat, in order that he may bless you before he dies." 11] Jacob answered his mother Rebekah, "But my brother Esau is a hairy man and I am smooth-skinned. 12] If my father touches me, I shall appear to him as a trickster and bring upon myself a curse, not a blessing." 13] But his mother said to him, "Your curse, my son, be upon me! Just do as I say and go fetch them for me."

14] He got them and brought them to his mother, and his mother prepared a tasty dish such as his father liked. 15] Rebekah then took the best clothes of her older son Esau, which were there in the house, and had her younger son Jacob put them on; 16] and she covered his hands and the hairless part of his neck with

יז יָדָיו וְעַל חֶלְקַת צַוָּארָיו: וַתִּתֵּן אֶת־הַמַּטְעַמִּים וְאֶת־

יח הַלֶּחֶם אֲשֶׁר עָשָׂתָה בְּיַד יַעֲקֹב בְּנָהּ: וַיָּבֹא אֶל־אָבִיו

יט וַיֹּאמֶר אָבִי וַיֹּאמֶר הִנֶּנִּי מִי אַתָּה בְּנִי: וַיֹּאמֶר יַעֲקֹב

אֶל־אָבִיו אָנֹכִי עֵשָׂו בְּכֹרֶךָ עָשִׂיתִי כַּאֲשֶׁר דִּבַּרְתָּ

אֵלָי קוּם־נָא שְׁבָה וְאָכְלָה מִצֵּידִי בַּעֲבוּר תְּבָרֲכַנִּי

כ נַפְשֶׁךָ: וַיֹּאמֶר יִצְחָק אֶל־בְּנוֹ מַה־זֶּה מִהַרְתָּ לִמְצֹא

כא בְּנִי וַיֹּאמֶר כִּי הִקְרָה יְהֹוָה אֱלֹהֶיךָ לְפָנָי: וַיֹּאמֶר

יִצְחָק אֶל־יַעֲקֹב גְּשָׁה־נָּא וַאֲמֻשְׁךָ בְּנִי הַאַתָּה זֶה בְּנִי

כב עֵשָׂו אִם־לֹא: וַיִּגַּשׁ יַעֲקֹב אֶל־יִצְחָק אָבִיו וַיְמֻשֵּׁהוּ

כג וַיֹּאמֶר הַקֹּל קוֹל יַעֲקֹב וְהַיָּדַיִם יְדֵי עֵשָׂו: וְלֹא הִכִּירוֹ

כד כִּי־הָיוּ יָדָיו כִּידֵי עֵשָׂו אָחִיו שְׂעִרֹת וַיְבָרֲכֵהוּ: וַיֹּאמֶר

כה אַתָּה זֶה בְּנִי עֵשָׂו וַיֹּאמֶר אָנִי: וַיֹּאמֶר הַגִּשָׁה לִּי

Genesis 27

17–25

the skins of the kids.   17] Then she put in the hands of her son Jacob the tasty dish and the bread that she had prepared.

18] He went to his father and said, "Father." And he said, "Yes, which of my sons are you?"   19] Jacob said to his father, "I am Esau, your first-born; I have done as you told me. Pray sit up and eat of my game, that you may give me your innermost blessing."   20] Isaac said to his son, "How did you succeed so quickly, my son?" And he said, "Because the Lord your God granted me good fortune."

21] Isaac said to Jacob, "Come closer that I may feel you, my son—whether you are really my son Esau or not."   22] So Jacob drew close to his father Isaac, who said as he felt him, "The voice is the voice of Jacob, but the hands are the hands of Esau."   23] He did not recognize him because his hands were hairy like those of his brother Esau. As he prepared to bless him,   24] he asked, "Are you really my son Esau?" And when he said, "I am,"   25] he said, "Serve me and let me eat of

וְאָכְלָה מִצֵּיד בְּנִי לְמַעַן תְּבָרֶכְךָ נַפְשִׁי וַיַּגֶּשׁ־לוֹ וַיֹּאכַל

כו וַיָּבֵא לוֹ יַיִן וַיֵּשְׁתְּ: וַיֹּאמֶר אֵלָיו יִצְחָק אָבִיו גְּשָׁה־נָּא

כז וּשְׁקָה־לִּי בְּנִי: וַיִּגַּשׁ וַיִּשַּׁק־לוֹ וַיָּרַח אֶת־רֵיחַ בְּגָדָיו

וַיְבָרְכֵהוּ וַיֹּאמֶר רְאֵה רֵיחַ בְּנִי כְּרֵיחַ שָׂדֶה אֲשֶׁר

כח בֵּרֲכוֹ יְהוָה: וְיִתֶּן־לְךָ הָאֱלֹהִים מִטַּל הַשָּׁמַיִם וּמִשְׁמַנֵּי

כט הָאָרֶץ וְרֹב דָּגָן וְתִירֹשׁ: יַעַבְדוּךָ עַמִּים וְיִשְׁתַּחוּ* לְךָ

לְאֻמִּים הֱוֵה גְבִיר לְאַחֶיךָ וְיִשְׁתַּחֲווּ לְךָ בְּנֵי אִמֶּךָ

ל אֹרְרֶיךָ אָרוּר וּמְבָרֲכֶיךָ בָּרוּךְ: וַיְהִי כַּאֲשֶׁר כִּלָּה

יִצְחָק לְבָרֵךְ אֶת־יַעֲקֹב וַיְהִי אַךְ יָצֹא יָצָא יַעֲקֹב

לא מֵאֵת פְּנֵי יִצְחָק אָבִיו וְעֵשָׂו אָחִיו בָּא מִצֵּידוֹ: וַיַּעַשׂ

גַּם־הוּא מַטְעַמִּים וַיָּבֵא לְאָבִיו וַיֹּאמֶר לְאָבִיו יָקֻם

* כט וישתחוו קרי.

my son's game that I may give you my innermost blessing." So he served him and he ate, and he brought him wine and he drank.   26] Then his father Isaac said to him, "Come close and kiss me, my son";   27] and he went up and kissed him. And he smelled his clothes and he blessed him, saying, "See, the smell of my son / Is as the smell of the field / That the LORD has blessed. / 28] May God give you / Of the dew of heaven and the fat of the earth, / Abundance of new grain and wine. / 29] Let peoples serve you, / And nations bow to you; / Be master over your brothers, / And let your mother's sons bow to you. / Cursed be they who curse you, / Blessed be they who bless you."

30] No sooner had Jacob left the presence of his father Isaac—after Isaac had finished blessing Jacob—than his brother Esau came back from his hunt.   31] He too prepared a tasty dish and brought it to his father. And he said to his father,

29] *Bow to you.* The younger one. This had been predicted by the birth oracle (Gen. 25:23).

לב אָבִי וְיֹאכַל מִצֵּיד בְּנוֹ בַּעֲבֻר תְּבָרֲכַנִּי נַפְשֶׁךָ: וַיֹּאמֶר
לוֹ יִצְחָק אָבִיו מִי־אָתָּה וַיֹּאמֶר אֲנִי בִּנְךָ בְכֹרְךָ
לג עֵשָׂו: וַיֶּחֱרַד יִצְחָק חֲרָדָה גְּדֹלָה עַד־מְאֹד וַיֹּאמֶר
מִי־אֵפוֹא הוּא הַצָּד־צַיִד וַיָּבֵא לִי וָאֹכַל מִכֹּל בְּטֶרֶם
לד תָּבוֹא וָאֲבָרֲכֵהוּ גַּם־בָּרוּךְ יִהְיֶה: כִּשְׁמֹעַ עֵשָׂו אֶת־
דִּבְרֵי אָבִיו וַיִּצְעַק צְעָקָה גְּדֹלָה וּמָרָה עַד־מְאֹד
לה וַיֹּאמֶר לְאָבִיו בָּרֲכֵנִי גַם־אָנִי אָבִי: וַיֹּאמֶר בָּא אָחִיךָ
לו בְּמִרְמָה וַיִּקַּח בִּרְכָתֶךָ: וַיֹּאמֶר הֲכִי קָרָא שְׁמוֹ יַעֲקֹב
וַיַּעְקְבֵנִי זֶה פַעֲמַיִם אֶת־בְּכֹרָתִי לָקָח וְהִנֵּה עַתָּה
לז לָקַח בִּרְכָתִי וַיֹּאמַר הֲלֹא־אָצַלְתָּ לִּי בְּרָכָה: וַיַּעַן

Genesis 27
32–37

"Let my father sit up and eat of his son's game, so that you may give me your inner-most blessing." **32]** His father Isaac said to him, "Who are you?" And he said, "Esau, your first-born!" **33]** Isaac was seized with very violent trembling. "Who was it then," he demanded, "that hunted game and brought it to me? Moreover, I ate of it before you came, and I blessed him; now he must remain blessed!" **34]** When Esau heard his father's words, he burst into wild and bitter sobbing, and said to his father, "Bless me too, Father!" **35]** But he answered, "Your brother came with guile and took away your blessing." **36]** [Esau] said, "Was he then named Jacob that he might supplant me these two times? First he took away my birthright and now he has taken away my blessing!" And he added, "Have you not reserved a blessing for me?" **37]** Isaac answered, saying to Esau, "But I have

35] *Came with guile.* In retribution guile will in turn be visited on Jacob (see Gen. 29:25).

36] *Supplant me.* יַעְקְבֵנִי connected with יַעֲקֹב (Jacob); see Gen. 25:26. Esau is saying, "Just be-cause he was named Jacob is no reason to take my rights away" [3]. A second word play is בְּכֹרָתִי־בִּרְכָתִי (my birthright—my blessing). Esau now implies that he was also cheated at the sale of the birthright.

יִצְחָק וַיֹּאמֶר לְעֵשָׂו הֵן גְּבִיר שַׂמְתִּיו לָךְ וְאֶת־כָּל־
אֶחָיו נָתַתִּי לוֹ לַעֲבָדִים וְדָגָן וְתִירֹשׁ סְמַכְתִּיו וּלְכָה

לח אֵפוֹא מָה אֶעֱשֶׂה בְּנִי: וַיֹּאמֶר עֵשָׂו אֶל־אָבִיו הַבְרָכָה
אַחַת הִוא־לְךָ אָבִי בָּרֲכֵנִי גַם־אָנִי אָבִי וַיִּשָּׂא עֵשָׂו

לט קֹלוֹ וַיֵּבְךְּ: וַיַּעַן יִצְחָק אָבִיו וַיֹּאמֶר אֵלָיו הִנֵּה מִשְׁמַנֵּי

מ הָאָרֶץ יִהְיֶה מוֹשָׁבֶךָ וּמִטַּל הַשָּׁמַיִם מֵעָל: וְעַל־חַרְבְּךָ
תִחְיֶה וְאֶת־אָחִיךָ תַּעֲבֹד וְהָיָה כַּאֲשֶׁר תָּרִיד וּפָרַקְתָּ

מא עֻלּוֹ מֵעַל צַוָּארֶךָ: וַיִּשְׂטֹם עֵשָׂו אֶת־יַעֲקֹב עַל־הַבְּרָכָה
אֲשֶׁר בֵּרֲכוֹ אָבִיו וַיֹּאמֶר עֵשָׂו בְּלִבּוֹ יִקְרְבוּ יְמֵי אֵבֶל

מב אָבִי וְאַהַרְגָה אֶת־יַעֲקֹב אָחִי: וַיֻּגַּד לְרִבְקָה אֶת־דִּבְרֵי

Genesis 27
38–42

made him master over you: I have given him all his brothers for servants, and sustained him with grain and wine. What, then, can I still do for you, my son?" 38] And Esau said to his father, "Have you but one blessing, Father? Bless me too, Father!" And Esau wept aloud.   39] And his father Isaac answered, saying to him, "See, your abode shall enjoy the fat of the earth / And the dew of heaven above. / 40] Yet by your sword you shall live, / And you shall serve your brother; / But when you grow restive, / You shall break his yoke from your neck."

41] Now Esau harbored a grudge against Jacob because of the blessing which his father had given him, and Esau said to himself, "Let but the mourning period of my father come, and I will kill my brother Jacob."   42] When the words of

38] *Bless me too, Father.* After these words the Septuagint adds a dramatic touch: ". . . and Isaac was silent."

39] *Enjoy the fat of the earth and.* The Hebrew is not clear. Others translate as "Be away from the fat of the earth and from," referring to the rocky soil of Edom.

40] *When you grow restive.* The meaning of the Hebrew text is unclear. B. Jacob translates: "When you grow rightly restive," meaning "when Israel becomes unjust." Best perhaps is Rashi's explanation: "When you shall suffer" [4].   Some hold that the blessing stems from later times, possibly Solomon's, when Edom broke loose from Israelite subjection.

עֵשָׂו בְּנָהּ הַגָּדֹל וַתִּשְׁלַח וַתִּקְרָא לְיַעֲקֹב בְּנָהּ הַקָּטָן
וַתֹּאמֶר אֵלָיו הִנֵּה עֵשָׂו אָחִיךָ מִתְנַחֵם לְךָ לְהָרְגֶךָ:

מג וְעַתָּה בְנִי שְׁמַע בְּקֹלִי וְקוּם בְּרַח־לְךָ אֶל־לָבָן אָחִי

מד חָרָנָה: וְיָשַׁבְתָּ עִמּוֹ יָמִים אֲחָדִים עַד אֲשֶׁר־תָּשׁוּב

מה חֲמַת אָחִיךָ: עַד־שׁוּב אַף־אָחִיךָ מִמְּךָ וְשָׁכַח אֵת
אֲשֶׁר־עָשִׂיתָ לּוֹ וְשָׁלַחְתִּי וּלְקַחְתִּיךָ מִשָּׁם לָמָה אֶשְׁכַּל

מו גַּם־שְׁנֵיכֶם יוֹם אֶחָד: וַתֹּאמֶר רִבְקָה אֶל־יִצְחָק קַצְתִּי
בְחַיַּי מִפְּנֵי בְּנוֹת חֵת אִם־לֹקֵחַ יַעֲקֹב אִשָּׁה מִבְּנוֹת־
חֵת כָּאֵלֶּה מִבְּנוֹת הָאָרֶץ לָמָה לִּי חַיִּים:

א וַיִּקְרָא יִצְחָק אֶל־יַעֲקֹב וַיְבָרֶךְ אֹתוֹ וַיְצַוֵּהוּ וַיֹּאמֶר לוֹ

Genesis 27; 28
43–46; 1

* מו ק' זעירא.

her older son Esau were reported to Rebekah, she sent for her younger son Jacob
and said to him, "Your brother Esau is consoling himself by planning to kill you.
43] Now then, my son, listen to me. Flee at once to Haran, to my brother Laban.
44] Stay with him a while, until your brother's fury subsides— 45] until your
brother's anger against you subsides—and he forgets what you have done to him.
Then I will fetch you from there. Let me not lose you both in one day!"

46] Rebekah said to Isaac, "I am disgusted with my life because of the Hittite
women. If Jacob marries a Hittite woman like these, from among the native
women, what good will life be to me?"   1] So Isaac sent for Jacob and blessed
him. He instructed him, saying, "You shall not take a wife from among the Canaanite

45] *Lose you both.* If Esau killed Jacob, he in turn
would become a fugitive.

46] *Rebekah said to Isaac.* What follows was most
likely adapted from another tradition (usually
assigned to the P-school). Jacob is not rebuffed
for his behavior nor is he sent away to escape

Esau. The reason for his departure is escape from
a bad marriage. Further, in this tradition, no
deathbed declaration is involved since Isaac will
live another eighty years.
/Rasbham explains the discrepancy by saying that
Rebekah suggested a pretext to have Jacob sent
away. See also the commentary below, pp. 274 f./

ב לֹא־תִקַּח אִשָּׁה מִבְּנוֹת כְּנָעַן: קוּם לֵךְ פַּדֶּנָה אֲרָם

בֵּיתָה בְתוּאֵל אֲבִי אִמֶּךָ וְקַח־לְךָ מִשָּׁם אִשָּׁה מִבְּנוֹת

ג לָבָן אֲחִי אִמֶּךָ: וְאֵל שַׁדַּי יְבָרֵךְ אֹתְךָ וְיַפְרְךָ וְיַרְבֶּךָ

ד וְהָיִיתָ לִקְהַל עַמִּים: וְיִתֶּן־לְךָ אֶת־בִּרְכַּת אַבְרָהָם

לְךָ וּלְזַרְעֲךָ אִתָּךְ לְרִשְׁתְּךָ אֶת־אֶרֶץ מְגֻרֶיךָ אֲשֶׁר־

ה נָתַן אֱלֹהִים לְאַבְרָהָם: וַיִּשְׁלַח יִצְחָק אֶת־יַעֲקֹב וַיֵּלֶךְ

פַּדֶּנָה אֲרָם אֶל־לָבָן בֶּן־בְּתוּאֵל הָאֲרַמִּי אֲחִי רִבְקָה

ו אֵם יַעֲקֹב וְעֵשָׂו: וַיַּרְא עֵשָׂו כִּי־בֵרַךְ יִצְחָק אֶת־יַעֲקֹב

וְשִׁלַּח אֹתוֹ פַּדֶּנָה אֲרָם לָקַחַת־לוֹ מִשָּׁם אִשָּׁה בְּבָרְכוֹ

אֹתוֹ וַיְצַו עָלָיו לֵאמֹר לֹא־תִקַּח אִשָּׁה מִבְּנוֹת

ז כְּנָעַן: וַיִּשְׁמַע יַעֲקֹב אֶל־אָבִיו וְאֶל־אִמּוֹ וַיֵּלֶךְ פַּדֶּנָה

women.   2] Up, go to Paddan-aram, to the house of Bethuel, your mother's father, and take a wife there from among the daughters of Laban, your mother's brother. 3] May El Shaddai bless you, make you fertile and numerous, so that you become a community of peoples.   4] May He grant you the blessing of Abraham, to you and your offspring; that you may possess the land where you are sojourning, which God gave to Abraham."

5] Then Isaac sent Jacob off, and he went to Paddan-aram, to Laban the son of Bethuel the Aramean, the brother of Rebekah, mother of Jacob and Esau.

6] When Esau saw that Isaac had blessed Jacob and sent him off to Paddan-aram to take a wife from there, charging him, as he blessed him, "You shall not take a wife from among the Canaanite women,"   7] and that Jacob had obeyed his

28:3] *Make you fertile.* Isaac has already bestowed on Jacob four other blessings: agricultural fertility, governmental sovereignty, and physical and spiritual salubrity. Only the final biblical category of blessings, military sovereignty, is withheld from Jacob. This is reserved for Esau, although given to him in an equivocal manner (Gen. 27:40) [5].

ח אֲרָם: וַיַּרְא עֵשָׂו כִּי רָעוֹת בְּנוֹת כְּנָעַן בְּעֵינֵי יִצְחָק

ט אָבִיו: וַיֵּלֶךְ עֵשָׂו אֶל־יִשְׁמָעֵאל וַיִּקַּח אֶת־מַחֲלַת

בַּת־יִשְׁמָעֵאל בֶּן־אַבְרָהָם אֲחוֹת נְבָיוֹת עַל־נָשָׁיו לוֹ

לְאִשָּׁה:

ח–ט

Haftarah Toledot, p. 539

father and mother and gone to Paddan-aram,   8] Esau realized that the Canaanite women displeased his father Isaac.   9] So Esau went to Ishmael and took to wife, in addition to the wives he had, Mahalath the daughter of Ishmael, sister of Nebaioth.

9] *Sister of Nebaioth.* Nebaioth is Ishmael's first-born (Gen. 25:13). Esau marries his first cousin.

The Deception

This story is bound to leave us with the same moral questions we asked at the sale of the birthright (Gen. 25:29–34). Again, Jacob does not come off very well. He practices outrageous deceit on a helpless father and a guileless brother, and he is rewarded for his deed. It has therefore been suggested that (as in the story of the birthright) the tale was originally told as a comedy: a goat cooked to taste like venison, the kid-skinned hands, the bumbling old father, the mother behind the door, and the inevitable dénouement. Such deception is said to have been an acceptable means of achieving God's purpose, because when these stories were first told morality and religion were presumably not yet clearly fixed or closely connected.[1]

But pathos rather than comedy is the story's main characteristic, and, moreover, Jacob's immorality does find its implicit judgment in the unfolding of his life, which turns into a prolonged tragedy (see p. 251). Jacob bears the burden of guilt all his lifetime and pays dearly for Esau's tears.[2] Ancient Jewish commentators even suggested that Jacob's entire heritage was weighted with this memory [9].

Ironically, Jacob and Rebekah involve themselves in moral turpitude in order to achieve what God would have brought to pass in any case. Here, too, lies the deeper issue of so many biblical stories: How free is man within the context of God's purposes? The Bible gives no explicit answer but implies that man is free to act morally or immorally. While what he does may not ultimately alter events, he is judged only on intent and deed, not on success or failure.

Was Isaac Really Deceived?

As we read the story with close attention to the personality of Isaac, we are led to conclude that throughout the episode he is subconsciously aware of Jacob's identity. However, since he is unable to admit this knowledge, he pretends to be deceived. Seen in this context, the tale contains a plot within a plot; Rebekah and Jacob lay elaborate plans for deceiving Isaac, while unknown to them Isaac looks for ways to deceive himself, in order that he might carry out God's design (though he does not really want to do it), namely, to bless his less-loved son [10].

Isaac is old, but not senile; his blessings are highly sophisticated. He has no doubts about Esau's identity; the latter's single word הִנֵּנִי (here I am) in chapter 27, verse 1 is enough to establish it, while Jacob's single word אָבִי (father) in verse 18 arouses doubt, so that no amount of play-acting, false skins, and goat-disguised-as-venison can really deceive Isaac. But he *wants* to be misled; in his heart he has long known that Esau cannot carry the burden of Abraham and that, instead, his quiet and complicated younger son must be chosen. Weak and indecisive man and father that he is, Isaac does not have the courage to face Esau with the truth. His own blindness and the ruse of Rebekah come literally as a godsend.[3] Consciously he cannot admit to knowing the identity of Jacob in verse 23; subconsciously he is relieved. So he proceeds and, as a start, gives a blessing of material goods to Jacob. Then comes the hardest part, the pathetic confrontation with Esau—the father trembling and the son weeping bitterly. Only when this is past can

---

[1] So Gunkel, who says tendentiously that "the hearers [of the story] are the happy heirs of the deceivers" [6]. The Church Fathers, like the Rabbis, excused the ruse. Jerome called it a laudable lie; others like Theodoret and Aquinas noted that Jacob, having acquired the birthright, was entitled to the blessing. Augustine saw Jacob as Jesus disguised: Jacob supplants Esau, as Jesus will assist the Gentiles to supplant the Jews; hence "it is not a deception but a divine mystery" [7].

[2] One view suggests that Esau's tears made Israel's exile bitter [8].

[3] Rashi says that Isaac grew dim-eyed so that Jacob might get the blessing.

Isaac call Jacob without anxiety and complete the blessing by invoking the memory of Abraham. Note that Isaac does not reprimand Jacob, for how can he who deceived himself be angry at deceit! In a sense, no one, not even Esau, is deceived, for he too knows that Jacob and not he is the chosen one [11].

Even in this reading of the story, however, the problem of Jacob's morality remains the same, for Jacob believes that he is deceiving his father and he acts on this belief.

Rebekah

The biblical text yields enough information about Rebekah to allow the reader to draw her personality in some detail. Her behavior at the well shows her basic qualities: She is utterly courteous, she is concerned for man and beast, she is modest, and she is deferential to her own family. She is also beautiful and appears self-assured and at ease with the stranger who meets her at the well. In other words, she is the perfect picture of a desirable and virtuous young woman.

She marries a man who sees in her a mother substitute (see p. 261) and who wants to be dominated. Indeed, she appears to manage both husband and household together [12].

Faced with a strong and independent son, Esau, she leaves him to his father, while she favors her younger son, who remains at home and gives promise of being as submissive as his father. She has little compunction in doing what she thinks ought to be done and, therefore, on the spur of the moment, invents a deception that she hopes will help her husband do the right thing.

Rebekah is what natural gifts and her marriage to Isaac have made her—clever, strong-willed, and clear-eyed, a mother who loves both of her children (Gen. 27:45) but loves them differently, a woman who finds herself in the chain of greatness and who attempts to shape a fate that she glimpses but perhaps cannot fully comprehend.

Rebekah is the most fully delineated of the four Matriarchs. Of Leah we learn little; we receive some insight into Rachel's personality; while Sarah's character is known to us primarily through the manner in which she deals with Hagar and Ishmael, although even these problematic incidents do not allow us a full view of her. Biblical stories deal usually with men, and only occasionally, as in the tales of Rebekah and Tamar, are a woman's intuition and ingenuity given a place of preeminence.

GLEANINGS

The Nature of Isaac's Blessings

Blessings like curses are ultimately prayers that God might translate them into reality, even as the Psalmist says: "Let them curse, but bless Thou" [109:28].

To be sure, there are scholars who see in Scripture, and especially in the blessing of Isaac, instances of magic, in that what has been said cannot be taken back. However, here too we have not magic but prayer, for it was not Isaac's intention to force God to do something against His will. The blessing cannot stand unless it represents God's will to begin with.   UMBERTO CASSUTO [13]

The Dilemma of Divine Choice

Apparently even God must select imperfect instruments to fulfil His purposes. He must choose between Jacob—a man who desires the birthright so deeply he will cheat to secure it—and Esau who so lightly esteems it that he forfeits the birthright for a bowl of lentils. Jacob's calculated cunning must be weighed against Esau's undisciplined craving for immediate self-gratification. Working with "human material" involved God in a difficult but inescapable choice, and God decides: It is better to care too much than too little.

SAMUEL E. KARFF [14]

He Knew

Think you he was so easily misled
That blindness made confusion possible
Between the son he thought he loved and
  him
Whom he must bless? . . . He blessed because
  he must,
Because God wrought in him. At such a
  time
Could our cheap trickery prevail? He knew.
This was the blessing of the chosen son,
Cross-purposed and reversing, it might seem,
The destiny of generations; strange
And repetitious are God's ways with man.

AMY K. BLANK [15]

God Uses Jacob

No, it *is* a deception which is reported by Scripture without being approved by it. The mystery is that of God's action who uses for His ends even human faults yet remains completely sovereign in His choice. He had preferred Jacob over Esau even before their birth.

ROLAND DE VAUX [16]

The Voice of Jacob

When Isaac said, "The voice is the voice of Jacob, yet the hands are the hands of Esau" [Gen. 27:22], he spoke prophetically. "The voice of Jacob" means learning and truth; "the hands of Esau" means force and violence. As long as the voice of Jacob is heard in the houses of prayer and learning, the hands of Esau will not prevail against him.   MIDRASH [17]

Jacob's Dream

The narrative now comes to focus entirely on Jacob. He has his father's blessing and is on his way to his relatives in Haran. He will fall in love and be himself deceived. He will serve a master, yet his wages will be uncertain. While these stories of classical charm speak to us of human thoughts and deeds, it is God's master plan, revealed to Jacob in his first encounter with God, that determines their underlying theme.

ס ס ס

יא וַיֵּצֵא יַעֲקֹב מִבְּאֵר שָׁבַע וַיֵּלֶךְ חָרָנָה: וַיִּפְגַּע בַּמָּקוֹם
וַיָּלֶן שָׁם כִּי־בָא הַשֶּׁמֶשׁ וַיִּקַּח מֵאַבְנֵי הַמָּקוֹם וַיָּשֶׂם
יב מְרַאֲשֹׁתָיו וַיִּשְׁכַּב בַּמָּקוֹם הַהוּא: וַיַּחֲלֹם וְהִנֵּה סֻלָּם
מֻצָּב אַרְצָה וְרֹאשׁוֹ מַגִּיעַ הַשָּׁמָיְמָה וְהִנֵּה מַלְאֲכֵי
יג אֱלֹהִים עֹלִים וְיֹרְדִים בּוֹ: וְהִנֵּה יְהוָה נִצָּב עָלָיו
וַיֹּאמַר אֲנִי יְהוָה אֱלֹהֵי אַבְרָהָם אָבִיךָ וֵאלֹהֵי יִצְחָק
הָאָרֶץ אֲשֶׁר אַתָּה שֹׁכֵב עָלֶיהָ לְךָ אֶתְּנֶנָּה וּלְזַרְעֶךָ:
יד וְהָיָה זַרְעֲךָ כַּעֲפַר הָאָרֶץ וּפָרַצְתָּ יָמָּה וָקֵדְמָה
וְצָפֹנָה וָנֶגְבָּה וְנִבְרְכוּ בְךָ כָּל־מִשְׁפְּחֹת הָאֲדָמָה
טו וּבְזַרְעֶךָ: וְהִנֵּה אָנֹכִי עִמָּךְ וּשְׁמַרְתִּיךָ בְּכֹל אֲשֶׁר־

Genesis 28

10–15

10] Jacob left Beer-sheba, and set out for Haran.   11] He came upon a certain place and stopped there for the night, for the sun had set. Taking one of the stones of that place, he put it under his head and lay down in that place.   12] He had a dream; a stairway was set on the ground and its top reached to the sky, and angels of God were going up and down on it.   13] And the LORD was standing beside him and He said, "I am the LORD, the God of your father Abraham and the God of Isaac: the ground on which you are lying I will give to you and to your offspring. 14] Your descendants shall be as the dust of the earth; you shall spread out to the west and to the east, to the north and to the south. All the families of the earth shall bless themselves by you and your descendants.   15] Remember, I am with you:

28:12] *A dream.* On the subject of dreams, see p. 388.

   Stairway. Or "ramp," or "ladder." The סֻלָּם (*sulam*) of Jacob's dream reflects an ancient belief in a cosmic bond between heaven and earth [1].

13] *Beside him.* עָלָיו. Compare with Gen. 18:8. / This translation follows Luzzatto in that עָלָיו refers to Jacob, not to the stairway. /

   Your father Abraham. Abraham is mentioned here because of the earlier promise made to him.

תֵּלֵךְ וַהֲשִׁבֹתִיךָ אֶל־הָאֲדָמָה הַזֹּאת כִּי לֹא אֶעֱזָבְךָ

טז עַד אֲשֶׁר אִם־עָשִׂיתִי אֵת אֲשֶׁר־דִּבַּרְתִּי לָךְ: וַיִּיקַץ
יַעֲקֹב מִשְּׁנָתוֹ וַיֹּאמֶר אָכֵן יֵשׁ יְהוָה בַּמָּקוֹם הַזֶּה

יז וְאָנֹכִי לֹא יָדָעְתִּי: וַיִּירָא וַיֹּאמַר מַה־נּוֹרָא הַמָּקוֹם
הַזֶּה אֵין זֶה כִּי אִם־בֵּית אֱלֹהִים וְזֶה שַׁעַר הַשָּׁמָיִם:

יח וַיַּשְׁכֵּם יַעֲקֹב בַּבֹּקֶר וַיִּקַּח אֶת־הָאֶבֶן אֲשֶׁר־שָׂם
מְרַאֲשֹׁתָיו וַיָּשֶׂם אֹתָהּ מַצֵּבָה וַיִּצֹק שֶׁמֶן עַל־רֹאשָׁהּ:

יט וַיִּקְרָא אֶת־שֵׁם־הַמָּקוֹם הַהוּא בֵּית־אֵל וְאוּלָם לוּז שֵׁם־

Genesis 28

16–19

I will protect you wherever you go and will bring you back to this land. I will not leave you until I have done what I have promised you."

16] Jacob awoke from his sleep and said, "Surely the LORD is present in this place, and I did not know it!"   17] Shaken, he said, "How awesome is this place! This is none other than the abode of God, and that is the gateway to heaven." 18] Early in the morning, Jacob took the stone that he had put under his head and set it up as a pillar and poured oil on the top of it.   19] He named that site Bethel; but previously the name of the city had been Luz.

17] *Shaken.* וַיִּירָא. "Awestruck" would better express the Hebrew word play with "awesome" (נוֹרָא).

Gateway to heaven. Similar to the "bond [or rope] of heaven and earth" in Babylonian texts.

18] *A pillar.* Many ancient peoples believed that gods lived in stones. It is therefore not surprising that Jacob also believed this at this stage of his life. Pillars such as the one mentioned here have been found at Gezer, Hazor, and other places. In later times the Torah forbade the use of stone markers (מַצֵּבוֹת) for worship purposes and ordered those of the pagans to be destroyed (Exod.

23:24; Lev. 26:1; Deut. 16:22). When Jacob returns from Haran he will revisit this place (Gen. 35:14).

19] *Bethel.* House of God. Abraham built an altar there previously (Gen. 12:8; 13:3–4), and it will be here that Jacob's name will be changed to Israel (Gen. 35:10–15). Excavations have shown that Bethel was founded about 2000 B.C.E. To the Canaanites, it was a sanctuary city dedicated to the god El, and the association with Jacob gave it added importance [2]. It is more frequently mentioned in the Bible than any other town except Jerusalem. The Prophets later condemned the altars of Bethel (e.g., Hos. 10:15; Amos 3:14).

כ הָעִיר לָרִאשֹׁנָה: וַיִּדַּר יַעֲקֹב נֶדֶר לֵאמֹר אִם־יִהְיֶה אֱלֹהִים עִמָּדִי וּשְׁמָרַנִי בַּדֶּרֶךְ הַזֶּה אֲשֶׁר אָנֹכִי הוֹלֵךְ

כא וְנָתַן־לִי לֶחֶם לֶאֱכֹל וּבֶגֶד לִלְבֹּשׁ: וְשַׁבְתִּי בְשָׁלוֹם

כב אֶל־בֵּית אָבִי וְהָיָה יְהֹוָה לִי לֵאלֹהִים: וְהָאֶבֶן הַזֹּאת אֲשֶׁר־שַׂמְתִּי מַצֵּבָה יִהְיֶה בֵּית אֱלֹהִים וְכֹל אֲשֶׁר תִּתֶּן־לִי עַשֵּׂר אֲעַשְּׂרֶנּוּ לָךְ:

20] Jacob then made a vow, saying, "If God remains with me, if He protects me on this journey that I am making, and gives me bread to eat and clothing to wear, 21] and if I return safe to my father's house—the LORD shall be my God.   22] And this stone, which I have set up as a pillar, shall be God's abode; and of all that You give me, I will always set aside a tithe for You."

Trial and Trembling

On awakening from his dream, Jacob promises that if God will be His protector, he in turn will worship God, build a shrine for Him, and offer Him a tithe.[1] This formal promise or vow (נֶדֶר) is conditional, and, although other such vows are found in the Bible (e.g., Judg. 11:30–31; I Sam. 1:11), it appears at first sight rather unusual.[2] Jacob bargains with God: if God performs properly—and performs first—Jacob will accept Him as his God. Readers often find this a highly objectionable way of dealing with the Almighty, especially since Jacob is shown doubting God's word. One ancient commentator, R. Jonathan, so despaired of explaining Jacob's words that he concluded that the text must somehow be in disarray. [4].

Indeed, Jacob at Bethel is not yet the man of faith who wrestles with the angel. He is only at the beginning of his quest. This is his first experience with trial. Understandably, in anxiety he cries that he will do anything if only someone will help. Jacob, to be sure, does not deliver a "proper" prayer. He prays realistically, from the heart. The vow is his human response to the covenant that God has offered him. It is the expression of his experience, not of his philosophy, and in similar ways men have always prayed and promised when in moments of crisis God appears as the only help.[3]

Jacob's first encounter with God produces fear and trembling. The forefather foreshadows the mystery of chosenness that will rest in his descendants: They too will dream of angels and wondrous things, but when they awake and face the realities of the world they too will tremble and find the service of God filled with terror.

---

[1] The sense of this passage would be seriously altered if Gen. 28:21–22 were read: "...and if I return safe to my father's house and the Lord shall be my God, then this stone, etc." The Hebrew permits this interpretation [3].

[2] The usual vow demonstrated devotion without condition, often involving abstinence and special sacrifice. The Torah devotes many passages to rules about vows. See Lev. 27; Num. 6.

[3] The Psalms show that vow and fulfilment are but a worshiper's way of moving from anxiety to thanksgiving: "I will pay Thee my vows, / That which my lips uttered / And my mouth promised when I was in trouble" (Ps. 66:13–14). Also see Pss. 22:26; 61:6; and 116:14, 18 [5].

GLEANINGS

The Dream

The stairway (סֻלָּם) was a symbol of Sinai (סִינַי). Both have the same numerical values (130). [6]

God showed Jacob the giving of the Torah and said: "If your descendants observe this Torah, they will ascend like these angels; if not, they will descend like them." MIDRASH [7]

This Place

The "place," observe: *any* place where God lets down the ladder. And how are you to know where that will be? Or how are you to determine where it may be, but by being ready for it always? JOHN RUSKIN [8]

Ha-Makom

In post-biblical usage הַמָּקוֹם (the place) was a name for God, so that (Gen. 28:11) "He came upon a certain place" could be read "He came upon God." Is God then a place? In a way, say the Rabbis, in that He encompasses the whole world: "God is the place of the world, but the world is not His place." [9]

The Gate of Heaven

Praying at any place is like standing at the very foot of God's throne of glory, for the gate of heaven is there and the door is open for prayer to be heard. MIDRASH [10]

I Did Not Know (Gen. 28:16)

When can man experience God's nearness? Only when he is suffused by "I don't know," when he himself knows that he does not know and does not pretend to have wisdom and insight.

PANIM YAFOT [11]

Thy Holy Choice

Here—Lord—I lie, Jacob, whom Thou didst call—
Chosen by Thee—and yet . . . child of this earth!
Lord, what Thy will imposes soon or late—
I'll bear it not as yoke—but as a crown!
If Thou didst choose my blood to be a torch
Which flaming burns above the nations' ways,
Let none that from my blood come forth forget,
Ever forget, my God, Thy holy choice!
But if they should forget—in weariness
Drop on their way—let not their heart be faint—

RICHARD BEER-HOFMANN [12]

Jacob in Haran

Jacob now tastes the fruit of deception and faces long service; he suffers and matures. This section deals with family life—with conception and birth, both human and animal. In the interplay of these biological forces, the Torah sees the working of God's plan.

In reading these accounts we should keep in mind that the Torah is interested less in describing the correct origin of names than it is in the background of the tribes, which these names represent. It answered questions for ancient Israel that in different form are asked by most groups: Who were our ancestors? How did we come to have our tribal and national structure?

א וַיִּשָּׂא יַעֲקֹב רַגְלָיו וַיֵּלֶךְ אַרְצָה בְנֵי־קֶדֶם: וַיַּרְא וְהִנֵּה
ב בְאֵר בַּשָּׂדֶה וְהִנֵּה־שָׁם שְׁלֹשָׁה עֶדְרֵי־צֹאן רֹבְצִים
עָלֶיהָ כִּי מִן־הַבְּאֵר הַהִוא יַשְׁקוּ הָעֲדָרִים וְהָאֶבֶן
ג גְּדֹלָה עַל־פִּי הַבְּאֵר: וְנֶאֶסְפוּ־שָׁמָּה כָל־הָעֲדָרִים
וְגָלְלוּ אֶת־הָאֶבֶן מֵעַל פִּי הַבְּאֵר וְהִשְׁקוּ אֶת־הַצֹּאן
ד וְהֵשִׁיבוּ אֶת־הָאֶבֶן עַל־פִּי הַבְּאֵר לִמְקֹמָהּ: וַיֹּאמֶר
לָהֶם יַעֲקֹב אַחַי מֵאַיִן אַתֶּם וַיֹּאמְרוּ מֵחָרָן אֲנָחְנוּ:
ה וַיֹּאמֶר לָהֶם הַיְדַעְתֶּם אֶת־לָבָן בֶּן־נָחוֹר וַיֹּאמְרוּ
ו יָדָעְנוּ: וַיֹּאמֶר לָהֶם הֲשָׁלוֹם לוֹ וַיֹּאמְרוּ שָׁלוֹם וְהִנֵּה
ז רָחֵל בִּתּוֹ בָּאָה עִם־הַצֹּאן: וַיֹּאמֶר הֵן עוֹד הַיּוֹם
גָּדוֹל לֹא־עֵת הֵאָסֵף הַמִּקְנֶה הַשְׁקוּ הַצֹּאן וּלְכוּ רְעוּ:

Genesis 29

1–7

1] Jacob resumed his journey and came to the land of the Easterners. 2] There before his eyes was a well in the open. Three flocks of sheep were lying there beside it, for the flocks were watered from that well. The stone on the mouth of the well was large. 3] When all the flocks were gathered there, the stone would be rolled from the mouth of the well and the sheep watered; then the stone would be put back in its place on the mouth of the well.

4] Jacob said to them, "My friends, where are you from?" And they said, "We are from Haran." 5] He said to them, "Do you know Laban the son of Nahor?" And they said, "Yes, we do." 6] He continued, "Is he well?" They answered, "He is; and there is his daughter Rachel, coming with the flock." 7] He said, "It is still broad daylight, too early to round up the animals; water the flock and take

29:1] *Resumed his journey.* Literally, "lifted up his feet."

7] *Water the flock.* Jacob is the son of a rich man and is used to giving commands. Apparently he is listened to with respect even though he is a stranger.

287

ח וַיֹּאמְרוּ לֹא נוּכַל עַד אֲשֶׁר יֵאָסְפוּ כָּל־הָעֲדָרִים וְגָלְלוּ אֶת־הָאֶבֶן מֵעַל פִּי הַבְּאֵר וְהִשְׁקִינוּ הַצֹּאן:

ט עוֹדֶנּוּ מְדַבֵּר עִמָּם וְרָחֵל בָּאָה עִם־הַצֹּאן אֲשֶׁר לְאָבִיהָ כִּי רֹעָה הִוא: וַיְהִי כַּאֲשֶׁר רָאָה יַעֲקֹב אֶת־

י רָחֵל בַּת־לָבָן אֲחִי אִמּוֹ וְאֶת־צֹאן לָבָן אֲחִי אִמּוֹ וַיִּגַּשׁ יַעֲקֹב וַיָּגֶל אֶת־הָאֶבֶן מֵעַל פִּי הַבְּאֵר וַיַּשְׁקְ אֶת־

יא צֹאן לָבָן אֲחִי אִמּוֹ: וַיִּשַּׁק יַעֲקֹב לְרָחֵל וַיִּשָּׂא אֶת־

יב קֹלוֹ וַיֵּבְךְּ: וַיַּגֵּד יַעֲקֹב לְרָחֵל כִּי אֲחִי אָבִיהָ הוּא וְכִי

יג בֶן־רִבְקָה הוּא וַתָּרָץ וַתַּגֵּד לְאָבִיהָ: וַיְהִי כִשְׁמֹעַ לָבָן אֶת־שֵׁמַע יַעֲקֹב בֶּן־אֲחֹתוֹ וַיָּרָץ לִקְרָאתוֹ וַיְחַבֶּק־לוֹ וַיְנַשֶּׁק־לוֹ וַיְבִיאֵהוּ אֶל־בֵּיתוֹ וַיְסַפֵּר לְלָבָן אֵת

Genesis 29
8–13

them to pasture." 8] But they said, "We cannot, until all the flocks are rounded up; then the stone is rolled off the mouth of the well and we water the sheep."

9] While he was still speaking with them, Rachel came with her father's flock; for she was a shepherdess. 10] And when Jacob saw Rachel, the daughter of Laban his mother's brother, and the flock of Laban his mother's brother, Jacob went up and rolled the stone off the mouth of the well, and watered the flock of Laban, his mother's brother. 11] Then Jacob kissed Rachel, and broke into tears. 12] Jacob told Rachel that he was her father's kinsman, that he was Rebekah's son; and she ran and told her father. 13] On hearing the news of his sister's son Jacob, Laban ran to greet him; he embraced him and kissed him, and took him into his

10] *Uncle.* Literally, "his mother's brother."
Rolled the stone. Lifting and throwing heavy stones was an old way of proving prowess [1]. Jacob demonstrates his strength in order to im-press the lovely girl.

11] *Kissed Rachel.* A formal greeting, here offered with deep emotion.

יד כָּל־הַדְּבָרִים הָאֵלֶּה: וַיֹּאמֶר לוֹ לָבָן אַךְ עַצְמִי

טו וּבְשָׂרִי אָתָּה וַיֵּשֶׁב עִמּוֹ חֹדֶשׁ יָמִים: וַיֹּאמֶר לָבָן

לְיַעֲקֹב הֲכִי־אָחִי אַתָּה וַעֲבַדְתַּנִי חִנָּם הַגִּידָה לִּי מַה־

טז מַּשְׂכֻּרְתֶּךָ: וּלְלָבָן שְׁתֵּי בָנוֹת שֵׁם הַגְּדֹלָה לֵאָה וְשֵׁם

יז הַקְּטַנָּה רָחֵל: וְעֵינֵי לֵאָה רַכּוֹת וְרָחֵל הָיְתָה יְפַת־

יח תֹּאַר וִיפַת מַרְאֶה: וַיֶּאֱהַב יַעֲקֹב אֶת־רָחֵל וַיֹּאמֶר

יט אֶעֱבָדְךָ שֶׁבַע שָׁנִים בְּרָחֵל בִּתְּךָ הַקְּטַנָּה: וַיֹּאמֶר

לָבָן טוֹב תִּתִּי אֹתָהּ לָךְ מִתִּתִּי אֹתָהּ לְאִישׁ אַחֵר

כ שְׁבָה עִמָּדִי: וַיַּעֲבֹד יַעֲקֹב בְּרָחֵל שֶׁבַע שָׁנִים

וַיִּהְיוּ בְעֵינָיו כְּיָמִים אֲחָדִים בְּאַהֲבָתוֹ אֹתָהּ:

Genesis 29

14–20

house. He told Laban all that had happened.   14] Laban then said to him, "You are truly my bone and flesh."

When he had stayed with him a month's time,   15] Laban said to Jacob, "Just because you are my kinsman, should you serve me for nothing? Tell me, what shall your wages be?"   16] Now Laban had two daughters; the name of the older one was Leah, and the name of the younger was Rachel.   17] Leah had weak eyes; Rachel was shapely and beautiful.   18] Jacob loved Rachel; so he answered, "I will serve you seven years for your younger daughter Rachel."   19] Laban said, "Better that I give her to you than that I should give her to an outsider. Stay with me."   20] So Jacob served seven years for Rachel and they seemed to him but a few days because of his love for her.

17] *Weak eyes.* It seems preferable to translate this as "tender eyes" [2], for the contrast is not between ugliness and beauty but between two types of attraction.

18] *I will serve you seven years.* Jacob's offer of seven years is so extreme that Laban is bound to accept. Service or performance of some kind to obtain a wife is a recurring biblical motif (see Josh. 15:16; Judg. 1:12).

כא וַיֹּאמֶר יַעֲקֹב אֶל־לָבָן הָבָה אֶת־אִשְׁתִּי כִּי מָלְאוּ יָמָי
כב וְאָבוֹאָה אֵלֶיהָ: וַיֶּאֱסֹף לָבָן אֶת־כָּל־אַנְשֵׁי הַמָּקוֹם וַיַּעַשׂ
כג מִשְׁתֶּה: וַיְהִי בָעֶרֶב וַיִּקַּח אֶת־לֵאָה בִתּוֹ וַיָּבֵא אֹתָהּ
כד אֵלָיו וַיָּבֹא אֵלֶיהָ: וַיִּתֵּן לָבָן לָהּ אֶת־זִלְפָּה שִׁפְחָתוֹ
כה לְלֵאָה בִתּוֹ שִׁפְחָה: וַיְהִי בַבֹּקֶר וְהִנֵּה־הִוא לֵאָה
וַיֹּאמֶר אֶל־לָבָן מַה־זֹּאת עָשִׂיתָ לִּי הֲלֹא בְרָחֵל
כו עָבַדְתִּי עִמָּךְ וְלָמָּה רִמִּיתָנִי: וַיֹּאמֶר לָבָן לֹא־יֵעָשֶׂה
כז כֵן בִּמְקוֹמֵנוּ לָתֵת הַצְּעִירָה לִפְנֵי הַבְּכִירָה: מַלֵּא
שְׁבֻעַ זֹאת וְנִתְּנָה לְךָ גַּם־אֶת־זֹאת בַּעֲבֹדָה אֲשֶׁר

21] Then Jacob said to Laban, "Give me my wife, for my time is fulfilled, that I may consort with her."   **22]** And Laban gathered all the people of the place and made a feast.   **23]** When evening came, he took his daughter Leah and brought her to him; and he cohabited with her.— **24]** Laban had given his maidservant Zilpah to his daughter Leah as her maid.— **25]** When morning came, there was Leah! So he said to Laban, "What is this you have done to me? Was it not for Rachel that I have been in your service? Why did you deceive me?"   **26]** Laban said, "It is not the practice in our place to marry off the younger before the older.   **27]** Wait until the bridal week of this one is over and we will give you that one too, provided

22] *A feast.* This was not only a testimony to the family's approval of the match, it also provided the opportunity to introduce the veiled bride into the marriage chamber; the subsequent marital relations would consummate the marriage. Once the feast was over, Leah would be considered married unless Jacob repudiated her. To prevent this, Laban asks Jacob to stay the week with her, before taking Rachel, too, as his wife. Laban's concern and cordiality last only one month [3].

24] *Maidservant.* According to Hurrian custom, high-status women received maidservants as part of their dowry.

25] *Deceive me.* Jacob uses the same Hebrew word (רִמִּיתָנִי) that Isaac used when he complained about being deceived (Gen. 27:35).

26] *The younger before the older.* Laban's remark makes it clear that Jacob has no right to complain, for he now receives retribution for having himself overtaken his older brother Esau [4].

כח תַּעֲבֹד עִמָּדִי עוֹד שֶׁבַע־שָׁנִים אֲחֵרוֹת: וַיַּעַשׂ יַעֲקֹב

כֵּן וַיְמַלֵּא שְׁבֻעַ זֹאת וַיִּתֶּן־לוֹ אֶת־רָחֵל בִּתּוֹ לוֹ לְאִשָּׁה:

כט וַיִּתֵּן לָבָן לְרָחֵל בִּתּוֹ אֶת־בִּלְהָה שִׁפְחָתוֹ לָהּ לְשִׁפְחָה:

ל וַיָּבֹא גַּם אֶל־רָחֵל וַיֶּאֱהַב גַּם־אֶת־רָחֵל מִלֵּאָה וַיַּעֲבֹד

לא עִמּוֹ עוֹד שֶׁבַע־שָׁנִים אֲחֵרוֹת: וַיַּרְא יְהוָה כִּי־שְׂנוּאָה

לב לֵאָה וַיִּפְתַּח אֶת־רַחְמָהּ וְרָחֵל עֲקָרָה: וַתַּהַר לֵאָה

וַתֵּלֶד בֵּן וַתִּקְרָא שְׁמוֹ רְאוּבֵן כִּי אָמְרָה כִּי־רָאָה

לג יְהוָה בְּעָנְיִי כִּי עַתָּה יֶאֱהָבַנִי אִישִׁי: וַתַּהַר עוֹד וַתֵּלֶד

בֵּן וַתֹּאמֶר כִּי־שָׁמַע יְהוָה כִּי־שְׂנוּאָה אָנֹכִי וַיִּתֶּן־לִי

Genesis 29

28–33

you serve me another seven years." **28]** Jacob did so: he waited out the bridal week of the one, and then he gave him his daughter Rachel as wife.— **29]** Laban had given his maidservant Bilhah to his daughter Rachel as her maid.— **30]** And Jacob cohabited with Rachel also; indeed, he loved Rachel more than Leah. And he served him another seven years.

31] The LORD saw that Leah was unloved and he opened her womb; but Rachel was barren. **32]** Leah conceived and bore a son, and named him Reuben; for she declared, "It means: 'The LORD has seen my affliction'; it also means: 'Now my husband will love me.'" **33]** She conceived again and bore a son, and declared, "This is because the LORD heard that I was unloved and has given me this one also";

28] *Gave him his daughter Rachel.* Marrying two sisters in this fashion was later forbidden (Lev. 18:18).

32] *Has seen.* רָאָה (*ra-ah*), connected with רְאוּ (*re-u*), which is the first part of Reuben.

Will love me. יֶאֱהָבַנִי (*ye-ehevani*) apparently meant as an assonance with בֵּן (*ben*), last part of Reuben. Note that it is the women who give the names (see p. 129).

33] *Heard.* שָׁמַע (*shama*), connected with שִׁמְעוֹן (*shim-on*). The real origin of the name is probably found in a word similar to the Arabic *sim'u* (wolf-hyena), a cognomen that would be descriptive of Simeon's violent nature. Examples of other personal names referring to animals are Rachel (ewe), Yael (mountain goat), Jonah (dove), Shaphan (rock-rabbit), Deborah (bee), and Hamor (donkey).

לד גַּם־אֶת־זֶה וַתִּקְרָא שְׁמוֹ שִׁמְעוֹן: וַתַּהַר עוֹד וַתֵּלֶד בֵּן בראשית כט; ל

לד–לה; א–ד

וַתֹּאמֶר עַתָּה הַפַּעַם יִלָּוֶה אִישִׁי אֵלַי כִּי־יָלַדְתִּי לוֹ

לה שְׁלֹשָׁה בָנִים עַל־כֵּן קָרָא־שְׁמוֹ לֵוִי: וַתַּהַר עוֹד וַתֵּלֶד

בֵּן וַתֹּאמֶר הַפַּעַם אוֹדֶה אֶת־יְהוָה עַל־כֵּן קָרְאָה

שְׁמוֹ יְהוּדָה וַתַּעֲמֹד מִלֶּדֶת:

א וַתֵּרֶא רָחֵל כִּי לֹא יָלְדָה לְיַעֲקֹב וַתְּקַנֵּא רָחֵל

בַּאֲחֹתָהּ וַתֹּאמֶר אֶל־יַעֲקֹב הָבָה־לִּי בָנִים וְאִם־אַיִן

ב מֵתָה אָנֹכִי: וַיִּחַר־אַף יַעֲקֹב בְּרָחֵל וַיֹּאמֶר הֲתַחַת

ג אֱלֹהִים אָנֹכִי אֲשֶׁר־מָנַע מִמֵּךְ פְּרִי־בָטֶן: וַתֹּאמֶר הִנֵּה

Genesis 29; 30

34–35; 1–4

אֲמָתִי בִלְהָה בֹּא אֵלֶיהָ וְתֵלֵד עַל־בִּרְכַּי וְאִבָּנֶה גַם־

ד אָנֹכִי מִמֶּנָּה: וַתִּתֶּן־לוֹ אֶת־בִּלְהָה שִׁפְחָתָהּ לְאִשָּׁה

so she named him Simeon.   34] Again she conceived and bore a son and declared, "This time my husband will become attached to me, for I have borne him three sons." Therefore he was named Levi.   35] She conceived again and bore a son, and declared, "This time I will praise the LORD." Therefore she named him Judah. Then she stopped bearing.

1] When Rachel saw that she had borne Jacob no children, she became envious of her sister; and Rachel said to Jacob, "Give me children, or I shall die."   2] Jacob was incensed at Rachel, and said, "Can I take the place of God, who has denied you fruit of the womb?"   3] She said, "Here is my maid Bilhah. Consort with her, that she may bear on my knees and that through her I too may have children."   4] So she gave him her maid Bilhah as concubine, and Jacob cohabited with her.

34] *Attached.* יִלָּוֶה, connected with לֵוִי.
35] *I will praise.* אוֹדֶה, connected with יְהוּדָה. Note Leah's pathetic hope that by giving him sons Jacob will come to love her.

30:3] *Here is my maid.* Sarah's dilemma is re-enacted (Gen. 16:2). Rachel performs the ancient custom of establishing the child's legitimacy or of adopting him by placing him on her knee.

ה וַיָּבֹא אֵלֶיהָ יַעֲקֹב: וַתַּהַר בִּלְהָה וַתֵּלֶד לְיַעֲקֹב בֵּן:

ו וַתֹּאמֶר רָחֵל דָּנַנִּי אֱלֹהִים וְגַם שָׁמַע בְּקֹלִי וַיִּתֶּן־לִי

ז בֵּן עַל־כֵּן קָרְאָה שְׁמוֹ דָּן: וַתַּהַר עוֹד וַתֵּלֶד בִּלְהָה

ח שִׁפְחַת רָחֵל בֵּן שֵׁנִי לְיַעֲקֹב: וַתֹּאמֶר רָחֵל נַפְתּוּלֵי

אֱלֹהִים נִפְתַּלְתִּי עִם־אֲחֹתִי גַּם־יָכֹלְתִּי וַתִּקְרָא שְׁמוֹ

ט נַפְתָּלִי: וַתֵּרֶא לֵאָה כִּי עָמְדָה מִלֶּדֶת וַתִּקַּח אֶת־

י זִלְפָּה שִׁפְחָתָהּ וַתִּתֵּן אֹתָהּ לְיַעֲקֹב לְאִשָּׁה: וַתֵּלֶד

יא זִלְפָּה שִׁפְחַת לֵאָה לְיַעֲקֹב בֵּן: וַתֹּאמֶר לֵאָה בָּגָד*

יב וַתִּקְרָא אֶת־שְׁמוֹ גָּד: וַתֵּלֶד זִלְפָּה שִׁפְחַת לֵאָה בֵּן

Genesis 30

5–12

* יא בא גד קרי.

5] Bilhah conceived and bore Jacob a son.   6] And Rachel said, "God has vindicated me; indeed, He has heeded my plea and given me a son." Therefore she named him Dan.   7] Rachel's maid Bilhah conceived again and bore Jacob a second son. 8] And Rachel said, "A fateful contest I waged with my sister; yes, and I have prevailed." So she named him Naphtali.

9] When Leah saw that she had stopped bearing, she took her maid Zilpah and gave her to Jacob as concubine.   10] And when Leah's maid Zilpah bore Jacob a son,   11] Leah said, "What luck!" So she named him Gad.   12] When Leah's

---

Henceforth she speaks of Bilhah's children as "mine."
/This procedure is attested to in Babylonian, Hittite, Hurrian, and Greek laws./

6] *Vindicated me.* דָּנַנִּי is connected with דָּן (judged).

8] *A fateful contest I waged.* נַפְתּוּלֵי...נִפְתַּלְתִּי is connected with נַפְתָּלִי. Literally, "a contest of God," suggesting that an ordeal was involved.

11] *What luck.* The written text is בְּגָד (bagad), while the understood text is בָּא גָד (ba gad), "luck has come," connected with Gad. This practice of reading the text differently from the written word constituted tradition's way of occasionally correcting the text without actually changing the spelling of the letters (which were meticulously copied even when obviously wrong). In cases of such correction the written text is referred to as כְּתִיב (ketiv), the understood and pronounced word as קְרֵי (kerey).

יג שֵׁנִי לְיַעֲקֹב: וַתֹּאמֶר לֵאָה בְּאָשְׁרִי כִּי אִשְּׁרוּנִי בָּנוֹת

יד וַתִּקְרָא אֶת־שְׁמוֹ אָשֵׁר: וַיֵּלֶךְ רְאוּבֵן בִּימֵי קְצִיר־

חִטִּים וַיִּמְצָא דוּדָאִים בַּשָּׂדֶה וַיָּבֵא אֹתָם אֶל־לֵאָה

אִמּוֹ וַתֹּאמֶר רָחֵל אֶל־לֵאָה תְּנִי־נָא לִי מִדּוּדָאֵי

טו בְּנֵךְ: וַתֹּאמֶר לָהּ הַמְעַט קַחְתֵּךְ אֶת־אִישִׁי וְלָקַחַת

גַּם אֶת־דּוּדָאֵי בְּנִי וַתֹּאמֶר רָחֵל לָכֵן יִשְׁכַּב עִמָּךְ

טז הַלַּיְלָה תַּחַת דּוּדָאֵי בְנֵךְ: וַיָּבֹא יַעֲקֹב מִן־הַשָּׂדֶה

בָּעֶרֶב וַתֵּצֵא לֵאָה לִקְרָאתוֹ וַתֹּאמֶר אֵלַי תָּבוֹא כִּי

שָׂכֹר שְׂכַרְתִּיךָ בְּדוּדָאֵי בְּנִי וַיִּשְׁכַּב עִמָּהּ בַּלַּיְלָה

יז הוּא: וַיִּשְׁמַע אֱלֹהִים אֶל־לֵאָה וַתַּהַר וַתֵּלֶד לְיַעֲקֹב

---

maid Zilpah bore Jacob a second son,   13] Leah declared, "What fortune!" meaning, "Women will deem me fortunate." So she named him Asher.

14] Once, at the time of the wheat harvest, Reuben came upon some mandrakes in the field and brought them to his mother Leah. Rachel said to Leah, "Please give me some of your son's mandrakes."   15] But she said to her, "Was it not enough for you to take away my husband, that you would also take my son's mandrakes?" Rachel replied, "Then let him lie with you tonight, in return for your son's mandrakes."   16] When Jacob came home from the field in the evening, Leah went out to meet him and said, "You are to sleep with me, for I have hired you with my son's mandrakes." And he lay with her that night.   17] And God

---

13] *What fortune.* בְּאָשְׁרִי is connected with אָשֵׁר. This translation is more exact than "happy."

14] *Mandrakes.* A plant whose potato-like bulbs sometimes look like faces. (The ancient belief in the mandrake as a sexual stimulant has persisted into modern times.) The potion fails for Rachel, while Leah, who does not use it, becomes pregnant. The intended meaning, then, is that only God can grant relief from barrenness.
/Rashi translates "jasmine"; similarly B. Jacob, who denies that a potion was involved. Rather, Rachel wanted Leah's flowers to give to her husband. So also Luzzatto [5]./

יח בֶּן חֲמִישִׁי: וַתֹּאמֶר לֵאָה נָתַן אֱלֹהִים שְׂכָרִי אֲשֶׁר־

יט נָתַתִּי שִׁפְחָתִי לְאִישִׁי וַתִּקְרָא שְׁמוֹ יִשָּׂשכָר: וַתַּהַר עוֹד

כ לֵאָה וַתֵּלֶד בֵּן־שִׁשִּׁי לְיַעֲקֹב: וַתֹּאמֶר לֵאָה זְבָדַנִי

אֱלֹהִים אֹתִי זֵבֶד טוֹב הַפַּעַם יִזְבְּלֵנִי אִישִׁי כִּי־יָלַדְתִּי

כא לוֹ שִׁשָּׁה בָנִים וַתִּקְרָא אֶת־שְׁמוֹ זְבֻלוּן: וְאַחַר יָלְדָה

כב בַת וַתִּקְרָא אֶת־שְׁמָהּ דִּינָה: וַיִּזְכֹּר אֱלֹהִים אֶת־רָחֵל

כג וַיִּשְׁמַע אֵלֶיהָ אֱלֹהִים וַיִּפְתַּח אֶת־רַחְמָהּ: וַתַּהַר וַתֵּלֶד

כד בֵּן וַתֹּאמֶר אָסַף אֱלֹהִים אֶת־חֶרְפָּתִי: וַתִּקְרָא אֶת־

כה שְׁמוֹ יוֹסֵף לֵאמֹר יֹסֵף יְהֹוָה לִי בֵּן אַחֵר: וַיְהִי כַּאֲשֶׁר

יָלְדָה רָחֵל אֶת־יוֹסֵף וַיֹּאמֶר יַעֲקֹב אֶל־לָבָן שַׁלְּחֵנִי

Genesis 30
18–25

heeded Leah, and she conceived and bore him a fifth son. 18] And Leah said, "God has given me my reward for having given my maid to my husband." So she named him Issachar. 19] When Leah conceived again and bore Jacob a sixth son, 20] Leah said, "God has given me a choice gift; this time my husband will give me presents, for I have borne him six sons." So she named him Zebulun. 21] Lastly, she bore him a daughter, and named her Dinah.

22] Now God remembered Rachel; God heeded her and opened her womb. 23] She conceived and bore a son, and said, "God has taken away my disgrace." 24] So she named him Joseph, which is to say, "May the LORD add another son for me."

25] After Rachel had borne Joseph, Jacob said to Laban, "Give me leave to go

---

18] *Issachar.* The text derives the name both from שָׂכוֹר שְׂכַרְתִּיךָ (I have hired you) in Gen. 30:16 and from שְׂכָרִי (my reward).

20] *Zebulun.* Two derivations are offered: זֵבֶד (a choice gift) and יִזְבְּלֵנִי. The meaning of the second is uncertain. The two explanations appear to stem from separate traditions. /Some scholars derive the name from the Akkadian

zubullu (bridegroom's gift), others link the name to the Ugaritic *zbl*, a divine epithet [6]./

22] *God remembered Rachel.* Stressing that He, not a potion, opened her womb.

24] *Joseph.* Again, two explanations are given for the name: אָסַף (has taken away) and יֹסֵף (may [He] add).

כו וְאֵלְכָה אֶל־מְקוֹמִי וּלְאַרְצִי: תְּנָה אֶת־נָשַׁי וְאֶת־יְלָדַי
אֲשֶׁר עָבַדְתִּי אֹתְךָ בָּהֵן וְאֵלֵכָה כִּי אַתָּה יָדַעְתָּ אֶת־
כז עֲבֹדָתִי אֲשֶׁר עֲבַדְתִּיךָ: וַיֹּאמֶר אֵלָיו לָבָן אִם־נָא
מָצָאתִי חֵן בְּעֵינֶיךָ נִחַשְׁתִּי וַיְבָרֲכֵנִי יְהוָה בִּגְלָלֶךָ:
כט וַיֹּאמַר נָקְבָה שְׂכָרְךָ עָלַי וְאֶתֵּנָה: וַיֹּאמֶר אֵלָיו אַתָּה
יָדַעְתָּ אֵת אֲשֶׁר עֲבַדְתִּיךָ וְאֵת אֲשֶׁר־הָיָה מִקְנְךָ אִתִּי:
ל כִּי מְעַט אֲשֶׁר־הָיָה לְךָ לְפָנַי וַיִּפְרֹץ לָרֹב וַיְבָרֶךְ
יְהוָה אֹתְךָ לְרַגְלִי וְעַתָּה מָתַי אֶעֱשֶׂה גַם־אָנֹכִי לְבֵיתִי:
לא וַיֹּאמֶר מָה אֶתֶּן־לָךְ וַיֹּאמֶר יַעֲקֹב לֹא־תִתֶּן־לִי מְאוּמָה
אִם־תַּעֲשֶׂה־לִּי הַדָּבָר הַזֶּה אָשׁוּבָה אֶרְעֶה צֹאנְךָ
לב אֶשְׁמֹר: אֶעֱבֹר בְּכָל־צֹאנְךָ הַיּוֹם הָסֵר מִשָּׁם כָּל־שֶׂה

back to my own homeland.   26] Give me my wives and my children, for whom I have served you, that I may go; for well you know how I have served you."   27] But Laban said to him, "If you will indulge me, I have learned by divination that the LORD has blessed me on your account."   28] And he continued, "Name the wages due from me, and I will pay you."   29] But he said, "You well know how I have served you and how your livestock has fared with me.   30] For the little you had before I came has grown to much, since the LORD has blessed you wherever I turned. And now, when shall I make provision for my own household?"   31] He said, "What shall I pay you?" And Jacob said, "Pay me nothing! If you will do this thing for me, I will again pasture and keep your flocks.   32] Let me pass through

26] *Give me.* Jacob is Laban's son-in-law but also very much the servant who entreats his master for the wages due him.

27] *Indulge me.* Literally, "if I have found favor in your eyes."

I have learned by divination. Laban apparently

thought that many of his black sheep looked like goats, which was considered a good omen [7].

The Lord has blessed me. A deferential mention of Jacob's God by the wily Laban, who is polite to the extreme.

/However, other versions have אֱלֹהִים./

נָקֹד וְטָלוּא וְכָל־שֶׂה־חוּם בַּכְּשָׂבִים וְטָלוּא וְנָקֹד

לג בָּעִזִּים וְהָיָה שְׂכָרִי: וְעָנְתָה־בִּי צִדְקָתִי בְּיוֹם מָחָר כִּי־תָבוֹא עַל־שְׂכָרִי לְפָנֶיךָ כֹּל אֲשֶׁר־אֵינֶנּוּ נָקֹד וְטָלוּא

לד בָּעִזִּים וְחוּם בַּכְּשָׂבִים גָּנוּב הוּא אִתִּי: וַיֹּאמֶר לָבָן

לה הֵן לוּ יְהִי כִדְבָרֶךָ: וַיָּסַר בַּיּוֹם הַהוּא אֶת־הַתְּיָשִׁים הָעֲקֻדִּים וְהַטְּלֻאִים וְאֵת כָּל־הָעִזִּים הַנְּקֻדּוֹת וְהַטְּלֻאֹת כֹּל אֲשֶׁר־לָבָן בּוֹ וְכָל־חוּם בַּכְּשָׂבִים וַיִּתֵּן בְּיַד־בָּנָיו:

לו וַיָּשֶׂם דֶּרֶךְ שְׁלֹשֶׁת יָמִים בֵּינוֹ וּבֵין יַעֲקֹב וְיַעֲקֹב רֹעֶה

לז אֶת־צֹאן לָבָן הַנּוֹתָרֹת: וַיִּקַּח־לוֹ יַעֲקֹב מַקַּל לִבְנֶה לח לַח וְלוּז וְעַרְמוֹן וַיְפַצֵּל בָּהֵן פְּצָלוֹת לְבָנוֹת מַחְשֹׂף הַלָּבָן אֲשֶׁר עַל־הַמַּקְלוֹת: וַיַּצֵּג אֶת־הַמַּקְלוֹת אֲשֶׁר

Genesis 30
33–38

your whole flock today, removing from there every speckled and spotted animal—every dark-colored sheep and every spotted and speckled goat. Such shall be my wages. 33] In the future when you go over my wages, let my honesty toward you testify for me: if there are among my goats any that are not speckled or spotted or any sheep that are not dark-colored, they got there by theft." 34] And Laban said, "Very well, let it be as you say."

35] But that same day he removed the streaked and spotted he-goats and all the speckled and spotted she-goats—every one that had white on it—and all the dark-colored sheep, and left them in the charge of his sons. 36] And he put a distance of three days' journey between himself and Jacob, while Jacob was pasturing the rest of Laban's flock.

37] Jacob then got fresh shoots of poplar, and of almond and plane, and peeled white stripes in them, laying bare the white of the shoots. 38] The rods that he

36] In the Samaritan version, the dream sequence related in Gen. 31:10-13 is inserted after this verse, which improves the sense of otherwise difficult passages.

פְּצֵל בָּרְהָטִים בְּשִׁקֲתוֹת הַמָּיִם אֲשֶׁר תָּבֹאןָ הַצֹּאן

לט לִשְׁתּוֹת לְנֹכַח הַצֹּאן וַיֵּחַמְנָה בְּבֹאָן לִשְׁתּוֹת: וַיֶּחֱמוּ

הַצֹּאן אֶל־הַמַּקְלוֹת וַתֵּלַדְןָ הַצֹּאן עֲקֻדִּים נְקֻדִּים

מ וּטְלֻאִים: וְהַכְּשָׂבִים הִפְרִיד יַעֲקֹב וַיִּתֵּן פְּנֵי הַצֹּאן

אֶל־עָקֹד וְכָל־חוּם בְּצֹאן לָבָן וַיָּשֶׁת לוֹ עֲדָרִים לְבַדּוֹ

מא וְלֹא שָׁתָם עַל־צֹאן לָבָן: וְהָיָה בְּכָל־יַחֵם הַצֹּאן

הַמְקֻשָּׁרוֹת וְשָׂם יַעֲקֹב אֶת־הַמַּקְלוֹת לְעֵינֵי הַצֹּאן

מב בָּרְהָטִים לְיַחְמֵנָּה בַּמַּקְלוֹת: וּבְהַעֲטִיף הַצֹּאן לֹא

מג יָשִׂים וְהָיָה הָעֲטֻפִים לְלָבָן וְהַקְּשֻׁרִים לְיַעֲקֹב: וַיִּפְרֹץ

הָאִישׁ מְאֹד מְאֹד וַיְהִי־לוֹ צֹאן רַבּוֹת וּשְׁפָחוֹת וַעֲבָדִים

וּגְמַלִּים וַחֲמֹרִים:

had peeled he set up in front of the flocks in troughs—the water receptacles that the flocks came to drink from; their mating occurred when they came to drink. **39]** Since the goats mated by the rods, the goats brought forth streaked, speckled, and spotted young.   **40]** The ewes, on the other hand, Jacob kept apart and made these animals face the streaked or wholly dark-colored animals in Laban's flocks. And so he produced special flocks for himself, which he did not put with Laban's flocks.   **41]** Moreover, when the sturdier animals were mating, Jacob would place the rods in the troughs, in full view of the animals, so that they mated by the rods; **42]** but with the feebler animals he would not place them there. Thus the feeble ones went to Laban and the sturdy to Jacob.   **43]** So the man grew exceedingly prosperous, and came to own large flocks, maidservants and menservants, camels and asses.

39] *Goats.* Literally, "flocks" [8].   42] *Feebler.* Or "late-breeding."
41] *Sturdier.* Or "early-breeding."

The Tribal Ancestors

The births of Jacob's sons are described in great detail because the Torah depicts the twelve tribes of Israel as having originated from the twelve sons of Jacob. This genealogical conception of Israel's history is an important feature of the biblical tradition, for it traces the background not merely of kings but of the whole people. This conception is also reflected in the recurrent emphasis on descent, on the "lines" of the Patriarchs.

Some scholars have suggested that these ancestral figures were the projection of later generations, reflecting the time of the Judges, when the tribes were linked in a sacral confederation, or amphictyony. In this view of Israel's history, the tribes were related to the twelve calendar months, and each tribe made a monthly contribution to or participated in rites at the cultic center, as did the Mesopotamians and Greeks. Popular saga later transferred the story of the varying fortunes and characteristics of the tribes to the legendary ancestors and to one common forefather, Jacob-Israel. This reconstruction of Israel's history is, however, challenged by other scholars [9].

Whatever the precise nature of the process by which the biblical tradition was established, we may not overlook the fact that the Torah presents the ancestral figures as identifiable persons in their own age. The secret of the lasting vitality of these biblical tales is indeed to be found in this personalization, for the ancestors are now felt to be "not the reflection of Israelite fortunes in a specific period of time but as the poetic presentation of ever-recurring human fortunes and characteristics" [10].

Biology and Faith

The biblical account tells us the following: Sheep and goats were generally either white or dark, hence Jacob's offer to take only speckled animals meant that he was prepared to take merely a small portion of the flock. Laban agreed, but being suspicious of Jacob he wanted to make sure of his advantage and proceeded to cheat Jacob even of the few animals he had requested. Laban did not reckon with Jacob's plan to crossbreed white and dark animals by means of visual stimulation [11]. It was believed that the color of the offspring would be influenced by the color of the staves the animal had seen at mating time. Jacob ascribed his knowledge to divine inspiration, which helped him to overcome Laban's guile and to receive his just reward.

The section presents, therefore, more than an insight into ancient ideas of biology. Along with other biblical texts that deal with administrative, commercial, and legal matters, it connects everyday affairs with theology.[1] In this, the biblical accounts differ markedly from Babylonian texts. The vast number of sources that have been preserved in cuneiform rarely unite religious and historical-legal matters organically.

The final purpose of the story is to show Jacob's deepening faith in God's promise [12]. He comes to know God not only in His immediate manifestations but also in the long-range processes of nature. God is concerned with Jacob and the latter knows this concern, which here is expressed in a non-miraculous way: Jacob is favored in that he learns the secrets of nature and utilizes them in accordance with God's will.[2]

---

[1] This will be especially apparent in Leviticus.

[2] We may note that contemporary religious humanism would put the relation between God, man, and nature in a similar way: To know God means to use the laws of nature in the right way.

GLEANINGS

It Is Still Broad Daylight (Gen. 29:7)

How could a stranger like Jacob reprimand the shepherds? Learn from this that if one visits a strange place and sees a wrong being perpetrated it is his duty to prevent it. One must not say, "It is no business of mine."   MIDRASH [13]

Jacob Kissed Rachel

John Calvin thought that Moses, in saying that Rachel accepted a kiss from a stranger, must here have made an error in editing the Torah; for how could one believe that Rachel behaved otherwise than sixteenth-century morality demanded! [14]

It Is Not the Practice in Our Place (Gen. 29:26)

No one understood this better than Jacob, for he himself as the younger son had crossed the finishing line before his older brother. Thus the narrator shows how a serious nemesis is at work.   GERHARD VON RAD [15]

Laban

A masterful characterization: A selfish, greedy, exploiting, suspicious man of wealth, who never fails to observe good manners.   BENNO JACOB

Jacob the Shepherd

Before Jacob, Moses, David, Amos, or Ezekiel were made great, they were first tested as shepherds. Labor is beloved, for all the Prophets engaged in it.   MIDRASH [16]

Mandrakes

Because of the resemblance of its root to the human form, the mandrake is almost universally credited with magical powers. Dioscorides, the Greek physician, calls it "Circe's plant" (kirkeion), and among modern Arabs it is known as the "apple of the jinns" and is used in concocting philtres. Theophrastus says that it is an antidote against spells and enchantments, and Josephus records the popular belief that it expels demons. Indeed, it has been suggested that the drug named moly which Hermes supplied to Odysseus in order to counteract the magic potions brewed by Circe was really the mandrake.

The plant is used especially, as in our biblical narrative, as an aphrodisiac and as an antidote to barrenness. It is thus mentioned, for example, by the Greek comic dramatist Alexis (fourth century B.C.), and Aphrodite, the goddess of love, was sometimes styled, "Our Lady of the Mandrake." The Hebrew word rendered "mandrake" is indeed connected with a verbal root meaning "to love" and has its English counterpart in the popular term, "love-apple." In the Song of Songs (7:14), when the maiden invites her lover to enjoy her favors, she adds to her inducements the statement that she has stored up for him fragrant mandrakes. In Jewish folklore, the mandrake was long believed to relieve barrenness; while in Germany and some other parts of Europe it was customary to place mandrakes under a bridal bed.

THEODOR H. GASTER [17]

[The plants are still carried as aphrodisiacs in some pharmacies, although there is no medical evidence for their efficacy.]

Jacob's Departure from Haran

Jacob and his household leave Haran and Laban's sphere of influence. As the parting takes place, the last act of deception is perpetrated—but this time by neither Jacob nor Laban. This time both are being deceived. Laban is cheated of his household deities and Jacob, through his wife's theft, unknowingly exposes her to unforeseen danger. Thus, deception returns to visit its perpetrators.

At times the text appears disjointed. Critics distinguish two traditions—the J-school and the E-school (for example, in chapter 31 compare verses 1 with 2 and 46–50 with 51–54).

א וַיִּשְׁמַע אֶת־דִּבְרֵי בְנֵי־לָבָן לֵאמֹר לָקַח יַעֲקֹב אֵת
כָּל־אֲשֶׁר לְאָבִינוּ וּמֵאֲשֶׁר לְאָבִינוּ עָשָׂה אֵת כָּל־
ב הַכָּבֹד הַזֶּה: וַיַּרְא יַעֲקֹב אֶת־פְּנֵי לָבָן וְהִנֵּה אֵינֶנּוּ עִמּוֹ
ג כִּתְמוֹל שִׁלְשׁוֹם: וַיֹּאמֶר יְהוָה אֶל־יַעֲקֹב שׁוּב אֶל־אֶרֶץ
ד אֲבוֹתֶיךָ וּלְמוֹלַדְתֶּךָ וְאֶהְיֶה עִמָּךְ: וַיִּשְׁלַח יַעֲקֹב
ה וַיִּקְרָא לְרָחֵל וּלְלֵאָה הַשָּׂדֶה אֶל־צֹאנוֹ: וַיֹּאמֶר לָהֶן
רֹאֶה אָנֹכִי אֶת־פְּנֵי אֲבִיכֶן כִּי־אֵינֶנּוּ אֵלַי כִּתְמֹל
ו שִׁלְשֹׁם וֵאלֹהֵי אָבִי הָיָה עִמָּדִי: וְאַתֵּנָה יְדַעְתֶּן כִּי
ז בְּכָל־כֹּחִי עָבַדְתִּי אֶת־אֲבִיכֶן: וַאֲבִיכֶן הֵתֶל בִּי
וְהֶחֱלִף אֶת־מַשְׂכֻּרְתִּי עֲשֶׂרֶת מֹנִים וְלֹא־נְתָנוֹ אֱלֹהִים
ח לְהָרַע עִמָּדִי: אִם־כֹּה יֹאמַר נְקֻדִּים יִהְיֶה שְׂכָרֶךָ
וְיָלְדוּ כָל־הַצֹּאן נְקֻדִּים וְאִם־כֹּה יֹאמַר עֲקֻדִּים

Genesis 31
1–8

1] Now he heard the things that Laban's sons were saying: "Jacob has taken all that was our father's and from that which should be our father's he has built up all this wealth." 2] Jacob also saw that Laban's manner toward him was not as it had been in the past. 3] Then the LORD said to Jacob, "Return to the land of your fathers where you were born, and I will be with you." 4] Jacob had Rachel and Leah called to the field, where his flock was, 5] and said to them, "I see that your father's manner toward me is not as it has been in the past; but the God of my father has been with me. 6] As you know, I have served your father with all my might; 7] but your father has cheated me, changing my wages time and again. God, however, would not let him do me harm. 8] If he said thus, 'The speckled shall be your wages,' then all the flocks would drop speckled young; and

31:4] *To the field.* To speak privately to them. Rachel is named first because she came first in Jacob's affection and because he had stayed on for her sake [1]. In the Book of Ruth (4:11) and in the Sabbath blessing of daughters, Rachel also precedes Leah.

7] *Time and again.* Literally, "ten times" [2] (see also Gen. 31:41).

ט יִהְיֶה שְׂכָרֶךָ וְיָלְדוּ כָל־הַצֹּאן עֲקֻדִּים: וַיַּצֵּל אֱלֹהִים

י אֶת־מִקְנֵה אֲבִיכֶם וַיִּתֶּן־לִי: וַיְהִי בְּעֵת יַחֵם הַצֹּאן

וָאֶשָּׂא עֵינַי וָאֵרֶא בַּחֲלוֹם וְהִנֵּה הָעַתֻּדִים הָעֹלִים

יא עַל־הַצֹּאן עֲקֻדִּים נְקֻדִּים וּבְרֻדִּים: וַיֹּאמֶר אֵלַי

יב מַלְאַךְ הָאֱלֹהִים בַּחֲלוֹם יַעֲקֹב וָאֹמַר הִנֵּנִי: וַיֹּאמֶר

שָׂא־נָא עֵינֶיךָ וּרְאֵה כָּל־הָעַתֻּדִים הָעֹלִים עַל־הַצֹּאן

עֲקֻדִּים נְקֻדִּים וּבְרֻדִּים כִּי רָאִיתִי אֵת כָּל־אֲשֶׁר

יג לָבָן עֹשֶׂה לָּךְ: אָנֹכִי הָאֵל בֵּית־אֵל אֲשֶׁר מָשַׁחְתָּ שָּׁם

מַצֵּבָה אֲשֶׁר נָדַרְתָּ לִּי שָׁם נֶדֶר עַתָּה קוּם צֵא מִן

יד הָאָרֶץ הַזֹּאת וְשׁוּב אֶל־אֶרֶץ מוֹלַדְתֶּךָ: וַתַּעַן רָחֵל

וְלֵאָה וַתֹּאמַרְנָה לוֹ הַעוֹד לָנוּ חֵלֶק וְנַחֲלָה בְּבֵית

טו אָבִינוּ: הֲלוֹא נָכְרִיּוֹת נֶחְשַׁבְנוּ לוֹ כִּי מְכָרָנוּ וַיֹּאכַל

if he said thus, 'The streaked shall be your wages,' then all the flocks would drop streaked young.   9] God has taken away your father's livestock and given it to me.

10] "Once, at the mating time of the flocks, I had a dream in which I saw that the he-goats in the flock, as they mated, were streaked, speckled, and mottled. 11] And in the dream an angel of God said to me, 'Jacob!' 'Here,' I answered. 12] And he said, 'Note well that all the he-goats in the flock which are mating are streaked, speckled, and mottled; for I have noted all that Laban has been doing to you.   13] I am the God of Bethel, where you anointed a pillar and where you made a vow to Me. Up, then, leave this land and return to the land of your birth.'"

14] Then Rachel and Leah answered him, saying, "Have we still a share in the inheritance of our father's house?   15] Are we not reckoned by him as outsiders?

10] *I had a dream.* Literally, "I raised my eyes and saw in a dream, behold."

13] *God of Bethel.* A reference to the events told in Gen. 28:10-15.

15] *Outsiders.* Or foreigners. According to many ancient laws, foreigners did not have the same rights as other members of the family. Leah and Rachel believe that their father now considers

טו גַּם־אָכוֹל אֶת־כַּסְפֵּנוּ: כִּי כָל־הָעֹשֶׁר אֲשֶׁר הִצִּיל

אֱלֹהִים מֵאָבִינוּ לָנוּ הוּא וּלְבָנֵינוּ וְעַתָּה כֹּל אֲשֶׁר

יז אָמַר אֱלֹהִים אֵלֶיךָ עֲשֵׂה: וַיָּקׇם יַעֲקֹב וַיִּשָּׂא אֶת־

יח בָּנָיו וְאֶת־נָשָׁיו עַל־הַגְּמַלִּים: וַיִּנְהַג אֶת־כָּל־מִקְנֵהוּ

וְאֶת־כָּל־רְכֻשׁוֹ אֲשֶׁר רָכָשׁ מִקְנֵה קִנְיָנוֹ אֲשֶׁר רָכַשׁ

יט בְּפַדַּן אֲרָם לָבוֹא אֶל־יִצְחָק אָבִיו אַרְצָה כְּנָעַן: וְלָבָן

הָלַךְ לִגְזֹז אֶת־צֹאנוֹ וַתִּגְנֹב רָחֵל אֶת־הַתְּרָפִים אֲשֶׁר

כ לְאָבִיהָ: וַיִּגְנֹב יַעֲקֹב אֶת־לֵב לָבָן הָאֲרַמִּי עַל־בְּלִי

כא הִגִּיד לוֹ כִּי בֹרֵחַ הוּא: וַיִּבְרַח הוּא וְכָל־אֲשֶׁר־לוֹ

וַיָּקׇם וַיַּעֲבֹר אֶת־הַנָּהָר וַיָּשֶׂם אֶת־פָּנָיו הַר הַגִּלְעָד:

כב וַיֻּגַּד לְלָבָן בַּיּוֹם הַשְּׁלִישִׁי כִּי בָרַח יַעֲקֹב: וַיִּקַּח אֶת־
כג

Genesis 31

16–23

For he sold us and then used up our purchase price.   16] Truly, all the wealth that God has taken away from our father belongs to us and to our children. Now then, do just as God has told you."

17] Thereupon Jacob put his children and wives on camels;   18] and he drove off all his livestock and all the wealth that he had amassed, the livestock in his possession that he had acquired in Paddan-aram, to go to his father Isaac in the land of Canaan.

19] Meanwhile Laban had gone to shear his sheep, and Rachel appropriated her father's household idols.   20] Jacob kept Laban the Aramean in the dark, not telling him that he was fleeing,   21] and fled with all that he had. Soon he was across the Euphrates and heading toward the hill country of Gilead.

22] On the third day, Laban was told that Jacob had fled.   23] So he took his

them foreigners because of their marriage to Jacob and that their dowry, set aside by their father, is "eaten up" or lost.

20] *Kept . . . in the dark.* Literally, "stole the mind of"; similarly Gen. 31:26.

21] *Euphrates.* הַנָּהָר. Literally, "*the* river."

אֶחָיו עִמּוֹ וַיִּרְדֹּף אַחֲרָיו דֶּרֶךְ שִׁבְעַת יָמִים וַיַּדְבֵּק

כד אֹתוֹ בְּהַר הַגִּלְעָד: וַיָּבֹא אֱלֹהִים אֶל־לָבָן הָאֲרַמִּי

בַּחֲלֹם הַלַּיְלָה וַיֹּאמֶר לוֹ הִשָּׁמֶר לְךָ פֶּן־תְּדַבֵּר

כה עִם־יַעֲקֹב מִטּוֹב עַד־רָע: וַיַּשֵּׂג לָבָן אֶת־יַעֲקֹב וְיַעֲקֹב

תָּקַע אֶת־אָהֳלוֹ בָּהָר וְלָבָן תָּקַע אֶת־אֶחָיו בְּהַר

כו הַגִּלְעָד: וַיֹּאמֶר לָבָן לְיַעֲקֹב מֶה עָשִׂיתָ וַתִּגְנֹב אֶת־

כז לְבָבִי וַתְּנַהֵג אֶת־בְּנֹתַי כִּשְׁבֻיוֹת חָרֶב: לָמָּה נַחְבֵּאתָ

לִבְרֹחַ וַתִּגְנֹב אֹתִי וְלֹא־הִגַּדְתָּ לִּי וָאֲשַׁלֵּחֲךָ בְּשִׂמְחָה

כח וּבְשִׁרִים בְּתֹף וּבְכִנּוֹר: וְלֹא נְטַשְׁתַּנִי לְנַשֵּׁק לְבָנַי

כט וְלִבְנֹתָי עַתָּה הִסְכַּלְתָּ עֲשׂוֹ: יֶשׁ־לְאֵל יָדִי לַעֲשׂוֹת

Genesis 31

24–29

kinsmen with him and pursued him a distance of seven days, catching up with him in the hill country of Gilead.   24] But God appeared to Laban the Aramean in a dream by night and said to him, "Beware of attempting anything with Jacob, good or bad."

25] Laban overtook Jacob. Jacob had pitched his tent on the Height, and Laban with his kinsmen encamped in the hill country of Gilead.   26] And Laban said to Jacob, "What did you mean by keeping me in the dark and carrying off my daughters like captives of the sword?   27] Why did you flee in secrecy and mislead me and not tell me? I would have sent you off with festive music, with timbrel and lyre.   28] You did not even let me kiss my sons and daughters good-by! It was a foolish thing for you to do.   29] I have it in my power to do

24] *God appeared to Laban.* As He had, for instance, appeared to Abimelech. Biblical tradition does not restrict divine communication to Abraham and his descendants.

Laban the Aramean. Laban spoke Aramaic

(Gen. 31:47) and lived in Paddan-aram. The Patriarchs were also later referred to as Arameans because they had come from this area (see p. 247 and Deut. 26:5).

עִמָּכֶם רָע וֵאלֹהֵי אֲבִיכֶם אֶמֶשׁ אָמַר אֵלַי לֵאמֹר

ל הִשָּׁמֶר לְךָ מִדַּבֵּר עִם־יַעֲקֹב מִטּוֹב עַד־רָע: וְעַתָּה הָלֹךְ הָלַכְתָּ כִּי־נִכְסֹף נִכְסַפְתָּה לְבֵית אָבִיךָ לָמָּה

לא גָנַבְתָּ אֶת־אֱלֹהָי: וַיַּעַן יַעֲקֹב וַיֹּאמֶר לְלָבָן כִּי יָרֵאתִי

לב כִּי אָמַרְתִּי פֶּן־תִּגְזֹל אֶת־בְּנוֹתֶיךָ מֵעִמִּי: עִם אֲשֶׁר תִּמְצָא אֶת־אֱלֹהֶיךָ לֹא יִחְיֶה נֶגֶד אַחֵינוּ הַכֶּר־לְךָ מָה עִמָּדִי וְקַח־לָךְ וְלֹא־יָדַע יַעֲקֹב כִּי רָחֵל גְּנָבָתַם:

לג וַיָּבֹא לָבָן בְּאֹהֶל־יַעֲקֹב וּבְאֹהֶל לֵאָה וּבְאֹהֶל שְׁתֵּי הָאֲמָהֹת וְלֹא מָצָא וַיֵּצֵא מֵאֹהֶל לֵאָה וַיָּבֹא בְּאֹהֶל

לד רָחֵל: וְרָחֵל לָקְחָה אֶת־הַתְּרָפִים וַתְּשִׂמֵם בְּכַר הַגָּמָל

Genesis 31
30–34

you harm; but the God of your father said to me last night, 'Beware of attempting anything with Jacob, good or bad.'   30] Very well, you had to leave because you were longing for your father's house; but why did you steal my gods?"

31] Jacob answered Laban, saying, "I was frightened at the thought that you would take your daughters from me by force.   32] But anyone with whom you find your gods shall not remain alive! In the presence of our kinsmen, point out what I have of yours and take it." Jacob, of course, did not know that Rachel had appropriated them.

33] So Laban went into Jacob's tent and Leah's tent and the tents of the two maidservants; but he did not find them. Leaving Leah's tent, he entered Rachel's tent.   34] Rachel, meanwhile, had taken the idols and placed them in the camel

30] *Leave . . . longing.* The simple translation does not convey that in the Hebrew text each verb is provided with an added infinitive, providing special emphasis to Laban's words. A colloquial rendering might be: "So you wanted to leave—leave already! You longed for your father's house, all right! But why did you have to steal my gods?" In his dis-

cussion of biblical meanings, R. Ishmael (second century C.E.) cited this verse as proof that "the Torah speaks in the language of men" [3].

34] *Camel cushion.* The idea that a woman might sit on the *teraphim* during her menstrual period (*niddah*) subtly indicates the Torah's contempt for

וַתֵּשֶׁב עֲלֵיהֶם וַיְמַשֵּׁשׁ לָבָן אֶת־כָּל־הָאֹהֶל וְלֹא מָצָא:

לה וַתֹּאמֶר אֶל־אָבִיהָ אַל־יִחַר בְּעֵינֵי אֲדֹנִי כִּי לוֹא אוּכַל לָקוּם מִפָּנֶיךָ כִּי־דֶרֶךְ נָשִׁים לִי וַיְחַפֵּשׂ וְלֹא מָצָא אֶת־הַתְּרָפִים:

לו וַיִּחַר לְיַעֲקֹב וַיָּרֶב בְּלָבָן וַיַּעַן יַעֲקֹב וַיֹּאמֶר לְלָבָן מַה־פִּשְׁעִי מַה חַטָּאתִי כִּי דָלַקְתָּ אַחֲרָי:

לז כִּי־מִשַּׁשְׁתָּ אֶת־כָּל־כֵּלַי מַה־מָּצָאתָ מִכֹּל כְּלֵי־בֵיתֶךָ שִׂים כֹּה נֶגֶד אַחַי וְאַחֶיךָ וְיוֹכִיחוּ בֵּין שְׁנֵינוּ:

לח זֶה עֶשְׂרִים שָׁנָה אָנֹכִי עִמָּךְ רְחֵלֶיךָ וְעִזֶּיךָ לֹא שִׁכֵּלוּ וְאֵילֵי צֹאנְךָ לֹא אָכָלְתִּי:

לט טְרֵפָה לֹא־הֵבֵאתִי אֵלֶיךָ אָנֹכִי אֲחַטֶּנָּה מִיָּדִי תְּבַקְשֶׁנָּה גְּנֻבְתִי יוֹם וּגְנֻבְתִי לָיְלָה:

cushion and sat on them; and Laban rummaged through the tent without finding them.   35] For she said to her father, "Let not my lord take it amiss that I cannot rise before you, for the period of women is upon me." Thus he searched, but could not find the household gods.

36] Now Jacob became incensed and took up his grievance with Laban. Jacob spoke up and said to Laban, "What is my crime, what is my guilt that you should pursue me?   37] You rummaged through all my things; what have you found of all your household objects? Set it here, before my kinsmen and yours, and let them decide between us two.

38] "These twenty years I have spent in your service, your ewes and she-goats never miscarried, nor did I feast on rams from your flock.   39] That which was torn by beasts I never brought to you; I myself made good the loss; you exacted it

---

the idols. Biblical law prevented men from coming close to menstruating women [4].
/Hertz translates כַּר as "palanquin."/

37] *Household objects*. Jacob derisively calls Laban's *teraphim* "objects."

38] *These twenty years*. His long pent-up anger begins to emerge.

39] *I never brought*. The legal obligations of a shepherd were set forth in detail in the Code of Hammurabi. For instance: "If a visitation of God

מ הָיִיתִי בַיּוֹם אֲכָלַנִי חֹרֶב וְקֶרַח בַּלָּיְלָה וַתִּדַּד שְׁנָתִי

מא מֵעֵינָי: זֶה־לִּי עֶשְׂרִים שָׁנָה בְּבֵיתֶךָ עֲבַדְתִּיךָ אַרְבַּע־
עֶשְׂרֵה שָׁנָה בִּשְׁתֵּי בְנֹתֶיךָ וְשֵׁשׁ שָׁנִים בְּצֹאנֶךָ וַתַּחֲלֵף

מב אֶת־מַשְׂכֻּרְתִּי עֲשֶׂרֶת מֹנִים: לוּלֵי אֱלֹהֵי אָבִי אֱלֹהֵי
אַבְרָהָם וּפַחַד יִצְחָק הָיָה לִי כִּי עַתָּה רֵיקָם שִׁלַּחְתָּנִי
אֶת־עָנְיִי וְאֶת־יְגִיעַ כַּפַּי רָאָה אֱלֹהִים וַיּוֹכַח אָמֶשׁ:

מג וַיַּעַן לָבָן וַיֹּאמֶר אֶל־יַעֲקֹב הַבָּנוֹת בְּנֹתַי וְהַבָּנִים בָּנַי
וְהַצֹּאן צֹאנִי וְכֹל אֲשֶׁר־אַתָּה רֹאֶה לִי־הוּא וְלִבְנֹתַי

מד מָה־אֶעֱשֶׂה לָאֵלֶּה הַיּוֹם אוֹ לִבְנֵיהֶן אֲשֶׁר יָלָדוּ: וְעַתָּה
לְכָה נִכְרְתָה בְרִית אֲנִי וָאָתָּה וְהָיָה לְעֵד בֵּינִי וּבֵינֶךָ:

Genesis 31

40–44

of me, whether snatched by day or snatched by night.   40] Often, scorching heat ravaged me by day and frost by night; and sleep fled from my eyes.   41] Of the twenty years that I spent in your household, I served you fourteen years for your two daughters, and six years for your flocks, since you changed my wages time and again.   42] Had not the God of my father, the God of Abraham and the Fear of Isaac, been with me, you would have sent me away empty-handed. But God took notice of my plight and the toil of my hands, and He gave judgment last night."

43] Then Laban spoke up and said to Jacob, "The daughters are my daughters, the children are my children, and the flocks are my flocks; all that you see is mine. Yet what can I do now about my daughters or the children they have borne? 44] Come, then, let us make a pact, you and I, that there may be a witness between

has occurred in a sheepfold or a lion has made a kill, the shepherd shall prove himself innocent in the presence of God, but the owner of the sheepfold shall receive from him the animal stricken in the fold" [5].   Jacob indicates that he has more than complied with the law (see p. 313).

42] *Fear of Isaac.* פַּחַד יִצְחָק. Also in Gen. 31:53.

The meaning is obscure. Isaiah, too, refers to God as "your fear" and "your dread" (8:13).

43] *The daughters are my daughters.* Laban places Jacob's marriages in a special Assyrian legal category, *erebu,* in which the husband lived with his wife's family; if he left he could not take his wife or her belongings with him [6].

מה וַיִּקַּח יַעֲקֹב אָבֶן וַיְרִימֶהָ מַצֵּבָה: וַיֹּאמֶר יַעֲקֹב
לְאֶחָיו לִקְטוּ אֲבָנִים וַיִּקְחוּ אֲבָנִים וַיַּעֲשׂוּ־גָל וַיֹּאכְלוּ

מו שָׁם עַל־הַגָּל: וַיִּקְרָא־לוֹ לָבָן יְגַר שָׂהֲדוּתָא וְיַעֲקֹב

מז קָרָא לוֹ גַּלְעֵד: וַיֹּאמֶר לָבָן הַגַּל הַזֶּה עֵד בֵּינִי וּבֵינֶךָ

מח הַיּוֹם עַל־כֵּן קָרָא־שְׁמוֹ גַּלְעֵד: וְהַמִּצְפָּה אֲשֶׁר אָמַר

נ יִצֶף יְהוָה בֵּינִי וּבֵינֶךָ כִּי נִסָּתֵר אִישׁ מֵרֵעֵהוּ: אִם־

תְּעַנֶּה אֶת־בְּנֹתַי וְאִם־תִּקַּח נָשִׁים עַל־בְּנֹתַי אֵין אִישׁ

נא עִמָּנוּ רְאֵה אֱלֹהִים עֵד בֵּינִי וּבֵינֶךָ: וַיֹּאמֶר לָבָן

לְיַעֲקֹב הִנֵּה הַגַּל הַזֶּה וְהִנֵּה הַמַּצֵּבָה אֲשֶׁר יָרִיתִי

נב בֵּינִי וּבֵינֶךָ: עֵד הַגַּל הַזֶּה וְעֵדָה הַמַּצֵּבָה אִם־אָנִי

you and me." **45]** Thereupon Jacob took a stone and set it up as a pillar. **46]** And Jacob said to his kinsmen, "Gather stones." So they took stones and made a mound; and they partook of a meal there by the mound. **47]** Laban named it Yegar-sahadutha, but Jacob named it Gal-ed. **48]** And Laban declared, "This mound is a witness between you and me this day." That is why it was named Gal-ed; **49]** also Mizpah, because he said, "May the LORD watch between you and me, when we are out of sight of each other. **50]** If you ill-treat my daughters or take other wives besides my daughters—though no one else be about, God Himself will be witness between you and me."

51] And Laban said to Jacob, "Here is this mound and here the pillar which I have set up between you and me: **52]** this mound shall be witness and this pillar

---

Yet what can I do. He gives in, knowing that his daughters want to leave.

47] *Yegar-sahadutha.* The only Aramaic words in the Torah, meaning "mound [or, stone-heap] of witness."

Gal-ed. A translation of Yegar-sahadutha into Hebrew. It reflects a popular etymology of the name Gilead, which occurs in Gen. 31:23.

48] *This mound.* Nothing was written down; the stones were symbols of the covenant.

49] *Watch.* יִצֶף (*yitzef*), associated with Mizpah. This is not a benediction but a warning: "Let God watch over us that we may not break our covenant" [7].

לֹא־אֶעֱבֹר אֵלֶיךָ אֶת־הַגַּל הַזֶּה וְאִם־אַתָּה לֹא־תַעֲבֹר
אֵלַי אֶת־הַגַּל הַזֶּה וְאֶת־הַמַּצֵּבָה הַזֹּאת לְרָעָה: אֱלֹהֵי
אַבְרָהָם וֵאלֹהֵי נָחוֹר יִשְׁפְּטוּ בֵינֵינוּ אֱלֹהֵי אֲבִיהֶם
וַיִּשָּׁבַע יַעֲקֹב בְּפַחַד אָבִיו יִצְחָק: וַיִּזְבַּח יַעֲקֹב זֶבַח
בָּהָר וַיִּקְרָא לְאֶחָיו לֶאֱכָל־לָחֶם וַיֹּאכְלוּ לֶחֶם וַיָּלִינוּ
בָּהָר:

וַיַּשְׁכֵּם לָבָן בַּבֹּקֶר וַיְנַשֵּׁק לְבָנָיו וְלִבְנוֹתָיו וַיְבָרֶךְ
אֶתְהֶם וַיֵּלֶךְ וַיָּשָׁב לָבָן לִמְקֹמוֹ: וְיַעֲקֹב הָלַךְ לְדַרְכּוֹ
וַיִּפְגְּעוּ־בוֹ מַלְאֲכֵי אֱלֹהִים: וַיֹּאמֶר יַעֲקֹב כַּאֲשֶׁר רָאָם
מַחֲנֵה אֱלֹהִים זֶה וַיִּקְרָא שֵׁם־הַמָּקוֹם הַהוּא מַחֲנָיִם:

Genesis 31; 32

53–54; 1–3

Haftarah Vayetze, p. 546

---

shall be witness that I am not to cross to you past this mound, and that you are not to cross to me past this mound and this pillar, with hostile intent.   **53]** May the God of Abraham and the god of Nahor"—their ancestral deities—"judge between us." And Jacob swore by the Fear of his father Isaac.   **54]** Jacob then offered up a sacrifice on the Height, and invited his kinsmen to partake of the meal. After the meal, they spent the night on the Height.

1] Early in the morning, Laban kissed his sons and daughters and bade them good-by; then Laban left on his journey homeward.   **2]** Jacob went on his way, and angels of God encountered him.   **3]** When he saw them, Jacob said, "This is God's camp." So he named that place Mahanaim.

53] *Their ancestral deities.* A parenthetical note. The Bible uses the word "elohim" generically, for Israel's Lord as well as pagan gods. In official Egyptian correspondence the writers bless Pharaoh in the name of his and their own gods.

54] *The Height.* The mount where the covenant was concluded.

32:1–3] The brevity of this account is puzzling; the three verses may have been part of a larger story now lost. They serve here as a postscript and conclusion to Jacob's wanderings. Angels met him when he first set out (Gen. 28:12) and meet him again here as if to signify that his exile for the past twenty years has always been guided by God.

3] *Mahanaim.* Connected with מַחֲנֶה (*machaneh*, camp, troup). The place is mentioned in later history (e.g., II Sam. 2:8).

Rachel's Theft

Rachel's theft of the household idols (*teraphim*), Laban's angry concern, and Jacob's extravagant denial all point to the great importance that ancient man attached to these objects. They were figurines, usually small and in the shape of men (see I Sam. 19:13, 16). Their use in Israel continued into the days of the Judges (17:5) and the Prophets (Hos. 3:4–5). Josephus reported that even in his day (first century C.E.) it was the custom "among all the people in that country to have objects of worship in their house and to take them along when going abroad" [8]. Rachel, therefore, may have felt it necessary to take household deities along on her journey and decided to appropriate her father's idols. By doing this, however, she left him without proper protection—hence his great anger [9].

Another interpretation gives legal rather than religious reasons for Rachel's action. Nuzi records indicate that *teraphim* were often symbols of property rights and family status. Their possession could indicate that certain privileges had been confirmed by transmitting the ownership of the *teraphim* (cf. the symbolism of the scepter or of keys to a house). Thus, Jacob's possession of the *teraphim* might prove that he was no longer Laban's servant and that he was, therefore, entitled to a part of the latter's estate. If Jacob had not in law attained this position, Rachel by her theft meant to assure it for him. Biblical tradition viewed Rachel as a resolute woman who did not hesitate to take the law—or what she believed to be the law—into her own hands [10]. She knew her husband's rights and she had ample reason to doubt that Laban would voluntarily and formally transfer the images. That she might proceed in this fashion apparently never occurred to Jacob. He either did not know the intricacies of Hurrian law or he was not aware of his wife's capacity for action.[1]

We have already learned of Rachel's consideration and charm at the time of her first meeting with Jacob, of her agony over her long barrenness, her jealousy over her sister's good fortune, and of her attempt to utilize aphrodisiacs. We now see her to be an independent woman. With the rift between Laban and Jacob widening, she took the lead over her sister in siding with her husband instead of her father, and in the moment of parting it was she again who was stirred to decisive action. However, her impetuousness caused Jacob to make an extreme and tragic oath.

Here the theme of retribution may again be glimpsed. For while the Torah passes no explicit judgment on Rachel's behavior, its tragic consequences will all too soon become evident. The commentators who exculpate Rachel[2] are therefore wide of the mark. Jacob's oath that whoever may be found with the *teraphim* should not remain alive (Gen. 31:32) is exacted—not by Laban, as expected, but by God himself. Rachel dies in her next childbirth and is buried by the roadside (Gen. 35:16–20). She is the only Matriarch not interred in Machpelah, the grave site of the other Matriarchs and Patriarchs.[3] She died at a young age because she had been disloyal to her father, which to the ancients was a cardinal sin. Jacob by his rash oath unwittingly brought on his beloved's destruction, a plot found also in Greek tragedies.

---

[1] It is, of course, possible that if her marriage was of the *erebu* type (see note at Gen. 31:43) Laban and not she was in the right.

[2] She stole the idols to keep Laban from idolatry [11]. They were a means of divination and Rachel feared Laban would discover her leaving [12].

[3] So, the Midrash on the Ten Commandments: Because she stole the *teraphim* she was not buried in Machpelah.

GLEANINGS

Jewish Law

Gen. 31:40 became an object lesson for defining the limitations of a paid watchman's responsibilities. Jewish law provides that a watchman engaged to guard property in the city must guard his charge constantly, while in the countryside he may be excused occasionally. Jacob's description of his own extreme attention to duty shows that he did more than the law required.   TALMUD [13]

Stealing the Heart

Rebeccah appropriates (or steals) Laban's household gods while Jacob keeps Laban in the dark about his impending departure (literally, "he stole the heart of Laban," 31:20).

The expression preserves an interesting piece of folklore. In ancient times the heart was considered, as it still is among primitive peoples, the seat not only of the emotions but also of the mental processes. Alike among the Hebrews and the Babylonians, for example, a common expression for "to think" was "to say in the heart." The heart was thus symbolic of the total self, and in moments, such as sleep or trance, when a man had temporarily lost consciousness, the heart was believed temporarily to have departed from him. It could even be enticed out of him by magic or by the action of demons. To "steal the heart" meant, therefore, more than to bemuse the emotions; it meant to gain complete control over a person's self-direction. In the Egyptian Pyramid Texts mention is made of a class of demons called "stealers of the heart" who were thought to divest the dead of consciousness.   THEODOR H. GASTER [14]

The Cairn

The custom of erecting cairns as witnesses is apparently not extinct in Syria even now. One of the most famous shrines of the country is that of Aaron on Mount Hor. The prophet's tomb on the mountain is visited by pilgrims, who pray the saint to intercede for the recovery of sick friends and pile up heaps of stones as witnesses (*meshhad*) of the vows they make on behalf of the sufferers.

JAMES G. FRAZER [15]

Greek Parallel

To thee doth Troy commend her household gods;
Now take them as companions of thy fate.

VERGIL [16]

Jacob Becomes Israel

Jacob's exile draws to a close. But he cannot go home without first settling accounts with his brother. Twenty years have elapsed since the frightened young man deceived Esau. Twenty years have changed him greatly, and they have changed Esau, too. The time has come to face the past and, in doing so, to secure the future. As Jacob prepares to meet Esau, he also meets his God. A "man" wrestles with him one night, and when morning breaks Jacob has become Israel. This story provides the background to the tale of reconciliation and raises important questions about the nature and meaning of the name "Israel."

פ   פ   פ

בראשית לב
ד–ט

ד וַיִּשְׁלַח יַעֲקֹב מַלְאָכִים לְפָנָיו אֶל־עֵשָׂו אָחִיו אַרְצָה
שֵׂעִיר שְׂדֵה אֱדוֹם: וַיְצַו אֹתָם לֵאמֹר כֹּה תֹאמְרוּן ה
לַאדֹנִי לְעֵשָׂו כֹּה אָמַר עַבְדְּךָ יַעֲקֹב עִם־לָבָן גַּרְתִּי
וָאֵחַר עַד־עָתָּה: וַיְהִי־לִי שׁוֹר וַחֲמוֹר צֹאן וְעֶבֶד ו
וְשִׁפְחָה וָאֶשְׁלְחָה לְהַגִּיד לַאדֹנִי לִמְצֹא־חֵן בְּעֵינֶיךָ:
וַיָּשֻׁבוּ הַמַּלְאָכִים אֶל־יַעֲקֹב לֵאמֹר בָּאנוּ אֶל־אָחִיךָ ז
אֶל־עֵשָׂו וְגַם הֹלֵךְ לִקְרָאתְךָ וְאַרְבַּע־מֵאוֹת אִישׁ עִמּוֹ:
וַיִּירָא יַעֲקֹב מְאֹד וַיֵּצֶר לוֹ וַיַּחַץ אֶת־הָעָם אֲשֶׁר־ ח
אִתּוֹ וְאֶת־הַצֹּאן וְאֶת־הַבָּקָר וְהַגְּמַלִּים לִשְׁנֵי מַחֲנוֹת:
וַיֹּאמֶר אִם־יָבוֹא עֵשָׂו אֶל־הַמַּחֲנֶה הָאַחַת וְהִכָּהוּ ט
וְהָיָה הַמַּחֲנֶה הַנִּשְׁאָר לִפְלֵיטָה:

Genesis 32
4–9

4] Jacob sent messengers ahead to his brother Esau in the land of Seir, the country of Edom, 5] and instructed them as follows, "Thus shall you say, 'To my lord Esau, thus says your servant Jacob: I stayed with Laban and remained until now; 6] I have acquired cattle, asses, sheep, and male and female slaves; and I send this message to my lord in the hope of gaining your favor.'" 7] The messengers returned to Jacob, saying, "We came to your brother Esau; he himself is coming to meet you, and there are four hundred men with him." 8] Jacob was greatly frightened; in his anxiety, he divided the people with him, and the flocks and herds and camels, into two camps, 9] thinking, "If Esau comes to the one camp and attacks it, the other camp may yet escape."

32:5] *Thus shall you say.* Jacob's instructions reflect a formula found in Sumerian and Akkadian letters.
/By punctuating the Hebrew text differently, we can read: "Thus shall you say to my Lord Esau, 'Thus says your servant Jacob'" [1]./

6] *In the hope.* Jacob does not pretend to make his gift out of pure love [2].

317

וַיֹּאמֶר יַעֲקֹב אֱלֹהֵי

אָבִי אַבְרָהָם וֵאלֹהֵי אָבִי יִצְחָק יְהוָה הָאֹמֵר אֵלַי

יא שׁוּב לְאַרְצְךָ וּלְמוֹלַדְתְּךָ וְאֵיטִיבָה עִמָּךְ: קָטֹנְתִּי

מִכֹּל הַחֲסָדִים וּמִכָּל־הָאֱמֶת אֲשֶׁר עָשִׂיתָ אֶת־עַבְדֶּךָ

כִּי בְמַקְלִי עָבַרְתִּי אֶת־הַיַּרְדֵּן הַזֶּה וְעַתָּה הָיִיתִי

יב לִשְׁנֵי מַחֲנוֹת: הַצִּילֵנִי נָא מִיַּד אָחִי מִיַּד עֵשָׂו כִּי־יָרֵא

אָנֹכִי אֹתוֹ פֶּן־יָבוֹא וְהִכַּנִי אֵם עַל־בָּנִים: וְאַתָּה אָמַרְתָּ

יג הֵיטֵב אֵיטִיב עִמָּךְ וְשַׂמְתִּי אֶת־זַרְעֲךָ כְּחוֹל הַיָּם

יד אֲשֶׁר לֹא־יִסָּפֵר מֵרֹב: וַיָּלֶן שָׁם בַּלַּיְלָה הַהוּא וַיִּקַּח

מִן־הַבָּא בְיָדוֹ מִנְחָה לְעֵשָׂו אָחִיו: עִזִּים מָאתַיִם

טו וּתְיָשִׁים עֶשְׂרִים רְחֵלִים מָאתַיִם וְאֵילִים עֶשְׂרִים:

טז גְּמַלִּים מֵינִיקוֹת וּבְנֵיהֶם שְׁלֹשִׁים פָּרוֹת אַרְבָּעִים

10] Then Jacob said, "O God of my father Abraham and God of my father Isaac, O LORD, who said to me, 'Return to your native land and I will deal bountifully with you'! 11] I am unworthy of all the kindness that you have so steadfastly shown Your servant: with my staff alone I crossed this Jordan, and now I have become two camps. 12] Deliver me, I pray, from the hand of my brother, from the hand of Esau; else, I fear, he may come and strike me down, mothers and children alike. 13] Yet You have said, 'I will deal bountifully with you and make your offspring as the sands of the sea, which are too numerous to count.'"

14] After spending the night there, he selected from what was at hand these presents for his brother Esau: 15] 200 she-goats and 20 he-goats; 200 ewes and 20 rams; 16] 30 milch camels with their colts; 40 cows and 10 bulls; 20 she-asses

12] *Deliver me.* This is one of the few prayers recorded in the Torah.
14] *Presents for his brother.* The gifts are extremely generous. The numbers (like others of this type) probably had some symbolic significance that is no longer clear.

יז וּפָרִים עֲשָׂרָה אֲתֹנֹת עֶשְׂרִים וַעְיָרִם עֲשָׂרָה: וַיִּתֵּן
בְּיַד־עֲבָדָיו עֵדֶר עֵדֶר לְבַדּוֹ וַיֹּאמֶר אֶל־עֲבָדָיו
יח עִבְרוּ לְפָנַי וְרֶוַח תָּשִׂימוּ בֵּין עֵדֶר וּבֵין עֵדֶר: וַיְצַו
אֶת־הָרִאשׁוֹן לֵאמֹר כִּי יִפְגָּשְׁךָ עֵשָׂו אָחִי וּשְׁאֵלְךָ
לֵאמֹר לְמִי־אַתָּה וְאָנָה תֵלֵךְ וּלְמִי אֵלֶּה לְפָנֶיךָ:
יט וְאָמַרְתָּ לְעַבְדְּךָ לְיַעֲקֹב מִנְחָה הִוא שְׁלוּחָה לַאדֹנִי
לְעֵשָׂו וְהִנֵּה גַם־הוּא אַחֲרֵינוּ: וַיְצַו גַּם אֶת־הַשֵּׁנִי גַּם
אֶת־הַשְּׁלִישִׁי גַּם אֶת־כָּל־הַהֹלְכִים אַחֲרֵי הָעֲדָרִים
לֵאמֹר כַּדָּבָר הַזֶּה תְּדַבְּרוּן אֶל־עֵשָׂו בְּמֹצַאֲכֶם אֹתוֹ:
כא וַאֲמַרְתֶּם גַּם הִנֵּה עַבְדְּךָ יַעֲקֹב אַחֲרֵינוּ כִּי־אָמַר
אֲכַפְּרָה פָנָיו בַּמִּנְחָה הַהֹלֶכֶת לְפָנָי וְאַחֲרֵי־כֵן אֶרְאֶה
כב פָנָיו אוּלַי יִשָּׂא פָנָי: וַתַּעֲבֹר הַמִּנְחָה עַל־פָּנָיו וְהוּא
לָן בַּלַּיְלָה־הַהוּא בַּמַּחֲנֶה:

Genesis 32
17–22

and 10 he-asses. **17]** These he put in the charge of his servants, drove by drove, and he told his servants, "Go on ahead, and keep a distance between droves." **18]** He instructed the one in front as follows, "When my brother Esau meets you and asks you, 'Whose man are you? Where are you going? And whose [animals] are these ahead of you?' **19]** you shall answer, 'Your servant Jacob's; they are a gift sent to my lord Esau; and [Jacob] himself is right behind us.'" **20]** He gave similar instructions to the second one, and the third, and all the others who followed the droves, namely, "Thus and so shall you say to Esau when you reach him. **21]** And you shall add, 'And your servant Jacob himself is right behind us.'" For he reasoned, "If I propitiate him with presents in advance, and then face him, perhaps he will show me favor." **22]** And so the gift went on ahead, while he remained in camp that night.

כג וַיָּקָם בַּלַּיְלָה הוּא וַיִּקַּח אֶת־שְׁתֵּי נָשָׁיו וְאֶת־שְׁתֵּי שִׁפְחֹתָיו וְאֶת־אַחַד עָשָׂר

כד יְלָדָיו וַיַּעֲבֹר אֵת מַעֲבַר יַבֹּק: וַיִּקָּחֵם וַיַּעֲבִרֵם אֶת־

כה הַנָּחַל וַיַּעֲבֵר אֶת־אֲשֶׁר־לוֹ: וַיִּוָּתֵר יַעֲקֹב לְבַדּוֹ וַיֵּאָבֵק

כו אִישׁ עִמּוֹ עַד עֲלוֹת הַשָּׁחַר: וַיַּרְא כִּי לֹא יָכֹל לוֹ

וַיִּגַּע בְּכַף־יְרֵכוֹ וַתֵּקַע כַּף־יֶרֶךְ יַעֲקֹב בְּהֵאָבְקוֹ עִמּוֹ:

כז וַיֹּאמֶר שַׁלְּחֵנִי כִּי עָלָה הַשָּׁחַר וַיֹּאמֶר לֹא אֲשַׁלֵּחֲךָ

כח כִּי אִם־בֵּרַכְתָּנִי: וַיֹּאמֶר אֵלָיו מַה־שְּׁמֶךָ וַיֹּאמֶר יַעֲקֹב:

כט וַיֹּאמֶר לֹא יַעֲקֹב יֵאָמֵר עוֹד שִׁמְךָ כִּי אִם־יִשְׂרָאֵל

ל כִּי־שָׂרִיתָ עִם־אֱלֹהִים וְעִם־אֲנָשִׁים וַתּוּכָל: וַיִּשְׁאַל
יַעֲקֹב וַיֹּאמֶר הַגִּידָה־נָּא שְׁמֶךָ וַיֹּאמֶר לָמָּה זֶּה תִּשְׁאַל

Genesis 32
23–30

23] That same night he arose, and taking his two wives, his two maidservants, and his eleven children, he crossed the ford of the Jabbok.   **24]** After taking them across the stream, he sent across all his possessions.   **25]** Jacob was left alone. And a man wrestled with him until the break of dawn.   **26]** When he saw that he had not prevailed against him, he wrenched Jacob's hip at its socket, so that the socket of his hip was strained as he wrestled with him.   **27]** Then he said, "Let me go, for dawn is breaking." But he answered, "I will not let you go, unless you bless me."   **28]** Said the other, "What is your name?" He replied, "Jacob."   **29]** Said he, "Your name shall no longer be Jacob, but Israel, for you have striven with beings divine and human, and have prevailed."   **30]** Jacob asked, "Pray tell me your name." But he said, "You must not ask my name!" And he took leave of him there.

23] *Eleven children.* That is, eleven sons. Benjamin was not yet born and Dinah was not included in the count (some commentators suggest that this narrative did not know of Dinah).

Jabbok. An eastern tributary of the Jordan, joining it about twenty-six miles north of the Dead Sea. Its steep banks make it a natural boundary: It divided the countries of Sihon and Og and, later, north and south Gilead.

29] *Striven.* שָׂרִיתָ (*sarita*), connected with the first part of יִשְׂרָאֵל (*Yisrael*).

Beings divine. Or "God" (אֱלֹהִים), explaining the syllable אֵל (*el*) in יִשְׂרָאֵל (*Yisrael*).

לא לִשְׁמִי וַיְבָרֶךְ אֹתוֹ שָׁם: וַיִּקְרָא יַעֲקֹב שֵׁם הַמָּקוֹם
פְּנִיאֵל כִּי־רָאִיתִי אֱלֹהִים פָּנִים אֶל־פָּנִים וַתִּנָּצֵל
לב נַפְשִׁי: וַיִּזְרַח־לוֹ הַשֶּׁמֶשׁ כַּאֲשֶׁר עָבַר אֶת־פְּנוּאֵל וְהוּא
לג צֹלֵעַ עַל־יְרֵכוֹ: עַל־כֵּן לֹא יֹאכְלוּ בְנֵי־יִשְׂרָאֵל אֶת־גִּיד
הַנָּשֶׁה אֲשֶׁר עַל־כַּף הַיָּרֵךְ עַד הַיּוֹם הַזֶּה כִּי נָגַע
בְּכַף־יֶרֶךְ יַעֲקֹב בְּגִיד הַנָּשֶׁה:
א וַיִּשָּׂא יַעֲקֹב עֵינָיו וַיַּרְא וְהִנֵּה עֵשָׂו בָּא וְעִמּוֹ אַרְבַּע
מֵאוֹת אִישׁ וַיַּחַץ אֶת־הַיְלָדִים עַל־לֵאָה וְעַל־רָחֵל
ב וְעַל שְׁתֵּי הַשְּׁפָחוֹת: וַיָּשֶׂם אֶת־הַשְּׁפָחוֹת וְאֶת־יַלְדֵיהֶן
רִאשֹׁנָה וְאֶת־לֵאָה וִילָדֶיהָ אַחֲרֹנִים וְאֶת־רָחֵל וְאֶת־
ג יוֹסֵף אַחֲרֹנִים: וְהוּא עָבַר לִפְנֵיהֶם וַיִּשְׁתַּחוּ אַרְצָה

31] So Jacob named the place Peniel, meaning, "I have seen a divine being face to face, yet my life has been preserved." **32]** The sun rose upon him as he passed Peniel, limping on his hip. **33]** That is why the children of Israel to this day do not eat the thigh muscle that is on the socket of the hip, since Jacob's hip socket was wrenched at the thigh muscle.

1] Looking up, Jacob saw Esau coming accompanied by four hundred men. He divided the children among Leah, Rachel, and the two maids, **2]** putting the maids and their children first, Leah and her children next, and Rachel and Joseph last. **3]** He himself went on ahead and bowed low to the ground seven times

31] *Peniel.* Understood as "face of God." Compare: "We shall surely die for we have seen Elohim" (Judg. 13:22). A different tradition (Gen. 35:10, 15) places the changing of the name at Bethel. There it is done freely by God himself, and not on demand by a "man," as here.

32] *Penuel.* Another version of Peniel; referred to in Judg. 8:8, 17.

33] *Do not eat.* The abstinence was apparently so generally observed that it was not mentioned specifically in the dietary codes of the Torah (Lev. 11; Deut. 12:15–27).

33:2] *Rachel and Joseph last.* These two, as Jacob's favorites, come last.

3] *Bowed . . . seven times.* This custom is also mentioned in other ancient documents [3].

ד שֶׁבַע פְּעָמִים עַד־גִּשְׁתּוֹ עַד־אָחִיו: וַיָּרָץ עֵשָׂו לִקְרָאתוֹ

ה וַיְחַבְּקֵהוּ וַיִּפֹּל עַל־צַוָּארָו֯ וַֽיִּשָּׁקֵהוּ וַיִּבְכּוּ: וַיִּשָּׂא אֶת־
עֵינָיו וַיַּרְא אֶת־הַנָּשִׁים וְאֶת־הַיְלָדִים וַיֹּאמֶר מִי־אֵלֶּה
לָּךְ וַיֹּאמַר הַיְלָדִים אֲשֶׁר־חָנַן אֱלֹהִים אֶת־עַבְדֶּךָ:

ו וַתִּגַּשְׁןָ הַשְּׁפָחוֹת הֵנָּה וְיַלְדֵיהֶן וַתִּשְׁתַּחֲוֶיןָ: וַתִּגַּשׁ גַּם־
לֵאָה וִילָדֶיהָ וַיִּשְׁתַּחֲווּ וְאַחַר נִגַּשׁ יוֹסֵף וְרָחֵל וַיִּשְׁתַּחֲווּ:

ח וַיֹּאמֶר מִי לְךָ כָּל־הַמַּחֲנֶה הַזֶּה אֲשֶׁר פָּגָשְׁתִּי וַיֹּאמֶר

ט לִמְצֹא־חֵן בְּעֵינֵי אֲדֹנִי: וַיֹּאמֶר עֵשָׂו יֶשׁ־לִי רָב אָחִי

י יְהִי לְךָ אֲשֶׁר־לָךְ: וַיֹּאמֶר יַעֲקֹב אַל־נָא אִם־נָא מָצָאתִי
חֵן בְּעֵינֶיךָ וְלָקַחְתָּ מִנְחָתִי מִיָּדִי כִּי עַל־כֵּן רָאִיתִי

יא פָנֶיךָ כִּרְאֹת פְּנֵי אֱלֹהִים וַתִּרְצֵנִי: קַח־נָא אֶת־בִּרְכָתִי

Genesis 33
4–11

* ד צואריו קרי.   נקוד על וישקהו.

until he was near his brother. **4]** Esau ran to greet him. He embraced him and, falling on his neck, he kissed him; and they wept. **5]** Looking about, he saw the women and the children. "Who," he asked, "are these with you?" He answered, "The children with whom God has favored your servant." **6]** Then the maids, with their children, came forward and bowed low; **7]** Leah too, with her children, came forward and bowed low; and lastly, Joseph and Rachel came forward and bowed low. **8]** And he asked, "What do you mean by all this company which I have met?" He answered, "To gain my lord's favor." **9]** Esau said, "I have enough, my brother; let what you have remain yours." **10]** But Jacob said, "No, I pray you; if you would do me this favor, accept from me this gift; for to see your face is like seeing the face of God, and you have received me favorably. **11]** Accept,

4] *Kissed him.* On the diacritical dots over the Hebrew word, see p. 326.

9] *I have enough.* It was an old custom to preface an acceptance of a large gift by first making a refusal.

10] *Like seeing the face of God.* Extreme flattery and at the same time a reference to the danger of seeing the face of God.

/Rashi: Jacob thought that he had met Esau's angel at night./

אֲשֶׁר הֻבֵאת לָּךְ כִּי־חַנַּנִי אֱלֹהִים וְכִי יֶשׁ־לִי־כֹל

יב וַיִּפְצַר־בּוֹ וַיִּקָּח: וַיֹּאמֶר נִסְעָה וְנֵלֵכָה וְאֵלְכָה לְנֶגְדֶּךָ:

יג וַיֹּאמֶר אֵלָיו אֲדֹנִי יֹדֵעַ כִּי־הַיְלָדִים רַכִּים וְהַצֹּאן
וְהַבָּקָר עָלוֹת עָלָי וּדְפָקוּם יוֹם אֶחָד וָמֵתוּ כָּל־
הַצֹּאן:

יד יַעֲבָר־נָא אֲדֹנִי לִפְנֵי עַבְדּוֹ וַאֲנִי אֶתְנָהֲלָה
לְאִטִּי לְרֶגֶל הַמְּלָאכָה אֲשֶׁר־לְפָנַי וּלְרֶגֶל הַיְלָדִים
עַד אֲשֶׁר־אָבֹא אֶל־אֲדֹנִי שֵׂעִירָה:

טו וַיֹּאמֶר עֵשָׂו אַצִּיגָה־
נָא עִמְּךָ מִן־הָעָם אֲשֶׁר אִתִּי וַיֹּאמֶר לָמָּה זֶּה אֶמְצָא־
חֵן בְּעֵינֵי אֲדֹנִי:

טז וַיָּשָׁב בַּיּוֹם הַהוּא עֵשָׂו לְדַרְכּוֹ
שֵׂעִירָה:

יז וְיַעֲקֹב נָסַע סֻכֹּתָה וַיִּבֶן לוֹ בָּיִת וּלְמִקְנֵהוּ
עָשָׂה סֻכֹּת עַל־כֵּן קָרָא שֵׁם־הַמָּקוֹם סֻכּוֹת: ס

Genesis 33
12–17

then, my offering which has been brought to you, for God has favored me and I have plenty." And when he urged him, he accepted.

12] And [Esau] said, "Let us start on our journey, and I will proceed at your pace." 13] But he said to him, "My lord knows that the children are frail and that the flocks and herds, which are nursing, are a care to me; if they are driven hard a single day, all the flocks will die. 14] Let my lord go on ahead of his servant, while I travel slowly, at the pace of the cattle before me and at the pace of the children, until I come to my lord in Seir."

15] Then Esau said, "Let me assign to you some of the men who are with me." But he said, "O no, my lord is too kind to me!" 16] So Esau started back that day on his way to Seir. 17] But Jacob journeyed on to Succoth, and built a house for himself and made stalls for his cattle; that is why the place was called Succoth.

14] *While I travel slowly.* Jacob wants reconciliation but not close association; he has no intention of going to his brother's home in Seir.
17] *Succoth.* Meaning "stalls," "huts," "booths."

The place was slightly north of the Jabbok (see Josh. 13:27; Judg. 8:5) and is not to be confused with the Succoth of Exod. 12:37, an Egyptian town.

The Struggle

Since ancient days crossing a river has been symbolic of overcoming hazard and going forward to new experience (note such expressions as "crossing the Rubicon"). In this sense, Jacob passing over the Jabbok to meet Esau crosses the watershed of his life. Everything that has happened to him since he obtained both birthright and parental blessing by doubtful means has been tainted with his own guilt and his brother's enmity. Jacob can fully face his own past only as he seeks reconciliation with Esau, and this he can do only as he becomes a different man. When Jacob becomes Israel he can achieve reconciliation with his brother.

Rivers, it was believed, were infested by demons. We may therefore infer that Jacob first thought that the "man" who met him during the night was a river demon—the assonance between the words יַבֹּק (the river Jabbok) and וַיֵּאָבֵק (he struggled) is not accidental. The man's urgent request, "Let me go for dawn is breaking," fortifies Jacob's belief that he has met a demonic being who must not be seen and who therefore must depart before sunrise [4]. Until that moment arrives Jacob is still his old self, albeit struggling to emerge into a new moral consciousness. As long as he can assume that his adversary is a demonic force, the old Jacob stands rooted in his past; it is only as the light breaks that he realizes it was not Satan but God whom he resisted—and now he sees his own past and present struggle in a new light and asks his adversary for a blessing. The struggle may be seen as a reenactment of the Eden theme: God wants man to conform to His will, yet He also wants him to be free even to oppose and struggle with Him. Jacob becomes Israel only after he has wrestled with God. The Torah says that there was also physical evidence of the struggle. The formerly self-assured and successful Jacob is now diminished in appearance; no longer with proud purposeful strides but with a hesitant limp will he greet his brother.[1]

Some interpreters say that Jacob struggled with no one but himself, emerging from the fight purified in soul.[2] However, this complete internalization of the struggle does not reflect the biblical intent. The text tells of God's role in Jacob's renewal; Jacob becomes Israel only with God's help, hence God's name is embedded in the cognomen that the forefather now bears and that his descendants will bear after him. Its etymology appears to proclaim "May God rule." Like Abram and Sarai, like a new king ascending the throne, Jacob receives a name which testifies that he is ready to assume his inheritance and that he has founded his life on the pledge he made at Bethel.

The Reconciliation

Esau's readiness to make peace with his brother comes as a surprising climax to the carefully prepared encounter. Esau's retainer of 400 armed men allows us to suppose that he did not originally come with peaceful intentions, especially since his scouts must have informed him that Jacob was unarmed. Esau expected to meet the old Jacob, the hated sibling who had overtaken him with

---

[1] See also the incident involving Moses (Exod. 4:24–26) and the simile of God attacking Israel (Hos. 13:7–8), which is assigned as the *Haftarah* to this section. The effect on Jacob's thigh muscle may be related to Greek stories of injured sexual organs.

In popular stories, spirits were usually portrayed as leaving before sunrise [5].

[2] Some scholars see the struggle as having taken place in a dream [6]. "There are things which become so fixed in one's mind that they leave a physical effect" [7]. In the Koran the dietary restriction relating to the incident is said to have been Jacob's own decision [8].

cleverness and guile. He was prepared for violence.

But in the brothers' fateful meeting all is suddenly changed—and hardly because of the gifts that Jacob brings, for Esau is a wealthy man in his own right. The reconciliation occurs because it is Israel, not Jacob, whom Esau meets, and Jacob is a new man who asks forgiveness, if not in words then in manner, who limps toward him with repentant air and not deceitful arrogance. He is not a man to be put to the sword, he is a man who can be loved as a brother. The essentially simple and uncomplicated Esau, who himself has matured, senses this at once and runs to kiss his newly found brother. The two are now at peace and Jacob-Israel, who has no further need to flee from Esau's wrath, settles down and builds a house.

GLEANINGS

Still Smaller

The letter ט in קְטֹנְתִּי [I am unworthy] [Gen. 32:11] is in some manuscripts written smaller than the rest of the word. This shows that though a man humbles himself, as Jacob did in prayer, he is usually still smaller than he makes himself out to be. In the midst of "unworthy" there is often something unworthier yet.　CHASIDIC [9]

Pious people think they are unworthy of God's gifts; while others think they are deserving of such gifts and even more.　SEFAT EMET [10]

The Demonic

Modern rationalism until recently regarded all allusion to demons merely as a vestige of ancient superstition. Now, however, we realize that to a large extent the ancient belief in demons was a crude way of accounting for the unconscious and almost uncontrollable forces in human nature itself, and the Torah teaching that God wards off from Israel the danger of the demons acquires a new relevance. The latest outbreak of the demonic forces in the world that left Israel limping is very much in need of being countered by the faith that Israel will not only survive but come away from the tragic experience with renewed strength and blessing. That is to be the meaning of the establishment of the State of Israel.

MORDECAI M. KAPLAN [11]

He Did Not Know

While he struggled, Jacob did not know the nature of his opponent. Perhaps that is the way it had to be, for when a man struggles with a force beyond himself he can, at the moment, not be sure whether it is God or Satan who is his adversary, whether a divine or demonic force [12]. Both will engage him almost past endurance. The great agony of the soul is precisely that during the struggle we are in doubt and "the man" may get away before we know his name. Only afterwards, in the full light of day, may we know what we saw, whether it was God whom we met face to face. The mystery may never be completely unraveled; this is part of the ambiguity of man's meeting with God.

Two Kinds of Fear

It says that Jacob suffered both fright and anxiety [Gen. 32:8]. Fright—that he might be killed by Esau; anxiety—that he himself might be led to kill.　RASHI [13]

He Kissed Him

The Hebrew vocalized text has dots over each letter of that expression [Gen. 33:4]. One tradition says that this means that Esau's kiss was not genuine, while another holds that it was because in the meeting Esau's latent love broke through.

RASHI [14]

Another tradition, which is roundly condemned by Ibn Ezra, states that Esau "bit" Jacob–a word play on נָשַׁק (kiss) and נָשַׁךְ (bite). [15]

Thigh Muscle

The halachah forbids the eating of that part of the thigh of large and small cattle which is served by the sciatic nerve. Birds are excluded from this prohibition. [16]

The process of cutting away the sinew, forbidden fat, and certain other parts is called porging (נִקּוּר), and because experts in porging were not always available many Jewish communities refrained from eating any part of an animal's hindquarter.

Prefiguration

The conquest of the Promised Land starts at the place where Jacob wrestled with the man (Num. 21:24). This is an added sign that the forefather prefigures his people: like him they will wrestle with a God who gets away from their grasp yet will leave them with a blessing.

Alone with Thee

Each one of us alone with God:
Behind the mask of face and deed
Each wrestles with an angel.

JESSIE SAMPTER [17]

O wrestlin' Jacob, Jacob day's a-breakin',
  I will not let thee go!
O wrestlin' Jacob, Jacob day's a-breakin',
  He will not let me go!
O, I hold my brudder wid a tremblin' hand;
  I would not let him go!
I hold my sister wid a tremblin' hand;
  I would not let her go!

SPIRITUAL [18]

Limping

By morning I was lame. Yet I did not let go until with the coming of the new day I had wrested the blessing of reassurance from my creator; then I rose up knowing that I had striven with God and with men and that I had prevailed. And I named the place Peniel because I knew that there I had truly seen *God face to face* and my life was preserved. And as the sun rose again upon me I went limping down to the ford thinking how unlike my youthful encounter with the God of my fathers on that journey out to Haran was this one. Then I had traveled in aweful wonder, now it was in painful and fearful perplexity. Then in the arrogant aspiration of my youth I had dreamed of a radiant ladder to distant divinity. Now in my maturer intention my God came down to me and I struggled with him as man with man. Then in my eager ignorant search for security I had bargained with him for his support. Now in my wrestling with him I tested my own powers. Both times I came away with renewed self-confidence, but then I had gone striding toward the bright beckoning future, now I was limping back to deal with the imperfect past.

I woke to the fact that a new day was come: the sun was rising; the rising wind tossed the night-stilled branches of the trees, adding its endless music to that of the irrevocable stream.

IRVING FINEMAN [19]

The Rape of Dinah

This story of rape and cruel retribution puts Jacob's family in a different light. While the basic theme also occurs in other literatures (e.g., the tale of Helen of Troy), the biblical tale reflects a particular aspect of Israel's tribal history and fits into the overall pattern of the Jacob tragedy, with deception once again playing a central role.

An introduction of three verses (Gen. 33:18–20) forms the link between this section and the preceding. Jacob has now settled down and, since his children are seen as adults, much time has elapsed since he and Esau met at the river Jabbok.

יח וַיָּבֹא יַעֲקֹב שָׁלֵם עִיר שְׁכֶם אֲשֶׁר בְּאֶרֶץ כְּנַעַן בְּבֹאוֹ

יט מִפַּדַּן אֲרָם וַיִּחַן אֶת־פְּנֵי הָעִיר: וַיִּקֶן אֶת־חֶלְקַת

הַשָּׂדֶה אֲשֶׁר נָטָה־שָׁם אָהֳלוֹ מִיַּד בְּנֵי־חֲמוֹר אֲבִי

כ שְׁכֶם בְּמֵאָה קְשִׂיטָה: וַיַּצֶּב־שָׁם מִזְבֵּחַ וַיִּקְרָא־לוֹ אֵל

אֱלֹהֵי יִשְׂרָאֵל: ס

א וַתֵּצֵא דִינָה בַּת־לֵאָה אֲשֶׁר יָלְדָה לְיַעֲקֹב לִרְאוֹת

ב בִּבְנוֹת הָאָרֶץ: וַיַּרְא אֹתָהּ שְׁכֶם בֶּן־חֲמוֹר הַחִוִּי נְשִׂיא

ג הָאָרֶץ וַיִּקַּח אֹתָהּ וַיִּשְׁכַּב אֹתָהּ וַיְעַנֶּהָ: וַתִּדְבַּק נַפְשׁוֹ

Genesis 33; 34
18–20; 1–3

18] Jacob arrived safe in the city of Shechem which is in the land of Canaan—having come thus from Paddan-aram—and he encamped before the city.   19] The parcel of land where he pitched his tent he purchased from the children of Hamor, Shechem's father, for a hundred *kesitahs*.   20] He set up an altar there, and called it El-elohe-yisrael.

1] Now Dinah, the daughter whom Leah had borne to Jacob, went out to visit the daughters of the land.   2] Shechem son of Hamor the Hivite, chief of the country, saw her, and took her and lay with her by force.   3] Being strongly drawn to

---

33:18] *Shechem.* An old Canaanite city, which had been visited previously by Abraham (Gen. 12:6). In later Israelite history it became an important religious and cultural center of the tribal confederacy (Josh. 24:1). Shechem, Hebrew for shoulder, is located in the area of today's Nablus, thirty-two miles north of Jerusalem, and is built on the slope of a large rise that is part of Mount Gerizim. Recent excavations show that the site was occupied as early as 4000 B.C.E.

19] *Shechem's father.* Shechem is also the name of the king's son, a major figure in the Dinah story.

A hundred kesitahs. Monetary unit of unknown value.

/In Job 42:11 the giving of a *kesitah* resembles the payment to a victor in Sumerian verbal disputations./

20] *El-elohe-yisrael.* El, God of Israel.

34:2] *Hivite.* The Septuagint has "Horite" (see note at Gen. 36:2).

By force. Literally, "lay with her and forced her." Such an offense brought guilt on the offender's whole community (Gen. 20:9; Deut. 24:4).

/According to Jewish law (Deut. 22:28–29), if a man has violated a virgin, he has to marry her and is prohibited from ever divorcing her. In addition, her father is to receive compensation./

בְּדִינָה בַּת־יַעֲקֹב וַיֶּאֱהַב אֶת־הַנַּעֲרָ* וַיְדַבֵּר עַל־לֵב

ד הַנַּעֲרָ*׃ וַיֹּאמֶר שְׁכֶם אֶל־חֲמוֹר אָבִיו לֵאמֹר קַח־לִי

ה אֶת־הַיַּלְדָּה הַזֹּאת לְאִשָּׁה׃ וְיַעֲקֹב שָׁמַע כִּי טִמֵּא

אֶת־דִּינָה בִתּוֹ וּבָנָיו הָיוּ אֶת־מִקְנֵהוּ בַּשָּׂדֶה וְהֶחֱרִשׁ

ו יַעֲקֹב עַד־בֹּאָם׃ וַיֵּצֵא חֲמוֹר אֲבִי־שְׁכֶם אֶל־יַעֲקֹב

ז לְדַבֵּר אִתּוֹ׃ וּבְנֵי יַעֲקֹב בָּאוּ מִן־הַשָּׂדֶה כְּשָׁמְעָם

וַיִּתְעַצְּבוּ הָאֲנָשִׁים וַיִּחַר לָהֶם מְאֹד כִּי־נְבָלָה עָשָׂה

ח בְיִשְׂרָאֵל לִשְׁכַּב אֶת־בַּת־יַעֲקֹב וְכֵן לֹא יֵעָשֶׂה׃ וַיְדַבֵּר

חֲמוֹר אִתָּם לֵאמֹר שְׁכֶם בְּנִי חָשְׁקָה נַפְשׁוֹ בְּבִתְּכֶם

ט תְּנוּ נָא אֹתָהּ לוֹ לְאִשָּׁה׃ וְהִתְחַתְּנוּ אֹתָנוּ בְּנֹתֵיכֶם

י תִּתְּנוּ־לָנוּ וְאֶת־בְּנֹתֵינוּ תִּקְחוּ לָכֶם׃ וְאִתָּנוּ תֵּשֵׁבוּ

Genesis 34
4–10

* ג הנערה קרי.   הנערה קרי.

Dinah daughter of Jacob, and in love with the maiden, he spoke to the maiden tenderly.   **4]** So Shechem said to his father Hamor, "Get me this girl as a wife."

5] Jacob heard that he had defiled his daughter Dinah; but since his sons were in the field with his cattle, Jacob kept silent until they came home.   **6]** Then Shechem's father Hamor came out to Jacob to speak to him.   **7]** Meanwhile Jacob's sons, having heard the news, came in from the field. The men were distressed and very angry, because he had committed an outrage in Israel by lying with Jacob's daughter—a thing not to be done.

8] And Hamor spoke with them, saying, "My son Shechem longs for your daughter. Please give her to him in marriage.   **9]** Intermarry with us: give your daughters to us, and take our daughters for yourselves.   **10]** You will dwell among us, and

---

5] *In the field.* Most probably they did not return home every night.

7] *Outrage in Israel.* An idiomatic term (cf. Deut. 22:21; Jer. 29:23) that is an anachronism here, since Israel did not yet exist.

10] *Move about.* The verb סָחַר (sachar) has a dual

וְהָאָ֣רֶץ תִּהְיֶ֣ה לִפְנֵיכֶ֗ם שְׁבוּ֙ וּסְחָר֔וּהָ וְהֵֽאָחֲז֖וּ בָּֽהּ׃

יא וַיֹּ֤אמֶר שְׁכֶם֙ אֶל־אָבִ֣יהָ וְאֶל־אַחֶ֔יהָ אֶמְצָא־חֵ֖ן בְּעֵינֵיכֶ֑ם

יב וַאֲשֶׁ֛ר תֹּאמְר֥וּ אֵלַ֖י אֶתֵּֽן׃ הַרְבּ֨וּ עָלַ֤י מְאֹד֙ מֹ֣הַר וּמַתָּ֔ן

וְאֶ֨תְּנָ֔ה כַּאֲשֶׁ֥ר תֹּאמְר֖וּ אֵלָ֑י וּתְנוּ־לִ֥י אֶת־הַֽנַּעֲרָ֖* לְאִשָּֽׁה׃

יג וַיַּעֲנ֨וּ בְנֵֽי־יַעֲקֹ֜ב אֶת־שְׁכֶ֨ם וְאֶת־חֲמ֥וֹר אָבִ֖יו בְּמִרְמָ֑ה

יד וַיְדַבֵּ֕רוּ אֲשֶׁ֣ר טִמֵּ֔א אֵ֖ת דִּינָ֣ה אֲחֹתָ֑ם׃ וַיֹּאמְר֣וּ אֲלֵיהֶ֗ם

לֹ֤א נוּכַל֙ לַעֲשׂוֹת֙ הַדָּבָ֣ר הַזֶּ֔ה לָתֵת֙ אֶת־אֲחֹתֵ֔נוּ לְאִ֖ישׁ

טו אֲשֶׁר־ל֣וֹ עָרְלָ֑ה כִּֽי־חֶרְפָּ֥ה הִ֖וא לָ֑נוּ׃ אַךְ־בְּזֹ֖את נֵא֣וֹת

טז לָכֶ֑ם אִ֚ם תִּהְי֣וּ כָמֹ֔נוּ לְהִמֹּ֥ל לָכֶ֖ם כָּל־זָכָֽר׃ וְנָתַ֨נּוּ

אֶת־בְּנֹתֵ֜ינוּ לָכֶ֗ם וְאֶת־בְּנֹֽתֵיכֶם֙ נִֽקַּֽח־לָ֔נוּ וְיָשַׁ֥בְנוּ אִתְּכֶֽם

Genesis 34

11–16

* יב הנערה קרי.

the land will be open before you; settle, move about, and acquire holdings in it." **11]** Then Shechem said to her father and brothers, "Do me this favor, and I will pay whatever you tell me. **12]** Ask of me a bride price ever so high, and I will pay what you tell me; only give me the maiden for a wife."

13] Jacob's sons answered Shechem and his father Hamor—speaking with guile because he had defiled their sister Dinah— **14]** and said to them, "We cannot do this thing, to give our sister to a man who is uncircumcised, for that is a disgrace among us. **15]** Only on this condition will we agree with you: that you will become like us in that every male among you is circumcised. **16]** Then we will give our daughters to you and take your daughters to ourselves; and we will dwell among

meaning, "to move about" and "to trade." It reflects ancient social conditions when to move about also meant a license to trade [1].

12] *Bride price.* Not "dowry" (money the bride brings to the groom), as מֹהַר is often translated.

13] *Jacob's sons.* Probably led by Simeon and Levi. The others may have assented by silence (see Gen. 34:25).

Guile. מִרְמָה (mirmah), a key word in the Jacob story (see Gen. 27:35).

יז וְהָיִינוּ לְעַם אֶחָד: וְאִם־לֹא תִשְׁמְעוּ אֵלֵינוּ לְהִמּוֹל

יח וְלָקַחְנוּ אֶת־בִּתֵּנוּ וְהָלָכְנוּ: וַיִּיטְבוּ דִבְרֵיהֶם בְּעֵינֵי

יט חֲמוֹר וּבְעֵינֵי שְׁכֶם בֶּן־חֲמוֹר: וְלֹא־אֵחַר הַנַּעַר לַעֲשׂוֹת

הַדָּבָר כִּי־חָפֵץ בְּבַת־יַעֲקֹב וְהוּא נִכְבָּד מִכֹּל בֵּית

כ אָבִיו: וַיָּבֹא חֲמוֹר וּשְׁכֶם בְּנוֹ אֶל־שַׁעַר עִירָם וַיְדַבְּרוּ

כא אֶל־אַנְשֵׁי עִירָם לֵאמֹר: הָאֲנָשִׁים הָאֵלֶּה שְׁלֵמִים הֵם

אִתָּנוּ וְיֵשְׁבוּ בָאָרֶץ וְיִסְחֲרוּ אֹתָהּ וְהָאָרֶץ הִנֵּה רַחֲבַת־

יָדַיִם לִפְנֵיהֶם אֶת־בְּנֹתָם נִקַּח־לָנוּ לְנָשִׁים וְאֶת־בְּנֹתֵינוּ

כב נִתֵּן לָהֶם: אַךְ־בְּזֹאת יֵאֹתוּ לָנוּ הָאֲנָשִׁים לָשֶׁבֶת

אִתָּנוּ לִהְיוֹת לְעַם אֶחָד בְּהִמּוֹל לָנוּ כָּל־זָכָר כַּאֲשֶׁר

כג הֵם נִמֹּלִים: מִקְנֵהֶם וְקִנְיָנָם וְכָל־בְּהֶמְתָּם הֲלוֹא לָנוּ

you and become as one kindred.   17] But if you will not listen to us and become circumcised, we will take our daughter and go."

18] Their words pleased Hamor and Hamor's son Shechem.   19] And the youth lost no time in doing the thing, for he wanted Jacob's daughter. Now he was the most respected in his father's house.   20] So Hamor and his son Shechem went to the public place of their town and spoke to their fellow townsmen, saying, 21] "These people are our friends; let them settle in the land and move about in it, for the land is large enough for them; we will take their daughters to ourselves as wives and give our daughters to them.   22] But only on this condition will the men agree with us to dwell among us and be as one kindred: that all our males become circumcised as they are circumcised.   23] Would not their cattle and substance

20] *Public place.* Literally, "gate."

23] *If we only agree.* In his attempt to persuade his people, Schechem is careful to depict the advantages of attracting Jacob's family but passes over his own involvement with Dinah.

כד הֵ֗ם אַ֤ךְ נֵא֙וֹתָה֙ לָהֶ֔ם וַיֵּשְׁב֖וּ אִתָּ֑נוּ׃ וַיִּשְׁמְע֣וּ אֶל־חֲמ֗וֹר
וְאֶל־שְׁכֶ֣ם בְּנ֔וֹ כָּל־יֹצְאֵ֖י שַׁ֣עַר עִיר֑וֹ וַיִּמֹּ֙לוּ֙ כָּל־זָכָ֔ר

כה כָּל־יֹצְאֵ֖י שַׁ֣עַר עִיר֑וֹ׃ וַיְהִ֤י בַיּוֹם֙ הַשְּׁלִישִׁ֔י בִּהְיוֹתָ֣ם
כֹּֽאֲבִ֗ים וַיִּקְח֣וּ שְׁנֵֽי־בְנֵֽי־יַ֠עֲקֹב שִׁמְע֨וֹן וְלֵוִ֜י אֲחֵ֤י דִינָה֙
אִ֣ישׁ חַרְבּ֔וֹ וַיָּבֹ֥אוּ עַל־הָעִ֖יר בֶּ֑טַח וַיַּֽהַרְג֖וּ כָּל־זָכָֽר׃

כו וְאֶת־חֲמוֹר֙ וְאֶת־שְׁכֶ֣ם בְּנ֔וֹ הָרְג֖וּ לְפִי־חָ֑רֶב וַיִּקְח֣וּ אֶת־
דִּינָ֛ה מִבֵּ֥ית שְׁכֶ֖ם וַיֵּצֵֽאוּ׃

כז בְּנֵ֣י יַעֲקֹ֗ב בָּ֚אוּ עַל־הַ֣חֲלָלִ֔ים
וַיָּבֹ֖זּוּ הָעִ֑יר אֲשֶׁ֥ר טִמְּא֖וּ אֲחוֹתָֽם׃

כח אֶת־צֹאנָ֥ם וְאֶת־
בְּקָרָ֖ם וְאֶת־חֲמֹרֵיהֶ֑ם וְאֵ֧ת אֲשֶׁר־בָּעִ֛יר וְאֶת־אֲשֶׁ֥ר

כט בַּשָּׂדֶ֖ה לָקָֽחוּ׃ וְאֶת־כָּל־חֵילָ֤ם וְאֶת־כָּל־טַפָּ֖ם וְאֶת־
נְשֵׁיהֶ֖ם שָׁב֑וּ וַיָּבֹ֕זּוּ וְאֵ֖ת כָּל־אֲשֶׁ֥ר בַּבָּֽיִת׃

and all their beasts be ours? Let us then agree with them, that they may dwell among us." **24]** All the fighting men in his community heeded Hamor and his son Shechem, and all males, the fighting men in his community were circumcised.

25] On the third day, when they were in pain, Simeon and Levi, two of Jacob's sons, brothers of Dinah, took each his sword, came upon the city unmolested, and slew all the males. **26]** They put Hamor and his son Schechem to the sword, took Dinah out of Shechem's house, and went away. **27]** The other sons of Jacob came upon the slain and plundered the town, because their sister had been defiled. **28]** They seized their flocks and herds and asses, all that was inside the town and outside; **29]** all their wealth, all their children, and their wives, all that was in the houses, they took as captives and booty.

24] *All who went.* That is, all his fellow townsmen.
25] *Simeon and Levi.* Full brothers of Dinah. They probably had their personal retinue with them.

Unmolested. Literally, "in peace," referring to the brothers. Others translate as "unawares," referring to the inhabitants [2].
27] *The other sons.* At the end of his life, Jacob will

ל וַיֹּאמֶר יַעֲקֹב אֶל־שִׁמְעוֹן וְאֶל־לֵוִי עֲכַרְתֶּם אֹתִי
לְהַבְאִישֵׁנִי בְּיֹשֵׁב הָאָרֶץ בַּכְּנַעֲנִי וּבַפְּרִזִּי וַאֲנִי מְתֵי
מִסְפָּר וְנֶאֶסְפוּ עָלַי וְהִכּוּנִי וְנִשְׁמַדְתִּי אֲנִי וּבֵיתִי:
לא וַיֹּאמְרוּ הַכְזוֹנָה יַעֲשֶׂה אֶת־אֲחוֹתֵנוּ:   פ

* לֹא ז׳ רבתי.

30] Jacob said to Simeon and Levi, "You have brought trouble on me, making me odious among the inhabitants of the land, the Canaanites and the Perizzites; my men are few in number, so that if they unite against me and attack me, I and my house will be destroyed."   31] But they answered, "Should our sister be treated like a whore?"

---

blame only Simeon and Levi for the slaughter of Shechem and his people (Gen. 49:5–7).

30] *You have brought trouble on me.* Or "you have muddied what was clear," a reference to his reputation [3].

31] *Our sister.* Thereafter, nothing further is heard of Dinah.

/Tradition has her variously as the mother of Saul the Canaanite (cf. Gen. 46:10), as Job's second wife, or as the mother of Asenath [4]./

The Tragic Element

Obviously, the Bible does not retell this violent tale of rape and murder merely "because it happened." Many other incidents in the rich and varied lives of the Patriarchs were probably forgotten. Why not this one?

A partial answer lies in the fact that this incident would later serve to explain the landless status of Simeon and Levi. The Levites became hereditary temple servants without a territory of their own (Num. 18:20), while a portion of the tribe of Simeon seems to have intermingled with the tribe of Judah and also with the Canaanites. This may explain the startling difference between the census figures in Num. 1 (59,300) and Num. 26 (22,200) and the complete omission of Simeon in the blessing of Moses (Deut. 33). The story of the rape of Dinah may thus have helped to provide a moral explanation for certain geopolitical realities of later centuries.

The incident at Shechem must also be seen as another chapter in the Jacob tragedy. As a youth, Jacob had practiced deceit; now two of his sons dishonor themselves and him by deceiving the people of Shechem. Dinah, Simeon, and Levi are the first three children with whom Jacob has profound trouble; Judah, Reuben, and Joseph will follow in time. Jacob has become Israel but this fact has not erased the tragic element from his life. Quite the contrary, his perception and deep sensitivity have brought him a greater capacity for suffering. His children, who represent his future, will bring him untold agony. This long-range retribution visited on Jacob also underscores the Bible's condemnation of the hypocritical concern for religion with which Jacob's sons induced Shechem and his people to submit to circumcision. The story of Dinah exposes this pretense of faith in all its ugliness [5].

The Reprimand

Jacob's castigation of his sons is so weak that it is puzzling. He seems worried only that his own reputation will suffer. To be sure, he will speak more strongly on his deathbed (Gen. 49:5–7), but how is it possible that he would view the unwarranted killing of so many people merely as having brought trouble to himself?

Some critics say that there were two separate strands of the Dinah story. Jacob's response, they say, belonged to a tradition (attributed to J) that told of the slaying of only Hamor and Shechem, an act that could have appeared as justifiable retribution and that would elicit the reprimand now found in the text. The story of the killing of the city's inhabitants, they say, stems from another tradition (P), one which had no record of Jacob's reaction. But however persuasive this argument seems, we must approach the text as it is now. And it here portrays the biblical Jacob as a man who makes no moral judgment on his sons.

Jacob is silent because he has in fact nothing to say. He has already become the object of events and has entered the twilight of his life. He is still young enough to become a father once more, but he is already too old to be in sole command of his fate. The divine blessings that follow (in chapter 35) merely reiterate what has already been vouchsafed to him in the past, and Jacob returns to Bethel as if symbolically to revisit the earlier stages of his life. This is what men do when growing old. In Jacob's case, however, old age will betoken not serenity but further trials. It thus becomes painfully clear that "Israel" was merely a name, not a reward; a potential, not a fulfilment. Literally and figuratively, Jacob will limp through the remainder of his life.

GLEANINGS

Exculpation

Later tradition attempted to explain the guile and cruelty of the brothers: Why were the men of Shechem slain along with Hamor, the offending leader? Because they countenanced the crime or were incapable of restraining their leadership, either of which rendered them co-responsible. [6]

The Prayer of Judith

[In the Book of Judith, probably of the second century B.C.E., the deed of the brothers was seen as pious retribution.]

O Lord, God of my father Simeon, into whose hand You gave a sword to take vengeance on the strangers who loosened the girdle of a virgin to defile her.... [Your dear children] were moved with zeal for You and abhorred the pollution of their blood and called upon You for aid. O God, O my God, hear me also who am a widow.

JUDITH [7]

Dinah

How was Shechem attracted to the young girl? One tradition says that she went out to see the pagan revelries; another, that she pranced about bedecked with jewelry—and jewelry ought to be worn only inside the house. [8]

Goethe called her "this foolish Dinah who runs about in the land." [9]

The Deed

I am not one of those people who profess to be able to distinguish between good and bad warfare, who say that good fighters are those who observe certain humanitarian rules according to which warfare should be regulated. And combatants when they make excuses for their brutal or tricky reprisals by pointing to the cruelty or unscrupulousness of their opponents seem to me as absurd as were your brothers when they said it was because Shechem had "defiled" Dinah, their sister, that they did this. For war between men, no matter how it is waged, is abominable....

...It was a brutal deed of my sons there in Shechem, and I, innocently thinking I was doing good, had been a party to its inception. Nor could I put a stop to it once it was under way; much as I abhorred what they were doing I could hardly make war on my own sons. But, when I looked upon the foul thing they had done after all my teaching, I thought how like it was to the behavior of a child who, left unwatched, will break the careful training of its mother and befoul itself.

IRVING FINEMAN [10]

Births and Deaths

These two chapters comprise the end of the Isaac cycle. The careful attention given to the lineages (תּוֹלְדוֹת) of the Patriarchs is an important characteristic of the Book of Genesis (see p. 19). The "line of Esau," the older brother, precedes the "line of Jacob," just as the genealogy of Ishmael preceded that of his younger brother Isaac.

This section contains a number of difficult textual problems. Some of the names and circumstances referred to are no longer fully understandable.

א וַיֹּאמֶר אֱלֹהִים אֶל־יַעֲקֹב קוּם עֲלֵה בֵית־אֵל וְשֶׁב־
שָׁם וַעֲשֵׂה־שָׁם מִזְבֵּחַ לָאֵל הַנִּרְאֶה אֵלֶיךָ בְּבָרְחֲךָ

ב מִפְּנֵי עֵשָׂו אָחִיךָ: וַיֹּאמֶר יַעֲקֹב אֶל־בֵּיתוֹ וְאֶל כָּל־
אֲשֶׁר עִמּוֹ הָסִרוּ אֶת־אֱלֹהֵי הַנֵּכָר אֲשֶׁר בְּתֹכְכֶם

ג וְהִטַּהֲרוּ וְהַחֲלִיפוּ שִׂמְלֹתֵיכֶם: וְנָקוּמָה וְנַעֲלֶה בֵּית־
אֵל וְאֶעֱשֶׂה־שָּׁם מִזְבֵּחַ לָאֵל הָעֹנֶה אֹתִי בְּיוֹם צָרָתִי

ד וַיְהִי עִמָּדִי בַּדֶּרֶךְ אֲשֶׁר הָלָכְתִּי: וַיִּתְּנוּ אֶל־יַעֲקֹב אֵת
כָּל־אֱלֹהֵי הַנֵּכָר אֲשֶׁר בְּיָדָם וְאֶת־הַנְּזָמִים אֲשֶׁר
בְּאָזְנֵיהֶם וַיִּטְמֹן אֹתָם יַעֲקֹב תַּחַת הָאֵלָה אֲשֶׁר עִם־

Genesis 35

1–4

1] God said to Jacob, "Go up promptly to Bethel and remain there; and build an altar there to the God who appeared to you when you were fleeing from your brother Esau." 2] So Jacob said to his household and to all who were with him, "Rid yourselves of the alien gods in your midst, purify yourselves, and change your garments. 3] Let us promptly go up to Bethel, and I will build an altar there to the God who answered me when I was in distress and who has been with me wherever I have gone." 4] They gave to Jacob all the alien gods that they had, and the rings that were in their ears, and Jacob buried them under the terebinth that was near

35:1] *Go up.* In the sense of pilgrimage, just as later one always "went up" to the Land of Israel. Jacob's journey to Bethel brings to a close the story of his exile.

2] *Alien gods.* Acquired either in Shechem or, through Rachel, in Haran. This is the only time in Genesis that foreign gods are contrasted with the God of the Patriarchs [1].

Purify yourselves. A ritual process that involved washing the body and clothes (cf. Exod. 19:10).

4] *Buried them.* Apparently there was an ancient taboo against destroying holy objects of any kind. Unlike Gideon, who used the golden earrings to fashion an object of idolatry (Judg. 8:24–27), Jacob does not allow the idols to become a snare [2].

/The Jewish practice of burying unusable Torah scrolls, phylacteries, and prayer books [3], or preserving them in a "Genizah," is based on the prohibition against destroying anything that has God's name written on it./

The terebinth. See note at Gen. 12:6.

ה שְׁכֶם: וַיִּסָּעוּ וַיְהִי חִתַּת אֱלֹהִים עַל־הֶעָרִים אֲשֶׁר

ו סְבִיבוֹתֵיהֶם וְלֹא רָדְפוּ אַחֲרֵי בְּנֵי יַעֲקֹב: וַיָּבֹא

יַעֲקֹב לוּזָה אֲשֶׁר בְּאֶרֶץ כְּנַעַן הִוא בֵּית־אֵל הוּא וְכָל־

ז הָעָם אֲשֶׁר־עִמּוֹ: וַיִּבֶן שָׁם מִזְבֵּחַ וַיִּקְרָא לַמָּקוֹם אֵל

בֵּית־אֵל כִּי שָׁם נִגְלוּ אֵלָיו הָאֱלֹהִים בְּבָרְחוֹ מִפְּנֵי

ח אָחִיו: וַתָּמָת דְּבֹרָה מֵינֶקֶת רִבְקָה וַתִּקָּבֵר מִתַּחַת

לְבֵית־אֵל תַּחַת הָאַלּוֹן וַיִּקְרָא שְׁמוֹ אַלּוֹן בָּכוּת: פ

ט וַיֵּרָא אֱלֹהִים אֶל־יַעֲקֹב עוֹד בְּבֹאוֹ מִפַּדַּן אֲרָם

י וַיְבָרֶךְ אֹתוֹ: וַיֹּאמֶר־לוֹ אֱלֹהִים שִׁמְךָ יַעֲקֹב לֹא־

Genesis 35
5–10

Shechem.   5] As they set out, a terror from God fell on the cities round about, so that they did not pursue the sons of Jacob.

6] Thus Jacob came to Luz—that is, Bethel—in the land of Canaan, he and all the people who were with him.   7] There he built an altar and named the site El-Bethel, for it was there that God had revealed Himself to him when he was fleeing from his brother.

8] Deborah, Rebekah's nurse, died, and was buried under the oak below Bethel; so it was named Allon-bacuth.

9] God appeared again to Jacob on his arrival from Paddan-aram, and He blessed him.   10] God said to him, "You whose name is Jacob, / You shall be

5] *Terror from God.* Compare this to the story of the angels in Sodom (Gen. 19:11) for a similar case of divine intervention.

6] *El-bethel.* The God of Bethel. Since no reference is made to the fact that Jacob had already named the site Bethel (Gen. 28:19), some commentators suggest that the two passages arose from separate traditions [4].

8] *Deborah.* If she is the nurse mentioned in Gen. 24:59, she would have to be very old here.

Allon-bacuth. Understood as "the oak of weeping."

9–15] This tradition is not aware of Jacob's wrestling bout with the angel (see note at Gen. 32:31) nor of the site having been named El-bethel. / Traditional explanation: God confirms what His angel has done "in the heat of the contest" [5]. /

10] *Jacob no more.* But in fact the appellation Jacob continues at once. Critics have attempted to distinguish between an "Israel tradition" and a

יָקָרֵא שִׁמְךָ עוֹד יַעֲקֹב כִּי אִם־יִשְׂרָאֵל יִהְיֶה שְׁמֶךָ

יא וַיִּקְרָא אֶת־שְׁמוֹ יִשְׂרָאֵל: וַיֹּאמֶר לוֹ אֱלֹהִים אֲנִי אֵל

שַׁדַּי פְּרֵה וּרְבֵה גּוֹי וּקְהַל גּוֹיִם יִהְיֶה מִמֶּךָּ וּמְלָכִים

יב מֵחֲלָצֶיךָ יֵצֵאוּ: וְאֶת־הָאָרֶץ אֲשֶׁר נָתַתִּי לְאַבְרָהָם

וּלְיִצְחָק לְךָ אֶתְּנֶנָּה וּלְזַרְעֲךָ אַחֲרֶיךָ אֶתֵּן אֶת־הָאָרֶץ:

יג וַיַּעַל מֵעָלָיו אֱלֹהִים בַּמָּקוֹם אֲשֶׁר־דִּבֶּר אִתּוֹ: וַיַּצֵּב

יד יַעֲקֹב מַצֵּבָה בַּמָּקוֹם אֲשֶׁר־דִּבֶּר אִתּוֹ מַצֶּבֶת אָבֶן

טו וַיַּסֵּךְ עָלֶיהָ נֶסֶךְ וַיִּצֹק עָלֶיהָ שָׁמֶן: וַיִּקְרָא יַעֲקֹב

אֶת־שֵׁם הַמָּקוֹם אֲשֶׁר דִּבֶּר אִתּוֹ שָׁם אֱלֹהִים בֵּית־אֵל:

טז וַיִּסְעוּ מִבֵּית אֵל וַיְהִי־עוֹד כִּבְרַת־הָאָרֶץ לָבוֹא

Genesis 35

11–16

called Jacob no more, / But Israel shall be your name." Thus He named him Israel.

11] And God said to him, "I am El Shaddai. / Be fertile and increase; / A nation, yea an assembly of nations, / Shall descend from you. / Kings shall issue from your loins. / 12] The land that I gave to Abraham and Isaac / I give to you; / And to your offspring to come / Will I give the land." 13] God parted from him at the spot where He had spoken to him. 14] And Jacob set up a pillar at the site where He had spoken to him, a pillar of stone, and he offered a libation on it and poured oil upon it. 15] And Jacob gave the site, where God had spoken to him, the name of Bethel.

16] They set out from Bethel; but when they were still some distance short of

"Jacob tradition." If these ever existed, they have been thoroughly interwoven, and the names have now become interchangeable.

/B. Jacob has attempted, however, to show that each particular usage has a purpose. His analysis covers the forty-five times "Jacob" is used and the thirty-four times "Israel" is written from here to the end of Genesis. "Israel" is said to be used whenever the spiritual side of the Patriarch is emphasized, "Jacob" when material and physical aspects are involved [6]./

11] *El Shaddai.* The name of God as He appeared to Abraham (Gen. 17:1).

16] *Short of Ephrath.* Verse 19 identifies this as

יז אֶפְרָתָה וַתֵּלֶד רָחֵל וַתְּקַשׁ בְּלִדְתָּהּ: וַיְהִי בְהַקְשֹׁתָהּ
בְּלִדְתָּהּ וַתֹּאמֶר לָהּ הַמְיַלֶּדֶת אַל־תִּירְאִי כִּי־גַם־זֶה
יח לָךְ בֵּן: וַיְהִי בְּצֵאת נַפְשָׁהּ כִּי מֵתָה וַתִּקְרָא שְׁמוֹ בֶּן־
יט אוֹנִי וְאָבִיו קָרָא־לוֹ בִנְיָמִין: וַתָּמָת רָחֵל וַתִּקָּבֵר
כ בְּדֶרֶךְ אֶפְרָתָה הִוא בֵּית לָחֶם: וַיַּצֵּב יַעֲקֹב מַצֵּבָה
כא עַל־קְבֻרָתָהּ הִוא מַצֶּבֶת קְבֻרַת־רָחֵל עַד־הַיּוֹם: וַיִּסַּע
כב יִשְׂרָאֵל וַיֵּט אָהֳלֹה מֵהָלְאָה לְמִגְדַּל־עֵדֶר: וַיְהִי בִּשְׁכֹּן
יִשְׂרָאֵל בָּאָרֶץ הַהִוא וַיֵּלֶךְ רְאוּבֵן וַיִּשְׁכַּב אֶת־בִּלְהָה
פִּילֶגֶשׁ אָבִיו וַיִּשְׁמַע יִשְׂרָאֵל פ

Ephrath, Rachel was in childbirth, and she had hard labor. 17] When her labor was at its hardest, the midwife said to her, "Have no fear, for it is another boy for you." 18] As she was breathing her last—for she was dying—she named him Ben-oni; but his father called him Benjamin. 19] Thus Rachel died. She was buried on the road to Ephrath—now Bethlehem. 20] Over her grave Jacob set up a pillar; it is the pillar at Rachel's grave to this day. 21] Israel journeyed on, and pitched his tent beyond Migdal-eder.

22] While Israel stayed in that land, Reuben went and lay with Bilhah, his father's concubine; and Israel found out.

Bethlehem. Rachel's tomb may be seen not far from that city. However, according to I Sam. 10:2, the grave was farther north [7]. And one authority holds it was originally near the Jaffa-Jerusalem road at Kiryat Yearim [8].

18] Ben-oni. Understood as "son of my suffering [or, strength]."

Benjamin. That is, "son of the south." Others interpret the name as "son of the right hand," which was the favored side. Still others interpret

Benjamin as "son of old age" (ben-yamim) [9]. Whatever the meaning, Jacob apparently did not want his son to live with the name Ben-oni, which recalled grief.

22] Reuben . . . Bilhah. This incident may hint at a revolt by the first-born against his father. (The revolt of Absalom against David takes the same form, II Sam. 16:20–22). Even though Jacob makes no immediate comment, the action will later on cost Reuben his birthright (Gen. 49:4). There is a

כג וַיִּהְיוּ בְנֵי־יַעֲקֹב שְׁנֵים עָשָׂר: בְּנֵי לֵאָה בְּכוֹר יַעֲקֹב

כד רְאוּבֵן וְשִׁמְעוֹן וְלֵוִי וִיהוּדָה וְיִשָּׂשכָר וּזְבֻלוּן: בְּנֵי

כה רָחֵל יוֹסֵף וּבִנְיָמִן: וּבְנֵי בִלְהָה שִׁפְחַת רָחֵל דָּן

כו וְנַפְתָּלִי: וּבְנֵי זִלְפָּה שִׁפְחַת לֵאָה גָּד וְאָשֵׁר אֵלֶּה בְּנֵי

כז יַעֲקֹב אֲשֶׁר יֻלַּד־לוֹ בְּפַדַּן אֲרָם: וַיָּבֹא יַעֲקֹב אֶל־

יִצְחָק אָבִיו מַמְרֵא קִרְיַת הָאַרְבַּע הִוא חֶבְרוֹן

כח אֲשֶׁר־גָּר־שָׁם אַבְרָהָם וְיִצְחָק: וַיִּהְיוּ יְמֵי יִצְחָק מְאַת

כט שָׁנָה וּשְׁמֹנִים שָׁנָה: וַיִּגְוַע יִצְחָק וַיָּמָת וַיֵּאָסֶף אֶל־

עַמָּיו זָקֵן וּשְׂבַע יָמִים וַיִּקְבְּרוּ אֹתוֹ עֵשָׂו וְיַעֲקֹב

בָּנָיו: פ

Genesis 35
23–29

Now the sons of Jacob were twelve in number. **23]** The sons of Leah: Reuben—Jacob's first-born—Simeon, Levi, Judah, Issachar, and Zebulun. **24]** The sons of Rachel: Joseph and Benjamin. **25]** The sons of Bilhah, Rachel's maid: Dan and Naphtali. **26]** And the sons of Zilpah, Leah's maid: Gad and Asher. These are the sons of Jacob who were born to him in Paddan-aram.

27] And Jacob came to his father Isaac at Mamre, at Kiriath-arba—now Hebron—where Abraham and Isaac had sojourned. **28]** Isaac was a hundred and eighty years old **29]** when he breathed his last and died. He was gathered to his kin in ripe old age; and he was buried by his sons Esau and Jacob.

blank space and double accentuation in the Hebrew text, suggesting that this verse presented some problem to the ancients; possibly the original story told of the incident in greater detail. / The Mishnah says that this verse is to be read from the Torah in public but not to be translated. The accentuation causes verses 22 and 23 to be read as one, so as to pass quickly over the passage [10]. The Tal-

mud, however, explains Reuben's action away [11]./ 28-29] Isaac's death is as quiet as his life. Most probably he died earlier [12] but the death notice is placed here to complete the patriarchal cycle before attention shifts to Joseph.

28] *One hundred and eighty years old.* On the relation of this age to the years of Abraham and Jacob, see p. 241.

א וְאֵלֶּה תֹּלְדוֹת עֵשָׂו הוּא אֱדוֹם: עֵשָׂו לָקַח אֶת־נָשָׁיו
ב מִבְּנוֹת כְּנָעַן אֶת־עָדָה בַּת־אֵילוֹן הַחִתִּי וְאֶת־
ג אָהֳלִיבָמָה בַּת־עֲנָה בַּת־צִבְעוֹן הַחִוִּי: וְאֶת־בָּשְׂמַת
ד בַּת־יִשְׁמָעֵאל אֲחוֹת נְבָיוֹת: וַתֵּלֶד עָדָה לְעֵשָׂו אֶת־
ה אֱלִיפָז וּבָשְׂמַת יָלְדָה אֶת־רְעוּאֵל: וְאָהֳלִיבָמָה יָלְדָה
אֶת־יְעִישׁ* וְאֶת־יַעְלָם וְאֶת־קֹרַח אֵלֶּה בְּנֵי עֵשָׂו אֲשֶׁר
ו יֻלְּדוּ־לוֹ בְּאֶרֶץ כְּנָעַן: וַיִּקַּח עֵשָׂו אֶת־נָשָׁיו וְאֶת־בָּנָיו
וְאֶת־בְּנֹתָיו וְאֶת־כָּל־נַפְשׁוֹת בֵּיתוֹ וְאֶת־מִקְנֵהוּ וְאֶת־
כָּל־בְּהֶמְתּוֹ וְאֵת כָּל־קִנְיָנוֹ אֲשֶׁר רָכַשׁ בְּאֶרֶץ כְּנָעַן
ז וַיֵּלֶךְ אֶל־אֶרֶץ מִפְּנֵי יַעֲקֹב אָחִיו: כִּי־הָיָה רְכוּשָׁם רָב
מִשֶּׁבֶת יַחְדָּו וְלֹא יָכְלָה אֶרֶץ מְגוּרֵיהֶם לָשֵׂאת אֹתָם

* ה יעוש קרי.

1] This is the line of Esau—that is, Edom.

2] Esau took his wives from among the Canaanite women—Adah daughter of Elon the Hittite, and Oholibamah daughter of Anah daughter of Zibeon the Hivite— 3] and also Basemath daughter of Ishmael and sister of Nebaioth. 4] Adah bore to Esau Eliphaz; Basemath bore Reuel; 5] and Oholibamah bore Jeush, Jalam, and Korah. Those were the sons of Esau, who were born to him in the land of Canaan.

6] Esau took his wives, his sons and daughters, and all the members of his household, his cattle and all his livestock, and all the property that he had acquired in the land of Canaan, and went to another land because of his brother Jacob. 7] For their possessions were too many for them to dwell together, and the land where

36:1] *Esau—that is, Edom.* Also called Seir. The land is southeast of the Dead Sea.

2] *Hivite.* Called Horite (חֹרִי) in Gen. 36:20, a Canaanite group of the same name as the Hori (Hurrians) in the north [13]. (Compare the dual use of "Cush" in the Bible, or "Indian" in our time.)

מִפְּנֵי מִקְנֵיהֶם: וַיֵּשֶׁב עֵשָׂו בְּהַר שֵׂעִיר עֵשָׂו הוּא ח

אֱדוֹם: וְאֵלֶּה תֹּלְדוֹת עֵשָׂו אֲבִי אֱדוֹם בְּהַר שֵׂעִיר: ט

אֵלֶּה שְׁמוֹת בְּנֵי־עֵשָׂו אֱלִיפַז בֶּן־עָדָה אֵשֶׁת עֵשָׂו י

רְעוּאֵל בֶּן־בָּשְׂמַת אֵשֶׁת עֵשָׂו: וַיִּהְיוּ בְּנֵי אֱלִיפָז יא

תֵּימָן אוֹמָר צְפוֹ וְגַעְתָּם וּקְנַז: וְתִמְנַע הָיְתָה פִילֶגֶשׁ יב

לֶאֱלִיפַז בֶּן־עֵשָׂו וַתֵּלֶד לֶאֱלִיפַז אֶת־עֲמָלֵק אֵלֶּה בְּנֵי

עָדָה אֵשֶׁת עֵשָׂו: וְאֵלֶּה בְּנֵי רְעוּאֵל נַחַת וָזֶרַח שַׁמָּה יג

וּמִזָּה אֵלֶּה הָיוּ בְּנֵי בָשְׂמַת אֵשֶׁת עֵשָׂו: וְאֵלֶּה הָיוּ בְּנֵי יד

אָהֳלִיבָמָה בַת־עֲנָה בַּת־צִבְעוֹן אֵשֶׁת עֵשָׂו וַתֵּלֶד

לְעֵשָׂו אֶת־יְעִישׁ* וְאֶת־יַעְלָם וְאֶת־קֹרַח: אֵלֶּה אַלּוּפֵי טו

בְּנֵי־עֵשָׂו בְּנֵי אֱלִיפַז בְּכוֹר עֵשָׂו אַלּוּף תֵּימָן אַלּוּף

Genesis 36
8–15

* יד יעוש קרי.

they sojourned could not support them because of their livestock.   8] So Esau settled in the hill country of Seir—Esau being Edom.

9] This, then, is the line of Esau, the ancestor of the Edomites, in the hill country of Seir.

10] These are the names of Esau's sons: Eliphaz, the son of Esau's wife Adah; Reuel, the son of Esau's wife Basemath.   11] The sons of Eliphaz were Teman, Omar, Zepho, Gatam, and Kenaz.   12] Timna was a concubine of Esau's son Eliphaz; she bore Amalek to Eliphaz. Those were the descendants of Esau's wife Adah. 13] And these were the sons of Reuel: Nahath, Zerah, Shammah, and Mizzah. Those were the descendants of Esau's wife Basemath.   14] And these were the sons of Esau's wife Oholibamah, daughter of Anah daughter of Zibeon: she bore to Esau Jeush, Jalam, and Korah.

15] These are the clans of the children of Esau. The descendants of Esau's first-

15] *Clans.* Better than "chiefs" of older translations [14].

טז אוֹמָר אַלּוּף צְפוֹ אַלּוּף קְנַז: אַלּוּף קֹרַח אַלּוּף
גַּעְתָּם אַלּוּף עֲמָלֵק אֵלֶּה אַלּוּפֵי אֱלִיפַז בְּאֶרֶץ
אֱדוֹם אֵלֶּה בְּנֵי עָדָה: וְאֵלֶּה בְּנֵי רְעוּאֵל בֶּן־עֵשָׂו
יז אַלּוּף נַחַת אַלּוּף זֶרַח אַלּוּף שַׁמָּה אַלּוּף מִזָּה אֵלֶּה
אַלּוּפֵי רְעוּאֵל בְּאֶרֶץ אֱדוֹם אֵלֶּה בְּנֵי בָשְׂמַת אֵשֶׁת
יח עֵשָׂו: וְאֵלֶּה בְּנֵי אָהֳלִיבָמָה אֵשֶׁת עֵשָׂו אַלּוּף יְעוּשׁ
אַלּוּף יַעְלָם אַלּוּף קֹרַח אֵלֶּה אַלּוּפֵי אָהֳלִיבָמָה
יט בַּת־עֲנָה אֵשֶׁת עֵשָׂו: אֵלֶּה בְנֵי־עֵשָׂו וְאֵלֶּה אַלּוּפֵיהֶם
כ הוּא אֱדוֹם: ס אֵלֶּה בְנֵי־שֵׂעִיר הַחֹרִי יֹשְׁבֵי הָאָרֶץ
כא לוֹטָן וְשׁוֹבָל וְצִבְעוֹן וַעֲנָה: וְדִשׁוֹן וְאֵצֶר וְדִישָׁן
אֵלֶּה אַלּוּפֵי הַחֹרִי בְּנֵי שֵׂעִיר בְּאֶרֶץ אֱדוֹם:
כב וַיִּהְיוּ בְנֵי־לוֹטָן חֹרִי וְהֵימָם וַאֲחוֹת לוֹטָן תִּמְנָע:

born Eliphaz: the clans Teman, Omar, Zepho, Kenaz, 16] Korah, Gatam, and Amalek; these are the clans of Eliphaz in the land of Edom. Those are the descendants of Adah. 17] And these are the descendants of Esau's son Reuel: the clans Nahath, Zerah, Shammah, and Mizzah; these are the clans of Reuel in the land of Edom. Those are the descendants of Esau's wife Basemath. 18] And these are the descendants of Esau's wife Oholibamah: the clans of Jeush, Jalam, and Korah; these are the clans of Esau's wife Oholibamah, the daughter of Anah. 19] Those were the sons of Esau—that is, Edom—and those are their clans.

20] These were the sons of Seir the Horite, who were settled in the land: Lotan, Shobal, Zibeon, Anah, 21] Dishon, Ezer, and Dishan. Those are the clans of the Horites, the descendants of Seir, in the land of Edom.

22] The sons of Lotan were Hori and Hemam; and Lotan's sister was Timna.

כג וְאֵלֶּה בְּנֵי שׁוֹבָל עַלְוָן וּמָנַחַת וְעֵיבָל שְׁפוֹ וְאוֹנָם: וְאֵלֶּה
בְנֵי־צִבְעוֹן וְאַיָּה וַעֲנָה הוּא עֲנָה אֲשֶׁר מָצָא אֶת־הַיֵּמִם
כה בַּמִּדְבָּר בִּרְעֹתוֹ אֶת־הַחֲמֹרִים לְצִבְעוֹן אָבִיו: וְאֵלֶּה
כו בְנֵי־עֲנָה דִּשֹׁן וְאָהֳלִיבָמָה בַּת־עֲנָה: וְאֵלֶּה בְּנֵי דִישָׁן
חֶמְדָּן וְאֶשְׁבָּן וְיִתְרָן וּכְרָן: אֵלֶּה בְּנֵי־אֵצֶר בִּלְהָן
כח וְזַעֲוָן וַעֲקָן: אֵלֶּה בְנֵי־דִישָׁן עוּץ וַאֲרָן: אֵלֶּה אַלּוּפֵי
כט הַחֹרִי אַלּוּף לוֹטָן אַלּוּף שׁוֹבָל אַלּוּף צִבְעוֹן אַלּוּף
ל עֲנָה: אַלּוּף דִּשֹׁן אַלּוּף אֵצֶר אַלּוּף דִּישָׁן אֵלֶּה
אַלּוּפֵי הַחֹרִי לְאַלֻּפֵיהֶם בְּאֶרֶץ שֵׂעִיר: פ
לא וְאֵלֶּה הַמְּלָכִים אֲשֶׁר מָלְכוּ בְּאֶרֶץ אֱדוֹם לִפְנֵי

Genesis 36
23–31

23] The sons of Shobal were these: Alvan, Manahath, Ebal, Shepho, and Onam.
24] The sons of Zibeon were these: Aiah and Anah—that was the Anah who discovered the hot springs in the wilderness while pasturing the asses of his father Zibeon.   25] The children of Anah were these: Dishon and Anah's daughter Oholibamah.   26] The sons of Dishon were these: Hemdan, Eshban, Ithran, and Cheran.
27] The sons of Ezer were these: Bilhan, Zaavan, and Akan.   28] And the sons of Dishan were these: Uz and Aran.

29] These are the clans of the Horites: the clans Lotan, Shobal, Zibeon, Anah,
30] Dishon, Ezer, and Dishan. Those are the clans of the Horites, clan by clan, in the land of Seir.

31] These are the kings who reigned in the land of Edom before any king reigned

24] *Aiah.* The Hebrew says "and Aiah."
Hot springs. The meaning of יֵמִם is uncertain. /This verse has given rise to much comment and speculation. Anah may be a word play on "female donkey": what Anah discovered was not "hot springs" but the crossbreeding of animals [15]./

26] *Dishon.* Spelled variously דִּישֹׁן (*Dishon*) and רִישֹׁן (*Rishon*). Compare Gen. 36:21, 25, 28; I Chron. 1:41.

31] *Before any king reigned over the Israelites.* The conclusion suggests itself that either this phrase

לב מְלָךְ־מֶלֶךְ לִבְנֵי יִשְׂרָאֵל: וַיִּמְלֹךְ בֶּאֱדוֹם בֶּלַע בֶּן־

לג בְּעוֹר וְשֵׁם עִירוֹ דִּנְהָבָה: וַיָּמָת בָּלַע וַיִּמְלֹךְ תַּחְתָּיו

לד יוֹבָב בֶּן־זֶרַח מִבָּצְרָה: וַיָּמָת יוֹבָב וַיִּמְלֹךְ תַּחְתָּיו

לה חֻשָׁם מֵאֶרֶץ הַתֵּימָנִי: וַיָּמָת חֻשָׁם וַיִּמְלֹךְ תַּחְתָּיו הֲדַד

בֶּן־בְּדַד הַמַּכֶּה אֶת־מִדְיָן בִּשְׂדֵה מוֹאָב וְשֵׁם עִירוֹ

לו עֲוִית: וַיָּמָת הֲדָד וַיִּמְלֹךְ תַּחְתָּיו שַׂמְלָה מִמַּשְׂרֵקָה:

לז וַיָּמָת שַׂמְלָה וַיִּמְלֹךְ תַּחְתָּיו שָׁאוּל מֵרְחֹבוֹת הַנָּהָר:

לח וַיָּמָת שָׁאוּל וַיִּמְלֹךְ תַּחְתָּיו בַּעַל חָנָן בֶּן־עַכְבּוֹר:

לט וַיָּמָת בַּעַל חָנָן בֶּן־עַכְבּוֹר וַיִּמְלֹךְ תַּחְתָּיו הֲדַר וְשֵׁם

Genesis 36

32–39

over the Israelites. **32]** Bela son of Beor reigned in Edom, and the name of his city was Dinhabah. **33]** When Bela died, Jobab son of Zerah, from Bozrah, succeeded him as king. **34]** When Jobab died, Husham of the land of the Temanites succeeded him as king. **35]** When Husham died, Hadad son of Bedad, who defeated the Midianites in the country of Moab, succeeded him as king; the name of his city was Avith. **36]** When Hadad died, Samlah of Masrekah succeeded him as king. **37]** When Samlah died, Saul of Rehoboth-on-the-river succeeded him as king. **38]** When Saul died, Baal-hanan son of Achbor succeeded him as king. **39]** And when Baal-hanan son of Achbor died, Hadar succeeded him as king; the name of

or the entire section was added after the establishment of the Israelite monarchy. The verse was a stumbling block to traditional interpreters who had to maintain that "the king" was Moses or that Moses wrote this as a prophecy. However, as early as 1000 C.E., the Spanish commentator Isaac ben Yashush (Yitzchaki) wrote that this verse had been added in the ninth century B.C.E., in the reign of King Jehoshaphat. Ibn Ezra was careful to let his readers know of this view (apparently a way of venting his own doubts) but then added piously:

"God forbid that he be right. His book deserves to be burnt."

37] *Saul.* שָׁאוּל (*Shaul*). Note that the name of this Edomite will be the name of Israel's first king.

Rehoboth-on-the-river. The location is uncertain. It has no connection with today's Rehovot.

39] *Hadar.* Elsewhere called Hadad (I Chron. 1:50).

עִירוֹ פָּעוּ וְשֵׁם אִשְׁתּוֹ מְהֵיטַבְאֵל בַּת־מַטְרֵד בַּת מֵי זָהָב:

מ וְאֵלֶּה שְׁמוֹת אַלּוּפֵי עֵשָׂו לְמִשְׁפְּחֹתָם לִמְקֹמֹתָם

מא בִּשְׁמֹתָם אַלּוּף תִּמְנָע אַלּוּף עַלְוָה אַלּוּף יְתֵת: אַלּוּף

מב אָהֳלִיבָמָה אַלּוּף אֵלָה אַלּוּף פִּינֹן: אַלּוּף קְנַז אַלּוּף

מג תֵּימָן אַלּוּף מִבְצָר: אַלּוּף מַגְדִּיאֵל אַלּוּף עִירָם

אֵלֶּה אַלּוּפֵי אֱדוֹם לְמֹשְׁבֹתָם בְּאֶרֶץ אֲחֻזָּתָם הוּא

עֵשָׂו אֲבִי אֱדוֹם:

Genesis 36

40–43

Haftarah Vayishlach, p. 552

his city was Pau, and his wife's name was Mehetabel daughter of Matred daughter of Me-zahab.

40] These are the names of the clans of Esau, each with its families and locality, name by name: the clans Timna, Alvah, Jetheth,   41] Oholibamah, Elah, Pinon, 42] Kenaz, Teman, Mibzar,   43] Magdiel, and Iram. Those are the clans of Edom— that is, of Esau, father of the Edomites—in their settlements in the land which they hold.

The Edomites

This section presents a number of difficulties. Scholars have not yet been successful in sorting out all the historical and geographical identities mentioned, especially since the Bible remains our only major source of knowledge in regard to the Edomites. Nothing remains of the language of Edom except proper names, and these suggest that the Edomites' tongue was similar to Hebrew [16]. There is no other written record of this people, and archeological discoveries have thus far been of no assistance. We have here an instance where traditions that were once meaningful to listener and reader and that carried nuances and references clear in their own time have become mere names and lists.

While this is not the first point at which the Bible discusses the Edomites, parts of this section appear to be based on traditions different from those recorded earlier. For instance, Basemath is here called the daughter of Ishmael (Gen. 36:3) but was earlier called the daughter of Elon (Gen. 26:34); Esau is married to Adah, daughter of Elon (Gen. 36:2), while earlier his wife is called Judith, daughter of Beeri (Gen. 26:34). Because of such inconsistencies and contradictions, the famous Bible scholar and critic Julius Wellhausen thought of chapter 36 as a show window for biblical criticism and said that either varying traditions stand here side by side or the whole system of biblical criticism must be pronounced invalid.[1]

The Character of Esau

Although the Bible relates many uncomplimentary incidents about Jacob, it records on the whole praiseworthy accounts of Esau. Nevertheless, Jacob-Israel became the chosen, Esau-Edom the rejected. Because of this, traditional interpreters felt compelled to whitewash Jacob's character and to blacken the name of Esau. After the Roman conquest of Judea (first century B.C.E.), "Edom" came to signify Rome, oppression, and evil. Not only was this a case of prejudicial stereotyping, it was also a misreading of the biblical intent. For Esau emerges from the text as a generally admirable man.

While he thought little of his birthright and contracted marriages displeasing to his parents, Esau was otherwise attentive to his father. One midrash even conceded that because he showed more respect to him than duty demanded he was mentioned first at the burial of his father (Gen. 35:29) [18]. Certainly his behavior at the reconciliation with Jacob was exemplary—he was generous and forgiving.

No wonder Isaac loved this outdoor man and skilful hunter who exuded strength. Yet precisely because Esau was the physical man, little concerned with things of the spirit, he could not be the inheritor of Abraham's and Isaac's blessings. Even before his birth (Gen. 25:23) it was foretold that God's mysterious choice would be Jacob, the complex and difficult man whose moral fibers needed building and strengthening, the man who ran from and toward fate, who would suffer deep pain and find the coveted blessing a source of bitter agony.

---

[1] Following ancient tradition, which saw in Esau the embodiment of evil, these passages have been called a "labyrinth of immoral connections," i.e., a somewhat veiled description of the presumed immorality of Edom [17].

GLEANINGS

Change Your Clothes (Gen. 35:2)

From this we learn that every Jew, when he goes to a place appointed for prayer, must be clean in body and clothes. IBN EZRA

Pillars

מַצֵּבוֹת served the ancients for worship and as tombstones, as in the case of Rachel. In talmudic times, when funds were collected to pay for burials, the surplus was applied to the purchase of a tombstone. However, R. Simeon ben Gamaliel, in order to prevent the erection of ostentatious markers, discouraged their use by teaching: "Tombstones are not erected for the righteous, since their teachings are their memorials." [19]

While the Patriarchs erected pillars for worship, this was later forbidden and gave way to altars at which cultic rites were to be performed. Why? Pillars were symbols of generalized faith; altars were symbols of faith plus *mitzvot*, i.e., Judaism.

RAV KUK [20]

The Burden

Because he [Jacob] moves forever shadowed by
  deep questioning,
And you [Esau] rejoice, happy and safe and
  sated ...
Because he does not shroud his God in distant
  heavens,
But wrestles with him daily, heart to heart!
Because you can but hunt, make offering,
  murder ...

He bears the blessing—and the blessing's burden. RICHARD BEER-HOFMANN [21]

Edom and Israel

In rabbinical tradition Esau and Edom came to symbolize Rome, the colossal, temporal, material power, which sought to crush nations, which overran the earth with warfare and bloodshed, and found its highest pleasure in murderous gladiatorial combats. And Jacob continued to represent Israel, the spiritual people, the servant of the Lord, whose mission was to bind up the bleeding wounds of cruelty and oppression and to bring law and order, peace and brotherhood, and the knowledge of God unto all mankind.

JULIAN MORGENSTERN [22]

The Meeting

Rebecca's twin sons were at this time fifty-five years old: the sweet-smelling grass and the prickly plant, as they had been known in all the countryside between Hebron and Beersheba. But the sweet-smelling grass, the smooth man, Jacob, had never behaved very youthful; a tent-dweller, thoughtful and timid, he had shown himself even as a boy. And now he was a ripe man, with much experience, heavy with goods that had accrued unto him, preoccupied in spirit, bearing with dignity the weight of events. And on the other hand Esau, though like his brother grey-haired, seemed still to be as of yore, the same feckless insignificant child of nature.

THOMAS MANN [23]

PART V

The Line of Jacob

The last part of Genesis begins with the "line of Jacob" (37:2) for, with Isaac dead, Jacob is now, technically, the leading figure. In effect, however, the Patriarch at once fades into the background. His life provides the framework for the Joseph saga, which is distinguished from the preceding sections of Genesis in a number of ways: its length as a continuing account and the absence both of divine revelation (except in Gen. 46:2–4) and of specific references in the most important parts (neither Goshen nor Pharaoh is further identified) [1].

The effective impact of Joseph's biography is created by the device of what Aristotle called "dramatic reversal," which he considered essential to good drama [2] and which is often found in Greek writing. Fate thwarts the will of man by turning the effect of his actions to its own purposes rather than to his. Joseph is sold by his brothers so that they may be rid of the dreamer, yet the dreams come true, the slave becomes master, hatred turns to love, and the rejected one saves his brothers' lives. In sum, man cannot alter the overriding purposes of divine power.

The prominence of Joseph in these tales should not let us forget the continuing tragedy of Jacob. He who chased after the birthright and secured its blessings in deceitful fashion pays heavily for the privilege. His children will cause him anxieties and agonies, and he will end his life in exile, a pensioner of his son.

Young Joseph

The apparent calm of a wealthy shepherd's pastoral existence forms the setting of the opening chapter of the Joseph cycle, but parental preference, youthful conceit, and sibling envy will create a bitter drama. Dreams play an important role and hint at unusual developments. And once again there is a descent into Egypt. Abraham had gone there to escape a famine; Joseph makes the journey as a slave.

בראשית לז

א-ה

א וַיֵּשֶׁב יַעֲקֹב בְּאֶרֶץ מְגוּרֵי אָבִיו בְּאֶרֶץ כְּנָעַן: אֵלֶּה

תֹּלְדוֹת יַעֲקֹב יוֹסֵף בֶּן־שְׁבַע־עֶשְׂרֵה שָׁנָה הָיָה רֹעֶה

אֶת־אֶחָיו בַּצֹּאן וְהוּא נַעַר אֶת־בְּנֵי בִלְהָה וְאֶת־בְּנֵי

זִלְפָּה נְשֵׁי אָבִיו וַיָּבֵא יוֹסֵף אֶת־דִּבָּתָם רָעָה אֶל־

ג אֲבִיהֶם: וְיִשְׂרָאֵל אָהַב אֶת־יוֹסֵף מִכָּל־בָּנָיו כִּי־בֶן־

ד זְקֻנִים הוּא לוֹ וְעָשָׂה לוֹ כְּתֹנֶת פַּסִּים: וַיִּרְאוּ אֶחָיו

כִּי־אֹתוֹ אָהַב אֲבִיהֶם מִכָּל־אֶחָיו וַיִּשְׂנְאוּ אֹתוֹ וְלֹא

ה יָכְלוּ דַּבְּרוֹ לְשָׁלֹם: וַיַּחֲלֹם יוֹסֵף חֲלוֹם וַיַּגֵּד לְאֶחָיו

Genesis 37

1–5

1] Now Jacob was settled in the land where his father had resided, the land of Canaan.   2] This, then, is the line of Jacob.

At seventeen years of age, Joseph tended the flocks with his brothers, as a helper to the sons of his father's wives Bilhah and Zilpah. And Joseph brought bad reports of them to their father.   3] Now Israel loved Joseph best of all his sons, for he was the child of his old age; and he had made him an ornamented tunic.   4] And when his brothers saw that their father loved him more than any of his brothers, they hated him so that they could not speak a friendly word to him.

5] Joseph had a dream which he told to his brothers; and they hated him even

---

37:1–2] The first verse and half of the second form a literary bridge. They conclude the core of the Jacob story and provide an introduction to the Joseph cycle (see Gen. 2:4, which has a similar function in connecting the two creation stories).

2] *Joseph brought bad reports.* He was a tale-bearer. Traditional commentators attempt to whitewash Joseph's behavior by saying that he merely did his job and reported what he saw.

3] *Ornamented tunic.* The meaning is not clear.

Others translate as "a coat of many colors," or "a robe with sleeves." In II Sam. 13:18, the same term signifies special distinction; perhaps it marked those who did not have to work [1].   Jacob's affection for Joseph most likely sprang from his love for Rachel, whose first-born he was. Later, after Joseph's presumed death, Jacob's preference is transferred to Benjamin, Rachel's second son.

5] *Joseph had a dream.* Six dreams (two by Joseph, two by the prisoners, and two by Pharaoh) lend suspense to the story. While dreams are now

י וַיּוֹסִפוּ עוֹד שְׂנֹא אֹתוֹ: וַיֹּאמֶר אֲלֵיהֶם שִׁמְעוּ־נָא

ז הַחֲלוֹם הַזֶּה אֲשֶׁר חָלָמְתִּי: וְהִנֵּה אֲנַחְנוּ מְאַלְּמִים

אֲלֻמִּים בְּתוֹךְ הַשָּׂדֶה וְהִנֵּה קָמָה אֲלֻמָּתִי וְגַם־נִצָּבָה

וְהִנֵּה תְסֻבֶּינָה אֲלֻמֹּתֵיכֶם וַתִּשְׁתַּחֲוֶיןָ לַאֲלֻמָּתִי:

ח וַיֹּאמְרוּ לוֹ אֶחָיו הֲמָלֹךְ תִּמְלֹךְ עָלֵינוּ אִם־מָשׁוֹל

תִּמְשֹׁל בָּנוּ וַיּוֹסִפוּ עוֹד שְׂנֹא אֹתוֹ עַל־חֲלֹמֹתָיו וְעַל־

ט דְּבָרָיו: וַיַּחֲלֹם עוֹד חֲלוֹם אַחֵר וַיְסַפֵּר אֹתוֹ לְאֶחָיו

וַיֹּאמֶר הִנֵּה חָלַמְתִּי חֲלוֹם עוֹד וְהִנֵּה הַשֶּׁמֶשׁ וְהַיָּרֵחַ

י וְאַחַד עָשָׂר כּוֹכָבִים מִשְׁתַּחֲוִים לִי: וַיְסַפֵּר אֶל־אָבִיו

וְאֶל־אֶחָיו וַיִּגְעַר־בּוֹ אָבִיו וַיֹּאמֶר לוֹ מָה הַחֲלוֹם הַזֶּה

אֲשֶׁר חָלָמְתָּ הֲבוֹא נָבוֹא אֲנִי וְאִמְּךָ וְאַחֶיךָ לְהִשְׁתַּחֲוֺת

יא לְךָ אָרְצָה: וַיְקַנְאוּ־בוֹ אֶחָיו וְאָבִיו שָׁמַר אֶת־הַדָּבָר:

Genesis 37

6–11

more. 6] He said to them, "Hear this dream which I have dreamed: 7] In it, we were binding sheaves in the field, when suddenly my sheaf stood up and remained upright; then your sheaves gathered around and bowed low to my sheaf." 8] His brothers answered, "Do you mean to reign over us? Do you mean to rule over us?" And they hated him even more for his talk about his dreams.

9] He dreamed another dream and told it to his brothers, saying, "Look, I have had another dream: And this time, the sun, the moon, and eleven stars were bowing down to me." 10] And when he told it to his father and brothers, his father berated him. "What," he said to him, "is this dream you have dreamed? Are we to come, I and your mother and your brothers, and bow low to you to the ground?" 11] So his brothers were wrought up at him, and his father kept the matter in mind.

studied as keys to hidden layers of personality, they were formerly thought to be prophetic. An Egyptian manual of the time gives instructions on how to interpret such premonitory dreams (see p. 388).

11] *Kept the matter in mind.* Because he believed that as a dream it revealed the future.

יב וַיֵּלְכוּ אֶחָיו לִרְעוֹת אֶת־צֹאן אֲבִיהֶם בִּשְׁכֶם: וַיֹּאמֶר

יִשְׂרָאֵל אֶל־יוֹסֵף הֲלוֹא אַחֶיךָ רֹעִים בִּשְׁכֶם לְכָה

וְאֶשְׁלָחֲךָ אֲלֵיהֶם וַיֹּאמֶר לוֹ הִנֵּנִי: וַיֹּאמֶר לוֹ לֶךְ־נָא

רְאֵה אֶת־שְׁלוֹם אַחֶיךָ וְאֶת־שְׁלוֹם הַצֹּאן וַהֲשִׁבֵנִי

טו דָּבָר וַיִּשְׁלָחֵהוּ מֵעֵמֶק חֶבְרוֹן וַיָּבֹא שְׁכֶמָה: וַיִּמְצָאֵהוּ

אִישׁ וְהִנֵּה תֹעֶה בַּשָּׂדֶה וַיִּשְׁאָלֵהוּ הָאִישׁ לֵאמֹר מַה־

טז תְּבַקֵּשׁ: וַיֹּאמֶר אֶת־אַחַי אָנֹכִי מְבַקֵּשׁ הַגִּידָה־נָּא לִי

יז אֵיפֹה הֵם רֹעִים: וַיֹּאמֶר הָאִישׁ נָסְעוּ מִזֶּה כִּי שָׁמַעְתִּי

אֹמְרִים נֵלְכָה דֹּתָיְנָה וַיֵּלֶךְ יוֹסֵף אַחַר אֶחָיו וַיִּמְצָאֵם

יח בְּדֹתָן: וַיִּרְאוּ אֹתוֹ מֵרָחֹק וּבְטֶרֶם יִקְרַב אֲלֵיהֶם

* יא נקוד על את.

Genesis 37

12–18

12] One time, when his brothers had gone to pasture their father's flock at Shechem,   13] Israel said to Joseph, "Your brothers are pasturing at Shechem. Come, I will send you to them." He answered, "I am ready."   14] And he said to him, "Go now, see how your brothers are and how the flocks are faring, and bring me back word." So he sent him from the valley of Hebron.

When he reached Shechem,   15] a man came upon him wandering in the fields. The man asked him, "What are you looking for?"   16] He answered, "I am looking for my brothers. Could you tell me where they are pasturing?" 17] The man said, "They have gone from here, for I heard them say: Let us go to Dothan." So Joseph followed his brothers and found them at Dothan.

18] They saw him from afar, and before he came close to them they conspired

14] *From the valley of Hebron.* Joseph will not return here, but hundreds of years later his remains will reach Shechem once again (Josh. 24:32).
/ The Talmud connects the passage with Gen. 15:13 and following, which predict enslavement in a foreign land and return to Canaan after 400 years [2]./

15] *A man.* His namelessness suggests a comparison with the nameless man who wrestled with Jacob.

17] *Dothan.* Today's Tell Dothan, north of Shechem. The city, excavated in 1953–1960, dates back to 3000 B.C.E.

וַיִּתְנַכְּלוּ אֹתוֹ לַהֲמִיתוֹ: וַיֹּאמְרוּ אִישׁ אֶל־אָחִיו הִנֵּה
בַּעַל הַחֲלֹמוֹת הַלָּזֶה בָּא: וְעַתָּה לְכוּ וְנַהַרְגֵהוּ
וְנַשְׁלִכֵהוּ בְּאַחַד הַבֹּרוֹת וְאָמַרְנוּ חַיָּה רָעָה אֲכָלָתְהוּ
וְנִרְאֶה מַה־יִּהְיוּ חֲלֹמֹתָיו: וַיִּשְׁמַע רְאוּבֵן וַיַּצִּלֵהוּ
מִיָּדָם וַיֹּאמֶר לֹא נַכֶּנּוּ נָפֶשׁ: וַיֹּאמֶר אֲלֵהֶם רְאוּבֵן
אַל־תִּשְׁפְּכוּ־דָם הַשְׁלִיכוּ אֹתוֹ אֶל־הַבּוֹר הַזֶּה אֲשֶׁר
בַּמִּדְבָּר וְיָד אַל־תִּשְׁלְחוּ־בוֹ לְמַעַן הַצִּיל אֹתוֹ מִיָּדָם
לַהֲשִׁיבוֹ אֶל־אָבִיו: וַיְהִי כַּאֲשֶׁר־בָּא יוֹסֵף אֶל־אֶחָיו
וַיַּפְשִׁיטוּ אֶת־יוֹסֵף אֶת־כֻּתָּנְתּוֹ אֶת־כְּתֹנֶת הַפַּסִּים אֲשֶׁר
עָלָיו: וַיִּקָּחֻהוּ וַיַּשְׁלִכוּ אֹתוֹ הַבֹּרָה וְהַבּוֹר רֵק אֵין בּוֹ
מָיִם: וַיֵּשְׁבוּ לֶאֱכָל־לֶחֶם וַיִּשְׂאוּ עֵינֵיהֶם וַיִּרְאוּ וְהִנֵּה
אֹרְחַת יִשְׁמְעֵאלִים בָּאָה מִגִּלְעָד וּגְמַלֵּיהֶם נֹשְׂאִים

Genesis 37
19–25

to kill him.   **19]** They said to one another, "Here comes that dreamer!   **20]** Come now, let us kill him and throw him into one of the pits; and we can say, 'A wild beast has devoured him.' We will see what comes of his dreams!"   **21]** But when Reuben heard it, he tried to save him from them. He said, "Let us not take his life."   **22]** And Reuben went on, "Shed no blood! Cast him into that pit out in the wilderness, but do not touch him yourselves"—intending to save him from them and restore him to his father.   **23]** When Joseph came up to his brothers, they stripped Joseph of his tunic, the ornamented tunic that he was wearing,   **24]** and took him and cast him into the pit. The pit was empty; there was no water in it.

25] Then they sat down to a meal. Looking up, they saw a caravan of Ishmaelites coming from Gilead, their camels bearing gum, balm, and ladanum to be taken to

25] *Ishmaelites.* Later the traders are called Midianites (Gen. 37:28, 36; see p. 367).

Ladanum. Or labdanum, a resinous juice used in the manufacture of perfume.

כו נְכֹאת וּצְרִי וָלֹט הוֹלְכִים לְהוֹרִיד מִצְרָיְמָה: וַיֹּאמֶר
יְהוּדָה אֶל־אֶחָיו מַה־בֶּצַע כִּי נַהֲרֹג אֶת־אָחִינוּ וְכִסִּינוּ
כז אֶת־דָּמוֹ: לְכוּ וְנִמְכְּרֶנּוּ לַיִּשְׁמְעֵאלִים וְיָדֵנוּ אַל־תְּהִי־
כח בוֹ כִּי־אָחִינוּ בְשָׂרֵנוּ הוּא וַיִּשְׁמְעוּ אֶחָיו: וַיַּעַבְרוּ
אֲנָשִׁים מִדְיָנִים סֹחֲרִים וַיִּמְשְׁכוּ וַיַּעֲלוּ אֶת־יוֹסֵף מִן
הַבּוֹר וַיִּמְכְּרוּ אֶת־יוֹסֵף לַיִּשְׁמְעֵאלִים בְּעֶשְׂרִים כָּסֶף
כט וַיָּבִיאוּ אֶת־יוֹסֵף מִצְרָיְמָה: וַיָּשָׁב רְאוּבֵן אֶל־הַבּוֹר
ל וְהִנֵּה אֵין־יוֹסֵף בַּבּוֹר וַיִּקְרַע אֶת־בְּגָדָיו: וַיָּשָׁב אֶל־
לא אֶחָיו וַיֹּאמַר הַיֶּלֶד אֵינֶנּוּ וַאֲנִי אָנָה אֲנִי־בָא: וַיִּקְחוּ
אֶת־כְּתֹנֶת יוֹסֵף וַיִּשְׁחֲטוּ שְׂעִיר עִזִּים וַיִּטְבְּלוּ אֶת־
לב הַכֻּתֹּנֶת בַּדָּם: וַיְשַׁלְּחוּ אֶת־כְּתֹנֶת הַפַּסִּים וַיָּבִיאוּ
אֶל־אֲבִיהֶם וַיֹּאמְרוּ זֹאת מָצָאנוּ הַכֶּר־נָא הַכְּתֹנֶת

Genesis 37
26–32

Egypt. **26]** Then Judah said to his brothers, "What do we gain by killing our brother and covering up his blood? **27]** Come, let us sell him to the Ishmaelites, but let us not do away with him ourselves. After all, he is our brother, our own flesh." His brothers agreed. **28]** When Midianite traders passed by, they pulled Joseph up out of the pit. They sold Joseph for twenty pieces of silver to the Ishmaelites, who brought Joseph to Egypt.

29] When Reuben returned to the pit and saw that Joseph was not in the pit, he rent his clothes. **30]** Returning to his brothers, he said, "The boy is gone! Now, what am I to do?" **31]** Then they took Joseph's tunic, slaughtered a kid, and dipped the tunic in the blood. **32]** They had the ornamented tunic taken to their father, and they said, "We found this. Please examine it; is it your son's tunic

26] *Covering up his blood.* The traces of the crime (cf. Gen. 4:10).

28] *Twenty pieces of silver.* The redemption price for a five- to twenty-year-old male (Lev. 27:5).

30] *Now, what am I to do?* As the oldest, Reuben feels himself responsible to his father.

וַיַּכִּירָהּ וַיֹּאמֶר כְּתֹנֶת בְּנִי חַיָּה
רָעָה אֲכָלָתְהוּ טָרֹף טֹרַף יוֹסֵף: וַיִּקְרַע יַעֲקֹב
שִׂמְלֹתָיו וַיָּשֶׂם שַׂק בְּמָתְנָיו וַיִּתְאַבֵּל עַל־בְּנוֹ יָמִים
רַבִּים: וַיָּקֻמוּ כָל־בָּנָיו וְכָל־בְּנֹתָיו לְנַחֲמוֹ וַיְמָאֵן
לְהִתְנַחֵם וַיֹּאמֶר כִּי־אֵרֵד אֶל־בְּנִי אָבֵל שְׁאֹלָה וַיֵּבְךְּ
אֹתוֹ אָבִיו: וְהַמְּדָנִים מָכְרוּ אֹתוֹ אֶל־מִצְרָיִם לְפוֹטִיפַר
סְרִיס פַּרְעֹה שַׂר הַטַּבָּחִים: פ

or not?" **33]** He recognized it, and said, "My son's tunic! A wild beast devoured him! Joseph was torn by a beast!" **34]** Jacob rent his clothes, put sackcloth on his loins, and observed mourning for his son many days. **35]** All his sons and daughters sought to comfort him; but he refused to be comforted, saying, "No, I will go down mourning to my son in Sheol." Thus his father bewailed him.

36] The Midianites, meanwhile, sold him in Egypt to Potiphar, a courtier of Pharaoh and his chief steward.

35] *Sheol.* The place where dead spirits were believed to reside. It was not, like Hades, a frightening abode. The term Sheol occurs often in the Bible but is not further defined.

36] *Potiphar.* From the Egyptian *Pa-di-pa-re* (He whom Re [the sun god] has given) [3].
Pharaoh. Egyptian *per-aa* (great house).

Reuben and Judah

The charm and suspense of the Joseph story are appealing in any language and to any age. In the Hebrew, however, there are touches of literary artistry that escape the powers of the translator.

It is clear that originally two traditions existed: In one, Reuben is the protector and Joseph is sold to the Midianites (Gen. 37:18–24, 29–36); in the other, Judah protects his brother from being killed but also suggests his sale and Joseph is surrendered to the Ishmaelites (Gen. 37:25–27). In verse 28 the traditions are joined. This fusion is facilitated by the fact that by the time the text assumed its present form the terms "Ishmaelites" and "Midianites" were used as synonyms (cf. Judg. 8:24, 26). The term "Medanites" (as it occurs in the Hebrew of Gen. 37:36) was a third synonym that had the additional connotation of "quarrelsome people." All three expressions also signified "traders"—so that to the Hebrew ear the text was further filled with literary nuances [4].

We must also remember that the Reuben and Judah versions of the story had a strong political flavor in their day. Like the Tamar episode, which follows (Gen. 38), they cast a special light both on the tribal fathers and on the tribes themselves. Listeners of ancient days most likely compared the merits of the biblical Reuben and Judah with the latter day fates and fortunes of the Reuben and Judah tribes. Thus, these patriarchal stories spoke to them with special contemporary overtones not easily heard by later generations.

GLEANINGS

Nemesis

The beginning of the story of Joseph still stands under the shadow of Jacob–Israel's guilt, which had clung to the old man since his youth. Just as he had once deceived his father and robbed the brother whom his father had preferred, so Jacob is now in turn deceived by his sons who have sidetracked his favorite son.　　OTTO PROCKSCH

The Story in Moslem Tradition

In revealing to thee this Koran, one of the most beautiful of narratives will we narrate to thee, of which thou hast hitherto been regardless.

When Joseph said to his father, "O my father! verily I beheld eleven stars and the sun and the moon—beheld them make obeisance to me!"

He said, "O my son! tell not thy vision to thy brethren, lest they plot a plot against thee: for Satan is the manifest foe of man.

"It is thus that thy Lord shall choose thee and will teach thee the interpretation of dark sayings and will perfect His favours on thee and on the family of Jacob, as of old He perfected it on thy fathers Abraham and Isaac; verily thy Lord is Knowing, Wise!"

Now in Joseph and his brethren are signs for the enquirers;

When they said, "Surely better loved by our father than we, who are more in number, is Joseph and his brother; verily, our father hath clearly erred.

"Slay ye Joseph! or drive him to some other land, and on you alone shall your father's face be set! and after this, ye shall live as upright persons."

One of them said, "Slay not Joseph, but cast him down to the bottom of the well: if ye do so, some wayfarers will take him up."

They said, "O our father! why dost thou not entrust us with Joseph? indeed we mean him well.

"Send him with us to-morrow that he may enjoy himself and sport: we will surely keep him safely."

He said, "Verily, your taking him away will grieve me; and I fear lest while ye are heedless of him the wolf devour him."

They said, "Surely if the wolf devour him, and we so many, we must in that case be weak indeed."

And when they went away with him they agreed to place him at the bottom of the well. And we revealed to him, "Thou wilt yet tell them of this their deed, when they shall not know thee."

And they came at nightfall to their father weeping.

They said, "O our father! of a truth, we went to run races, and we left Joseph with our clothes, and the wolf devoured him: but thou wilt not believe us even though we speak the truth."

And they brought his shirt with false blood upon it. He said, "Nay, but yourselves have managed this affair. But patience is seemly: and the help of God is to be implored that I may bear what you tell me."

And wayfarers came and sent their drawer of water, and he let down his bucket. "Good news!" said he. "This is a youth!" And they kept his case secret, to make merchandise of him. But God knew what they did.　　KORAN [5]

Tamar

The story of Tamar is a complete unit that tells of various old traditions in meticulous detail. It is likely that we have here not only a personal vignette but also a tale of wider implications—Judah is represented as an individual, but he is also the ancestor of the Davidic line.[1]

This interlude interrupts the story of Joseph at a point of rising suspense. It covers many years and thus allows the Bible to take up the tale of Joseph again after the boy has grown into manhood.[2]

---

[1] Through his son Perez (Gen. 46:12; Ruth 4:18) [1]. Possibly the account of the rape of Tamar, David's daughter (II Sam. 13), is also to be read in the light of the Genesis story. [2] It is not possible, however, to integrate the names and figures in this chapter with the Jacob-Joseph story. There, the grandsons of Tamar and Judah migrate to Egypt (Gen. 46:12), yet only twenty-two years have elapsed from the time of Joseph's sale to the time of the migration. Hence these traditions were originally independent of the Tamar tradition.

א וַיְהִי בָּעֵת הַהִוא וַיֵּרֶד יְהוּדָה מֵאֵת אֶחָיו וַיֵּט עַד־אִישׁ

ב עֲדֻלָּמִי וּשְׁמוֹ חִירָה: וַיַּרְא־שָׁם יְהוּדָה בַּת־אִישׁ כְּנַעֲנִי

ג וּשְׁמוֹ שׁוּעַ וַיִּקָּחֶהָ וַיָּבֹא אֵלֶיהָ: וַתַּהַר וַתֵּלֶד בֵּן

ד וַיִּקְרָא אֶת־שְׁמוֹ עֵר: וַתַּהַר עוֹד וַתֵּלֶד בֵּן וַתִּקְרָא

ה אֶת־שְׁמוֹ אוֹנָן: וַתֹּסֶף עוֹד וַתֵּלֶד בֵּן וַתִּקְרָא אֶת־שְׁמוֹ

ו שֵׁלָה וְהָיָה בִכְזִיב בְּלִדְתָּהּ אֹתוֹ: וַיִּקַּח יְהוּדָה אִשָּׁה

ז לְעֵר בְּכוֹרוֹ וּשְׁמָהּ תָּמָר: וַיְהִי עֵר בְּכוֹר יְהוּדָה רַע

ח בְּעֵינֵי יְהוָה וַיְמִתֵהוּ יְהוָה: וַיֹּאמֶר יְהוּדָה לְאוֹנָן בֹּא

ט אֶל־אֵשֶׁת אָחִיךָ וְיַבֵּם אֹתָהּ וְהָקֵם זֶרַע לְאָחִיךָ: וַיֵּדַע

אוֹנָן כִּי לֹּא לוֹ יִהְיֶה הַזָּרַע וְהָיָה אִם־בָּא אֶל־אֵשֶׁת

Genesis 38
1–9

1] About that time Judah left his brothers and camped near a certain Adullamite whose name was Hirah.   2] There Judah saw the daughter of a certain Canaanite whose name was Shua, and he married her and cohabited with her.   3] She conceived and bore a son, and he named him Er.   4] She conceived again and bore a son, and named him Onan.   5] Once again she bore a son, and named him Shelah; he was at Chezib when she bore him.

6] Judah got a wife for Er his first-born; her name was Tamar.   7] But Er, Judah's first-born, was displeasing to the LORD, and the LORD took his life.   8] Then Judah said to Onan, "Join with your brother's wife and do your duty by her as a brother-in-law, and provide offspring for your brother."   9] But Onan, knowing that the seed would not count as his, let it go to waste whenever he joined with his

---

38:2] *Canaanite.* Some translate this as "trafficker" (as in Zech. 14:21) or "merchant" and thereby deny that intermarriage was involved [2].

5] *Chezib.* Possibly the same as Achzib (Josh. 15:44), a city southwest of Jerusalem.

6] *Tamar.* Palm tree.

8] *Do your duty.* A reference to levirate marriage (from the Latin *levir* [brother-in-law]). When a man died without male offspring his brother was obliged to marry the widow, and a son born of this union was considered the son of the dead man (see Deut. 25:5; Ruth, chapters 3 and 4; and p. 377).

9] *Go to waste.* Literally, "spoil on the ground."

אָחִיו וְשִׁחֵת אַרְצָה לְבִלְתִּי נְתָן־זֶרַע לְאָחִיו: וַיֵּרַע
בְּעֵינֵי יְהֹוָה אֲשֶׁר עָשָׂה וַיָּמֶת גַּם־אֹתוֹ: וַיֹּאמֶר יְהוּדָה
לְתָמָר כַּלָּתוֹ שְׁבִי אַלְמָנָה בֵית־אָבִיךְ עַד־יִגְדַּל שֵׁלָה
בְנִי כִּי אָמַר פֶּן־יָמוּת גַּם־הוּא כְּאֶחָיו וַתֵּלֶךְ תָּמָר
וַתֵּשֶׁב בֵּית אָבִיהָ: וַיִּרְבּוּ הַיָּמִים וַתָּמָת בַּת־שׁוּעַ
אֵשֶׁת־יְהוּדָה וַיִּנָּחֶם יְהוּדָה וַיַּעַל עַל־גֹּזְזֵי צֹאנוֹ הוּא
וְחִירָה רֵעֵהוּ הָעֲדֻלָּמִי תִּמְנָתָה: וַיֻּגַּד לְתָמָר לֵאמֹר
הִנֵּה חָמִיךְ עֹלֶה תִמְנָתָה לָגֹז צֹאנוֹ: וַתָּסַר בִּגְדֵי
אַלְמְנוּתָהּ מֵעָלֶיהָ וַתְּכַס בַּצָּעִיף וַתִּתְעַלָּף וַתֵּשֶׁב

brother's wife, so as not to provide offspring for his brother.   10] What he did was displeasing to the LORD, and He took his life also.   11] Then Judah said to his daughter-in-law Tamar, "Stay as a widow in your father's house until my son Shelah grows up"—for he thought, "He too might die like his brothers." So Tamar went to live in her father's house.

12] A long time afterward, Shua's daughter, the wife of Judah, died. When his period of sorrow was over, Judah went up to Timnah to his sheepshearers, together with his friend Hirah the Adullamite.   13] And Tamar was told, "Your father-in-law is coming up to Timnah for the sheepshearing."   14] So she took off her widow's garb, covered her face with a veil and, wrapping herself up, sat down at

10] *What he did.* Namely, to have evaded his levirate duty. Later, all spilling of seed (called onanism), especially masturbation, was considered "displeasing to the Lord."

11] *For he thought.* Judah thought that if Tamar were removed from the house Shelah's duty to marry her might become less pressing as time passed. Judah may also have been influenced by the belief that one should not tempt fate three times.

/ In Jewish legal tradition, a woman whose first two husbands died was considered a poor candidate for a third marriage and should not be wedded again [3]./

12] *When his period of mourning was over.* Literally, "when he was comforted."

13] *To Timnah for the sheepshearing.* And the festivities that were held on such occasions. The Timnah here referred to was located in the hill country south of Jerusalem (cf. Josh. 15:10). It was not the Timnah near the seacoast mentioned in the Samson story (Judg. 14:1).

14] *Enaim.* Probably the Enam of Josh. 15:34 [4].

בְּפֶתַח עֵינַיִם אֲשֶׁר עַל־דֶּרֶךְ תִּמְנָתָה כִּי רָאֲתָה כִּי־

טו גָדַל שֵׁלָה וְהִוא לֹא־נִתְּנָה לוֹ לְאִשָּׁה: וַיִּרְאֶהָ יְהוּדָה

טז וַיַּחְשְׁבֶהָ לְזוֹנָה כִּי כִסְּתָה פָּנֶיהָ: וַיֵּט אֵלֶיהָ אֶל־

הַדֶּרֶךְ וַיֹּאמֶר הָבָה־נָּא אָבוֹא אֵלַיִךְ כִּי לֹא יָדַע כִּי

כַלָּתוֹ הִוא וַתֹּאמֶר מַה־תִּתֶּן־לִי כִּי תָבוֹא אֵלָי: וַיֹּאמֶר

יז אָנֹכִי אֲשַׁלַּח גְּדִי־עִזִּים מִן־הַצֹּאן וַתֹּאמֶר אִם־תִּתֵּן

יח עֵרָבוֹן עַד שָׁלְחֶךָ: וַיֹּאמֶר מָה הָעֵרָבוֹן אֲשֶׁר אֶתֶּן־

לָךְ וַתֹּאמֶר חֹתָמְךָ וּפְתִילֶךָ וּמַטְּךָ אֲשֶׁר בְּיָדֶךָ וַיִּתֶּן־

יט לָהּ וַיָּבֹא אֵלֶיהָ וַתַּהַר לוֹ: וַתָּקָם וַתֵּלֶךְ וַתָּסַר צְעִיפָהּ

מֵעָלֶיהָ וַתִּלְבַּשׁ בִּגְדֵי אַלְמְנוּתָהּ:

Genesis 38
15–19

the entrance to Enaim, which is on the road to Timnah; for she saw that Shelah was grown up, yet she had not been given to him as wife. **15]** When Judah saw her, he took her for a harlot; she had covered her face. **16]** So he turned aside to her by the road and said, "Here, let me sleep with you"—for he did not know that she was his daughter-in-law. And she said, "What will you pay for sleeping with me?" **17]** He said, "I will send a kid from my flock." She replied, "But you must leave a pledge until you have sent it." **18]** And he said, "What pledge shall I give you?" She replied, "Your seal and cord, and the staff which you carry." So he gave them to her and joined with her, and she conceived by him. **19]** Then she went on her way. She took off her veil and again put on her widow's garb.

Others suggest it means "open place" or "at the crossroad." There is a word play here: Tamar covers her face (her eyes, Hebrew *enaim*) while sitting at Enaim.

18] *Seal.* It was usually of cylindrical shape, mounted on a pin, suspended by a cord, and worn by the owner as part of his public attire. Imprints of the seal were used as signatures, to represent the owner.

The staff. Often it was personalized and served as a symbol of transmission in sales proceedings.

כ וַיִּשְׁלַח יְהוּדָה אֶת־גְּדִי הָעִזִּים בְּיַד רֵעֵהוּ הָעֲדֻלָּמִי

כא לָקַחַת הָעֵרָבוֹן מִיַּד הָאִשָּׁה וְלֹא מְצָאָהּ: וַיִּשְׁאַל אֶת־

אַנְשֵׁי מְקֹמָהּ לֵאמֹר אַיֵּה הַקְּדֵשָׁה הִוא בָעֵינַיִם עַל־

כב הַדָּרֶךְ וַיֹּאמְרוּ לֹא־הָיְתָה בָזֶה קְדֵשָׁה: וַיָּשָׁב אֶל־יְהוּדָה

וַיֹּאמֶר לֹא מְצָאתִיהָ וְגַם אַנְשֵׁי הַמָּקוֹם אָמְרוּ לֹא־הָיְתָה

כג בָזֶה קְדֵשָׁה: וַיֹּאמֶר יְהוּדָה תִּקַּח־לָהּ פֶּן נִהְיֶה לָבוּז הִנֵּה

כד שָׁלַחְתִּי הַגְּדִי הַזֶּה וְאַתָּה לֹא מְצָאתָהּ: וַיְהִי כְּמִשְׁלֹשׁ

חֳדָשִׁים וַיֻּגַּד לִיהוּדָה לֵאמֹר זָנְתָה תָּמָר כַּלָּתֶךָ וְגַם

הִנֵּה הָרָה לִזְנוּנִים וַיֹּאמֶר יְהוּדָה הוֹצִיאוּהָ וְתִשָּׂרֵף:

כה הִוא מוּצֵאת וְהִיא שָׁלְחָה אֶל־חָמִיהָ לֵאמֹר לְאִישׁ

20] Judah sent the kid by his friend the Adullamite, to redeem the pledge from the woman; but he could not find her.   21] He inquired of the people of that town, "Where is the cult prostitute, the one at Enaim, by the road?" But they said, "There has been no prostitute here."   22] So he returned to Judah and said, "I could not find her; moreover, the townspeople said: There has been no prostitute here."   23] Judah said, "Let her keep them, lest we become a laughingstock. I did send her this kid, but you did not find her."

24] About three months later, Judah was told, "Your daughter-in-law Tamar has played the harlot; what is more, she is with child by harlotry." "Bring her out," said Judah, "and let her be burned."   25] As she was being brought out, she sent this message to her father-in-law, "I am with child by the man to whom these

21] *Cult prostitute.* Judah uses this term, rather than "harlot" (as in Gen. 38:15), to give the relationship a somewhat more acceptable status. Ritual prostitutes participated in fertility cults in many ancient countries [5].

23] *A laughingstock.* His relationship with a prosti-

tute would become a matter for public discussion and mocking comment.

24] *Let her be burned.* The laws of adultery included engaged people, and Tamar was considered engaged to Shelah. Judah, as head of the family, had judicial powers.

אֲשֶׁר־אֵלֶּה לּוֹ אָנֹכִי הָרָה וַתֹּאמֶר הַכֶּר־נָא לְמִי
כו הַחֹתֶמֶת וְהַפְּתִילִים וְהַמַּטֶּה הָאֵלֶּה: וַיַּכֵּר יְהוּדָה
וַיֹּאמֶר צָדְקָה מִמֶּנִּי כִּי־עַל־כֵּן לֹא־נְתַתִּיהָ לְשֵׁלָה בְנִי
כז וְלֹא־יָסַף עוֹד לְדַעְתָּהּ: וַיְהִי בְּעֵת לִדְתָּהּ וְהִנֵּה
כח תְאוֹמִים בְּבִטְנָהּ: וַיְהִי בְלִדְתָּהּ וַיִּתֶּן־יָד וַתִּקַּח
הַמְיַלֶּדֶת וַתִּקְשֹׁר עַל־יָדוֹ שָׁנִי לֵאמֹר זֶה יָצָא רִאשֹׁנָה:
כט וַיְהִי כְּמֵשִׁיב יָדוֹ וְהִנֵּה יָצָא אָחִיו וַתֹּאמֶר מַה־פָּרַצְתָּ
ל עָלֶיךָ פָּרֶץ וַיִּקְרָא שְׁמוֹ פָּרֶץ: וְאַחַר יָצָא אָחִיו
אֲשֶׁר עַל־יָדוֹ הַשָּׁנִי וַיִּקְרָא שְׁמוֹ זָרַח: ס

Genesis 38

26–30

belong." And she added, "Examine these: whose seal and cord and staff are these?"
26] Judah recognized them, and said, "She is more in the right than I, inasmuch as I did not give her to my son Shelah." And he was not intimate with her again.

27] When the time came for her to give birth, there were twins in her womb! **28]** While she was in labor, one of them put out his hand, and the midwife tied a crimson thread on that hand, to signify: This one came out first. **29]** But just then he drew back his hand, and out came his brother; and she said, "What a breach you have made for yourself!" So he was named Perez. **30]** Afterwards his brother came out, on whose hand was the crimson thread; he was named Zerah.

/ The Torah law in this case (Deut. 22:23–24) provides for stoning, not burning. Even as a ritual prostitute she was subject to punishment, for such a woman was not supposed to have children of her own [6]./

26] *Not intimate . . . again.* Although Tamar was now considered Judah's wife, her previous relation to his sons made further intimacy undesirable.

28] *Crimson thread.* To make sure which was the first-born. The color was an allusion to harlotry: Red bands, like red lights in modern times, were the mark of prostitution (cf. Josh. 2:18) [7].

29] *Perez.* Breach.

30] *Zerah.* Brightness, perhaps alluding to the crimson thread [8].

Destiny

Why was the Tamar story included in the Jacob–Joseph cycle and why was it preserved with such careful attention to detail?

Perhaps the intriguing nature of the incident played a role, but the major reason does not lie in historical, literary, or dramatic factors. The chief figures are Tamar and Judah, and Judah is the ultimate preserver of the house of Israel. From the union of the tribal progenitor and his daughter-in-law, Perez is born, and from him will descend the person and the house of David. The Tamar tale thus became an important part of the David saga, just as the Book of Ruth did in later days. We are told that Ruth and Boaz would be forebears of the king and that Boaz traced his line to Perez, son of Tamar and Judah (Ruth 4:12–22).

Both accounts together emphasize that King David stemmed from a strange and non-indigenous line: Tamar and Ruth were not Israelites, both were widows, and both claimed a son by dint of the levirate tradition. David thus arises out of the most unlikely configurations. After tragedy had marred their lives, it appeared that Tamar and Ruth would remain childless, but God in His wisdom turned fate to His own design. The Judah–Tamar interlude is, therefore, not merely an old tribal tale but an important link in the main theme: to show the steady, though not always readily visible, guiding hand of God who never forgets His people and their destiny [9].

In this story, Tamar is His unlikely tool. She is a Canaanite, a daughter of the very people against whom Abraham had warned and whom the children of Israel would later displace. Tamar is treated with respect; her desperate deed draws no condemnation from the Torah. What she did fulfilled the requirements of Hebrew law and, in addition, appeared to serve the higher purposes of God.

GLEANINGS

The Burden of Leadership

It says that "about that time Judah left his brothers" [Gen. 38:1]. Why? It was in consequence of the sale of Joseph. The brothers suddenly appreciated the depth of their father's grief. Then they blamed Judah and said: "You suggested that we sell Joseph and we followed you. Had you suggested to set Joseph free we would have followed you also." That is when "Judah left his brothers." MIDRASH [10]

The Levirate

In earlier ages, the duty of a man to marry the widow of his brother could probably not be evaded; such an obligatory union was called *yibum* in Jewish legal tradition. In later times, the brother could refuse *yibum* by making a public declaration to this effect through the ceremony of *chalitzah* (Deut. 25:5–10). Still later, *chalitzah* became mandatory and *yibum* was frowned upon, which is essentially the position of Jewish law today. In fact, the chief rabbinate of the State of Israel issued a decree (*takanah*) in 1950 prohibiting *yibum* and making *chalitzah* obligatory. The court may under certain circumstances compel the *levir* to grant *chalitzah*. [11]

Human Sin and Divine Guidance

The beginnings of the tribe of Judah were shaped by the remarkable interaction of human sin and divine guidance. How simple are the images of Israel's ancestors! They have almost more shadow than light. National ambition did not add to them or change them. No trace of an idealizing myth is noticeable. The nobleness of these figures consists in the fact that they conquer in the strength of the grace granted to them and, when defeated, they arise again and again. Their mistakes are the foils of their greatness for sacred history. By the yardstick of the Old Testament even Tamar, with all her going astray, is a saint because of her wisdom, her tenderness, her nobility. FRANZ DELITZSCH [12]

Judah's Confession

Tamar threw the pledges before the feet of the judges, with the words: "By the man whose these are am I with child but, though I perish in the flames, I will not betray him. I hope in the Lord of the world that He will turn the heart of the man, so that he will make confession thereof." Then Judah rose up, and said: "With your permission, my brethren, and ye men of my father's house, I make it known that with what measure a man metes it shall be measured unto him, be it for good or for evil, but happy the man that acknowledgeth his sins. Because I took the coat of Joseph, and colored it with the blood of a kid, and then laid it at the feet of my father, saying, Know now whether it be thy son's coat or not, therefore must I now confess, before the court, unto whom belongeth this signet, this mantle, and this staff." MIDRASH [13]

As for the insertion of 38 at exactly this point in the story (and not between 39 and 40, or 40 and 41), one can only protest (a) between chapters 37 and 39 there is a natural pause in the action and (b) certain coincidental features of chapter 38 bind it to chapters 37 and 39. Among the latter one may note the similarity between Judah in 38 and Jacob in 37: both are patriarchs, both are deceived, both are obliged to give legal recognition to a piece of evidence. Between Tamar and Potiphar's wife on the other hand there is a marked contrast; the former is an honorable woman faithful to the interests of her husband, while the latter is adulterous, malevolent, and contemptuous of her husband. DONALD B. REDFORD [14]

Joseph in Egypt

"The Lord was with Joseph" (Gen. 39:2)—this is the key to the developing drama that now takes up the thread temporarily dropped because of the Tamar interlude. God's presence is constantly visible in the background, both when Joseph is tempted or in trouble and when he is successful: "Upon the Lord's word was he tried, until His word was fulfilled" (Ps. 105:19). God guides Joseph in his relationships and gives him the wisdom to interpret dreams. The divine power reaches to the men and the fate of Egypt, a theme that returns time and again in prophetic literature.

The traditions reflected in these chapters have an authentic ring. The descriptions are realistic, and the text contains numerous Egyptian loan words [1]. Still, all attempts to assign a precise historical setting to the Joseph cycle have failed. Neither the name of the Pharaoh whom Joseph served nor that of a Pharaoh in Exodus is given (Pharaoh is a title, not a name). Egyptian records show high officials with Semitic names such as Ben-Horen and Ben-Anath, but none with a name that would fit Joseph. The word יְאֹר (*ye-or*, river), which occurs in the Joseph tale to describe the Nile, appears in Egyptian use after the sixteenth century B.C.E., and cyclical seven-year famines are also mentioned—but without precise dating.

Some scholars believe that Jacob's migration to Egypt took place during the period of Hyksos rule, i.e., before the middle of the second millennium B.C.E.[1] The Hyksos were probably an ethnically composite group who invaded Canaan and then Egypt,[2] where they succeeded in establishing themselves [3]. However, the data at our disposal are not sufficient to link them securely to the Jacob–Joseph stories or to suppose, as has been suggested, that Jacob's sons—described throughout as עִבְרִים (*ivrim*)[3]— were invited to settle in Egypt because their talents and experiences, already amply demonstrated by Joseph, would prove useful to the Hyksos [4].

[1] A more definite time assignment should be related to one's opinion about the date of the Abraham saga (see p. 111).

[2] The capital was Avaris (or Tanis, the Hebrew Zoan). The Hyksos apparently spoke a Semitic tongue, possibly with Hurrian and Indo-European admixtures. One theory identifies the Hyksos as Amorites [2].

[3] On the term and its meaning as a group characteristic, see p. 140.

א וְיוֹסֵף הוּרַד מִצְרָיְמָה וַיִּקְנֵהוּ פּוֹטִיפַר סְרִיס פַּרְעֹה
שַׂר הַטַּבָּחִים אִישׁ מִצְרִי מִיַּד הַיִּשְׁמְעֵאלִים אֲשֶׁר
ב הוֹרִדֻהוּ שָׁמָּה: וַיְהִי יְהוָה אֶת־יוֹסֵף וַיְהִי אִישׁ מַצְלִיחַ
ג וַיְהִי בְּבֵית אֲדֹנָיו הַמִּצְרִי: וַיַּרְא אֲדֹנָיו כִּי יְהוָה אִתּוֹ
ד וְכֹל אֲשֶׁר־הוּא עֹשֶׂה יְהוָה מַצְלִיחַ בְּיָדוֹ: וַיִּמְצָא
יוֹסֵף חֵן בְּעֵינָיו וַיְשָׁרֶת אֹתוֹ וַיַּפְקִדֵהוּ עַל־בֵּיתוֹ
ה וְכָל־יֶשׁ־לוֹ נָתַן בְּיָדוֹ: וַיְהִי מֵאָז הִפְקִיד אֹתוֹ בְּבֵיתוֹ
וְעַל כָּל־אֲשֶׁר יֶשׁ־לוֹ וַיְבָרֶךְ יְהוָה אֶת־בֵּית הַמִּצְרִי
בִּגְלַל יוֹסֵף וַיְהִי בִּרְכַּת יְהוָה בְּכָל־אֲשֶׁר יֶשׁ־לוֹ
ו בַּבַּיִת וּבַשָּׂדֶה: וַיַּעֲזֹב כָּל־אֲשֶׁר־לוֹ בְּיַד יוֹסֵף וְלֹא־
יָדַע אִתּוֹ מְאוּמָה כִּי אִם־הַלֶּחֶם אֲשֶׁר־הוּא אוֹכֵל

Genesis 39
1–6

1] When Joseph was taken down to Egypt, a certain Egyptian, Potiphar, a courtier of Pharaoh and his chief steward, bought him from the Ishmaelites who had brought him there.   2] The Lord was with Joseph, and he was a successful man. He remained in the house of his Egyptian master;   3] and when his master saw that the Lord was with him and that the Lord lent success to everything he undertook,   4] he took a liking to Joseph. He made him his personal attendant and put him in charge of his household, placing in his hands all that he owned.   5] And from the time that the Egyptian put him in charge of his household and of all that he owned, the Lord blessed his house for Joseph's sake, so that the blessing of the Lord was upon everything that he owned, in the house and outside.   6] He left all that he had in Joseph's hands and, with him there, he paid attention to

39:1] *Egyptian.* Also mentioned in verses 2 and 5. This triple emphasis suggests that Potiphar's background deserved special mention, possibly because an Egyptian civil servant among the ruling Hyksos was an oddity worth noting.

6] *Attention to nothing save the food.* As a Hebrew, Joseph could have nothing to do with food because of the dietary taboos observed by Egyptians (see Gen. 43:32 and comment there) [5].

ז וַיְהִי יוֹסֵף יְפֵה־תֹאַר וִיפֵה מַרְאֶה: וַיְהִי אַחַר הַדְּבָרִים
הָאֵלֶּה וַתִּשָּׂא אֵשֶׁת־אֲדֹנָיו אֶת־עֵינֶיהָ אֶל־יוֹסֵף וַתֹּאמֶר

ח שִׁכְבָה עִמִּי: וַיְמָאֵן וַיֹּאמֶר אֶל־אֵשֶׁת אֲדֹנָיו הֵן אֲדֹנִי
לֹא־יָדַע אִתִּי מַה־בַּבָּיִת וְכֹל אֲשֶׁר־יֶשׁ־לוֹ נָתַן בְּיָדִי:

ט אֵינֶנּוּ גָדוֹל בַּבַּיִת הַזֶּה מִמֶּנִּי וְלֹא־חָשַׂךְ מִמֶּנִּי מְאוּמָה
כִּי אִם־אוֹתָךְ בַּאֲשֶׁר אַתְּ־אִשְׁתּוֹ וְאֵיךְ אֶעֱשֶׂה הָרָעָה

י הַגְּדֹלָה הַזֹּאת וְחָטָאתִי לֵאלֹהִים: וַיְהִי כְּדַבְּרָהּ אֶל־
יוֹסֵף יוֹם יוֹם וְלֹא־שָׁמַע אֵלֶיהָ לִשְׁכַּב אֶצְלָהּ לִהְיוֹת

יא עִמָּהּ: וַיְהִי כְּהַיּוֹם הַזֶּה וַיָּבֹא הַבַּיְתָה לַעֲשׂוֹת מְלַאכְתּוֹ

יב וְאֵין אִישׁ מֵאַנְשֵׁי הַבַּיִת שָׁם בַּבָּיִת: וַתִּתְפְּשֵׂהוּ בְּבִגְדוֹ
לֵאמֹר שִׁכְבָה עִמִּי וַיַּעֲזֹב בִּגְדוֹ בְּיָדָהּ וַיָּנָס וַיֵּצֵא

Genesis 39

7–12

nothing save the food that he ate. Now Joseph was well built and hand-some.

7] After a time, his master's wife cast her eyes upon Joseph and said, "Lie with me." **8]** But he refused. He said to his master's wife, "Look, with me here, my master gives no thought to anything in this house, and all that he owns he has placed in my hands. **9]** He wields no more authority in this house than I, and he has withheld nothing from me except yourself, since you are his wife. How then could I do this most wicked thing, and sin before God?" **10]** And much as she coaxed Joseph day after day, he did not yield to her request to lie beside her, to be with her.

11] One such day, he came into the house to do his work. None of the household being there inside, **12]** she caught hold of him by his coat and said, "Lie with me!"

7] *His master's wife.* Her name is not stated. Later tradition called her Zuleika [6]. The old Egyptian "Tale of Two Brothers" is based on the same plot of attempted seduction and subsequent false accusation; thereafter, however, the two stories diverge completely (see p. 349).

יג הַחוּצָה: וַיְהִי כִּרְאוֹתָהּ כִּי־עָזַב בִּגְדוֹ בְּיָדָהּ וַיָּנָס

יד הַחוּצָה: וַתִּקְרָא לְאַנְשֵׁי בֵיתָהּ וַתֹּאמֶר לָהֶם לֵאמֹר

רְאוּ הֵבִיא לָנוּ אִישׁ עִבְרִי לְצַחֶק בָּנוּ בָּא אֵלַי

טו לִשְׁכַּב עִמִּי וָאֶקְרָא בְּקוֹל גָּדוֹל: וַיְהִי כְשָׁמְעוֹ כִּי־

הֲרִימֹתִי קוֹלִי וָאֶקְרָא וַיַּעֲזֹב בִּגְדוֹ אֶצְלִי וַיָּנָס וַיֵּצֵא

טז הַחוּצָה: וַתַּנַּח בִּגְדוֹ אֶצְלָהּ עַד־בּוֹא אֲדֹנָיו אֶל־בֵּיתוֹ:

יז וַתְּדַבֵּר אֵלָיו כַּדְּבָרִים הָאֵלֶּה לֵאמֹר בָּא אֵלַי

יח הָעֶבֶד הָעִבְרִי אֲשֶׁר־הֵבֵאתָ לָּנוּ לְצַחֶק בִּי: וַיְהִי

כַּהֲרִימִי קוֹלִי וָאֶקְרָא וַיַּעֲזֹב בִּגְדוֹ אֶצְלִי וַיָּנָס הַחוּצָה:

יט וַיְהִי כִשְׁמֹעַ אֲדֹנָיו אֶת־דִּבְרֵי אִשְׁתּוֹ אֲשֶׁר דִּבְּרָה

אֵלָיו לֵאמֹר כַּדְּבָרִים הָאֵלֶּה עָשָׂה לִי עַבְדֶּךָ וַיִּחַר

כ אַפּוֹ: וַיִּקַּח אֲדֹנֵי יוֹסֵף אֹתוֹ וַיִּתְּנֵהוּ אֶל־בֵּית הַסֹּהַר

Genesis 39

13–20

But he left his coat in her hand and got away and fled outside.   13] When she saw that he had left his coat in her hand and had fled outside,   14] she called out to her servants and said to them, "Look, he had to bring us a Hebrew to dally with us! This one came to lie with me; but I screamed loud.   15] And when he heard me screaming at the top of my voice, he left his coat with me and got away and fled outside."   16] She kept his coat beside her, until his master came home.   17] Then she told him the same story, saying, "The Hebrew slave, whom you brought into our house, came to me to dally with me;   18] but when I screamed at the top of my voice, he left his coat with me and fled outside."

19] When his master heard the story that his wife told him, namely, "Thus and so your slave did to me," he was furious.   20] So Joseph's master had him put in

14] *To dally with us.* The Hebrew לְצַחֶק (letzachek) has the additional meaning of "to mock."

20] *Prison.* סֹהַר (sohar), which appears in the Bible only in Genesis, was probably a special place where important prisoners were confined. Joseph was put in prison rather than punished in the usual way, by death; perhaps Potiphar was aware of his

כא הַסֹּהַר: וַיְהִי יְהוָה אֶת־יוֹסֵף וַיֵּט אֵלָיו חָסֶד וַיִּתֵּן חִנּוֹ כא–כג; א–ג

כב בְּעֵינֵי שַׂר בֵּית־הַסֹּהַר: וַיִּתֵּן שַׂר בֵּית־הַסֹּהַר בְּיַד־יוֹסֵף אֵת כָּל־הָאֲסִירִם אֲשֶׁר בְּבֵית הַסֹּהַר וְאֵת כָּל־אֲשֶׁר

כג עֹשִׂים שָׁם הוּא הָיָה עֹשֶׂה: אֵין שַׂר בֵּית־הַסֹּהַר רֹאֶה אֶת־כָּל־מְאוּמָה בְּיָדוֹ בַּאֲשֶׁר יְהוָה אִתּוֹ וַאֲשֶׁר־הוּא עֹשֶׂה יְהוָה מַצְלִיחַ: פ

א וַיְהִי אַחַר הַדְּבָרִים הָאֵלֶּה חָטְאוּ מַשְׁקֵה מֶלֶךְ־

ב מִצְרַיִם וְהָאֹפֶה לַאֲדֹנֵיהֶם לְמֶלֶךְ מִצְרָיִם: וַיִּקְצֹף פַּרְעֹה עַל שְׁנֵי סָרִיסָיו עַל שַׂר הַמַּשְׁקִים וְעַל שַׂר

ג הָאוֹפִים: וַיִּתֵּן אֹתָם בְּמִשְׁמַר בֵּית שַׂר הַטַּבָּחִים אֶל־

Genesis 39; 40

21–23; 1–3

* כ אסירי קרי.

prison, where the king's prisoners were confined. But even while he was there in prison, **21]** the LORD was with Joseph: He extended kindness to him and disposed the chief jailer favorably toward him. **22]** The chief jailer put in Joseph's charge all the prisoners who were in that prison, and he was the one to carry out everything that was done there. **23]** The chief jailer did not supervise anything that was in Joseph's charge, because the LORD was with him, and whatever he did the LORD made successful.

1] Sometime later, the cupbearer and the baker of the king of Egypt gave offense to their lord the king of Egypt. **2]** Pharaoh was angry with his two officials, the chief cupbearer and the chief baker, **3]** and put them in custody, in the house of

wife's roving eyes and not at all sure of Joseph's guilt [7].

23] *In Joseph's charge.* Literally, "his charge."

40:2] *Cupbearer.* The royal taster, an important government official.

Chief baker. The Egyptians were renowned gourmets and knew fifty-seven varieties of bread and thirty-eight different kinds of cakes [8].

ד בֵּית הַסֹּהַר מְקוֹם אֲשֶׁר יוֹסֵף אָסוּר שָׁם: וַיִּפְקֹד שַׂר
הַטַּבָּחִים אֶת־יוֹסֵף אִתָּם וַיְשָׁרֶת אֹתָם וַיִּהְיוּ יָמִים
ה בְּמִשְׁמָר: וַיַּחַלְמוּ חֲלוֹם שְׁנֵיהֶם אִישׁ חֲלֹמוֹ בְּלַיְלָה
אֶחָד אִישׁ כְּפִתְרוֹן חֲלֹמוֹ הַמַּשְׁקֶה וְהָאֹפֶה אֲשֶׁר
ו לְמֶלֶךְ מִצְרַיִם אֲשֶׁר אֲסוּרִים בְּבֵית הַסֹּהַר: וַיָּבֹא
ז אֲלֵיהֶם יוֹסֵף בַּבֹּקֶר וַיַּרְא אֹתָם וְהִנָּם זֹעֲפִים: וַיִּשְׁאַל
אֶת־סְרִיסֵי פַרְעֹה אֲשֶׁר אִתּוֹ בְמִשְׁמַר בֵּית אֲדֹנָיו
ח לֵאמֹר מַדּוּעַ פְּנֵיכֶם רָעִים הַיּוֹם: וַיֹּאמְרוּ אֵלָיו
חֲלוֹם חָלַמְנוּ וּפֹתֵר אֵין אֹתוֹ וַיֹּאמֶר אֲלֵהֶם יוֹסֵף
ט הֲלוֹא לֵאלֹהִים פִּתְרֹנִים סַפְּרוּ־נָא לִי: וַיְסַפֵּר שַׂר־
הַמַּשְׁקִים אֶת־חֲלֹמוֹ לְיוֹסֵף וַיֹּאמֶר לוֹ בַּחֲלוֹמִי וְהִנֵּה־
י גֶּפֶן לְפָנָי: וּבַגֶּפֶן שְׁלֹשָׁה שָׂרִיגִם וְהִוא כְפֹרַחַת עָלְתָה

Genesis 40
4–10

the chief steward, in the same prison house where Joseph was confined.   4] The chief steward assigned Joseph to them, and he attended them.

When they had been in custody for some time,   5] both of them—the cupbearer and the baker of the king of Egypt, who were confined in the prison—dreamed in the same night, each his own dream and each dream with its own meaning. 6] When Joseph came to them in the morning, he saw that they were distraught. 7] He asked Pharaoh's officials, who were with him in custody in his master's house, saying, "Why do you appear downcast today?"   8] And they said to him, "We had dreams, and there is no one to interpret them." So Joseph said to them, "Do not interpretations come from God? Tell me about it."

9] Then the chief cupbearer told his dream to Joseph. He said to him, "In my dream, there was a vine in front of me.   10] On the vine were three branches. It

4] *Chief steward.* Potiphar, who had charge of the prison.

נִצָּהּ הִבְשִׁילוּ אַשְׁכְּלֹתֶיהָ עֲנָבִים: וְכוֹס פַּרְעֹה בְּיָדִי

וָאֶקַּח אֶת־הָעֲנָבִים וָאֶשְׂחַט אֹתָם אֶל־כּוֹס פַּרְעֹה

יב וָאֶתֵּן אֶת־הַכּוֹס עַל־כַּף פַּרְעֹה: וַיֹּאמֶר לוֹ יוֹסֵף זֶה

יג פִּתְרֹנוֹ שְׁלֹשֶׁת הַשָּׂרִגִים שְׁלֹשֶׁת יָמִים הֵם: בְּעוֹד

שְׁלֹשֶׁת יָמִים יִשָּׂא פַרְעֹה אֶת־רֹאשֶׁךָ וַהֲשִׁיבְךָ עַל־

כַּנֶּךָ וְנָתַתָּ כוֹס־פַּרְעֹה בְּיָדוֹ כַּמִּשְׁפָּט הָרִאשׁוֹן אֲשֶׁר

יד הָיִיתָ מַשְׁקֵהוּ: כִּי אִם־זְכַרְתַּנִי אִתְּךָ כַּאֲשֶׁר יִיטַב לָךְ

וְעָשִׂיתָ־נָּא עִמָּדִי חָסֶד וְהִזְכַּרְתַּנִי אֶל־פַּרְעֹה וְהוֹצֵאתַנִי

טו מִן־הַבַּיִת הַזֶּה: כִּי־גֻנֹּב גֻּנַּבְתִּי מֵאֶרֶץ הָעִבְרִים וְגַם־

טז פֹּה לֹא־עָשִׂיתִי מְאוּמָה כִּי־שָׂמוּ אֹתִי בַּבּוֹר: וַיַּרְא

שַׂר־הָאֹפִים כִּי טוֹב פָּתָר וַיֹּאמֶר אֶל־יוֹסֵף אַף־אֲנִי

Genesis 40
11–16

had barely budded, when out came its blossoms, and its clusters ripened into grapes.
11] Pharaoh's cup was in my hand, and I took the grapes, pressed them into Pharaoh's cup, and placed the cup in Pharaoh's hand." **12]** Joseph said to him, "This is its interpretation: The three branches are three days. **13]** In three days Pharaoh will pardon you and restore you to your post; you will place Pharaoh's cup in his hand, as was your custom formerly when you were his cupbearer. **14]** But think of me when all is well with you again, and do me the kindness of mentioning me to Pharaoh, so as to free me from this place. **15]** For in truth, I was kidnaped from the land of the Hebrews; nor have I done anything here that they should have put me in the dungeon."

16] When the chief baker saw how favorably he had interpreted, he said to

---

13] *Pardon you.* Literally, "lift up your head." A word play on יִשָּׂא. The same expression is used in verse 19 in a literal sense (to behead), and in verse 20 in a third sense (to single out).

16] *Open-work baskets.* Others translate as "baskets with white bread" or "white baskets." Meaning of Hebrew is uncertain.

יז בַּחֲלוֹמִי וְהִנֵּה שְׁלֹשָׁה סַלֵּי חֹרִי עַל־רֹאשִׁי: וּבַסַּל
הָעֶלְיוֹן מִכֹּל מַאֲכַל פַּרְעֹה מַעֲשֵׂה אֹפֶה וְהָעוֹף
יח אֹכֵל אֹתָם מִן־הַסַּל מֵעַל רֹאשִׁי: וַיַּעַן יוֹסֵף וַיֹּאמֶר
יט זֶה פִּתְרֹנוֹ שְׁלֹשֶׁת הַסַּלִּים שְׁלֹשֶׁת יָמִים הֵם: בְּעוֹד
שְׁלֹשֶׁת יָמִים יִשָּׂא פַרְעֹה אֶת־רֹאשְׁךָ מֵעָלֶיךָ וְתָלָה
כ אוֹתְךָ עַל־עֵץ וְאָכַל הָעוֹף אֶת־בְּשָׂרְךָ מֵעָלֶיךָ: וַיְהִי
בַּיּוֹם הַשְּׁלִישִׁי יוֹם הֻלֶּדֶת אֶת־פַּרְעֹה וַיַּעַשׂ מִשְׁתֶּה
לְכָל־עֲבָדָיו וַיִּשָּׂא אֶת־רֹאשׁ שַׂר הַמַּשְׁקִים וְאֶת־רֹאשׁ
כא שַׂר הָאֹפִים בְּתוֹךְ עֲבָדָיו: וַיָּשֶׁב אֶת־שַׂר הַמַּשְׁקִים
כב עַל־מַשְׁקֵהוּ וַיִּתֵּן הַכּוֹס עַל־כַּף פַּרְעֹה: וְאֵת שַׂר
כג הָאֹפִים תָּלָה כַּאֲשֶׁר פָּתַר לָהֶם יוֹסֵף: וְלֹא־זָכַר שַׂר־
הַמַּשְׁקִים אֶת־יוֹסֵף וַיִּשְׁכָּחֵהוּ:

Genesis 40
17–23

Haftarah Vayeshev, p. 558

Joseph, "In my dream, similarly, **there were three open-work** baskets on my head.
17] In the uppermost basket were all kinds of food for Pharaoh that a baker prepares; and the birds were eating it out of the basket above my head."   18] Joseph
answered, "This is its interpretation: The three baskets are three days.   19] In
three days Pharaoh will lift off your head and impale you upon a pole; and the
birds will pick off your flesh."

20] On the third day—his birthday—Pharaoh made a banquet for all his officials,
and he singled out his chief cupbearer and his chief baker from among his officials.
21] He restored the chief cupbearer to his cupbearing, and he placed the cup in
Pharaoh's hand;   22] but the chief baker he impaled—just as Joseph had interpreted to them.

23] Yet the chief cupbearer did not think of Joseph; he forgot him.

19] *Lift off*. Literal meaning; see verse 13.   20] *Singled out*. A word play; see verse 13.

The Temptation

In his response to Potiphar's wife Joseph says that yielding to her invitation to commit adultery would be a "sin before God" (Gen. 39:9). In many other cultures adultery was merely a proprietary misdemeanor; a wife was considered property, and injury to a man's possessions drew punishment thought adequate to the act (Deut. 22:29) [9]. Joseph speaks in true accents of the Bible, which regards marriage as more than a relationship of civil law. Marital trust has divine sanction and is so fundamental to human relationships that Jewish tradition considers the command against adultery as one of the Noahide laws that every man is bound to observe [10].

Dreams

From ancient times, dreams have tantalized men with their secrets. Today dreams are used to explore the inner chambers of the dreamer's mind. In antiquity, however, dreams were thought to be signs from divine powers exposing their intent. While occasionally dreams contained a direct divine message (as in Gen. 15:13 when God appeared to Abraham in a dream), they usually were considered coded visions [11] to which a key was needed.[1]

Professional dream interpreters who claimed to possess the proper keys were prominent in Mesopotamia and especially in Egypt. An Egyptian manual of dreams (ca. 1300 B.C.E.) contains over 200 interpretations.[2] The ancient Israelites no doubt shared many of the prevailing ideas about dreams and considered them a legitimate source of divine guidance.[3] On the whole, however, the Bible says remarkably little on the subject of dream interpretation. Only Joseph and Daniel engage in it, and both give the credit unreservedly to God (see Dan. 2).

To be sure, there is a similarity between the superstitions of a dream book, which provides mechanical rules for divining the future, and the belief that God's will needs the interpretations of a qualified and pious man. Joseph and Daniel used no book; they used their imaginations, and both merely exposed to the eye that which was already ordained. Of course, this kind of activity could encourage fatalism and weaken one of the basic assumptions of the Bible, namely, that man has a share in shaping his fate. We may understand, therefore, the reticence of the Bible to give added room to the "science of dreams." Only because Joseph and Daniel were in the service of pagan powers and acted within a foreign mental and religious framework were their dream interpretations recorded with approbation.[4]

---

[1] But note the saying: "Man sees in his dreams only the stirrings of his own heart."

[2] Example: Seeing a large cat meant a large harvest. Dreams figured prominently in "Gilgamesh." There was also an Assyrian dream book [12].

[3] As were Urim, I Sam. 28:6.

[4] Note that Joseph does not interpret his own dreams; he merely relates them to his family. In post-biblical Judaism, however, dream interpretation played a significant role [13].

GLEANINGS

God Was with Joseph

Human friends can always be found when a man is successful, but in time of trouble they tend to forsake him. Not so God: He was with Joseph when he was a slave, when he was in prison, and also when he was viceroy.   MIDRASH [14]

Bread and Wife

It says that Potiphar "paid attention to nothing save the food that he ate" [Gen. 39:6]. This is a hint at what is to follow; for לֶחֶם [food or bread] is here a synonym for "wife," as in: "Bread of falsehood is sweet to a man" [Prov. 20:17].
MIDRASH [15]

The Temptation

The musical note *shalshelet* over the word "he refused" was introduced in the text to indicate delay: The woman insisted again and again and Joseph refused again and again.   MIDRASH [16]

Joseph did consider yielding, but the image of his father appeared to him, that is to say, he thought, "What would my father say?"
MIDRASH [17]

His Master's Wife

Why does it say expressly that Joseph refused "his master's wife"? Because as a servant, Joseph was obligated to obey her; still he chose to obey God's law instead. In the conflict between human duty and conscience he chose the latter.
NACHMANIDES

An Egyptian Parallel

[The "Story of Two Brothers" features an aggressive woman who lusts after her husband's younger brother.]

Then she stood up and took hold of him and said to him: "Come, let's spend an hour sleeping together! This will do you good, because I shall make fine clothes for you!" Then the lad became like a leopard with great rage at the wicked suggestion which she had made to him, and she was very, very much frightened. Then he argued with her, saying: "See here—you are like a mother to me, and your husband is like a father to me! Because—being older than I—he was the one who brought me up. What is this great crime which you have said to me? Don't say it to me again!"

But the wife of his elder brother was afraid because of the suggestion which she had made. Then she took fat and grease, and she became like one who had been criminally beaten, wanting to tell her husband: "It was your younger brother who did the beating!" So her husband said to her: "Who has been talking with you?" Then she said to him: "Not one person has been talking with me except your younger brother. He said to me: 'Come, let's spend an hour sleeping together! Put on your curls!' So he spoke to me. But I wouldn't listen to him: 'Aren't I your mother?—for your elder brother is like a father to you!' So I spoke to him. But he was afraid, and he beat me, so as not to let me tell you."

Then his elder brother became like a leopard, and he made his lance sharp, and stood behind the door of his stable to kill his younger brother when he came back in the evening to put his cattle in the stable.   OLD EGYPTIAN FOLKTALE [18]

The Elevation of Joseph;
The Brothers' First Visit

The scene shifts to Pharaoh's court and to the dramatic elevation of the poor Hebrew boy to the vice-regal office of Egypt. As Joseph had predicted, seven years of plenty are followed by famine. Now the stage is set for the first meeting with his brothers. As they arrive in court, Joseph's adolescent dreams are realized, and in the stress and strain of reunion we can see the character of the dreamer clearly delineated.

Again, as the story progresses and reaches its midpoint, the reader is made aware that a grand design is being fulfilled.

בראשית מא
א–ח

א וַיְהִי מִקֵּץ שְׁנָתַיִם יָמִים וּפַרְעֹה חֹלֵם וְהִנֵּה עֹמֵד עַל־

ב הַיְאֹר: וְהִנֵּה מִן־הַיְאֹר עֹלֹת שֶׁבַע פָּרוֹת יְפוֹת מַרְאֶה

ג וּבְרִיאֹת בָּשָׂר וַתִּרְעֶינָה בָּאָחוּ: וְהִנֵּה שֶׁבַע פָּרוֹת

אֲחֵרוֹת עֹלוֹת אַחֲרֵיהֶן מִן־הַיְאֹר רָעוֹת מַרְאֶה וְדַקּוֹת

בָּשָׂר וַתַּעֲמֹדְנָה אֵצֶל הַפָּרוֹת עַל־שְׂפַת הַיְאֹר:

ד וַתֹּאכַלְנָה הַפָּרוֹת רָעוֹת הַמַּרְאֶה וְדַקֹּת הַבָּשָׂר אֵת

שֶׁבַע הַפָּרוֹת יְפֹת הַמַּרְאֶה וְהַבְּרִיאֹת וַיִּיקַץ פַּרְעֹה:

ה וַיִּישָׁן וַיַּחֲלֹם שֵׁנִית וְהִנֵּה שֶׁבַע שִׁבֳּלִים עֹלוֹת בְּקָנֶה

י אֶחָד בְּרִיאוֹת וְטֹבוֹת: וְהִנֵּה שֶׁבַע שִׁבֳּלִים דַּקּוֹת

ז וּשְׁדוּפֹת קָדִים צֹמְחוֹת אַחֲרֵיהֶן: וַתִּבְלַעְנָה הַשִּׁבֳּלִים

הַדַּקּוֹת אֵת שֶׁבַע הַשִּׁבֳּלִים הַבְּרִיאוֹת וְהַמְּלֵאוֹת

ח וַיִּיקַץ פַּרְעֹה וְהִנֵּה חֲלוֹם: וַיְהִי בַבֹּקֶר וַתִּפָּעֶם רוּחוֹ

וַיִּשְׁלַח וַיִּקְרָא אֶת־כָּל־חַרְטֻמֵּי מִצְרַיִם וְאֶת־כָּל־

Genesis 41
1–8

1] After two years' time, Pharaoh dreamed that he was standing up the Nile,
2] when out of the Nile there came up seven cows, handsome and sturdy, and they grazed in the reed grass.   3] But presently, seven other cows came up from the Nile close behind them, ugly and gaunt, and stood beside the cows on the bank of the Nile;   4] and the ugly gaunt cows ate up the seven handsome sturdy cows. And Pharaoh awoke.

5] He fell asleep and dreamed a second time: Seven ears of grain, solid and healthy, grew on a single stalk.   6] But close behind them sprouted seven ears, thin and scorched by the east wind.   7] And the thin ears swallowed up the seven solid and full ears. Then Pharaoh awoke: it was a dream!

8] Next morning, his spirit was agitated, and he sent for all the magicians of

חֲכָמֶיהָ וַיְסַפֵּר פַּרְעֹה לָהֶם אֶת־חֲלֹמוֹ וְאֵין־פּוֹתֵר

ט אוֹתָם לְפַרְעֹה: וַיְדַבֵּר שַׂר הַמַּשְׁקִים אֶת־פַּרְעֹה

י לֵאמֹר אֶת־חֲטָאַי אֲנִי מַזְכִּיר הַיּוֹם: פַּרְעֹה קָצַף עַל־

עֲבָדָיו וַיִּתֵּן אֹתִי בְּמִשְׁמַר בֵּית שַׂר הַטַּבָּחִים אֹתִי וְאֵת

יא שַׂר הָאֹפִים: וַנַּחַלְמָה חֲלוֹם בְּלַיְלָה אֶחָד אֲנִי וָהוּא

יב אִישׁ כְּפִתְרוֹן חֲלֹמוֹ חָלָמְנוּ: וְשָׁם אִתָּנוּ נַעַר עִבְרִי

עֶבֶד לְשַׂר הַטַּבָּחִים וַנְּסַפֶּר־לוֹ וַיִּפְתָּר־לָנוּ אֶת־

יג חֲלֹמֹתֵינוּ אִישׁ כַּחֲלֹמוֹ פָּתָר: וַיְהִי כַּאֲשֶׁר פָּתַר־לָנוּ

יד כֵּן הָיָה אֹתִי הֵשִׁיב עַל־כַּנִּי וְאֹתוֹ תָלָה: וַיִּשְׁלַח

פַּרְעֹה וַיִּקְרָא אֶת־יוֹסֵף וַיְרִיצֻהוּ מִן־הַבּוֹר וַיְגַלַּח

טו וַיְחַלֵּף שִׂמְלֹתָיו וַיָּבֹא אֶל־פַּרְעֹה: וַיֹּאמֶר פַּרְעֹה אֶל־

Genesis 41
9–15

Egypt and all its wise men; and Pharaoh told them his dreams, but none could interpret them for Pharaoh.

9] The chief cupbearer then spoke up and said to Pharaoh, "I must make mention today of my offenses. 10] Once Pharaoh was angry with his servants, and placed me in custody in the house of the chief steward, together with the chief baker. 11] We had dreams the same night, he and I, each of us a dream with a meaning of its own. 12] A Hebrew youth was there with us, a servant of the chief steward; and when we told him our dreams, he interpreted them for us, telling each the meaning of his dream. 13] And as he interpreted for us, so it came to pass: I was restored to my post, and the other was impaled."

14] Thereupon Pharaoh sent for Joseph, and he was rushed from the dungeon. He had his hair cut, he changed his clothes, and he appeared before Pharaoh. 15] And

41:9] *My offenses.* Those committed against Pharaoh and those committed against Joseph, by forgetting the promise he had made to him (Gen. 40:23).

יוֹסֵף חֲלוֹם חָלַמְתִּי וּפֹתֵר אֵין אֹתוֹ וַאֲנִי שָׁמַעְתִּי

טז עָלֶיךָ לֵאמֹר תִּשְׁמַע חֲלוֹם לִפְתֹּר אֹתוֹ: וַיַּעַן יוֹסֵף

אֶת־פַּרְעֹה לֵאמֹר בִּלְעָדָי אֱלֹהִים יַעֲנֶה אֶת־שְׁלוֹם

יז פַּרְעֹה: וַיְדַבֵּר פַּרְעֹה אֶל־יוֹסֵף בַּחֲלֹמִי הִנְנִי עֹמֵד

יח עַל־שְׂפַת הַיְאֹר: וְהִנֵּה מִן־הַיְאֹר עֹלֹת שֶׁבַע פָּרוֹת

יט בְּרִיאוֹת בָּשָׂר וִיפֹת תֹּאַר וַתִּרְעֶינָה בָּאָחוּ: וְהִנֵּה

שֶׁבַע־פָּרוֹת אֲחֵרוֹת עֹלוֹת אַחֲרֵיהֶן דַּלּוֹת וְרָעוֹת

תֹּאַר מְאֹד וְרַקּוֹת בָּשָׂר לֹא־רָאִיתִי כָהֵנָּה בְּכָל־אֶרֶץ

כ מִצְרַיִם לָרֹעַ: וַתֹּאכַלְנָה הַפָּרוֹת הָרַקּוֹת וְהָרָעוֹת אֵת

כא שֶׁבַע הַפָּרוֹת הָרִאשֹׁנוֹת הַבְּרִיאֹת: וַתָּבֹאנָה אֶל־

קִרְבֶּנָה וְלֹא נוֹדַע כִּי־בָאוּ אֶל־קִרְבֶּנָה וּמַרְאֵיהֶן רַע

כב כַּאֲשֶׁר בַּתְּחִלָּה וָאִיקָץ: וָאֵרֶא בַּחֲלֹמִי וְהִנֵּה שֶׁבַע

Genesis 41

16–22

Pharaoh said to Joseph, "I have had a dream, but no one can interpret it. Now I have heard it said of you that for you to hear a dream is to tell its meaning." **16]** Joseph answered Pharaoh, saying, "Not I! God will see to Pharaoh's welfare."

17] Then Pharaoh said to Joseph, "In my dream, I was standing on the bank of the Nile, **18]** when out of the Nile came up seven sturdy and well-formed cows and grazed in the reed grass. **19]** Presently there followed them seven other cows, scrawny, ill-formed, and emaciated—never had I seen their likes for ugliness in all the land of Egypt! **20]** And the seven lean and ugly cows ate up the first seven cows, the sturdy ones; **21]** but when they had consumed them, no one could tell that they had consumed them, for they looked just as bad as before. And I awoke. **22]** In

16] *Not I!* Joseph again gives honor to God and at the same time makes it clear that he is not a professional soothsayer (cf. Dan. 2:28).

כג שִׁבֲּלִים עֹלֹת בְּקָנֶה אֶחָד מְלֵאֹת וְטֹבוֹת: וְהִנֵּה שֶׁבַע
שִׁבֲּלִים צְנֻמוֹת דַּקּוֹת שְׁדֻפוֹת קָדִים צֹמְחוֹת אַחֲרֵיהֶם:

כד וַתִּבְלַעְןָ הַשִׁבֲּלִים הַדַּקּוֹת אֵת שֶׁבַע הַשִׁבֲּלִים הַטֹּבוֹת

כה וָאֹמַר אֶל־הַחַרְטֻמִּים וְאֵין מַגִּיד לִי: וַיֹּאמֶר יוֹסֵף
אֶל־פַּרְעֹה חֲלוֹם פַּרְעֹה אֶחָד הוּא אֵת אֲשֶׁר הָאֱלֹהִים

כו עֹשֶׂה הִגִּיד לְפַרְעֹה: שֶׁבַע פָּרֹת הַטֹּבֹת שֶׁבַע שָׁנִים
הֵנָּה וְשֶׁבַע הַשִׁבֲּלִים הַטֹּבֹת שֶׁבַע שָׁנִים הֵנָּה חֲלוֹם

כז אֶחָד הוּא: וְשֶׁבַע הַפָּרוֹת הָרַקּוֹת וְהָרָעֹת הָעֹלֹת
אַחֲרֵיהֶן שֶׁבַע שָׁנִים הֵנָּה וְשֶׁבַע הַשִׁבֲּלִים הָרֵקוֹת

כח שְׁדֻפוֹת הַקָּדִים יִהְיוּ שֶׁבַע שְׁנֵי רָעָב: הוּא הַדָּבָר
אֲשֶׁר דִּבַּרְתִּי אֶל־פַּרְעֹה אֲשֶׁר הָאֱלֹהִים עֹשֶׂה הֶרְאָה

כט אֶת־פַּרְעֹה: הִנֵּה שֶׁבַע שָׁנִים בָּאוֹת שָׂבָע גָּדוֹל בְּכָל־

ל אֶרֶץ מִצְרָיִם: וְקָמוּ שֶׁבַע שְׁנֵי רָעָב אַחֲרֵיהֶן וְנִשְׁכַּח

Genesis 41

23–30

my other dream, I saw seven ears of grain, full and healthy, growing on a single stalk;   23] but right behind them sprouted seven ears, shriveled, thin, and scorched by the east wind.   24] And the thin ears swallowed the seven healthy ears. I have told my magicians, but none has an explanation for me."

25] And Joseph said to Pharaoh, "Pharaoh's dreams are one and the same: God has told Pharaoh what He is about to do.   26] The seven healthy cows are seven years, and the seven healthy ears are seven years; it is the same dream.   27] The seven lean and ugly cows that followed are seven years, as are also the seven empty ears scorched by the east wind; they are seven years of famine.   28] It is just as I have told Pharaoh: God has revealed to Pharaoh what He is about to do. 29] Immediately ahead are seven years of great abundance in all the land of Egypt. 30] After them will come seven years of famine, and all the abundance in the land

כָּל־הַשָּׂבָע בָּאֶרֶץ מִצְרָיִם וְכִלָּה הָרָעָב אֶת־הָאָרֶץ:

לא וְלֹא־יִוָּדַע הַשָּׂבָע בָּאָרֶץ מִפְּנֵי הָרָעָב הַהוּא אַחֲרֵי־

לב כֵן כִּי־כָבֵד הוּא מְאֹד: וְעַל הִשָּׁנוֹת הַחֲלוֹם אֶל־

פַּרְעֹה פַּעֲמָיִם כִּי־נָכוֹן הַדָּבָר מֵעִם הָאֱלֹהִים וּמְמַהֵר

לג הָאֱלֹהִים לַעֲשֹׂתוֹ: וְעַתָּה יֵרֶא פַרְעֹה אִישׁ נָבוֹן וְחָכָם

לד וִישִׁיתֵהוּ עַל־אֶרֶץ מִצְרָיִם: יַעֲשֶׂה פַרְעֹה וְיַפְקֵד פְּקִדִים

עַל־הָאָרֶץ וְחִמֵּשׁ אֶת־אֶרֶץ מִצְרַיִם בְּשֶׁבַע שְׁנֵי הַשָּׂבָע:

לה וְיִקְבְּצוּ אֶת־כָּל־אֹכֶל הַשָּׁנִים הַטֹּבוֹת הַבָּאֹת הָאֵלֶּה

וְיִצְבְּרוּ־בָר תַּחַת יַד־פַּרְעֹה אֹכֶל בֶּעָרִים וְשָׁמָרוּ:

לו וְהָיָה הָאֹכֶל לְפִקָּדוֹן לָאָרֶץ לְשֶׁבַע שְׁנֵי הָרָעָב אֲשֶׁר

תִּהְיֶיןָ בְּאֶרֶץ מִצְרָיִם וְלֹא־תִכָּרֵת הָאָרֶץ בָּרָעָב:

Genesis 41
31–36

of Egypt will be forgotten. As the land is ravaged by famine,   **31]** no trace of the abundance will be left in the land because of the famine thereafter, for it will be very severe.   **32]** As for Pharaoh having had the same dream twice, it means that the matter has been determined by God, and that God will soon carry it out.

33] "Accordingly, let Pharaoh find a man of discernment and wisdom, and set him over the land of Egypt.   **34]** And let Pharaoh take steps to appoint overseers over the land, and organize the land of Egypt in the seven years of plenty.   **35]** Let all the food of these good years that are coming be gathered, and let the grain be collected under Pharaoh's authority as food to be stored in the cities.   **36]** Let that food be a reserve for the land for the seven years of famine which will come upon the land of Egypt, so that the land may not perish in the famine."

34] *Organize.* Others translate as "take a fifth part of."

לז   וַיִּיטַב הַדָּבָר בְּעֵינֵי פַרְעֹה וּבְעֵינֵי כָּל־עֲבָדָיו:

לח   וַיֹּאמֶר פַּרְעֹה אֶל־עֲבָדָיו הֲנִמְצָא כָזֶה אִישׁ אֲשֶׁר

רוּחַ אֱלֹהִים בּוֹ: וַיֹּאמֶר פַּרְעֹה אֶל־יוֹסֵף אַחֲרֵי

הוֹדִיעַ אֱלֹהִים אוֹתְךָ אֶת־כָּל־זֹאת אֵין־נָבוֹן וְחָכָם

מ   כָּמוֹךָ: אַתָּה תִּהְיֶה עַל־בֵּיתִי וְעַל־פִּיךָ יִשַּׁק כָּל־עַמִּי

מא   רַק הַכִּסֵּא אֶגְדַּל מִמֶּךָּ: וַיֹּאמֶר פַּרְעֹה אֶל־יוֹסֵף רְאֵה

מב   נָתַתִּי אֹתְךָ עַל כָּל־אֶרֶץ מִצְרָיִם: וַיָּסַר פַּרְעֹה אֶת־

טַבַּעְתּוֹ מֵעַל יָדוֹ וַיִּתֵּן אֹתָהּ עַל־יַד יוֹסֵף וַיַּלְבֵּשׁ אֹתוֹ

מג   בִּגְדֵי־שֵׁשׁ וַיָּשֶׂם רְבִד הַזָּהָב עַל־צַוָּארוֹ: וַיַּרְכֵּב אֹתוֹ

בְּמִרְכֶּבֶת הַמִּשְׁנֶה אֲשֶׁר־לוֹ וַיִּקְרְאוּ לְפָנָיו אַבְרֵךְ

Genesis 41

37–43

37] The plan pleased Pharaoh and all his courtiers.   38] And Pharaoh said to his courtiers, "Could we find another like him, a man in whom is the spirit of God?" 39] So Pharaoh said to Joseph, "Since God has made all this known to you, there is none so discerning and wise as you.   40] You shall be in charge of my court, and by your command shall all my people be directed; only with respect to the throne shall I be superior to you."   41] Pharaoh further said to Joseph, "See, I put you in charge of all the land of Egypt."   42] And removing his signet ring from his hand, Pharaoh put it on Joseph's hand; and he had him dressed in robes of fine linen, and put a gold chain about his neck.   43] He had him ride in the chariot of his second-

40] *Directed.* Others translate as "order themselves," or "pay homage." As vizier, Joseph had direct access to Pharaoh.

42] *Signet ring.* The vizier was called "Seal Bearer of the King." Impressing a document with the ring was equivalent to an authorized signature.

Gold chain. An ancient symbol of investiture still in use today in British Commonwealth countries and elsewhere.

43] *Abrek.* Either an Egyptian word of unknown meaning or an Assyrian title.
/ The Akkadian word *abarakku* means "temple steward" or "steward of the royal household," which raises the question of how an Assyrian title came to be attached to the Joseph story. See W. W. Hallo's introductory essay above, pp. xxxii./

מד וְנָתוֹן אֹתוֹ עַל כָּל־אֶרֶץ מִצְרָיִם: וַיֹּאמֶר פַּרְעֹה אֶל־
יוֹסֵף אֲנִי פַרְעֹה וּבִלְעָדֶיךָ לֹא־יָרִים אִישׁ אֶת־יָדוֹ
מה וְאֶת־רַגְלוֹ בְּכָל־אֶרֶץ מִצְרָיִם: וַיִּקְרָא פַרְעֹה שֵׁם־
יוֹסֵף צָפְנַת פַּעְנֵחַ וַיִּתֶּן־לוֹ אֶת־אָסְנַת בַּת־פּוֹטִי פֶרַע
מו כֹּהֵן אֹן לְאִשָּׁה וַיֵּצֵא יוֹסֵף עַל־אֶרֶץ מִצְרָיִם: וְיוֹסֵף
בֶּן־שְׁלֹשִׁים שָׁנָה בְּעָמְדוֹ לִפְנֵי פַּרְעֹה מֶלֶךְ־מִצְרָיִם
וַיֵּצֵא יוֹסֵף מִלִּפְנֵי פַרְעֹה וַיַּעֲבֹר בְּכָל־אֶרֶץ מִצְרָיִם:
מז וַתַּעַשׂ הָאָרֶץ בְּשֶׁבַע שְׁנֵי הַשָּׂבָע לִקְמָצִים: וַיִּקְבֹּץ
אֶת־כָּל־אֹכֶל שֶׁבַע שָׁנִים אֲשֶׁר הָיוּ בְּאֶרֶץ מִצְרַיִם

Genesis 41
44–48

in-command, and they cried before him, "Abrek!" Thus he placed him over all the land of Egypt.

44] Pharaoh said to Joseph, "I am Pharaoh; yet without you, no one shall lift up hand or foot in all the land of Egypt." **45]** Pharaoh then gave Joseph the name Zaphenath-paneah; and he gave him for a wife Asenath daughter of Poti-phera priest of On. Thus Joseph emerged in charge of the land of Egypt.— **46]** Joseph was thirty years old when he entered the service of Pharaoh king of Egypt.—Leaving Pharaoh's presence, Joseph traveled through all the land of Egypt.

47] During the seven years of plenty, the land produced in abundance. **48]** And he gathered all the grain of the seven years that the land of Egypt was enjoying,

45] *Zaphenath-paneah.* Egyptian for "God speaks; He lives" or "Creator of life." Joseph is no longer the "Hebrew youth" (Gen. 41:12); his new name signifies his acceptance into official society. / Targum: "He to whom hidden matters are revealed" [1]. /
Poti-phera. A fuller form of Potiphar, but here a different person, unless this passage represents a second tradition that remembers Joseph not as the steward of Potiphar but as his son-in-law.

On. Later Heliopolis, the "Sun-city," near today's Cairo.
In charge of the land. He probably bore the title found in Egyptian records, "Chief of the Entire Land."
46] *Thirty years old.* His servitude thus lasted thirteen years. Apparently Joseph's youth was not a hindrance to his high appointment.
48] *The seven years.* Literally, "...that were in the land."

וַיִּתֶּן־אֹכֶל בֶּעָרִים אֹכֶל שְׂדֵה־הָעִיר אֲשֶׁר סְבִיבֹתֶיהָ

מט נָתַן בְּתוֹכָהּ: וַיִּצְבֹּר יוֹסֵף בָּר כְּחוֹל הַיָּם הַרְבֵּה

נ מְאֹד עַד כִּי־חָדַל לִסְפֹּר כִּי־אֵין מִסְפָּר: וּלְיוֹסֵף

יֻלַּד שְׁנֵי בָנִים בְּטֶרֶם תָּבוֹא שְׁנַת הָרָעָב אֲשֶׁר יָלְדָה־

נא לּוֹ אָסְנַת בַּת־פּוֹטִי פֶרַע כֹּהֵן אוֹן: וַיִּקְרָא יוֹסֵף אֶת־

שֵׁם הַבְּכוֹר מְנַשֶּׁה כִּי־נַשַּׁנִי אֱלֹהִים אֶת־כָּל־עֲמָלִי

נב וְאֵת כָּל־בֵּית אָבִי: וְאֵת שֵׁם הַשֵּׁנִי קָרָא אֶפְרָיִם כִּי־

נג הִפְרַנִי אֱלֹהִים בְּאֶרֶץ עָנְיִי: וַתִּכְלֶינָה שֶׁבַע שְׁנֵי הַשָּׂבָע

נד אֲשֶׁר הָיָה בְּאֶרֶץ מִצְרָיִם: וַתְּחִלֶּינָה שֶׁבַע שְׁנֵי הָרָעָב

לָבוֹא כַּאֲשֶׁר אָמַר יוֹסֵף וַיְהִי רָעָב בְּכָל־הָאֲרָצוֹת

נה וּבְכָל־אֶרֶץ מִצְרַיִם הָיָה לָחֶם: וַתִּרְעַב כָּל־אֶרֶץ

Genesis 41
49–55

and stored the grain in the cities; he put in each city the grain of the fields around it.   **49]** So Joseph collected produce in very large quantity, like the sands of the sea, until he ceased to measure it, for it could not be measured.

50] Before the years of famine came, Joseph became the father of two sons, whom Asenath daughter of Poti-phera, priest of On, bore to him.   **51]** Joseph named the first-born Manasseh, meaning, "God has made me forget completely my hardship and my parental home."   **52]** And the second he named Ephraim, meaning, "God has made me fertile in the land of my affliction."

53] The seven years of abundance that the land of Egypt enjoyed came to an end,   **54]** and the seven years of famine set in, just as Joseph had foretold. There was famine in all lands, but throughout the land of Egypt there was bread.   **55]** And

---

51] *God has made me forget.* נַשַּׁנִי, a word play on   **52]** *God has made me fertile.* הִפְרַנִי, a word play on מְנַשֶּׁה. On the implications of this sentiment, see   אֶפְרָיִם. p. 408.

מִצְרַיִם וַיִּצְעַק הָעָם אֶל־פַּרְעֹה לַלֶּחֶם וַיֹּאמֶר פַּרְעֹה
לְכָל־מִצְרַיִם לְכוּ אֶל־יוֹסֵף אֲשֶׁר־יֹאמַר לָכֶם תַּעֲשׂוּ:
נו וְהָרָעָב הָיָה עַל כָּל־פְּנֵי הָאָרֶץ וַיִּפְתַּח יוֹסֵף אֶת־כָּל־
אֲשֶׁר בָּהֶם וַיִּשְׁבֹּר לְמִצְרַיִם וַיֶּחֱזַק הָרָעָב בְּאֶרֶץ
נז מִצְרָיִם: וְכָל־הָאָרֶץ בָּאוּ מִצְרַיְמָה לִשְׁבֹּר אֶל־יוֹסֵף
כִּי־חָזַק הָרָעָב בְּכָל־הָאָרֶץ:
א וַיַּרְא יַעֲקֹב כִּי יֶשׁ־שֶׁבֶר בְּמִצְרָיִם וַיֹּאמֶר יַעֲקֹב
ב לְבָנָיו לָמָּה תִּתְרָאוּ: וַיֹּאמֶר הִנֵּה שָׁמַעְתִּי כִּי יֶשׁ־שֶׁבֶר
בְּמִצְרָיִם רְדוּ־שָׁמָּה וְשִׁבְרוּ־לָנוּ מִשָּׁם וְנִחְיֶה וְלֹא
ג נָמוּת: וַיֵּרְדוּ אֲחֵי־יוֹסֵף עֲשָׂרָה לִשְׁבֹּר בָּר מִמִּצְרָיִם:
ד וְאֶת־בִּנְיָמִין אֲחִי יוֹסֵף לֹא־שָׁלַח יַעֲקֹב אֶת־אֶחָיו כִּי
ה אָמַר פֶּן־יִקְרָאֶנּוּ אָסוֹן: וַיָּבֹאוּ בְּנֵי יִשְׂרָאֵל לִשְׁבֹּר

Genesis 41; 42
56–57; 1–5

when all the land of Egypt felt the hunger, the people cried out to Pharaoh for bread; and Pharaoh said to all the Egyptians, "Go to Joseph; whatever he tells you, you shall do."— 56] The famine spread over the whole world.—When the famine became severe in the land of Egypt, Joseph laid open all that was within, and rationed out grain to the Egyptians.   57] And all the world came to Joseph in Egypt to buy grain, for the famine had become severe throughout the world.

1] When Jacob saw that there were food rations to be had in Egypt, he said to his sons, "Why do you keep looking at one another?   2] Now I hear," he went on, "that there are rations to be had in Egypt. Go down and obtain rations for us there, that we may live and not die."   3] So ten of Joseph's brothers went down to get grain rations in Egypt;   4] for Jacob did not send Joseph's brother Benjamin with his brothers, since he feared that he might suffer disaster.   5] Thus the sons of

57] *All the world.* Everyone from Canaan and perhaps even from Mesopotamia.

א בְּתוֹךְ הַבָּאִים כִּי־הָיָה הָרָעָב בְּאֶרֶץ כְּנָעַן: וְיוֹסֵף
הוּא הַשַּׁלִּיט עַל־הָאָרֶץ הוּא הַמַּשְׁבִּיר לְכָל־עַם
הָאָרֶץ וַיָּבֹאוּ אֲחֵי יוֹסֵף וַיִּשְׁתַּחֲווּ־לוֹ אַפַּיִם אָרְצָה:

ז וַיַּרְא יוֹסֵף אֶת־אֶחָיו וַיַּכִּרֵם וַיִּתְנַכֵּר אֲלֵיהֶם וַיְדַבֵּר
אִתָּם קָשׁוֹת וַיֹּאמֶר אֲלֵהֶם מֵאַיִן בָּאתֶם וַיֹּאמְרוּ

ח מֵאֶרֶץ כְּנַעַן לִשְׁבָּר־אֹכֶל: וַיַּכֵּר יוֹסֵף אֶת־אֶחָיו וְהֵם

ט לֹא הִכִּרֻהוּ: וַיִּזְכֹּר יוֹסֵף אֵת הַחֲלֹמוֹת אֲשֶׁר חָלַם
לָהֶם וַיֹּאמֶר אֲלֵהֶם מְרַגְּלִים אַתֶּם לִרְאוֹת אֶת־עֶרְוַת

י הָאָרֶץ בָּאתֶם: וַיֹּאמְרוּ אֵלָיו לֹא אֲדֹנִי וַעֲבָדֶיךָ בָּאוּ

יא לִשְׁבָּר־אֹכֶל: כֻּלָּנוּ בְּנֵי אִישׁ־אֶחָד נָחְנוּ כֵּנִים אֲנַחְנוּ

Genesis 42
6–11

Israel were among those who came to get rations, for the famine extended to the land of Canaan.

6] Now Joseph was the vizier of the land; it was he who dispensed rations to all the people of the land. And Joseph's brothers came and bowed low to him, with their faces to the ground.   **7]** When Joseph saw his brothers, he recognized them; but he acted like a stranger toward them and spoke harshly to them. He asked them, "Where do you come from?" And they said, "From the land of Canaan, to buy food."   **8]** For though Joseph recognized his brothers, they did not recognize him.   **9]** And Joseph recalled the dreams that he had dreamed about them.

He said to them, "You are spies, you have come to see the land in its nakedness." **10]** But they said to him, "No, my lord! Truly, your servants have come to procure food.   **11]** We are all of us sons of the same man; we are honest men; your servants

---

42:9] *Nakedness.* Joseph refers to Egypt's military exposure from the Sinai peninsula, where the country was most vulnerable. Garrisons trans- mitted daily reports detailing the entry and exit of all strangers.

לֹא־הָיוּ עֲבָדֶיךָ מְרַגְּלִים: וַיֹּאמֶר אֲלֵהֶם לֹא כִּי־עֶרְוַת

הָאָרֶץ בָּאתֶם לִרְאוֹת: וַיֹּאמְרוּ שְׁנֵים עָשָׂר עֲבָדֶיךָ

אַחִים אֲנַחְנוּ בְּנֵי אִישׁ־אֶחָד בְּאֶרֶץ כְּנָעַן וְהִנֵּה הַקָּטֹן

אֶת־אָבִינוּ הַיּוֹם וְהָאֶחָד אֵינֶנּוּ: וַיֹּאמֶר אֲלֵהֶם יוֹסֵף

הוּא אֲשֶׁר דִּבַּרְתִּי אֲלֵכֶם לֵאמֹר מְרַגְּלִים אַתֶּם:

בְּזֹאת תִּבָּחֵנוּ חֵי פַרְעֹה אִם־תֵּצְאוּ מִזֶּה כִּי אִם־בְּבוֹא

אֲחִיכֶם הַקָּטֹן הֵנָּה: שִׁלְחוּ מִכֶּם אֶחָד וְיִקַּח אֶת־

אֲחִיכֶם וְאַתֶּם הֵאָסְרוּ וְיִבָּחֲנוּ דִּבְרֵיכֶם הַאֱמֶת אִתְּכֶם

וְאִם־לֹא חֵי פַרְעֹה כִּי מְרַגְּלִים אַתֶּם: וַיֶּאֱסֹף אֹתָם

אֶל־מִשְׁמָר שְׁלֹשֶׁת יָמִים: וַיֹּאמֶר אֲלֵהֶם יוֹסֵף בַּיּוֹם

הַשְּׁלִישִׁי זֹאת עֲשׂוּ וִחְיוּ אֶת־הָאֱלֹהִים אֲנִי יָרֵא: אִם־

כֵּנִים אַתֶּם אֲחִיכֶם אֶחָד יֵאָסֵר בְּבֵית מִשְׁמַרְכֶם

Genesis 42

12–19

have never been spies!"   12] And he said to them, "No, you have come to see the land in its nakedness!"   13] And they replied, "We your servants were twelve brothers, sons of a certain man in the land of Canaan; the youngest, however, is now with our father, and one is no more."   14] But Joseph said to them, "It is just as I have told you: You are spies!   15] By this you shall be put to the test: unless your youngest brother comes here, by Pharaoh, you shall not depart from this place!   16] Let one of you go and bring your brother, while the rest of you remain confined, that your words may be put to the test whether there is truth in you. Else, by Pharaoh, you are nothing but spies!"   17] And he confined them in the guardhouse for three days.

18] On the third day Joseph said to them, "Do this and you shall live, for I am a God-fearing man.   19] If you are honest men, let one of you brothers be held

18] *On the third day.* Joseph changes his mind and comes up with a more workable scheme.

וְאַתֶּם לְכוּ הָבִיאוּ שֶׁבֶר רַעֲבוֹן בָּתֵּיכֶם: וְאֶת־אֲחִיכֶם
הַקָּטֹן תָּבִיאוּ אֵלַי וְיֵאָמְנוּ דִבְרֵיכֶם וְלֹא תָמוּתוּ
וַיַּעֲשׂוּ־כֵן: וַיֹּאמְרוּ אִישׁ אֶל־אָחִיו אֲבָל אֲשֵׁמִים אֲנַחְנוּ
עַל־אָחִינוּ אֲשֶׁר רָאִינוּ צָרַת נַפְשׁוֹ בְּהִתְחַנְנוֹ אֵלֵינוּ
וְלֹא שָׁמָעְנוּ עַל־כֵּן בָּאָה אֵלֵינוּ הַצָּרָה הַזֹּאת: וַיַּעַן
רְאוּבֵן אֹתָם לֵאמֹר הֲלוֹא אָמַרְתִּי אֲלֵיכֶם לֵאמֹר
אַל־תֶּחֶטְאוּ בַיֶּלֶד וְלֹא שְׁמַעְתֶּם וְגַם־דָּמוֹ הִנֵּה נִדְרָשׁ:
וְהֵם לֹא יָדְעוּ כִּי שֹׁמֵעַ יוֹסֵף כִּי הַמֵּלִיץ בֵּינֹתָם: וַיִּסֹּב
מֵעֲלֵיהֶם וַיֵּבְךְּ וַיָּשָׁב אֲלֵהֶם וַיְדַבֵּר אֲלֵהֶם וַיִּקַּח
מֵאִתָּם אֶת־שִׁמְעוֹן וַיֶּאֱסֹר אֹתוֹ לְעֵינֵיהֶם: וַיְצַו יוֹסֵף
וַיְמַלְאוּ אֶת־כְּלֵיהֶם בָּר וּלְהָשִׁיב כַּסְפֵּיהֶם אִישׁ אֶל־

בראשית מב

Genesis 42
20–25

in your place of detention, while the rest of you go and take home rations for your starving households; 20] but you must bring me your youngest brother, that your words may be verified and that you may not die." And they did accordingly. 21] They said to one another, "Alas, we are being punished on account of our brother, because we looked on at his anguish, yet paid no heed as he pleaded with us. That is why this distress has come upon us." 22] Then Reuben spoke up and said to them, "Did I not tell you, 'Do no wrong to the boy'? But you paid no heed. Now comes the reckoning for his blood." 23] They did not know that Joseph understood, for there was an interpreter between him and them. 24] He turned away from them and wept. But he came back to them and spoke to them; and he took Simeon from among them and had him bound before their eyes. 25] Then Joseph gave orders to fill their bags with grain, return each one's money to his sack, and

22] *Did I not tell you?* They assume that Joseph is dead and are now assailed by a sense of blood guilt (see Gen. 9:6).

404

כו שַׂקּוֹ וְלָתֵת לָהֶם צֵדָה לַדָּרֶךְ וַיַּעַשׂ לָהֶם כֵּן: וַיִּשְׂאוּ

כז אֶת־שִׁבְרָם עַל־חֲמֹרֵיהֶם וַיֵּלְכוּ מִשָּׁם: וַיִּפְתַּח הָאֶחָד

אֶת־שַׂקּוֹ לָתֵת מִסְפּוֹא לַחֲמֹרוֹ בַּמָּלוֹן וַיַּרְא אֶת־

כח כַּסְפּוֹ וְהִנֵּה־הוּא בְּפִי אַמְתַּחְתּוֹ: וַיֹּאמֶר אֶל־אֶחָיו

הוּשַׁב כַּסְפִּי וְגַם הִנֵּה בְאַמְתַּחְתִּי וַיֵּצֵא לִבָּם וַיֶּחֶרְדוּ

אִישׁ אֶל־אָחִיו לֵאמֹר מַה־זֹּאת עָשָׂה אֱלֹהִים לָנוּ:

כט וַיָּבֹאוּ אֶל־יַעֲקֹב אֲבִיהֶם אַרְצָה כְּנָעַן וַיַּגִּידוּ לוֹ אֵת

ל כָּל־הַקֹּרֹת אֹתָם לֵאמֹר: דִּבֶּר הָאִישׁ אֲדֹנֵי הָאָרֶץ

לא אִתָּנוּ קָשׁוֹת וַיִּתֵּן אֹתָנוּ כִּמְרַגְּלִים אֶת־הָאָרֶץ: וַנֹּאמֶר

לב אֵלָיו כֵּנִים אֲנָחְנוּ לֹא הָיִינוּ מְרַגְּלִים: שְׁנֵים־עָשָׂר

אֲנַחְנוּ אַחִים בְּנֵי אָבִינוּ הָאֶחָד אֵינֶנּוּ וְהַקָּטֹן הַיּוֹם

לג אֶת־אָבִינוּ בְּאֶרֶץ כְּנָעַן: וַיֹּאמֶר אֵלֵינוּ הָאִישׁ אֲדֹנֵי

הָאָרֶץ בְּזֹאת אֵדַע כִּי כֵנִים אַתֶּם אֲחִיכֶם הָאֶחָד

Genesis 42
26–33

give them provisions for the journey; and this was done for them. **26]** So they loaded their asses with the rations and departed from there.

27] As one of them was opening his sack to give feed to his ass at the night encampment, he saw his money right there at the mouth of his bag. **28]** And he said to his brothers, "My money has been returned! It is here in my bag!" Their hearts sank; and, trembling, they turned to one another, saying, "What is this that God has done to us?"

29] When they came to their father Jacob in the land of Canaan, they told him all that had befallen them, saying, **30]** "The man who is lord of the land spoke harshly to us and accused us of spying on the land. **31]** We said to him, 'We are honest men; we have never been spies! **32]** There were twelve of us brothers, sons by the same father; but one is no more, and the youngest is now with our father in the land of Canaan.' **33]** But the man who is lord of the land said to us, 'By this I shall know that you are honest men: leave one of your brothers with me,

לד הַנִּיחוּ אִתִּי וְאֶת־רַעֲבוֹן בָּתֵּיכֶם קְחוּ וָלֵכוּ: וְהָבִיאוּ
אֶת־אֲחִיכֶם הַקָּטֹן אֵלַי וְאֵדְעָה כִּי לֹא מְרַגְּלִים
אַתֶּם כִּי כֵנִים אַתֶּם אֶת־אֲחִיכֶם אֶתֵּן לָכֶם וְאֶת־
לה הָאָרֶץ תִּסְחָרוּ: וַיְהִי הֵם מְרִיקִים שַׂקֵּיהֶם וְהִנֵּה־אִישׁ
צְרוֹר־כַּסְפּוֹ בְּשַׂקּוֹ וַיִּרְאוּ אֶת־צְרֹרוֹת כַּסְפֵּיהֶם הֵמָּה
לו וַאֲבִיהֶם וַיִּירָאוּ: וַיֹּאמֶר אֲלֵהֶם יַעֲקֹב אֲבִיהֶם אֹתִי
שִׁכַּלְתֶּם יוֹסֵף אֵינֶנּוּ וְשִׁמְעוֹן אֵינֶנּוּ וְאֶת־בִּנְיָמִן תִּקָּחוּ
לז עָלַי הָיוּ כֻלָּנָה: וַיֹּאמֶר רְאוּבֵן אֶל־אָבִיו לֵאמֹר אֶת־
שְׁנֵי בָנַי תָּמִית אִם־לֹא אֲבִיאֶנּוּ אֵלֶיךָ תְּנָה אֹתוֹ עַל־
לח יָדִי וַאֲנִי אֲשִׁיבֶנּוּ אֵלֶיךָ: וַיֹּאמֶר לֹא־יֵרֵד בְּנִי עִמָּכֶם
כִּי־אָחִיו מֵת וְהוּא לְבַדּוֹ נִשְׁאָר וּקְרָאָהוּ אָסוֹן בַּדֶּרֶךְ
אֲשֶׁר תֵּלְכוּ־בָהּ וְהוֹרַדְתֶּם אֶת־שֵׂיבָתִי בְּיָגוֹן שְׁאוֹלָה:

and take something for your starving households and be off.   34] And bring your
youngest brother to me, that I may know that you are not spies but honest men. I will
then restore your brother to you, and you shall be free to move about in the land.'"

35] As they were emptying their sacks, there, in each one's sack was his money-
bag! When they and their father saw their money-bags, they were dismayed.
36] Their father Jacob said to them, "It is always me that you bereave: Joseph is no
more and Simeon is no more, and now you would take away Benjamin. These things
always happen to me!"   37] Then Reuben said to his father, "You may kill my
two sons if I do not bring him back to you. Put him in my care, and I will return
him to you."   38] But he said, "My son must not go down with you, for his brother
is dead and he alone is left. If he meets with disaster on the journey you are taking,
you will send my white head down to Sheol in grief."

37] *You may kill my two sons.* A hyperbole: "I swear I will bring him back."

A Man in Conflict

The attempts by older traditions to portray Joseph as a persistently noble character do injustice to the text and to its artistry.

Thirteen years as a slave, even though at times a privileged one, left their mark on the young man. He had been his father's favorite, a pampered youth, who told tales on his brothers and who overwhelmed his family with his ambitious dreams. But the trauma of near-death and his subsequent sale into slavery apparently brought on a profound change. Gone were the ornamented tunic and with it the easy arrogance. Bitterness over his lot, then a brief period of success followed by temptation and by imprisonment with long hours of solitude—all these combined to bring out Joseph's latent powers. The gifted son of Jacob developed a sense of humility, and with it his basic qualities of religious sentiment began to emerge.

Joseph was the first Hebrew who lived, so to speak, in Diaspora (גָּלוּת). He became thoroughly assimilated, adopted the customs of his environment, changed his name, wore Egyptian clothes, swore by Pharaoh's name (Gen. 42:15), and married an Egyptian wife.[1] In Potiphar's house and in prison he was still "the Hebrew"; as an Egyptian official, he became wholly Egyptian. He entered a new life of affluence and power, and the past seemed far away. He was moved to call his first-born Manasseh because "God has made me forget completely my hardship and my parental home" (Gen. 41:51).

The forgetting, of course, was only on the surface, in his everyday existence. His past would not and could not go away. He would have been more than human if he did not think how some day he would let his brothers know of his great position, put them to shame, and arouse their envy. But why did he not communicate with his father? Why did he not make inquiry through Pharaoh's subordinates in Canaan whether Jacob was still alive?

This failure hints at a severely strained relationship between son and father. Jacob doubtlessly loved Rachel's first-born son with a fierce and possessive love. He saw in Joseph (as he would later in Benjamin) a surrogate for Rachel, his dead wife. It is altogether possible that the ornamented tunic may have served to feminize young Joseph who, according to a midrash, curled his hair and painted his eyebrows [3]. The boy must have suffered deep agony in this intense relationship, and, when he was separated from his father, he must have found it easier to suppress the memory of Jacob than to face it with maturity.[2]

The turning point came with the sudden appearance of his brothers. At first, and understandably, Joseph thought of revenge, but, when he saw them from his new and elevated position, he glimpsed them—perhaps for the first time in his life—as human beings in need of help, as brothers. And now, inevitably, he had to think of his father.

Literary artistry here introduces a delay that heightens suspense and reflects Joseph's own inner conflict. He still wants revenge more than he wants love, and so he proceeds to imprison the most aggressive of his brothers and to subject his father to the severest trial: giving up his new Rachel-substitute, the beloved Benjamin. Only after this will the final act of the drama emerge. Only after this will Joseph have reached his full potential and be able to say, "I am Joseph" and "Is my father still well?" (Gen. 45:3).

---

[1] An apocryphal tale of Joseph and Asenath has been preserved in Greek, but not in Hebrew or Aramaic [2].
[2] Nachmanides calls Joseph's decision to keep his father ignorant of the situation a grave sin, while Abarbanel excuses it on grounds of political prudence.

GLEANINGS

The Dreams

Joseph interprets to Pharaoh not his dreams but his duties. BENNO JACOB

Famine in Egypt

I was in distress on the Great Throne, and those who are in the palace were in heart's affliction from a very great evil, since the Nile had not come in my time for a space of seven years. Grain was scant, fruits were dried up, and everything which they eat was short. Every man robbed his companion. They moved without going ahead. The infant was wailing; the youth was waiting; the heart of the old men was in sorrow, their legs were bent, crouching on the ground, their arms were folded. The courtiers were in need. The temples were shut up; the sanctuaries held nothing but air. Everything was found empty.

A PHARAONIC RECORD [4]

Simeon

Joseph took his brother Simeon as a hostage, possibly because he was the one who had suggested that Joseph be killed. Thus punishment is exacted and the scales of justice begin to balance.

MIDRASH [5]

Double-Entendre

The word שֶׁבֶר (shever, rations) is used often in this story. Since the tale was probably first told by the tribe of Ephraim who pronounced "sh" as "s" [the Shibboleth-Sibboleth story, Judg. 12:6] they heard שֶׁבֶר (shever) as שֵׂבֶר (sever, i.e., hope). We have here an artistic double-entendre: Jacob means "food in Egypt," but the listener knows already that there is also "hope in Egypt." [6]

An Old Egyptian Proverb

A foreigner who drinks of the waters of the Nile forgets his native land.

Joseph

The nakedness of Joseph before Pharaoh
was the nakedness of an elm tree in winter.

Not like the pine, whose branches hold the snow
and bend and break in the cold, but like the elm
stood Joseph, stripped of his colored garments,
the ornaments of his youthful summer,
stripped of his pride as favorite son
and his pretensions to rule his brothers;
yet rooted in the teachings of his father,
as the elm tree is rooted in the deep earth
Joseph stood before the king of Egypt
as his father, Jacob, had stood before the
    Wrestler.

The nakedness of bare branches and deep roots
is the nakedness of the Jew before history.

RUTH BRIN [7]

The Second Visit

As the story of Joseph and his brothers advances to its climax, it becomes clear that Joseph is testing his brothers' feelings toward Benjamin and is working out his own new relationship to them.

In this section Judah rather than the first-born Reuben plays the commanding role. Critics have assigned this "Judah-strand" to the J-school and the "Reuben-strand" to the E-tradition. Another reason for supposing that we have varying traditions is that in this portion of the story Jacob seems to disregard the fate of the imprisoned Simeon. But the final text has woven the strands together so artfully that the flow of the tale and its emotional impact on the reader are not in the least diminished.

אַ וְהָרָעָב כָּבֵד בָּאָרֶץ: וַיְהִי כַּאֲשֶׁר כִּלּוּ לֶאֱכֹל אֶת־
הַשֶּׁבֶר אֲשֶׁר הֵבִיאוּ מִמִּצְרָיִם וַיֹּאמֶר אֲלֵיהֶם אֲבִיהֶם
גַ שֻׁבוּ שִׁבְרוּ־לָנוּ מְעַט־אֹכֶל: וַיֹּאמֶר אֵלָיו יְהוּדָה
לֵאמֹר הָעֵד הֵעִד בָּנוּ הָאִישׁ לֵאמֹר לֹא־תִרְאוּ פָנַי
בִּלְתִּי אֲחִיכֶם אִתְּכֶם: אִם־יֶשְׁךָ מְשַׁלֵּחַ אֶת־אָחִינוּ
אִתָּנוּ נֵרְדָה וְנִשְׁבְּרָה לְךָ אֹכֶל: וְאִם־אֵינְךָ מְשַׁלֵּחַ
לֹא נֵרֵד כִּי־הָאִישׁ אָמַר אֵלֵינוּ לֹא־תִרְאוּ פָנַי
בִּלְתִּי אֲחִיכֶם אִתְּכֶם: וַיֹּאמֶר יִשְׂרָאֵל לָמָה הֲרֵעֹתֶם
לִי לְהַגִּיד לָאִישׁ הַעוֹד לָכֶם אָח: וַיֹּאמְרוּ שָׁאוֹל
שָׁאַל־הָאִישׁ לָנוּ וּלְמוֹלַדְתֵּנוּ לֵאמֹר הַעוֹד אֲבִיכֶם
חַי הֲיֵשׁ לָכֶם אָח וַנַּגֶּד־לוֹ עַל־פִּי הַדְּבָרִים
הָאֵלֶּה הֲיָדוֹעַ נֵדַע כִּי יֹאמַר הוֹרִידוּ אֶת־אֲחִיכֶם:

Genesis 43
1–7

1] But the famine in the land was severe.   2] And when they had eaten up the rations which they had brought from Egypt, their father said to them, "Go again and procure some grain for us."   3] But Judah said to him, "The man warned us, 'Do not let me see your faces unless your brother is with you.'   4] If you will let our brother go with us, we will go down and procure food for you;   5] but if you will not let him go, we will not go down, for the man said to us, 'Do not let me see your faces unless your brother is with you.'"   6] And Israel said, "Why did you serve me so ill as to tell the man that you had another brother?"   7] They replied, "But the man kept asking about us and our family, saying, 'Is your father still living? Have you another brother?' And we answered him accordingly. How were we to know that he would say, 'Bring your brother here'?"

43:3] *Do not let me see your faces.* Reversing the literal Hebrew,
"do not see my face."

411

ח וַיֹּאמֶר יְהוּדָה אֶל־יִשְׂרָאֵל אָבִיו שִׁלְחָה הַנַּעַר אִתִּי
וְנָקוּמָה וְנֵלֵכָה וְנִחְיֶה וְלֹא נָמוּת גַּם־אֲנַחְנוּ גַם־אַתָּה גַּם־
ט טַפֵּנוּ: אָנֹכִי אֶעֶרְבֶנּוּ מִיָּדִי תְּבַקְשֶׁנּוּ אִם־לֹא הֲבִיאֹתִיו
י אֵלֶיךָ וְהִצַּגְתִּיו לְפָנֶיךָ וְחָטָאתִי לְךָ כָּל־הַיָּמִים: כִּי לוּלֵא
יא הִתְמַהְמָהְנוּ כִּי־עַתָּה שַׁבְנוּ זֶה פַעֲמָיִם: וַיֹּאמֶר אֲלֵהֶם
יִשְׂרָאֵל אֲבִיהֶם אִם־כֵּן אֵפוֹא זֹאת עֲשׂוּ קְחוּ מִזִּמְרַת
הָאָרֶץ בִּכְלֵיכֶם וְהוֹרִידוּ לָאִישׁ מִנְחָה מְעַט צֳרִי
יב וּמְעַט דְּבַשׁ נְכֹאת וָלֹט בָּטְנִים וּשְׁקֵדִים: וְכֶסֶף
מִשְׁנֶה קְחוּ בְיֶדְכֶם וְאֶת־הַכֶּסֶף הַמּוּשָׁב בְּפִי
יג אַמְתְּחֹתֵיכֶם תָּשִׁיבוּ בְיֶדְכֶם אוּלַי מִשְׁגֶּה הוּא: וְאֶת־

8] Then Judah said to his father Israel, "Send the boy in my care, and let us be on our way, that we may live and not die—you and we and our children. **9]** I myself will be surety for him; you may hold me responsible: if I do not bring him back to you and set him before you, I shall stand condemned before you forever. **10]** For we could have been there and back twice if we had not delayed."

11] Then their father Israel said to them, "If it must be so, do this: take some of the choice products of the land in your baggage, and carry them down as a gift for the man—some balm and some honey, gum, ladanum, pistachio nuts, and almonds. **12]** And take with you double the money, carrying back with you the money that was replaced in the mouths of your bags; perhaps it was a mistake. **13]** Take

9] *Surety.* A legal term denoting personal responsibility for someone else's performance.

10] *If we had not dawdled.* Because of Benjamin.

11] *Do this.* Once Jacob realizes the inevitable, he acts quickly and firmly.

12] *Double the money . . . perhaps it was a mistake.* These have similar sounds in Hebrew: מִשְׁגֶּה and מִשְׁנֶה (*mishgeh* and *mishneh*).

13] *Your brother.* A subtle literary and psychological change of expression. Until then Jacob has said of Benjamin "my son" (Gen. 42:38); now he

יד אֲחִיכֶם קְחוּ וְקוּמוּ שׁוּבוּ אֶל־הָאִישׁ: וְאֵל שַׁדַּי יִתֵּן לָכֶם רַחֲמִים לִפְנֵי הָאִישׁ וְשִׁלַּח לָכֶם אֶת־אֲחִיכֶם

טו אַחֵר וְאֶת־בִּנְיָמִין וַאֲנִי כַּאֲשֶׁר שָׁכֹלְתִּי שָׁכָלְתִּי: וַיִּקְחוּ הָאֲנָשִׁים אֶת־הַמִּנְחָה הַזֹּאת וּמִשְׁנֶה־כֶּסֶף לָקְחוּ בְיָדָם וְאֶת־בִּנְיָמִן וַיָּקֻמוּ וַיֵּרְדוּ מִצְרַיִם וַיַּעַמְדוּ לִפְנֵי יוֹסֵף:

טז וַיַּרְא יוֹסֵף אִתָּם אֶת־בִּנְיָמִין וַיֹּאמֶר לַאֲשֶׁר עַל־בֵּיתוֹ הָבֵא אֶת־הָאֲנָשִׁים הַבָּיְתָה וּטְבֹחַ טֶבַח וְהָכֵן כִּי אִתִּי יֹאכְלוּ הָאֲנָשִׁים בַּצָּהֳרָיִם: וַיַּעַשׂ הָאִישׁ כַּאֲשֶׁר אָמַר

יז יוֹסֵף וַיָּבֵא הָאִישׁ אֶת־הָאֲנָשִׁים בֵּיתָה יוֹסֵף: וַיִּירְאוּ

יח הָאֲנָשִׁים כִּי הוּבְאוּ בֵּית יוֹסֵף וַיֹּאמְרוּ עַל־דְּבַר הַכֶּסֶף הַשָּׁב בְּאַמְתְּחֹתֵינוּ בַּתְּחִלָּה אֲנַחְנוּ מוּבָאִים

Genesis 43
14–18

your brother too; and go back at once to the man.   14] And may El Shaddai dispose the man to mercy toward you, that he may release to you your other brother, as well as Benjamin. As for me, if I am to be bereaved, I shall be bereaved."

15] So the men took the present, and they took with them double the money, as well as Benjamin. They made their way down to Egypt, where they presented themselves to Joseph.   16] When Joseph saw Benjamin with them, he said to his house steward, "Take the men into the house; slaughter and prepare an animal, for the men will dine with me at noon."   17] The man did as Joseph said, and he brought the men into Joseph's house.   18] But the men were frightened at being brought into Joseph's house. "It must be," they thought, "because of the money replaced in our bags the first time that we have been brought inside, as a

shifts the responsibility for the boy and says "your brother."

18] *With our pack animals.* Even though their personal liberty is at stake, the brothers are still concerned about their possessions—a timeless, universal trait [1].

לְהִתְגֹּלֵל עָלֵינוּ וּלְהִתְנַפֵּל עָלֵינוּ וְלָקַחַת אֹתָנוּ

יט לַעֲבָדִים וְאֶת־חֲמֹרֵינוּ: וַיִּגְּשׁוּ אֶל־הָאִישׁ אֲשֶׁר עַל־

כ בֵּית יוֹסֵף וַיְדַבְּרוּ אֵלָיו פֶּתַח הַבָּיִת: וַיֹּאמְרוּ בִּי

כא אֲדֹנִי יָרֹד יָרַדְנוּ בַּתְּחִלָּה לִשְׁבָּר־אֹכֶל: וַיְהִי כִּי־בָאנוּ

אֶל־הַמָּלוֹן וַנִּפְתְּחָה אֶת־אַמְתְּחֹתֵינוּ וְהִנֵּה כֶסֶף־אִישׁ

בְּפִי אַמְתַּחְתּוֹ כַּסְפֵּנוּ בְּמִשְׁקָלוֹ וַנָּשֶׁב אֹתוֹ בְּיָדֵנוּ:

כב וְכֶסֶף אַחֵר הוֹרַדְנוּ בְיָדֵנוּ לִשְׁבָּר־אֹכֶל לֹא יָדַעְנוּ

כג מִי־שָׂם כַּסְפֵּנוּ בְּאַמְתְּחֹתֵינוּ: וַיֹּאמֶר שָׁלוֹם לָכֶם אַל־

תִּירָאוּ אֱלֹהֵיכֶם וֵאלֹהֵי אֲבִיכֶם נָתַן לָכֶם מַטְמוֹן

בְּאַמְתְּחֹתֵיכֶם כַּסְפְּכֶם בָּא אֵלָי וַיּוֹצֵא אֲלֵהֶם אֶת־

כד שִׁמְעוֹן: וַיָּבֵא הָאִישׁ אֶת־הָאֲנָשִׁים בֵּיתָה יוֹסֵף וַיִּתֶּן־

כה מַיִם וַיִּרְחֲצוּ רַגְלֵיהֶם וַיִּתֵּן מִסְפּוֹא לַחֲמֹרֵיהֶם: וַיָּכִינוּ

pretext to attack us and seize us as slaves, with our pack animals." **19]** So they went up to Joseph's house steward and spoke to him at the entrance of the house. **20]** "If you please, my lord," they said, "we came down once before to procure food. **21]** But when we arrived at the night encampment and opened our bags, there was each one's money in the mouth of his bag, our money in full. So we have brought it back with us. **22]** And we have brought down with us other money to procure food. We do not know who put the money in our bags." **23]** He replied, "All is well with you; do not be afraid. Your God and the God of your father must have put treasure in your bags for you. I got your payment." And he brought out Simeon to them.

24] Then the man brought the men into Joseph's house; he gave them water to bathe their feet, and he provided feed for their asses. **25]** They laid out their

21] *Money in full.* Literally, "by its weight."

414

אֶת־הַמִּנְחָה עַד־בּוֹא יוֹסֵף בַּצׇּהֳרָיִם כִּי שָׁמְעוּ כִּי־שָׁם

כו] יֹאכְלוּ לָחֶם: וַיָּבֹא יוֹסֵף הַבַּיְתָה וַיָּבִיאוּ לוֹ אֶת־

הַמִּנְחָה אֲשֶׁר־בְּיָדָם הַבָּיְתָה וַיִּשְׁתַּחֲווּ־לוֹ אָרְצָה:

כז] וַיִּשְׁאַל לָהֶם לְשָׁלוֹם וַיֹּאמֶר הֲשָׁלוֹם אֲבִיכֶם הַזָּקֵן

כח] אֲשֶׁר אֲמַרְתֶּם הַעוֹדֶנּוּ חָי: וַיֹּאמְרוּ שָׁלוֹם לְעַבְדְּךָ

כט] לְאָבִינוּ עוֹדֶנּוּ חָי וַיִּקְּדוּ וַיִּשְׁתַּחֲו*וּ: וַיִּשָּׂא עֵינָיו וַיַּרְא

אֶת־בִּנְיָמִין אָחִיו בֶּן־אִמּוֹ וַיֹּאמֶר הֲזֶה אֲחִיכֶם הַקָּטֹן

ל] אֲשֶׁר אֲמַרְתֶּם אֵלָי וַיֹּאמַר אֱלֹהִים יׇחְנְךָ בְּנִי: וַיְמַהֵר

יוֹסֵף כִּי־נִכְמְרוּ רַחֲמָיו אֶל־אָחִיו וַיְבַקֵּשׁ לִבְכּוֹת

לא] וַיָּבֹא הַחַדְרָה וַיֵּבְךְּ שָׁמָּה: וַיִּרְחַץ פָּנָיו וַיֵּצֵא וַיִּתְאַפַּק

לב] וַיֹּאמֶר שִׂימוּ לָחֶם: וַיָּשִׂימוּ לוֹ לְבַדּוֹ וְלָהֶם לְבַדָּם

Genesis 43
26–32

* כח וישתחוו קרי.

gifts to await Joseph's arrival at noon, for they had heard that they were to dine there.

26] When Joseph came home, they presented to him the gifts that they had brought with them into the house, bowing low before him to the ground.   27] He greeted them, and he said, "How is your aged father, of whom you spoke? Is he still in good health?"   28] They replied, "It is well with your servant our father; he is still in good health." And they bowed and made obeisance.

29] Looking about, he saw his brother Benjamin, his mother's son, and asked, "Is this your youngest brother, of whom you spoke to me?" And he went on, "May God be gracious to you, my boy."   30] With that, Joseph hurried out, for he was overcome with feeling toward his brother and wanted to cry; he went into a room and wept there.   31] Then he washed his face, reappeared, and—now in control of himself—gave the order, "Serve the meal."   32] They served him by himself,

30] *Overcome with feeling.* A pale translation of the Hebrew, which literally says "his innards were burning up."

32] *By himself.* Joseph ate alone, which apparently was befitting his rank [2].

Abhorrent to the Egyptians. The Egyptians dis-

וְלַמִּצְרִים הָאֹכְלִים אִתּוֹ לְבַדָּם כִּי לֹא יוּכְלוּן **בְּרֵאשִׁית** מג; מד
הַמִּצְרִים לֶאֱכֹל אֶת־הָעִבְרִים לֶחֶם כִּי־תוֹעֵבָה הִוא לג-לד; א-ג

לג לַמִּצְרִים: וַיֵּשְׁבוּ לְפָנָיו הַבְּכֹר כִּבְכֹרָתוֹ וְהַצָּעִיר
לד כִּצְעִרָתוֹ וַיִּתְמְהוּ הָאֲנָשִׁים אִישׁ אֶל־רֵעֵהוּ: וַיִּשָּׂא
מַשְׂאֹת מֵאֵת פָּנָיו אֲלֵהֶם וַתֵּרֶב מַשְׂאַת בִּנְיָמִן מִמַּשְׂאֹת
כֻּלָּם חָמֵשׁ יָדוֹת וַיִּשְׁתּוּ וַיִּשְׁכְּרוּ עִמּוֹ:

א וַיְצַו אֶת־אֲשֶׁר עַל־בֵּיתוֹ לֵאמֹר מַלֵּא אֶת־אַמְתְּחֹת
הָאֲנָשִׁים אֹכֶל כַּאֲשֶׁר יוּכְלוּן שְׂאֵת וְשִׂים כֶּסֶף־אִישׁ
ב בְּפִי אַמְתַּחְתּוֹ: וְאֶת־גְּבִיעִי גְּבִיעַ הַכֶּסֶף תָּשִׂים בְּפִי
אַמְתַּחַת הַקָּטֹן וְאֵת כֶּסֶף שִׁבְרוֹ וַיַּעַשׂ כִּדְבַר יוֹסֵף
ג אֲשֶׁר דִּבֵּר: הַבֹּקֶר אוֹר וְהָאֲנָשִׁים שֻׁלְּחוּ הֵמָּה

Genesis 43; 44
33–34; 1–3

and them by themselves, and the Egyptians who ate with him by themselves; for the Egyptians could not dine with the Hebrews, since that would be abhorrent to the Egyptians.   33] As they were seated by his direction, from the oldest in the order of his seniority to the youngest in the order of his youth, the men looked at one another in astonishment.   34] Portions were served them from his table; but Benjamin's portion was several times that of anyone else. And they feasted and drank with him.

1] Then he instructed his house steward as follows, "Fill the men's bags with food, as much as they can carry, and put each one's money in the mouth of his bag. 2] Put my silver goblet in the mouth of the bag of the youngest one, together with his money for the rations." And he did as Joseph told him.

3] With the first light of morning, the men were sent off with their pack

liked eating with strangers. Herodotus once noted that Egyptians despised the Greek habit of using utensils while eating [3].
33] *In astonishment.* That Joseph had mysteriously

seated them exactly in the order of their seniority.
34] *Several times.* Literally, "five times."
They drank their fill. Literally, "they drank and became drunk." This episode ends on a note

ד וַחֲמֹרֵיהֶם: הֵם יָצְאוּ אֶת־הָעִיר לֹא הִרְחִיקוּ וְיוֹסֵף
אָמַר לַאֲשֶׁר עַל־בֵּיתוֹ קוּם רְדֹף אַחֲרֵי הָאֲנָשִׁים
וְהִשַּׂגְתָּם וְאָמַרְתָּ אֲלֵהֶם לָמָּה שִׁלַּמְתֶּם רָעָה תַּחַת

ה טוֹבָה: הֲלוֹא זֶה אֲשֶׁר יִשְׁתֶּה אֲדֹנִי בּוֹ וְהוּא נַחֵשׁ

ו יְנַחֵשׁ בּוֹ הֲרֵעֹתֶם אֲשֶׁר עֲשִׂיתֶם: וַיַּשִּׂגֵם וַיְדַבֵּר אֲלֵהֶם

ז אֶת־הַדְּבָרִים הָאֵלֶּה: וַיֹּאמְרוּ אֵלָיו לָמָּה יְדַבֵּר אֲדֹנִי
כַּדְּבָרִים הָאֵלֶּה חָלִילָה לַעֲבָדֶיךָ מֵעֲשׂוֹת כַּדָּבָר

ח הַזֶּה: הֵן כֶּסֶף אֲשֶׁר מָצָאנוּ בְּפִי אַמְתְּחֹתֵינוּ הֱשִׁיבֹנוּ
אֵלֶיךָ מֵאֶרֶץ כְּנָעַן וְאֵיךְ נִגְנֹב מִבֵּית אֲדֹנֶיךָ כֶּסֶף אוֹ

ט זָהָב: אֲשֶׁר יִמָּצֵא אִתּוֹ מֵעֲבָדֶיךָ וָמֵת וְגַם־אֲנַחְנוּ נִהְיֶה

י לַאדֹנִי לַעֲבָדִים: וַיֹּאמֶר גַּם־עַתָּה כְדִבְרֵיכֶם כֶּן־הוּא

Genesis 44
4–10

animals.   4] They had just left the city and had not gone far, when Joseph said to his steward, "Up, go after the men! And when you overtake them, say to them, 'Why did you repay good with evil?   5] It is the very one from which my master drinks and which he uses for divination. It was a wicked thing for you to do!' "

6] He overtook them and spoke those words to them.   7] And they said to him, "Why does my lord say such things? Far be it from your servants to do anything of that kind!   8] Here we brought back to you from the land of Canaan the money that we found in the mouths of our bags. How then could we have stolen any silver or gold from your master's house!   9] Whichever of your servants it is found with shall die; the rest of us, moreover, shall become slaves to my lord."   10] He replied, "Although what you are proposing is right,

of conviviality, in sharp contrast to what is to follow.   44:10] *My* slave. The servant speaks for Joseph.

אֲשֶׁר יִמָּצֵא אִתּוֹ יִהְיֶה־לִּי עָבֶד וְאַתֶּם תִּהְיוּ נְקִיִּם:

יא וַיְמַהֲרוּ וַיּוֹרִדוּ אִישׁ אֶת־אַמְתַּחְתּוֹ אָרְצָה וַיִּפְתְּחוּ

יב אִישׁ אַמְתַּחְתּוֹ: וַיְחַפֵּשׂ בַּגָּדוֹל הֵחֵל וּבַקָּטֹן כִּלָּה

יג וַיִּמָּצֵא הַגָּבִיעַ בְּאַמְתַּחַת בִּנְיָמִן: וַיִּקְרְעוּ שִׂמְלֹתָם

יד וַיַּעֲמֹס אִישׁ עַל־חֲמֹרוֹ וַיָּשֻׁבוּ הָעִירָה: וַיָּבֹא יְהוּדָה

וְאֶחָיו בֵּיתָה יוֹסֵף וְהוּא עוֹדֶנּוּ שָׁם וַיִּפְּלוּ לְפָנָיו

טו אָרְצָה: וַיֹּאמֶר לָהֶם יוֹסֵף מָה־הַמַּעֲשֶׂה הַזֶּה אֲשֶׁר

עֲשִׂיתֶם הֲלוֹא יְדַעְתֶּם כִּי־נַחֵשׁ יְנַחֵשׁ אִישׁ אֲשֶׁר

טז כָּמֹנִי: וַיֹּאמֶר יְהוּדָה מַה־נֹּאמַר לַאדֹנִי מַה־נְּדַבֵּר

וּמַה־נִּצְטַדָּק הָאֱלֹהִים מָצָא אֶת־עֲוֹן עֲבָדֶיךָ הִנֶּנּוּ

עֲבָדִים לַאדֹנִי גַּם־אֲנַחְנוּ גַּם אֲשֶׁר־נִמְצָא הַגָּבִיעַ בְּיָדוֹ:

Genesis 44

11–16

only the one with whom it is found shall be my slave; but the rest of you shall go free."

11] So each one hastened to lower his bag to the ground, and each one opened his bag. **12]** He searched, beginning with the oldest and ending with the youngest; and the goblet turned up in Benjamin's bag. **13]** At this they rent their clothes. Each reloaded his pack animal, and they returned to the city. **14]** When Judah and his brothers re-entered the house of Joseph, who was still there, they threw themselves on the ground before him. **15]** Joseph said to them, "What is this deed that you have done? Do you not know that a man like me practices divination?" **16]** Judah replied, "What can we say to my lord? How can we plead, how can we prove our innocence? God has uncovered the crime of your servants. Here we are, then, slaves of my lord, the rest of us as much as he in whose

16] *God has uncovered the crime.* They never directly admit Benjamin's guilt, but they accept the whole calamity as somehow being God's will because of the *real* crime, the sale of Joseph [4].

וַיֹּאמֶר חָלִילָה לִּי מֵעֲשׂוֹת זֹאת הָאִישׁ אֲשֶׁר נִמְצָא ⁱ⁶
הַגָּבִיעַ בְּיָדוֹ הוּא יִהְיֶה־לִּי עָבֶד וְאַתֶּם עֲלוּ לְשָׁלוֹם
אֶל־אֲבִיכֶם: 17

Genesis 44

Haftarah Miketz, p. 564

possession the goblet was found." **17]** But **he replied,** "Far be it from me to act thus! Only he in whose possession the goblet was found shall be my slave; the rest of you may go back unhindered to your father."

On Divination

Joseph is referred to as one who practices divination, that is to say, one who foretells events by certain external signs, sounds, or movements—here, by the surface motion of wine in a special cup. This practice, called hydromancy by the Greeks, was well known in the ancient Near East, as were numerous other forms of divination. The Bible itself mentions several: the shaking of arrows and the inspection of livers and various forms of astrological prognostication (Ezek. 21:26; Isa. 47:13; Jer. 10:2). Joseph's activity is described as *nachesh*, which may come from the Hebrew word for serpent (*nachash*), which in turn suggests that one of the early forms of divination was to prophesy from the hissing of a snake.

These and other forms of soothsaying came under severe attack from Torah law and the Prophets and were called "abhorrent practices." Deuteronomy warns: "Let no one be found among you who consigns his son or daughter to the fire, or who is an augur, a soothsayer, a diviner, a sorcerer, one who casts spells, or one who consults ghosts or familiar spirits, or who inquires of the dead" (18:10–11). The frequent repetition of these prohibitions bears witness to the continued popularity of such superstitions [5]. The Talmud enumerates a whole series of persistent (and condemned) divining practices:

"Who may be said to be practicing divination? Someone who draws conclusions from events such as these: a piece of food dropped out of his mouth by eating; a cane fell from his hand; a child called him from behind his back; a deer ran across his way; he saw a snake on his right or a fox on his left, and so forth" [6].

While the spread of modern science has reduced many forms of superstition, it has not succeeded in eliminating them entirely. At the root of such practices remains the human desire to know the future and the belief that this foreknowledge must somehow be available to men.

GLEANINGS

Jacob's Dilemma

You may learn from the story of Jacob that it is a man's worst trial to have his children ask him for food when he has nothing to give.

MIDRASH [7]

The Feast

The nagging anxiety which has befallen the brothers before the strange Egyptian prince is now replaced by an equally inexplicable sense of well-being. Meanwhile Joseph—still unknown to the brothers, yet so well-known to the reader—holds the key to the mystery and looks on with delight on the dearest of his guests whom God has led to him.

FRANZ DELITZSCH [8]

Go Back in Peace (Gen. 44:17)

Joseph really says "Go back *toward* peace" (לְשָׁלוֹם) rather than "in peace" (בְּשָׁלוֹם). For to say לְשָׁלוֹם always means to go forward to a peaceful life, while בְּשָׁלוֹם is associated with eternal peace, i.e., death (e.g., Gen. 15:15). [9]

Hence, Joseph's subtlety foretells the happy outcome.

[This is also the meaning of לְשָׁלוֹם in the Sabbath hymn שָׁלוֹם עֲלֵיכֶם.]

A Game

To Joseph had been granted, side by side with stupendous practical abilities, the unanalyzable and fatal gift of personal magnetism. He had that mysterious power to bewitch or to wound, which in contact with others gave him that advantage in the psychic field which a Samson has in the physical. The possession of either kind of strength is of course accompanied by the overwhelming need to make use of it. . . . He played with individuals. Individuals were to him material for psychic exercise, therefore material for dramatic exploitation and the enhancement of his personality. He was an actor who always had to "upstage" his fellow actors, and he expected them to like it.

MAURICE SAMUEL [10]

Joseph Reveals His Identity

The traditional weekly portion (*sidrah*) takes up the tale at its most dramatic point, Judah's superbly persuasive plea—"the most complete pattern of genuine natural eloquence," as Sir Walter Scott called it. The plea is followed by the long-postponed but finally inevitable climax, the self-disclosure of Joseph. However often we read these thirty-two verses, we are struck by the literary mastery of the text. "We know the outcome, yet we tremble—this is art at its highest" [1].

But more than art is involved. At first in the background and now emerging ever more clearly is the guiding hand of God. The human story has a link with divine purpose. Four times in succession Joseph avers that it was not he but God who brought these events to pass. The promise to Abraham will not be denied: "God has sent me ahead of you to insure your survival on earth, and to save your lives in an extraordinary deliverance" (Gen. 45:7). The tale here foreshadows slavery and exodus; what happens between Joseph and his brothers is therefore an introduction to the story of deliverance that will occupy the second book of the Torah.

The invitation to Jacob's family to settle in Egypt was not without parallel. A thirteenth-century-B.C.E. document records a similar event, probably under the Pharaoh Mernephtah and probably in the region of Goshen: Some Edomite Bedouin were permitted to settle in order "to keep them alive and to keep their cattle alive" [2].

בראשית מד
יח–כה

יח וַיִּגַּשׁ אֵלָיו יְהוּדָה וַיֹּאמֶר בִּי אֲדֹנִי יְדַבֶּר־נָא עַבְדְּךָ
דָבָר בְּאָזְנֵי אֲדֹנִי וְאַל־יִחַר אַפְּךָ בְּעַבְדֶּךָ כִּי כָמוֹךָ
יט כְּפַרְעֹה: אֲדֹנִי שָׁאַל אֶת־עֲבָדָיו לֵאמֹר הֲיֵשׁ־לָכֶם
כ אָב אוֹ־אָח: וַנֹּאמֶר אֶל־אֲדֹנִי יֶשׁ־לָנוּ אָב זָקֵן וְיֶלֶד
זְקֻנִים קָטָן וְאָחִיו מֵת וַיִּוָּתֵר הוּא לְבַדּוֹ לְאִמּוֹ וְאָבִיו
כא אֲהֵבוֹ: וַתֹּאמֶר אֶל־עֲבָדֶיךָ הוֹרִדֻהוּ אֵלָי וְאָשִׂימָה
כב עֵינִי עָלָיו: וַנֹּאמֶר אֶל־אֲדֹנִי לֹא־יוּכַל הַנַּעַר לַעֲזֹב
כג אֶת־אָבִיו וְעָזַב אֶת־אָבִיו וָמֵת: וַתֹּאמֶר אֶל־עֲבָדֶיךָ
אִם־לֹא יֵרֵד אֲחִיכֶם הַקָּטֹן אִתְּכֶם לֹא תֹסִפוּן לִרְאוֹת
כד פָּנָי: וַיְהִי כִּי עָלִינוּ אֶל־עַבְדְּךָ אָבִי וַנַּגֶּד־לוֹ אֵת
כה דִּבְרֵי אֲדֹנִי: וַיֹּאמֶר אָבִינוּ שֻׁבוּ שִׁבְרוּ־לָנוּ מְעַט־אֹכֶל:

Genesis 44
18–25

18] Then Judah went up to him and said, "Please, my lord, let your servant appeal to my lord, and do not be impatient with your servant, you who are the equal of Pharaoh.   19] My lord asked his servants, 'Have you a father or another brother?'   20] We told my lord, 'We have an old father, and there is a child of his old age, the youngest; his full brother is dead, so that he alone is left of his mother. and his father dotes on him.'   21] Then you said to your servants, 'Bring him down to me, that I may set eyes on him.'   22] We said to my lord, 'The boy cannot leave his father; if he were to leave him, his father would die.'   23] But you said to your servants, 'Unless your youngest brother comes down with you, do not let me see your faces.'   24] When we came back to your servant my father, we reported my lord's words to him.

25] "Later our father said, 'Go back and procure some food for us.'

44:20] *Dead.* From their father's point of view.

425

כו וַנֹּאמֶר לֹא נוּכַל לָרֶדֶת אִם־יֵשׁ אָחִינוּ הַקָּטֹן אִתָּנוּ
וְיָרַדְנוּ כִּי־לֹא נוּכַל לִרְאוֹת פְּנֵי הָאִישׁ וְאָחִינוּ

כז הַקָּטֹן אֵינֶנּוּ אִתָּנוּ: וַיֹּאמֶר עַבְדְּךָ אָבִי אֵלֵינוּ אַתֶּם

כח יְדַעְתֶּם כִּי שְׁנַיִם יָלְדָה־לִּי אִשְׁתִּי: וַיֵּצֵא הָאֶחָד מֵאִתִּי

כט וָאֹמַר אַךְ טָרֹף טֹרָף וְלֹא רְאִיתִיו עַד־הֵנָּה: וּלְקַחְתֶּם
גַּם־אֶת־זֶה מֵעִם פָּנַי וְקָרָהוּ אָסוֹן וְהוֹרַדְתֶּם אֶת־

ל שֵׂיבָתִי בְּרָעָה שְׁאֹלָה: וְעַתָּה כְּבֹאִי אֶל־עַבְדְּךָ אָבִי

לא וְהַנַּעַר אֵינֶנּוּ אִתָּנוּ וְנַפְשׁוֹ קְשׁוּרָה בְנַפְשׁוֹ: וְהָיָה
כִּרְאוֹתוֹ כִּי־אֵין הַנַּעַר וָמֵת וְהוֹרִידוּ עֲבָדֶיךָ אֶת־

לב שֵׂיבַת עַבְדְּךָ אָבִינוּ בְּיָגוֹן שְׁאֹלָה: כִּי עַבְדְּךָ עָרַב
אֶת־הַנַּעַר מֵעִם אָבִי לֵאמֹר אִם־לֹא אֲבִיאֶנּוּ אֵלֶיךָ

Genesis 44
26–32

26] We answered, 'We cannot go down; only if our youngest brother is with us can we go down, for we may not show our faces to the man unless our youngest brother is with us.'   27] Your servant my father said to us, 'As you know, my wife bore me two sons.   28] But one is gone from me, and I said: Alas, he was torn by a beast! Nor have I seen him since.   29] If you take this one from me, too, and he meets with disaster, you will send my white head down to Sheol in grief.'

30] "Now, if I come to your servant my father and the boy is not with us—since his own life is so bound up with his— 31] when he sees that the boy is not with us, he will die, and your servants will send the white head of your servant our father down to Sheol in grief.   32] Now your servant has pledged himself for the boy to my father, saying, "If I do not bring him back to you, I shall stand guilty before

---

26] *Show our faces to the man.* Literally, "see the man's face."
28] *Torn by a beast.* Joseph now learns what his fate is said to have been. Judah's obvious and touching concern for Benjamin and Jacob prepares Joseph for his own disclosure.

לג וְחָטָאתִי לְאָבִי כָּל־הַיָּמִים: וְעַתָּה יֵשֶׁב־נָא עַבְדְּךָ

לד תַּחַת הַנַּעַר עֶבֶד לַאדֹנִי וְהַנַּעַר יַעַל עִם־אֶחָיו: כִּי־

אֵיךְ אֶעֱלֶה אֶל־אָבִי וְהַנַּעַר אֵינֶנּוּ אִתִּי פֶּן אֶרְאֶה

בָרָע אֲשֶׁר יִמְצָא אֶת־אָבִי:

א וְלֹא־יָכֹל יוֹסֵף לְהִתְאַפֵּק לְכֹל הַנִּצָּבִים עָלָיו וַיִּקְרָא

הוֹצִיאוּ כָל־אִישׁ מֵעָלָי וְלֹא־עָמַד אִישׁ אִתּוֹ בְּהִתְוַדַּע

ב יוֹסֵף אֶל־אֶחָיו: וַיִּתֵּן אֶת־קֹלוֹ בִּבְכִי וַיִּשְׁמְעוּ מִצְרַיִם

ג וַיִּשְׁמַע בֵּית פַּרְעֹה: וַיֹּאמֶר יוֹסֵף אֶל־אֶחָיו אֲנִי יוֹסֵף

הַעוֹד אָבִי חָי וְלֹא־יָכְלוּ אֶחָיו לַעֲנוֹת אֹתוֹ כִּי נִבְהֲלוּ

ד מִפָּנָיו: וַיֹּאמֶר יוֹסֵף אֶל־אֶחָיו גְּשׁוּ־נָא אֵלַי וַיִּגְּשׁוּ

Genesis 44; 45

33–34; 1–4

my father forever.' **33]** Therefore, please let your servant remain as a slave to my lord instead of the boy, and let the boy go back with his brothers. **34]** For how can I go back to my father unless the boy is with me? Let me not be witness to the woe that would overtake my father!"

1] Joseph could no longer control himself before all his attendants, and he cried out, "Have everyone withdraw from me!" So there was no one else about when Joseph made himself known to his brothers. **2]** His sobs were so loud that the Egyptians could hear, and so the news reached Pharaoh's palace.

3] Joseph said to his brothers, "I am Joseph. Is my father still well?" But his brothers could not answer him, so dumbfounded were they on account of him.

4] Then Joseph said to his brothers, "Come forward to me." And when they

---

33] *Let the boy go back.* This offer marks Judah as a man of exceptional character. He speaks for himself and also for his brothers; he speaks in accents of love and not of sibling hatred.

45:1] *Have everyone withdraw.* The revelation will be made in private; Joseph will not shame his brothers [3].

3] *Is my father still well?* Or "Is he *really* alive?" (see Gen. 43:27).

וַיֹּאמֶר אֲנִי יוֹסֵף אֲחִיכֶם אֲשֶׁר־מְכַרְתֶּם אֹתִי מִצְרָיְמָה:

ה וְעַתָּה אַל־תֵּעָצְבוּ וְאַל־יִחַר בְּעֵינֵיכֶם כִּי־מְכַרְתֶּם

י אֹתִי הֵנָּה כִּי לְמִחְיָה שְׁלָחַנִי אֱלֹהִים לִפְנֵיכֶם: כִּי־זֶה

שְׁנָתַיִם הָרָעָב בְּקֶרֶב הָאָרֶץ וְעוֹד חָמֵשׁ שָׁנִים אֲשֶׁר

אֵין־חָרִישׁ וְקָצִיר: וַיִּשְׁלָחֵנִי אֱלֹהִים לִפְנֵיכֶם לָשׂוּם

לָכֶם שְׁאֵרִית בָּאָרֶץ וּלְהַחֲיוֹת לָכֶם לִפְלֵיטָה גְּדֹלָה:

ה וְעַתָּה לֹא־אַתֶּם שְׁלַחְתֶּם אֹתִי הֵנָּה כִּי הָאֱלֹהִים

וַיְשִׂימֵנִי לְאָב לְפַרְעֹה וּלְאָדוֹן לְכָל־בֵּיתוֹ וּמֹשֵׁל

ט בְּכָל־אֶרֶץ מִצְרָיִם: מַהֲרוּ וַעֲלוּ אֶל־אָבִי וַאֲמַרְתֶּם

אֵלָיו כֹּה אָמַר בִּנְךָ יוֹסֵף שָׂמַנִי אֱלֹהִים לְאָדוֹן

י לְכָל־מִצְרָיִם רְדָה אֵלַי אַל־תַּעֲמֹד: וְיָשַׁבְתָּ בְאֶרֶץ־

גֹּשֶׁן וְהָיִיתָ קָרוֹב אֵלַי אַתָּה וּבָנֶיךָ וּבְנֵי בָנֶיךָ וְצֹאנְךָ

came forward, he said, "I am your brother Joseph, he whom you sold into Egypt. **5]** Now, do not be distressed or reproach yourselves because you sold me hither; it was to save life that God sent me ahead of you. **6]** It is now two years that there has been famine in the land, and there are still five years to come in which there shall be no yield from tilling. **7]** God has sent me ahead of you to insure your survival on earth, and to save your lives in an extraordinary deliverance. **8]** So, it was not you who sent me here, but God; and He has made me a father to Pharaoh, lord of all his household, and ruler over the whole land of Egypt.

9] "Hurry back, then, to my father and say to him: Thus says your son Joseph, 'God has made me lord of all Egypt; come down to me without delay. **10]** You will dwell in the region of Goshen, where you will be near me—you and your chil-

8] *Father to Pharaoh.* That is, vizier. This and the two subsequent descriptions are translations of official Egyptian titles. Joseph speaks to his broth-ers in his native tongue without the help of in-terpreters.

10] *Goshen.* The area of Wadi Tumilat, in the

יא וּבְקָרְךָ וְכָל־אֲשֶׁר־לָךְ: וְכִלְכַּלְתִּי אֹתְךָ שָׁם כִּי־עוֹד
חָמֵשׁ שָׁנִים רָעָב פֶּן־תִּוָּרֵשׁ אַתָּה וּבֵיתְךָ וְכָל־אֲשֶׁר־
יב לָךְ: וְהִנֵּה עֵינֵיכֶם רֹאוֹת וְעֵינֵי אָחִי בִנְיָמִין כִּי־פִי
יג הַמְדַבֵּר אֲלֵיכֶם: וְהִגַּדְתֶּם לְאָבִי אֶת־כָּל־כְּבוֹדִי
בְּמִצְרַיִם וְאֵת כָּל־אֲשֶׁר רְאִיתֶם וּמִהַרְתֶּם וְהוֹרַדְתֶּם
יד אֶת־אָבִי הֵנָּה: וַיִּפֹּל עַל־צַוְּארֵי בִנְיָמִן־אָחִיו וַיֵּבְךְּ
טו וּבִנְיָמִן בָּכָה עַל־צַוָּארָיו: וַיְנַשֵּׁק לְכָל־אֶחָיו וַיֵּבְךְּ
עֲלֵהֶם וְאַחֲרֵי כֵן דִּבְּרוּ אֶחָיו אִתּוֹ:

Genesis 45
11–15

dren and your grandchildren, your flocks and herds, and all that is yours. **11]** There I will provide for you—for there are yet five years of famine to come—that you and your household and all that is yours may not suffer want.' **12]** You can see for yourselves, and my brother Benjamin for himself, that it is indeed I who am speaking to you. **13]** And you must tell my father everything about my high station in Egypt and all that you have seen; and bring my father here with all speed."

14] With that he embraced his brother Benjamin around the neck and wept, and Benjamin wept on his neck. **15]** He kissed all his brothers and wept upon them; only then were his brothers able to talk to him.

eastern Nile delta, between today's Port Said and Suez. It was a region, not a specific place in Egypt.

that his use of Hebrew was additional proof of his identity [4].

12] *It is indeed I who am speaking.* Perhaps inferring

14] *Embraced.* Literally, "fell on."

A Test

The Midrash and many subsequent commentaries have dwelt on the theme of testing that underlies the story. Joseph first faces his brothers in bitterness and devises a cat-and-mouse game in order to have his revenge, but in the end, having worked out his own feelings toward his father and brothers, he is ready for reconciliation [5]. However, before this can take place, the brothers, too, must be ready, and Joseph wants to make certain that the new brotherly relationship will be mutual. Thus, the elaborate device of deception and delay that serves to heighten the suspense provides at the same time a sound motivational framework for the story. When the brothers' affection for each other and for their father becomes evident, when they hint that now they consider their sale of Joseph a crime, and when finally Judah offers himself as a slave to save Benjamin, the scales are balanced and Joseph can speak as the brother.[1] The test is over, for him as well as for them [7].

Yet more than human testing is at stake, more than revenge and repentance. The delays Joseph introduces strengthen not only his conviction about the changes in his brothers' attitude but also his conviction about God's incessant watchfulness over the seed of Abraham. Joseph believes that he is a tool of destiny, that as a child of his father he partakes of the heritage and the promise. When events single him out as a key factor in the covenant and everything begins to point to the validity of the promise, he becomes humble and thereby underscores his fitness as God's chosen servant. The heritage and its bearers had been in danger, but God has turned impending calamity into salvation. In Genesis this thread of rescue-and-deliverance becomes visible in the stories of Noah, Lot, Sarah, and Rebekah. Now, in the Joseph tale, the ground is laid for transferring the theme from the individual onto the nation.

---

[1] The expression וְעַתָּה in Gen. 45:5 is said always to refer to repentance [6].

GLEANINGS

Judah

The word וַיִּגַּשׁ [went up], which opens the section [Gen. 44:18], occurs as an introduction to three different kinds of action: to do battle [II Sam. 10:13], to conciliate [Josh. 14:6], to pray [I Kings 18:36]. The three are strangely related: Men are usually ready for any one of the three. So was Judah when he "went up."   MIDRASH [8]

וַיִּגַּשׁ יְהוּדָה can also be translated: "Then Judah drew near." To whom? To himself, for only when Judah became himself at his best was he able to speak as he did.   CHASIDIC [9]

At first Judah spoke softly and humbly, for he remembered his own crime against Joseph. But when punishment was to fall on the innocent Benjamin, Judah dropped all caution and spoke angrily and so loudly that his voice resounded throughout Egypt.   MIDRASH [10]

I Am Your Brother Joseph (Gen. 45:4)

These were the words with which, in October 1960, Pope John XXIII greeted a group of 130 Jewish leaders—Joseph being his baptismal name.

Jewish Survival

The story of the children of Israel had hardly begun, and already survival was the issue (Gen. 45:7). It was to remain the issue in Egypt and the desert, in Canaan and Palestine, Diaspora and re-turn. This is the way Jewish history was shaped from its inception, and from Joseph's day down to modern times the children of Israel have looked into the abyss and, later, experienced the "extra-ordinary deliverance."

The Plea

[The following is the beginning of a long ora-tion, hortatory in tone, put by Flavius Josephus into the mouth of Judah.]

But Judah who had persuaded their father to send the lad from him, being otherwise also a very bold and active man, determined to hazard him-self for the preservation of his brother. "It is true," said he, "O governor, that we have been very wicked with regard to thee and, on that account, deserve punishment; even all of us may justly be punished, although the theft were not committed by all but only by one of us, and he the youngest also: but yet there remains some hope for us who otherwise must be under despair on his account, and this from thy goodness which promises us a deliverance out of our present danger. And now I beg thou wilt not look at us, or at that great crime we have been guilty of, but at thy own excellent nature and take advice of thine own virtue, in-stead of that wrath thou hast against us; which passion those that otherwise are of lower character indulge as they do their strength, and that not only on great but also on very trifling occasions. Over-come, Sir, that passion and be not subdued by it."

JOSEPHUS [11]

Jacob Goes to Egypt

After Joseph's emotion-filled disclosure the narrative resumes a leisurely pace. The text turns to the last act of the drama—Jacob's descent into Egypt, the reunion, and the deaths of Jacob and Joseph. The aged father learns that his son is still alive and elaborate preparations are made for the journey to Canaan. It is a moving scene described with the fewest of words.

The Egyptian sojourn begins with a vision, the last to be recounted in Genesis and in many ways one of the most important, for it speaks of God's part in exile and exodus.

טז וַיִּקֹּל נִשְׁמַע בֵּית פַּרְעֹה לֵאמֹר בָּאוּ אֲחֵי יוֹסֵף וַיִּיטַב
יז בְּעֵינֵי פַרְעֹה וּבְעֵינֵי עֲבָדָיו: וַיֹּאמֶר פַּרְעֹה אֶל־יוֹסֵף
אֱמֹר אֶל־אַחֶיךָ זֹאת עֲשׂוּ טַעֲנוּ אֶת־בְּעִירְכֶם וּלְכוּ־
יח בֹאוּ אַרְצָה כְּנָעַן: וּקְחוּ אֶת־אֲבִיכֶם וְאֶת־בָּתֵּיכֶם וּבֹאוּ
אֵלָי וְאֶתְּנָה לָכֶם אֶת־טוּב אֶרֶץ מִצְרַיִם וְאִכְלוּ אֶת־
יט חֵלֶב הָאָרֶץ: וְאַתָּה צֻוֵּיתָה זֹאת עֲשׂוּ קְחוּ־לָכֶם מֵאֶרֶץ
מִצְרַיִם עֲגָלוֹת לְטַפְּכֶם וְלִנְשֵׁיכֶם וּנְשָׂאתֶם אֶת־אֲבִיכֶם
כ וּבָאתֶם: וְעֵינְכֶם אַל־תָּחֹס עַל־כְּלֵיכֶם כִּי־טוּב כָּל־
כא אֶרֶץ מִצְרַיִם לָכֶם הוּא: וַיַּעֲשׂוּ־כֵן בְּנֵי יִשְׂרָאֵל וַיִּתֵּן
לָהֶם יוֹסֵף עֲגָלוֹת עַל־פִּי פַרְעֹה וַיִּתֵּן לָהֶם צֵדָה

Genesis 45

16–21

16] The news reached Pharaoh's palace: "Joseph's brothers have come." Pharaoh and his courtiers were pleased.   17] And Pharaoh said to Joseph, "Say to your brothers, 'Do as follows: load up your beasts and go at once to the land of Canaan.   18] Take your father and your households and come to me; I will give you the best of the land of Egypt and you shall live off the fat of the land.' 19] And you are bidden [to add], 'Do as follows: take from the land of Egypt wagons for your children and your wives, and bring your father here.   20] And never mind your belongings, for the best of all the land of Egypt shall be yours.' "

21] The sons of Israel did so; Joseph gave them wagons as Pharaoh had com-

45:16] *Were pleased.* A simple statement showing how highly Joseph was esteemed. Yet some generations later his contribution was no longer remembered (Exod. 1:8).

17] *And Pharaoh said.* Pharaoh now officially confirms the invitation Joseph has already extended.

It is to his advantage to have his vizier's family settle in Egypt; he will make Joseph a permanent resident [1].

19] *[To add].* Septuagint and Vulgate supply these words, which do not appear in the Hebrew text.

לַדָּרֶךְ: לְכֻלָּם נָתַן לָאִישׁ חֲלִפוֹת שְׂמָלֹת וּלְבִנְיָמִן

נָתַן שְׁלֹשׁ־מֵאוֹת כֶּסֶף וְחָמֵשׁ חֲלִפֹת שְׂמָלֹת: וּלְאָבִיו

שָׁלַח כְּזֹאת עֲשָׂרָה חֲמֹרִים נֹשְׂאִים מִטּוּב מִצְרָיִם

וְעֶשֶׂר אֲתֹנֹת נֹשְׂאֹת בָּר וָלֶחֶם וּמָזוֹן לְאָבִיו לַדָּרֶךְ:

וַיְשַׁלַּח אֶת־אֶחָיו וַיֵּלֵכוּ וַיֹּאמֶר אֲלֵהֶם אַל־תִּרְגְּזוּ

בַדָּרֶךְ: וַיַּעֲלוּ מִמִּצְרָיִם וַיָּבֹאוּ אֶרֶץ כְּנַעַן אֶל־יַעֲקֹב

אֲבִיהֶם: וַיַּגִּדוּ לוֹ לֵאמֹר עוֹד יוֹסֵף חַי וְכִי־הוּא

מֹשֵׁל בְּכָל־אֶרֶץ מִצְרָיִם וַיָּפָג לִבּוֹ כִּי לֹא־הֶאֱמִין

לָהֶם: וַיְדַבְּרוּ אֵלָיו אֵת כָּל־דִּבְרֵי יוֹסֵף אֲשֶׁר דִּבֶּר

אֲלֵהֶם וַיַּרְא אֶת־הָעֲגָלוֹת אֲשֶׁר־שָׁלַח יוֹסֵף לָשֵׂאת

manded, and he supplied them with provisions for the journey.   22] To each of them, moreover, he gave a change of clothing; but to Benjamin he gave three hundred pieces of silver and several changes of clothing.   23] And to his father he sent the following: ten he-asses laden with the best things of Egypt, and ten she-asses laden with grain, bread, and provisions for his father on the journey.   24] As he sent his brothers off on their way, he told them, "Do not be quarrelsome on the way."

25] They went up from Egypt and came to their father Jacob in the land of Canaan.   26] And they told him, "Joseph is still alive; yes, he is ruler over the whole land of Egypt." His heart went numb, for he did not believe them.   27] But when they recounted all that Joseph had said to them, and when he saw the wagons that

22] *Three hundred.* Also used as a round number [2].   Should be understood as "a large sum."
Several. Literally, "five" (see Gen. 43:34).

24] *Do not be quarrelsome.* Joseph realizes his brothers will have to tell Jacob the full story of the sale. He cautions them not to blame one

another [3].
/ Another interpretation: "Don't be afraid of robbers" (seeing you carry such wealth, for God will protect you) [4]./

27] *When they recounted.* The text is gently silent about what they said and also about the way in

כח אֹתוֹ וַתְּחִי רוּחַ יַעֲקֹב אֲבִיהֶם: וַיֹּאמֶר יִשְׂרָאֵל רַב
עוֹד־יוֹסֵף בְּנִי חָי אֵלְכָה וְאֶרְאֶנּוּ בְּטֶרֶם אָמוּת:

א וַיִּסַּע יִשְׂרָאֵל וְכָל־אֲשֶׁר־לוֹ וַיָּבֹא בְּאֵרָה שֶּׁבַע וַיִּזְבַּח

ב זְבָחִים לֵאלֹהֵי אָבִיו יִצְחָק: וַיֹּאמֶר אֱלֹהִים לְיִשְׂרָאֵל
בְּמַרְאֹת הַלַּיְלָה וַיֹּאמֶר יַעֲקֹב יַעֲקֹב וַיֹּאמֶר הִנֵּנִי:

ג וַיֹּאמֶר אָנֹכִי הָאֵל אֱלֹהֵי אָבִיךָ אַל־תִּירָא מֵרְדָה

ד מִצְרַיְמָה כִּי־לְגוֹי גָּדוֹל אֲשִׂימְךָ שָׁם: אָנֹכִי אֵרֵד עִמְּךָ
מִצְרַיְמָה וְאָנֹכִי אַעַלְךָ גַם־עָלֹה וְיוֹסֵף יָשִׁית יָדוֹ

ה עַל־עֵינֶיךָ: וַיָּקָם יַעֲקֹב מִבְּאֵר שָׁבַע וַיִּשְׂאוּ בְּנֵי־
יִשְׂרָאֵל אֶת־יַעֲקֹב אֲבִיהֶם וְאֶת־טַפָּם וְאֶת־נְשֵׁיהֶם

Genesis 45; 46
28; 1–5

Joseph had sent to transport him, the spirit of their father Jacob revived.
28] "Enough!" said Israel, "My son Joseph is still alive! I must go and see him before I die."

1] So Israel set out with all that was his, and he came to Beer-sheba, where he offered sacrifices to the God of his father Isaac. **2]** God called to Israel in a vision by night: "Jacob! Jacob!" He answered, "Here." **3]** And He said, "I am God, the God of your father. Fear not to go down to Egypt, for there I will make you a great nation. **4]** I Myself will go down with you to Egypt, and I Myself will also bring you back; and Joseph's hand shall close your eyes."

5] So Jacob set out from Beer-sheba. The sons of Israel put their father Jacob and their children and their wives in the wagons which Pharaoh had sent to trans-

which they made a clean breast of their past sins [5].

46:1] *He came to Beer-sheba.* Probably from Hebron.

2] *Israel.* He is called Israel in his response though he remains Jacob. The fusion of past and present is complete [6] (see Gen. 35:10 and p. 324).

4] *Bring you back.* That is, your descendants.

Joseph's hand shall close your eyes. Jewish tradition [7] demands that the eyes of the deceased be closed, preferably, by a son.

/Others render the biblical text figuratively: "He will take care of you" [8]./

י בָּעֲגָלוֹת אֲשֶׁר־שָׁלַח פַּרְעֹה לָשֵׂאת אֹתוֹ: וַיִּקְחוּ אֶת־
מִקְנֵיהֶם וְאֶת־רְכוּשָׁם אֲשֶׁר רָכְשׁוּ בְּאֶרֶץ כְּנַעַן וַיָּבֹאוּ

ז מִצְרָיְמָה יַעֲקֹב וְכָל־זַרְעוֹ אִתּוֹ: בָּנָיו וּבְנֵי בָנָיו אִתּוֹ
בְּנֹתָיו וּבְנוֹת בָּנָיו וְכָל־זַרְעוֹ הֵבִיא אִתּוֹ מִצְרָיְמָה: ס

ח וְאֵלֶּה שְׁמוֹת בְּנֵי־יִשְׂרָאֵל הַבָּאִים מִצְרַיְמָה יַעֲקֹב

ט וּבָנָיו בְּכֹר יַעֲקֹב רְאוּבֵן: וּבְנֵי רְאוּבֵן חֲנוֹךְ וּפַלּוּא

י וְחֶצְרֹן וְכַרְמִי: וּבְנֵי שִׁמְעוֹן יְמוּאֵל וְיָמִין וְאֹהַד וְיָכִין

יא וְצֹחַר וְשָׁאוּל בֶּן־הַכְּנַעֲנִית: וּבְנֵי לֵוִי גֵּרְשׁוֹן קְהָת

יב וּמְרָרִי: וּבְנֵי יְהוּדָה עֵר וְאוֹנָן וְשֵׁלָה וָפֶרֶץ וָזָרַח
וַיָּמָת עֵר וְאוֹנָן בְּאֶרֶץ כְּנַעַן וַיִּהְיוּ בְנֵי־פֶרֶץ חֶצְרֹן

יג וְחָמוּל: וּבְנֵי יִשָּׂשכָר תּוֹלָע וּפֻוָּה וְיוֹב וְשִׁמְרֹן:

Genesis 46

6–13

port him;   6] and they took along their livestock and the wealth that they had amassed in the land of Canaan. Thus Jacob and all his offspring with him came to Egypt: 7] he brought with him to Egypt his sons and grandsons, his daughters and granddaughters—all his offspring.

8] These are the names of the Israelites, Jacob and his descendants, who came to Egypt.

Jacob's first-born Reuben;   9] Reuben's sons: Enoch, Pallu, Hezron, and Carmi. 10] Simeon's sons: Jemuel, Jamin, Ohad, Jachin, Zohar, and Saul the son of a Canaanite woman.   11] Levi's sons: Gershon, Kohath, and Merari.   12] Judah's sons: Er, Onan, Shelah, Perez, and Zerah—but Er and Onan had died in the land of Canaan; and Perez's sons were Hezron and Hamul.   13] Issachar's sons: Tola,

8–27] The list of descendants is probably from another tradition; its insertion here creates some difficulties and discrepancies; e.g., that Perez and Benjamin are reported to have children, although they are too young to be fathers.

9] *Enoch.* The usual English rendering of חֲנוֹךְ.

10] *Jemuel.* Called Nemuel in Num. 26:12; I Chron. 4:24.

Saul. The usual English rendering of שָׁאוּל.

13] *Iob.* Called Jashub in Num. 26:24 and several ancient versions.

יד וּבְנֵי זְבֻלוּן סֶרֶד וְאֵלוֹן וְיַחְלְאֵל: אֵלֶּה בְּנֵי לֵאָה אֲשֶׁר
יָלְדָה לְיַעֲקֹב בְּפַדַּן אֲרָם וְאֵת דִּינָה בִתּוֹ כָּל־נֶפֶשׁ
טו בָּנָיו וּבְנוֹתָיו שְׁלֹשִׁים וְשָׁלֹשׁ: וּבְנֵי גָד צִפְיוֹן וְחַגִּי שׁוּנִי
טז וְאֶצְבֹּן עֵרִי וַאֲרוֹדִי וְאַרְאֵלִי: וּבְנֵי אָשֵׁר יִמְנָה וְיִשְׁוָה
יז וְיִשְׁוִי וּבְרִיעָה וְשֶׂרַח אֲחֹתָם וּבְנֵי בְרִיעָה חֶבֶר
יח וּמַלְכִּיאֵל: אֵלֶּה בְּנֵי זִלְפָּה אֲשֶׁר־נָתַן לָבָן לְלֵאָה
יט בִתּוֹ וַתֵּלֶד אֶת־אֵלֶּה לְיַעֲקֹב שֵׁשׁ עֶשְׂרֵה נָפֶשׁ: בְּנֵי
כ רָחֵל אֵשֶׁת יַעֲקֹב יוֹסֵף וּבִנְיָמִן: וַיִּוָּלֵד לְיוֹסֵף בְּאֶרֶץ
מִצְרַיִם אֲשֶׁר יָלְדָה־לּוֹ אָסְנַת בַּת־פּוֹטִי פֶרַע כֹּהֵן
כא אֹן אֶת־מְנַשֶּׁה וְאֶת־אֶפְרָיִם: וּבְנֵי בִנְיָמִן בֶּלַע וָבֶכֶר

Genesis 46

14–21

Puvah, Iob, and Shimron.   14] Zebulun's sons: Sered, Elon, and Jahleel.
15] Those were the sons whom Leah bore to Jacob in Paddan-aram, in addition to
his daughter Dinah. Persons in all, male and female: 33.

16] Gad's sons: Ziphion, Haggi, Shuni, Ezbon, Eri, Arodi, and Areli.   17] Asher's
sons: Imnah, Ishvah, Ishvi, and Beriah, and their sister Serah. Beriah's sons: Heber
and Malchiel.   18] These were the descendants of Zilpah, whom Laban had given
to his daughter Leah. These she bore to Jacob—16 persons.

19] The sons of Jacob's wife Rachel were Joseph and Benjamin.   20] To Joseph
were born in the land of Egypt Manasseh and Ephraim, whom Asenath daughter
of Poti-phera priest of On bore to him.   21] Benjamin's sons: Bela, Becher, Ashbel,

15] *Persons in all . . . 33.* Including Jacob [9].

17] *Their sister Serah.* The insertion of her name
in an all-male list gave rise to many midrashic
speculations, especially that Serah was the one who
first told Jacob of Joseph's survival [10].

19] *Jacob's wife Rachel.* The favorite one. Leah is

simply called by name.

21] *Benjamin's sons.* Benjamin here has ten sons;
in Num. 26:38–40, only five. The Septuagint gives
him three and also grandchildren; further differences (suggesting different traditions) appear in
I Chron. 8:1–5.

כב וְאַשְׁבֵּל גֵּרָא וְנַעֲמָן אֵחִי וָרֹאשׁ מֻפִּים וְחֻפִּים וָאָרְדְּ׃
אֵלֶּה בְּנֵי רָחֵל אֲשֶׁר יֻלַּד לְיַעֲקֹב כָּל־נֶפֶשׁ אַרְבָּעָה

כג עָשָׂר׃ וּבְנֵי־דָן חֻשִׁים׃ וּבְנֵי נַפְתָּלִי יַחְצְאֵל וְגוּנִי וְיֵצֶר

כה וְשִׁלֵּם׃ אֵלֶּה בְּנֵי בִלְהָה אֲשֶׁר־נָתַן לָבָן לְרָחֵל בִּתּוֹ

כו וַתֵּלֶד אֶת־אֵלֶּה לְיַעֲקֹב כָּל־נֶפֶשׁ שִׁבְעָה׃ כָּל־הַנֶּפֶשׁ
הַבָּאָה לְיַעֲקֹב מִצְרַיְמָה יֹצְאֵי יְרֵכוֹ מִלְּבַד נְשֵׁי

כז בְנֵי־יַעֲקֹב כָּל־נֶפֶשׁ שִׁשִּׁים וָשֵׁשׁ׃ וּבְנֵי יוֹסֵף אֲשֶׁר־
יֻלַּד־לוֹ בְמִצְרַיִם נֶפֶשׁ שְׁנָיִם כָּל־הַנֶּפֶשׁ לְבֵית־יַעֲקֹב
הַבָּאָה מִצְרַיְמָה שִׁבְעִים׃ ס

Gera, Naaman, Ehi, Rosh, Muppim, Huppim, and Ard. **22]** These were the descendants of Rachel, who were born to Jacob—14 persons in all.

23] Dan's son: Hushim. **24]** Naphtali's sons: Jahzeel, Guni, Jezer, and Shillem. **25]** These were the descendants of Bilhah, whom Laban had given to his daughter Rachel. These she bore to Jacob—7 persons in all.

26] All the persons who came with Jacob to Egypt—his own issue, aside from the wives of Jacob's sons—all these persons numbered 66. **27]** And Joseph's sons who were born to him in Egypt were two in number. Thus the total of Jacob's household who came to Egypt was 70 persons.

23] *Dan's son.* In Hebrew "sons," a formulaic plural [11].

26] *All the persons.* Here exclusive of Jacob, Joseph, and his two sons.

27] *Total . . . 70 persons.* The entire family, here including Jacob and Joseph. The belabored method of counting represents an attempt to reconcile varying traditions [12]. It is also possible that "seventy" represented a round or "good" number as with Gideon's seventy sons (Judg. 8:30).

A Paradox

Quite obviously the biblical authors believed that God willed Jacob's descent into Egypt. They envisioned Him saying, "I Myself will go down with you to Egypt, and I Myself will also bring you back" (Gen. 46:4). Yet the Rabbis pictured Jacob pondering whether to remain in Canaan or to settle in Egypt. Had God not expressly forbidden Isaac to go there? And had Abraham not encountered grave dangers in Egypt? Should he, Jacob, now be the one to forsake the Promised Land? The Midrash says that he finally decided to leave because the decision was God's and not his [13].

The Torah appears to explain the foundations of Israel's existence through this interplay of divine plan and human decision. It shows God knowingly sending His children into Egypt and into subsequent oppression. Had not Abraham already been informed: "Know well that your offspring shall be strangers in a land not theirs, and they shall be enslaved and oppressed four hundred years" (Gen. 15:13).

The biblical authors offer no explanation why this should have been so. We may infer, however, that in their view God *had* to do what the human situation required; in Canaan the people of Israel could not or would not become what they were destined to be. In Canaan lurked the dangers of intermingling and absorption; in Goshen there would be isolation and segregation, both of which would provide fertile soil for the development of particular national characteristics [14]. If oppression, too, would be part of the experience, this would be the price the people-to-be would have to pay.

We meet here a paradox intrinsic in the biblical view of God's relation to Israel. He loves His people, yet they undergo deep suffering. God guards Israel, yet their freedom to act limits God's own knowledge of the future. Biblical man accepted this paradox as inevitable, for logic could not resolve the inaccessibility of God's ultimate nature (see p. 46).[1] Nowhere is this paradox of God's relationship to Israel better portrayed than in the old saying that God was exiled with His people and that as they wept He wept with them [16].[2]

---

[1] Note Rabbi Akiba's saying: "All is foreseen, yet freedom is given" [15].

[2] The Zohar compares God with Rachel in that both weep for their children [17]. Note also the rabbinic concept of "chastisements of divine love" (יִסּוּרִין שֶׁל אַהֲבָה) [18].

GLEANINGS

The News Reached Pharaoh's Palace (Gen. 45:16)

The word for news, קֹל [literally, "voice"], is written without the usual ו, that is, in a constricted fashion. For it is the voice that is small which is often heard more than any other. This also teaches us to pray silently, for God hears the prayer of the heart.   ZOHAR [19]

Pharaoh Was Pleased

Why? He was pleased to learn that Joseph after all had fine family connections.

MIDRASH [20]

Full Circle

The gift of clothing and the preference shown to Benjamin are Joseph's subtle hint that the old quarrel over the ornamented tunic is shown to have been futile.   TOLEDOT YITSCHAK

Jacob Did Not Believe Them

When the brothers lied and told him Joseph was dead he believed them; when they spoke the truth and said that Joseph was alive he disbelieved them. This is the punishment of liars: even when they speak the truth they are not believed.

MIDRASH [21]

Exile

Jacob's descent into Egypt was Israel's first Diaspora.   MIDRASH [22]

Jacob Hears the News

But when they arrived at home, and told their father their story about their brother, which was so apparently incredible and beyond all his hopes, he did not much believe them; for even though those who brought the account were trustworthy, still the greatness and extraordinary character of the circumstances which they reported did not allow him to believe them easily: but when the old man saw the vast preparation, and the supplies of all necessary things, at such a time, in such abundance, corresponding to the good fortune of his son which they were reporting to him, he praised God that he had made complete that part of his house which seemed to be deficient; but his joy immediately begat fear again in his soul, respecting his departure from his national laws and customs; for he knew that youth is by nature prone to fall and that in foreign nations there is great indulgence given to error and especially in the country of Egypt, a land in a state of utter blindness respecting the true God, in consequence of their making created and mortal things into gods.

Moreover, the addition of riches and glory is a snare to weak minds, and he also recollected that he had been left to himself, as no one had gone forth out of his father's house with him to keep him in the right way, but he had been left solitary and destitute of all good instructions and might therefore be supposed to be ready to change and adopt their foreign customs. Therefore, when that Being, who alone is able to behold the invisible soul, saw him in this frame of mind, he took pity on him and, appearing unto him by night while he was lying asleep, said unto him: "Fear nothing about your departure into Egypt; I myself will guide you on your way and will give you a safe and pleasant journey; and I will restore to you your long lamented son, who was once many years ago believed by you to have died but who is not only alive but is even governor of all that mighty country."   PHILO [23]

Jacob in Egypt

Jacob and Joseph meet at last. The Bible describes the fateful moment in very few words, leaving much to the reader's imagination. Next, Pharaoh is introduced to Joseph's family, and while here, too, the text understates the situation the recorded words are extremely revealing.

We learn about the effects of the famine and, so it seems to many, the morally puzzling aspects of Joseph's economic and political management. Israel now dwells in Goshen, and a new chapter in his people's history is about to begin.

וְאֶת־יְהוּדָה שָׁלַח לְפָנָיו אֶל־יוֹסֵף לְהוֹרֹת לְפָנָיו גֹּשְׁנָה וַיָּבֹאוּ אַרְצָה
גֹּשֶׁן: כח וַיֶּאְסֹר יוֹסֵף מֶרְכַּבְתּוֹ וַיַּעַל לִקְרַאת־יִשְׂרָאֵל כט
אָבִיו גֹּשְׁנָה וַיֵּרָא אֵלָיו וַיִּפֹּל עַל־צַוָּארָיו וַיֵּבְךְּ עַל־
צַוָּארָיו עוֹד: וַיֹּאמֶר יִשְׂרָאֵל אֶל־יוֹסֵף אָמוּתָה הַפָּעַם ל
אַחֲרֵי רְאוֹתִי אֶת־פָּנֶיךָ כִּי עוֹדְךָ חָי: וַיֹּאמֶר יוֹסֵף לא
אֶל־אֶחָיו וְאֶל־בֵּית אָבִיו אֶעֱלֶה וְאַגִּידָה לְפַרְעֹה
וְאֹמְרָה אֵלָיו אַחַי וּבֵית־אָבִי אֲשֶׁר בְּאֶרֶץ־כְּנַעַן בָּאוּ
אֵלָי: וְהָאֲנָשִׁים רֹעֵי צֹאן כִּי־אַנְשֵׁי מִקְנֶה הָיוּ וְצֹאנָם לב
וּבְקָרָם וְכָל־אֲשֶׁר לָהֶם הֵבִיאוּ: וְהָיָה כִּי־יִקְרָא לָכֶם לג

Genesis 46
28–33

28] He had sent Judah ahead of him to Joseph, to point the way before him to Goshen. So when they came to the region of Goshen, 29] Joseph ordered his chariot and went to Goshen to meet his father Israel; he presented himself to him and, embracing him around the neck, he wept on his neck a good while. 30] Then Israel said to Joseph, "Now I can die, having seen for myself that you are still alive."

31] Then Joseph said to his brothers and to his father's household, "I will go up and tell the news to Pharaoh, and say to him, 'My brothers and my father's household, who were in the land of Canaan, have come to me. 32] The men are shepherds, having long been keepers of livestock, and they have brought with them their flocks and herds and all that is theirs.' 33] So when Pharaoh summons you

46:28] *Judah.* He is chosen by Jacob and now replaces Reuben as the leader. Simeon and Levi are likewise passed over. The reason will become clear in Jacob's blessing (Gen. 49:5–7).

29] *Ordered.* Literally "hitched."
Presented himself. The Hebrew expression

וַיֵּרָא (va-yera) is used in other biblical passages in reference to God in the sense of "He appeared." Here the text implies that Joseph suddenly stood before his father, as if in a vision.

/Some commentators feel that Jacob and not Joseph is the subject of the sentence [1]./

445

לד פַּרְעֹה וְאָמַר מַה־מַּעֲשֵׂיכֶם: וַאֲמַרְתֶּם אַנְשֵׁי מִקְנֶה בראשית מו; מז
הָיוּ עֲבָדֶיךָ מִנְּעוּרֵינוּ וְעַד־עַתָּה גַּם־אֲנַחְנוּ גַּם־אֲבֹתֵינוּ לד; א—ד
בַּעֲבוּר תֵּשְׁבוּ בְּאֶרֶץ גֹּשֶׁן כִּי־תוֹעֲבַת מִצְרַיִם כָּל־
רֹעֵה צֹאן:

א וַיָּבֹא יוֹסֵף וַיַּגֵּד לְפַרְעֹה וַיֹּאמֶר אָבִי וְאַחַי וְצֹאנָם
וּבְקָרָם וְכָל־אֲשֶׁר לָהֶם בָּאוּ מֵאֶרֶץ כְּנָעַן וְהִנָּם

ב בְּאֶרֶץ גֹּשֶׁן: וּמִקְצֵה אֶחָיו לָקַח חֲמִשָּׁה אֲנָשִׁים וַיַּצִּגֵם

ג לִפְנֵי פַרְעֹה: וַיֹּאמֶר פַּרְעֹה אֶל־אֶחָיו מַה־מַּעֲשֵׂיכֶם
וַיֹּאמְרוּ אֶל־פַּרְעֹה רֹעֵה צֹאן עֲבָדֶיךָ גַּם־אֲנַחְנוּ גַּם־

ד אֲבוֹתֵינוּ: וַיֹּאמְרוּ אֶל־פַּרְעֹה לָגוּר בָּאָרֶץ בָּאנוּ כִּי־

Genesis 46; 47
34; 1–4

and asks, 'What is your occupation?'   34] you shall answer, 'Your servants have been keepers of livestock from the start until now, both we and our fathers'—so that you may stay in the region of Goshen. For all shepherds are abhorrent to Egyptians."

1] Then Joseph came and reported to Pharaoh, saying, "My father and my brothers, with their flocks and herds and all that is theirs, have come from the land of Canaan and are now in the region of Goshen."   2] And selecting a few of his brothers, he presented them to Pharaoh.   3] Pharaoh said to his brothers, "What is your occupation?" They answered Pharaoh, "We your servants are shepherds, as were also our fathers.   4] We have come," they said to Pharaoh, "to sojourn in this

34] *Shepherds are abhorrent.* Egyptian sources do not support this statement.
/The attempt has been made to connect this reported attitude toward shepherds with the Egyptian's dislike for the Hyksos. This goes back to Manethos who understood the term Hyksos to mean "shepherd kings" [2].   In fact, it means "foreign rulers."/

47:2] *A few.* Literally, "five" (cf. Gen. 43:34; 45:22). The Bible does not say whom he picked; some interpreters say that he chose the weakest lest Pharaoh draft them for his army [3],   others say he chose the strongest in order to make a good impression [4].

אֵין מִרְעֶה לַצֹּאן אֲשֶׁר לַעֲבָדֶיךָ כִּי־כָבֵד הָרָעָב
בְּאֶרֶץ כְּנָעַן וְעַתָּה יֵשְׁבוּ־נָא עֲבָדֶיךָ בְּאֶרֶץ גֹּשֶׁן:
ה וַיֹּאמֶר פַּרְעֹה אֶל־יוֹסֵף לֵאמֹר אָבִיךָ וְאַחֶיךָ בָּאוּ
אֵלֶיךָ: אֶרֶץ מִצְרַיִם לְפָנֶיךָ הִוא בְּמֵיטַב הָאָרֶץ
הוֹשֵׁב אֶת־אָבִיךָ וְאֶת־אַחֶיךָ יֵשְׁבוּ בְּאֶרֶץ גֹּשֶׁן וְאִם־
יָדַעְתָּ וְיֶשׁ־בָּם אַנְשֵׁי־חַיִל וְשַׂמְתָּם שָׂרֵי מִקְנֶה עַל־
אֲשֶׁר־לִי: וַיָּבֵא יוֹסֵף אֶת־יַעֲקֹב אָבִיו וַיַּעֲמִדֵהוּ לִפְנֵי
פַרְעֹה וַיְבָרֶךְ יַעֲקֹב אֶת־פַּרְעֹה: וַיֹּאמֶר פַּרְעֹה אֶל־
יַעֲקֹב כַּמָּה יְמֵי שְׁנֵי חַיֶּיךָ: וַיֹּאמֶר יַעֲקֹב אֶל־פַּרְעֹה
יְמֵי שְׁנֵי מְגוּרַי שְׁלֹשִׁים וּמְאַת שָׁנָה מְעַט וְרָעִים הָיוּ
יְמֵי שְׁנֵי חַיַּי וְלֹא הִשִּׂיגוּ אֶת־יְמֵי שְׁנֵי חַיֵּי אֲבֹתַי בִּימֵי

Genesis 47
5–9

land, for there is no pasture for your servants' flocks, the famine being severe in the land of Canaan. Pray, then, let your servants stay in the region of Goshen."
5] Then Pharaoh said to Joseph, "Now that your father and your brothers have come to you,   6] the land of Egypt is open before you; settle your father and your brothers in the best part of the land; let them stay in the region of Goshen. And if you know any capable men among them, put them in charge of my livestock."

7] Joseph then brought his father Jacob and presented him to Pharaoh; and Jacob greeted Pharaoh.   8] Pharaoh asked Jacob, "How many are the years of your life?"   9] And Jacob answered Pharaoh, "The years of my sojourn [on earth] are one hundred and thirty. Few and hard have been the years of my life, nor do they come up to the life-spans of my fathers during their

---

5] *Then Pharaoh said.* This and the following verse are possibly disarranged. The Septuagint reads differently from the Masoretic text.

9] *My sojourn* [on earth]. Literally, "wanderings." Jacob answers Pharaoh's quantitative question qualitatively as well and speaks of the essential tragedy and transitoriness of his years.

מְגוּרֵיהֶם: וַיְבָרֶךְ יַעֲקֹב אֶת־פַּרְעֹה וַיֵּצֵא מִלִּפְנֵי

פַרְעֹה: וַיּוֹשֵׁב יוֹסֵף אֶת־אָבִיו וְאֶת־אֶחָיו וַיִּתֵּן לָהֶם

אֲחֻזָּה בְּאֶרֶץ מִצְרַיִם בְּמֵיטַב הָאָרֶץ בְּאֶרֶץ רַעְמְסֵס

כַּאֲשֶׁר צִוָּה פַרְעֹה: וַיְכַלְכֵּל יוֹסֵף אֶת־אָבִיו וְאֶת־

אֶחָיו וְאֵת כָּל־בֵּית אָבִיו לֶחֶם לְפִי הַטָּף: וְלֶחֶם אֵין

בְּכָל־הָאָרֶץ כִּי־כָבֵד הָרָעָב מְאֹד וַתֵּלַהּ אֶרֶץ מִצְרַיִם

וְאֶרֶץ כְּנַעַן מִפְּנֵי הָרָעָב: וַיְלַקֵּט יוֹסֵף אֶת־כָּל־הַכֶּסֶף

הַנִּמְצָא בְאֶרֶץ־מִצְרַיִם וּבְאֶרֶץ כְּנַעַן בַּשֶּׁבֶר אֲשֶׁר־

הֵם שֹׁבְרִים וַיָּבֵא יוֹסֵף אֶת־הַכֶּסֶף בֵּיתָה פַרְעֹה:

וַיִּתֹּם הַכֶּסֶף מֵאֶרֶץ מִצְרַיִם וּמֵאֶרֶץ כְּנַעַן וַיָּבֹאוּ כָל־

Genesis 47
10–15

sojourns." **10]** Then Jacob bade Pharaoh farewell, and left Pharaoh's presence.

11] So Joseph settled his father and his brothers, giving them holdings in the choicest part of the land of Egypt, in the region of Rameses, as Pharaoh had commanded. **12]** Joseph sustained his father, and his brothers, and all his father's household with food, down to the little ones.

13] Now there was no bread in all the world, for the famine was very severe; both the land of Egypt and the land of Canaan languished because of the famine. **14]** Joseph gathered in all the money that was to be found in the land of Egypt and in the land of Canaan, as payment for the rations that were being procured, and Joseph brought the money into Pharaoh's palace. **15]** And when the money gave out in the land of Egypt and in the land of Canaan, all the Egyptians came to

10] *Bade Pharaoh farewell.* Others translate as "he blessed." Both translations together render the Hebrew best. Compare this with the English "he bid Godspeed."

11] *Region of Rameses.* As Goshen later became known; named for Rameses II, who lived after Jacob.

מִצְרַיִם אֶל־יוֹסֵף לֵאמֹר הָבָה־לָּנוּ לֶחֶם וְלָמָּה נָמוּת

נֶגְדֶּךָ כִּי אָפֵס כָּסֶף: וַיֹּאמֶר יוֹסֵף הָבוּ מִקְנֵיכֶם

וְאֶתְּנָה לָכֶם בְּמִקְנֵיכֶם אִם־אָפֵס כָּסֶף: וַיָּבִיאוּ אֶת־

מִקְנֵיהֶם אֶל־יוֹסֵף וַיִּתֵּן לָהֶם יוֹסֵף לֶחֶם בַּסּוּסִים

וּבְמִקְנֵה הַצֹּאן וּבְמִקְנֵה הַבָּקָר וּבַחֲמֹרִים וַיְנַהֲלֵם

בַּלֶּחֶם בְּכָל־מִקְנֵהֶם בַּשָּׁנָה הַהִוא: וַתִּתֹּם הַשָּׁנָה הַהִוא

וַיָּבֹאוּ אֵלָיו בַּשָּׁנָה הַשֵּׁנִית וַיֹּאמְרוּ לוֹ לֹא־נְכַחֵד

מֵאֲדֹנִי כִּי אִם־תַּם הַכֶּסֶף וּמִקְנֵה הַבְּהֵמָה אֶל־אֲדֹנִי

לֹא נִשְׁאַר לִפְנֵי אֲדֹנִי בִּלְתִּי אִם־גְּוִיָּתֵנוּ וְאַדְמָתֵנוּ:

לָמָּה נָמוּת לְעֵינֶיךָ גַּם־אֲנַחְנוּ גַּם־אַדְמָתֵנוּ קְנֵה־אֹתָנוּ

וְאֶת־אַדְמָתֵנוּ בַּלָּחֶם וְנִהְיֶה אֲנַחְנוּ וְאַדְמָתֵנוּ עֲבָדִים

לְפַרְעֹה וְתֶן־זֶרַע וְנִחְיֶה וְלֹא נָמוּת וְהָאֲדָמָה לֹא תֵשָׁם:

Genesis 47
16–19

Joseph and said, "Give us bread, lest we die before your very eyes; for the money is gone!"   **16]** And Joseph said, "Bring your livestock, and I will sell to you against your livestock, if the money is gone."   **17]** So they brought their livestock to Joseph, and Joseph sold them bread in exchange for horses, for the stocks of sheep and cattle, and for asses; thus he provided them with bread that year in exchange for all their livestock.   **18]** And when that year was ended, they came to him the next year and said to him, "We cannot hide from my lord that, with all the money and animal stocks consigned to my lord, nothing is left at my lord's disposal save our persons and our farm land.   **19]** Let us not perish before your eyes, both we and our land. Take us and our land in exchange for bread, and we with our land will be serfs to Pharaoh; provide the seed, that we may live and not die, and that the land may not become a waste."

17] *Brought their livestock.* Probably not in a literal sense, but by signing over ownership to Pharaoh.

449

וַיִּקֶן יוֹסֵף אֶת־כָּל־אַדְמַת מִצְרַיִם לְפַרְעֹה כִּי־
מָכְרוּ מִצְרַיִם אִישׁ שָׂדֵהוּ כִּי־חָזַק עֲלֵהֶם הָרָעָב
וַתְּהִי הָאָרֶץ לְפַרְעֹה: וְאֶת־הָעָם הֶעֱבִיר אֹתוֹ לֶעָרִים
מִקְצֵה גְבוּל־מִצְרַיִם וְעַד־קָצֵהוּ: רַק אַדְמַת הַכֹּהֲנִים
לֹא קָנָה כִּי חֹק לַכֹּהֲנִים מֵאֵת פַּרְעֹה וְאָכְלוּ אֶת־
חֻקָּם אֲשֶׁר נָתַן לָהֶם פַּרְעֹה עַל־כֵּן לֹא מָכְרוּ אֶת־
אַדְמָתָם: וַיֹּאמֶר יוֹסֵף אֶל־הָעָם הֵן קָנִיתִי אֶתְכֶם
הַיּוֹם וְאֶת־אַדְמַתְכֶם לְפַרְעֹה הֵא־לָכֶם זֶרַע וּזְרַעְתֶּם
אֶת־הָאֲדָמָה: וְהָיָה בַּתְּבוּאֹת וּנְתַתֶּם חֲמִישִׁית לְפַרְעֹה
וְאַרְבַּע הַיָּדֹת יִהְיֶה לָכֶם לְזֶרַע הַשָּׂדֶה וּלְאָכְלְכֶם

20] So Joseph gained possession of all the farm land of Egypt for Pharaoh, every Egyptian having sold his field because the famine was too much for them; thus the land passed over to Pharaoh.   21] And he removed the population town by town, from one end of Egypt's border to the other.   22] Only the land of the priests he did not take over, for the priests had an allotment from Pharaoh, and they lived off the allotment which Pharaoh had made to them; therefore they did not sell their land.

23] Then Joseph said to the people, "Since I have this day acquired you and your land for Pharaoh, here is seed for you to sow the land.   24] And when harvest comes, you shall give one fifth to Pharaoh, and four fifths shall be yours as seed for the fields and as food for you and those in your households, and as nourishment

---

21] *Town by town.* A wholesale removal of the population seems unlikely. הֶעֱבִיר ... לֶעָרִים is obscure. By reading הֶעֱבִיד ... לַעֲבָדִים, we get the likely rendering, "He reduced them to servitude."

22] *An allotment.* In money or kind [5], so they did not have to sell their property. Landed clergy were found among many peoples, in contradistinction to the landless priesthood in Israel.

450

כה וְלַאֲשֶׁר בְּבָתֵּיכֶם וְלֶאֱכֹל לְטַפְּכֶם: וַיֹּאמְרוּ הֶחֱיִתָנוּ
כו נִמְצָא־חֵן בְּעֵינֵי אֲדֹנִי וְהָיִינוּ עֲבָדִים לְפַרְעֹה: וַיָּשֶׂם
אֹתָהּ יוֹסֵף לְחֹק עַד־הַיּוֹם הַזֶּה עַל־אַדְמַת מִצְרַיִם
לְפַרְעֹה לַחֹמֶשׁ רַק אַדְמַת הַכֹּהֲנִים לְבַדָּם לֹא הָיְתָה
כז לְפַרְעֹה: וַיֵּשֶׁב יִשְׂרָאֵל בְּאֶרֶץ מִצְרַיִם בְּאֶרֶץ גֹּשֶׁן
וַיֵּאָחֲזוּ בָהּ וַיִּפְרוּ וַיִּרְבּוּ מְאֹד:

Genesis 47
25–27

Haftarah Vayigash, p. 567

for your children." 25] And they said, "You have saved our lives! If it please my lord, we shall be serfs to Pharaoh." 26] And Joseph made it into a land law in Egypt, which is still valid, that a fifth should be Pharaoh's; only the land of the priests did not become Pharaoh's.

27] Thus Israel settled in the country of Egypt, in the region of Goshen; they acquired holdings in it, and increased greatly in numbers.

The Shepherds

Joseph carefully rehearses his brothers before they speak to Pharaoh and his court. It is obvious that he wants to make certain that his brothers mention their profession, even though "all shepherds are abhorrent to Egyptians" (Gen. 46:34). In essence, what Joseph wants his brothers to convey to Pharaoh is that they are ready to do unpopular labor and that like Joseph they are reliable and will be useful to the ruler. They can, therefore, be trusted with the sensitive border province of Goshen [6].

They subtly emphasize their point by hinting that the land itself is less important to them than who they are and the work they can do. They convey this by repeating the word אֶרֶץ (eretz, land) in three different senses in their carefully phrased statement (Gen. 47:4). Pharaoh understands the implications; he admits the newcomers and at once gives them important supervisory positions. When not long after Joseph's death the rulers (according to some, the Hyksos) were overthrown and a new kingdom was established, a Pharaoh ascended the throne "who did not know Joseph" (Exod. 1:8). He had no use for associates of the previous dynasty and therefore took no time in enslaving them in the very land of Goshen to which they had come to make their home. The experience of Joseph was to be repeated through many centuries of Jewish history: As long as the Jew was useful to the host country, he was tolerated and even elevated; but often when political circumstances changed, he was offered to the masses as a convenient scapegoat.

Later generations, no longer aware of the subtleties and political overtones of Joseph's advice to his brothers, praised him for displaying great character. Even though his family pursued a trade despised by the Egyptians, he was not, they said, ashamed of his kin and insisted that his father and brethren be presented to the Pharaoh precisely for what they were. Joseph, they claimed, was not one to dissemble his background [7].

Political Morality

Because of the careful and unemotional accounting of the disenfranchisement of the Egyptian people and the apparent approval of Joseph's role in it, this section has been made "a show piece of anti-Semitic polemic" [8]. Here is the Bible, it has been said, Jewry's sacred book, and look at the morality that, by its exaltation of Joseph, it obviously endorses [9].[1]

To reach a proper understanding of the text, we must approach it in its own context. Famine and depression endanger any regime, and it may be assumed that the rulers of that time, whether they were Hyksos or not, probably found a great deal of resistance to their policies among those likely to be their most severe critics: the aristocracy and local officials. The governmental loans of which the story speaks were probably made primarily to these groups. When the famine persisted and the rulers called in their pledges, they managed to ruin their chief debtors and antagonists. The Pharaoh did this with the help of a cadre of civil servants who, like Joseph and his clan, had been imported from abroad (see p. 379). The powerful priests were apparently not touched.

The economic and political changes initiated at that time were part of the country's complex economic and political development. "That they should be credited in this narrative to Joseph is part and parcel of his

---

[1] It has been pointed out that a rental payment of one-fifth to the king was, if anything, a *modest* percentage judged by ancient as well as later standards.

Under Syrian rule the Jews paid the king one-third of their seed and one-half of their fruits [10].

idealized historical image. Pharaonic Egypt followed its own due course regardless of ancient visitors or modern moralizers" [11].

To superimpose twentieth-century ideas of social and political morality on this story is, therefore, not helpful. Joseph served Pharaoh in his struggle with the Egyptian hierarchy. In so doing he saved the multitudes from starvation, and apparently this was worth any price to them—including a mortgage on their freedom. And it is altogether possible that they thought little of their freedom anyway. Jewish tradition sensed, long ago, that Joseph's actions might not have met with the same success had the Egyptians valued their liberty more highly. The Bible calls Egypt the "house of bondage" not only because Israel was enslaved there but also because its people accepted their own bondage as a normal condition of life.[2]

[2] However, Joseph's participation in bringing about this condition left later generations with a sense of uneasiness, a trace of which may be found in the way the people of Egypt were treated in biblical literature. Egypt never became a pejorative term like Moab or Edom. One can even detect a vague sense of kinship with the people of Egypt, an affinity most notably expressed by Isaiah (19:25) who envisions God as saying, "Egypt, My people" [12].

GLEANINGS

He Sent Judah to Point the Way (Gen. 46:28)

But the other brothers knew the way! Some say that Judah was really sent לְהוֹרֹת [to teach], that is, to establish a school for the new arrivals. Our father Jacob teaches us that the first thing a Jew must consider in a new dwelling place is facilities for learning.   MIDRASH [13]

Jacob before Pharaoh

I stand before you, Pharaoh, yet I turn
Toward the past, the counting of my days.
Stretched out before my face I see my life,
I see the hungry hills, the well's dusty lips,
The long journeyings; and over-arching all,
Even from first to last of generations spanned,
The God who blessed my way . . .

The moonlight almost spent
Upon the river,
The stars spread far apart—
Jacob, the father, thought into the future:
"My hope is far removed."
The lissome Pharaoh thought:
"My hope is long fulfilled."
Deep silence fell
Upon the two old men who understood
Each other's separate earth and separate heaven.
                    AMY K. BLANK [14]

Joseph the Statesman

Joseph was one of the earliest economic statesmen in history. Apparently he put the farmers on the relief rolls until the drought was over and then gave them back the use of their land in exchange for a very low rent . . . The cry "You cannot regiment nature," while true enough, is the cry of little men lost in primitive superstition. Joseph had a bigger vision than they. He didn't regiment nature but he prepared for the whims of nature.   HENRY A. WALLACE [15]

They Acquired Holdings (Gen. 47:27)

Although the brothers had come to Egypt as sojourners, they now became residents in a land not their own. Had they not acquired holdings and thereby become land-bound, they would not have become slaves.   KELI YEKAR

Joseph's Honesty

And the young man, Joseph, displayed such excessive good faith and honesty in all his dealings that, though the time and the circumstances of the time gave him innumerable opportunities of making money so that he might, in a short period, have become the richest man of that age or kingdom, he still so truly honoured genuine riches before illegitimate wealth, and the treasure which sees rather than that which is blind, that he stored up all the silver and gold which he collected as the price of the corn in the king's treasury, not appropriating a single drachm of it to his own use, but being satisfied with nothing beyond the gifts which the king bestowed on him voluntarily in acknowledgment of his services.   PHILO [16]

The Blessing of Ephraim
and Manasseh

This section concentrates on the special blessings given to two of Jacob's grandsons. It is a subtle replay of the blessings given by Isaac: Jacob, too, cannot see, but unlike his father he gives his preferential blessing to the younger child consciously. As in his own case, the theme of the younger brother taking precedence over the older reappears.

In reading this highly emotional and poetically graceful account, we must remember that the ancients saw in Ephraim and Manasseh more than long-departed primal ancestors. For when these stories were told and retold in the days of settlement in Canaan, both narrator and listener must have related Jacob's blessing to the circumstances of their own day, when the tribe of Ephraim enjoyed numerical and economic superiority over Manasseh. We may be sure that many Israelites of that time believed the comparative strength of the two tribes within the tribal confederation to be directly related to Jacob's blessing.

כח וַיְחִי יַעֲקֹב בְּאֶרֶץ מִצְרַיִם שְׁבַע עֶשְׂרֵה שָׁנָה וַיְהִי יְמֵי־
יַעֲקֹב שְׁנֵי חַיָּיו שֶׁבַע שָׁנִים וְאַרְבָּעִים וּמְאַת שָׁנָה:
כט וַיִּקְרְבוּ יְמֵי־יִשְׂרָאֵל לָמוּת וַיִּקְרָא לִבְנוֹ לְיוֹסֵף וַיֹּאמֶר
לוֹ אִם־נָא מָצָאתִי חֵן בְּעֵינֶיךָ שִׂים־נָא יָדְךָ תַּחַת
יְרֵכִי וְעָשִׂיתָ עִמָּדִי חֶסֶד וֶאֱמֶת אַל־נָא תִקְבְּרֵנִי
ל בְּמִצְרָיִם: וְשָׁכַבְתִּי עִם־אֲבֹתַי וּנְשָׂאתַנִי מִמִּצְרַיִם
וּקְבַרְתַּנִי בִּקְבֻרָתָם וַיֹּאמַר אָנֹכִי אֶעֱשֶׂה כִדְבָרֶךָ:
לא וַיֹּאמֶר הִשָּׁבְעָה לִי וַיִּשָּׁבַע לוֹ וַיִּשְׁתַּחוּ יִשְׂרָאֵל עַל־
רֹאשׁ הַמִּטָּה: פ

Genesis 47

28–31

28] Jacob lived seventeen years in the land of Egypt, so that the span of Jacob's life came to one hundred and forty-seven years.   **29]** And when the time approached for Israel to die, he summoned his son Joseph and said to him, "If you would please me, place your hand under my thigh as a pledge of your steadfast loyalty: pray do not bury me in Egypt.   **30]** When I lie down with my fathers, take me up from Egypt and bury me in their burial-place." And he said, "I will do as you have spoken."   **31]** And he said, "Swear to me." And he swore to him. Then Israel bowed at the head of the bed.

47:28] *Seventeen years.* The figure corresponds to the first seventeen years of Joseph's life, which Jacob had enjoyed with his son.
/As Jacob sustained Joseph for seventeen years, so now Joseph sustains Jacob for the same length of time [1]./
    One hundred and forty-seven. On the schematic nature of this figure (3×7^2), see p. 241.

29] *Under my thigh.* To stress the importance of the oath (see Gen. 24:2). Jacob knew that carrying a body to Canaan would be a matter of considerable difficulty (even today internment in another country is a complicated matter). Jacob also knew

that such an act could conceivably cast some doubt on Joseph's full identification with and loyalty to Egypt. By making his son take an oath, Jacob made it possible for Joseph to say to Pharaoh: "My father made me swear" (see Gen. 50:4–6) [2].
    Steadfast loyalty. חֶסֶד וֶאֱמֶת (*chesed ve-emet*); today often the name for a free burial society.

30] *Burial-place.* Machpelah (see Gen. 23:17–20).

31] *Israel bowed.* A gesture of gratitude; but it is not clear whether he bowed to God [3] or to Joseph [4].
/"The *Shechinah* appears at the head of a sick per-

א וַיְהִי אַחֲרֵי הַדְּבָרִים הָאֵלֶּה וַיֹּאמֶר לְיוֹסֵף הִנֵּה אָבִיךָ חֹלֶה וַיִּקַּח אֶת־שְׁנֵי בָנָיו עִמּוֹ אֶת־מְנַשֶּׁה וְאֶת־

ב אֶפְרָיִם: וַיַּגֵּד לְיַעֲקֹב וַיֹּאמֶר הִנֵּה בִּנְךָ יוֹסֵף בָּא

ג אֵלֶיךָ וַיִּתְחַזֵּק יִשְׂרָאֵל וַיֵּשֶׁב עַל־הַמִּטָּה: וַיֹּאמֶר יַעֲקֹב אֶל־יוֹסֵף אֵל שַׁדַּי נִרְאָה־אֵלַי בְּלוּז בְּאֶרֶץ כְּנָעַן

ד וַיְבָרֶךְ אֹתִי: וַיֹּאמֶר אֵלַי הִנְנִי מַפְרְךָ וְהִרְבִּיתִךָ וּנְתַתִּיךָ לִקְהַל עַמִּים וְנָתַתִּי אֶת־הָאָרֶץ הַזֹּאת לְזַרְעֲךָ

ה אַחֲרֶיךָ אֲחֻזַּת עוֹלָם: וְעַתָּה שְׁנֵי־בָנֶיךָ הַנּוֹלָדִים לְךָ בְּאֶרֶץ מִצְרַיִם עַד־בֹּאִי אֵלֶיךָ מִצְרַיְמָה לִי־הֵם

ו אֶפְרַיִם וּמְנַשֶּׁה כִּרְאוּבֵן וְשִׁמְעוֹן יִהְיוּ־לִי: וּמוֹלַדְתְּךָ אֲשֶׁר־הוֹלַדְתָּ אַחֲרֵיהֶם לְךָ יִהְיוּ עַל שֵׁם אֲחֵיהֶם

Genesis 48
1–6

1] Some time afterward, Joseph was told, "Your father is ill." So he took with him his two sons, Manasseh and Ephraim.   2] When Jacob was told, "Your son Joseph has come to see you," Israel summoned his strength and sat up in bed.

3] And Jacob said to Joseph, "El Shaddai appeared to me at Luz in the land of Canaan, and He blessed me,   4] and said to me, 'I will make you fertile and numerous, making of you a community of peoples; and I will give this land to your offspring to come for an everlasting possession.'   5] Now, your two sons, who were born to you in the land of Egypt before I came to you in Egypt, shall be mine; Ephraim and Manasseh shall be mine no less than Reuben and Simeon.   6] But progeny born to you after them shall be yours; they shall be recorded instead of

son" [5]. The Septuagint appears to read מַטֶּה (staff) instead of מִטָּה (bed) [6]./

48:5] *Shall be mine*. Jacob here adopts the two boys in a formal way, by placing them on his

knees (verse 12). They now are like his own sons, hence Ephraim and Manasseh are reckoned among the tribes with Jacob's other sons.

6] *Instead*. Literally, "by the name"

ז יִקָּרְאוּ בְּנַחֲלָתָם: וַאֲנִי בְּבֹאִי מִפַּדָּן מֵתָה עָלַי רָחֵל בְּאֶרֶץ כְּנַעַן בַּדֶּרֶךְ בְּעוֹד כִּבְרַת־אֶרֶץ לָבֹא אֶפְרָתָה

ח וָאֶקְבְּרֶהָ שָּׁם בְּדֶרֶךְ אֶפְרָת הִוא בֵּית לָחֶם: וַיַּרְא

ט יִשְׂרָאֵל אֶת־בְּנֵי יוֹסֵף וַיֹּאמֶר מִי־אֵלֶּה: וַיֹּאמֶר יוֹסֵף אֶל־אָבִיו בָּנַי הֵם אֲשֶׁר־נָתַן־לִי אֱלֹהִים בָּזֶה וַיֹּאמַר

י קָחֶם־נָא אֵלַי וַאֲבָרְכֵם: וְעֵינֵי יִשְׂרָאֵל כָּבְדוּ מִזֹּקֶן לֹא יוּכַל לִרְאוֹת וַיַּגֵּשׁ אֹתָם אֵלָיו וַיִּשַּׁק לָהֶם וַיְחַבֵּק

יא לָהֶם: וַיֹּאמֶר יִשְׂרָאֵל אֶל־יוֹסֵף רְאֹה פָנֶיךָ לֹא פִלָּלְתִּי וְהִנֵּה הֶרְאָה אֹתִי אֱלֹהִים גַּם אֶת־זַרְעֶךָ:

יב וַיּוֹצֵא יוֹסֵף אֹתָם מֵעִם בִּרְכָּיו וַיִּשְׁתַּחוּ לְאַפָּיו אָרְצָה:

Genesis 48

7–12

their brothers in their inheritance.   **7]** I [do this because], when I was returning from Paddan, Rachel died, to my sorrow, while I was journeying in the land of Canaan, when still some distance short of Ephrath; and I buried her there on the road to Ephrath"—now Bethlehem.

8] Noticing Joseph's sons, Israel asked, "Who are these?"   **9]** And Joseph said to his father, "They are my sons, whom God has given me here." "Bring them up to me," he said, "that I may bless them."   **10]** Now Israel's eyes were dim with age; he could not see. So [Joseph] brought them close to him, and he kissed them and embraced them.   **11]** And Israel said to Joseph, "I never expected to see you again, and here God has let me see your children as well."

12] Joseph then removed them from his knees, and bowed low with his face to

---

7] *Paddan.* Short for Paddan-aram. The reason for this verse is much disputed [7]. It is perhaps an aside: "I am doing this for you, Rachel, since your early death prevented you from bearing more children."

9] *Bless them.* The expression could also mean, "place them on my knees," a gesture of adoption.

יג וַיִּקַּח יוֹסֵף אֶת־שְׁנֵיהֶם אֶת־אֶפְרַיִם בִּימִינוֹ מִשְּׂמֹאל
יִשְׂרָאֵל וְאֶת־מְנַשֶּׁה בִשְׂמֹאלוֹ מִימִין יִשְׂרָאֵל וַיַּגֵּשׁ
יד אֵלָיו: וַיִּשְׁלַח יִשְׂרָאֵל אֶת־יְמִינוֹ וַיָּשֶׁת עַל־רֹאשׁ
אֶפְרַיִם וְהוּא הַצָּעִיר וְאֶת־שְׂמֹאלוֹ עַל־רֹאשׁ מְנַשֶּׁה
טו שִׂכֵּל אֶת־יָדָיו כִּי מְנַשֶּׁה הַבְּכוֹר: וַיְבָרֶךְ אֶת־יוֹסֵף
וַיֹּאמַר הָאֱלֹהִים אֲשֶׁר הִתְהַלְּכוּ אֲבֹתַי לְפָנָיו אַבְרָהָם
וְיִצְחָק הָאֱלֹהִים הָרֹעֶה אֹתִי מֵעוֹדִי עַד־הַיּוֹם הַזֶּה:
טז הַמַּלְאָךְ הַגֹּאֵל אֹתִי מִכָּל־רָע יְבָרֵךְ אֶת־הַנְּעָרִים
וְיִקָּרֵא בָהֶם שְׁמִי וְשֵׁם אֲבֹתַי אַבְרָהָם וְיִצְחָק וְיִדְגּוּ
יז לָרֹב בְּקֶרֶב הָאָרֶץ: וַיַּרְא יוֹסֵף כִּי־יָשִׁית אָבִיו יַד־

the ground.   13] Joseph took the two of them, Ephraim with his right hand—to Israel's left—and Manasseh with his left hand—to Israel's right—and brought them close to him.   14] But Israel stretched out his right hand and laid it on Ephraim's head, though he was the younger, and his left hand on Manasseh's head—thus crossing his hands—although Manasseh was the first-born.   15] And he blessed Joseph, saying, "The God in whose ways my fathers Abraham and Isaac walked, / The God who has been my shepherd from my birth to this day— / 16] The Angel who has redeemed me from all harm— / Bless the lads. / In them may my name be recalled, / And the names of my fathers Abraham and Isaac, / And may they be teeming multitudes upon the earth."

17] When Joseph saw that his father was placing his right hand on Ephraim's

14] *Crossing his hands.* A subtle word play in Hebrew, for the same word can also mean to act wisely, and the like-sounding סִכֵּל means to act foolishly [8]. Later Torah law prohibited such preference of the younger son (Deut. 21:15–17).

16] *The Angel.* In this moment, when past and future blend into one, Jacob recalls his dream at Bethel, when angels symbolized God's everlasting protection.

17] *He thought it wrong.* Knowing that deathbed

יְמִינוֹ עַל־רֹאשׁ אֶפְרַיִם וַיֵּרַע בְּעֵינָיו וַיִּתְמֹךְ יַד־אָבִיו לְהָסִיר אֹתָהּ מֵעַל רֹאשׁ־אֶפְרַיִם עַל־רֹאשׁ מְנַשֶּׁה:

יח וַיֹּאמֶר יוֹסֵף אֶל־אָבִיו לֹא־כֵן אָבִי כִּי־זֶה הַבְּכֹר

יט שִׂים יְמִינְךָ עַל־רֹאשׁוֹ: וַיְמָאֵן אָבִיו וַיֹּאמֶר יָדַעְתִּי בְנִי יָדַעְתִּי גַּם־הוּא יִהְיֶה־לְּעָם וְגַם־הוּא יִגְדָּל וְאוּלָם אָחִיו הַקָּטֹן יִגְדַּל מִמֶּנּוּ וְזַרְעוֹ יִהְיֶה מְלֹא־הַגּוֹיִם:

כ וַיְבָרֲכֵם בַּיּוֹם הַהוּא לֵאמוֹר בְּךָ יְבָרֵךְ יִשְׂרָאֵל לֵאמֹר יְשִׂמְךָ אֱלֹהִים כְּאֶפְרַיִם וְכִמְנַשֶּׁה וַיָּשֶׂם אֶת־אֶפְרַיִם לִפְנֵי מְנַשֶּׁה:

כא וַיֹּאמֶר יִשְׂרָאֵל אֶל־יוֹסֵף הִנֵּה אָנֹכִי מֵת וְהָיָה אֱלֹהִים עִמָּכֶם וְהֵשִׁיב אֶתְכֶם אֶל־

Genesis 48

18–21

head, he thought it wrong; so he took hold of his father's hand to move it from Ephraim's head to Manasseh's. 18] "Not so, Father," Joseph said to his father, "for the other is the first-born; place your right hand on his head." 19] But his father objected, saying, "I know, my son, I know. He too shall become a people, and he too shall be great. Yet his younger brother shall be greater than he, and his offspring shall be plentiful enough for nations." 20] So he blessed them that day, saying, "By you shall Israel invoke blessings, saying: God make you like Ephraim and Manasseh." Thus he put Ephraim before Manasseh.

21] Then Israel said to Joseph, "I am about to die; but God will be with you and

blessings were irrevocable, Joseph tries to stop Jacob before he comes to the specific blessings for the two sons. In most cultures the right hand takes linguistic and emotional preference over the left, e.g., in English "right" also means just; while "left" has negative meanings (left-handed, gauche; the word sinister comes from the Latin word for "left").

20] *By you shall Israel invoke blessings.* Jacob here uses his other name to foreshadow the future. "The veil parts, the nation Israel appears before the breaking view of the old man" [9]. Jacob's words are the traditional formula with which a Jewish father blesses his sons on Sabbath eve.

bring you back to the land of your fathers.   **22]** And now, I give you one portion more than to your brothers, which I wrested from the Amorites with my sword and bow."

22] *One portion.* שְׁכֶם (shechem); the meaning is uncertain. Some scholars maintain that this refers to the mountain slope of Shechem and that it is here deeded to Joseph as a burial place [10].

Wrested. In no other place has Jacob been portrayed as a military person. This notation is, therefore, either a remnant of another tradition [11] or "bow and sword" may be an idiom for "through my own labor," a reference to Jacob's purchase of property at Shechem with hard-earned money (Gen. 33:19) [12].

/The Midrash says that prayer was Jacob's bow and sword [13]. Another view is that bow and sword were *mitzvot* and good deeds [14]./

The Blessing

Every blessing bestowed by man is at the core a prayer, since it asks God to help him accomplish what he by himself cannot. Yet the blessing is more than prayer, for it assigns a decisive role to the one who pronounces it. Placing his hands in the solemn act, the Patriarch sees himself as God's co-worker and as an essential link between the generations. Man cannot take God's place; but neither can God take the place of parents and grandparents in the shaping of the children's future.

Jacob's blessing has often served as a classic example of prayer: It begins with adoration, it proceeds to thanksgiving, and only then turns to the petition. Jacob speaks of the God of his fathers; this is his link with the past. God is his Lord because of tradition—but not only because of tradition. He is his God also through personal experience and relationship. This remains the basic nature of Jewish worship: God is approached as the God of history, especially Jewish history, but beyond that each generation has to rediscover for itself the God who was the God of the Fathers.[1]

Jacob sees his life spread before him. He is aware of the continued presence of God and acknowledges it with deep feeling. Past and future are now fused. He knows in this moment that his own complex life is crowned with hope, a hope that is represented by the God of his fathers and by the two boys at his side. His life is completed; the blessing of Abraham, which Isaac had bestowed on him, has now passed down to his children's children.

---

[1] This is the traditional interpretation given to the beginning of the Eighteen Benedictions: "Praised be Thou, O Lord, our God [i.e., of the present] and God of our Fathers [i.e., of the past], God of Abraham, God of Isaac, and God of Jacob [i.e., of each generation separately] . . ."

GLEANINGS

Respect

Why does the *sidrah* start with verse 28 when it would have been more logical to start with verse 27? The reason is that in that case the previous *sidrah* would have concluded with Gen. 47:26 which speaks of the Egyptians surrendering their land to Pharaoh. Our congregations did not want to conclude that *sidrah* with the plight of the Egyptians. RALBAG

Jacob Lived (Gen. 47:28)

Of how few men can we repeat a phrase like "Jacob *lived*"? When a man dies, a death notice appears in the press. In reality, it is a life notice; because but for it the world would never have known that the man had ever been alive. Only he who has been a force for human goodness can be said to have *lived*. JOSEPH H. HERTZ

[The Romans also said *vixit* (he has lived) in reporting the death of a prominent man.]

Visiting the Sick

It is written that Joseph took his two sons to see Jacob when he heard that his father was ill. From this we learn the *mitzvah* of visiting the sick. MIDRASH [15]

Deathbed Testament

The words of a dying man are as binding as a deed which is written and delivered.

TALMUD [16]

The End of Days

Why should Jacob have wanted to reveal the date of the end of days to his sons?

Because exile is easier to bear if one knows in advance when it will end. But God wanted Israel's exile to be difficult, and therefore He closed Jacob's vision from him so that the Children of Israel should not learn the date of their final redemption.

R. SIMCHAH BUNAM [17]

"And He Blessed Joseph" (Gen. 48:15)

The blessing that follows was actually addressed not to Joseph but only to Joseph's two sons. Why, then, does Scripture say that Jacob blessed Joseph?

In order to show that there is no greater blessing for a father than the wish that his children should take after him and become good people. Hence Jacob's blessing to Manasseh and Ephraim "The angel who has redeemed me from all evil, bless the lads and let my name be named in them and the name of my fathers, Abraham and Isaac" (verse 16) is the greatest blessing Joseph, their father, could possibly have received.

R. ISAIAH HOROWITZ [18]

Jacob's Testament

Jacob's final words to his assembled sons are a combination of prayer, blessing, curse, warning, psychological assessment, parable, recollection, and hope.[1] They are presented in poetic form; and like much other poetry, ancient and modern, their meaning is not always readily accessible.

Traditional commentators have looked at the testament as a prophetic utterance pronounced by the dying forefather (see note to Gen. 49:1). It is more likely, however, that the testament is a collection of old tribal songs and memories, which were welded into a poem and then incorporated into the life story of Jacob. Historical references suggest that the chapter as it stands now was written during the period of the Judges, or some time before the year 1000 B.C.E., at a time when the tribes were already in Canaan, although not yet a nation, when differences were still keenly felt and old animosities were not yet forgotten.[2]

It was a time when the tribe of Levi fell far short of the position of priestly importance that the blessing of Moses (Deut. 33) assigned to it and when the tribe of Simeon (not named in Deuteronomy and later absorbed into the tribe of Judah) was still worthy of mention [3]. The

---

[1] For a full comparison with the blessing of Moses, see Deut. 33. The testament of Jacob may also be considered in the light of the recurrent patterns of blessings and curses in Genesis (1:28; 3:14; 9:12–17, 25; 12:1–3; 14:19; 24:60; 27:27, 39; 48:16, 20) [1].

[2] Some scholars believe that the twelve sons here represent the signs of the zodiac. Others say that they reveal traces of totemism, a social system based on belief in kinship with animals (or plants), for many of the tribes are here compared to animals [2].

reader might also compare this testament with the song of Deborah (Judg. 5), which comes from about the same general epoch, although it deals with a special military constellation rather than a general view of the tribal confederacy.

וַיִּקְרָא יַעֲקֹב אֶל־בָּנָיו וַיֹּאמֶר הֵאָסְפוּ וְאַגִּידָה לָכֶם א

אֵת אֲשֶׁר־יִקְרָא אֶתְכֶם בְּאַחֲרִית הַיָּמִים: הִקָּבְצוּ ב

וְשִׁמְעוּ בְּנֵי יַעֲקֹב וְשִׁמְעוּ אֶל־יִשְׂרָאֵל אֲבִיכֶם: רְאוּבֵן ג

בְּכֹרִי אַתָּה כֹּחִי וְרֵאשִׁית אוֹנִי יֶתֶר שְׂאֵת וְיֶתֶר עָז:

פַּחַז כַּמַּיִם אַל־תּוֹתַר כִּי עָלִיתָ מִשְׁכְּבֵי אָבִיךָ אָז ד

חִלַּלְתָּ יְצוּעִי עָלָה: פ

שִׁמְעוֹן וְלֵוִי אַחִים כְּלֵי חָמָס מְכֵרֹתֵיהֶם: בְּסֹדָם אַל־ ה ו

תָּבֹא נַפְשִׁי בִּקְהָלָם אַל־תֵּחַד כְּבֹדִי כִּי בְאַפָּם הָרְגוּ

Genesis 49

1–6

1] And Jacob called his sons and said, "Come together that I may tell you what is to befall you in days to come.

2] Assemble and hearken, O sons of Jacob; / Hearken to Israel your father:

3] Reuben, you are my first-born, / My might and first fruit of my vigor, / Exceeding in rank / And exceeding in honor. / **4]** Unstable as water, you shall excel no longer; / For when you mounted your father's bed, / You brought disgrace—my couch he mounted!

5] Simeon and Levi are a pair; / Their weapons are tools of lawlessness. / **6]** Let not my person enter their council; / Or my being be joined to their company. /

49:1] *In days to come.* Not a reference to messianic days as older translations ("In the end of days") suggest [4].

4] *Your father's bed.* Reuben had cohabited with Jacob's concubine (Gen. 35:22).

My couch he mounted! An aside to himself or to the assembled children to explain why Reuben will no longer enjoy the rights of the first-born [5].

/In the song of Deborah, Reuben is chastised for egotism and lack of cooperation; the blessing of Moses voices fear that the tribe may disappear altogether (Judg. 5:16 and Deut. 33:6, respectively), as in fact it did under the monarchy when Moab occupied the Trans-Jordanian territory of Reuben./

5] *A pair.* אַחִים (*achim*), literally, "brothers," here meaning "two of a kind" [6].

Weapons. The Hebrew is obscure [7].

6] *My being.* That is, "what I represent." Jacob had no part in their violence at Shechem and does not want his name connected with what the two sons might do in the future.

They maim oxen. Delighting in cruelty and senseless, wanton destruction.

/Redak, however, gives the verse a different sense by

אִישׁ וּבִרְצֹנָם עִקְּרוּ־שׁוֹר: אָרוּר אַפָּם כִּי עָז וְעֶבְרָתָם

כִּי קָשָׁתָה אֲחַלְּקֵם בְּיַעֲקֹב וַאֲפִיצֵם בְּיִשְׂרָאֵל: פ

יְהוּדָה אַתָּה יוֹדוּךָ אַחֶיךָ יָדְךָ בְּעֹרֶף אֹיְבֶיךָ יִשְׁתַּחֲווּ

לְךָ בְּנֵי אָבִיךָ: גּוּר אַרְיֵה יְהוּדָה מִטֶּרֶף בְּנִי עָלִיתָ

כָּרַע רָבַץ כְּאַרְיֵה וּכְלָבִיא מִי יְקִימֶנּוּ: לֹא־יָסוּר

שֵׁבֶט מִיהוּדָה וּמְחֹקֵק מִבֵּין רַגְלָיו עַד כִּי־יָבֹא שִׁילֹה

וְלוֹ יִקְּהַת עַמִּים: אֹסְרִי לַגֶּפֶן עִירֹה וְלַשֹּׂרֵקָה בְּנִי

* יא עירו קרי.

For when angry they slay men, / And when pleased they maim oxen. / **7]** Cursed be their anger so fierce, / And their wrath so relentless. / I will divide them in Jacob, / Scatter them in Israel.

8] You, O Judah, your brothers shall praise; / Your hand shall be on the nape of your foes; / Your father's sons shall bow low to you. / **9]** Judah is a lion's whelp; / On prey, my son, have you grown. / He crouches, lies down like a lion, / Like the king of beasts—who dare rouse him? / **10]** The scepter shall not depart from Judah, / Nor the ruler's staff from between his feet; / So that tribute shall come to him / And the homage of peoples be his. / **11]** He tethers his ass to a vine, / His ass's foal

taking "ox" (שׁוֹר) as figurative for Hamor, son of Shechem. This would then refer to the Dinah incident and provide a parallel with the first half of the verse./

9] *Lion's whelp.* In Deut. 33:22, Dan is given this ascription.

10] *Tribute shall come to him.* עַד כִּי־יָבֹא שִׁילֹה, literally, "until he comes to Shiloh," or "until Shiloh comes." The Hebrew is obscure; the above translation reads the text as if it were שַׁי לוֹ (שַׁי meaning "tribute" and לֹה, an alternate form for לוֹ, meaning "to him") [8].

Shiloh was an important religious center and pre-Jerusalem sanctuary located in the territory of Ephraim. One Jewish tradition, taking Jacob's blessing to be a prophecy for the end of time (see verse 1), interpreted "Shiloh" to mean the Messiah, a new David who would come out of the house of Judah [9]. Christianity expanded this interpretation into a direct reference to Jesus, especially since verse 11 alludes to the ruler riding an ass, as Jesus did when he entered Jerusalem [10]. If we abide by the Masoretic text it may be best to interpret: "Until Judah will come to worship at Shiloh," that is, "until the northern and southern kingdoms will be reunited."

יב אָתְנוֹ כִּבֵּס בַּיַּיִן לְבֻשׁוֹ וּבְדַם־עֲנָבִים סוּתֹה:* חַכְלִילִי
עֵינַיִם מִיָּיִן וּלְבֶן־שִׁנַּיִם מֵחָלָב: פ

יג זְבוּלֻן לְחוֹף יַמִּים יִשְׁכֹּן וְהוּא לְחוֹף אֳנִיֹּת וְיַרְכָתוֹ
עַל־צִידֹן: פ

יד יִשָּׂשכָר חֲמֹר גָּרֶם רֹבֵץ בֵּין הַמִּשְׁפְּתָיִם: וַיַּרְא מְנֻחָה
טו כִּי טוֹב וְאֶת־הָאָרֶץ כִּי נָעֵמָה וַיֵּט שִׁכְמוֹ לִסְבֹּל וַיְהִי
לְמַס־עֹבֵד: ס טז דָּן יָדִין עַמּוֹ כְּאַחַד שִׁבְטֵי יִשְׂרָאֵל:

יז יְהִי־דָן נָחָשׁ עֲלֵי־דֶרֶךְ שְׁפִיפֹן עֲלֵי־אֹרַח הַנֹּשֵׁךְ עִקְּבֵי־
סוּס וַיִּפֹּל רֹכְבוֹ אָחוֹר:

Genesis 49
12–17

* יא סוּתֹה קרי.

---

to a choice vine; / He washes his garment in wine, / His robe in blood of grapes. / **12]** His eyes are darker than wine; / His teeth are whiter than milk.

13] Zebulun shall dwell by the seashore; / He shall be a haven for ships, / And his flank shall rest on Sidon.

14] Issachar is a strong-boned ass, / Crouching between the saddlebags. / **15]** When he saw how good was security, / And how pleasant was the country, / He bent his shoulder to the burden, / And became a toiling serf.

16] Dan shall govern his people, / At one with the tribes of Israel. / **17]** Dan shall be a serpent by the road, / A viper by the path / That bites the horse's heels / So that his rider is thrown backward.

12] *Darker than wine.* Or "dark from wine."
Whiter than milk. Or "white from milk." Judah is to have such abundance that he can even afford to wash his clothes in wine (we would say, bathe in champagne) and to tie his ass to a vine (ordinarily not done because the animal would consume it).

13] *By the seashore.* In this poem Zebulon's territory is seen situated on the coast, from today's Haifa northward into Lebanon, a picture contrary to all other (and probably later) attestation (cf. Josh. 19:10–16).

15] *Toiling serf.* A castigation of the tribe. At the time of the Judges it had apparently traded freedom for comfort and was subjected by the Canaanites.

16] *Dan shall govern.* A word play or possibly a

לִישׁוּעָתְךָ קִוִּיתִי יְהוָֹה: ס

יט גָּד גְּדוּד יְגוּדֶנּוּ וְהוּא יָגֻד עָקֵב: ס כ מֵאָשֵׁר שְׁמֵנָה

כא לַחְמוֹ וְהוּא יִתֵּן מַעֲדַנֵּי־מֶלֶךְ: ס נַפְתָּלִי אַיָּלָה

כב שְׁלֻחָה הַנֹּתֵן אִמְרֵי־שָׁפֶר: ס בֵּן פֹּרָת יוֹסֵף בֵּן

כג פֹּרָת עֲלֵי־עָיִן בָּנוֹת צָעֲדָה עֲלֵי־שׁוּר: וַיְמָרֲרֻהוּ וָרֹבּוּ

כד וַיִּשְׂטְמֻהוּ בַּעֲלֵי חִצִּים: וַתֵּשֶׁב בְּאֵיתָן קַשְׁתּוֹ וַיָּפֹזּוּ

זְרֹעֵי יָדָיו מִידֵי אֲבִיר יַעֲקֹב מִשָּׁם רֹעֶה אֶבֶן יִשְׂרָאֵל:

כה מֵאֵל אָבִיךָ וְיַעְזְרֶךָ וְאֵת שַׁדַּי וִיבָרֲכֶךָ בִּרְכֹת שָׁמַיִם

Genesis 49
18–25

18] I wait for Your deliverance, O LORD!

19] Gad shall be raided by raiders, / But he shall raid at their heels.

20] Asher's bread shall be rich, / And he shall yield royal dainties.

21] Naphtali is a hind let loose, / Which yields lovely fawns.

22] Joseph is a wild ass, / A wild ass by a spring / —Wild colts on a hillside. / 23] Archers bitterly assailed him; / They shot at him and harried him. / 24] Yet his bow stayed taut, / And his arms were made firm / By the hands of the Mighty One of Jacob— / There, the Shepherd, the Rock of Israel— / 25] The God of your father who helps you, / And Shaddai who blesses you / With blessings of heaven

reference to the Danite Samson and his rule [11]. In the early days of settlement Dan's territory was southeast of modern Tel Aviv but was later in northern Galilee; hence the expression, "From Dan to Beer-sheba."

18] *I wait.* Another aside.
/ Many other explanations have been offered, e.g., "For your salvation [O Dan] I trust in the Lord" [12]./

19] *Raided.* A quadruple word play in Hebrew on "Gad" and "raid," in praise of the tribe's bravery.

20] *Yield.* Produce and export to the neighboring Phoenicians.

21] *A hind let loose.* The simile expresses the feelings of exhilaration bred by the spaciousness of Upper Galilee [13].

22] *Joseph is a wild ass.* Others render as "Joseph is a fruitful bough, a fruitful bough by a spring, its branches run over a wall." The simile from the animal world is more in consonance with the rest of the poem [14].

24] *His bow stayed taut.* Making him able to withstand the onslaughts of other men's designs—those of his brothers, of Potiphar's wife, and presumably of enemies at court.

מֵעַל בִּרְכֹת תְּהוֹם רֹבֶצֶת תָּחַת בִּרְכֹת שָׁדַיִם וָרָחַם:

כו בִּרְכֹת אָבִיךָ גָּבְרוּ עַל־בִּרְכֹת הוֹרַי עַד־תַּאֲוַת גִּבְעֹת עוֹלָם תִּהְיֶיןָ לְרֹאשׁ יוֹסֵף וּלְקָדְקֹד נְזִיר אֶחָיו: פ

כז בִּנְיָמִין זְאֵב יִטְרָף בַּבֹּקֶר יֹאכַל עַד וְלָעֶרֶב יְחַלֵּק שָׁלָל:

above, / Blessings of the deep that couches below, / Blessings of the breast and womb. / 26] The blessings of your father / Surpass the blessings of my ancestors, / To the utmost bounds of the eternal hills. / May they rest on the head of Joseph, / On the brow of the elect of his brothers.

27] Benjamin is a ravenous wolf; / In the morning he consumes the foe, / And in the evening he divides the spoil."

/Some old commentators believe the expression to be a circumlocution for sexual temptation [15]./

His arms. Or "the sinews of his hands" [16].

26] *Surpass.* The first half of the verse is obscure.

27] *Ravenous wolf.* Benjamin's warlike temperament is here characterized. Two famous warriors, Ehud the Judge and Saul the King, were of this tribe.

Foe. Others translate as "booty."

The Vision of Jacob

If we look at Jacob's testament as a picture of the Israelites at the time of the Judges, as biblical scholars are generally wont to do, we recognize twelve tribes as different from each other as twelve sons could be. Their temperaments vary widely, from the war-loving Benjamin to the security-loving Issachar; from the morally unstable Reuben to the self-disciplined Joseph; from the violent natures of Simeon and Levi to the calm judgment of Judah. It is obvious that the tribes are still in a state of ferment, and it is equally remarkable that they seemingly have little cohesion. What unites them is not a sense of national purpose or identity; neither is in evidence. If anything binds them, it is their sense of common ancestry and the memory of an old covenant.

We would not do justice to the poem, however, were we to examine it only as a characterization of the twelve tribes at a certain point in later history. The poem also serves as a climax to the Book of Genesis and as an echo of its underlying purpose. Genesis follows one basic theme: God's guidance of His world and His special love of and promise to Abraham and his seed. Now the book comes to a close, and the next act in the great drama is about to open. The testament is to be seen as a bridge between the past and the future, and both are beheld through the eyes of Jacob.

Jacob's has not been a happy life and he cannot but reflect on his deep disappointments over his three oldest sons. Yet now, as death nears, a better future rises before his inner eye. This future is tied to Judah and Joseph, and these two he addresses directly (the others, with the exception of the first-born Reuben, are only spoken about).

Joseph has always had the deep affection of his father, whose grateful words pronounce praise and blessing and form a fitting summary of the life of his great son. The ultimate focus, however, is on Judah. It is through him that God's mysterious designs will be carried on. When the poem turns to Judah it turns resolutely to the future. It may not, in its enigmatic Shiloh passage, speak of the end of time, but it does reach into days to come. At whatever period these stanzas were composed, they looked forward in the sense of prophecy, and in the light of history the prophecy turned out to be remarkably accurate. It was Judah's tribe that survived destruction and deportation by the Babylonians (586 B.C.E.) and that provided continuity for the children of Israel. It was from Judah that the Jew took his name.

Thus Genesis concludes with a vision that looks to "the eternal hills" (Gen. 49:26). Perhaps the words that are now verse 18 and stand near the middle of the testament once formed the poem's concluding line and summary: "I wait for Your deliverance, O Lord!"

GLEANINGS

Joseph

Joseph is the ideal manifested, as the union of darkness and light, feeling and mind, the primitive and the civilized, wisdom and the happy heart—in short as the humanized mystery we call man.

THOMAS MANN [17]

The Man of Faith

[The Koran devotes an entire Sura to Joseph (Yusuf). It elaborates on the biblical tale and puts Mohammed's doctrines in his mouth.]

This is part of what my Lord has taught me; for I have abandoned the religion of those who do not believe in God and who deny the life-to-come. I follow the religion of my fathers Abraham, Isaac, and Jacob: We may not associate anything with God.... Judgment belongs to God alone. He has bidden you to worship none but Him. This is the right faith, but most men know it not.

KORAN [18]

The Blessing of Judah

Here we touch on one of those deep, sure insights which make the Jewish Bible incomparable among ancient writings and full of truth, which no modern conditions can outgrow. The great nation has for its hero the highest type of man. It was the instinct which felt this that made Israel unique ... Israel has endured because of that inheritance.

WALTER R. BOWIE [19]

Joseph and Disraeli

He has been called the Disraeli of the ancient world. The comparison goes much further than is usually perceived, and if it has not yet been done someone should write two Plutarchian parallel lives of Victoria's prime minister and Pharaoh's vizier. There are many differences between the two men, but the similarities are astonishing. Both were brilliant, and brilliant alike in their ability to irritate and to charm. Both were "foreigners," though Disraeli was second-generation English-born. Both were democratic conservatives, concerned with the welfare of the masses as much as with the retention of the traditional authority.

MAURICE SAMUEL [20]

The Deaths of Jacob and Joseph

We now reach the end of the last division of Genesis and of the "line of Jacob." The finale of the book focuses on the death of Jacob, with the story of Joseph's death as a kind of epilogue. We obtain a brief insight into Egyptian burial customs, and the relationship of Joseph to his brothers receives its last test.

The main theme of Genesis emerges once more: God has guided the descendants of Abraham and has brought them to the land of Egypt. Thus, the conclusion of Genesis is an introduction to Exodus, where we read how God's guidance is manifested before the whole world as He leads His chosen ones from Egypt back to the Promised Land.

כח כָּל־אֵלֶּה שִׁבְטֵי יִשְׂרָאֵל שְׁנֵים עָשָׂר וְזֹאת אֲשֶׁר־
דִּבֶּר לָהֶם אֲבִיהֶם וַיְבָרֶךְ אוֹתָם אִישׁ אֲשֶׁר כְּבִרְכָתוֹ
כט בֵּרַךְ אֹתָם: וַיְצַו אוֹתָם וַיֹּאמֶר אֲלֵהֶם אֲנִי נֶאֱסָף
אֶל־עַמִּי קִבְרוּ אֹתִי אֶל־אֲבֹתָי אֶל־הַמְּעָרָה אֲשֶׁר
ל בִּשְׂדֵה עֶפְרוֹן הַחִתִּי: בַּמְּעָרָה אֲשֶׁר בִּשְׂדֵה הַמַּכְפֵּלָה
אֲשֶׁר־עַל־פְּנֵי מַמְרֵא בְּאֶרֶץ כְּנָעַן אֲשֶׁר קָנָה אַבְרָהָם
לא אֶת־הַשָּׂדֶה מֵאֵת עֶפְרֹן הַחִתִּי לַאֲחֻזַּת־קָבֶר: שָׁמָּה
קָבְרוּ אֶת־אַבְרָהָם וְאֵת שָׂרָה אִשְׁתּוֹ שָׁמָּה קָבְרוּ אֶת־
יִצְחָק וְאֵת רִבְקָה אִשְׁתּוֹ וְשָׁמָּה קָבַרְתִּי אֶת־לֵאָה:
לב מִקְנֵה הַשָּׂדֶה וְהַמְּעָרָה אֲשֶׁר־בּוֹ מֵאֵת בְּנֵי־חֵת: וַיְכַל
לג יַעֲקֹב לְצַוֺּת אֶת־בָּנָיו וַיֶּאֱסֹף רַגְלָיו אֶל־הַמִּטָּה וַיִּגְוַע
וַיֵּאָסֶף אֶל־עַמָּיו:

Genesis 49
28–33

28] All these were the tribes of Israel, twelve in number, and this is what their father said to them as he bade them farewell, addressing to each a parting word appropriate to him.

29] Then he instructed them, saying to them, "I am about to be gathered to my kin. Bury me with my fathers in the cave which is in the field of Ephron the Hittite, 30] the cave which is in the field of Machpelah, facing Mamre, in the land of Canaan, the field that Abraham bought from Ephron the Hittite for a burial site— 31] there Abraham and his wife Sarah were buried; there Isaac and his wife Rebekah were buried; and there I buried Leah— 32] the field and the cave in it, bought from the Hittites." 33] When Jacob finished his instructions to his sons, he drew his feet into the bed and, breathing his last, he was gathered to his people.

49:28] *All these.* The verse serves as a conclusion to the testament and as an introduction to the final words of Genesis.

33] *Drew his feet . . . gathered to.* Hebrew assonances on the word Joseph (וַיֵּאָסֶף . . . וַיֶּאֱסֹף).

א וַיִּפֹּל יוֹסֵף עַל־פְּנֵי אָבִיו וַיֵּבְךְּ עָלָיו וַיִּשַּׁק־לוֹ: וַיְצַו
ב יוֹסֵף אֶת־עֲבָדָיו אֶת־הָרֹפְאִים לַחֲנֹט אֶת־אָבִיו וַיַּחַנְטוּ
ג הָרֹפְאִים אֶת־יִשְׂרָאֵל: וַיִּמְלְאוּ־לוֹ אַרְבָּעִים יוֹם כִּי
כֵּן יִמְלְאוּ יְמֵי הַחֲנֻטִים וַיִּבְכּוּ אֹתוֹ מִצְרַיִם שִׁבְעִים
ד יוֹם: וַיַּעַבְרוּ יְמֵי בְכִיתוֹ וַיְדַבֵּר יוֹסֵף אֶל־בֵּית פַּרְעֹה
לֵאמֹר אִם־נָא מָצָאתִי חֵן בְּעֵינֵיכֶם דַּבְּרוּ־נָא בְּאָזְנֵי
ה פַרְעֹה לֵאמֹר: אָבִי הִשְׁבִּיעַנִי לֵאמֹר הִנֵּה אָנֹכִי
מֵת בְּקִבְרִי אֲשֶׁר כָּרִיתִי לִי בְּאֶרֶץ כְּנַעַן שָׁמָּה
תִּקְבְּרֵנִי וְעַתָּה אֶעֱלֶה־נָּא וְאֶקְבְּרָה אֶת־אָבִי וְאָשׁוּבָה:

1] Joseph flung himself upon his father's face and wept over him and kissed him. 2] Then Joseph ordered the physicians in his service to embalm his father, and the physicians embalmed Israel.   3] It required forty days, for such is the full period of embalming. The Egyptians bewailed him seventy days;   4] and when the wailing period was over, Joseph spoke to Pharaoh's court, saying, "Do me this favor, and lay this appeal before Pharaoh: 5] 'My father made me swear, saying, "I am about to die. Be sure to bury me in the grave which I made ready for myself in the land of Canaan." Now, therefore, let me go up and bury my father; then I shall

---

50:2] *Embalm.* The purpose of embalming, widely practiced in Egypt, was to preserve the body for the eventual return of the soul. It involved removing the brain and filling the skull with spices; removing the entrails and cleaning the cavity with alcohol, then filling it with myrrh and similar substances; placing the whole body in a nitric solution for many days; washing and wrapping it, and finally sealing it with a rubber paste. There were elaborate and quite costly mummifications as well as others more cursory and less expensive [1].

The physicians. Who specialized in embalming.

3] *Seventy days.* Almost as many as the seventy-two days of mourning customarily set aside for the Pharaoh. Jacob receives a quasi-royal treatment. The mourning period was characterized by official public observances.

4] *Pharaoh's court.* Joseph does not approach Pharaoh directly, perhaps because he had touched the corpse and was, therefore, considered unclean.

וַיֹּאמֶר פַּרְעֹה עֲלֵה וּקְבֹר אֶת־אָבִיךָ כַּאֲשֶׁר הִשְׁבִּיעֶךָ: ו

וַיַּעַל יוֹסֵף לִקְבֹּר אֶת־אָבִיו וַיַּעֲלוּ אִתּוֹ כָּל־עַבְדֵי ז

פַרְעֹה זִקְנֵי בֵיתוֹ וְכֹל זִקְנֵי אֶרֶץ־מִצְרָיִם: וְכֹל בֵּית ח

יוֹסֵף וְאֶחָיו וּבֵית אָבִיו רַק טַפָּם וְצֹאנָם וּבְקָרָם

עָזְבוּ בְּאֶרֶץ גֹּשֶׁן: וַיַּעַל עִמּוֹ גַּם־רֶכֶב גַּם־פָּרָשִׁים וַיְהִי ט

הַמַּחֲנֶה כָּבֵד מְאֹד: וַיָּבֹאוּ עַד־גֹּרֶן הָאָטָד אֲשֶׁר י

בְּעֵבֶר הַיַּרְדֵּן וַיִּסְפְּדוּ־שָׁם מִסְפֵּד גָּדוֹל וְכָבֵד מְאֹד

וַיַּעַשׂ לְאָבִיו אֵבֶל שִׁבְעַת יָמִים: וַיַּרְא יוֹשֵׁב הָאָרֶץ יא

return.' " **6]** And Pharaoh said, "Go up and bury your father, as he made you promise on oath."

7] So Joseph went up to bury his father; and with him went up all the officials of Pharaoh, the senior members of his court, and all of Egypt's dignitaries, **8]** together with all of Joseph's household, his brothers, and his father's household; only their children, their flocks, and their herds were left in the region of Goshen. **9]** Chariots, too, and horsemen went up with him; it was a very large troop.

10] When they came to Goren ha-Atad, which is beyond the Jordan, they held there a very great and solemn lamentation; and he observed a mourning period of seven days for his father. **11]** And when the Canaanite inhabitants of the land

10] *Goren ha-Atad.* Others "the threshing floor of Atad."

Beyond the Jordan. East of the Jordan (see also verse 11). The procession took a circuitous route around the Dead Sea and approached Hebron from the north. Was the funeral an opportunity to impress as many people as possible? Or was it, in the context of the biblical scheme, a prefiguration of what would happen when the bones of Joseph would make the same journey, so that Jacob even in death showed his descendants the road to the Promised Land? [2].

Seven days. In Jewish tradition the basic time of mourning (*shivah,* seven).

/A talmudic passage derives the custom of *shivah* from this verse [3]./

11] *Abel-mizraim.* Interpreted as "the mourning of the Egyptians."

הַכְּנַעֲנִי אֶת־הָאֵבֶל בְּגֹרֶן הָאָטָד וַיֹּאמְרוּ אֵבֶל־כָּבֵד
זֶה לְמִצְרָיִם עַל־כֵּן קָרָא שְׁמָהּ אָבֵל מִצְרַיִם אֲשֶׁר
יב בְּעֵבֶר הַיַּרְדֵּן: וַיַּעֲשׂוּ בָנָיו לוֹ כֵּן כַּאֲשֶׁר צִוָּם: וַיִּשְׂאוּ
אֹתוֹ בָנָיו אַרְצָה כְּנַעַן וַיִּקְבְּרוּ אֹתוֹ בִּמְעָרַת שְׂדֵה
הַמַּכְפֵּלָה אֲשֶׁר קָנָה אַבְרָהָם אֶת־הַשָּׂדֶה לַאֲחֻזַּת־
יד קֶבֶר מֵאֵת עֶפְרֹן הַחִתִּי עַל־פְּנֵי מַמְרֵא: וַיָּשָׁב יוֹסֵף
מִצְרַיְמָה הוּא וְאֶחָיו וְכָל־הָעֹלִים אִתּוֹ לִקְבֹּר אֶת־
טו אָבִיו אַחֲרֵי קָבְרוֹ אֶת־אָבִיו: וַיִּרְאוּ אֲחֵי־יוֹסֵף כִּי־מֵת
אֲבִיהֶם וַיֹּאמְרוּ לוּ יִשְׂטְמֵנוּ יוֹסֵף וְהָשֵׁב יָשִׁיב לָנוּ אֵת
טז כָּל־הָרָעָה אֲשֶׁר גָּמַלְנוּ אֹתוֹ: וַיְצַוּוּ אֶל־יוֹסֵף לֵאמֹר
יז אָבִיךָ צִוָּה לִפְנֵי מוֹתוֹ לֵאמֹר: כֹּה־תֹאמְרוּ לְיוֹסֵף
אָנָּא שָׂא נָא פֶּשַׁע אַחֶיךָ וְחַטָּאתָם כִּי־רָעָה גְמָלוּךָ
וְעַתָּה שָׂא נָא לְפֶשַׁע עַבְדֵי אֱלֹהֵי אָבִיךָ וַיֵּבְךְּ יוֹסֵף

Genesis 50

12–17

saw the mourning at Goren ha-Atad, they said, "This is a solemn mourning on the part of the Egyptians." That is why it was named Abel-mizraim, which is beyond the Jordan. **12]** Thus his sons did for him as he had instructed them. **13]** His sons carried him to the land of Canaan, and buried him in the cave of the field of Machpelah, the field near Mamre which Abraham had bought for a burial site from Ephron the Hittite. **14]** After burying his father, Joseph returned to Egypt, he and his brothers and all who had gone up with him to bury his father.

15] When Joseph's brothers saw that their father was dead, they said, "What if Joseph seeks to pay us back for all the wrong that we did him!" **16]** So they sent this message to Joseph, "Before his death your father left this instruction: **17]** So shall you say to Joseph, 'Forgive, I urge you, the offense and guilt of your brothers who treated you so harshly.' Therefore, please forgive the offense of the servants of the God of your father." And Joseph was in tears as they spoke to him.

בְּדַבְּרָם אֵלָיו: וַיֵּלְכוּ גַּם־אֶחָיו וַיִּפְּלוּ לְפָנָיו וַיֹּאמְרוּ ‏יח

הִנֶּנּוּ לְךָ לַעֲבָדִים: וַיֹּאמֶר אֲלֵהֶם יוֹסֵף אַל־תִּירָאוּ ‏יט

כִּי הֲתַחַת אֱלֹהִים אָנִי: וְאַתֶּם חֲשַׁבְתֶּם עָלַי רָעָה ‏כ

אֱלֹהִים חֲשָׁבָהּ לְטֹבָה לְמַעַן עֲשֹׂה כַּיּוֹם הַזֶּה לְהַחֲיֹת

עַם־רָב: וְעַתָּה אַל־תִּירָאוּ אָנֹכִי אֲכַלְכֵּל אֶתְכֶם ‏כא

וְאֶת־טַפְּכֶם וַיְנַחֵם אוֹתָם וַיְדַבֵּר עַל־לִבָּם: וַיֵּשֶׁב ‏כב

יוֹסֵף בְּמִצְרַיִם הוּא וּבֵית אָבִיו וַיְחִי יוֹסֵף מֵאָה

וָעֶשֶׂר שָׁנִים: וַיַּרְא יוֹסֵף לְאֶפְרַיִם בְּנֵי שִׁלֵּשִׁים גַּם ‏כג

בְּנֵי מָכִיר בֶּן־מְנַשֶּׁה יֻלְּדוּ עַל־בִּרְכֵּי יוֹסֵף: וַיֹּאמֶר ‏כד

יוֹסֵף אֶל־אֶחָיו אָנֹכִי מֵת וֵאלֹהִים פָּקֹד יִפְקֹד אֶתְכֶם

וְהֶעֱלָה אֶתְכֶם מִן־הָאָרֶץ הַזֹּאת אֶל־הָאָרֶץ אֲשֶׁר

Genesis 50

18–24

18] His brothers went to him themselves, flung themselves before him, and said, "We are prepared to be your slaves." 19] But Joseph said to them, "Have no fear! Am I a substitute for God? 20] Besides, although you intended me harm, God intended it for good, so as to bring about the present result—the survival of many people. 21] And so, fear not. I will sustain you and your children." Thus he reassured them, speaking kindly to them.

22] Joseph remained in Egypt, he and his father's household. Joseph lived one hundred and ten years. 23] Joseph lived to see children of the third generation of Ephraim; the children of Machir son of Manasseh were likewise born upon Joseph's knees. 24] At length, Joseph said to his brothers, "I am about to die. God will surely take notice of you and bring you up from this land to the land which

22] *One hundred and ten years.* Considered the ideal life span in Egypt.
/Joshua, who will bring Joseph's bones back to Canaan, will also live 110 years [4]./
23] *Upon Joseph's knees.* Either to indicate Joseph's long life, which saw great-grandchildren, or the record of an adoption. Joseph may have adopted

Machir as his son as Jacob adopted Ephraim and Manasseh. In the time of the Judges the clan of Machir became virtually equated with one-half of Manassesh and was renowned for its administrative abilities (Judg. 5:14), thus resembling Joseph.
24] *To Abraham, to Isaac, and to Jacob.* In this

כה נִשְׁבַּע לְאַבְרָהָם לְיִצְחָק וְלְיַעֲקֹב׃ וַיַּשְׁבַּע יוֹסֵף אֶת־
בְּנֵי יִשְׂרָאֵל לֵאמֹר פָּקֹד יִפְקֹד אֱלֹהִים אֶתְכֶם
כו וְהַעֲלִתֶם אֶת־עַצְמֹתַי מִזֶּה׃ וַיָּמָת יוֹסֵף בֶּן־מֵאָה וָעֶשֶׂר
שָׁנִים וַיַּחַנְטוּ אֹתוֹ וַיִּישֶׂם בָּאָרוֹן בְּמִצְרָיִם׃

Haftarah Vayechi, p. 571

He promised on oath to Abraham, to Isaac, and to Jacob." 25] So Joseph made the sons of Israel swear, saying, "When God has taken notice of you, you shall carry up my bones from here."

26] Joseph died at the age of one hundred and ten years; and he was embalmed and placed in a coffin in Egypt.

passage the Patriarchs are mentioned together for the first time.

25] *Carry my bones.* The promise will be fulfilled by Moses and Joshua (Exod. 13:19; Josh. 24:32).

26] *In Egypt.* The last word of Genesis is a bridge to Exodus, a reminder also that much of the book is set outside of Canaan, and that Israel's beginnings belonged to a nomadic or semi-nomadic past.

Measure of a Man

The last chapter of Genesis once again brings the character of Joseph into focus. In his devotion to his father and in his warm affection for his brothers, we see a full picture of this man who is "the true son, the true brother, the true servant . . . loyal and faithful, disinterested and sincere, modest and considerate" [5].[1] But while he is the obvious hero of the tale, the reader realizes that behind the man, behind the friend of Pharaoh and the guide of Egypt, stands God, the Friend of Abraham and the Guardian of Israel.

Joseph's greatness is in a large measure due to his own awareness that he is serving a higher destiny. Egypt has been good to him, it has given him everything a man could hope for. Still, to him it represents exile; his home is elsewhere. It is to a land not yet his that his bones will be taken; as his people wander, he will wander; as they find a home, he will find his home with them. Joseph is a man who in many ways represents the Jew-to-be, who remains a son of his father and of his people, who wants to return to his origins, and who even in death will not be separated from the fate of his descendants. A monument in Egypt is little to him when compared to the monument he will have erected in the hearts of his people; the survival about which he speaks is not his own so much as that of his heritage.

"Am I a substitute for God?" (Gen. 50:19) he asks and thereby shows himself the prototype of the religious man. He acknowledges his human limitations in the midst of affluence and power and, at the same time, acknowledges the ultimate power of God. This is true greatness fashioned out of suffering and hardship; it is great will and deep devotion fashioned out of ability and humility.

Thus ends the Book of Genesis. It opened with "When God began to create" and then turned to the story of the Fathers. It is a book that reaches from the creation of the world to the creation of the people of Israel. The Midrash says that God created the Torah even before He formed the world. Now, in Egyptian exile and slavery, a people will arise to whom He can entrust this precious gift.

---

[1] In assessing these qualities, one scholar finds Joseph the ideal of the Jewish "wisdom school" [6].

GLEANINGS

Hatred

The brethren of Joseph could never have done him so much good with their love and favor as they did with their malice and hatred.

THOMAS MORE [7]

A White Lie

The brothers told Joseph about Jacob's last instructions of which, however, nothing is recorded [Gen. 50:16, 17]. Said R. Ilaa: "A person may tell a white lie for the sake of peace." R. Simeon b. Gamaliel taught: "Great is peace, for even the tribal ancestors resorted to a fabrication in order to make peace between Joseph and themselves."

TALMUD [8]

Joseph's Kindness

The Rabbis taught: "He who shows himself merciful to his fellow men proves thereby that he is a descendant of Abraham, Isaac, and Jacob; and he who is cruel to his fellow man proves that he is no descendant of theirs."

MIDRASH [9]

Coffin and Ark

The word for both is אָרוֹן [aron, a word no-where else in the Bible used for coffin]. Why? So that in their wanderings through the desert the children of Israel would carry with them both the aron of Joseph and the aron containing the Tablets of the Law, to show that in one aron was a man who fulfilled the commandments contained in the other. The Torah is indeed in the reach of man.

TALMUD [10]

Summation

And he lived a hundred and ten years and then died at a good old age, having enjoyed the greatest perfection of beauty, and wisdom, and eloquence of speech. The beauty of his person is testified to by the violent love with which he inflamed the wife of the eunuch; his wisdom by the evenness of his conduct in the indescribable variety of circumstances that attended the whole of his life, by which he wrought regularity among things that were irregular and harmony among things that were discordant. His eloquence of speech is displayed in his interpretation of the dreams, in his affability in ordinary conversation, and by the persuasion which followed his words; in consequence of which his subjects all obeyed him cheerfully and voluntarily rather than from any compulsion.

Of these hundred and ten years he spent seventeen, till the expiration of his boyhood, in his father's house; and thirteen he passed amid unforeseen events, being plotted against, and sold, and becoming a slave, and having false accusations brought against him, and being thrown into prison; and the remaining eighty years he spent in authority and in all manner of prosperity, being the most excellent manager and administrator, both of scarcity and plenty, and the most competent of all men to manage affairs under either complexion of circumstances.

PHILO [11]

REFERENCE NOTES

BIBLIOGRAPHY

Reference Notes

Creation GEN. 1:1—2:3

1. See *Interpreter's Dictionary* (4 vols., New York and Nashville: Abingdon, 1962), Vol. I, p. 728, and literature cited on p. 732. On בְּרֵאשִׁית see the study by Menahem Naor, *Beth Mikra*, 46, 3 (June 1971), pp. 306 ff.

2. See *Notes on the New Translation of the Torah*, ed. H. Orlinsky (Philadelphia: Jewish Publication Society, 1969), especially on Philo's influence on the interpretation of this verse. [Hereafter this work will be referred to as JPS *Notes*.]

    The translation here follows the Septuagint; Targum. Also see Hagiga 12a for what was created on the first day.

3. See A. Jeremias, *Das Alte Testament* (Leipzig: J. C. Hinrich, 1916), pp. 49 ff., for a detailed analysis.

4. Compare Isa. 51:9, 10; Ps. 89:11; Job 26:10–12; and also rabbinic sources, e.g., B. B. 74b.

5. So Jonathan ben Uzziel; Sanh. 38b; Ibn Ezra. Luzzatto: an Aramaism; Nachmanides: God and Earth together; Pirke de-R. Eliezer 11: God addresses the Torah. Also, cf. Epistle of Barnabas 5:5; 6:12, where God is represented as consulting Christ.

6. Mishnah Yeb. 6:6. See J. M. Epstein, Aruch ha-Shulchan, Even ha-Ezer 1:11.

7. See Rashi; Ibn Ezra.

8. Gen. R. 1:1, 2; 12:2.

9. See Abarbanel.

10. Gen. R. 8:10.

11. Maimonides, *Guide of the Perplexed*, I, 52–53. For a linguistic study of the terms "image" and "likeness," see J. Maxwell Miller, *JBL*, 99 (Sept. 1972), pp. 289–304.

12. Sifre Deuteronomy Ekev, 49, ed. Friedmann; similarly Sota 14a.

13. Leo Baeck, *Das Wesen des Judentums* (5th ed.; Frankfurt: J. Kauffmann, 1922), p. 166; Eng. ed.: *The Essence of Judaism* (rev. ed.; New York: Schocken, 1948), p. 152.

14. Cassuto, *A Commentary on the Book of Genesis*, 2 parts (Jerusalem: Magnes Press, 1961, 1964), *passim*. Some have taken this theory to extremes. For instance, the letters in וַיֹּאמֶר אֱלֹהִים ("God said"), when taken at their numerical value (see p. 142), amount to 343, which is 7 x 7 x 7.

15. Revelations 1:10.

16. Gen. R. 9:2.

17. Gottfried von Leibnitz, *Theodicee* 1:8. Compare Voltaire's satire on "the best of all possible worlds" in *Candide*, Ch. 1.

18. Benno Jacob, *Das erste Buch der Tora, Genesis* (Berlin: Schocken, 1934).

19. Franz Rosenzweig, *Stern der Erlösung* (2d ed.; Frankfurt: J. Kauffmann, 1930), pp. 196 f. Eng. ed.: *The Star of Redemption*, trans. William W. Hallo (New York: Holt, Rinehart & Winston, 1970–1971), p. 154. [Hereafter reference is to Eng. ed.]

20. *Ethics of the Fathers* 3:18.

21. Mishnah Sanh. 4:5.

22. *Ibid.*

23. Buber, *Die chassidischen Bücher* (Berlin: Schocken, 1927), p. 157.

24. Pritchard, *ANET*, pp. 60 f.

25. *Interpreter's Dictionary*, Vol. I, p. 726.

26. Karl Barth, *Church Dogmatics* (Edinburgh: T. & T. Clark, 1958), Vol. III, p. 215.

27. Rosenzweig, *op. cit.*, pp. 313 f.

28. R. Simchah Bunam, quoted by Louis I. Newman, *The Hasidic Anthology* (New York: Bloch, 1944), p. 61.

29. Robert Gordis, *Congress bi-Weekly*, 38, 5 (April 1971), p. 12. Man as God's co-partner: Sab. 10a. Further on ecology and Jewish tradition, see J. I. Helfand, *Judaism*, 20, 3 (Summer 1971), pp. 330–335.

30. Fackenheim, Emil L., in his B. G. Rudolph Lecture at Syracuse University, *Congress bi-Weekly*, 39, 7 (April 1972), p. 6. Based on the midrash in Gen. R. 8:5.

1. See JPS *Notes*.

2. See Theodor H. Gaster, *Myth, Legend and Custom in the Old Testament* (New York: Harper & Row, 1969), p. 27.

3. *Ibid.*; also see D. Ershal, *Beth Mikra*, 40, 1 (Dec. 1969), pp. 100 ff.

4. Yeb. 63a; also see Ibn Ezra on Exod. 1:1.

5. Pritchard, *ANET*, "Enuma Elish," pp. 60 f.

6. *Ibid.*, "Enki and Ninhursag," p. 38.

7. Rashi, based on Sanh. 38a–b.

8. B. Jacob, with reference to Ps. 139:16.

9. Gen. R. 8:1.

10. There probably was a separate midrashic collection about the original Adam, which has survived only in comments and quotations, interpretations and speculations, found in other sources. Among these are the writings of Philo, the Christian Scripture, the Gnostics; Mishnah and Talmud; the writings of Islam and the Druses; and medieval Jewish mystical books. See Gershom Scholem, *On the Kabbalah and Its Symbolism* (New York: Schocken, 1965), pp. 159–165. For a modern interpretation, see Joseph B. Soloveitchik, *Tradition*, 7, 2 (Summer 1965), pp. 5 f.

11. Philo, summarized by Samuel Sandmel, *Philo's Place in Judaism* (New York: Ktav, 1971), pp. xxi, 100.

12. Shakespeare, *The Merchant of Venice*, Act 4, Scene 1.

13. Buber, *Werke* (Munich: Kösel Verlag, 1964), Vol. II, p. 877.

14. Unpublished manuscript. By permission of the author.

15. "From Depatriarchalizing in Biblical Interpretation," *Journal of the American Academy of Religion*, XLI, I (March 1973), pp. 30–48. The article reevaluates the role of woman in the Genesis story.

The Expulsion from Eden GEN. 3

1. Wisdom of Solomon 2:24.

2. See JPS *Notes*.

3. Gen. R. 15:7.

4. Buber, *The Prophetic Faith* (New York: Macmillan, 1949), p. 90.

5. Pes. 118a.

6. See E. O. James, *The Tree of Life* (Leiden: E. J. Brill, 1966), for a full treatment of this subject.

7. II Esd. 7:118; but, in contrast, see Baruch 4:1.

8. Rom. 5:12, 18.

9. Compare JPS *Notes* and von Rad, *op. cit.*, p. 79. See also the discussion by W. Malcolm Clark, *JBL*, 88 (Sept. 1969), pp. 266–278.

10. Consult *Interpreter's Dictionary*, Vol. II, p. 235, under "Fall" for bibliography.

11. Maimonides, *Guide*, I, 2.

12. Rashi; see Gen. R. 22:2.

13. For a summary of opinions, see John A. Bailey, *JBL*, 89 (June 1970), pp. 144 ff.

14. See Rosenzweig, *op. cit.*, p. 266.

15. Friedrich von Schiller, from his poem *Kassandra*.

16. Compare Mech. to Exod. 14:29.

17. Tanch. Vayeshev 46b; Gen. R. 9:5 (based on a tradition that R. Meir had a Torah scroll in which Gen. 1:31 read טוֹב מוֹת instead of טוֹב מְאֹד, or which had a marginal note to that effect).

18. Sab. 55b.

19. Pritchard, *ANET*, "Gilgamesh," p. 75.

20. Philo, *On the Creation of the World*, #56.

21. Sanh. 29a.

22. C. F. von Weizsäcker, quoted in V. Gollancz, *Man and God* (Boston: Houghton Mifflin, 1951), pp. 190 f.

23. Tanch. Tazri'a 1:9.

24. Pirke de-R. Eliezer 14.

25. John Milton, *Paradise Lost*, opening stanzas.

26. Henry S. Slonimsky, *Essays* (Cincinnati, Ohio: Hebrew Union College Press, 1967), p. 53.

27. Erub. 13b.

28. Moshe Mordecai Epstein, quoted in *Ma'yanah shel Torah*, ed. A. Z. Friedman (5 vols., Tel Aviv: Pe'er, 1955–56), Vol. I, p. 26; Eng. trans. *Wellsprings of Torah* (2 vols., New York: Judaica Press, 1969), p. 11. The passage is a comment on Rashi, *ad loc.*

29. *Joseph and His Brothers*, transl. H. T. Lowe-Porter (New York: Alfred A. Knopf, 1966), p. 27.

1. This theory has been elaborately developed and illustrated by Gaster, *op. cit.*, pp. 51 ff.

2. See JPS *Notes*.

3. So Ephraim A. Speiser, *Genesis* (Garden City: Doubleday, 1964), *ad loc.*; also New English Bible.

4. Similarly, Targum Yerushalmi.

5. Compare II Chron. 1:2, for a similar ellipsis.

6. Compare Maimonides, Hilch. Rotse'ach 1:4.

7. See JPS *Notes*.

8. For a complete analysis of this difficult passage, see Samuel Sandmel, *Hebrew Union College Annual*, 32 (1961), pp. 19 ff. [Hereafter this journal will be referred to as *HUCA*.]

9. S. R. Hirsch and others.

10. Cyrus H. Gordon, *Before the Bible* (New York: Harper & Row, 1962), p. 16. Rabbinic sources deal with the whole question of Cain's repentance. See Lev. R. 10:5; Tanch. 1:25; and literature quoted in Louis Ginzberg, *The Legends of the Jews* (Philadelphia: Jewish Publication Society, 1909–1946), Vol. V, p. 141, note 26. For a comprehensive discussion, see C. L. Gvaryahu, *Beth Mikra*, 32 (Oct. 1967), pp. 27 ff. The Koran, too, speaks of Cain's repentance, Sura V:36 (The Table).

11. Yehezkel Kaufmann, *The Religion of Israel* (Chicago: University of Chicago Press, 1960), p. 295.

12. Gen. R. 22:9.

13. Hul. 7b; see also R. Simchah Bunam, quoted in *Ma'yanah shel Torah*, Vol. I, p. 31.

14. Also see Gen. R. 22:8.

15. Ben Sira 15:12.

16. *Ethics of the Fathers* 4:1.

17. Maimonides, Hilch. Teshuvah 5:4.

18. Mishnah Sanh. 4:5. See Maimonides, Hilch. Rotse'ach 4:9; and Rashi.

19. Avot de-R. Nathan 31, also quoted in the Koran, Sura V:36 (The Table).

20. Mordecai M. Kaplan, unpublished manuscript.

21. Elie Wiesel, *A Beggar in Jerusalem* (New York: Random House, 1970), p. 111.

22. Westermann, *Genesis* 1–11 (Darmstadt: Wissenschaftliche Buchhandlung, 1972), p. 59.

Primeval Man GEN. 5:1—6:8

1. See B. B. 17a. Buber (*Werke*, Vol. II, p. 887) denies, however, that the expression "walked with God" is a moral judgment in either Enoch's or Moses' case but means these men were able to participate in God's governance, His own "movement."

2. See JPS *Notes*; see also Westermann, *op. cit.*, pp. 68–76.

3. See Enoch 6–8; see also Ginzberg, *op. cit.*, Vol. V, p. 153, note 57.

4. Julian Morgenstern, *HUCA*, 14 (1939), pp. 29–40, 114 ff.

5. Bernard Bamberger, *Fallen Angels* (Philadelphia: Jewish Publication Society, 1952), p. 263, note 1.

6. So Mendelssohn; Hirsch.

7. So various midrashim, e.g., Sifre Beha'alotecha 86; Rashi; Ibn Ezra; B. Jacob. See also Augustine who derives the Civitas Dei from the children of Seth, and Civitas Terrestra from Cain.

8. The figure 120 occurs frequently in the Bible; see Num. 7:86; I Kings 9:14; 10:10; II Chron. 5:12. See also the use of 120,000 in Judg. 8:10; I Kings 8:63; I Chron. 12:37; II Chron. 7:5; 28:6.

9. Rashi. The whole subject of these numbers is explored by E. Dhorme, *Revue Biblique*, 33 (1924), pp. 532–556; 35 (1926), pp. 66–82; 223–239; 532–556.

10. Morgenstern, *HUCA*, 14 (1939), p. 85.

11. *Rediscovering Judaism*, ed. A. J. Wolf (Chicago: Quadrangle Press, 1965), editor's essay, pp. 142 ff.

12. Gen. R. 23:3.

13. See William W. Hallo, *Journal of Cuneiform Studies*, 23, 3 (1971), pp. 57–67.

14. Speiser, *op. cit.*, p. 41.

15. Luzzatto, following Redak.

16. Kaplan, unpublished manuscript.

17. Jer. Ned. 9:4, 41c, which portrays the Torah as saving Israel.

18. M. M. Kasher, in *Encyclopedia of Biblical Interpretation* (New York: American Biblical Encyclopedic Society, 1953), Vol. I, p. 245. Also see Nachmanides and Bachya; and Rabad, Commentary on Sifra Kedoshim 4:12.

19. Avot de-R. Nathan 31; Sanh. 37a (see Munich manuscript and Dikduke Sofrim). Quoted also in the Koran, Sura V:36 (The Table), in connection with Abel's death.

20. Based on Gen. R. 26:7.

The Flood GEN. 6:9—8:14

1. So Rashi who cites a similar use of אֶת in Exod. 9:33 and I Kings 15:23.

2. See Sanh. 108b; Ginzberg, *op. cit.*, Vol. V, p. 175, note 20.

3. Tanch. Bereshit 12; Sanh. 108a. Further references in Ginzberg, *op. cit.*, Vol. V, p. 173, notes 15, 17.

4. Sefer ha-Yashar.

5. Compare Matt. 24:37 ff.; Luke 17:26 ff.

6. I Pet. 3:20–21. See Jack P. Lewis, *A Study of the Interpretation of Noah and the Flood in Jewish and Christian Literature* (Leiden: E. J. Brill, 1968).

7. Sanh. 108a.

8. See Gordis, *op. cit.*, pp. 9 ff.

9. See Ginzberg, *op. cit.*, Vol. V, p. 180, note 32.

10. Pritchard, *ANET*, "Atrahasis," p. 104.

11. *Ibid.*, "Gilgamesh," pp. 94 f.

12. *Ibid.*, p. 93.

13. Tanchuma; Midrash ha-Gadol; Sanh. 108a–b; and Ginzberg, *op. cit.*, Vol. V, p. 174, note 19, where old Christian sources are also cited.

14. Koran, Sura VII:57–62 (Al Araf).

15. Morris Adler, *The Voice Still Speaks* (New York: Bloch, 1969), pp. 19, 21.

16. Buber, *Werke*, Vol. II, p. 884.

After the Flood GEN. 8:15—9:29

1. See Targum. The anthropomorphism of this expression was discussed by the Church Father Clementine, *Homilies* 3:39. R. Rendtorff (*Kerygma und Dogma*, 7 [1961], pp. 69–78) sees in 8:21 the original end of the Urgeschichte, with blessing now taking the place of the Eden curse (Gen. 3).

2. Pritchard, *ANET*, "Gilgamesh," p. 95.

3. See Mishnah B. K. 1:4.

4. Speiser.

5. Compare Malbim; Cassuto.

6. Sanh. 70a.

7. Pesikta Zutarti; see also Redak.

8. Ned. 31a.

9. Sanh. 56b.

10. Sanh. 56a–b; Maimonides, Hilch. Melachim 8:11, 9:1 ff.; Judah Halevi, *Kuzari* 3:73.

11. Acts 15:20, 29.

12. H. Revel, *Universal Jewish Encyclopedia* (New York: Universal Jewish Encyclopedia Inc., 1939–1943), Vol. VIII, pp. 227–228. Hermann Cohen, in *Die Religion der Vernunft aus den Quellen des Judentums* (Leipzig: G. Fock, 1919, pp. 143 f.), has shown how Hugo Grotius and others developed the rabbinic approach to Noahide law into a system of natural law.

13. Samuel Atlas, *Dimensions*, 1, 2 (1967), p. 22.

14. Yore De'ah 7:1, 2. See also Acts 15:29; and Koran, Sura II:168, v. 4.

15. See Saadia; Rashi. For a divergent view, see Ibn Ezra.

16. Pes. 25a–b; Sanh. 74a.

17. Sanh. 57b.

18. Sanh. 59b; cf. Maharsha; Yeb. 62a.

19. Sanh. 70a.

20. John Skinner, *Genesis* (New York: Scribner's, 1910), *ad loc.*

The Nations GEN. 10

1. Targum Yerushalmi.

2. See also the connection of Cushan and Midian in Hab. 3:7.

3. Speiser.

4. Rabbi Meir of Rothenburg, Responsum No. 27. For a fuller discussion, see Solomon B. Freehof, *A Treasury of Responsa* (Philadelphia: Jewish Publication Society, 1963), pp. 216 ff., with a responsum by Ezekiel Landau. Also see Lev. 17:13.

5. Acts 2:9.

6. Speiser.

7. Erub. 53a; Sifre Bechukotai 2.

8. Midrash ha-Gadol 11:28; Gen. R. 38:13. There is also a special midrash dealing with Nimrod and Abraham: Jellinek, *Bet ha-Midrash* 1:25 ff.

9. Following Targum Jonathan.

10. Kaplan, unpublished manuscript.

11. Borowitz, *Journal of Ecumenical Studies*, 8, 3 (Summer 1971), p. 566.

Babel and after: The End of Prehistory GEN. 11:1–26

1. Pritchard, *ANET*, pp. 68 f.

2. Herodotus, *History*, Vol. I, p. 179.

3. See William F. Albright, *JBL*, 43 (1924), pp. 363–393, esp. p. 385.

4. But Albright, in *Yahweh and the Gods of Canaan* (Garden City, N. Y.: Doubleday, 1968, p. 99), denies that the biblical tower can have referred to Etemenanki.

5. So Josephus, *Jewish Antiquities*, I, 4:1; B. Jacob; Cassuto.

6. B. Jacob, commentary, *ad loc.*

7. See the analysis by Ch. Gevaryahu, *Beth Mikra*, 32, 1 (Oct. 1967), pp. 27–36.

8. A. Koestler, in accepting the Sonning Prize, University of Copenhagen, quoted in *Toronto Globe and Mail* (May 6, 1968), p. 7.

9. Gen. R. 38:7.

10. Tanch. Noah 18; Rashi.

11. See also Cassuto on Gen. 11:5 who calls the verse "a satirical allusion."

12. Midrash ha-Gadol 11:3.

13. See also Apocalypse of Baruch (Greek version) 3:5.

14. Midrash ha-Gadol 11:9; Rashi.

15. John Ruskin, *Lecture on Architecture and Painting*, quoted in Solomon Goldman, *In the Beginning* (Philadelphia: Jewish Publication Society, 1949), p. 518.

16. Edna St. Vincent Millay, *Conversation at Midnight* (New York: Harper & Row, 1937), p. 100.

17. See Gordon, *Before Columbus* (New York: Crown, 1971), pp. 164 f.

Part III *The Line of Terah. Abraham*

1. William F. Albright and Nelson Glueck choose the earlier age; Ephraim A. Speiser and Cyrus H. Gordon, the later.

2. Von Rad., *op. cit.*, p. 166.

3. Kaufmann, *op. cit.*, pp. 221 ff.

4. *Hebrew Origins* (New York: Harper and Brothers, rev. ed. 1950), pp. 184 ff.

The Call of Abraham GEN. 11:27—12:9

1. Tanch. Lech Lecha 9.

2. See, e.g., Sota 34a; Gen. R. 70:6; Ibn Ezra on Gen. 9:18, 31:42.

3. Gordon, *Before the Bible*, p. 287.

4. See Nachmanides.

5. See Hermann Gunkel, *Genesis* (Göttingen: Vandenhoeck & Ruprecht, 1901), *ad loc.*; Speiser.

6. See *Entsiklopedyah Mikra'it* (Jerusalem: Mosad Bialik, from 1955 on), Vol. I, cols. 328–29.

7. Spinoza, *Theological Tractate* 8.

8. Maharal (commentary on Rashi). For a Christian point of view, see von Rad, *op. cit.*, pp. 155 f.

9. Kaufmann, *op. cit.*, p. 60.

10. Avot de-R. Nathan 33; Pirke de-R. Eliezer 26; Gunkel, *op. cit.*, p. 164.

11. A. M. Klein, *Poems* (Philadelphia: Jewish Publication Society, 1944), p. 46.

12. Gen. R. 38:13, *et al.*, especially *Ma'aseh Avraham Avinu* (Jellinek, *Bet ha-Midrash* 1:25 ff.); Jubilees 11, 12, 20. Philo considered Abraham's opposition to the Babylonian astrologers the reason for his emigration. The Koran, Sura XXI:53 (The Prophets), utilizes these tales.

13. Buber, *Prophetic Faith*, p. 88.

14. Millay, *op. cit.*, pp. 43, 46.

15. *Itture Torah*, comp. and ed., Aaron Jacob Greenberg (Tel Aviv: Yavneh, from 1965 on), Vol. I, p. 83.

16. Gen. R. 39:2.

17. Philo, *On the Migration of Abraham*, 9.

18. Kaufmann, *op. cit.*, p. 222.

19. *Joseph and His Brothers*, pp. 6–7.

1. Nelson Glueck, *The River Jordan* (Philadelphia: Jewish Publication Society, 1946), p. 73.

2. See Earle Bennett Cross, *The Hebrew Family: A Study in Historical Sociology* (Chicago: University of Chicago Press, 1927).

3. This interpretation is proposed by Speiser, *op. cit.*, pp. 91 ff. See also Sandmel, *JBL*, 80 (June 1961), pp. 105–122.

4. Redak; Sforno; Luzzatto.

5. Nachmanides.

6. Josephus, *op. cit.*, Vol. I, 8:1, 2.

7. Gunkel.

8. Klaus Koch, *The Growth of the Biblical Tradition* (New York: Scribner's, 1969), p. 127.

9. Pes. 25b; Sanh. 74a.

10. N. Avigad and Y. Yadin, *A Genesis Apocryphon* (Jerusalem: Magnes Press of the Hebrew University, 1956), cols. 20:6 f. (For the Christian Scripture, see Rom. 4:19; 9:9; Heb. 11:11; I Pet. 3:6.) The quotation is a small part of an extravagant description of Sarah's beauty. Also see the tale in Gen. R. 40:5 which is similar to the opening story in the *Arabian Nights*.

11. Henry Wadsworth Longfellow, *The Divine Tragedy*, The First Passover, III.

12. Quoted in M. M. Kasher, *Torah Shelemah* (3rd ed., New York; beginning with Vol. 20, Jerusalem: Machon Torah Shelemah, from 1949 on), 12:145, 565. [Hereafter this work will be referred to as *TS*.]

13. As told by Ginzberg, *op. cit.*, Vol. I, pp. 221–222.

14. Vol. XI, p. 57.

The War of the Four against the Five GEN. 14

1. The majority of scholars assume a historical incident, but some deny it, especially Gunkel, *op. cit.*, pp. 262 ff. See *Biblical Motifs*, ed. A. Altmann (Cambridge, Mass.: Harvard University Press, 1966), pp. 65 ff. There is a dispute also over the usual assumption of different sources. For instance, Engnell (*op. cit.*, p. 54, note 6) strongly maintains the unity of 14:17 and 18.

2. See J. Simons, *The Geographical and Topographical Texts of the Old Testament* (Leiden: E. J. Brill, 1959), p. 86.

3. See *Entsiklopedyah Mikra'it*, Vol. III, p. 272.

4. So Gordon, *Journal of Near Eastern Studies*, 13 (1954), p. 57. [Hereafter this journal will be referred to as *JNES*.]

5. Glueck, *op. cit.*, p. 74.

6. So Gordon, *Before the Bible*, p. 286.

7. So Albright, *op. cit.*, who further supports the theory that Eber and Arab are essentially the same terms.

8. However, see R. de Vaux, *JNES*, 27 (1968), pp. 221–228, who discusses the "ethnic" theory.

9. For a study of terms and relationships, see Mary Gray, *HUCA*, 29 (1958), pp. 135–202.

10. See also Gen. 39:14; 41:12 where Joseph is called a Hebrew, or coming from the land of the Hebrews (Gen. 40:15).

11. Compare Adonizedek; Josh. 10:1. See Roy A. Rosenberg, *HUCA*, 36 (1965), pp. 161 ff.

12. Heb. 5:6–11.

13. Heb. 7:1–3.

14. Targum. See also Josephus, *op. cit.*, Vol. I, 10:2.

15. See further, *Interpreter's Dictionary*, Vol. III, p. 343; and Ginzberg, *op. cit.*, Vol. V, p. 225, note 102.

16. Lev. R. 28:4.

17. Gen. R. 42:8.

18. Quoted in Mordecai Hacohen, *Al ha-Torah* (Jerusalem: Reuben Mass, 1962), Vol. I, p. 48.

19. *Joseph and His Brothers*, p. 288.

The Covenant between the Pieces; The Birth of Ishmael GEN. 15—16

1. Albright, *Yahweh and the Gods of Canaan*, pp. 65–66.

2. Rom. 4:2, 3; Gal. 3:6–11.

3. James 2:23–26.

4. See Simons, *op. cit.*, pp. 15 ff. Kaufmann, *op. cit.*, pp. 201 ff., distinguishes a series of different concep-

tions about the shape of the Promised Land in the Bible. For a full discussion of this subject, see Num. 34:1 ff.

5. Gen. R. 45:2.

6. Pritchard, *ANET*, Code of Hammurabi 146, p. 172.

7. Quoted by Speiser, *op. cit.*, p. 120.

8. On the question of concubine and slave wife, see Louis Epstein, *Marriage Laws in the Bible and Talmud* (Cambridge, Mass.: Harvard University Press, 1942), pp. 55 ff.

9. Compare Wellhausen; Tur-Sinai.

10. Nahum Sarna, *Understanding Genesis* (New York: McGraw Hill, 1966), p. 127.

11. See James Frazer, quoted in Gaster, *op. cit.*, pp. 140 ff., where arguments for various theories are marshaled. For Greek parallels, see Gordon, *Before the Bible*, p. 96.

12. Koran, Sura IV:124 (The Women).

13. Brichto, *HUCA*, 39 (1968), pp. 44 f.

14. John Ruskin, *Fors Clavigera*, Letter 65, quoted in Goldman, *op. cit.*, p. 541.

15. Leo Baeck, *This People Israel* (Philadelphia: Jewish Publication Society, 1965), p. 12.

16. Note on Shulchan Aruch, Even ha-Ezer 1:3 and 154:10. The relevant law is based on Yeb. 64a and Tosefta Yeb. 8:4. For a detailed treatment, see P. Dickstein, *Dine nisu'in vegerushin* (Tel Aviv: Yavneh, 1956), Ch. XI.

The Covenant of Circumcision GEN. 17

1. Speiser.

2. R. H. 16b.

3. So Rashi.

4. So Gen. R. 47:4.

5. Zohar 1:93b.

6. For a general survey of the practice, see *Encyclopedia of Religion and Ethics*, ed. James Hastings (New York: Scribner's, 1924–27), Vol. III, pp. 659 ff., under "Circumcision." Also Morgenstern, *Rites of Birth, Marriage, Death and Kindred Occasions* (Cincinnati, Ohio: Hebrew Union College Press, 1966), pp. 48 ff.

7. Herodotus, *op. cit.*, Vol. II, 36, 104; Maimonides, *Guide*, II, 49.

8. Mishnah Nid. 5:3; Jer. Ned. 3 to end (38b).

9. Tanch. Lech Lecha 20.

10. Gen. R. 11:6. Also see Ned. 31b; Rashi; Baruch Epstein, *Torah Temimah* on Gen. 17:1.

11. See Isserles to Shulchan Aruch, Yoreh De'ah 335:10.

12. See Freehof, *Reform Jewish Practice* (Cincinnati, Ohio: Hebrew Union College Press, 1944), Vol. II, pp. 113 f.

13. See the discussion in Sab. 132a; Freehof, *Reform Responsa* (Cincinnati, Ohio: Hebrew Union College Press, 1960), pp. 90 ff.

14. Freehof, *Current Reform Responsa* (Cincinnati, Ohio: Hebrew Union College Press, 1963), p. 95.

15. The laws are conveniently summarized in Hyman Goldin, *HaMadrikh* (rev. ed.; New York: Hebrew Publishing Company, 1956), pp. 27 ff.

16. Pes. R. 23:4.

The Messengers GEN. 18:1–15

1. Maimonides, *Guide*, II, 42. For a Greek parallel to the tale, see Homer, *Odyssey*, XVII, 485 ff.; also see, Gunkel, *op. cit.*, p. 200.

2. Nachmanides.

3. Luzzatto.

4. Gen. R. 48:14.

5. See Ginzberg, *op. cit.*, Vol. V, p. 235, note 140.

6. Ovid, *Fasti*, V, 493–544.

7. Also see Bamberger.

8. Gordon, *Before the Bible*, p. 291.

9. B. M. 86b.

10. Gen. R. 48:9; Midrash ha-Gadol 1:267.

11. Avot de-R. Nathan 13; Gen. R. 48:13.

12. The original source of the story is not known. See Bamberger, *Proselytism in the Talmudic Period* (Cincinnati, Ohio: Hebrew Union College Press, 1939), p. 209, note 17.

13. Based on the quotation in *On Jewish Learning*, ed. Nahum Glatzer (New York: Schocken, 1955), p. 124.

14. B. M. 87a. See also Yeb. 65b.

Sodom and Gomorrah GEN. 18:16—19:38

1. Mishnah Bik. 1:4 and Bertinoro thereto; differently, Jer. Bik. 1:4, 64a. Also see Tosafot to B. B. 81a; Maimonides, Hilch. Bikurim 4:3, and his letter to the convert Obadiah.
2. See Gleanings and notes 10 and 11.
3. On this subject, see Arthur Marmorstein, *The Doctrine of Merits in Old Rabbinical Literature* (London: Jew's College, 1920).
4. Mishnah Sanh. 1:6.
5. Pirke de-R. Eliezer 25; Zohar Vayera 108b–109a.
6. Gen. R. 49:6.
7. Sheldon H. Blank, *Prophetic Faith in Isaiah* (New York: Harper & Row, 1958), pp. 199 ff.
8. See Gen. R. 50:9.
9. See Zohar, *loc. cit.*; Pirke de-R. Eliezer 25; Sefer ha-Yashar 62 on the legend of a "Procrustean bed" in Sodom.
10. Wisdom of Solomon 10:6–8. Deuteronomy 29:23 mentions four cities (adding Admah and Zeboiim), while Wisdom and other ancient sources also count Zoar in the number, making it five altogether.
11. *Views of the Biblical World* (Chicago and New York: Jordan Publishing Company, 1959–1961), Vol. I, pp. 60–61; Josephus, *Antiquities*, I, 11:4; *The Jewish War*, IV, 8:4.

Crises GEN. 20—21

1. Jer. Meg. 1:9, 71d.
2. See Rashi; Rashbam; Sforno.
3. Hallo, *JAOS*, 88 (1968), pp. 71–89.
4. Ket. 60a; II Macc. 7:29.
5. See Rashi; note Nachmanides' rejoinder.
6. Pritchard, *ANET*, p. 160.
7. Maimonides, *Guide*, I, 44.
8. Speiser.
9. Ta'an. 14b.
10. Zvi Adar, *The Biblical Narrative* (Jerusalem: World Zionist Organization, 1959), p. 123.
11. Gen. R. 52:13.
12. See Galatians 4:21–5:1.
13. *Handwörterbuch des Islam*, ed. A. J. Wensick and H. J. Kramer (Leiden: E. J. Brill, 1941), under "Islam."
14. Koran, Sura XIX:55 (Mary). Enoch (Idris) is described in the same fashion. It may be noted that both here and in Sura XXI:85 (The Prophets) Enoch is listed *after* Ishmael.
15. Gen. R. 53:14.
16. See Ginzberg, *op. cit.*, Vol. V, p. 248, note 225.
17. Louis Isaac Rabinowitz, *Jerusalem Post* (Nov. 3, 1969), p. 13.
18. As told by Ginzberg, *op. cit.*, Vol. I, p. 239, based on Gen. R. 45:5–8; 46:3, and other sources; see *ibid.*, Vol. V, pp. 232–233, notes 122 and 123.

The Akedah GEN. 22

1. Gen. R. 56:8.
2. See Josephus, *Antiquities*, I, 13:2; Jubilees 18:13.
3. Speiser.
4. Reproduced in *From Adam to Daniel*, ed. G. Cornfeld (New York: Macmillan, 1962), p. 75.
5. Compare Euripides' play, *Iphigenia at Aulis*. On the use of the Akedah in ancient decorations, see Bernard Goldman, *The Sacred Portal* (Detroit: Wayne State University Press, 1966), pp. 53 ff.
6. Eduard Meyer, *Die Israeliten und ihre Nachbarstämme* (Halle: M. Niemeyer, 1906), p. 241.
7. Jer. Sota 5:8, 20c. This was, however, a minority opinion. The majority held that Job was a contemporary of Moses; see B. B. 14b.
8. See Morgenstern, *Rites of Birth, Marriage, Death and Kindred Occasions*, p. 182.
9. John 3:16.
10. R. Graves and R. Patai, *Hebrew Myths* (London: Cassell, 1963–1964), p. 176.
11. Heb. 11:17–19; Jas. 2:21 f.
12. Zohar 1:119b.
13. IV Macc. 14:20.
14. *Ethics of the Fathers* 5:3; Pirke de-R. Eliezer 26.
15. Maimonides, *Guide*, III, 24; Nachmanides. See also Nehama Leibowitz, *Iyyunim Besefer Bereshit* (Jerusalem: Ha-Histadrut ha-Tsiyonit Ha-Olamit, 1966), p. 134.
16. Rosenzweig, *op. cit.*, p. 266.

17. Gen. R. 56:8; see also Rashi and Bachya on text.

18. Gen. R. 56:8.

19. See Ta'an. 16a and Tosafot. Also Shalom Spiegel, *The Last Trial* (Philadelphia: Jewish Publication Society, 1968), who devotes an entire volume to this tradition.

20. Based on the midrashim cited in previous note.

21. Divre Hayyim 9, quoted in *Itture Torah*, Vol. I, p. 161.

22. R. H. 16a where the ceremony is described.

23. Shulchan Aruch shel ha-Rav, quoted by Shmuel Y. Agnon, *Days of Awe* (New York: Schocken, 1965), pp. 68–69.

24. Saadia, quoted by Agnon, *op. cit.*, pp. 71–72.

25. Ikkarim 3:36, based on Sanh. 89b and Rashi.

26. *Musaf* service.

27. Koran, Sura XXXVII:100–109 (The Ranks).

28. Kaplan, unpublished manuscript.

29. S. R. Driver, *Genesis* (New York: Edwin S. Gorham, 1904), p. 222.

30. Erich Auerbach, *Mimesis* (Garden City, N. Y.: Doubleday, 1957), pp. 6–7.

31. Sören Kierkegaard, *Fear and Trembling* (Princeton, N.J.: Princeton University Press, 1945), pp. xvi, 89–90.

32. Fackenheim, *Quest for Past and Future* (Bloomington: Indiana University Press, 1968), pp. 64 f.

33. Wellisch, *Isaac and Oedipus* (London: Routledge and Kegan Paul, 1954), pp. 114 ff.

The Death of Sarah GEN. 23

1. Von Rad. Compare also M. Noth, *Überlieferungsgeschichte des Pentateuchs* (Stuttgart: W. Kohlhammer, 2nd ed., 1960), p. 170.

2. Compare Herbert Petschow, *Journal of Cuneiform Studies*, 19, 4 (1965), pp. 103 ff.; Gene M. Tucker, *JBL*, 85 (March 1966), pp. 77 ff.

3. The antiquity of the grave stones is discussed by Yosef Breslavi, *Beth Mikra*, 36, 1 (Jan. 1969), pp. 50 ff.

4. Gen. R. 58:1; Midrash ha-Gadol.

5. Gen. R. 79:7.

6. Sanh. 91a.

7. *TS*, Vol. IV, p. 918, note 5.

8. *Ibid.*; Midrash Mishle 31. See also Ginzberg, *op. cit.*, Vol. V, p. 258.

9. M. K. 27b.

10. Avot de-R. Nathan 44.

11. *Itture Torah*, Vol. I, p. 180.

12. See *Encyclopaedia Judaica*, Vol. 11, cols. 670–674.

Rebekah at the Well GEN. 24:1—25:18

1. See *Jewish Encyclopedia*, (New York: Funk & Wagnalls, 1901–1906), Vol. VIII, pp. 335 ff., for polygamy and monogamy in Jewish history.

2. So Speiser.

3. Nachmanides.

4. Mishnah Ket. 5:2.

5. Gen. R. 61:4; Rashi. Ibn Ezra denies this.

6. Gen. R. 68:4.

7. Sota 2a.

8. Medieval commentators discussed this problem in detail: cf., especially, Abarbanel, *ad loc.*; Nachmanides at the end of sidra בֹּא; Maimonides, Hilch. Akkum 11:4; and Rabad's critique thereon.

9. Sarna, *op. cit.*, pp. 84–85.

10. Gen. R. 65:9, 59:6.

11. Compare Rashi; Hacohen, *op. cit.*, Vol. I, p. 69.

12. As told by Ginzberg, *op. cit.*, Vol. I, pp. 305–306, based on "The Testament of Abraham," a pseudepigraphic work.

The Line of Isaac GEN. 25:19–34

1. Pritchard, *ANET*, "Gilgamesh," p. 74.

2. Speiser; Cassuto.

3. Jeremias, *op. cit.*, p. 315.

4. Jeremias, *op. cit.*, p. 316.

5. Tur-Sinai.

6. So B. Jacob.

7. Reference and sources in Sarna, *op. cit.*, pp. 185 ff.

8. Compare *TS* 1037:210.

9. Rashbam; Sforno; but see Nachmanides.

10. So, especially, Gunkel, *ad loc.* The term "games-manship" is applied by Speiser.

11. See Rashi; Sforno.

12. So von Rad.

13. Gen. R. 63:6 ff.

14. Ginzberg, *op. cit.*, Vol. V, p. 278, note 51.

15. John Bunyan, *The Pilgrim's Progress*, quoted by S. Goldman, *op. cit.*, p. 596.

16. Roger Williams, letter to Major Mason, June 22, 1670, quoted in S. Goldman, *op. cit.*, p. 399.

17. Sarna, *op. cit.*, p. 188.

18. So Cassuto. See *Entsiklopedyah Mikra'it*, Vol. III, p. 722.

19. IV Esdras 6:8–10.

20. Maurice Samuel, *Certain People of the Book* (New York: Alfred A. Knopf, 1955), p. 163.

21. Henry E. Kagan, lecture delivered at UAHC Biennial, Chicago, Nov. 16, 1963.

The Life of Isaac GEN. 26

1. Speiser.

2. She was so characterized by Samuel, *op. cit.*, pp. 130–185. Also see p. 275. For a characterization of Isaac, see also Adar, *op. cit.*, pp. 70 ff.

3. Leibowitz, *op. cit.*, p. 183.

4. Hacohen, *op. cit.*, Vol. I, p. 80.

5. Adler, *op. cit.*, p. 105.

6. R. Beer-Hofmann, *Jacob's Dream*, trans. I. B. Wynn (Philadelphia: Jewish Publication Society, 1946), p. 85.

Isaac Blesses His Sons GEN. 27:1—28:9

1. Similarly Redak.

2. Malbim.

3. Sforno; Rashbam.

4. So also Nachmanides and Rashbam.

5. Stanley Gevirtz, *Patterns in the Early Poetry of Israel* (Chicago: University of Chicago Press, 1963), pp. 35–47.

6. Gunkel, *ad loc.*

7. See de Vaux, *Genèse* (Paris: Les Editions du Cerf, 1953), p. 125, note d.

8. Zohar, Gen. 145a.

9. See Tanch. Toledot 171.

10. See the detailed discussion by W. Gunther Plaut, *CCAR Journal* (June 1960), pp. 30 ff.

11. See Thomas Mann, *Joseph and His Brothers*, p. 131. Similarly, Samuel, *op. cit.*, p. 166.

12. See Naphtali Berlin in his comment on Gen. 24:65.

13. *Entsiklopedyah Mikra'it*, Vol. II, p. 357; see *ibid.* for literature. Also see *Interpreter's Dictionary*, Vol. I, pp. 446 ff.

14. Samuel E. Karff, manuscript work, by permission.

15. Amy K. Blank, *The Spoken Choice* (Cincinnati, Ohio: Hebrew Union College Press, 1959), pp. 11 ff.

16. De Vaux, *Genèse*, p. 126.

17. Gen. R. 65:20; Bachya; Malbim.

Jacob's Dream GEN. 28:10–22

1. On parallels to this image see *Interpreter's Dictionary*, Vol. I, p. 130, under "Angel"; H. A. Hoffner, Jr., *JBL*, 86 (December 1967), p. 397. Note that the staircase of the Babylonian *zikkurrat* is called *simmiltu*, possibly—by transposition—from the same root as *sullam*.

2. See Kaufmann, *op. cit.*, p. 259.

3. So, e.g., Malbim.

4. Gen. R. 70:4. See the commentary of Z. W. Einhorn (Maharzu).

5. On the subject of vows in Psalms, see especially H. Gunkel and J. Begrich, *Einleitung in die Psalmen* (Göttingen: Vandenhoek & Ruprecht, 1933), pp. 247–250.

6. Gen. R. 68:12. See the commentary of S. Straschun (Hareshash), note 6.

7. Gen. R. 68:12; Lev. R. 29:2.

8. John Ruskin, *The Crown of Wild Olive*, quoted by S. Goldman, *op. cit.*, p. 611.

9. Gen. R. 68:9; Pirke de-R. Eliezer 35.

10. Pirke de-R. Eliezer 35.

11. Quoted by Hacohen, *op. cit.*, Vol. I, pp. 91 f.

12. Beer-Hofmann, *op. cit.*, pp. 170 f.

Jacob in Haran GEN. 29—30

1. Compare Homer, *Iliad*, XII, 451.

2. Targum; Sforno: "beautiful eyes."

3. Speiser.

4. Buber and Rosenzweig, *Die Schrift und ihre Verdeutschung* (Berlin: Schocken, 1936), pp. 224 ff. Also see p. 274.

5. Also see Rabinowitz, *Jerusalem Post* (Nov. 28, 1968; Jan. 13 and Jan. 20, 1970).

6. See also JPS *Notes*.

7. Speiser. In Gen. 44:5, 15, Joseph is also reported to have practiced divination.

8. See JPS *Notes*.

9. Martin Noth, *The History of Israel* (New York: Harper & Row, 1956), pp. 85 ff., suggests the existence of an amphictyony, but this is disputed by others.

See also John Bright, "Early Israel," in *Old Testament Issues*, ed. Sandmel (New York-Evanston-London: Harper & Row, 1968), pp. 159 ff.

10. See Otto Eissfeldt, *The Old Testament* (New York: Harper & Row, 1965), p. 40, with further references. See also p. 472.

11. See Gen. R. 73:10.

12. See Bachya on Gen. 30:38.

13. Midrash Lekach Tov.

14. John Calvin, *Commentaries*, trans. John King (Grand Rapids, Mich.: Eerdmans, 1948–1950), Vol. II, p. 128.

15. Von Rad, *op. cit.*, p. 268.

16. Midrash Yelammedenu and Midrash Lekach Tov.

17. Gaster, *op. cit.*, p. 200.

Jacob's Departure from Haran GEN. 31:1—32:3

1. Rashi.

2. See JPS *Notes*.

3. Jer. Sab. 17a.

4. Nachmanides; see also B. Jacob.

5. Pritchard, *ANET*, p. 177. For an actual court case in Hurrian law, see Hallo, *JAOS*, 87 (1967), p. 64, note 1.

6. Gordon, *Before the Bible*, pp. 249 ff. See also above, note to Gen. 2:24.

7. See Driver.

8. Josephus, *Antiquities*, XVIII, 9:5.

9. Moshe Greenberg, *JBL*, 81 (1962), p. 239 ff.; so also Gunkel, *op. cit.*, pp. 344 ff. On the etymology of תְּרָפִים see Hoffner, Jr., *JNES*, 27, 1 (1968), pp. 61 ff.

10. Speiser, *op. cit.*, p. 250.

11. So Gen. R. 74:5.

12. So Rashbam; Ibn Ezra; based on Tanch. Vayetse 12.

13. B. M. 93b.

14. Gaster, *op. cit.*, p. 201.

15. Quoted in Gaster, *op. cit.*, p. 204.

16. Vergil, *Aeneid*, II, 293 f.

Jacob Becomes Israel GEN. 32:4—33:17

1. So Speiser; see JPS *Notes*.

2. See also Nachmanides and Sforno on Gen. 32:21.

3. El-Amarna letters and Ugarit.

4. For Mesopotamian and Greek parallels, cf. Gunkel, *op. cit.*, pp. 363 f.; Graves and Patai, *op. cit.*, pp. 227 f.

5. Compare Shakespeare, *Hamlet*, Act I, Scene 1; Plautus, *Amphitryon*, Act I, Scene 3.

6. Morgenstern, *Book of Genesis*, pp. 270 ff.; Maimonides, *Guide*, II, 42; also Ralbag, *Commentary, ad loc.*; and Milch. ha-Shem 6.

7. Abarbanel.

8. Koran, Sura III:87 (The Family of Imran).
9. Quoted in *Ma'yanah shel Torah*, Vol. I, p. 148.
10. Quoted in *Itture Torah*, Vol. I. p. 293.
11. Kaplan, unpublished manuscript.
12. The ambiguity recurs in II Sam. 24:1 and I Chron. 21:1. Compare Gen. R. 77:3 (the man was Esau's protective angel) and sources quoted in *TS* 32:116, note (he was Samael). In Beer-Hofmann, *op. cit.*, angels as well as Samael wrestle with him. See also A. J. Wolf, *CCAR Journal* (Oct. 1961), p. 47; von Rad, *op. cit.*, p. 316.

13. Based on Gen. R. 76:2.
14. Based on Sifre Beha'alotecha.
15. Gen. R. 78:9.
16. Hull. 89b ff.; Yoreh De'ah 65:5–7.
17. Jessie Sampter, *Brand Plucked from the Fire* (Philadelphia: Jewish Publication Society, 1937), p. 170.
18. From *An Anthology of American Negro Literature*, ed. S. C. Watkins (New York: Modern Library, 1944), p. 144.
19. *Jacob* (New York: Random House, 1941), pp. 179–180.

The Rape of Dinah GEN. 33:18—34:31

1. See JPS *Notes*.
2. Rashi favors the former; Rashbam the latter interpretation.
3. See Gen. R. 80:12.
4. Gen. R. 80:11; B. B. 15b; Pirke de-R. Eliezer 38.
5. B. Jacob. Gunkel, in line with his general assessment of biblical morality, thinks that the Torah relates the incident "with satisfaction," *ad* Gen. 34:28. See also, W. R. Bowie, *Interpreter's Bible, ad loc.*
6. See Midrash ha-Chefets 9; in *TS* 34:59.
7. Judith 9:2 ff.
8. Koh. R. 10:8; Tanch. Vayishlach 5.
9. Johann Wolfgang von Goethe, Letter to Sara von Grothuss, 1812; quoted in S. Goldman, *op. cit.*, p. 634.
10. *Jacob*, pp. 208–209.

Births and Deaths GEN. 35—36

1. On this see B. Gemser, *O. T. Studien*, 12 (1958), pp. 1 ff.
2. See E. C. Kingsbury, *HUCA*, 38 (1967), p. 136.
3. See Orach Chayim, Yoreh De'ah 282.
4. J-source, Ch. 28; E-source, Ch. 35.
5. J. H. Hertz.
6. B. Jacob, *op. cit.*, p. 664.
7. Note Gen. R. 82:10; also Rashi; Biur.
8. M. Tsevat, *HUCA*, 33 (1962), pp. 107 ff.
9. So the Samaritan version; Hertz. At Mari a major tribe was known as "Sons of the South" (*Maru-Yamina*).
10. Meg. 4:10.
11. Sab. 55b. Note the parallel in the *Iliad*, Vol. IX, 446 ff.
12. Rashi.

13. For a full discussion of this question, see de Vaux, *Revue Biblique*, 74 (1967), pp. 481–503.
14. See JPS *Notes*.
15. See Jer. Ber. 8:5, 12b; Pes. 54a; and Rabbenu Tam's comment on B. B. 115b.
16. Driver.
17. B. Jacob.
18. Midrash Or ha-Afelah 9, quoted in *TS* 35:110.
19. Jer. Shek. 2:5, 47a; and Gen. R. 82:10.
20. Abraham Isaac Kuk, *Iggerot Re'ayah* (1st ed.; Jerusalem: Hotsa'at Yerushalayim, 1923), Vol. I, p. 190.
21. Beer-Hofmann, *op. cit.*, pp. 60–61.
22. Morgenstern, *Book of Genesis*, p. 229.
23. *Joseph and His Brothers*, p. 94.

Part V *The Line of Jacob*

1. For an extensive analysis of the entire story, see Donald B. Redford, *A Study of the Biblical Story of Joseph* (Leiden: E. J. Brill, 1970).

2. Aristotle's term is "Peripety" which, when combined with "Discovery" (as in the Joseph story), produces the most effective drama; see *Poetics*, XII.

Young Joseph GEN. 37

1. Gunkel. See JPS *Notes* for a summary of interpretations. Also Gaster, *op. cit.*, p. 216, who believes it was a coat of extra length reaching to the ankles.
2. Sota 11a.
3. J. Vergote, *Joseph en Egypte* (Louvain: Publications Universitaires, 1959), pp. 146 ff.

4. For a detailed analysis, see Plaut, *CCAR Journal* (April 1969), pp. 65 ff. See also Gen. R. 84:18. The Joseph story is retold, with special additions, in the Koran, Sura XII (Joseph, Peace Be on Him); for an excerpt, see p. 368.
5. Sura XII:2–19 (Joseph, Peace Be on Him).

Tamar GEN. 38

1. Compare Gen. R. 85:1.
2. Targum; Rashi.
3. See Even ha-Ezer 9:1.
4. So Ibn Ezra; Luzzatto; Gunkel.
5. Herodotus, *op. cit.*, Vol. I, 199, tells of the widespread observance of this custom in Babylonia.
6. This is explained by Michael C. Astour, *JBL*, 85 (1966), pp. 185 ff.
7. Graves and Patai, *op. cit.*, p. 247, quote also an Ethiopian seduction tale.

8. So Rashbam; Redak; Hizkuni.
9. Compare Midrash Lekach Tov.
10. *TS* 38:6–8.
11. Shulchan Aruch, Even ha-Ezer 165:1; see also *Encyclopaedia Judaica*, Vol. 11, cols. 122 ff.
12. F. Delitzsch, quoted by von Rad, *op. cit.*, p. 35, note.
13. As told by Ginzberg, *op. cit.*, Vol. II, pp. 35–36.
14. *A Study of the Biblical Story of Joseph*, p. 18.

Joseph in Egypt GEN. 39—40

1. T. O. Lambdin, *JAOS*, 73 (1953), pp. 145 ff.
2. See *Interpreter's Dictionary*, Vol. II, p. 667.
3. Gordon, *Before the Bible*, p. 114.
4. Compare Orlinsky, *Ancient Israel*, pp. 32 ff.
5. So Ibn Ezra; Redak; Hizkuni; and others. In Gen. R. 86:6 "bread" has a sexual connotation.
6. Sefer ha-Yashar.
7. Abarbanel and Sforno make this point. Gunkel, *op. cit.*, citing Diodorus, suggests that castration would have been another and more likely punishment.
8. See Vergote, *op. cit.*, pp. 35 ff.
9. Compare W. Kornfeld, *Revue Biblique*, 57 (1950), pp. 92 ff.
10. Sanh. 56a–b; see p. 85 and see Rashi on Gen. 39:9.
11. See Ber. 55b.

12. Pritchard, *ANET*, p. 495. See also Oppenheim on interpretation of dreams in the ancient Near East, *Transactions of the American Philosophical Society*, 46, 3 (1956). And see "Mesopotamia" in *Entsiklopedyah Mikra'it*, Vol. V, cols. 59 ff.
13. See Ber. 55–57.
14. *TS* 39:18 ff.
15. Midrash ha-Gadol; Zohar 1:246a; Rashi; Abarbanel.
16. *TS* 39:18 ff.; Gen. R. 98:20. On the *shalshelet* and other rare accents in the light of Midrash, see D. B. Weisberg, *Jewish Quarterly Review*, 57 (1966), p. 64. See also note to Gen. 24:12.
17. Midrash Or ha-Afelah.
18. Pritchard, *ANET*, p. 24.

The Elevation of Joseph: The Brothers' First Visit GEN. 41—42

1. Targum Onkelos.
2. See *Joseph et Aseneth*, ed. M. Philonenko (Leiden: E. J. Brill, 1968); *Jewish Encyclopedia*, Vol. II, pp. 172 ff.
3. Gen. R. 84:7.
4. Pritchard, *ANET*, pp. 31–32. The record claims

to stem from the Pharaoh Djoser (*ca.* 2800 B.C.E.).
5. After Sefer ha-Yashar.
6. Gen. R. 91:1 preserved this implication.
7. Ruth Brin, *A Rag of Love* (Minneapolis, Minn.: Emmett, 1969), p. 41.

The Second Visit GEN. 43:1—44:17

1. Compare Maimonides, *Guide*, III, 40.
2. Biur; Luzzatto.
3. Herodotus, *op. cit.*, Vol. I, 241.
4. Compare von Rad.
5. For further references, see the survey in *Jewish Encyclopedia*, Vol. IV, pp. 623-624.
6. Sanh. 65b. See also Maimonides, Hilch. Akkum 11:4; and Kesef Mishneh, *ad loc*.
7. Midrash ha-Gadol.
8. Quoted by Gunkel.
9. Berachot, end.
10. *Certain People of the Book*, pp. 309-310.

Joseph Reveals His Identity GEN. 44:18—45:15

1. B. Jacob.
2. Pritchard, *ANET*, p. 259.
3. Rashi; Nachmanides; *et al.*
4. Rashi.
5. See p. 407.
6. Gen. R. 21:6.
7. This emphasis is made by Josephus, *Antiquities*, II, 6:7; Jubilees 42:25; and sources quoted in TS 44:14.
8. Gen. R. 93:6.
9. *Itture Torah*, Vol. I, p. 389.
10. Gen. R. 93:7; Rashi; and see Alshech.
11. *Antiquities*, II, 6:8.

Jacob Goes to Egypt GEN. 45:16—46:27

1. Sforno.
2. See Hul. 90b.
3. Rashi and Ibn Ezra.
4. Nachmanides and Rashbam.
5. See sources quoted in TS 45:88 on midrashic elaborations of this scene.
6. Compare B. Jacob.
7. Zohar Vayechi 226a; Chochmat Adam 157:9. Nowadays the mitzvah of closing the eyes is usually fulfilled by the burial society. Mishnah Sab. 23:5 prohibits such closing on the Sabbath.
8. Rashbam; Hizkuni; Sforno. See also JPS *Notes*.
9. See JPS *Notes* for a discussion of this counting.
10. Midrash ha-Gadol; Sefer ha-Yashar.
11. Speiser.
12. Compare Gen. R. 94:9 for a sample of how the Midrash dealt with the problem.
13. Midrash ha-Gadol; Midrash Lekach Tov; see also von Rad, *op. cit.*, p. 397.
14. Sforno follows this line of reasoning.
15. *Ethics of the Fathers* 3:16.
16. Mech. Pischa 14.
17. Zohar Vayigash 1:210a.
18. See, e.g., Ber. 5a; Sanh. 101a,b; Ta'an. 8a.
19. Zohar Vayigash 210a.
20. Midrash Lekach Tov; cf. Nachmanides.
21. Reported in the name of R. Simeon (Avot de-R. Nathan 30) and R. Hiya (Gen. R. 94:3).
22. Mech. Shira 3.
23. *On Joseph*, XLII.

Jacob in Egypt GEN. 46:28—47:27

1. So, e.g., B. Jacob.
2. See T. Reinach, *Textes des Auteurs Grecs et Romains Relatifs au Judaisme* (Paris: Ernest Leroux, 1895), p. 23.
3. Rashi, following B. K. 92a and Gen. R. 95:4.
4. Ehrlich; Speiser.
5. See the use of the term in Prov. 30:8, 31:15. On priestly privilege in antiquity, see Diodorus, *Historical Library*, Vol. I, 54, 73 f.; Herodotus, *op. cit.*, Vol. II, 168 f.
6. See Speiser.
7. Hertz.
8. Von Rad, *op. cit.*, p. 404.
9. See, e.g., Gunkel.
10. I Macc. 10:30; other details in Driver, *op. cit.*, *ad loc*.
11. Speiser, *op. cit.*, p. 353.
12. See Plaut, *CCAR Journal* (Oct. 1961), pp. 29 ff.
13. Gen. R. 95:3; Rashi; *Itture Torah*, p. 420.
14. Amy K. Blank, *op. cit.*, pp. 21, 25, excerpts.
15. *Democracy Reborn*, quoted by S. Goldman, *op. cit.*, pp. 685 f.
16. *On Joseph*, XLIII.

The Blessing of Ephraim and Manasseh GEN. 47:28—48:22

1. Bachya; Midrash ha-Gadol.
2. So Midrash ha-Gadol; Nachmanides; Bachya.
3. So Rashi, following the Talmud, Meg. 16b.
4. So Ibn Ezra; Sforno. See Tanch. Vayechi 3.
5. Midrash Aggadah.
6. Also in Heb. 11:21.
7. See *TS* and Driver, *op. cit., ad loc.*
8. The textual translation "crossing his hands" follows the Septuagint. See JPS *Notes* for further discussion and references.
9. O. Procksch, *Die Genesis übersetzt und erklärt* (Leipzig: A. Deichert, 1913), *ad loc.*

10. B. Jacob, in reference to Josh. 24:32, which states that Joseph was buried at Shechem, "in the parcel of ground which Jacob bought," and that this property became the inheritance of the children of Joseph.
11. Jubilees 34:1–9 notes such a tradition which may itself be an outflow of Gen. 48:22.
12. So Abarbanel; Ehrlich. See also John 4:5.
13. Mech. Beshallach 3.
14. Gen. R. 97:6.
15. Midrash ha-Chefets.
16. Gittin 13a.
17. Quoted in *Wellsprings of Torah*, pp. 93–94.
18. *Ibid.*, p. 95.

Jacob's Testament GEN. 49:1–27

1. Compare Gevirtz, *op. cit.*, pp. 35 ff.
2. Compare Jeremias, *op. cit.*, pp. 343 ff.
3. Josh. 19:1; Judg. 1:3.
4. See the discussion in JPS *Notes*.
5. So Hizkuni; Delitzsch; B. Jacob.
6. Following Rashi. On this passage and the verses to follow (Gen. 49:5–7, 8–12), see the discussion by C. M. Carmichael, *JBL*, 88 (Dec. 1969), Part IV, pp. 435–444.
7. The translation follows Rashi and Tanchuma. The derivation from the Greek, there suggested, is however in error. Compare M. Dahood, *Catholic Biblical Quarterly*, 23 (1961), pp. 54–56, who translates "circumcision blades."
8. Isa. 18:7; Pss. 68:30, 76:12 have the word שַׁי meaning tribute or present. See also Gen. R. 97 (new version). There exists a large body of literature devoted to an interpretation of this single phrase; cf. Driver, *op. cit.*, pp. 410 ff.; Gunkel, Skinner, and

B. Jacob, *ad loc.*; also Eissfeldt, Supplement to *Vetus Testamentum*, 4 (1957), pp. 138–147. For a contemporary interpretation, see Monford Harris, in *Rediscovering Judaism*, ed. Wolf, pp. 99 ff.
9. See Targum Onkelos; Sanh. 98b; Gen. R. 97 (new version); Zohar 1:25b.
10. Matth. 21:5, in connection with Zech. 9:9.
11. Yalkut Shimoni 161.
12. Ibn Ezra; Redak; *et al.* Ehrlich thinks that Gen. 49:18 is an ejaculation by the falling rider.
13. Delitzsch.
14. See JPS *Notes* for discussion and reference.
15. Jer. Hor. 2:5, 46d; Gen. R. 98:20.
16. Compare Rashbam.
17. Mann, *I Believe*, ed. Clifton Fadiman (New York: Simon and Schuster, 1939), pp. 189–194.
18. Koran, Sura XII:37–40 (Joseph, Peace Be on Him).
19. Bowie, *Interpreter's Bible*, pp. 821–822.
20. *Certain People of the Book*, pp. 344–345.

The Deaths of Jacob and Joseph GEN. 49:28—50:26

1. Herodotus, *op. cit.*, Vol. II, 86 ff.; Diodorus, *op. cit.*, Vol. I, 72, 91.
2. See B. Jacob.
3. Jer. M. K. 3:5, 82c. See also Gen. R. 100:7.
4. Josh. 24:29. See Speiser; Gaster, *op. cit.*, p. 222.
5. Driver, *op. cit.*, p. 400.

6. Von Rad, *op. cit.*, pp. 428 ff.
7. Thomas More, *Godly Meditation*, quoted by S. Goldman, *op. cit.*, p. 700.
8. Yeb. 65b; Gen. R. 100:8. See also B. M. 87a.
9. Midrash Lekach Tov.
10. After Sota 13a, b; Mech. to Exod. 13:19.
11. *On Joseph*, XLIV.

Biblical and Talmudic Abbreviations

Biblical Books

Chron.	Chronicles	Lam.	Lamentations
Deut.	Deuteronomy	Lev.	Leviticus
Eccl.	Ecclesiastes (Koheleth)	Mal.	Malachi
Exod.	Exodus	Neh.	Nehemiah
Ez.	Ezekiel	Numb.	Numbers
Gen.	Genesis	Ob.	Obadiah
Hab.	Habakkuk	Prov.	Proverbs
Hos.	Hosea	Ps.	Psalms
Isa.	Isaiah	Sam.	Samuel
Jer.	Jeremiah	Song	Song of Songs
Josh.	Joshua	Zech.	Zechariah
Jud.	Judges	Zeph.	Zephaniah

Mishnah and Gemara (Talmud)

(An English edition of the Babylonian Talmud has been published by Soncino Press, London, 1948.)

A.Z.	Avodah Zarah	Meg.	Megillah
B.B.	Bava Batra	M.K.	Mo'ed katan
B.K.	Bava Kamma	Ned.	Nedarim
B.M.	Bava Metzia	Nid.	Nidda
Ber.	Berachot	Pes.	Pesachim
Erub.	Eruvin	R.H.	Rosh Hashanah
Git.	Gittin	Sab.	Shabbat
Hag.	Chagiga	Sanh.	Sanhedrin
Hul.	Chullin	Shev.	Shevuot
Ket.	Ketubot	Ta'an.	Ta'anit
Kid.	Kiddushin	Yeb.	Yevamot
Mak.	Makkot		

Other Hebrew sources (not as yet translated into English) have been listed in the manner familiar to students of such texts.

Bible Translations

frequently consulted in the preparation of this commentary

SEPTUAGINT (attributed to seventy-two translators), third–second centuries B.C.E., Greek.

PESHITTA, about first–second centuries C.E., Syriac.

TARGUM (attributed to Onkelos), second century C.E., Aramaic.

VULGATE, by Jerome, fourth–fifth centuries C.E., Latin.

TARGUM YERUSHALMI, probably fifth–sixth centuries C.E., Aramaic.

JONATHAN (attributed to Jonathan ben Uzziel), about eighth century C.E., Aramaic.

DOUAI, 1609–1610, English.

KJV, KING JAMES (also called "Authorized") Version, 1611, English.

MENDELSSOHN, 1780–1783, German.

JPS, Jewish Publication Society (first) version, 1917, American.

BUBER-ROSENZWEIG, from 1926 on, German.

DE VAUX, 1953, French.

RSV, Revised Standard Version, 1953, American.

NJPS (The Torah), New Jewish Publication Society version, revised ed., 1967, American.

NEB, New English Bible, 1970, English.

Midrashic and Post-Midrashic Collections

frequently quoted; available wholly or in part in English

AVOT DE-R. NATHAN. Edited by Judah Goldin. New Haven: Yale University Press, 1955.

DEUT. R. Deuteronomy Rabbah. *The Midrash*, Vol. 7. London: Soncino Press, 1939.

EXOD. R. Exodus Rabbah. *The Midrash*, Vol. 3. London: Soncino Press, 1939.

GEN. R. Genesis Rabbah. *The Midrash*, Vols. 1 and 2. London: Soncino Press, 1939.

GINZBERG, LOUIS. *The Legends of the Jews.* 7 vols. Philadelphia: JPS, 1933.

LEV. R. Leviticus Rabbah. *The Midrash*, Vol. 4. London: Soncino Press, 1939.

MA'YANAH SHEL TORAH. Alexander Zusia Friedman, *Wellsprings of Torah.* 2 vols. New York: Judaica Press, 1969.

MECH. Mechilta de-R. Yishmael. Edited by Jacob Z. Lauterbach. Philadelphia: JPS, 1933.

NUMB. R. Numbers Rabbah. *The Midrash*, Vols. 5 and 6. London: Soncino Press, 1939.

PIRKE DE-R. ELIEZER. English edition by Gerald Friedlander, reprinted New York: Hermon Press, 1965.

T. S. (TORAH SHELEMAH). M. M. Kasher, 3rd edition, from 1949: partial English edition, *Encyclopedia of Biblical Interpretation.* New York: American Biblical Encyclopedia Society, from 1953.

ZOHAR. English edition, London: Soncino Press, 1931.

Commentaries on Genesis

Unless otherwise stated, *ad loc.* indicates the verse under discussion; thus, when our commentary treats of 12:3 and cites Rashi as a source, it means Rashi's own comment on this verse.

The following list of commentaries contains only those works most frequently referred to in the preparation of this book. English commentaries or those available fully or partially in English translation are marked by an asterisk. English excerpts from traditional Hebrew commentaries may be found in *The Soncino Chumash*, ed. A. Cohen (Hindhead, Surrey: Soncino Press, 1947).

Commentaries of Earlier Centuries

*Rashi (Rabbi *Shelomoh Itzchaki*), France, 1040–1105.

Rashbam (Rabbi *Shemuel ben* Meir), his grandson, c. 1085–1158.

Ibn Ezra (Abraham), Spain, 1092–1167.

Lek. Tov (Lekach Tov, by Tobiah ben Eliezer), Bulgaria, c. eleventh century.

Sechel Tov (Menachem b. Solomon), Italy, twelfth century.

Redak (Rabbi *David Kimchi*), France, 1160–1235.

Nachmanides (Rabbi Moses ben Nachman), Spain, 1194–1270.

Hizkuni (Chizkiya ben Mano'ach), France, thirteenth century.

Ralbag (Rabbi *Levi ben* Gershon), France, 1288–1344.

Bachya (ben Asher), Spain, died 1340.

Abarbanel (Isaac), Spain–Italy, 1437–1508.

Sforno, Obadiah ben Jacob, Italy, c. 1475–1550.

*Calvin, John, Switzerland, 1509–1564.

Biur (commentary by Solomon of Dubno on the German translation of Moses Mendelssohn), Russia–Germany, 1738–1813.

Reggio, Isaac Samuel, Italy, 1784–1855.

Ha-ketav veha-kabbalah (commentary by J. Z. Meklenburg), Poland, 1785–1865.

Luzzatto, Samuel David, Italy, 1800–1865.

Malbim (Meir *Lev ben* Yechiel Michael), Russia, 1809–1879.

*Hirsch (Samson Raphael), Germany, 1808–1888.

Commentaries of the Twentieth Century

Gunkel, Hermann. Germany. Göttingen: Vandenhoeck und Ruprecht, 1901.

Kahana, Abraham. Russia–Palestine. Zhitomir: publ. by author, 1903.

*Driver, Samuel R. England. New York: Edwin G. Gorham, 1904.

*Skinner, John. England. New York: Charles Scribner's Sons, 1910.

Procksch, Otto. Germany. Leipzig: A. Deichert, 1913.

*Morgenstern, Julian. U.S.A. Cincinnati: Union of American Hebrew Congregations, 1919.

*Hertz, Joseph H., ed. England. Oxford: Oxford University Press, 1929.

Jacob, Benno. Germany. Berlin: Schocken, 1934.

*Cassuto, Umberto. Italy–Israel, 1949. (English edition, Jerusalem: Magnes Press, 1961–64.)

De Vaux, Raoul. France. Paris: Editions du Cerf, 1953.

*Von Rad, Gerhard. Germany, 1956. (English edition, Philadelphia: Westminster Press, 1961.)

*Interpreter's Bible. U.S.A. New York and Nashville: Abingdon Press, 1957.

*Speiser, Ephraim A. U.S.A. Garden City: Doubleday, 1964.

*Jerome Bible Commentary. U.S.A. Englewood Cliffs: Prentice-Hall, 1968.

Commentary Aids

Ehrlich, Arnold B. *Mikra Kifeshuto*. 1899. (Reprinted New York: Ktav, 1966.)

Tur-Sinai, N. H. *Peshuto shel mikra*. Jerusalem: Kiryat Sefer, 1962.

*[JPS Notes] *Notes on the New Translation of the Torah*. Edited by Harry M. Orlinsky. Philadelphia: Jewish Publication Society, 1969.

*[ANET] Pritchard, James B., ed. *Ancient Near Eastern Texts*, revised edition. Princeton: Princeton University Press, 1955. (Additional supplementary texts and pictures were published in 1969.)

Macmillan Bible Atlas. Edited by Y. Aharoni and M. Avi-Yonah. New York: Macmillan Co., 1968.

Selected General English Bibliography

Adam to Daniel (illustr.). Edited by G. Cornfeld. New York: Macmillan Co., 1961.

ADAR, ZVI. *The Biblical Narrative.* Jerusalem: W.Z.O., 1959.

ALBRIGHT, WILLIAM FOXWELL. *Yahweh and the Gods of Canaan.* Garden City: Doubleday, 1968.

————. *The Archeology of Palestine.* Harmondsworth: Penguin Books, 1949.

EISSFELDT, OTTO. *The Old Testament.* New York: Harper and Row, 1965.

Encyclopaedia Judaica. 16 vols. New York and Jerusalem: Macmillan Co., 1972. (The work appeared after our manuscript was completed and was referred to only in a few cases thereafter.)

FRAZER, JAMES G. *Folklore in the Old Testament.* 3 vols. London: Macmillan Co., 1919. Parts of this work have been updated and republished in Gaster's book (see below).

FREEHOF, SOLOMON B. *Preface to Scripture.* Cincinnati: Union of American Hebrew Congregations, 1950.

GASTER, THEODOR H. *Myth, Legend and Custom in the Old Testament.* New York: Harper and Row, 1969.

GLUECK, NELSON. *The Other Side of the Jordan.* New Haven: American School of Oriental Research, 1940.

————. *The River Jordan.* Philadelphia: Jewish Publication Society, 1946.

GOLDMAN, SOLOMON. *In the Beginning.* Philadelphia: Jewish Publication Society, 1949.

GORDON, CYRUS H. *Before the Bible.* New York: Harper and Row, 1962.

GRAVES, ROBERT, AND PATAI, RAPHAEL. *Hebrew Myths.* London: Cassel and Co., 1964.

————. *The Book of Genesis.* London: Cassel and Co., 1964.

Interpreter's Dictionary of the Bible. 4 vols. New York and Nashville: Abingdon Press, 1962.

JACOBSON, B. S. *Meditations on the Torah.* Tel Aviv: Sinai Publishing Co., 1956.

Jewish Encyclopedia. Edited by I. Singer. 12 vols. New York: Funk and Wagnalls Co., 1901–1904.

KAUFMANN, YEHEZKEL. *The Religion of Israel.* Translated and abridged by Moshe Greenberg. Chicago: University of Chicago Press, 1960.

*LEIBOWITZ, NECHAMA. *Iyyunim besefer bereshit.* Jerusalem: Hahistadrut ha-tsiyonit ha-olamit, 1966. English excerpts from 1958 on.

ORLINSKY, HARRY M. *Ancient Israel.* Ithaca: Cornell University Press, 1954.

SANDMEL, SAMUEL. *The Hebrew Scriptures.* New York: Knopf, 1963.

*SARNA, NAHUM M. *Understanding Genesis.* New York: McGraw-Hill, 1966.

SIMONS, J. *The Geographical and Topographical Texts of the Old Testament.* Leiden: E. J. Brill, 1959.

Universal Jewish Encyclopedia. Edited by I. Landman. 10 vols. New York: U.J.E. Co., 1939–1943.

Views of the Biblical World (illustr.). 5 vols. Chicago–New York: Jordan Publishing Co., 1959–1961.

הפטרות

HAFTAROT

Haftarah (meaning "conclusion"; plural, *Haftarot*) was originally a special reading from the Prophets which followed the weekly Torah reading and concluded the service. In the following, three *Haftarot* are provided for each Sabbath when Genesis is read. The first selections are the traditional ones, the second and third alternatives have been chosen by the author from a wider range of biblical sources.

The translations are taken from *The Holy Scriptures* Philadelphia: Jewish Publication Society, 1917. The Society's new translation of Psalms, which was available at the time of printing, was also utilized.

בְּרֵאשִׁית

FIRST SELECTION

Isaiah

42 : 5 - 21

Chapter 42

מב

5] Thus saith God the LORD
He that created the heavens, and stretched them
   forth,
He that spread forth the earth and that which
   cometh out of it,
He that giveth breath unto the people upon it,
And spirit to them that walk therein:

5] כֹּה־אָמַר הָאֵל | יְהֹוָה
בּוֹרֵא הַשָּׁמַיִם וְנוֹטֵיהֶם
רֹקַע הָאָרֶץ וְצֶאֱצָאֶיהָ
נֹתֵן נְשָׁמָה לָעָם עָלֶיהָ
וְרוּחַ לַהֹלְכִים בָּהּ:

6] I the LORD have called thee in righteousness,
And have taken hold of thy hand,
And kept thee, and set thee for a covenant of the
   people,
For a light of the nations;

6] אֲנִי יְהֹוָה קְרָאתִיךָ בְצֶדֶק
וְאַחְזֵק בְּיָדֶךָ
וְאֶצָּרְךָ וְאֶתֶּנְךָ לִבְרִית עָם
לְאוֹר גּוֹיִם:

7] To open the blind eyes,
To bring out the prisoners from the dungeon,
And them that sit in darkness out of the prison-
   house.

7] לִפְקֹחַ עֵינַיִם עִוְרוֹת
לְהוֹצִיא מִמַּסְגֵּר אַסִּיר
מִבֵּית כֶּלֶא יֹשְׁבֵי חֹשֶׁךְ:

8] I am the LORD, that is My name;
And My glory will I not give to another,
Neither My praise to graven images.

8] אֲנִי יְהֹוָה הוּא שְׁמִי
וּכְבוֹדִי לְאַחֵר לֹא־אֶתֵּן
וּתְהִלָּתִי לַפְּסִילִים:

9] Behold, the former things are come to pass,
And new things do I declare;
Before they spring forth I tell you of them.

9] הָרִאשֹׁנוֹת הִנֵּה־בָאוּ
וַחֲדָשׁוֹת אֲנִי מַגִּיד
בְּטֶרֶם תִּצְמַחְנָה אַשְׁמִיעַ אֶתְכֶם:

10] Sing unto the LORD a new song,
And His praise from the end of the earth;

10] שִׁירוּ לַיהֹוָה שִׁיר חָדָשׁ
תְּהִלָּתוֹ מִקְצֵה הָאָרֶץ

513

Ye that go down to the sea, and all that is therein,
The isles, and the inhabitants thereof.

11] Let the wilderness and the cities thereof lift
up their voice,
The villages that Kedar doth inhabit;
Let the inhabitants of Sela exult,
Let them shout from the top of the mountains.

12] Let them give glory unto the LORD,
And declare His praise in the islands.

13] The LORD will go forth as a mighty man,
He will stir up jealousy like a man of war;
He will cry, yea, He will shout aloud,
He will prove Himself mighty against His enemies.

14] I have long time held My peace,
I have been still, and refrained Myself;
Now will I cry like a travailing woman,
Gasping and panting at once.

15] I will make waste mountains and hills,
And dry up all their herbs;
And I will make the rivers islands,
And I will dry up the pools.

16] And I will bring the blind by a way that they
knew not,
In paths that they knew not will I lead them;
I will make darkness light before them,
And rugged places plain.
These things will I do,
And I will not leave them undone.

17] They shall be turned back, greatly ashamed,
That trust in graven images,

יוֹרְדֵי הַיָּם וּמְלֹאוֹ
אִיִּים וְיֹשְׁבֵיהֶם:

11] יִשְׂאוּ מִדְבָּר וְעָרָיו
חֲצֵרִים תֵּשֵׁב קֵדָר
יָרֹנּוּ יֹשְׁבֵי סֶלַע
מֵרֹאשׁ הָרִים יִצְוָחוּ:

12] יָשִׂימוּ לַיהוָה כָּבוֹד
וּתְהִלָּתוֹ בָּאִיִּים יַגִּידוּ:

13] יְהוָה כַּגִּבּוֹר יֵצֵא
כְּאִישׁ מִלְחָמוֹת יָעִיר קִנְאָה
יָרִיעַ אַף־יַצְרִיחַ
עַל־אֹיְבָיו יִתְגַּבָּר:

14] הֶחֱשֵׁיתִי מֵעוֹלָם
אַחֲרִישׁ אֶתְאַפָּק
כַּיּוֹלֵדָה אֶפְעֶה
אֶשֹּׁם וְאֶשְׁאַף יָחַד:

15] אַחֲרִיב הָרִים וּגְבָעוֹת
וְכָל־עֶשְׂבָּם אוֹבִישׁ
וְשַׂמְתִּי נְהָרוֹת לָאִיִּים
וַאֲגַמִּים אוֹבִישׁ:

16] וְהוֹלַכְתִּי עִוְרִים בְּדֶרֶךְ לֹא יָדְעוּ
בִּנְתִיבוֹת לֹא־יָדְעוּ אַדְרִיכֵם
אָשִׂים מַחְשָׁךְ לִפְנֵיהֶם לָאוֹר
וּמַעֲקַשִּׁים לְמִישׁוֹר
אֵלֶּה הַדְּבָרִים עֲשִׂיתִם
וְלֹא עֲזַבְתִּים:

17] נָסֹגוּ אָחוֹר יֵבֹשׁוּ בֹשֶׁת
הַבֹּטְחִים בַּפָּסֶל

514

That say unto molten images:
"Ye are our gods."

הָאֹמְרִים לְמַסֵּכָה
אַתֶּם אֱלֹהֵינוּ:

18] Hear, ye deaf,
And look, ye blind, that ye may see.

18] הַחֵרְשִׁים שְׁמָעוּ
וְהַעִוְרִים הַבִּיטוּ לִרְאוֹת:

19] Who is blind, but My servant?
Or deaf, as My messenger that I send?
Who is blind as he that is wholehearted,
And blind as the Lord's servant?

19] מִי עִוֵּר כִּי אִם־עַבְדִּי
וְחֵרֵשׁ כְּמַלְאָכִי אֶשְׁלָח
מִי עִוֵּר כִּמְשֻׁלָּם
וְעִוֵּר כְּעֶבֶד יְהֹוָה:

20] Seeing many things, thou observest not;
Opening the ears, he heareth not.

20] רָאִיתָ רַבּוֹת וְלֹא תִשְׁמֹר
פָּקוֹחַ אָזְנַיִם וְלֹא יִשְׁמָע:

21] The Lord was pleased, for His righteousness'
sake,
To make the teaching great and glorious.

21] יְהֹוָה חָפֵץ לְמַעַן צִדְקוֹ
יַגְדִּיל תּוֹרָה וְיַאְדִּיר:

SECOND SELECTION

Psalms
104 : 1-13

Psalm 104

קד

1] Bless the Lord, O my soul;
O Lord, my God, You are very great;
You are clothed in glory and majesty,

1] בָּרְכִי נַפְשִׁי אֶת־יְהֹוָה
יְהֹוָה אֱלֹהַי גָּדַלְתָּ מְּאֹד
הוֹד וְהָדָר לָבָשְׁתָּ:

2] wrapt in a robe of light;
You spread the heavens like a tent cloth.

2] עֹטֶה־אוֹר כַּשַּׂלְמָה
נוֹטֶה שָׁמַיִם כַּיְרִיעָה:

3] He sets the rafters of his lofts in the waters,
makes the clouds His chariot,
moves on the wings of the wind.

3] הַמְקָרֶה בַמַּיִם עֲלִיּוֹתָיו
הַשָּׂם־עָבִים רְכוּבוֹ
הַמְהַלֵּךְ עַל־כַּנְפֵי־רוּחַ:

4] He makes the winds His messengers,
fiery flames His servants.

4] עֹשֶׂה מַלְאָכָיו רוּחוֹת
מְשָׁרְתָיו אֵשׁ לֹהֵט:

v. 20. ראות ק'   v. 21. עד כאן לספרדים

5] He established the earth on its foundations,
so that it shall never totter.

6] You made the deep cover it as a garment;
the waters stood above the mountains.

7] They fled at Your blast,
rushed away at the sound of Your thunder,

8] up the mountains, down the valleys,
to the place You established for them.

9] You set bounds they must not pass
so that they never again cover the earth.

10] You make springs gush forth in torrents;
they make their way between the hills,

11] giving drink to all the wild beasts;
the wild asses slake their thirst.

12] The birds of the sky dwell beside them
and sing among the foliage.

13] You water the mountains from Your[a] lofts;
the earth is sated from the fruit of Your work.

יָסַד־אֶרֶץ עַל־מְכוֹנֶיהָ [5
בַּל־תִּמּוֹט עוֹלָם וָעֶד:

תְּהוֹם כַּלְּבוּשׁ כִּסִּיתוֹ [6
עַל־הָרִים יַעַמְדוּ־מָיִם:

מִן־גַּעֲרָתְךָ יְנוּסוּן [7
מִן־קוֹל רַעַמְךָ יֵחָפֵזוּן:

יַעֲלוּ הָרִים יֵרְדוּ בְקָעוֹת [8
אֶל־מְקוֹם זֶה | יָסַדְתָּ לָהֶם:

גְּבוּל־שַׂמְתָּ בַּל־יַעֲבֹרוּן [9
בַּל־יְשֻׁבוּן לְכַסּוֹת הָאָרֶץ:

הַמְשַׁלֵּחַ מַעְיָנִים בַּנְּחָלִים [10
בֵּין הָרִים יְהַלֵּכוּן:

יַשְׁקוּ כָּל־חַיְתוֹ שָׂדָי [11
יִשְׁבְּרוּ פְרָאִים צְמָאָם:

עֲלֵיהֶם עוֹף־הַשָּׁמַיִם יִשְׁכּוֹן [12
מִבֵּין עֳפָאיִם יִתְּנוּ־קוֹל:

מַשְׁקֶה הָרִים מֵעֲלִיּוֹתָיו [13
מִפְּרִי מַעֲשֶׂיךָ תִּשְׂבַּע הָאָרֶץ:

THIRD SELECTION

Psalms

19 : 1-15

Psalm 19

1] For the Leader.
A psalm of David.
2] The heavens declare the glory of God,
the sky proclaims His handiwork;

3] Day to day makes utterance,
night to night speaks out.

יט

לַמְנַצֵּחַ מִזְמוֹר לְדָוִד: [1
הַשָּׁמַיִם מְסַפְּרִים כְּבוֹד־אֵל [2
וּמַעֲשֵׂה יָדָיו מַגִּיד הָרָקִיעַ:

יוֹם לְיוֹם יַבִּיעַ אֹמֶר [3
וְלַיְלָה לְּלַיְלָה יְחַוֶּה־דָּעַת:

a Lit. "His"

4] There is no utterance,
there are no words,
a-whose sound goes unheard.-*a*

5] Their voice*b* carries throughout the earth,
their words to the end of the world.
He placed in them*c* a tent for the sun,

6] who is like a groom coming forth from the
chamber
like a hero, eager to run his course.

7] His rising-place is at one end of heaven,
and his circuit reaches the other;
nothing escapes his heat.

8] The teaching of the LORD is perfect, renewing
life;
the decrees of the LORD are enduring, making the
simple wise;

9] The precepts of the LORD are just, rejoicing the
heart;
the instruction of the LORD is lucid, *d*-restoring
strength.-*d*

10] The fear of the LORD is pure, abiding forever;
the judgments of the LORD are true, righteous
altogether,

11] more desirable than gold, than much fine gold;
sweeter than honey, than *e*-drippings of the comb.-*e*

12] Your servant pays them heed;
in obeying them there is much reward.

13] Who can be aware of errors? Clear me of
unperceived guilt,

14] and from *f*-willful sins-*f* keep Your servant;
let them not dominate me;
then shall I be blameless and clear of grave offense.

15] May the words of my mouth and the prayer
of my heart
be acceptable to You, O LORD, my rock and my
redeemer.

4 אֵין־אֹמֶר וְאֵין דְּבָרִים
בְּלִי נִשְׁמָע קוֹלָם:

5 בְּכָל־הָאָרֶץ ׀ יָצָא קַוָּם
וּבִקְצֵה תֵבֵל מִלֵּיהֶם
לַשֶּׁמֶשׁ שָׂם־אֹהֶל בָּהֶם:

6 וְהוּא כְּחָתָן יֹצֵא מֵחֻפָּתוֹ
יָשִׂישׂ כְּגִבּוֹר לָרוּץ אֹרַח:

7 מִקְצֵה הַשָּׁמַיִם ׀ מוֹצָאוֹ
וּתְקוּפָתוֹ עַל־קְצוֹתָם
וְאֵין נִסְתָּר מֵחַמָּתוֹ:

8 תּוֹרַת יְהוָה תְּמִימָה מְשִׁיבַת נָפֶשׁ
עֵדוּת יְהוָה נֶאֱמָנָה מַחְכִּימַת פֶּתִי:

9 פִּקּוּדֵי יְהוָה יְשָׁרִים מְשַׂמְּחֵי־לֵב
מִצְוַת יְהוָה בָּרָה מְאִירַת עֵינָיִם:

10 יִרְאַת יְהוָה ׀ טְהוֹרָה עוֹמֶדֶת לָעַד
מִשְׁפְּטֵי־יְהוָה אֱמֶת צָדְקוּ יַחְדָּו:

11 הַנֶּחֱמָדִים מִזָּהָב וּמִפַּז רָב
וּמְתוּקִים מִדְּבַשׁ וְנֹפֶת צוּפִים:

12 גַּם־עַבְדְּךָ נִזְהָר בָּהֶם
בְּשָׁמְרָם עֵקֶב רָב:

13 שְׁגִיאוֹת מִי־יָבִין
מִנִּסְתָּרוֹת נַקֵּנִי:

14 גַּם מִזֵּדִים ׀ חֲשֹׂךְ עַבְדֶּךָ
אַל־יִמְשְׁלוּ־בִי
אָז אֵיתָם וְנִקֵּיתִי מִפֶּשַׁע רָב:

15 יִהְיוּ לְרָצוֹן ׀ אִמְרֵי־פִי וְהֶגְיוֹן
לִבִּי לְפָנֶיךָ יְהוָה צוּרִי וְגֹאֲלִי:

a-a With Septuagint, Symmachus, and Vulgate; or "Their sound is not heard"
b Cf. Septuagint, Symmachus, and Vulgate; Arabic qawwa, "to shout"
d-d Lit. "Give light to my eyes"; cf. I Sam. 14.27–30; Ps. 38.11; Ezra 9.8
f-f Or "arrogant men"

c Viz. the heavens
e-e Meaning of Heb. uncertain

FIRST SELECTION

Isaiah

54 : 1-10

נד

Chapter 54

1] Sing, O barren, thou that didst not bear,
Break forth into singing, and cry aloud, thou that
   didst not travail;
For more are the children of the desolate
Than the children of the married wife, saith the
   LORD.

2] Enlarge the place of thy tent,
And let them stretch forth the curtains of thy
   habitations, spare not;
Lengthen thy cords, and strengthen thy stakes.

3] For thou shalt spread abroad on the right hand
   and on the left;
And thy seed shall possess the nations,
And make the desolate cities to be inhabited.

4] Fear not, for thou shalt not be ashamed.
Neither be thou confounded, for thou shalt not
   be put to shame;
For thou shalt forget the shame of thy youth,
And the reproach of thy widowhood shalt thou
   remember no more.

5] For thy Maker is thy husband,
The LORD of hosts is His name;
And the Holy One of Israel is thy Redeemer,
The God of the whole earth shall He be called.

6] For the LORD hath called thee
As a wife forsaken and grieved in spirit;

נד

1] רָנִּי עֲקָרָה לֹא יָלָדָה
פִּצְחִי רִנָּה וְצַהֲלִי לֹא־חָלָה
כִּי־רַבִּים בְּנֵי־שׁוֹמֵמָה
מִבְּנֵי בְעוּלָה אָמַר יְהוָה:

2] הַרְחִיבִי ׀ מְקוֹם אָהֳלֵךְ
וִירִיעוֹת מִשְׁכְּנוֹתַיִךְ יַטּוּ אַל־תַּחְשֹׂכִי
הַאֲרִיכִי מֵיתָרַיִךְ וִיתֵדֹתַיִךְ חַזֵּקִי:

3] כִּי־יָמִין וּשְׂמֹאול תִּפְרֹצִי
וְזַרְעֵךְ גּוֹיִם יִירָשׁ
וְעָרִים נְשַׁמּוֹת יוֹשִׁיבוּ:

4] אַל־תִּירְאִי כִּי־לֹא תֵבוֹשִׁי
וְאַל־תִּכָּלְמִי כִּי־לֹא תַחְפִּירִי
כִּי בֹשֶׁת עֲלוּמַיִךְ תִּשְׁכָּחִי
וְחֶרְפַּת אַלְמְנוּתַיִךְ לֹא תִזְכְּרִי־עוֹד:

5] כִּי בֹעֲלַיִךְ עֹשַׂיִךְ
יְהוָה צְבָאוֹת שְׁמוֹ
וְגֹאֲלֵךְ קְדוֹשׁ יִשְׂרָאֵל
אֱלֹהֵי כָל־הָאָרֶץ יִקָּרֵא:

6] כִּי־כְאִשָּׁה עֲזוּבָה
וַעֲצוּבַת רוּחַ קְרָאָךְ יְהוָה

מלא ו׳ .v. 3

518

And a wife of youth, can she be rejected?
Saith thy God.

וְאֵשֶׁת נְעוּרִים

כִּי תִמָּאֵס אָמַר אֱלֹהָיִךְ:

7] For a small moment have I forsaken thee;
But with great compassion will I gather thee.

7 בְּרֶגַע קָטֹן עֲזַבְתִּיךְ

וּבְרַחֲמִים גְּדוֹלִים אֲקַבְּצֵךְ:

8] In a little wrath I hid My face from thee for a
    moment;
But with everlasting kindness will I have compas-
    sion on thee,
Saith the Lord thy Redeemer.

8 בְּשֶׁצֶף קֶצֶף הִסְתַּרְתִּי פָנַי רֶגַע מִמֵּךְ

וּבְחֶסֶד עוֹלָם רִחַמְתִּיךְ

אָמַר גֹּאֲלֵךְ יְהֹוָה:

9] For this is as the waters of Noah unto Me;
For as I have sworn that the waters of Noah
Should no more go over the earth,
So have I sworn that I would not be wroth with
    thee,
Nor rebuke thee.

9 כִּי־מֵי נֹחַ זֹאת לִי

אֲשֶׁר נִשְׁבַּעְתִּי מֵעֲבֹר מֵי־נֹחַ

עוֹד עַל־הָאָרֶץ

כֵּן נִשְׁבַּעְתִּי

מִקְּצֹף עָלַיִךְ וּמִגְּעָר־בָּךְ:

10] For the mountains may depart,
And the hills be removed;
But my kindness shall not depart from thee,
Neither shall My covenant of peace be removed,
Saith the Lord that hath compassion on thee.

10 כִּי הֶהָרִים יָמוּשׁוּ

וְהַגְּבָעוֹת תְּמוּטֶינָה

וְחַסְדִּי מֵאִתֵּךְ לֹא־יָמוּשׁ

וּבְרִית שְׁלוֹמִי לֹא תָמוּט

אָמַר מְרַחֲמֵךְ יְהֹוָה:׃

SECOND SELECTION

Isaiah

44 : 1-8

מד

Chapter 44

1] Yet now hear, O Jacob My servant,
And Israel whom I have chosen;

1 וְעַתָּה שְׁמַע יַעֲקֹב עַבְדִּי

וְיִשְׂרָאֵל בָּחַרְתִּי בוֹ:

2] Thus saith the Lord that made thee,
And formed thee from the womb, who will help
    thee:
Fear not, O Jacob My servant,
And thou, Jeshurun, whom I have chosen.

2 כֹּה־אָמַר יְהֹוָה עֹשֶׂךָ

וְיֹצֶרְךָ מִבֶּטֶן יַעְזְרֶךָ

אַל־תִּירָא עַבְדִּי יַעֲקֹב

וִישֻׁרוּן בָּחַרְתִּי בוֹ:

3] For I will pour water upon the thirsty land,
And streams upon the dry ground;

3 כִּי אֶצָּק־מַיִם עַל־צָמֵא

וְנֹזְלִים עַל־יַבָּשָׁה

I will pour My spirit upon thy seed,
And My blessing upon thine offspring;

4] And they shall spring up among the grass,
As willows by the watercourses.

5] One shall say: "I am the Lord's";
And another shall call himself by the name o
Jacob;
And another shall subscribe with his hand unto
the Lord,
And surname himself by the name of Israel.

6] Thus saith the Lord, the King of Israel,
And his Redeemer the Lord of hosts:
I am the first, and I am the last,
And beside Me there is no God.

7] And who, as I, can proclaim—
Let him declare it, and set it in order for Me—
Since I appointed the ancient people?
And the things that are coming, and that shall
come to pass, let them declare.

8] Fear ye not, neither be afraid;
Have I not announced unto thee of old, and
declared it?
And ye are My witnesses.
Is there a God beside Me?
Yea, there is no Rock; I know not any.

THIRD SELECTION

Psalms

104 : 24 - 35

Psalm 104

24] How many are the things You have made,
O Lord;
You have made them all with wisdom;
the earth is full of Your creations.

אֶצֹּק רוּחִי עַל־זַרְעֶךָ

וּבִרְכָתִי עַל־צֶאֱצָאֶיךָ:

4] וְצָמְחוּ בְּבֵין חָצִיר

כַּעֲרָבִים עַל־יִבְלֵי־מָיִם:

5] זֶה יֹאמַר לַיהוָה אָנִי

וְזֶה יִקְרָא בְשֵׁם־יַעֲקֹב

וְזֶה יִכְתֹּב יָדוֹ לַיהוָה

וּבְשֵׁם יִשְׂרָאֵל יְכַנֶּה:

6] כֹּה־אָמַר יְהוָה מֶלֶךְ־יִשְׂרָאֵל

וְגֹאֲלוֹ יְהוָה צְבָאוֹת

אֲנִי רִאשׁוֹן וַאֲנִי אַחֲרוֹן

וּמִבַּלְעָדַי אֵין אֱלֹהִים:

7] וּמִי־כָמוֹנִי יִקְרָא

וְיַגִּידֶהָ וְיַעְרְכֶהָ לִי

מִשּׂוּמִי עַם־עוֹלָם

וְאֹתִיּוֹת וַאֲשֶׁר תָּבֹאנָה יַגִּידוּ לָמוֹ:

8] אַל־תִּפְחֲדוּ וְאַל־תִּרְהוּ

הֲלֹא מֵאָז הִשְׁמַעְתִּיךָ וְהִגַּדְתִּי

וְאַתֶּם עֵדָי

הֲיֵשׁ אֱלוֹהַּ מִבַּלְעָדַי

וְאֵין צוּר בַּל־יָדָעְתִּי:

קד

24] מָה־רַבּוּ מַעֲשֶׂיךָ | יְהוָה

כֻּלָּם בְּחָכְמָה עָשִׂיתָ

מָלְאָה הָאָרֶץ קִנְיָנֶךָ:

25] There is the sea, vast and wide,
with its creatures beyond number,
livings things, small and great.

26] There go the ships,
and Leviathan that You formed to sport with.

27] All of them look to You
to give them their food when it is due.

28] Give it to them, they gather it up;
open Your hand, they are well satisfied;

29] hide Your face, they are terrified;
take away their breath, they perish
and turn again into dust;

30] send back Your breath, they are created,
and You renew the face of the earth.

31] May the glory of the LORD endure forever;
may the LORD rejoice in His works!

32] He looks at the earth and it trembles;
He touches the mountains and they smoke.

33] I will sing to the LORD as long as I live;
all my life I will chant hymns to my God.

34] May my prayer be pleasing to Him;
I will rejoice in the LORD.

35] May sinners disappear from the earth,
and the wicked be no more.
Bless the LORD, O my soul.
Hallelujah.

25] זֶה ׀ הַיָּם גָּדוֹל וּרְחַב יָדָיִם
שָׁם־רֶמֶשׂ וְאֵין מִסְפָּר
חַיּוֹת קְטַנּוֹת עִם־גְּדֹלוֹת:

26] שָׁם אֳנִיּוֹת יְהַלֵּכוּן
לִוְיָתָן זֶה־יָצַרְתָּ לְשַׂחֶק־בּוֹ:

27] כֻּלָּם אֵלֶיךָ יְשַׂבֵּרוּן
לָתֵת אָכְלָם בְּעִתּוֹ:

28] תִּתֵּן לָהֶם יִלְקֹטוּן
תִּפְתַּח יָדְךָ יִשְׂבְּעוּן טוֹב:

29] תַּסְתִּיר פָּנֶיךָ יִבָּהֵלוּן
תֹּסֵף רוּחָם יִגְוָעוּן
וְאֶל־עֲפָרָם יְשׁוּבוּן:

30] תְּשַׁלַּח רוּחֲךָ יִבָּרֵאוּן
וּתְחַדֵּשׁ פְּנֵי אֲדָמָה:

31] יְהִי כְבוֹד יְהֹוָה לְעוֹלָם
יִשְׂמַח יְהֹוָה בְּמַעֲשָׂיו:

32] הַמַּבִּיט לָאָרֶץ וַתִּרְעָד
יִגַּע בֶּהָרִים וְיֶעֱשָׁנוּ:

33] אָשִׁירָה לַיהֹוָה בְּחַיָּי
אֲזַמְּרָה לֵאלֹהַי בְּעוֹדִי:

34] יֶעֱרַב עָלָיו שִׂיחִי
אָנֹכִי אֶשְׂמַח בַּיהֹוָה:

35] יִתַּמּוּ חַטָּאִים ׀ מִן־הָאָרֶץ
וּרְשָׁעִים ׀ עוֹד אֵינָם
בָּרְכִי נַפְשִׁי אֶת־יְהֹוָה
הַלְלוּיָהּ:

לך לך

FIRST SELECTION

Isaiah

40 : 27 – 41 : 16

Chapter 40

מ

27] Why sayest thou, O Jacob,
And speakest, O Israel:
"My way is hid from the Lord,
And my right is passed over from my God"?

27] לָמָּה תֹאמַר יַעֲקֹב
וּתְדַבֵּר יִשְׂרָאֵל
נִסְתְּרָה דַרְכִּי מֵיְהֹוָה
וּמֵאֱלֹהַי מִשְׁפָּטִי יַעֲבוֹר:

28] Hast thou not known? hast thou not heard
That the everlasting God, the Lord,
The Creator of the ends of the earth,
Fainteth not, neither is weary?
His discernment is past searching out.

28] הֲלוֹא יָדַעְתָּ אִם־לֹא שָׁמַעְתָּ
אֱלֹהֵי עוֹלָם | יְהֹוָה
בּוֹרֵא קְצוֹת הָאָרֶץ
לֹא יִיעַף וְלֹא יִיגָע
אֵין חֵקֶר לִתְבוּנָתוֹ:

29] He giveth power to the faint;
And to him that hath no might He increaseth
strength.

29] נֹתֵן לַיָּעֵף כֹּחַ
וּלְאֵין אוֹנִים עָצְמָה יַרְבֶּה:

30] Even the youths shall faint and be weary,
And the young men shall utterly fall;

30] וְיִעֲפוּ נְעָרִים וְיִגָעוּ
וּבַחוּרִים כָּשׁוֹל יִכָּשֵׁלוּ:

31] But they that wait for the Lord shall renew
their strength;
They shall mount up with wings as eagles;
They shall run, and not be weary;
They shall walk, and not faint.

31] וְקֹוֵי יְהֹוָה יַחֲלִיפוּ כֹחַ
יַעֲלוּ אֵבֶר כַּנְּשָׁרִים
יָרוּצוּ וְלֹא יִיגָעוּ
יֵלְכוּ וְלֹא יִיעָפוּ:

1] Keep silence before Me, O islands,
And let the peoples renew their strength;
Let them draw near, then let them speak;
Let us come near together to judgment.

2] Who hath raised up one from the east,
At whose steps victory attendeth?
He giveth nations before him,
And maketh him rule over kings;
His sword maketh them as the dust,
His bow as the driven stubble.

3] He pursueth them, and passeth on safely;
The way with his feet he treadeth not.

4] Who hath wrought and done it?
He that called the generations from the beginning.
I, the Lord, who am the first,
And with the last am the same.

5] The isles saw, and feared;
The ends of the earth trembled;
They drew near, and came.

6] They helped every one his neighbour;
And every one said to his brother:
"Be of good courage."

7] So the carpenter encouraged the goldsmith,
And he that smootheth with the hammer him that
    smiteth the anvil,
Saying of the soldering: "It is good";
And he fastened it with nails, that it should not be
    moved.

8] But thou, Israel, My servant,
Jacob whom I have chosen,
The seed of Abraham My friend;

[1] הַחֲרִישׁוּ אֵלַי אִיִּים

וּלְאֻמִּים יַחֲלִיפוּ כֹחַ

יִגְּשׁוּ אָז יְדַבֵּרוּ

יַחְדָּו לַמִּשְׁפָּט נִקְרָבָה:

[2] מִי הֵעִיר מִמִּזְרָח

צֶדֶק יִקְרָאֵהוּ לְרַגְלוֹ

יִתֵּן לְפָנָיו גּוֹיִם

וּמְלָכִים יַרְדְּ

יִתֵּן כֶּעָפָר חַרְבּוֹ

כְּקַשׁ נִדָּף קַשְׁתּוֹ:

[3] יִרְדְּפֵם יַעֲבוֹר שָׁלוֹם

אֹרַח בְּרַגְלָיו לֹא יָבוֹא:

[4] מִי־פָעַל וְעָשָׂה

קֹרֵא הַדֹּרוֹת מֵרֹאשׁ

אֲנִי יְהוָה רִאשׁוֹן

וְאֶת־אַחֲרֹנִים אֲנִי־הוּא:

[5] רָאוּ אִיִּים וְיִירָאוּ

קְצוֹת הָאָרֶץ יֶחֱרָדוּ

קָרְבוּ וַיֶּאֱתָיוּן:

[6] אִישׁ אֶת־רֵעֵהוּ יַעְזֹרוּ

וּלְאָחִיו יֹאמַר חֲזָק:

[7] וַיְחַזֵּק חָרָשׁ אֶת־צֹרֵף

מַחֲלִיק פַּטִּישׁ אֶת־הוֹלֶם פָּעַם

אֹמֵר לַדֶּבֶק טוֹב הוּא

וַיְחַזְּקֵהוּ בְמַסְמְרִים לֹא יִמּוֹט:

[8] וְאַתָּה יִשְׂרָאֵל עַבְדִּי

יַעֲקֹב אֲשֶׁר בְּחַרְתִּיךָ

זֶרַע אַבְרָהָם אֹהֲבִי:

9] Thou whom I have taken hold of from the ends
      of the earth,
   And called thee from the uttermost parts thereof,
   And said unto thee: "Thou art My servant,
   I have chosen thee and not cast thee away";

9] אֲשֶׁר הֶחֱזַקְתִּיךָ מִקְצוֹת הָאָרֶץ
וּמֵאֲצִילֶיהָ קְרָאתִיךָ
וָאֹמַר לְךָ עַבְדִּי־אַתָּה
בְּחַרְתִּיךָ וְלֹא מְאַסְתִּיךָ:

10] Fear thou not, for I am with thee,
   Be not dismayed, for I am thy God;
   I strengthen thee, yea, I help thee;
   Yea, I uphold thee with My victorious right hand.

10] אַל־תִּירָא כִּי־עִמְּךָ אָנִי
אַל־תִּשְׁתָּע כִּי־אֲנִי אֱלֹהֶיךָ
אִמַּצְתִּיךָ אַף־עֲזַרְתִּיךָ
אַף־תְּמַכְתִּיךָ בִּימִין צִדְקִי:

11] Behold, all they that were incensed against thee
   Shall be ashamed and confounded;
   They that strove with thee
   Shall be as nothing, and shall perish.

11] הֵן יֵבֹשׁוּ וְיִכָּלְמוּ
כֹּל הַנֶּחֱרִים בָּךְ
יִהְיוּ כְאַיִן וְיֹאבְדוּ
אַנְשֵׁי רִיבֶךָ:

12] Thou shalt seek them, and shalt not find them,
   Even them that contended with thee;
   They that warred against thee
   Shall be as nothing, and as a thing of nought.

12] תְּבַקְשֵׁם וְלֹא תִמְצָאֵם
אַנְשֵׁי מַצֻּתֶךָ
יִהְיוּ כְאַיִן וּכְאֶפֶס
אַנְשֵׁי מִלְחַמְתֶּךָ:

13] For I the LORD thy God
   Hold thy right hand,
   Who say unto thee: "Fear not,
   I help thee."

13] כִּי אֲנִי יְהֹוָה אֱלֹהֶיךָ
מַחֲזִיק יְמִינֶךָ
הָאֹמֵר לְךָ אַל־תִּירָא
אֲנִי עֲזַרְתִּיךָ:

14] Fear not, thou worm Jacob,
   And ye men of Israel;
   I help thee, saith the LORD,
   And thy Redeemer, the Holy One of Israel.

14] אַל־תִּירְאִי תּוֹלַעַת יַעֲקֹב
מְתֵי יִשְׂרָאֵל
אֲנִי עֲזַרְתִּיךְ נְאֻם־יְהֹוָה
וְגֹאֲלֵךְ קְדוֹשׁ יִשְׂרָאֵל:

15] Behold, I make thee a new threshing-sledge
   Having sharp teeth;
   Thou shalt thresh the mountains, and beat them
      small,
   And shalt make the hills as chaff.

15] הִנֵּה שַׂמְתִּיךְ לְמוֹרַג חָרוּץ חָדָשׁ
בַּעַל פִּיפִיּוֹת
תָּדוּשׁ הָרִים וְתָדֹק
וּגְבָעוֹת כַּמֹּץ תָּשִׂים:

524

16] Thou shalt fan them, and the wind shall carry
    them away,
And the whirlwind shall scatter them;
And thou shalt rejoice in the LORD,
Thou shalt glory in the Holy One of Israel.

[16 תִּזְרֵם וְרוּחַ תִּשָּׂאֵם

וּסְעָרָה תָּפִיץ אֹתָם

וְאַתָּה תָּגִיל בַּיהוָה

בִּקְדוֹשׁ יִשְׂרָאֵל תִּתְהַלָּל:

SECOND SELECTION

Joel

2 : 21 — 3 : 2

Chapter 2

ב

21] Fear not, O land, be glad and rejoice;
For the LORD hath done great things.

[21 אַל־תִּירְאִי אֲדָמָה גִּילִי וּשְׂמָחִי

כִּי־הִגְדִּיל יְהוָה לַעֲשׂוֹת:

22] Be not afraid, ye beasts of the field;
For the pastures of the wilderness do spring,
For the tree beareth its fruit,
The fig-tree and the vine do yield their strength.

[22 אַל־תִּירְאוּ בַּהֲמוֹת שָׂדַי

כִּי דָשְׁאוּ נְאוֹת מִדְבָּר

כִּי־עֵץ נָשָׂא פִרְיוֹ

תְּאֵנָה וָגֶפֶן נָתְנוּ חֵילָם:

23] Be glad then, ye children of Zion, and rejoice
In the LORD your God;
For He giveth you the former rain in just measure,
And He causeth to come down for you the rain,
The former rain and the latter rain, at the first.

[23 וּבְנֵי צִיּוֹן גִּילוּ וְשִׂמְחוּ

בַּיהוָה אֱלֹהֵיכֶם

כִּי־נָתַן לָכֶם אֶת־הַמּוֹרֶה לִצְדָקָה

וַיּוֹרֶד לָכֶם גֶּשֶׁם

מוֹרֶה וּמַלְקוֹשׁ בָּרִאשׁוֹן:

24] And the floors shall be full of corn,
And the vats shall overflow with wine and oil.

[24 וּמָלְאוּ הַגֳּרָנוֹת בָּר

וְהֵשִׁיקוּ הַיְקָבִים תִּירוֹשׁ וְיִצְהָר:

25] And I will restore to you the years that the lo-
    cust hath eaten,
The canker-worm, and the caterpillar, and the
    palmer-worm,
My great army which I sent among you.

[25 וְשִׁלַּמְתִּי לָכֶם אֶת־הַשָּׁנִים

אֲשֶׁר אָכַל הָאַרְבֶּה

הַיֶּלֶק וְהֶחָסִיל וְהַגָּזָם

חֵילִי הַגָּדוֹל אֲשֶׁר שִׁלַּחְתִּי בָּכֶם:

26] And ye shall eat in plenty and be satisfied,
And shall praise the name of the LORD your God,

[26 וַאֲכַלְתֶּם אָכוֹל וְשָׂבוֹעַ

וְהִלַּלְתֶּם אֶת־שֵׁם יְהוָה אֱלֹהֵיכֶם

That hath dealt wondrously with you;
And My people shall never be ashamed.

27] And ye shall know that I am in the midst of
Israel,
And that I am the LORD your God, and there is
none else;
And My people shall never be ashamed.

אֲשֶׁר־עָשָׂה עִמָּכֶם לְהַפְלִיא

וְלֹא־יֵבֹשׁוּ עַמִּי לְעוֹלָם:

27] וִידַעְתֶּם כִּי בְקֶרֶב יִשְׂרָאֵל אָנִי

וַאֲנִי יְהוָה אֱלֹהֵיכֶם וְאֵין עוֹד

וְלֹא־יֵבֹשׁוּ עַמִּי לְעוֹלָם:

Chapter 3

ג

1] And it shall come to pass afterward,
That I will pour out My spirit upon all flesh;
And your sons and your daughters shall prophesy,
Your old men shall dream dreams,
Your young men shall see visions;

1] וְהָיָה אַחֲרֵי־כֵן

אֶשְׁפּוֹךְ אֶת־רוּחִי עַל־כָּל־בָּשָׂר

וְנִבְּאוּ בְּנֵיכֶם וּבְנוֹתֵיכֶם

זִקְנֵיכֶם חֲלֹמוֹת יַחֲלֹמוּן

בַּחוּרֵיכֶם חֶזְיֹנוֹת יִרְאוּ:

2] And also upon the servants and upon the hand-
maids
In those days will I pour out My spirit.

2] וְגַם עַל־הָעֲבָדִים וְעַל־הַשְּׁפָחוֹת

בַּיָּמִים הָהֵמָּה אֶשְׁפּוֹךְ אֶת־רוּחִי:

THIRD SELECTION

Psalms

105 : 1-15

Psalm 105

קה

1] Praise the LORD; call on His name;
proclaim His deeds among the nations.

1] הוֹדוּ לַיהוָה קִרְאוּ בִשְׁמוֹ

הוֹדִיעוּ בָעַמִּים עֲלִילוֹתָיו:

2] Sing praises unto Him;
speak of all His wondrous acts.

2] שִׁירוּ־לוֹ זַמְּרוּ־לוֹ

שִׂיחוּ בְּכָל־נִפְלְאוֹתָיו:

3] Exult in His holy name;
let all who seek the LORD rejoice.

3] הִתְהַלְלוּ בְּשֵׁם קָדְשׁוֹ

יִשְׂמַח לֵב | מְבַקְשֵׁי יְהוָה:

4] Turn to the LORD, to His might;[a]
seek His presence constantly.

4] דִּרְשׁוּ יְהוָה וְעֻזּוֹ

בַּקְּשׁוּ פָנָיו תָּמִיד:

[a] *I.e., the ark; cf. Ps. 78, 61; 132,8*

5] Remember the wonders He has done;
His portents and the judgments He has pronounced,

6] O offspring of Abraham, His servant,
O descendants of Jacob, His chosen ones.

7] He is the LORD our God;
His judgments are throughout the earth.

8] He is ever mindful of His covenant,
the promise He gave for a thousand generations,

9] that He made with Abraham,
swore to Isaac,

10] and confirmed in a decree for Jacob,
for Israel, as an eternal covenant,

11] Saying, "To you I will give the land of Canaan
as your allotted heritage."

12] They were then few in number,
a handful, merely sojourning there,

13] wandering from nation to nation,
from one kingdom to another.

14] He allowed no one to oppress them;
He reproved kings on their account,

15] "Do not touch My anointed ones;
do not harm My prophets."

זִכְרוּ נִפְלְאוֹתָיו אֲשֶׁר־עָשָׂה [5
מֹפְתָיו וּמִשְׁפְּטֵי־פִיו:

זֶרַע אַבְרָהָם עַבְדּוֹ [6
בְּנֵי יַעֲקֹב בְּחִירָיו:

הוּא יְהוָה אֱלֹהֵינוּ [7
בְּכָל־הָאָרֶץ מִשְׁפָּטָיו:

זָכַר לְעוֹלָם בְּרִיתוֹ [8
דָּבָר צִוָּה לְאֶלֶף דּוֹר:

אֲשֶׁר כָּרַת אֶת־אַבְרָהָם [9
וּשְׁבוּעָתוֹ לְיִשְׂחָק:

וַיַּעֲמִידֶהָ לְיַעֲקֹב לְחֹק [10
לְיִשְׂרָאֵל בְּרִית עוֹלָם:

לֵאמֹר לְךָ אֶתֵּן אֶת־אֶרֶץ כְּנָעַן [11
חֶבֶל נַחֲלַתְכֶם:

בִּהְיוֹתָם מְתֵי מִסְפָּר [12
כִּמְעַט וְגָרִים בָּהּ:

וַיִּתְהַלְכוּ מִגּוֹי אֶל־גּוֹי [13
מִמַּמְלָכָה אֶל־עַם אַחֵר:

לֹא־הִנִּיחַ אָדָם לְעָשְׁקָם [14
וַיּוֹכַח עֲלֵיהֶם מְלָכִים:

אַל־תִּגְּעוּ בִמְשִׁיחָי [15
וְלִנְבִיאַי אַל־תָּרֵעוּ:

וירא

FIRST SELECTION

Second Kings

4 : 1-23

ד

1] וְאִשָּׁה אַחַת מִנְּשֵׁי בְנֵי־הַנְּבִיאִים צָעֲקָה אֶל־אֱלִישָׁע לֵאמֹר עַבְדְּךָ אִישִׁי מֵת וְאַתָּה יָדַעְתָּ כִּי עַבְדְּךָ הָיָה יָרֵא אֶת־יְהֹוָה וְהַנֹּשֶׁה בָּא לָקַחַת אֶת־שְׁנֵי יְלָדַי לוֹ לַעֲבָדִים: 2] וַיֹּאמֶר אֵלֶיהָ אֱלִישָׁע מָה אֶעֱשֶׂה־לָּךְ הַגִּידִי לִי מַה־יֶּשׁ־לָכִי בַּבָּיִת וַתֹּאמֶר אֵין לְשִׁפְחָתְךָ כֹל בַּבַּיִת כִּי אִם־אָסוּךְ שָׁמֶן: 3] וַיֹּאמֶר לְכִי שַׁאֲלִי־לָךְ כֵּלִים מִן־הַחוּץ מֵאֵת כָּל־שְׁכֵנָיְכִי כֵּלִים רֵקִים אַל־תַּמְעִיטִי: 4] וּבָאת וְסָגַרְתְּ הַדֶּלֶת בַּעֲדֵךְ וּבְעַד־בָּנַיִךְ וְיָצַקְתְּ עַל כָּל־ הַכֵּלִים הָאֵלֶּה וְהַמָּלֵא תַּסִּיעִי: 5] וַתֵּלֶךְ מֵאִתּוֹ וַתִּסְגֹּר הַדֶּלֶת בַּעֲדָהּ וּבְעַד בָּנֶיהָ הֵם מַגִּשִׁים אֵלֶיהָ וְהִיא מֵיצָקֶת: 6] וַיְהִי | כִּמְלֹאת הַכֵּלִים וַתֹּאמֶר אֶל־בְּנָהּ הַגִּישָׁה אֵלַי עוֹד כֶּלִי וַיֹּאמֶר אֵלֶיהָ אֵין עוֹד כֶּלִי וַיַּעֲמֹד הַשָּׁמֶן: 7] וַתָּבֹא וַתַּגֵּד לְאִישׁ הָאֱלֹהִים וַיֹּאמֶר לְכִי מִכְרִי אֶת־הַשֶּׁמֶן וְשַׁלְּמִי אֶת־נִשְׁיֵכִי וְאַתְּ בָּנַיְכִי תִחְיִי בַּנּוֹתָר: 8] וַיְהִי הַיּוֹם וַיַּעֲבֹר אֱלִישָׁע אֶל־שׁוּנֵם וְשָׁם אִשָּׁה גְדוֹלָה וַתַּחֲזֶק־בּוֹ לֶאֱכָל־לָחֶם וַיְהִי מִדֵּי

Chapter 4

1] Now there cried a certain woman of the wives of the sons of the prophets unto Elisha, saying: 'Thy servant my husband is dead; and thou knowest that thy servant did fear the Lord; and the creditor is come to take unto him my two children to be bondmen.'

2] And Elisha said unto her: 'What shall I do for thee? tell me; what hast thou in the house?' And she said: 'Thy handmaid hath not any thing in the house, save a pot of oil.' 3] Then he said: 'Go, borrow thee vessels abroad of all thy neighbours, even empty vessels; borrow not a few.

4] And thou shalt go in and shut the door upon thee and upon thy sons, and pour out into all those vessels; and thou shalt set aside that which is full.'

5] So she went from him, and shut the door upon her and upon her sons; they brought the vessels to her, and she poured out.

6] And it came to pass, when the vessels were full, that she said unto her son 'Bring me yet a vessel.' And he said unto her: 'There is not a vessel more.' And the oil stayed.

7] Then she came and told the man of God. And he said: 'Go, sell the oil, and pay thy debt, and live thou and thy sons of the rest.'

8] And it fell on a day, that Elisha passed to Shunem, where was a great woman; and she constrained him to eat bread. And so it was, that as

v. 2. לך ק׳. v. 3. שכניך ק׳. v. 5. מוצקת ק׳. v. 7. נשיך ק׳. v. 7. ובניך ק׳.

528

oft as he passed by, he turned in thither to eat bread.

9] And she said unto her husband: 'Behold now, I perceive that this is a holy man of God, that passeth by us continually.

10] Let us make, I pray thee, a little chamber on the roof; and let us set for him there a bed, and a table, and a stool, and a candlestick; and it shall be, when he cometh to us, that he shall turn in thither.'

11] And it fell on a day, that he came thither, and he turned into the upper chamber and lay there.

12] And he said to Gehazi his servant: 'Call this Shunammite.' And when he had called her, she stood before him.

13] And he said unto him: 'Say now unto her: Behold, thou hast been careful for us with all this care; what is to be done for thee? wouldest thou be spoken for to the king, or to the captain of the host?' And she answered: 'I dwell among mine own people.'

14] And he said: 'What then is to be done for her?' And Gehazi answered: 'Verily she hath no son, and her husband is old.' 15] And he said: 'Call her.' And when he had called her, she stood in the door.

16] And he said: 'At this season, when the time cometh round, thou shalt embrace a son.' And she said: 'Nay, my lord, thou man of God, do not lie unto thy handmaid.'

17] And the woman conceived, and bore a son at that season, when the time came round, as Elisha had said unto her.

18] And when the child was grown, it fell on a day, that he went out to his father to the reapers. 19] And he said unto his father: 'My head, my head.' And he said to his servant: 'Carry him to his mother.'

20] And when he had taken him, and brought him to his mother, he sat on her knees till noon, and then died.

21] And she went up, and laid him on the bed of the man of God, and shut the door upon him, and went out. 22] And she called unto her husband, and said: 'Send me, I pray thee, one of the servants, and one of the asses, that I may run to the man of God, and come back.'

עָבְרוֹ יָסֻר שָׁמָּה לֶאֱכָל־לָחֶם: 9 וַתֹּאמֶר אֶל־אִישָׁהּ הִנֵּה־נָא יָדַעְתִּי כִּי אִישׁ אֱלֹהִים קָדוֹשׁ הוּא עֹבֵר עָלֵינוּ תָּמִיד: 10 נַעֲשֶׂה־נָּא עֲלִיַּת־קִיר קְטַנָּה וְנָשִׂים לוֹ שָׁם מִטָּה וְשֻׁלְחָן וְכִסֵּא וּמְנוֹרָה וְהָיָה בְּבֹאוֹ אֵלֵינוּ יָסוּר שָׁמָּה: 11 וַיְהִי הַיּוֹם וַיָּבֹא שָׁמָּה וַיָּסַר אֶל־הָעֲלִיָּה וַיִּשְׁכַּב־שָׁמָּה: 12 וַיֹּאמֶר אֶל־גֵּחֲזִי נַעֲרוֹ קְרָא לַשּׁוּנַמִּית הַזֹּאת וַיִּקְרָא־לָהּ וַתַּעֲמֹד לְפָנָיו: 13 וַיֹּאמֶר לוֹ אֱמָר־נָא אֵלֶיהָ הִנֵּה חָרַדְתְּ | אֵלֵינוּ אֶת־כָּל־הַחֲרָדָה הַזֹּאת מֶה לַעֲשׂוֹת לָךְ הֲיֵשׁ לְדַבֶּר־לָךְ אֶל־הַמֶּלֶךְ אוֹ אֶל־שַׂר הַצָּבָא וַתֹּאמֶר בְּתוֹךְ עַמִּי אָנֹכִי יֹשָׁבֶת: 14 וַיֹּאמֶר וּמֶה לַעֲשׂוֹת לָהּ וַיֹּאמֶר גֵּחֲזִי אֲבָל בֵּן אֵין־לָהּ וְאִישָׁהּ זָקֵן: 15 וַיֹּאמֶר קְרָא־לָהּ וַיִּקְרָא־לָהּ וַתַּעֲמֹד בַּפָּתַח: 16 וַיֹּאמֶר לַמּוֹעֵד הַזֶּה כָּעֵת חַיָּה אַתְּי חֹבֶקֶת בֵּן וַתֹּאמֶר אַל־אֲדֹנִי אִישׁ הָאֱלֹהִים אַל־תְּכַזֵּב בְּשִׁפְחָתֶךָ: 17 וַתַּהַר הָאִשָּׁה וַתֵּלֶד בֵּן לַמּוֹעֵד הַזֶּה כָּעֵת חַיָּה אֲשֶׁר־דִּבֶּר אֵלֶיהָ אֱלִישָׁע: 18 וַיִּגְדַּל הַיָּלֶד וַיְהִי הַיּוֹם וַיֵּצֵא אֶל־אָבִיו אֶל־הַקֹּצְרִים: 19 וַיֹּאמֶר אֶל־אָבִיו רֹאשִׁי | רֹאשִׁי וַיֹּאמֶר אֶל־הַנַּעַר שָׂאֵהוּ אֶל־אִמּוֹ: 20 וַיִּשָּׂאֵהוּ וַיְבִיאֵהוּ אֶל־אִמּוֹ וַיֵּשֶׁב עַל־בִּרְכֶּיהָ עַד־הַצָּהֳרַיִם וַיָּמֹת: 21 וַתַּעַל וַתַּשְׁכִּבֵהוּ עַל־מִטַּת אִישׁ הָאֱלֹהִים וַתִּסְגֹּר בַּעֲדוֹ וַתֵּצֵא: 22 וַתִּקְרָא אֶל־אִישָׁהּ וַתֹּאמֶר שִׁלְחָה נָא לִי אֶחָד מִן־הַנְּעָרִים וְאַחַת הָאֲתֹנוֹת וְאָרוּצָה עַד־

23] And he said: 'Wherefore wilt thou go to him to-day? it is neither new moon nor sabbath.' And she said: 'It shall be well.'

וַיֹּאמֶר מַדּוּעַ [23] אִישׁ הָאֱלֹהִים וְאָשׁוּבָה: אַתִּי הֹלֶכֶת אֵלָיו הַיּוֹם לֹא־חֹדֶשׁ וְלֹא שַׁבָּת וַתֹּאמֶר שָׁלוֹם:

SECOND SELECTION

Job

5 : 17 – 27

Chapter 5

ה

17] Behold, happy is the man whom God correcteth;
Therefore despise not thou the chastening of the Almighty.

18] For He maketh sore, and bindeth up;
He woundeth, and His hands make whole.

[17] הִנֵּה אַשְׁרֵי אֱנוֹשׁ יוֹכִיחֶנּוּ אֱלוֹהַּ
וּמוּסַר שַׁדַּי אַל־תִּמְאָס:

[18] כִּי הוּא יַכְאִיב וְיֶחְבָּשׁ
יִמְחַץ וְיָדָו תִּרְפֶּינָה:

19] He will deliver thee in six troubles;
Yea, in seven there shall no evil touch thee.

[19] בְּשֵׁשׁ צָרוֹת יַצִּילֶךָ
וּבְשֶׁבַע לֹא־יִגַּע בְּךָ רָע:

20] In famine He will redeem thee from death;
And in war from the power of the sword.

[20] בְּרָעָב פָּדְךָ מִמָּוֶת
וּבְמִלְחָמָה מִידֵי חָרֶב:

21] Thou shalt be hid from the scourge of the tongue;
Neither shalt thou be afraid of destruction when it cometh.

22] At destruction and famine thou shalt laugh;
Neither shalt thou be afraid of the beasts of the earth.

[21] בְּשׁוֹט לָשׁוֹן תֵּחָבֵא
וְלֹא־תִירָא מִשֹּׁד כִּי יָבוֹא:

[22] לְשֹׁד וּלְכָפָן תִּשְׂחָק
וּמֵחַיַּת הָאָרֶץ אַל־תִּירָא:

23] For thou shalt be in league with the stones of the field;
And the beasts of the field shall be at peace with thee.

24] And thou shalt know that thy tent is in peace;
And thou shalt visit thy habitation, and shalt miss nothing.

[23] כִּי עִם־אַבְנֵי הַשָּׂדֶה בְרִיתֶךָ
וְחַיַּת הַשָּׂדֶה הָשְׁלְמָה־לָךְ:

[24] וְיָדַעְתָּ כִּי־שָׁלוֹם אָהֳלֶךָ
וּפָקַדְתָּ נָוְךָ וְלֹא תֶחֱטָא:

25] Thou shalt know also that thy seed shall be great,
And thine offspring as the grass of the earth.

[25] וְיָדַעְתָּ כִּי־רַב זַרְעֶךָ
וְצֶאֱצָאֶיךָ כְּעֵשֶׂב הָאָרֶץ:

עד כאן לספרדים v. 23.   הֹלֶכֶת ק' v. 23.   אַתְּ ק' v. 23.
וִידָיו ק' v. 18.

530

26] Thou shalt come to thy grave in ripe age,
Like as a shock of corn cometh in its season.

27] Lo this, we have searched it, so it is;
Hear it, and know thou it for thy good.

THIRD SELECTION

Psalms

111 : 1-10

Psalm 111

1] Hallelujah.
I praise the LORD with all my heart
in the assembled congregation of the upright.

2] The works of the LORD are great,
a-within reach of all who desire them.-*a*

3] His deeds are splendid and glorious;
His beneficence is everlasting;

4] He has won renown for His wonders.
The LORD is gracious and compassionate;

5] He gives food to those who fear Him;
He is ever mindful of His covenant.

6] He revealed to His people His powerful works,
in giving them the heritage of nations.

7] His handiwork is truth and justice;
all His precepts are enduring,

8] well-founded for all eternity,
wrought of truth and equity.

a-a Meaning of Heb. uncertain

תָּבוֹא בְכֶלַח אֱלֵי־קָבֶר 26[
כַּעֲלוֹת גָּדִישׁ בְּעִתּוֹ:

הִנֵּה־זֹאת חֲקַרְנוּהָ כֶּן־הִיא 27[
שְׁמָעֶנָּה וְאַתָּה דַע־לָךְ:

קיא

הַלְלוּיָהּ | 1[
אוֹדֶה יְהֹוָה בְּכָל־לֵבָב
בְּסוֹד יְשָׁרִים וְעֵדָה:

גְּדֹלִים מַעֲשֵׂי יְהֹוָה 2[
דְּרוּשִׁים לְכָל־חֶפְצֵיהֶם:

הוֹד־וְהָדָר פָּעֳלוֹ 3[
וְצִדְקָתוֹ עֹמֶדֶת לָעַד:

זֵכֶר עָשָׂה לְנִפְלְאוֹתָיו 4[
חַנּוּן וְרַחוּם יְהֹוָה:

טֶרֶף נָתַן לִירֵאָיו 5[
יִזְכֹּר לְעוֹלָם בְּרִיתוֹ:

כֹּחַ מַעֲשָׂיו הִגִּיד לְעַמּוֹ 6[
לָתֵת לָהֶם נַחֲלַת גּוֹיִם:

מַעֲשֵׂי יָדָיו אֱמֶת וּמִשְׁפָּט 7[
נֶאֱמָנִים כָּל־פִּקּוּדָיו:

סְמוּכִים לָעַד לְעוֹלָם 8[
עֲשׂוּיִם בֶּאֱמֶת וְיָשָׁר:

9] He sent redemption to His people;
He ordained His covenant for all time;
His name is holy and awesome.

רְדוּת | שָׁלַח לְעַמּוֹ [9
צִוָּה לְעוֹלָם בְּרִיתוֹ
קָדוֹשׁ וְנוֹרָא שְׁמוֹ:

10] The essence[b] of wisdom is the fear of the LORD;
[a]all who practice it gain sound understanding.[a]
Praise of Him is everlasting.

רֵאשִׁית חָכְמָה | יִרְאַת יְהֹוָה [10
שֵׂכֶל טוֹב לְכָל־עֹשֵׂיהֶם
תְּהִלָּתוֹ עֹמֶדֶת לָעַד:

---

[b] Or, "beginning"   [a-a] Meaning of Heb. uncertain

חיי שרה

FIRST SELECTION

First Kings

1 : 1-31

Chapter 1

1] Now king David was old and stricken in years; and they covered him with clothes, but he could get no heat.

2] Wherefore his servants said unto him: 'Let there be sought for my lord the king a young virgin; and let her stand before the king, and be a companion unto him: and let her lie in thy bosom, that my lord the king may get heat.

3] So they sought for a fair damsel throughout all the borders of Israel, and found Abishag the Shunammite, and brought her to the king.

4] And the damsel was very fair; and she became a companion unto the king, and ministered to him; but the king knew her not.

5] Now Adonijah the son of Haggith exalted himself, saying: 'I will be king'; and he prepared him chariots and horsemen, and fifty men to run before him.

6] And his father had not grieved him all his life in saying: 'Why hast thou done so?' and he was also a very goodly man; and he was born after Absalom.

7] And he conferred with Joab the son of Zeruiah, and with Abiathar the priest; and they following Adonijah helped him. 8] But Zadok the priest, and Benaiah the son of Jehoiada, and Nathan the prophet, and Shimei, and Rei, and the mighty men that belonged to David, were not with Adonijah.

9] And Adonijah slew sheep and oxen and fatlings by the stone of Zoheleth, which is beside En-rogel; and he called

א

1] וְהַמֶּלֶךְ דָּוִד זָקֵן בָּא בַּיָּמִים וַיְכַסֻּהוּ בַּבְּגָדִים וְלֹא יִחַם לוֹ: 2] וַיֹּאמְרוּ לוֹ עֲבָדָיו יְבַקְשׁוּ לַאדֹנִי הַמֶּלֶךְ נַעֲרָה בְתוּלָה וְעָמְדָה לִפְנֵי הַמֶּלֶךְ וּתְהִי־לוֹ סֹכֶנֶת וְשָׁכְבָה בְחֵיקֶךָ וְחַם לַאדֹנִי הַמֶּלֶךְ: 3] וַיְבַקְשׁוּ נַעֲרָה יָפָה בְּכֹל גְּבוּל יִשְׂרָאֵל וַיִּמְצְאוּ אֶת־אֲבִישַׁג הַשּׁוּנַמִּית וַיָּבִאוּ אֹתָהּ לַמֶּלֶךְ: 4] וְהַנַּעֲרָה יָפָה עַד־מְאֹד וַתְּהִי לַמֶּלֶךְ סֹכֶנֶת וַתְּשָׁרְתֵהוּ וְהַמֶּלֶךְ לֹא יְדָעָהּ:

5] וַאֲדֹנִיָּה בֶן־חַגִּית מִתְנַשֵּׂא לֵאמֹר אֲנִי אֶמְלֹךְ וַיַּעַשׂ לוֹ רֶכֶב וּפָרָשִׁים וַחֲמִשִּׁים אִישׁ רָצִים לְפָנָיו: 6] וְלֹא־עֲצָבוֹ אָבִיו מִיָּמָיו לֵאמֹר מַדּוּעַ כָּכָה עָשִׂיתָ וְגַם־הוּא טוֹב־תֹּאַר מְאֹד וְאֹתוֹ יָלְדָה אַחֲרֵי אַבְשָׁלוֹם: 7] וַיִּהְיוּ דְבָרָיו עִם יוֹאָב בֶּן־צְרוּיָה וְעִם אֶבְיָתָר הַכֹּהֵן וַיַּעְזְרוּ אַחֲרֵי אֲדֹנִיָּה: 8] וְצָדוֹק הַכֹּהֵן וּבְנָיָהוּ בֶן־יְהוֹיָדָע וְנָתָן הַנָּבִיא וְשִׁמְעִי וְרֵעִי וְהַגִּבּוֹרִים אֲשֶׁר לְדָוִד לֹא הָיוּ עִם־אֲדֹנִיָּהוּ: 9] וַיִּזְבַּח אֲדֹנִיָּהוּ צֹאן וּבָקָר וּמְרִיא עִם אֶבֶן הַזֹּחֶלֶת אֲשֶׁר־אֵצֶל עֵין רֹגֵל וַיִּקְרָא אֶת־כָּל־אֶחָיו בְּנֵי

all his brethren the king's sons, and all the men of Judah the king's servants;

10] but Nathan the prophet, and Benaiah, and the mighty men, and Solomon his brother, he called not.

11] Then Nathan spoke unto Bath-sheba, the mother of Solomon, saying: 'Hast thou not heard that Adonijah the son of Haggith doth reign, and David our lord knoweth it not?

12] Now therefore come, let me, I pray thee, give thee counsel, that thou mayest save thine own life, and the life of thy son Solomon.

13] Go and get thee in unto king David, and say unto him: Didst not thou, my lord, O king, swear unto thy handmaid, saying: Assuredly Solomon thy son shall reign after me, and he shall sit upon my throne? why then doth Adonijah reign?

14] Behold, while thou yet talkest there with the king, I also will come in after thee, and confirm thy words.'

15] And Bath-sheba went in unto the king into the chamber.—Now the king was very old; and Abishag the Shunammite ministered unto the king.—

16] And Bath-sheba bowed, and prostrated herself unto the king. And the king said: 'What wouldest thou?'

17] And she said unto him: 'My lord, thou didst swear by the LORD thy God unto thy handmaid: Assuredly Solomon thy son shall reign after me, and he shall sit upon my throne.

18] And now, behold, Adonijah reigneth; and thou, my lord the king, knowest it not.

19] And he hath slain oxen and fatlings and sheep in abundance, and hath called all the sons of the king, and Abiathar the priest, and Joab the captain of the host; but Solomon thy servant hath he not called.

20] And thou, my lord the king, the eyes of all Israel are upon thee, that thou shouldest tell them who shall sit on the throne of my lord the king after him.

21] Otherwise it will come to pass, when my lord the king shall sleep with his fathers, that I and my son Solomon shall be counted offenders.'

22] And, lo, while she yet talked with the king, Nathan the prophet came in.

הַמֶּלֶךְ וּלְכָל־אַנְשֵׁי יְהוּדָה עַבְדֵי הַמֶּלֶךְ:

10] וְאֶת־נָתָן הַנָּבִיא וּבְנָיָהוּ וְאֶת־הַגִּבּוֹרִים וְאֶת־שְׁלֹמֹה אָחִיו לֹא קָרָא:

11] וַיֹּאמֶר נָתָן אֶל־בַּת־שֶׁבַע אֵם־שְׁלֹמֹה לֵאמֹר הֲלוֹא שָׁמַעַתְּ כִּי מָלַךְ אֲדֹנִיָּהוּ בֶן־חַגִּית וַאֲדֹנֵינוּ דָוִד לֹא יָדָע: 12] וְעַתָּה לְכִי אִיעָצֵךְ נָא עֵצָה וּמַלְּטִי אֶת־נַפְשֵׁךְ וְאֶת־נֶפֶשׁ בְּנֵךְ שְׁלֹמֹה: 13] לְכִי וּבֹאִי | אֶל־הַמֶּלֶךְ דָּוִד וְאָמַרְתְּ אֵלָיו הֲלֹא־אַתָּה אֲדֹנִי הַמֶּלֶךְ נִשְׁבַּעְתָּ לַאֲמָתְךָ לֵאמֹר כִּי שְׁלֹמֹה בְנֵךְ יִמְלֹךְ אַחֲרַי וְהוּא יֵשֵׁב עַל־כִּסְאִי וּמַדּוּעַ מָלַךְ אֲדֹנִיָּהוּ: 14] הִנֵּה עוֹדָךְ מְדַבֶּרֶת שָׁם עִם־הַמֶּלֶךְ וַאֲנִי אָבוֹא אַחֲרַיִךְ וּמִלֵּאתִי אֶת־דְּבָרָיִךְ: 15] וַתָּבֹא בַת־שֶׁבַע אֶל־הַמֶּלֶךְ הַחַדְרָה וְהַמֶּלֶךְ זָקֵן מְאֹד וַאֲבִישַׁג הַשּׁוּנַמִּית מְשָׁרַת אֶת־הַמֶּלֶךְ: 16] וַתִּקֹּד בַּת־שֶׁבַע וַתִּשְׁתַּחוּ לַמֶּלֶךְ וַיֹּאמֶר הַמֶּלֶךְ מַה־לָּךְ: 17] וַתֹּאמֶר לוֹ אֲדֹנִי אַתָּה נִשְׁבַּעְתָּ בַּיהֹוָה אֱלֹהֶיךָ לַאֲמָתֶךָ כִּי־שְׁלֹמֹה בְנֵךְ יִמְלֹךְ אַחֲרָי וְהוּא יֵשֵׁב עַל־כִּסְאִי: 18] וְעַתָּה הִנֵּה אֲדֹנִיָּה מָלָךְ וְעַתָּה אֲדֹנִי הַמֶּלֶךְ לֹא יָדָעְתָּ: 19] וַיִּזְבַּח שׁוֹר וּמְרִיא־וְצֹאן לָרֹב וַיִּקְרָא לְכָל־בְּנֵי הַמֶּלֶךְ וּלְאֶבְיָתָר הַכֹּהֵן וּלְיֹאָב שַׂר הַצָּבָא וְלִשְׁלֹמֹה עַבְדְּךָ לֹא קָרָא: 20] וְאַתָּה אֲדֹנִי הַמֶּלֶךְ עֵינֵי כָל־יִשְׂרָאֵל עָלֶיךָ לְהַגִּיד לָהֶם מִי יֵשֵׁב עַל־כִּסֵּא אֲדֹנִי־הַמֶּלֶךְ אַחֲרָיו: 21] וְהָיָה כִּשְׁכַב אֲדֹנִי־הַמֶּלֶךְ עִם־אֲבֹתָיו וְהָיִיתִי אֲנִי וּבְנִי שְׁלֹמֹה חַטָּאִים:

22] וְהִנֵּה עוֹדֶנָּה מְדַבֶּרֶת עִם־הַמֶּלֶךְ וְנָתָן

23] And they told the king, saying: 'Behold Nathan the prophet.' And when he was come in before the king, he bowed down before the king with his face to the ground.

24] And Nathan said: 'My lord, O king, hast thou said: Adonijah shall reign after me, and he shall sit upon my throne?

25] For he is gone down this day, and hath slain oxen and fatlings and sheep in abundance, and hath called all the king's sons, and the captains of the host, and Abiathar the priest; and, behold, they eat and drink before him, and say: Long live king Adonijah.

26] But me, even me thy servant, and Zadok the priest, and Benaiah the son of Jehoiada, and thy servant Solomon, hath he not called.

27] Is this thing done by my lord the king, and thou hast not declared unto thy servant who should sit on the throne of my lord the king after him?'

28] Then king David answered and said: 'Call me Bath-sheba.' And she came into the king's presence, and stood before the king.

29] And the king swore and said: 'As the LORD liveth, who hath redeemed my soul out of all adversity, 30] verily as I swore unto thee by the LORD, the God of Israel, saying: Assuredly Solomon thy son shall reign after me, and he shall sit upon my throne in my stead; verily so will I do this day.'

31] Then Bath-sheba bowed with her face to the earth, and prostrated herself to the king, and said: 'Let my lord king David live for ever.'

23 וַיַּגִּידוּ לַמֶּלֶךְ לֵאמֹר הִנֵּה נָתָן הַנָּבִיא בָּא׃ וַיָּבֹא לִפְנֵי הַמֶּלֶךְ וַיִּשְׁתַּחוּ לַמֶּלֶךְ עַל־אַפָּיו אָרְצָה׃ 24 וַיֹּאמֶר נָתָן אֲדֹנִי הַמֶּלֶךְ אַתָּה אָמַרְתָּ אֲדֹנִיָּהוּ יִמְלֹךְ אַחֲרָי וְהוּא יֵשֵׁב עַל־כִּסְאִי׃ 25 כִּי יָרַד הַיּוֹם וַיִּזְבַּח שׁוֹר וּמְרִיא־וְצֹאן לָרֹב וַיִּקְרָא לְכָל־בְּנֵי הַמֶּלֶךְ וּלְשָׂרֵי הַצָּבָא וּלְאֶבְיָתָר הַכֹּהֵן וְהִנָּם אֹכְלִים וְשֹׁתִים לְפָנָיו וַיֹּאמְרוּ יְחִי הַמֶּלֶךְ אֲדֹנִיָּהוּ׃ 26 וְלִי אֲנִי־עַבְדֶּךָ וּלְצָדֹק הַכֹּהֵן וְלִבְנָיָהוּ בֶן־יְהוֹיָדָע וְלִשְׁלֹמֹה עַבְדְּךָ לֹא קָרָא׃ 27 אִם מֵאֵת אֲדֹנִי הַמֶּלֶךְ נִהְיָה הַדָּבָר הַזֶּה וְלֹא הוֹדַעְתָּ אֶת־עַבְדֶּיךָ מִי יֵשֵׁב עַל־כִּסֵּא אֲדֹנִי־הַמֶּלֶךְ אַחֲרָיו׃

28 וַיַּעַן הַמֶּלֶךְ דָּוִד וַיֹּאמֶר קִרְאוּ־לִי לְבַת־שָׁבַע וַתָּבֹא לִפְנֵי הַמֶּלֶךְ וַתַּעֲמֹד לִפְנֵי הַמֶּלֶךְ׃ 29 וַיִּשָּׁבַע הַמֶּלֶךְ וַיֹּאמַר חַי־יְהוָה אֲשֶׁר־פָּדָה אֶת־נַפְשִׁי מִכָּל־צָרָה׃ 30 כִּי כַּאֲשֶׁר נִשְׁבַּעְתִּי לָךְ בַּיהוָה אֱלֹהֵי יִשְׂרָאֵל לֵאמֹר כִּי־שְׁלֹמֹה בְנֵךְ יִמְלֹךְ אַחֲרַי וְהוּא יֵשֵׁב עַל־כִּסְאִי תַּחְתָּי כִּי כֵּן אֶעֱשֶׂה הַיּוֹם הַזֶּה׃ 31 וַתִּקֹּד בַּת־שֶׁבַע אַפַּיִם אֶרֶץ וַתִּשְׁתַּחוּ לַמֶּלֶךְ וַתֹּאמֶר יְחִי אֲדֹנִי הַמֶּלֶךְ דָּוִד לְעֹלָם׃

עבדך ק׳ v. 27.

535

Proverbs

31 : 10 - 31

Chapter 31   לא

א 10] A woman of valour who can find?   10] אֵשֶׁת חַיִל מִי יִמְצָא
For her price is far above rubies.   וְרָחֹק מִפְּנִינִים מִכְרָהּ:

ב 11] The heart of her husband doth safely trust   11] בָּטַח בָּהּ לֵב בַּעְלָהּ
in her,
And he hath no lack of gain.   וְשָׁלָל לֹא יֶחְסָר:

ג 12] She doeth him good and not evil   12] גְּמָלַתְהוּ טוֹב וְלֹא־רָע
All the days of her life.   כֹּל יְמֵי חַיֶּיהָ:

ד 13] She seeketh wool and flax,   13] דָּרְשָׁה צֶמֶר וּפִשְׁתִּים
And worketh willingly with her hands.   וַתַּעַשׂ בְּחֵפֶץ כַּפֶּיהָ:

ה 14] She is like the merchant-ships;   14] הָיְתָה כָּאֳנִיּוֹת סוֹחֵר
She bringeth her food from afar.   מִמֶּרְחָק תָּבִיא לַחְמָהּ:

ו 15] She riseth also while it is yet night,   15] וַתָּקָם ׀ בְּעוֹד לַיְלָה
And giveth food to her household,   וַתִּתֵּן טֶרֶף לְבֵיתָהּ
And a portion to her maidens.   וְחֹק לְנַעֲרֹתֶיהָ:

ז 16] She considereth a field, and buyeth it;   16] זָמְמָה שָׂדֶה וַתִּקָּחֵהוּ
With the fruit of her hands she planteth a vine-   מִפְּרִי כַפֶּיהָ נָטְעָ כָּרֶם:
yard.

ח 17] She girdeth her loins with strength,   17] חָגְרָה בְעוֹז מָתְנֶיהָ
And maketh strong her arms.   וַתְּאַמֵּץ זְרוֹעֹתֶיהָ:

ט 18] She perceiveth that her merchandise is good;   18] טָעֲמָה כִּי־טוֹב סַחְרָהּ
Her lamp goeth not out by night.   לֹא־יִכְבֶּה בַלַּיְלָ נֵרָהּ:

י 19] She layeth her hands to the distaff,   19] יָדֶיהָ שִׁלְּחָה בַכִּישׁוֹר
And her hands hold the spindle.   וְכַפֶּיהָ תָּמְכוּ פָלֶךְ:

כ	20]	She stretcheth out her hand to the poor. Yea, she reacheth forth her hands to the needy.	[20] כַּפָּהּ פָּרְשָׂה לֶעָנִי וְיָדֶיהָ שִׁלְּחָה לָאֶבְיוֹן:
ל	21]	She is not afraid of the snow for her house- hold; For all her household are clothed with scarlet.	[21] לֹא-תִירָא לְבֵיתָהּ מִשָּׁלֶג כִּי כָל-בֵּיתָהּ לָבֻשׁ שָׁנִים:
מ	22]	She maketh for herself coverlets; Her clothing is fine linen and purple.	[22] מַרְבַדִּים עָשְׂתָה-לָּהּ שֵׁשׁ וְאַרְגָּמָן לְבוּשָׁהּ:
נ	23]	Her husband is known in the gates, When he sitteth among the elders of the land.	[23] נוֹדָע בַּשְּׁעָרִים בַּעְלָהּ בְּשִׁבְתּוֹ עִם-זִקְנֵי-אָרֶץ:
ס	24]	She maketh linen garments and selleth them: And delivereth girdles unto the merchant.	[24] סָדִין עָשְׂתָה וַתִּמְכֹּר וַחֲגוֹר נָתְנָה לַכְּנַעֲנִי:
ע	25]	Strength and dignity are her clothing; And she laugheth at the time to come.	[25] עֹז-וְהָדָר לְבוּשָׁהּ וַתִּשְׂחַק לְיוֹם אַחֲרוֹן:
פ	26]	She openeth her mouth with wisdom; And the law of kindness is on her tongue.	[26] פִּיהָ פָּתְחָה בְחָכְמָה וְתוֹרַת-חֶסֶד עַל-לְשׁוֹנָהּ:
צ	27]	She looketh well to the ways of her house- hold, And eateth not the bread of idleness.	[27] צוֹפִיָּה הֲלִיכוֹת בֵּיתָהּ וְלֶחֶם עַצְלוּת לֹא תֹאכֵל:
ק	28]	Her children rise up, and call her blessed; Her husband also, and he praiseth her:	[28] קָמוּ בָנֶיהָ וַיְאַשְּׁרוּהָ בַּעְלָהּ וַיְהַלְלָהּ:
ר	29]	"Many daughters have done valiantly, But thou excellest them all."	[29] רַבּוֹת בָּנוֹת עָשׂוּ חָיִל וְאַתְּ עָלִית עַל-כֻּלָּנָה:
ש	30]	Grace is deceitful, and beauty is vain; But a woman that feareth the LORD, she shall be praised.	[30] שֶׁקֶר הַחֵן וְהֶבֶל הַיֹּפִי אִשָּׁה יִרְאַת-יְהֹוָה הִיא תִתְהַלָּל:
ת	31]	Give her of the fruit of her hands; And let her works praise her in the gates.	[31] תְּנוּ-לָהּ מִפְּרִי יָדֶיהָ וִיהַלְלוּהָ בַשְּׁעָרִים מַעֲשֶׂיהָ:

Psalms

15 : 1-5

Psalm 15

1] A psalm of David.
LORD, who may stay in Your tent,
who may reside on Your holy mountain?

1] מִזְמוֹר לְדָוִד
יְהֹוָה מִי־יָגוּר בְּאָהֳלֶךָ
מִי־יִשְׁכֹּן בְּהַר קָדְשֶׁךָ:

2] He who lives without blame, who does what is
right,
and in his heart acknowledges the truth;

2] הוֹלֵךְ תָּמִים וּפֹעֵל צֶדֶק
וְדֹבֵר אֱמֶת בִּלְבָבוֹ:

3] *a*-whose tongue is not given to evil;-*a*
who has never done harm to his fellow,
or borne reproach for [his act toward] his neighbor;

3] לֹא־רָגַל | עַל־לְשֹׁנוֹ
לֹא־עָשָׂה לְרֵעֵהוּ רָעָה
וְחֶרְפָּה לֹא־נָשָׂא עַל־קְרֹבוֹ:

4] for whom a contemptible man is abhorrent,
but who honors those who fear the LORD;
who stands by his oath even to his hurt;

4] נִבְזֶה | בְּעֵינָיו נִמְאָס
וְאֶת־יִרְאֵי יְהֹוָה יְכַבֵּד
נִשְׁבַּע לְהָרַע וְלֹא יָמִר:

5] who has never lent money at interest,
or accepted a bribe against the innocent;
the man who acts thus shall never be shaken.

5] כַּסְפּוֹ | לֹא־נָתַן בְּנֶשֶׁךְ
וְשֹׁחַד עַל־נָקִי לֹא־לָקָח
עֹשֵׂה אֵלֶּה לֹא יִמּוֹט לְעוֹלָם:

---

a-a Meaning of Heb. uncertain; or "Who has no slander upon his tongue"

תולדת

FIRST SELECTION

Malachi

1 : 1 – 2 : 7

Chapter 1

א

1] The burden of the word of the LORD to Israel by Malachi.

[1] מַשָּׂא דְבַר־יְהֹוָה אֶל־יִשְׂרָאֵל

בְּיַד מַלְאָכִי:

2] I have loved you, saith the LORD.
Yet ye say: 'Wherein hast Thou loved us?'
Was not Esau Jacob's brother?
Saith the LORD;
Yet I loved Jacob;

[2] אָהַבְתִּי אֶתְכֶם אָמַר יְהֹוָה

וַאֲמַרְתֶּם בַּמָּה אֲהַבְתָּנוּ

הֲלוֹא־אָח עֵשָׂו לְיַעֲקֹב

נְאֻם־יְהֹוָה

וָאֹהַב אֶת־יַעֲקֹב:

3] But Esau I hated,
And made his mountains a desolation,
And gave his heritage to the jackals of the wilderness.

[3] וְאֶת־עֵשָׂו שָׂנֵאתִי

וָאָשִׂים אֶת־הָרָיו שְׁמָמָה

וְאֶת־נַחֲלָתוֹ לְתַנּוֹת מִדְבָּר:

4] Whereas Edom saith:
'We are beaten down,
But we will return and build the waste places';
Thus saith the LORD of hosts:
They shall build, but I will throw down;
And they shall be called The border of wickedness,
And The people whom the LORD execrateth for ever.

[4] כִּי־תֹאמַר אֱדוֹם רֻשַּׁשְׁנוּ

וְנָשׁוּב וְנִבְנֶה חֳרָבוֹת

כֹּה אָמַר יְהֹוָה צְבָאוֹת

הֵמָּה יִבְנוּ וַאֲנִי אֶהֱרוֹס

וְקָרְאוּ לָהֶם גְּבוּל רִשְׁעָה

וְהָעָם אֲשֶׁר־זָעַם יְהֹוָה עַד־עוֹלָם:

5] And your eyes shall see,
And he shall say:
'The LORD is great beyond the border of Israel.'

[5] וְעֵינֵיכֶם תִּרְאֶינָה

וְאַתֶּם תֹּאמְרוּ יִגְדַּל יְהֹוָה

מֵעַל לִגְבוּל יִשְׂרָאֵל:

6] A son honoureth his father,
And a servant his master;
If then I be a father,
Where is My honour?
And if I be a master,
Where is My fear?
Saith the LORD of hosts
Unto you, O priests, that despise My name.
And ye say: 'Wherein have we despised Thy name?'

7] Ye offer polluted bread upon Mine altar.
And ye say: 'Wherein have we polluted Thee?'
In that ye say: 'The table of the LORD is
    contemptible.'

8] And when ye offer the blind for sacrifice, it is
    no evil!
And when ye offer the lame and sick, it is no evil!
Present it now unto thy governor;
Will he be pleased with thee?
Or will he accept thy person?
Saith the LORD of hosts.

9] And now, I pray you, entreat the favour of God
That He may be gracious unto us!—
This hath been of your doing.—
Will He accept any of your persons?
Saith the LORD of hosts.

10] Oh that there were even one among you that
    would shut the doors,
That ye might not kindle fire on Mine altar in
    vain!
I have no pleasure in you,
Saith the LORD of hosts,
Neither will I accept an offering at your hand.

11] For from the rising of the sun even unto the
    going down of the same
My name is great among the nations;

[6 בֵּן יְכַבֵּד אָב

וְעֶבֶד אֲדֹנָיו

וְאִם־אָב אָנִי

אַיֵּה כְבוֹדִי

וְאִם־אֲדוֹנִים אָנִי

אַיֵּה מוֹרָאִי

אָמַר | יְהֹוָה צְבָאוֹת

לָכֶם הַכֹּהֲנִים בּוֹזֵי שְׁמִי

וַאֲמַרְתֶּם בַּמֶּה בָזִינוּ אֶת־שְׁמֶךָ:

[7 מַגִּישִׁים עַל־מִזְבְּחִי לֶחֶם מְגֹאָל

וַאֲמַרְתֶּם בַּמֶּה גֵאַלְנוּךָ

בֶּאֱמָרְכֶם שֻׁלְחַן יְהֹוָה נִבְזֶה הוּא:

[8 וְכִי־תַגִּשׁוּן עִוֵּר לִזְבֹּחַ אֵין רָע

וְכִי תַגִּישׁוּ פִּסֵּחַ וְחֹלֶה אֵין רָע

הַקְרִיבֵהוּ נָא לְפֶחָתֶךָ

הֲיִרְצְךָ

אוֹ הֲיִשָּׂא פָנֶיךָ

אָמַר יְהֹוָה צְבָאוֹת:

[9 וְעַתָּה חַלּוּ־נָא פְנֵי־אֵל וִיחָנֵנוּ

מִיֶּדְכֶם הָיְתָה זֹּאת

הֲיִשָּׂא מִכֶּם פָּנִים

אָמַר יְהֹוָה צְבָאוֹת:

[10 מִי גַם־בָּכֶם וְיִסְגֹּר דְּלָתַיִם

וְלֹא־תָאִירוּ מִזְבְּחִי חִנָּם

אֵין־לִי חֵפֶץ בָּכֶם

אָמַר יְהֹוָה צְבָאוֹת

וּמִנְחָה לֹא־אֶרְצֶה מִיֶּדְכֶם:

[11 כִּי מִמִּזְרַח שֶׁמֶשׁ וְעַד־מְבוֹאוֹ

גָּדוֹל שְׁמִי בַּגּוֹיִם

And in every place offerings are presented unto
    My name,
Even pure oblations;
For My name is great among the nations,
Saith the Lord of hosts.

12] But ye profane it,
In that ye say:
'The table of the Lord is polluted,
And the fruit thereof, even the food thereof,
    is contemptible.'

13] Ye say also:
'Behold, what a weariness is it!'
And ye have snuffed at it,
Saith the Lord of hosts;
And ye have brought that which was taken by
    violence,
And the lame, and the sick;
Thus ye bring the offering;
Should I accept this of your hand?
Saith the Lord.

14] But cursed be he that dealeth craftily,
Whereas he hath in his flock a male,
And voweth, and sacrificeth unto the Lord a
    blemished thing;
For I am a great King,
Saith the Lord of hosts,
And My name is feared among the nations.

Chapter 2

1] And now, this commandment
Is for you, O ye priests.

2] If ye will not hearken, and if ye will not lay it
    to heart,
To give glory unto My name,
Saith the Lord of hosts,

וּבְכָל־מָקוֹם מֻקְטָר מֻגָּשׁ

לִשְׁמִי וּמִנְחָה טְהוֹרָה

כִּי־גָדוֹל שְׁמִי בַּגּוֹיִם

אָמַר יְהֹוָה צְבָאוֹת:

12] וְאַתֶּם מְחַלְּלִים אוֹתוֹ

בֶּאֱמָרְכֶם

שֻׁלְחַן אֲדֹנָי מְגֹאָל הוּא

וְנִיבוֹ נִבְזֶה אָכְלוֹ:

13] וַאֲמַרְתֶּם הִנֵּה מַתְּלָאָה

וְהִפַּחְתֶּם אוֹתוֹ אָמַר יְהֹוָה צְבָאוֹת

וַהֲבֵאתֶם גָּזוּל

וְאֶת־הַפִּסֵּחַ וְאֶת־הַחוֹלֶה

וַהֲבֵאתֶם אֶת־הַמִּנְחָה

הַאֶרְצֶה אוֹתָהּ

מִיֶּדְכֶם אָמַר יְהֹוָה:

14] וְאָרוּר נוֹכֵל וְיֵשׁ בְּעֶדְרוֹ זָכָר

וְנֹדֵר וְזֹבֵחַ מָשְׁחָת לַאדֹנָי

כִּי מֶלֶךְ גָּדוֹל אָנִי

אָמַר יְהֹוָה צְבָאוֹת

וּשְׁמִי נוֹרָא בַגּוֹיִם:

ב

1] וְעַתָּה אֲלֵיכֶם

הַמִּצְוָה הַזֹּאת הַכֹּהֲנִים:

2] אִם־לֹא תִשְׁמְעוּ

וְאִם־לֹא תָשִׂימוּ עַל־לֵב

לָתֵת כָּבוֹד לִשְׁמִי

אָמַר יְהֹוָה צְבָאוֹת

Then will I send the curse upon you,
And I will curse your blessings;
Yea, I curse them,
Because ye do not lay it to heart.

3] Behold, I will rebuke the seed for your hurt,
And will spread dung upon your faces,
Even the dung of your sacrifices;
And ye shall be taken away unto it.

4] Know then that I have sent
This commandment unto you,
That My covenant might be with Levi,
Saith the LORD of hosts.

5] My covenant was with him
Of life and peace, and I gave them to him,
And of fear, and he feared Me,
And was afraid of My name.

6] The law of truth was in his mouth,
And unrighteousness was not found in his lips;
He walked with Me in peace and uprightness,
And did turn many away from iniquity.

7] For the priest's lips should keep knowledge,
And they should seek the law at his mouth;
For he is the messenger of the LORD of hosts.

וְשָׁלַחְתִּי בָכֶם אֶת־הַמְּאֵרָה

וְאָרוֹתִי אֶת־בִּרְכוֹתֵיכֶם

וְגַם אָרוֹתִיהָ

כִּי אֵינְכֶם שָׂמִים עַל־לֵב:

3] הִנְנִי גֹעֵר לָכֶם אֶת־הַזֶּרַע

וְזֵרִיתִי פֶרֶשׁ עַל־פְּנֵיכֶם

פֶּרֶשׁ חַגֵּיכֶם

וְנָשָׂא אֶתְכֶם אֵלָיו:

4] וִידַעְתֶּם כִּי שִׁלַּחְתִּי אֲלֵיכֶם

אֵת הַמִּצְוָה הַזֹּאת

לִהְיוֹת בְּרִיתִי אֶת־לֵוִי

אָמַר יְהֹוָה צְבָאוֹת:

5] בְּרִיתִי | הָיְתָה אִתּוֹ

הַחַיִּים וְהַשָּׁלוֹם

וָאֶתְּנֵם־לוֹ מוֹרָא וַיִּירָאֵנִי

וּמִפְּנֵי שְׁמִי נִחַת הוּא:

6] תּוֹרַת אֱמֶת הָיְתָה בְּפִיהוּ

וְעַוְלָה לֹא־נִמְצָא בִשְׂפָתָיו

בְּשָׁלוֹם וּבְמִישׁוֹר הָלַךְ אִתִּי

וְרַבִּים הֵשִׁיב מֵעָוֹן:

7] כִּי־שִׂפְתֵי כֹהֵן יִשְׁמְרוּ־דַעַת

וְתוֹרָה יְבַקְשׁוּ מִפִּיהוּ

כִּי מַלְאַךְ יְהֹוָה־צְבָאוֹת הוּא:

Proverbs

4 : 1-13

Chapter 4

ד

1] Hear, ye children, the instruction of a father,
And attend to know understanding.

2] For I give you good doctrine;
Forsake ye not my teaching.

3] For I was a son unto my father,
Tender and an only one in the sight of my mother.

4] And he taught me, and said unto me:
'Let thy heart hold fast my words,
Keep my commandments, and live;

5] Get wisdom, get understanding;
Forget not, neither decline from the words of my
   mouth;

6] Forsake her not, and she will preserve thee;
Love her, and she will keep thee.

7] The beginning of wisdom is: Get wisdom;
Yea, with all thy getting get understanding.

8] Extol her, and she will exalt thee;
She will bring thee to honour, when thou dost
   embrace her.

9] She will give to thy head a chaplet of grace;
A crown of glory will she bestow on thee.'

10] Hear, O my son, and receive my sayings;
And the years of thy life shall be many.

11] I have taught thee in the way of wisdom;
I have led thee in paths of uprightness.

1] שִׁמְעוּ בָנִים מוּסַר אָב
וְהַקְשִׁיבוּ לָדַעַת בִּינָה:

2] כִּי לֶקַח טוֹב נָתַתִּי לָכֶם
תּוֹרָתִי אַל־תַּעֲזֹבוּ:

3] כִּי־בֵן הָיִיתִי לְאָבִי
רַךְ וְיָחִיד לִפְנֵי אִמִּי:

4] וַיֹּרֵנִי וַיֹּאמֶר לִי
יִתְמָךְ־דְּבָרַי לִבֶּךָ
שְׁמֹר מִצְוֹתַי וֶחְיֵה:

5] קְנֵה חָכְמָה קְנֵה בִינָה
אַל־תִּשְׁכַּח וְאַל־תֵּט מֵאִמְרֵי־פִי:

6] אַל־תַּעַזְבֶהָ וְתִשְׁמְרֶךָּ
אֱהָבֶהָ וְתִצְּרֶךָּ:

7] רֵאשִׁית חָכְמָה קְנֵה חָכְמָה
וּבְכָל־קִנְיָנְךָ קְנֵה בִינָה:

8] סַלְסְלֶהָ וּתְרוֹמְמֶךָּ
תְּכַבֵּדְךָ כִּי תְחַבְּקֶנָּה:

9] תִּתֵּן לְרֹאשְׁךָ לִוְיַת־חֵן
עֲטֶרֶת תִּפְאֶרֶת תְּמַגְּנֶךָּ:

10] שְׁמַע בְּנִי וְקַח אֲמָרָי
וְיִרְבּוּ לְךָ שְׁנוֹת חַיִּים:

11] בְּדֶרֶךְ חָכְמָה הֹרֵיתִיךָ
הִדְרַכְתִּיךָ בְּמַעְגְּלֵי־יֹשֶׁר:

12] When thou goest, thy step shall not be
  straitened;
And if thou runnest, thou shalt not stumble.

13] Take fast hold of instruction, let her not go;
Keep her, for she is thy life.

בְּלֶכְתְּךָ לֹא־יֵצַר צַעֲדֶךָ [12

וְאִם־תָּרוּץ לֹא תִכָּשֵׁל׃

הַחֲזֵק בַּמּוּסָר אַל־תֶּרֶף [13

נִצְּרֶהָ כִּי־הִיא חַיֶּיךָ׃

THIRD SELECTION

Psalms

5 : 1-13

Psalm 5

ה

1] ^{a-}For the leader; on *nehiloth.*^{-a}
A psalm of David.

לַמְנַצֵּחַ אֶל־הַנְּחִילוֹת מִזְמוֹר לְדָוִד׃ [1

2] Give ear to my speech, O LORD;
consider my utterance.

אֲמָרַי הַאֲזִינָה ׀ יְהֹוָה [2

בִּינָה הֲגִיגִי׃

3] Heed the sound of my cry, my king and God,
for I pray to You.

הַקְשִׁיבָה ׀ לְקוֹל שַׁוְעִי מַלְכִּי וֵאלֹהָי [3

כִּי־אֵלֶיךָ אֶתְפַּלָּל׃

4] Hear my voice, O LORD, at daybreak;
at daybreak I plead before You, and wait.

יְהֹוָה בֹּקֶר תִּשְׁמַע קוֹלִי [4

בֹּקֶר אֶעֱרָךְ־לְךָ וַאֲצַפֶּה׃

5] For You are not a god who desires wickedness;
evil cannot abide with You;

כִּי ׀ לֹא אֵל־חָפֵץ רֶשַׁע ׀ אָתָּה [5

לֹא יְגֻרְךָ רָע׃

6] wanton men cannot endure in Your sight.
You detest all evildoers;

לֹא־יִתְיַצְּבוּ הוֹלְלִים לְנֶגֶד עֵינֶיךָ [6

שָׂנֵאתָ כָּל־פֹּעֲלֵי אָוֶן׃

7] You doom those who speak lies;
murderous, deceitful men the LORD abhors.

תְּאַבֵּד דֹּבְרֵי כָזָב [7

אִישׁ־דָּמִים וּמִרְמָה יְתָעֵב ׀ יְהֹוָה׃

8] But I, through Your abundant love, enter Your
  house;
I bow down in awe at Your holy temple.

וַאֲנִי בְּרֹב חַסְדְּךָ אָבוֹא בֵיתֶךָ [8

אֶשְׁתַּחֲוֶה אֶל־הֵיכַל־קָדְשְׁךָ בְּיִרְאָתֶךָ׃

9] O LORD, ^{b-}lead me along Your righteous [path]^{-b}
because of my watchful foes;
make Your way straight before me.

יְהֹוָה ׀ נְחֵנִי בְצִדְקָתֶךָ לְמַעַן שׁוֹרְרָי [9

הוֹשַׁר לְפָנַי דַּרְכֶּךָ׃

---

^{a-a} *Meaning of Heb. uncertain*   ^{b-b} *Or "As You are righteous, lead me"*   הַיְשַׁר ק׳ v. 9.

10] For there is no sincerity on their lips;[c]
their heart is [filled with] malice;
their throat is an open grave;
their tongue slippery.
11] Condemn them, O God;
let them fall by their own devices;
cast them out for their many crimes,
for they defy You.

12] But let all who take refuge in You rejoice,
ever jubilant as You shelter them;
and let those who love Your name exult in You.

13] For You surely bless the righteous, O Lord,
encompassing him with favor like a shield.

10] כִּי אֵין בְּפִיהוּ נְכוֹנָה קִרְבָּם הַוּוֹת
קֶבֶר־פָּתוּחַ גְּרֹנָם לְשׁוֹנָם יַחֲלִיקוּן:
11] הַאֲשִׁימֵם ׀ אֱלֹהִים יִפְּלוּ
מִמֹּעֲצוֹתֵיהֶם
בְּרֹב פִּשְׁעֵיהֶם הַדִּיחֵמוֹ
כִּי־מָרוּ בָךְ:
12] וְיִשְׂמְחוּ כָל־חוֹסֵי בָךְ לְעוֹלָם יְרַנֵּנוּ
וְתָסֵךְ עָלֵימוֹ וְיַעְלְצוּ בְךָ
אֹהֲבֵי שְׁמֶךָ:
13] כִּי־אַתָּה תְּבָרֵךְ צַדִּיק יְהֹוָה
כַּצִּנָּה רָצוֹן תַּעְטְרֶנּוּ:

---

[c] Lit. "mouth"

FIRST SELECTION

Hosea

12 : 13 – 14 : 10

Chapter 12	**יב**

13] And Jacob fled into the field of Aram,
And Israel served for a wife,
And for a wife he kept sheep.

13] וַיִּבְרַח יַעֲקֹב שְׂדֵה אֲרָם
וַיַּעֲבֹד יִשְׂרָאֵל בְּאִשָּׁה
וּבְאִשָּׁה שָׁמָר:

14] And by a prophet the LORD brought Israel
up out of Egypt,
And by a prophet was he kept.

14] וּבְנָבִיא הֶעֱלָה יְהוָה
אֶת־יִשְׂרָאֵל מִמִּצְרָיִם
וּבְנָבִיא נִשְׁמָר:

15] Ephraim hath provoked most bitterly;
Therefore shall his blood be cast upon him,
And his reproach shall his Lord return unto him.

15] הִכְעִיס אֶפְרַיִם תַּמְרוּרִים
וְדָמָיו עָלָיו יִטּוֹשׁ
וְחֶרְפָּתוֹ יָשִׁיב לוֹ אֲדֹנָיו:

Chapter 13	**יג**

1] When Ephraim spoke, there was trembling,
He exalted himself in Israel;
But when he became guilty through Baal, he died.

1] כְּדַבֵּר אֶפְרַיִם רְתֵת
נָשָׂא הוּא בְּיִשְׂרָאֵל
וַיֶּאְשַׁם בַּבַּעַל וַיָּמֹת:

2] And now they sin more and more,
And have made them molten images of their silver,
According to their own understanding, even idols,
All of them the work of the craftsmen;

2] וְעַתָּה | יוֹסִפוּ לַחֲטֹא
וַיַּעֲשׂוּ לָהֶם מַסֵּכָה מִכַּסְפָּם
כִּתְבוּנָם עֲצַבִּים
מַעֲשֵׂה חָרָשִׁים כֻּלֹּה

נ״א בתבונם .v 2.

Of them they say:
'They that sacrifice men kiss calves.'

3] Therefore they shall be as the morning cloud,
And as the dew that early passeth away,
As the chaff that is driven with the wind out of the
    threshing-floor,
And as the smoke out of the window.

4] Yet I am the LORD thy God
From the land of Egypt;
And thou knowest no God but Me,
And beside Me there is no saviour.

5] I did know thee in the wilderness,
In the land of great drought.

6] When they were fed, they became full,
They were filled, and their heart was exalted;
Therefore have they forgotten Me.

7] Therefore am I become unto them as a lion;
As a leopard will I watch by the way;

8] I will meet them as a bear that is bereaved of
    her whelps,
And will rend the enclosure of their heart;
And there will I devour them like a lioness,
The wild beast shall tear them.

9] It is thy destruction, O Israel,
That thou art against Me, against thy help.

10] Ho, now, thy king,
That he may save thee in all thy cities!
And thy judges, of whom thou saidst:
'Give me a king and princes!'

לָהֶם הֵם אֹמְרִים
זֹבְחֵי אָדָם עֲגָלִים יִשָּׁקוּן:

3 לָכֵן יִהְיוּ כַּעֲנַן־בֹּקֶר
וְכַטַּל מַשְׁכִּים הֹלֵךְ
כְּמֹץ יְסֹעֵר מִגֹּרֶן
וּכְעָשָׁן מֵאֲרֻבָּה:

4 וְאָנֹכִי יְהֹוָה אֱלֹהֶיךָ
מֵאֶרֶץ מִצְרָיִם
וֵאלֹהִים זוּלָתִי לֹא תֵדָע
וּמוֹשִׁיעַ אַיִן בִּלְתִּי:

5 אֲנִי יְדַעְתִּיךָ בַּמִּדְבָּר
בְּאֶרֶץ תַּלְאֻבוֹת:

6 כְּמַרְעִיתָם וַיִּשְׂבָּעוּ
שָׂבְעוּ וַיָּרָם לִבָּם
עַל־כֵּן שְׁכֵחוּנִי:

7 וָאֱהִי לָהֶם כְּמוֹ־שָׁחַל
כְּנָמֵר עַל־דֶּרֶךְ אָשׁוּר:

8 אֶפְגְּשֵׁם כְּדֹב שַׁכּוּל
וְאֶקְרַע סְגוֹר לִבָּם
וְאֹכְלֵם שָׁם כְּלָבִיא
חַיַּת הַשָּׂדֶה תְּבַקְּעֵם:

9 שִׁחֶתְךָ יִשְׂרָאֵל
כִּי־בִי בְעֶזְרֶךָ:

10 אֱהִי מַלְכְּךָ אֵפוֹא
וְיוֹשִׁיעֲךָ בְּכָל־עָרֶיךָ
וְשֹׁפְטֶיךָ אֲשֶׁר אָמַרְתָּ
תְּנָה־לִּי מֶלֶךְ וְשָׂרִים:

11] I give thee a king in Mine anger,
And take him away in My wrath.

12] The iniquity of Ephraim is bound up;
His sin is laid up in store.

13] The throes of a travailing woman shall come
upon him;
He is an unwise son;
For it is time he should not tarry
In the place of the breaking forth of children.

14] Shall I ransom them from the power of the
nether-world?
Shall I redeem them from death?
Ho, thy plagues, O death!
Ho, thy destruction, O nether-world!
Repentance be hid from Mine eyes!

15] For though he be fruitful among the reed-
plants,
An east wind shall come, the wind of the LORD
coming up from the wilderness,
And his spring shall become dry, and his fountain
shall be dried up;
He shall spoil the treasure of all precious vessels.

Chapter 14

1] Samaria shall bear her guilt,
For she hath rebelled against her God;
They shall fall by the sword;
Their infants shall be dashed in pieces,
And their women with child shall be ripped up.

2] Return, O Israel, unto the LORD thy God;
For thou hast stumbled in thine iniquity.

3] Take with you words,
And return unto the LORD;

יא] אֶתֶּן־לְךָ מֶלֶךְ בְּאַפִּי
וְאֶקַּח בְּעֶבְרָתִי:

יב] צָרוּר עֲוֺן אֶפְרָיִם
צְפוּנָה חַטָּאתוֹ:

יג] חֶבְלֵי יוֹלֵדָה יָבֹאוּ לוֹ
הוּא־בֵן לֹא חָכָם
כִּי־עֵת לֹא־יַעֲמֹד
בְּמִשְׁבַּר בָּנִים:

יד] מִיַּד שְׁאוֹל אֶפְדֵּם
מִמָּוֶת אֶגְאָלֵם
אֱהִי דְבָרֶיךָ מָוֶת
אֱהִי קָטָבְךָ שְׁאוֹל
נֹחַם יִסָּתֵר מֵעֵינָי:

טו] כִּי הוּא בֵּין אַחִים יַפְרִיא
יָבוֹא קָדִים רוּחַ יְהֹוָה
מִמִּדְבָּר עֹלֶה
וְיֵבוֹשׁ מְקוֹרוֹ וְיֶחֱרַב מַעְיָנוֹ
הוּא יִשְׁסֶה אוֹצַר כָּל־כְּלִי חֶמְדָּה:

יד

א] תֶּאְשַׁם שֹׁמְרוֹן
כִּי מָרְתָה בֵּאלֹהֶיהָ
בַּחֶרֶב יִפֹּלוּ
עֹלְלֵיהֶם יְרֻטָּשׁוּ
וְהָרִיּוֹתָיו יְבֻקָּעוּ:

ב] שׁוּבָה יִשְׂרָאֵל עַד יְהֹוָה אֱלֹהֶיךָ
כִּי כָשַׁלְתָּ בַּעֲוֺנֶךָ:

ג] קְחוּ עִמָּכֶם דְּבָרִים
וְשׁוּבוּ אֶל־יְהֹוָה

548

Say unto Him: 'Forgive all iniquity,
And accept that which is good;
So will we render for bullocks the offering of our
    lips.

4] Asshur shall not save us;
We will not ride upon horses;
Neither will we call any more the work of our
    hands our gods;
For in Thee the fatherless findeth mercy.'

5] I will heal their backsliding,
I will love them freely;
For Mine anger is turned away from him.

6] I will be as the dew unto Israel;
He shall blossom as the lily,
And cast forth his roots as Lebanon.

7] His branches shall spread,
And his beauty shall be as the olive tree,
And his fragrance as Lebanon.

8] They that dwell under his shadow shall again
Make corn to grow,
And shall blossom as the vine;
The scent thereof shall be as the wine of Lebanon.

9] Ephraim [shall say]:
'What have I to do any more with idols?'
As for Me, I respond and look on him;
I am like a leafy cypress-tree;
From Me is thy fruit found.

10] Whoso is wise, let him understand these things,
Whoso is prudent, let him know them.
For the ways of the LORD are right,
And the just do walk in them;
But transgressors do stumble therein.

אִמְרוּ אֵלָיו כָּל־תִּשָּׂא עָוֹן
וְקַח־טוֹב
וּנְשַׁלְּמָה פָרִים שְׂפָתֵינוּ:
4] אַשּׁוּר ׀ לֹא יוֹשִׁיעֵנוּ
עַל־סוּס לֹא נִרְכָּב
וְלֹא־נֹאמַר עוֹד
אֱלֹהֵינוּ לְמַעֲשֵׂה יָדֵינוּ
אֲשֶׁר־בְּךָ יְרֻחַם יָתוֹם:
5] אֶרְפָּא מְשׁוּבָתָם אֹהֲבֵם נְדָבָה
כִּי שָׁב אַפִּי מִמֶּנּוּ:
6] אֶהְיֶה כַטַּל לְיִשְׂרָאֵל
יִפְרַח כַּשּׁוֹשַׁנָּה
וְיַךְ שָׁרָשָׁיו כַּלְּבָנוֹן:
7] יֵלְכוּ יֹנְקוֹתָיו
וִיהִי כַזַּיִת הוֹדוֹ
וְרֵיחַ לוֹ כַּלְּבָנוֹן:
8] יָשֻׁבוּ יֹשְׁבֵי בְצִלּוֹ יְחַיּוּ דָגָן
וְיִפְרְחוּ כַגָּפֶן
זִכְרוֹ כְּיֵין לְבָנוֹן:
9] אֶפְרַיִם מַה־לִּי עוֹד לַעֲצַבִּים
אֲנִי עָנִיתִי וַאֲשׁוּרֶנּוּ
אֲנִי כִּבְרוֹשׁ רַעֲנָן
מִמֶּנִּי פֶּרְיְךָ נִמְצָא:
10] מִי חָכָם וְיָבֵן אֵלֶּה
נָבוֹן וְיֵדָעֵם
כִּי־יְשָׁרִים דַּרְכֵי יְהוָה
וְצַדִּקִים יֵלְכוּ בָם
וּפֹשְׁעִים יִכָּשְׁלוּ בָם:

549

Proverbs

2 : 1 - 9

Chapter 2	ב

1] My son, if thou wilt receive my words,
And lay up my commandments with thee;

2] So that thou make thine ear attend unto wisdom,
And thy heart incline to discernment;

3] Yea, if thou call for understanding,
And lift up thy voice for discernment;

4] If thou seek her as silver,
And search for her as for hid treasures;

5] Then shalt thou understand the fear of the LORD,
And find the knowledge of God.

6] For the LORD giveth wisdom,
Out of His mouth cometh knowledge and discernment;

7] He layeth up sound wisdom for the upright,
He is a shield to them that walk in integrity;

8] That He may guard the paths of justice,
And preserve the way of His godly ones.

9] Then shalt thou understand righteousness and justice,
And equity, yea, every good path.

1] בְּנִי אִם־תִּקַּח אֲמָרָי
וּמִצְוֹתַי תִּצְפֹּן אִתָּךְ:

2] לְהַקְשִׁיב לַחָכְמָה אָזְנֶךָ
תַּטֶּה לִבְּךָ לַתְּבוּנָה:

3] כִּי אִם לַבִּינָה תִקְרָא
לַתְּבוּנָה תִּתֵּן קוֹלֶךָ:

4] אִם־תְּבַקְשֶׁנָּה כַכָּסֶף
וְכַמַּטְמוֹנִים תַּחְפְּשֶׂנָּה:

5] אָז תָּבִין יִרְאַת יְהֹוָה
וְדַעַת אֱלֹהִים תִּמְצָא:

6] כִּי־יְהֹוָה יִתֵּן חָכְמָה
מִפִּיו דַּעַת וּתְבוּנָה:

7] וְצָפַן לַיְשָׁרִים תּוּשִׁיָּה
מָגֵן לְהֹלְכֵי תֹם:

8] לִנְצֹר אָרְחוֹת מִשְׁפָּט
וְדֶרֶךְ חֲסִידָו יִשְׁמֹר:

9] אָז תָּבִין צֶדֶק וּמִשְׁפָּט
וּמֵישָׁרִים כָּל־מַעְגַּל־טוֹב:

Psalms

62 : 1-9

Psalm 62

1] For the leader.
For Jeduthun; [A psalm] of David.
2] Truly my soul waits quietly for God;
my deliverance comes from Him.

3] Truly He is my rock and deliverance,
my haven; I shall never be shaken.

4] How long will all of you attack*ᵃ* a man,
to crush*ᵃ* him, as though he were
a leaning wall, a tottering fence?

5] They lay plans to topple him from his rank;
they delight in falsehood;
they bless with their mouths,
while inwardly they curse.   *Selah*

6] Truly, wait quietly for God, O my soul,
for my hope comes from Him.

7] He is my rock and deliverance,
my haven; I shall not be shaken.

8] I rely on God, my deliverance and glory,
my rock of strength;
in God is my refuge.

9] Trust in Him at all times, O people;
pour out your heart before Him;
God is our refuge.

[1] לַמְנַצֵּחַ עַל־יְדוּתוּן מִזְמוֹר לְדָוִד:

[2] אַךְ אֶל־אֱלֹהִים דּוּמִיָּה נַפְשִׁי

מִמֶּנּוּ יְשׁוּעָתִי:

[3] אַךְ־הוּא צוּרִי וִישׁוּעָתִי

מִשְׂגַּבִּי לֹא־אֶמּוֹט רַבָּה:

[4] עַד־אָנָה ׀ תְּהוֹתְתוּ עַל־אִישׁ

תְּרָצְּחוּ כֻלְּכֶם

כְּקִיר נָטוּי גָּדֵר הַדְּחוּיָה:

[5] אַךְ מִשְּׂאֵתוֹ ׀ יָעֲצוּ לְהַדִּיחַ

יִרְצוּ כָזָב

בְּפִיו יְבָרֵכוּ

וּבְקִרְבָּם יְקַלְלוּ־סֶלָה:

[6] אַךְ לֵאלֹהִים דּוֹמִּי נַפְשִׁי

כִּי־מִמֶּנּוּ תִּקְוָתִי:

[7] אַךְ־הוּא צוּרִי וִישׁוּעָתִי

מִשְׂגַּבִּי לֹא אֶמּוֹט:

[8] עַל־אֱלֹהִים יִשְׁעִי וּכְבוֹדִי

צוּר־עֻזִּי מַחְסִי בֵּאלֹהִים:

[9] בִּטְחוּ בוֹ בְכָל־עֵת ׀ עָם

שִׁפְכוּ־לְפָנָיו לְבַבְכֶם

אֱלֹהִים מַחֲסֶה־לָּנוּ סֶלָה:

ᵃ Meaning of Heb. uncertain

וישלח

FIRST SELECTION

Hosea

11 : 7 – 12 : 12

Chapter 11

יא

7] And My people are in suspense about returning
    to Me;
And though they call them upwards,
None at all will lift himself up.

וְעַמִּי תְלוּאִים לִמְשׁוּבָתִי
וְאֶל־עַל יִקְרָאֻהוּ
יַחַד לֹא יְרוֹמֵם׃

8] How shall I give thee up, Ephraim?
How shall I surrender thee, Israel?
How shall I make thee as Admah?
How shall I set thee as Zeboim?
My heart is turned within Me,
My compassions are kindled together.

אֵיךְ אֶתֶּנְךָ אֶפְרַיִם
אֲמַגֶּנְךָ יִשְׂרָאֵל
אֵיךְ אֶתֶּנְךָ כְאַדְמָה
אֲשִׂימְךָ כִּצְבֹאִים
נֶהְפַּךְ עָלַי לִבִּי
יַחַד נִכְמְרוּ נִחוּמָי׃

9] I will not execute the fierceness of Mine anger,
I will not return to destroy Ephraim;
For I am God, and not man,
The Holy One in the midst of thee,
And I will not come in fury.

לֹא אֶעֱשֶׂה חֲרוֹן אַפִּי
לֹא אָשׁוּב לְשַׁחֵת אֶפְרָיִם
כִּי אֵל אָנֹכִי וְלֹא־אִישׁ
בְּקִרְבְּךָ קָדוֹשׁ
וְלֹא אָבוֹא בְּעִיר׃

10] They shall walk after the Lord,
Who shall roar like a lion;
For He shall roar,
And the children shall come trembling from the
    west.

אַחֲרֵי יְהֹוָה
יֵלְכוּ כְּאַרְיֵה יִשְׁאָג
כִּי־הוּא יִשְׁאַג
וְיֶחֶרְדוּ בָנִים מִיָּם׃

א׳ נחה v. 8.

552

1] They shall come trembling as a bird out of
    Egypt,
And as a dove out of the land of Assyria;
And I will make them to dwell in their houses,
Saith the LORD.

11] יֶחֶרְדוּ כְצִפּוֹר מִמִּצְרַיִם
וּכְיוֹנָה מֵאֶרֶץ אַשּׁוּר
וְהוֹשַׁבְתִּים עַל־בָּתֵּיהֶם
נְאֻם־יְהֹוָה:

Chapter 12

יב

1] Ephraim compasseth Me about with lies,
And the house of Israel with deceit;
And Judah is yet wayward towards God,
And towards the Holy One who is faithful.

1] סְבָבֻנִי בְכַחַשׁ אֶפְרַיִם
וּבְמִרְמָה בֵּית יִשְׂרָאֵל
וִיהוּדָה עֹד רָד עִם־אֵל
וְעִם־קְדוֹשִׁים נֶאֱמָן:

2] Ephraim striveth after wind, and followeth
    after the east wind;
All the day he multiplieth lies and desolation;
And they make a covenant with Assyria,
And oil is carried into Egypt.

2] אֶפְרַיִם רֹעֶה רוּחַ וְרֹדֵף קָדִים
כָּל־הַיּוֹם כָּזָב וָשֹׁד יַרְבֶּה
וּבְרִית עִם־אַשּׁוּר יִכְרֹתוּ
וְשֶׁמֶן לְמִצְרַיִם יוּבָל:

3] The LORD hath also a controversy with Judah,
And will punish Jacob according to his ways,
According to his doings will He recompense him.

3] וְרִיב לַיהֹוָה עִם־יְהוּדָה
וְלִפְקֹד עַל־יַעֲקֹב כִּדְרָכָיו
כְּמַעֲלָלָיו יָשִׁיב לוֹ:

4] In the womb he took his brother by the heel,
And by his strength he strove with a godlike being;

4] בַּבֶּטֶן עָקַב אֶת־אָחִיו
וּבְאוֹנוֹ שָׂרָה אֶת־אֱלֹהִים:

5] So he strove with an angel, and prevailed;
He wept, and made supplication unto him;
At Beth-el he would find him,
And there he would speak with us.

5] וַיָּשַׂר אֶל־מַלְאָךְ וַיֻּכָל
בָּכָה וַיִּתְחַנֶּן־לוֹ
בֵּית־אֵל יִמְצָאֶנּוּ
וְשָׁם יְדַבֵּר עִמָּנוּ:

6] But the LORD, the God of hosts,
The LORD is His name.

6] וַיהֹוָה אֱלֹהֵי הַצְּבָאוֹת יְהֹוָה זִכְרוֹ:

7] Therefore turn thou to thy God;
Keep mercy and justice,
And wait for thy God continually.

7] וְאַתָּה בֵּאלֹהֶיךָ תָשׁוּב
חֶסֶד וּמִשְׁפָּט שְׁמֹר
וְקַוֵּה אֶל־אֱלֹהֶיךָ תָּמִיד:

8] As for the trafficker, the balances of deceit are
  in his hand.
He loveth to oppress.

כְּנַעַן בְּיָדוֹ מֹאזְנֵי מִרְמָה [8
לַעֲשֹׁק אָהֵב:

9] And Ephraim said: 'Surely I am become rich,
I have found me wealth;
In all my labours they shall find in me
No iniquity that were sin.'

וַיֹּאמֶר אֶפְרַיִם אַךְ עָשַׁרְתִּי [9
מָצָאתִי אוֹן לִי
כָּל־יְגִיעַי לֹא יִמְצְאוּ־לִי
עָוֹן אֲשֶׁר־חֵטְא:

10] But I am the LORD thy God
From the land of Egypt;
I will yet again make thee to dwell in tents,
As in the days of the appointed season.

וְאָנֹכִי יְהֹוָה אֱלֹהֶיךָ [10
מֵאֶרֶץ מִצְרָיִם
עֹד אוֹשִׁיבְךָ בָאֳהָלִים
כִּימֵי מוֹעֵד:

11] I have also spoken unto the prophets,
And I have multiplied visions;
And by the ministry of the prophets have I used
  similitudes.

וְדִבַּרְתִּי עַל־הַנְּבִיאִים [11
וְאָנֹכִי חָזוֹן הִרְבֵּיתִי
וּבְיַד הַנְּבִיאִים אֲדַמֶּה:

12] If Gilead be given to iniquity
Becoming altogether vanity,
In Gilgal they sacrifice unto bullocks;
Yea, their altars shall be as heaps
In the furrows of the field.

אִם־גִּלְעָד אָוֶן [12
אַךְ־שָׁוְא הָיוּ
בַּגִּלְגָּל שְׁוָרִים זִבֵּחוּ
גַּם מִזְבְּחוֹתָם כְּגַלִּים
עַל תַּלְמֵי שָׂדָי:

SECOND SELECTION

Jeremiah

31 : 10-20

Chapter 31

לא

10] Hear the word of the LORD, O ye nations,
And declare it in the isles afar off, and say:
'He that scattered Israel doth gather him,
And keep him, as a shepherd doth his flock.'

שִׁמְעוּ דְבַר־יְהֹוָה גּוֹיִם וְהַגִּידוּ בָאִיִּים [10
מִמֶּרְחָק וְאִמְרוּ מְזָרֵה יִשְׂרָאֵל יְקַבְּצֶנּוּ וּשְׁמָרוֹ
כְּרֹעֶה עֶדְרוֹ:

11] For the LORD hath ransomed Jacob,
And He redeemeth him from the hand of him
  that is stronger than he.

כִּי־פָדָה יְהֹוָה אֶת־יַעֲקֹב וּגְאָלוֹ מִיַּד חָזָק [11
מִמֶּנּוּ:

554

12] And they shall come and sing in the height of
    Zion,
And shall flow unto the goodness of the LORD,
To the corn, and to the wine, and to the oil,
And to the young of the flock and of the herd;
And their soul shall be as a watered garden,
And they shall not pine any more at all.

13] Then shall the virgin rejoice in the dance,
And the young men and the old together;
For I will turn their mourning into joy,
And will comfort them, and make them rejoice
    from their sorrow.

14] And I will satiate the soul of the priests with
    fatness,
And My people shall be satisfied with My goodness,
Saith the LORD.

15] Thus saith the LORD:
A voice is heard in Ramah,
Lamentation, and bitter weeping,
Rachel weeping for her children;
She refuseth to be comforted for her children,
Because they are not.

16] Thus saith the LORD:
Refrain thy voice from weeping,
And thine eyes from tears;
For thy work shall be rewarded, saith the LORD;
And they shall come back from the land of the
    enemy.

17] And there is hope for thy future, saith the LORD;
And thy children shall return to their own border.

18] I have surely heard Ephraim bemoaning him-
    self:
'Thou hast chastised me, and I was chastised,
As a calf untrained;
Turn thou me, and I shall be turned,
For Thou art the LORD my God.

19] Surely after that I was turned, I repented,
And after that I was instructed, I smote upon my
    thigh;
I was ashamed, yea, even confounded,
Because I did bear the reproach of my youth.'

20] Is Ephraim a darling son unto Me?
Is he a child that is dandled?
For as often as I speak of him,
I do earnestly remember him still;
Therefore My heart yearneth for him,
I will surely have compassion upon him, saith the
    LORD.

[12] וּבָאוּ וְרִנְּנוּ בִמְרוֹם־צִיּוֹן וְנָהֲרוּ אֶל־טוּב
יְהֹוָה עַל־דָּגָן וְעַל־תִּירֹשׁ וְעַל־יִצְהָר וְעַל־בְּנֵי־
צֹאן וּבָקָר וְהָיְתָה נַפְשָׁם כְּגַן רָוֶה וְלֹא־יוֹסִיפוּ
לְדַאֲבָה עוֹד:

[13] אָז תִּשְׂמַח בְּתוּלָה בְּמָחוֹל וּבַחֻרִים וּזְקֵנִים
יַחְדָּו וְהָפַכְתִּי אֶבְלָם לְשָׂשׂוֹן וְנִחַמְתִּים
וְשִׂמַּחְתִּים מִיגוֹנָם:

[14] וְרִוֵּיתִי נֶפֶשׁ הַכֹּהֲנִים דָּשֶׁן וְעַמִּי אֶת־טוּבִי
יִשְׂבָּעוּ נְאֻם־יְהֹוָה:

[15] כֹּה | אָמַר יְהֹוָה קוֹל בְּרָמָה נִשְׁמָע נְהִי
בְּכִי תַמְרוּרִים רָחֵל מְבַכָּה עַל־בָּנֶיהָ מֵאֲנָה
לְהִנָּחֵם עַל־בָּנֶיהָ כִּי אֵינֶנּוּ:

[16] כֹּה | אָמַר יְהֹוָה מִנְעִי קוֹלֵךְ מִבֶּכִי וְעֵינַיִךְ
מִדִּמְעָה כִּי יֵשׁ שָׂכָר לִפְעֻלָּתֵךְ נְאֻם־יְהֹוָה
וְשָׁבוּ מֵאֶרֶץ אוֹיֵב:

[17] וְיֵשׁ־תִּקְוָה לְאַחֲרִיתֵךְ נְאֻם־יְהֹוָה וְשָׁבוּ בָנִים
לִגְבוּלָם:

[18] שָׁמוֹעַ שָׁמַעְתִּי אֶפְרַיִם מִתְנוֹדֵד יִסַּרְתַּנִי
וָאִוָּסֵר כְּעֵגֶל לֹא לֻמָּד הֲשִׁבֵנִי וְאָשׁוּבָה כִּי
אַתָּה יְהֹוָה אֱלֹהָי:

[19] כִּי־אַחֲרֵי שׁוּבִי נִחַמְתִּי וְאַחֲרֵי הִוָּדְעִי
סָפַקְתִּי עַל־יָרֵךְ בֹּשְׁתִּי וְגַם־נִכְלַמְתִּי כִּי נָשָׂאתִי
חֶרְפַּת נְעוּרָי:

[20] הֲבֵן יַקִּיר לִי אֶפְרַיִם אִם יֶלֶד שַׁעֲשׁוּעִים
כִּי־מִדֵּי דַבְּרִי בּוֹ זָכֹר אֶזְכְּרֶנּוּ עוֹד עַל־כֵּן
הָמוּ מֵעַי לוֹ רַחֵם אֲרַחֲמֶנּוּ נְאֻם־יְהֹוָה:

Psalms

27 : 1-14

Psalm 27

כז

1] [A psalm] of David.
The LORD is my light and my help;
whom should I fear?
The LORD is the stronghold of my life,
whom should I dread?

‎1] לְדָוִד ׀

‎יְהֹוָה ׀ אוֹרִי וְיִשְׁעִי מִמִּי אִירָא

‎יְהֹוָה מָעוֹז־חַיַּי מִמִּי אֶפְחָד:

2] When evil men assail me
to devour my flesh—
it is they, my foes and my enemies,
who stumble and fall.

‎2] בִּקְרֹב עָלַי ׀ מְרֵעִים

‎לֶאֱכֹל אֶת־בְּשָׂרִי

‎צָרַי וְאֹיְבַי לִי הֵמָּה כָּשְׁלוּ וְנָפָלוּ:

3] Should an army besiege me,
my heart would have no fear;
should war beset me,
still would I be confident.

‎3] אִם־תַּחֲנֶה עָלַי ׀ מַחֲנֶה לֹא־יִירָא לִבִּי

‎אִם־תָּקוּם עָלַי מִלְחָמָה

‎בְּזֹאת אֲנִי בוֹטֵחַ:

4] One thing I ask of the LORD,
only that do I seek:
to live in the house of the LORD
all the days of my life,
to gaze upon the beauty of the LORD,
to frequent His temple.

‎4] אַחַת ׀ שָׁאַלְתִּי מֵאֵת יְהֹוָה

‎אוֹתָהּ אֲבַקֵּשׁ

‎שִׁבְתִּי בְּבֵית־יְהֹוָה כָּל־יְמֵי חַיַּי

‎לַחֲזוֹת בְּנֹעַם־יְהֹוָה וּלְבַקֵּר בְּהֵיכָלוֹ:

5] He will shelter me in His pavilion
on an evil day,
grant me the protection of His tent,
raise me high upon a rock.

‎5] כִּי יִצְפְּנֵנִי ׀ בְּסֻכֹּה בְּיוֹם רָעָה

‎יַסְתִּרֵנִי בְּסֵתֶר אָהֳלוֹ

‎בְּצוּר יְרוֹמְמֵנִי:

6] Now is my head high
over my enemies roundabout;
I sacrifice in His tent with shouts of joy,
singing and chanting a hymn to the LORD.

‎6] וְעַתָּה יָרוּם רֹאשִׁי

‎עַל אֹיְבַי סְבִיבוֹתַי

‎וְאֶזְבְּחָה בְאָהֳלוֹ זִבְחֵי תְרוּעָה

‎אָשִׁירָה וַאֲזַמְּרָה לַיהֹוָה:

7] Hear, O LORD, when I cry aloud;
have mercy on me, answer me.

‎7] שְׁמַע־יְהֹוָה קוֹלִי אֶקְרָא

‎וְחָנֵּנִי וַעֲנֵנִי:

---

a-a Or "to slander me"; cf. Daniel 3.8; 6.25   *b-b* Meaning of Heb. uncertain   ‎בסכו ק' v. 5.

8] *In Your behalf* my heart says:
"Seek My face!"
O Lᴏʀᴅ, I seek Your face.

9] Do not hide Your face from me;
do not thrust aside Your servant in anger;
you have ever been my help.
Do not forsake me, do not abandon me,
O God, my deliverer.

10] Though my father and mother abandon me,
the Lᴏʀᴅ will take me in.

11] Show me Your way, O Lᴏʀᴅ,
and lead me on a level path
because of my watchful foes.

12] Do not subject me to the will of my foes,
for false witnesses and unjust accusers
have appeared against me.

13] Had I not the assurance
that I would enjoy the goodness of the Lᴏʀᴅ
in the land of the living....

14] Look to the Lᴏʀᴅ;
be strong and of good courage;
O look to the Lᴏʀᴅ!

8 לְךָ֨ ׀ אָמַ֣ר לִ֭בִּי בַּקְּשׁ֣וּ פָנָ֑י
אֶת־פָּנֶ֖יךָ יְהוָ֣ה אֲבַקֵּֽשׁ׃
9 אַל־תַּסְתֵּ֬ר פָּנֶ֨יךָ ׀ מִמֶּנִּי֮
אַל־תַּ֤ט בְּאַ֗ף עַ֫בְדֶּ֥ךָ עֶזְרָתִ֥י הָיִ֑יתָ
אַֽל־תִּטְּשֵׁ֥נִי וְֽאַל־תַּ֝עַזְבֵ֗נִי
אֱלֹהֵ֥י יִשְׁעִֽי׃
10 כִּי־אָבִ֣י וְאִמִּ֣י עֲזָב֑וּנִי
וַֽיהוָ֣ה יַֽאַסְפֵֽנִי׃
11 ה֤וֹרֵ֥נִי יְהוָ֗ה דַּ֫רְכֶּ֥ךָ
וּ֭נְחֵנִי בְּאֹ֣רַח מִישׁ֑וֹר לְ֝מַ֗עַן שׁוֹרְרָֽי׃
12 אַֽל־תִּ֭תְּנֵנִי בְּנֶ֣פֶשׁ צָרָ֑י
כִּ֥י קָמוּ־בִ֥י עֵֽדֵי־שֶׁ֝֗קֶר וִיפֵ֥חַ חָמָֽס׃
13 ל֭וּלֵא הֶ֭אֱמַנְתִּי לִרְא֥וֹת
בְּֽטוּב־יְהוָ֗ה בְּאֶ֣רֶץ חַיִּֽים׃
14 קַוֵּ֗ה אֶל־יְה֫וָ֥ה
חֲ֭זַק וְיַאֲמֵ֣ץ לִבֶּ֑ךָ
וְ֝קַוֵּ֗ה אֶל־יְהוָֽה׃

*Meaning of Heb. uncertain

וישב

FIRST SELECTION

Amos

2 : 6 – 3 : 8

Chapter 2

ב

6] Thus saith the Lord:
For three transgressions of Israel,
Yea, for four, I will not reverse it:
Because they sell the righteous for silver,
And the needy for a pair of shoes;

‫6[כֹּה אָמַר יְהֹוָה‬
‫עַל־שְׁלשָׁה פִּשְׁעֵי יִשְׂרָאֵל‬
‫וְעַל־אַרְבָּעָה לֹא אֲשִׁיבֶנּוּ‬
‫עַל־מִכְרָם בַּכֶּסֶף צַדִּיק‬
‫וְאֶבְיוֹן בַּעֲבוּר נַעֲלָיִם:‬

7] That pant after the dust of the earth on the head
    of the poor,
And turn aside the way of the humble;
And a man and his father go unto the same maid,
To profane My holy name;

‫7[הַשֹּׁאֲפִים עַל־עֲפַר־אֶרֶץ‬
‫בְּרֹאשׁ דַּלִּים‬
‫וְדֶרֶךְ עֲנָוִים יַטּוּ‬
‫וְאִישׁ וְאָבִיו יֵלְכוּ אֶל־הַנַּעֲרָה‬
‫לְמַעַן חַלֵּל אֶת־שֵׁם קָדְשִׁי:‬

8] And they lay themselves down beside every
    altar
Upon clothes taken in pledge,
And in the house of their God they drink
The wine of them that have been fined.

‫8[וְעַל־בְּגָדִים חֲבֻלִים יַטּוּ‬
‫אֵצֶל כָּל־מִזְבֵּחַ‬
‫וְיֵין עֲנוּשִׁים יִשְׁתּוּ בֵּית אֱלֹהֵיהֶם:‬

9] Yet destroyed I the Amorite before them,
Whose height was like the height of the cedars,
And he was strong as the oaks;
Yet I destroyed his fruit from above,
And his roots from beneath.

‫9[וְאָנֹכִי הִשְׁמַדְתִּי‬
‫אֶת־הָאֱמֹרִי מִפְּנֵיהֶם‬
‫אֲשֶׁר כְּגֹבַהּ אֲרָזִים גָּבְהוֹ‬
‫וְחָסֹן הוּא כָּאַלּוֹנִים‬
‫וָאַשְׁמִיד פִּרְיוֹ מִמַּעַל‬
‫וְשָׁרָשָׁיו מִתָּחַת:‬

10] Also I brought you up out of the land of Egypt,
And led you forty years in the wilderness,
To possess the land of the Amorite.

11] And I raised up of your sons for prophets,
And of your young men for Nazirites.
Is it not even thus, O ye children of Israel?
Saith the LORD.

12] But ye gave the Nazirites wine to drink;
And commanded the prophets, saying: 'Prophesy
    not.'

13] Behold, I will make it creak under you,
As a cart creaketh that is full of sheaves.

14] And flight shall fail the swift,
And the strong shall not exert his strength,
Neither shall the mighty deliver himself;

15] Neither shall he stand that handleth the bow;
And he that is swift of foot shall not deliver him-
    self;
Neither shall he that rideth the horse deliver
    himself;

16] And he that is courageous among the mighty
Shall flee away naked in that day,
Saith the LORD.

Chapter 3

1] Hear this word that the LORD hath spoken
against you, O children of Israel, against the whole
family which I brought up out of the land of
Egypt, saying:

10] וְאָנֹכִי הֶעֱלֵיתִי אֶתְכֶם
מֵאֶרֶץ מִצְרָיִם
וָאוֹלֵךְ אֶתְכֶם בַּמִּדְבָּר
אַרְבָּעִים שָׁנָה
לָרֶשֶׁת אֶת־אֶרֶץ הָאֱמֹרִי:

11] וָאָקִים מִבְּנֵיכֶם לִנְבִיאִים
וּמִבַּחוּרֵיכֶם לִנְזִרִים
הַאַף אֵין־זֹאת בְּנֵי יִשְׂרָאֵל
נְאֻם־יְהוָה:

12] וַתַּשְׁקוּ אֶת־הַנְּזִרִים יָיִן
וְעַל־הַנְּבִיאִים צִוִּיתֶם לֵאמֹר
לֹא תִּנָּבְאוּ:

13] הִנֵּה אָנֹכִי מֵעִיק תַּחְתֵּיכֶם
כַּאֲשֶׁר תָּעִיק הָעֲגָלָה
הַמְלֵאָה לָהּ עָמִיר:

14] וְאָבַד מָנוֹס מִקָּל
וְחָזָק לֹא־יְאַמֵּץ כֹּחוֹ
וְגִבּוֹר לֹא־יְמַלֵּט נַפְשׁוֹ:

15] וְתֹפֵשׂ הַקֶּשֶׁת לֹא יַעֲמֹד
וְקַל בְּרַגְלָיו לֹא יְמַלֵּט
וְרֹכֵב הַסּוּס לֹא יְמַלֵּט נַפְשׁוֹ:

16] וְאַמִּיץ לִבּוֹ בַּגִּבּוֹרִים
עָרוֹם יָנוּס בַּיּוֹם־הַהוּא נְאֻם־יְהוָה:

ג
1] שִׁמְעוּ אֶת־הַדָּבָר הַזֶּה אֲשֶׁר דִּבֶּר יְהוָה
עֲלֵיכֶם בְּנֵי יִשְׂרָאֵל עַל כָּל־הַמִּשְׁפָּחָה אֲשֶׁר
הֶעֱלֵיתִי מֵאֶרֶץ מִצְרָיִם לֵאמֹר:

2] You only have I known of all the families of the earth;
Therefore I will visit upon you all your iniquities.

רַק אֶתְכֶם יָדַעְתִּי [2
מִכֹּל מִשְׁפְּחוֹת הָאֲדָמָה
עַל־כֵּן אֶפְקֹד עֲלֵיכֶם
אֵת כָּל־עֲוֹנֹתֵיכֶם:

3] Will two walk together,
Except they have agreed?

הֲיֵלְכוּ שְׁנַיִם יַחְדָּו [3
בִּלְתִּי אִם־נוֹעָדוּ:

4] Will a lion roar in the forest,
When he hath no prey?
Will a young lion give forth his voice out of his
· den,
If he have taken nothing?

הֲיִשְׁאַג אַרְיֵה בַּיַּעַר וְטֶרֶף אֵין לוֹ [4
הֲיִתֵּן כְּפִיר קוֹלוֹ מִמְּעֹנָתוֹ
בִּלְתִּי אִם־לָכָד:

5] Will a bird fall in a snare upon the earth,
Where there is no lure for it?
Will a snare spring up from the ground,
And have taken nothing at all?

הֲתִפֹּל צִפּוֹר עַל־פַּח הָאָרֶץ [5
וּמוֹקֵשׁ אֵין לָהּ
הֲיַעֲלֶה־פַּח מִן־הָאֲדָמָה
וְלָכוֹד לֹא יִלְכּוֹד:

6] Shall the horn be blown in a city,
And the people not tremble?
Shall evil befall a city,
And the Lord hath not done it?

אִם־יִתָּקַע שׁוֹפָר בְּעִיר [6
וְעָם לֹא יֶחֱרָדוּ
אִם־תִּהְיֶה רָעָה בְּעִיר
וַיהֹוָה לֹא עָשָׂה:

7] For the Lord God will do nothing,
But He revealeth His counsel unto His servants the
prophets.

כִּי לֹא יַעֲשֶׂה אֲדֹנָי יֱהֹוִה דָּבָר [7
כִּי אִם־גָּלָה סוֹדוֹ
אֶל־עֲבָדָיו הַנְּבִיאִים:

8] The lion hath roared,
Who will not fear?
The Lord God hath spoken,
Who can but prophesy?

אַרְיֵה שָׁאָג מִי לֹא יִירָא [8
אֲדֹנָי יֱהֹוִה דִּבֶּר מִי לֹא יִנָּבֵא:

First Kings

3 : 5-15

Chapter 3

ג

5] In Gibeon the LORD appeared to Solomon in a dream by night; and God said: 'Ask what I shall give thee.'

6] And Solomon said: 'Thou hast shown unto Thy servant David my father great kindness, according as he walked before Thee in truth, and in righteousness, and in uprightness of heart with Thee; and Thou hast kept for him this great kindness, that Thou hast given him a son to sit on his throne, as it is this day.

7] And now, O LORD my God, Thou hast made Thy servant king instead of David my father; and I am but a little child; I know not how to go out or come in.

8] And Thy servant is in the midst of Thy people which Thou hast chosen, a great people, that cannot be numbered nor counted for multitude.

9] Give Thy servant therefore an understanding heart to judge Thy people, that I may discern between good and evil; for who is able to judge this Thy great people?'

10] And the speech pleased the LORD, that Solomon had asked this thing.

11] And God said unto him: 'Because thou hast asked this thing, and hast not asked for thyself long life; neither hast asked riches for thyself, nor hast asked the life of thine enemies; but hast asked for thyself understanding to discern justice;

12] behold, I have done according to thy word: lo, I have given thee a wise and an understanding heart; so that there hath been none like thee before thee, neither after thee shall any arise like unto thee.

13] And I have also given thee that which thou hast not asked, both riches and honour—so that there hath not been any among the kings like unto thee—all thy days.

14] And if thou wilt walk in My ways, to keep My statutes

5] בְּגִבְעוֹן נִרְאָה יְהֹוָה אֶל־שְׁלֹמֹה בַּחֲלוֹם הַלָּיְלָה וַיֹּאמֶר אֱלֹהִים שְׁאַל מָה אֶתֶּן־לָךְ: 6] וַיֹּאמֶר שְׁלֹמֹה אַתָּה עָשִׂיתָ עִם־עַבְדְּךָ דָוִד אָבִי חֶסֶד גָּדוֹל כַּאֲשֶׁר הָלַךְ לְפָנֶיךָ בֶּאֱמֶת וּבִצְדָקָה וּבְיִשְׁרַת לֵבָב עִמָּךְ וַתִּשְׁמָר־לוֹ אֶת־הַחֶסֶד הַגָּדוֹל הַזֶּה וַתִּתֶּן־לוֹ בֵן ישֵׁב עַל־כִּסְאוֹ כַּיּוֹם הַזֶּה: 7] וְעַתָּה יְהֹוָה אֱלֹהָי אַתָּה הִמְלַכְתָּ אֶת־עַבְדְּךָ תַּחַת דָּוִד אָבִי וְאָנֹכִי נַעַר קָטֹן לֹא אֵדַע צֵאת וָבֹא: 8] וְעַבְדְּךָ בְּתוֹךְ עַמְּךָ אֲשֶׁר בָּחָרְתָּ עַם־רָב אֲשֶׁר לֹא־יִמָּנֶה וְלֹא יִסָּפֵר מֵרֹב: 9] וְנָתַתָּ לְעַבְדְּךָ לֵב שֹׁמֵעַ לִשְׁפֹּט אֶת־עַמְּךָ לְהָבִין בֵּין־טוֹב לְרָע כִּי מִי יוּכַל לִשְׁפֹּט אֶת־עַמְּךָ הַכָּבֵד הַזֶּה: 10] וַיִּיטַב הַדָּבָר בְּעֵינֵי אֲדֹנָי כִּי שָׁאַל שְׁלֹמֹה אֶת־הַדָּבָר הַזֶּה: 11] וַיֹּאמֶר אֱלֹהִים אֵלָיו יַעַן אֲשֶׁר שָׁאַלְתָּ אֶת־הַדָּבָר הַזֶּה וְלֹא־שָׁאַלְתָּ לְּךָ יָמִים רַבִּים וְלֹא־שָׁאַלְתָּ לְּךָ עשֶׁר וְלֹא שָׁאַלְתָּ נֶפֶשׁ אֹיְבֶיךָ וְשָׁאַלְתָּ לְּךָ הָבִין לִשְׁמֹעַ מִשְׁפָּט: 12] הִנֵּה עָשִׂיתִי כִּדְבָרֶיךָ הִנֵּה | נָתַתִּי לְךָ לֵב חָכָם וְנָבוֹן אֲשֶׁר כָּמוֹךָ לֹא־הָיָה לְפָנֶיךָ וְאַחֲרֶיךָ לֹא־יָקוּם כָּמוֹךָ: 13] וְגַם אֲשֶׁר לֹא־שָׁאַלְתָּ נָתַתִּי לָךְ גַּם־עֹשֶׁר גַּם־כָּבוֹד אֲשֶׁר לֹא־הָיָה כָמוֹךָ אִישׁ בַּמְּלָכִים כָּל־יָמֶיךָ: 14] וְאִם | תֵּלֵךְ בִּדְרָכַי לִשְׁמֹר חֻקַּי וּמִצְוֹתַי כַּאֲשֶׁר הָלַךְ

and My commandments, as thy father David did
walk, then I will lengthen thy days.'

15] And Solo-
mon awoke, and, behold, it was a dream; and
he came to Jerusalem, and stood before the ark of
the covenant of the Lord, and offered up burnt-
offerings, and offered peace-offerings, and made a
feast to all his servants.

דָּוִיד אָבִיךָ וְהַאֲרַכְתִּי אֶת־יָמֶיךָ: 15] וַיִּקַץ
שְׁלֹמֹה וְהִנֵּה חֲלוֹם וַיָּבוֹא יְרוּשָׁלַם וַיַּעֲמֹד |
לִפְנֵי | אֲרוֹן בְּרִית־יְהוָֹה וַיַּעַל עֹלוֹת וַיַּעַשׂ
שְׁלָמִים וַיַּעַשׂ מִשְׁתֶּה לְכָל־עֲבָדָיו:

THIRD SELECTION

Psalms

63 : 1-12

Psalm 63

1] A psalm of David
when he was in the Wilderness of Judah.

2] God, You are my God;
I search for You,
my soul thirsts for You,
my body yearns for You,
as a parched and thirsty land that has no water.

3] I shall behold You in the sanctuary,
and see Your might and glory,

4] Truly Your faithfulness is better than life;
my lips declare Your praise.

5] I bless You all my life;
I lift up my hands, invoking Your name.

6] I am sated as with a ᵃ-rich feast,-ᵃ
I sing praises with joyful lips,

7] when I call You to mind upon my bed,
when I think of You in the watches of the night;

8] for You are my help,
and in the shadow of Your wings
I shout for joy.

סג

1] מִזְמוֹר לְדָוִד בִּהְיוֹתוֹ
בְּמִדְבַּר יְהוּדָה:

2] אֱלֹהִים | אֵלִי אַתָּה אֲשַׁחֲרֶךָּ
צָמְאָה לְךָ | נַפְשִׁי כָּמַהּ לְךָ בְשָׂרִי
בְּאֶרֶץ־צִיָּה וְעָיֵף בְּלִי־מָיִם:

3] כֵּן בַּקֹּדֶשׁ חֲזִיתִךָ
לִרְאוֹת עֻזְּךָ וּכְבוֹדֶךָ:

4] כִּי־טוֹב חַסְדְּךָ מֵחַיִּים
שְׂפָתַי יְשַׁבְּחוּנְךָ:

5] כֵּן אֲבָרֶכְךָ בְחַיָּי
בְּשִׁמְךָ אֶשָּׂא כַפָּי:

6] כְּמוֹ חֵלֶב וָדֶשֶׁן תִּשְׂבַּע נַפְשִׁי
וְשִׂפְתֵי רְנָנוֹת יְהַלֶּל־פִּי:

7] אִם־זְכַרְתִּיךָ עַל־יְצוּעָי
בְּאַשְׁמֻרוֹת אֶהְגֶּה־בָּךְ:

8] כִּי־הָיִיתָ עֶזְרָתָה לִּי
וּבְצֵל כְּנָפֶיךָ אֲרַנֵּן:

ᵃ⁻ᵃ Lit. "suet and fat"

562

9] My soul is attached to You;
Your right hand supports me.

10] May those who seek to destroy my life
enter the depths of the earth.

11] May they be gutted by the sword;
may they be prey to foxes.

12] But the king shall rejoice in God;
all who swear by Him shall exult,
when the mouth of liars is stopped.

9] דָּבְקָה נַפְשִׁי אַחֲרֶיךָ

בִּי תָּמְכָה יְמִינֶךָ:

10] וְהֵמָּה לְשׁוֹאָה יְבַקְשׁוּ נַפְשִׁי

יָבֹאוּ בְּתַחְתִּיּוֹת הָאָרֶץ:

11] יַגִּירֻהוּ עַל־יְדֵי־חָרֶב

מְנָת שֻׁעָלִים יִהְיוּ:

12] וְהַמֶּלֶךְ יִשְׂמַח בֵּאלֹהִים

יִתְהַלֵּל כָּל־הַנִּשְׁבָּע בּוֹ

כִּי יִסָּכֵר פִּי דוֹבְרֵי־שָׁקֶר:

מקץ

FIRST SELECTION

First Kings

3 : 15 – 4 : 1

Chapter 3

15] And Solomon awoke, and behold, it was a dream; and he came to Jerusalem, and stood before the ark of the covenant of the LORD, and offered up burnt-offerings, and offered peace-offerings, and made a feast to all his servants.

16] Then came there two women, that were harlots, unto the king, and stood before him. 17] And the one woman said: 'Oh, my lord, I and this woman dwell in one house; and I was delivered of a child with her in the house.

18] And it came to pass the third day after I was delivered, that this woman was delivered also; and we were together; there was no stranger with us in the house, save we two in the house. 19] And this woman's child died in the night; because she overlay it. 20] And she arose at midnight, and took my son from beside me, while thy handmaid slept, and laid it in her bosom, and laid her dead child in my bosom. 21] And when I rose in the morning to give my child suck, behold, it was dead; but when I had looked well at it in the morning, behold, it was not my son, whom I did bear.'

22] And the other woman said: 'Nay; but the living is my son, and the dead is thy son.' And this said: 'No; but the dead is thy son, and the living is my son.' Thus they spoke before the king.

23] Then said the king: 'The one saith: This is my son that liveth, and thy son is the dead; and the other saith: Nay; but thy son is the dead, and my son is the living.'

24] And the king said:

ג

15] וַיִּקַץ שְׁלֹמֹה וְהִנֵּה חֲלוֹם וַיָּבוֹא יְרוּשָׁלַ͏ִם וַיַּעֲמֹד | לִפְנֵי | אֲרוֹן בְּרִית־יְהֹוָה וַיַּעַל עֹלוֹת וַיַּעַשׂ שְׁלָמִים וַיַּעַשׂ מִשְׁתֶּה לְכָל־עֲבָדָיו:

16] אָז תָּבֹאנָה שְׁתַּיִם נָשִׁים זֹנוֹת אֶל־הַמֶּלֶךְ וַתַּעֲמֹדְנָה לְפָנָיו: 17] וַתֹּאמֶר הָאִשָּׁה הָאַחַת בִּי אֲדֹנִי אֲנִי וְהָאִשָּׁה הַזֹּאת יֹשְׁבֹת בְּבַיִת אֶחָד וָאֵלֵד עִמָּהּ בַּבָּיִת: 18] וַיְהִי בַּיּוֹם הַשְּׁלִישִׁי לְלִדְתִּי וַתֵּלֶד גַּם־הָאִשָּׁה הַזֹּאת וַאֲנַחְנוּ יַחְדָּו אֵין־זָר אִתָּנוּ בַּבַּיִת זוּלָתִי שְׁתַּיִם־אֲנַחְנוּ בַּבָּיִת: 19] וַיָּמָת בֶּן־הָאִשָּׁה הַזֹּאת לָיְלָה אֲשֶׁר שָׁכְבָה עָלָיו: 20] וַתָּקָם בְּתוֹךְ הַלַּיְלָה וַתִּקַּח אֶת־בְּנִי מֵאֶצְלִי וַאֲמָתְךָ יְשֵׁנָה וַתַּשְׁכִּיבֵהוּ בְּחֵיקָהּ וְאֶת־בְּנָהּ הַמֵּת הִשְׁכִּיבָה בְחֵיקִי: 21] וָאָקֻם בַּבֹּקֶר לְהֵינִיק אֶת־בְּנִי וְהִנֵּה־מֵת וָאֶתְבּוֹנֵן אֵלָיו בַּבֹּקֶר וְהִנֵּה לֹא־הָיָה בְנִי אֲשֶׁר יָלָדְתִּי: 22] וַתֹּאמֶר הָאִשָּׁה הָאַחֶרֶת לֹא כִי בְּנִי הַחַי וּבְנֵךְ הַמֵּת וְזֹאת אֹמֶרֶת לֹא כִי בְּנֵךְ הַמֵּת וּבְנִי הֶחָי וַתְּדַבֵּרְנָה לִפְנֵי הַמֶּלֶךְ: 23] וַיֹּאמֶר הַמֶּלֶךְ זֹאת אֹמֶרֶת זֶה־בְּנִי הַחַי וּבְנֵךְ הַמֵּת וְזֹאת אֹמֶרֶת לֹא כִי בְּנֵךְ הַמֵּת וּבְנִי הֶחָי: 24] וַיֹּאמֶר הַמֶּלֶךְ קְחוּ לִי־חָרֶב וַיָּבִאוּ

'Fetch me a sword.' And they brought a sword before the king.

25] And the king said: 'Divide the living child in two, and give half to the one, and half to the other.'

26] Then spoke the woman whose the living child was unto the king, for her heart yearned upon her son, and she said: 'Oh, my lord, give her the living child, and in no wise slay it.' But the other said: 'It shall be neither mine nor thine; divide it.'

27] Then the king answered and said: 'Give her the living child, and in no wise slay it; she is the mother thereof.'

28] And all Israel heard of the judgment which the king had judged; and they feared the king; for they saw that the wisdom of God was in him, to do justice.

הַחֶרֶב לִפְנֵי הַמֶּלֶךְ: 25] וַיֹּאמֶר הַמֶּלֶךְ גִּזְרוּ אֶת־הַיֶּלֶד הַחַי לִשְׁנָיִם וּתְנוּ אֶת־הַחֲצִי לְאַחַת וְאֶת־הַחֲצִי לְאֶחָת: 26] וַתֹּאמֶר הָאִשָּׁה אֲשֶׁר־בְּנָהּ הַחַי אֶל־הַמֶּלֶךְ כִּי־נִכְמְרוּ רַחֲמֶיהָ עַל־בְּנָהּ וַתֹּאמֶר | בִּי אֲדֹנִי תְּנוּ־לָהּ אֶת־הַיָּלוּד הַחַי וְהָמֵת אַל־תְּמִיתֻהוּ וְזֹאת אֹמֶרֶת גַּם־לִי גַם־לָךְ לֹא יִהְיֶה גְּזֹרוּ: 27] וַיַּעַן הַמֶּלֶךְ וַיֹּאמֶר תְּנוּ־לָהּ אֶת־הַיָּלוּד הַחַי וְהָמֵת לֹא תְמִיתֻהוּ הִיא אִמּוֹ: 28] וַיִּשְׁמְעוּ כָל־יִשְׂרָאֵל אֶת־הַמִּשְׁפָּט אֲשֶׁר שָׁפַט הַמֶּלֶךְ וַיִּרְאוּ מִפְּנֵי הַמֶּלֶךְ כִּי רָאוּ כִּי־חָכְמַת אֱלֹהִים בְּקִרְבּוֹ לַעֲשׂוֹת מִשְׁפָּט:

Chapter 4

1] And king Solomon was king over all Israel.

ד

1] וַיְהִי הַמֶּלֶךְ שְׁלֹמֹה מֶלֶךְ עַל־כָּל־יִשְׂרָאֵל:

SECOND SELECTION

Proverbs

10 : 1-7

Chapter 10

1] The proverbs of Solomon.
A wise son maketh a glad father;
But a foolish son is the grief of his mother.

2] Treasures of wickedness profit nothing;
But righteousness delivereth from death.

3] The Lord will not suffer the soul of the righteous to famish;
But He thrusteth away the desire of the wicked.

4] He becometh poor that dealeth with a slack hand;
But the hand of the diligent maketh rich.

י

1] מִשְׁלֵי שְׁלֹמֹה
בֵּן חָכָם יְשַׂמַּח־אָב
וּבֵן כְּסִיל תּוּגַת אִמּוֹ:

2] לֹא־יוֹעִילוּ אוֹצְרוֹת רֶשַׁע
וּצְדָקָה תַּצִּיל מִמָּוֶת:

3] לֹא־יַרְעִיב יְהוָֹה נֶפֶשׁ צַדִּיק
וְהַוַּת רְשָׁעִים יֶהְדֹּף:

4] רָאשׁ עֹשֶׂה כַף־רְמִיָּה
וְיַד חָרוּצִים תַּעֲשִׁיר:

5] A wise son gathereth in summer;
But a son that doeth shamefully sleepeth in harvest.

6] Blessings are upon the head of the righteous;
But the mouth of the wicked concealeth violence.

7] The memory of the righteous shall be for a blessing;
But the name of the wicked shall rot.

THIRD SELECTION

Psalms

67 : 1-8

Psalm 67

1] For the leader; with instrumental music.
A psalm, a song.

2] May God be gracious to us and bless us;
may He show us favor,   *Selah*

3] that Your way be known on earth,
Your deliverance among all nations.

4] Peoples will praise You, O God;
all peoples will praise You.

5] Nations will exult and shout for joy,
for You rule the peoples with equity,
guide the nations of the earth.   *Selah*

6] The peoples will praise You, O God;
all peoples will praise You.

7] May the earth yield its produce;
may God, our God, bless us.

8] May God bless us,
and be revered to the ends of the earth.

[5] אֹגֵר בַּקַּיִץ בֵּן מַשְׂכִּיל

נִרְדָּם בַּקָּצִיר בֵּן מֵבִישׁ:

[6] בְּרָכוֹת לְרֹאשׁ צַדִּיק

וּפִי רְשָׁעִים יְכַסֶּה חָמָס:

[7] זֵכֶר צַדִּיק לִבְרָכָה

וְשֵׁם רְשָׁעִים יִרְקָב:

סז

[1] לַמְנַצֵּחַ בִּנְגִינֹת

מִזְמוֹר שִׁיר:

[2] אֱלֹהִים יְחָנֵּנוּ וִיבָרְכֵנוּ

יָאֵר פָּנָיו אִתָּנוּ סֶלָה:

[3] לָדַעַת בָּאָרֶץ דַּרְכֶּךָ

בְּכָל־גּוֹיִם יְשׁוּעָתֶךָ:

[4] יוֹדוּךָ עַמִּים ׀ אֱלֹהִים

יוֹדוּךָ עַמִּים כֻּלָּם:

[5] יִשְׂמְחוּ וִירַנְּנוּ לְאֻמִּים

כִּי־תִשְׁפֹּט עַמִּים מִישֹׁר

וּלְאֻמִּים ׀ בָּאָרֶץ תַּנְחֵם סֶלָה:

[6] יוֹדוּךָ עַמִּים ׀ אֱלֹהִים

יוֹדוּךָ עַמִּים כֻּלָּם:

[7] אֶרֶץ נָתְנָה יְבוּלָהּ

יְבָרְכֵנוּ אֱלֹהִים אֱלֹהֵינוּ:

[8] יְבָרְכֵנוּ אֱלֹהִים

וְיִירְאוּ אֹתוֹ כָּל־אַפְסֵי־אָרֶץ:

וִיגַּשׁ

FIRST SELECTION

Ezekiel

37 : 15 - 28

Chapter 37

לז

15] And the word of the LORD came unto me, saying:

16] 'And thou, son of man, take thee one stick, and write upon it: For Judah, and for the children of Israel his companions; then take another stick, and write upon it: For Joseph, the stick of Ephraim, and of all the house of Israel his companions;

17] and join them for thee one to another into one stick, that they may become one in thy hand.

18] And when the children of thy people shall speak unto thee, saying: Wilt thou not tell us what thou meanest by these? 19] say unto them: Thus saith the LORD GOD: Behold, I will take the stick of Joseph, which is in the hand of Ephraim, and the tribes of Israel his companions; and I will put them unto him together with the stick of Judah, and make them one stick, and they shall be one in My hand. 20] And the sticks whereon thou writest shall be in thy hand before their eyes.

21] And say unto them: Thus saith the Lord GOD: Behold, I will take the children of Israel from among the nations, whither they are gone, and will gather them on every side, and bring them into their own land;

22] and I will make them one nation in the land, upon the mountains of Israel, and one king shall be king to them all; and they shall be no more two nations, neither shall they be divided into two kingdoms any more at all;

23] neither shall they defile themselves any more with their

15] וַיְהִי דְבַר־יְהֹוָה אֵלַי לֵאמֹר: 16] וְאַתָּה בֶן־אָדָם קַח־לְךָ עֵץ אֶחָד וּכְתֹב עָלָיו לִיהוּדָה וְלִבְנֵי יִשְׂרָאֵל חֲבֵרָו וּלְקַח עֵץ אֶחָד וּכְתוֹב עָלָיו לְיוֹסֵף עֵץ אֶפְרַיִם וְכָל־בֵּית יִשְׂרָאֵל חֲבֵרָו: 17] וְקָרַב אֹתָם אֶחָד אֶל־אֶחָד לְךָ לְעֵץ אֶחָד וְהָיוּ לַאֲחָדִים בְּיָדֶךָ: 18] וְכַאֲשֶׁר יֹאמְרוּ אֵלֶיךָ בְּנֵי עַמְּךָ לֵאמֹר הֲלוֹא־תַגִּיד לָנוּ מָה־אֵלֶּה לָּךְ: 19] דַּבֵּר אֲלֵהֶם כֹּה־אָמַר אֲדֹנָי יֱהֹוִה הִנֵּה אֲנִי לֹקֵחַ אֶת־עֵץ יוֹסֵף אֲשֶׁר בְּיַד־אֶפְרַיִם וְשִׁבְטֵי יִשְׂרָאֵל חֲבֵרָו וְנָתַתִּי אוֹתָם עָלָיו אֶת־עֵץ יְהוּדָה וַעֲשִׂיתִם לְעֵץ אֶחָד וְהָיוּ אֶחָד בְּיָדִי: 20] וְהָיוּ הָעֵצִים אֲשֶׁר תִּכְתֹּב עֲלֵיהֶם בְּיָדְךָ לְעֵינֵיהֶם: 21] וְדַבֵּר אֲלֵיהֶם כֹּה־אָמַר אֲדֹנָי יֱהֹוִה הִנֵּה אֲנִי לֹקֵחַ אֶת־בְּנֵי יִשְׂרָאֵל מִבֵּין הַגּוֹיִם אֲשֶׁר הָלְכוּ־שָׁם וְקִבַּצְתִּי אֹתָם מִסָּבִיב וְהֵבֵאתִי אוֹתָם אֶל־אַדְמָתָם: 22] וְעָשִׂיתִי אֹתָם לְגוֹי אֶחָד בָּאָרֶץ בְּהָרֵי יִשְׂרָאֵל וּמֶלֶךְ אֶחָד יִהְיֶה לְכֻלָּם לְמֶלֶךְ וְלֹא יִהְיֶה־עוֹד לִשְׁנֵי גוֹיִם וְלֹא יֵחָצוּ עוֹד לִשְׁתֵּי מַמְלָכוֹת עוֹד: 23] וְלֹא יִטַּמְּאוּ עוֹד

ישראל ק' v. 16. חבריו ק' v. 16. חבריו ק' v. 19. יהיו ק' v. 22.

567

idols, nor with their detestable things, nor with any of their transgressions; but I will save them out of all their dwelling-places, wherein they have sinned, and will cleanse them; so shall they be My people, and I will be their God.

24] And My servant David shall be king over them, and they all shall have one shepherd; they shall also walk in Mine ordinances, and observe My statutes, and do them.

25] And they shall dwell in the land that I have given unto Jacob My servant, wherein your fathers dwelt; and they shall dwell therein, they, and their children, and their children's children, for ever; and David My servant shall be their prince for ever.

26] Moreover I will make a covenant of peace with them—it shall be an everlasting covenant with them; and I will establish them, and multiply them, and will set My sanctuary in the midst of them for ever. 27] My dwelling-place also shall be over them; and I will be their God, and they shall be My people. 28] And the nations shall know that I am the Lord that sanctify Israel, when My sanctuary shall be in the midst of them for ever.'

בְּגִלּוּלֵיהֶם וּבְשִׁקּוּצֵיהֶם וּבְכֹל פִּשְׁעֵיהֶם וְהוֹשַׁעְתִּי אֹתָם מִכֹּל מוֹשְׁבֹתֵיהֶם אֲשֶׁר חָטְאוּ בָהֶם וְטִהַרְתִּי אוֹתָם וְהָיוּ־לִי לְעָם וַאֲנִי אֶהְיֶה לָהֶם לֵאלֹהִים: 24] וְעַבְדִּי דָוִד מֶלֶךְ עֲלֵיהֶם וְרוֹעֶה אֶחָד יִהְיֶה לְכֻלָּם וּבְמִשְׁפָּטַי יֵלֵכוּ וְחֻקֹּתַי יִשְׁמְרוּ וְעָשׂוּ אוֹתָם: 25] וְיָשְׁבוּ עַל־הָאָרֶץ אֲשֶׁר נָתַתִּי לְעַבְדִּי לְיַעֲקֹב אֲשֶׁר יָשְׁבוּ־בָהּ אֲבוֹתֵיכֶם וְיָשְׁבוּ עָלֶיהָ הֵמָּה וּבְנֵיהֶם וּבְנֵי בְנֵיהֶם עַד־עוֹלָם וְדָוִד עַבְדִּי נָשִׂיא לָהֶם לְעוֹלָם: 26] וְכָרַתִּי לָהֶם בְּרִית שָׁלוֹם בְּרִית עוֹלָם יִהְיֶה אוֹתָם וּנְתַתִּים וְהִרְבֵּיתִי אוֹתָם וְנָתַתִּי אֶת־מִקְדָּשִׁי בְּתוֹכָם לְעוֹלָם: 27] וְהָיָה מִשְׁכָּנִי עֲלֵיהֶם וְהָיִיתִי לָהֶם לֵאלֹהִים וְהֵמָּה יִהְיוּ־לִי לְעָם: 28] וְיָדְעוּ הַגּוֹיִם כִּי אֲנִי יְהֹוָה מְקַדֵּשׁ אֶת־יִשְׂרָאֵל בִּהְיוֹת מִקְדָּשִׁי בְּתוֹכָם לְעוֹלָם:

SECOND SELECTION

Amos

8 : 4-11

Chapter 8

4] Hear this, O ye that would swallow the needy,
And destroy the poor of the land,

5] Saying: 'When will the new moon be gone, that
we may sell grain?
And the sabbath, that we may set forth corn?
Making the ephah small, and the shekel great,
And falsifying the balances of deceit;

ח

4] שִׁמְעוּ־זֹאת הַשֹּׁאֲפִים אֶבְיוֹן
וְלַשְׁבִּית עֲנוּיֵ־אָרֶץ:

5] לֵאמֹר מָתַי יַעֲבֹר הַחֹדֶשׁ
וְנַשְׁבִּירָה שֶּׁבֶר
וְהַשַּׁבָּת וְנִפְתְּחָה־בָּר
לְהַקְטִין אֵיפָה וּלְהַגְדִּיל שֶׁקֶל
וּלְעַוֵּת מֹאזְנֵי מִרְמָה:

v. 4. עֲנִיֵי ק'

568

6] That we may buy the poor for silver,
And the needy for a pair of shoes,
And sell the refuse of the corn.'

7] The LORD hath sworn by the pride of Jacob:
Surely I will never forget any of their works.

8] Shall not the land tremble for this,
And every one mourn that dwelleth therein?
Yea, it shall rise up wholly like the River;
And it shall be troubled and sink again, like the
     River of Egypt.

9] And it shall come to pass in that day,
Saith the Lord GOD,
That I will cause the sun to go down at noon,
And I will darken the earth in the clear day.

10] And I will turn your feasts into mourning,
And all your songs into lamentation;
And I will bring up sackcloth upon all loins,
And baldness upon every head;
And I will make it as the mourning for an only
     son,
And the end thereof as a bitter day.

11] Behold, the days come, saith the Lord GOD,
That I will send a famine in the land,
Not a famine of bread, nor a thirst for water,
But of hearing the words of the LORD.

לִקְנוֹת בַּכֶּסֶף דַּלִּים 6[
וְאֶבְיוֹן בַּעֲבוּר נַעֲלָיִם
וּמַפַּל בַּר נַשְׁבִּיר:

נִשְׁבַּע יְהוָה בִּגְאוֹן יַעֲקֹב 7[
אִם־אֶשְׁכַּח לָנֶצַח כָּל־מַעֲשֵׂיהֶם:

הַעַל זֹאת לֹא־תִרְגַּז הָאָרֶץ 8[
וְאָבַל כָּל־יוֹשֵׁב בָּהּ
וְעָלְתָה כָאֹר כֻּלָּהּ
וְנִגְרְשָׁה וְנִשְׁקְ[עָ]ה כִּיאוֹר מִצְרָיִם:

וְהָיָה | בַּיּוֹם הַהוּא 9[
נְאֻם אֲדֹנָי יְהוִה
וְהֵבֵאתִי הַשֶּׁמֶשׁ בַּצָּהֳרָיִם
וְהַחֲשַׁכְתִּי לָאָרֶץ בְּיוֹם אוֹר:

וְהָפַכְתִּי חַגֵּיכֶם לְאֵבֶל 10[
וְכָל־שִׁירֵיכֶם לְקִינָה
וְהַעֲלֵיתִי עַל־כָּל־מָתְנַיִם שָׂק
וְעַל־כָּל־רֹאשׁ קָרְחָה
וְשַׂמְתִּיהָ כְּאֵבֶל יָחִיד
וְאַחֲרִיתָהּ כְּיוֹם מָר:

הִנֵּה | יָמִים בָּאִים נְאֻם אֲדֹנָי יְהוִה 11[
וְהִשְׁלַחְתִּי רָעָב בָּאָרֶץ
לֹא־רָעָב לַלֶּחֶם וְלֹא־צָמָא לַמַּיִם
כִּי אִם־לִשְׁמֹעַ אֵת דִּבְרֵי יְהוָה:

Psalms

72 : 1-7, 18-19

Psalm 72

עב

1] [A Psalm] of Solomon.
O God, endow the king with Your judgments,
the king's son with Your righteousness;

2] that he judge Your people rightly;
Your lowly ones, justly.

3] Let the mountains produce well-being for the
      people;
the hills, the reward of justice.

4] Let him champion the lowly among the people,
deliver the needy folk,
and crush those who wrong them.

5] Let them fear You as long as the sun shines,
while the moon lasts, generations on end.

6] Let him be like rain that falls on a mown field,
like a downpour of rain on the ground,

7] that the righteous may flourish in his time,
and well-being abound, till the moon is no more.

. . .

18] Blessed is the Lord God, God of Israel,
who alone does wondrous things;

19] Blessed is His glorious name forever,
and let His glory fill the whole world;
Amen and Amen.

1] לִשְׁלֹמֹה ׀

אֱלֹהִים מִשְׁפָּטֶיךָ לְמֶלֶךְ תֵּן

וְצִדְקָתְךָ לְבֶן־מֶלֶךְ:

2] יָדִין עַמְּךָ בְצֶדֶק

וַעֲנִיֶּיךָ בְמִשְׁפָּט:

3] יִשְׂאוּ הָרִים שָׁלוֹם לָעָם

וּגְבָעוֹת בִּצְדָקָה:

4] יִשְׁפֹּט ׀ עֲנִיֵּי־עָם

יוֹשִׁיעַ לִבְנֵי אֶבְיוֹן

וִידַכֵּא עוֹשֵׁק:

5] יִירָאוּךָ עִם־שָׁמֶשׁ

וְלִפְנֵי יָרֵחַ דּוֹר דּוֹרִים:

6] יֵרֵד כְּמָטָר עַל־גֵּז

כִּרְבִיבִים זַרְזִיף אָרֶץ:

7] יִפְרַח־בְּיָמָיו צַדִּיק

וְרֹב שָׁלוֹם עַד־בְּלִי יָרֵחַ:

. . .

18] בָּרוּךְ ׀ יְהֹוָה אֱלֹהִים אֱלֹהֵי יִשְׂרָאֵל

עֹשֵׂה נִפְלָאוֹת לְבַדּוֹ:

19] וּבָרוּךְ ׀ שֵׁם כְּבוֹדוֹ לְעוֹלָם

וְיִמָּלֵא כְבוֹדוֹ אֶת־כָּל־הָאָרֶץ

אָמֵן ׀ וְאָמֵן:

וִיְחִי

FIRST SELECTION

First Kings

2 : 1- 12

Chapter 2

1] Now the days of David drew nigh that he should die; and he charged Solomon his son, saying:

2] 'I go the way of all the earth; be thou strong therefore, and show thyself a man; 3] and keep the charge of the Lord thy God, to walk in His ways, to keep His statutes, and His commandments, and His ordinances, and His testimonies, according to that which is written in the law of Moses, that thou mayest prosper in all that thou doest, and whithersoever thou turnest thyself; 4] that the Lord may establish His word which He spoke concerning me, saying: If thy children take heed to their way, to walk before Me in truth with all their heart and with all their soul, there shall not fail thee, said He, a man on the throne of Israel.

5] Moreover thou knowest also what Joab the son of Zeruiah did unto me, even what he did to the two captains of the hosts of Israel, unto Abner the son of Ner and unto Amasa the son of Jether, whom he slew, and shed the blood of war in peace, and put the blood of war upon his girdle that was about his loins, and in his shoes that were on his feet.

6] Do therefore according to thy wisdom, and let not his hoar head go down to the grave in peace.

7] But show kindness unto the sons of Barzillai the Gileadite, and let them be of those that eat at thy table; for so they drew nigh unto me when I fled from Absalom thy brother.

8] And behold,

ב

1] וַיִּקְרְבוּ יְמֵי־דָוִד לָמוּת וַיְצַו אֶת־שְׁלֹמֹה בְנוֹ לֵאמֹר: 2] אָנֹכִי הֹלֵךְ בְּדֶרֶךְ כָּל־הָאָרֶץ וְחָזַקְתָּ וְהָיִיתָ לְאִישׁ: 3] וְשָׁמַרְתָּ אֶת־מִשְׁמֶרֶת ׀ יְהֹוָה אֱלֹהֶיךָ לָלֶכֶת בִּדְרָכָיו לִשְׁמֹר חֻקֹּתָיו מִצְוֺתָיו וּמִשְׁפָּטָיו וְעֵדְוֺתָיו כַּכָּתוּב בְּתוֹרַת מֹשֶׁה לְמַעַן תַּשְׂכִּיל אֵת כָּל־אֲשֶׁר תַּעֲשֶׂה וְאֵת כָּל־אֲשֶׁר תִּפְנֶה שָׁם: 4] לְמַעַן יָקִים יְהֹוָה אֶת־דְּבָרוֹ אֲשֶׁר דִּבֶּר עָלַי לֵאמֹר אִם־יִשְׁמְרוּ בָנֶיךָ אֶת־דַּרְכָּם לָלֶכֶת לְפָנַי בֶּאֱמֶת בְּכָל־לְבָבָם וּבְכָל־נַפְשָׁם לֵאמֹר לֹא־יִכָּרֵת לְךָ אִישׁ מֵעַל כִּסֵּא יִשְׂרָאֵל: 5] וְגַם אַתָּה יָדַעְתָּ אֵת אֲשֶׁר־עָשָׂה לִי יוֹאָב בֶּן־צְרוּיָה אֲשֶׁר עָשָׂה לִשְׁנֵי־שָׂרֵי צִבְאוֹת יִשְׂרָאֵל לְאַבְנֵר בֶּן־נֵר וְלַעֲמָשָׂא בֶן־יֶתֶר וַיַּהַרְגֵם וַיָּשֶׂם דְּמֵי־מִלְחָמָה בְּשָׁלֹם וַיִּתֵּן דְּמֵי מִלְחָמָה בַּחֲגֹרָתוֹ אֲשֶׁר בְּמָתְנָיו וּבְנַעֲלוֹ אֲשֶׁר בְּרַגְלָיו: 6] וְעָשִׂיתָ כְּחָכְמָתֶךָ וְלֹא־תוֹרֵד שֵׂיבָתוֹ בְּשָׁלֹם שְׁאֹל: 7] וְלִבְנֵי בַרְזִלַּי הַגִּלְעָדִי תַּעֲשֶׂה־חֶסֶד וְהָיוּ בְּאֹכְלֵי שֻׁלְחָנֶךָ כִּי־כֵן קָרְבוּ אֵלַי בְּבָרְחִי מִפְּנֵי אַבְשָׁלוֹם אָחִיךָ: 8] וְהִנֵּה עִמְּךָ שִׁמְעִי בֶן

there is with thee Shimei the son of Gera, the Benjamite, of Bahurim, who cursed me with a grievous curse in the day when I went to Mahanaim; but he came down to meet me at the Jordan, and I swore to him by the LORD, saying: I will not put thee to death with the sword.

9] Now therefore hold him not guiltless, for thou art a wise man; and thou wilt know what thou oughtest to do unto him and thou shalt bring his hoar head down to the grave with blood.'

10] And David slept with his fathers, and was buried in the city of David.

11] And the days that David reigned over Israel were forty years: seven years reigned he in Hebron, and thirty and three years reigned he in Jerusalem.

12] And Solomon sat upon the throne of David his father; and his kingdom was established firmly.

גֵּרָא בֶן־הַיְמִינִי מִבַּחֻרִים וְהוּא קִלְלַנִי קְלָלָה נִמְרֶצֶת בְּיוֹם לֶכְתִּי מַחֲנָיִם וְהוּא־יָרַד לִקְרָאתִי הַיַּרְדֵּן וָאֶשָּׁבַע לוֹ בַיהוָה לֵאמֹר אִם־אֲמִיתְךָ בֶּחָרֶב: 9 וְעַתָּה אַל־תְּנַקֵּהוּ כִּי אִישׁ חָכָם אָתָּה וְיָדַעְתָּ אֵת אֲשֶׁר תַּעֲשֶׂה־לּוֹ וְהוֹרַדְתָּ אֶת־שֵׂיבָתוֹ בְּדָם שְׁאוֹל:

10] וַיִּשְׁכַּב דָּוִד עִם־אֲבֹתָיו וַיִּקָּבֵר בְּעִיר דָּוִד: 11] וְהַיָּמִים אֲשֶׁר מָלַךְ דָּוִד עַל־יִשְׂרָאֵל אַרְבָּעִים שָׁנָה בְּחֶבְרוֹן מָלַךְ שֶׁבַע שָׁנִים וּבִירוּשָׁלַם מָלַךְ שְׁלֹשִׁים וְשָׁלֹשׁ שָׁנִים: 12] וּשְׁלֹמֹה יָשַׁב עַל־כִּסֵּא דָוִד אָבִיו וַתִּכֹּן מַלְכֻתוֹ מְאֹד:

SECOND SELECTION

First Chronicles

28 : 1-10

Chapter 28

1] And David assembled all the princes of Israel, the princes of the tribes, and the captains of the companies that served the king by course, and the captains of thousands, and the captains of hundreds, and the rulers over all the substance and cattle of the king and of his sons, with the officers, and the mighty men, even all the mighty men of valour, unto Jerusalem.

2] Then David the king stood up upon his feet, and said: 'Hear me, my brethren, and my people; as for me, it was in my heart to build a house of rest for the ark of the covenant of the LORD, and for the footstool of our God; and I had made ready for the building. 3] But God said unto me: Thou shalt not build a house for My name, because thou art a man of war, and hast shed blood.

4] Howbeit the LORD,

כח

1] וַיַּקְהֵל דָּוִיד אֶת־כָּל־שָׂרֵי יִשְׂרָאֵל שָׂרֵי הַשְּׁבָטִים וְשָׂרֵי הַמַּחְלְקוֹת הַמְשָׁרְתִים אֶת־ הַמֶּלֶךְ וְשָׂרֵי הָאֲלָפִים וְשָׂרֵי הַמֵּאוֹת וְשָׂרֵי כָל־רְכוּשׁ־וּמִקְנֶה לַמֶּלֶךְ וּלְבָנָיו עִם־הַסָּרִיסִים וְהַגִּבּוֹרִים וּלְכָל־גִּבּוֹר חָיִל אֶל־יְרוּשָׁלָם: 2] וַיָּקָם דָּוִיד הַמֶּלֶךְ עַל־רַגְלָיו וַיֹּאמֶר שְׁמָעוּנִי אַחַי וְעַמִּי אֲנִי עִם־לְבָבִי לִבְנוֹת בֵּית מְנוּחָה לַאֲרוֹן בְּרִית־יְהוָה וְלַהֲדֹם רַגְלֵי אֱלֹהֵינוּ וַהֲכִינוֹתִי לִבְנוֹת: 3] וְהָאֱלֹהִים אָמַר לִי לֹא־ תִבְנֶה בַיִת לִשְׁמִי כִּי אִישׁ מִלְחָמוֹת אַתָּה וְדָמִים שָׁפָכְתָּ: 4] וַיִּבְחַר יְהוָה אֱלֹהֵי יִשְׂרָאֵל

the God of Israel, chose me out of all the house of my father to be king over Israel for ever; for He hath chosen Judah to be prince, and in the house of Judah, the house of my father, and among the sons of my father He took pleasure in me to make me king over all Israel;

5] and of all my sons—for the LORD hath given me many sons—He hath chosen Solomon my son to sit upon the throne of the kingdom of the LORD over Israel.

6] And He said unto me: Solomon thy son, he shall build My house and My courts; for I have chosen him to be to Me for a son, and I will be to him for a father.

7] And I will establish his kingdom for ever, if he be constant to do My commandments and Mine ordinances, as at this day.

8] Now therefore, in the sight of all Israel, the congregation of the LORD, and in the hearing of our God, observe and seek out all the commandments of the LORD your God; that ye may possess this good land, and leave it for an inheritance to your children after you for ever.

9] And thou, Solomon my son, know thou the God of thy father, and serve Him with a whole heart and with a willing mind; for the LORD searcheth all hearts, and understandeth all the imaginations of the thoughts; if thou seek Him, He will be found of thee; but if thou forsake Him, He will cast thee off for ever.

10] Take heed now; for the LORD hath chosen thee to build a house for the sanctuary; be strong, and do it.'

בִּי מִכֹּל בֵּית־אָבִי לִהְיוֹת לְמֶלֶךְ עַל־יִשְׂרָאֵל לְעוֹלָם כִּי בִיהוּדָה בָּחַר לְנָגִיד וּבְבֵית יְהוּדָה בֵּית אָבִי וּבִבְנֵי אָבִי בִּי רָצָה לְהַמְלִיךְ עַל־כָּל־יִשְׂרָאֵל: 5] וּמִכָּל־בָּנַי כִּי רַבִּים בָּנִים נָתַן לִי יְהֹוָה וַיִּבְחַר בִּשְׁלֹמֹה בְנִי לָשֶׁבֶת עַל־כִּסֵּא מַלְכוּת יְהֹוָה עַל־יִשְׂרָאֵל: 6] וַיֹּאמֶר לִי שְׁלֹמֹה בִנְךָ הוּא יִבְנֶה בֵיתִי וַחֲצֵרוֹתָי כִּי־בָחַרְתִּי בוֹ לִי לְבֵן וַאֲנִי אֶהְיֶה־לּוֹ לְאָב: 7] וַהֲכִינוֹתִי אֶת־מַלְכוּתוֹ עַד־לְעוֹלָם אִם־יֶחֱזַק לַעֲשׂוֹת מִצְוֹתַי וּמִשְׁפָּטַי כַּיּוֹם הַזֶּה: 8] וְעַתָּה לְעֵינֵי כָל־יִשְׂרָאֵל קְהַל־יְהֹוָה וּבְאָזְנֵי אֱלֹהֵינוּ שִׁמְרוּ וְדִרְשׁוּ כָּל־מִצְוֹת יְהֹוָה אֱלֹהֵיכֶם לְמַעַן תִּירְשׁוּ אֶת־הָאָרֶץ הַטּוֹבָה וְהִנְחַלְתֶּם לִבְנֵיכֶם אַחֲרֵיכֶם עַד־עוֹלָם:

9] וְאַתָּה שְׁלֹמֹה־בְנִי דַּע אֶת־אֱלֹהֵי אָבִיךָ וְעָבְדֵהוּ בְּלֵב שָׁלֵם וּבְנֶפֶשׁ חֲפֵצָה כִּי כָל־לְבָבוֹת דּוֹרֵשׁ יְהֹוָה וְכָל־יֵצֶר מַחֲשָׁבוֹת מֵבִין אִם־תִּדְרְשֶׁנּוּ יִמָּצֵא לָךְ וְאִם־תַּעַזְבֶנּוּ יַזְנִיחֲךָ לָעַד: 10] רְאֵה | עַתָּה כִּי־יְהֹוָה בָּחַר בְּךָ לִבְנוֹת־בַּיִת לַמִּקְדָּשׁ חֲזַק וַעֲשֵׂה:

THIRD SELECTION

Psalms

22 : 24-32

Psalm 22

24] You who fear the LORD, praise Him!
All you offspring of Jacob, glorify Him!
Be in dread of Him, all you offspring of Israel!

כב

24] יִרְאֵי יְהֹוָה | הַלְלוּהוּ
כָּל־זֶרַע יַעֲקֹב כַּבְּדוּהוּ.
וְגוּרוּ מִמֶּנּוּ כָּל־זֶרַע יִשְׂרָאֵל:

25] For He did not scorn, He did not spurn
the plea[a] of the lowly;
he did not hide His face from him;
when he cried out to Him, He listened.

26] [b]Because of You I offer praise[b] in the great
congregations;
I pay my vows in the presence of His worshipers.

27] Let the lowly eat and be satisfied;
let all who seek the LORD praise Him.
Always be of good cheer!

28] Let all the ends of the earth, pay heed and turn
to the LORD,
and the peoples of all nations prostrate themselves
before You;

29] for kingship is the LORD's
and He rules the nations.

30] [c]All those in full vigor shall eat and prostrate
themselves
all those at death's door, whose spirits flag,
shall bend the knee before Him.[c]

31] Offspring shall serve Him;
the LORD's fame shall be proclaimed to the
generation

32] to come;
they shall tell of His beneficence
to people yet to be born,
for He has acted.

כה] כִּי לֹא־בָזָה וְלֹא שִׁקַּץ עֱנוּת עָנִי
וְלֹא־הִסְתִּיר פָּנָיו מִמֶּנּוּ
וּבְשַׁוְּעוֹ אֵלָיו שָׁמֵעַ:

כו] מֵאִתְּךָ תְהִלָּתִי בְּקָהָל רָב
נְדָרַי אֲשַׁלֵּם נֶגֶד יְרֵאָיו:

כז] יֹאכְלוּ עֲנָוִים | וְיִשְׂבָּעוּ
יְהַלְלוּ יְהוָה דֹּרְשָׁיו
יְחִי לְבַבְכֶם לָעַד:

כח] יִזְכְּרוּ | וְיָשֻׁבוּ אֶל־יְהוָה
כָּל־אַפְסֵי־אָרֶץ
וְיִשְׁתַּחֲווּ לְפָנֶיךָ כָּל־מִשְׁפְּחוֹת גּוֹיִם:

כט] כִּי לַיהוָה הַמְּלוּכָה
וּמֹשֵׁל בַּגּוֹיִם:

ל] אָכְלוּ וַיִּשְׁתַּחֲווּ | כָּל־דִּשְׁנֵי־אֶרֶץ
לְפָנָיו יִכְרְעוּ כָּל־יוֹרְדֵי עָפָר
וְנַפְשׁוֹ לֹא חִיָּה:

לא] זֶרַע יַעַבְדֶנּוּ
יְסֻפַּר לַאדֹנָי לַדּוֹר:

לב] יָבֹאוּ וְיַגִּידוּ צִדְקָתוֹ
לְעַם נוֹלָד כִּי עָשָׂה:

---

[a] Or "plight"   [b-b] Lit. "From You is my praise"
[c-c] Meaning of Heb. uncertain; others

"All the fat ones of the earth shall eat and worship;
all they that go down to the dust shall kneel before Him,
even he that cannot keep his soul alive"

FIRST SELECTION

Zechariah

2 : 14 – 4 : 7

Chapter 2

ב

14] 'Sing and rejoice, O daughter of Zion; for lo, I come, and I will dwell in the midst of thee, saith the LORD.

15] And many nations shall join themselves to the LORD in that day, and shall be My people, and I will dwell in the midst of thee'; and thou shalt know that the LORD of hosts hath sent me unto thee.

16] And the LORD shall inherit Judah as His portion in the holy land, and shall choose Jerusalem again. 17] Be silent, all flesh, before the LORD; for He is aroused out of His holy habitation.

‏14] רָנִּי וְשִׂמְחִי בַּת־צִיּוֹן כִּי הִנְנִי־בָא
וְשָׁכַנְתִּי בְתוֹכֵךְ נְאֻם־יְהֹוָה: 15] וְנִלְווּ גוֹיִם
רַבִּים אֶל־יְהֹוָה בַּיּוֹם הַהוּא וְהָיוּ לִי לְעָם
וְשָׁכַנְתִּי בְתוֹכֵךְ וְיָדַעַתְּ כִּי־יְהֹוָה צְבָאוֹת
שְׁלָחַנִי אֵלָיִךְ: 16] וְנָחַל יְהֹוָה אֶת־יְהוּדָה
חֶלְקוֹ עַל אַדְמַת הַקֹּדֶשׁ וּבָחַר עוֹד בִּירוּשָׁלָם:
17] הַס כָּל־בָּשָׂר מִפְּנֵי יְהֹוָה כִּי נֵעוֹר מִמְּעוֹן
קָדְשׁוֹ:

Chapter 3

ג

1] And he showed me Joshua the high priest standing before the angel of the LORD, and Satan standing at his right hand to accuse him.

2] And the LORD said unto Satan: 'The LORD rebuke thee, O Satan, yea, the LORD that hath chosen Jerusalem rebuke thee; is not this man a brand plucked out of the fire?'

3] Now Joshua was clothed with filthy garments, and stood before the angel.

4] And he answered and spoke unto those that stood before him, saying: 'Take the filthy garments from off him.' And unto him he said: 'Behold, I cause thine iniquity to pass from thee, and I will clothe thee with robes.'

‏1] וַיַּרְאֵנִי אֶת־יְהוֹשֻׁעַ הַכֹּהֵן הַגָּדוֹל עֹמֵד
לִפְנֵי מַלְאַךְ יְהֹוָה וְהַשָּׂטָן עֹמֵד עַל־יְמִינוֹ
לְשִׂטְנוֹ: 2] וַיֹּאמֶר יְהֹוָה אֶל־הַשָּׂטָן יִגְעַר
יְהֹוָה בְּךָ הַשָּׂטָן וְיִגְעַר יְהֹוָה בְּךָ הַבֹּחֵר
בִּירוּשָׁלָם הֲלוֹא זֶה אוּד מֻצָּל מֵאֵשׁ:
3] וִיהוֹשֻׁעַ הָיָה לָבוּשׁ בְּגָדִים צוֹאִים וְעֹמֵד
לִפְנֵי הַמַּלְאָךְ: 4] וַיַּעַן וַיֹּאמֶר אֶל־הָעֹמְדִים
לְפָנָיו לֵאמֹר הָסִירוּ הַבְּגָדִים הַצֹּאִים מֵעָלָיו
וַיֹּאמֶר אֵלָיו רְאֵה הֶעֱבַרְתִּי מֵעָלֶיךָ עֲוֹנֶךָ

575

said: 'Let them set a fair mitre upon his head.' So they set a fair mitre upon his head, and clothed him with garments; and the angel of the LORD stood by.

6] And the angel of the LORD forewarned Joshua, saying:

7] 'Thus saith the LORD of hosts: If thou wilt walk in My ways, and if thou wilt keep My charge, and wilt also judge My house, and wilt also keep My courts, then I will give thee free access among these that stand by. 8] Hear now, O Joshua the high priest, thou and thy fellows that sit before thee; for they are men that are a sign; for, behold, I will bring forth My servant the Shoot.

9] For behold the stone that I have laid before Joshua; upon one stone are seven facets: behold, I will engrave the graving thereof, saith the LORD of hosts: And I will remove the iniquity of that land in one day.

10] In that day, saith the LORD of hosts, shall ye call every man his neighbour under the vine and under the fig-tree.'

Chapter 4

1] And the angel that spoke with me returned, and waked me, as a man that is wakened out of his sleep.

2] And he said unto me: 'What seest thou?' And I said: 'I have seen, and behold a candlestick all of gold, with a bowl upon the top of it, and its seven lamps thereon; there are seven pipes, yea, seven, to the lamps, which are upon the top thereof;

3] and two olive-trees by it, one upon the right side of the bowl, and the other upon the left side thereof.'

4] And I answered and spoke to the angel that spoke with me, saying: 'What are these, my lord?'

5] Then the angel

וְהַלְבֵּשׁ אֹתְךָ מַחֲלָצוֹת: 5 וָאֹמַר יָשִׂימוּ צָנִיף טָהוֹר עַל־רֹאשׁוֹ וַיָּשִׂימוּ הַצָּנִיף הַטָּהוֹר עַל־רֹאשׁוֹ וַיַּלְבִּשֻׁהוּ בְּגָדִים וּמַלְאַךְ יְהֹוָה עֹמֵד:

6 וַיָּעַד מַלְאַךְ יְהֹוָה בִּיהוֹשֻׁעַ לֵאמֹר:

7 כֹּה־אָמַר יְהֹוָה צְבָאוֹת אִם־בִּדְרָכַי תֵּלֵךְ וְאִם אֶת־מִשְׁמַרְתִּי תִשְׁמֹר וְגַם־אַתָּה תָּדִין אֶת־בֵּיתִי וְגַם תִּשְׁמֹר אֶת־חֲצֵרָי וְנָתַתִּי לְךָ מַהְלְכִים בֵּין הָעֹמְדִים הָאֵלֶּה: 8 שְׁמַע־נָא יְהוֹשֻׁעַ הַכֹּהֵן הַגָּדוֹל אַתָּה וְרֵעֶיךָ הַיֹּשְׁבִים לְפָנֶיךָ כִּי־אַנְשֵׁי מוֹפֵת הֵמָּה כִּי־הִנְנִי מֵבִיא אֶת־עַבְדִּי צֶמַח: 9 כִּי הִנֵּה הָאֶבֶן אֲשֶׁר נָתַתִּי לִפְנֵי יְהוֹשֻׁעַ עַל־אֶבֶן אַחַת שִׁבְעָה עֵינָיִם הִנְנִי מְפַתֵּחַ פִּתֻּחָהּ נְאֻם יְהֹוָה צְבָאוֹת וּמַשְׁתִּי אֶת־עֲוֹן הָאָרֶץ־הַהִיא בְּיוֹם אֶחָד: 10 בַּיּוֹם הַהוּא נְאֻם יְהֹוָה צְבָאוֹת תִּקְרְאוּ אִישׁ לְרֵעֵהוּ אֶל־תַּחַת גֶּפֶן וְאֶל־תַּחַת תְּאֵנָה:

1 וַיָּשָׁב הַמַּלְאָךְ הַדֹּבֵר בִּי וַיְעִירֵנִי כְּאִישׁ אֲשֶׁר־יֵעוֹר מִשְּׁנָתוֹ: 2 וַיֹּאמֶר אֵלַי מָה אַתָּה רֹאֶה וָאֹמַר רָאִיתִי וְהִנֵּה מְנוֹרַת זָהָב כֻּלָּהּ וְגֻלָּהּ עַל־רֹאשָׁהּ וְשִׁבְעָה נֵרֹתֶיהָ עָלֶיהָ שִׁבְעָה וְשִׁבְעָה מוּצָקוֹת לַנֵּרוֹת אֲשֶׁר עַל־רֹאשָׁהּ: 3 וּשְׁנַיִם זֵיתִים עָלֶיהָ אֶחָד מִימִין הַגֻּלָּה וְאֶחָד עַל־שְׂמֹאלָהּ: 4 וָאַעַן וָאֹמַר אֶל־הַמַּלְאָךְ הַדֹּבֵר בִּי לֵאמֹר מָה אֵלֶּה אֲדֹנִי: 5 וַיַּעַן הַמַּלְאָךְ הַדֹּבֵר בִּי וַיֹּאמֶר אֵלַי הֲלוֹא יָדַעְתָּ

that spoke with me answered and said unto me: 'Knowest thou not what these are?' And I said: 'No, my lord.'

6] Then he answered and spoke unto me, saying: 'This is the word of the Lord unto Zerubbabel, saying: Not by might, nor by power, but by My spirit, saith the Lord of hosts. 7] Who art thou, O great mountain before Zerubbabel? thou shalt become a plain; and he shall bring forth the top stone with shoutings of Grace, grace, unto it.'

SECOND SELECTION

Amos

6 : 1-8

מָה־הֵמָּה אֵלֶּה וָאֹמַר לֹא אֲדֹנִי: 6] וַיַּעַן וַיֹּאמֶר אֵלַי לֵאמֹר זֶה דְּבַר־יְהֹוָה אֶל־זְרֻבָּבֶל לֵאמֹר לֹא בְחַיִל וְלֹא בְכֹחַ כִּי אִם־בְּרוּחִי אָמַר יְהֹוָה צְבָאוֹת: 7] מִי־אַתָּה הַר־הַגָּדוֹל לִפְנֵי זְרֻבָּבֶל לְמִישֹׁר וְהוֹצִיא אֶת־הָאֶבֶן הָרֹאשָׁה תְּשֻׁאוֹת חֵן | חֵן לָהּ:

Chapter 6

1] Woe to them that are at ease in Zion,
And to them that are secure in the mountain of
      Samaria,
The notable men of the first of the nations,
To whom the house of Israel come!

2] Pass ye unto Calneh, and see,
And from thence go ye to Hamath the great;
Then go down to Gath of the Philistines;
Are they better than these kingdoms?
Or is their border greater than your border?

3] Ye that put far away the evil day,
And cause the seat of violence to come near;

4] That lie upon beds of ivory,
And stretch themselves upon their couches,
And eat the lambs out of the flock,
And the calves out of the midst of the stall;

5] That thrum on the psaltery,
That devise for themselves instruments of music,
      like David;

ו

1] הוֹי הַשַּׁאֲנַנִּים בְּצִיּוֹן
וְהַבֹּטְחִים בְּהַר שֹׁמְרוֹן
נְקֻבֵי רֵאשִׁית הַגּוֹיִם
וּבָאוּ לָהֶם בֵּית יִשְׂרָאֵל:

2] עִבְרוּ כַלְנֵה וּרְאוּ
וּלְכוּ מִשָּׁם חֲמַת רַבָּה
וּרְדוּ גַת־פְּלִשְׁתִּים
הֲטוֹבִים מִן־הַמַּמְלָכוֹת הָאֵלֶּה
אִם־רַב גְּבוּלָם מִגְּבֻלְכֶם:

3] הַמְנַדִּים לְיוֹם רָע
וַתַּגִּישׁוּן שֶׁבֶת חָמָס:

4] הַשֹּׁכְבִים עַל־מִטּוֹת שֵׁן
וּסְרֻחִים עַל־עַרְשֹׂתָם
וְאֹכְלִים כָּרִים מִצֹּאן
וַעֲגָלִים מִתּוֹךְ מַרְבֵּק:

5] הַפֹּרְטִים עַל־פִּי הַנָּבֶל
כְּדָוִיד חָשְׁבוּ לָהֶם כְּלֵי־שִׁיר:

577

6] That drink wine in bowls,
And anoint themselves with the chief ointments;
But they are not grieved for the hurt of Joseph.

7] Therefore now shall they go captive at the head
   of them that go captive,
And the revelry of them that stretched themselves
   shall pass away.
8] The Lord GOD hath sworn by Himself,
Saith the LORD, the God of hosts:
I abhor the pride of Jacob,
And hate his palaces;
And I will deliver up the city with all that is therein.

6] הַשֹּׁתִים בְּמִזְרְקֵי יַיִן
וְרֵאשִׁית שְׁמָנִים יִמְשָׁחוּ
וְלֹא נֶחְלוּ עַל־שֵׁבֶר יוֹסֵף:

7] לָכֵן עַתָּה יִגְלוּ בְּרֹאשׁ גֹּלִים
וְסָר מִרְזַח סְרוּחִים:

8] נִשְׁבַּע אֲדֹנָי יֱהוִֹה בְּנַפְשׁוֹ
נְאֻם־יְהוָֹה אֱלֹהֵי צְבָאוֹת
מְתָאֵב אָנֹכִי אֶת־גְּאוֹן יַעֲקֹב
וְאַרְמְנֹתָיו שָׂנֵאתִי
וְהִסְגַּרְתִּי עִיר וּמְלֹאָהּ:

THIRD SELECTION

Psalms

101 : 1-8

Psalm 101

1] A psalm of David.
I will sing of faithfulness and justice;
I will chant a hymn to You, O LORD.

2] I will study the way of the blameless;
when shall I attain it?
I will live without blame within my house.

3] I will not set before my eyes anything base;
I hate crooked dealing;
I will have none of it.

4] Perverse thoughts will be far from me;
I will know nothing of evil.

קא

1] לְדָוִד מִזְמוֹר
חֶסֶד־וּמִשְׁפָּט אָשִׁירָה
לְךָ יְהוָֹה אֲזַמֵּרָה:

2] אַשְׂכִּילָה ׀ בְּדֶרֶךְ תָּמִים
מָתַי תָּבוֹא אֵלָי
אֶתְהַלֵּךְ בְּתָם־לְבָבִי
בְּקֶרֶב בֵּיתִי:

3] לֹא־אָשִׁית ׀ לְנֶגֶד עֵינַי
דְּבַר־בְּלִיָּעַל
עֲשֹׂה־סֵטִים שָׂנֵאתִי
לֹא יִדְבַּק בִּי:

4] לֵבָב עִקֵּשׁ יָסוּר מִמֶּנִּי
רָע לֹא אֵדָע:

578

5] He who slanders his friend in secret will I
destroy;
I cannot endure the haughty and presumptuous.

6] My eyes are on the trusty men of the land,
to have them at my side.
He who follows the way of the blameless,
will be in my service.

7] He who deals deceitfully
shall not live in my house;
he who speaks untruth
shall not stand before my eyes.

8] Each morning I will destroy
all the wicked of the land,
To rid the city of the Lord
of all evildoers.

5] מְלָשְׁנִי בַסֵּתֶר ׀ רֵעֵהוּ
אוֹתוֹ אַצְמִית
גְּבַהּ־עֵינַיִם וּרְחַב לֵבָב
אֹתוֹ לֹא אוּכָל:

6] עֵינַי ׀ בְּנֶאֶמְנֵי־אֶרֶץ
לָשֶׁבֶת עִמָּדִי
הֹלֵךְ בְּדֶרֶךְ תָּמִים
הוּא יְשָׁרְתֵנִי:

7] לֹא־יֵשֵׁב ׀ בְּקֶרֶב בֵּיתִי
עֹשֵׂה רְמִיָּה
דֹּבֵר שְׁקָרִים לֹא־יִכּוֹן לְנֶגֶד עֵינָי:

8] לַבְּקָרִים אַצְמִית כָּל־רִשְׁעֵי־אָרֶץ
לְהַכְרִית מֵעִיר־יְהֹוָה
כָּל־פֹּעֲלֵי אָוֶן:

FIRST SELECTION

First Kings

7 : 40 - 50

ז

Chapter 7

40] And ᵃHiram made the pots, and the shovels, and the basins.

So Hiram made an end of doing all the work that he wrought for king Solomon in the house of the LORD:

41] the two pillars, and the two bowls of the capitals that were on the top of the pillars; and the two networks to cover the two bowls of the capitals that were on the top of the pillars;

42] and the four hundred pomegranates for the two networks, two rows of pomegranates for each network, to cover the two bowls of the capitals that were upon the top of the pillars;

43] and the ten bases, and the ten lavers on the bases;

44] and the one sea, and the twelve oxen under the sea;

45] and the pots, and the shovels, and the basins; even all these vessels, which Hiram made for king Solomon, in the house of the LORD, were of burnished brass.

46] In the plain of the Jordan did the king cast them, in the clay ground between Succoth and Zarethan.

47] And Solomon left all the vessels unweighed, because they were exceeding many; the weight of the brass could not be found out.

40] וַיַּעַשׂ חִירוֹם אֶת־הַכִּירוֹת וְאֶת־הַיָּעִים וְאֶת־הַמִּזְרָקוֹת

וַיְכַל חִירָם לַעֲשׂוֹת אֶת־כָּל־הַמְּלָאכָה אֲשֶׁר עָשָׂה לַמֶּלֶךְ שְׁלֹמֹה בֵּית יְהוָה: 41] עַמֻּדִים שְׁנַיִם וְגֻלֹּת הַכֹּתָרֹת אֲשֶׁר־עַל־רֹאשׁ הָעַמּוּדִים שְׁתָּיִם וְהַשְּׂבָכוֹת שְׁתַּיִם לְכַסּוֹת אֶת־שְׁתֵּי גֻּלֹּת הַכֹּתָרֹת אֲשֶׁר עַל־רֹאשׁ הָעַמּוּדִים: 42] וְאֶת־הָרִמֹּנִים אַרְבַּע מֵאוֹת לִשְׁתֵּי הַשְּׂבָכוֹת שְׁנֵי־טוּרִים רִמֹּנִים לַשְּׂבָכָה הָאֶחָת לְכַסּוֹת אֶת־שְׁתֵּי גֻּלֹּת הַכֹּתָרֹת אֲשֶׁר עַל־פְּנֵי הָעַמּוּדִים: 43] וְאֶת־הַמְּכֹנוֹת עָשֶׂר וְאֶת־הַכִּיֹּרֹת עֲשָׂרָה עַל־הַמְּכֹנוֹת: 44] וְאֶת־הַיָּם הָאֶחָד וְאֶת־הַבָּקָר שְׁנֵים־עָשָׂר תַּחַת הַיָּם: 45] וְאֶת־הַסִּירוֹת וְאֶת־הַיָּעִים וְאֶת־הַמִּזְרָקוֹת וְאֵת כָּל־הַכֵּלִים הָאֹהֶל אֲשֶׁר עָשָׂה חִירָם לַמֶּלֶךְ שְׁלֹמֹה בֵּית יְהוָה נְחֹשֶׁת מְמֹרָט: 46] בְּכִכַּר הַיַּרְדֵּן יְצָקָם הַמֶּלֶךְ בְּמַעֲבֵה הָאֲדָמָה בֵּין סֻכּוֹת וּבֵין צָרְתָן: 47] וַיַּנַּח שְׁלֹמֹה אֶת־כָּל־הַכֵּלִים מֵרֹב מְאֹד מְאֹד לֹא נֶחְקַר מִשְׁקַל

ᵃ Heb. *Hirom*

48] And Solomon made all the vessels that were in the house of the LORD: the golden altar, and the table whereupon the showbread was, of gold;

49] and the candlesticks, five on the right side, and five on the left, before the Sanctuary, of pure gold; and the flowers, and the lamps, and the tongs, of gold;

50] and the cups, and the snuffers, and the basins, and the pans, and the fire-pans, of pure gold; and the hinges, both for the doors of the inner house, the most holy place, and for the doors of the house, that is, of the temple, of gold.

הַנְּחֹשֶׁת: 48] וַיַּעַשׂ שְׁלֹמֹה אֵת כָּל־הַכֵּלִים אֲשֶׁר בֵּית יְהוָה אֵת מִזְבַּח הַזָּהָב וְאֶת־הַשֻּׁלְחָן אֲשֶׁר עָלָיו לֶחֶם הַפָּנִים זָהָב: 49] וְאֶת־הַמְּנֹרוֹת חָמֵשׁ מִיָּמִין וְחָמֵשׁ מִשְּׂמֹאול לִפְנֵי הַדְּבִיר זָהָב סָגוּר וְהַפֶּרַח וְהַנֵּרֹת וְהַמֶּלְקָחַיִם זָהָב: 50] וְהַסִּפּוֹת וְהַמְזַמְּרוֹת וְהַמִּזְרָקוֹת וְהַכַּפּוֹת וְהַמַּחְתּוֹת זָהָב סָגוּר וְהַפֹּתוֹת לְדַלְתוֹת הַבַּיִת הַפְּנִימִי לְקֹדֶשׁ הַקֳּדָשִׁים לְדַלְתֵי הַבַּיִת לַהֵיכָל זָהָב:

SECOND SELECTION

Amos

5 : 1-9

Chapter 5	**ה**

1] Hear ye this word which I take up for a lamentation over you, O house of Israel:

1] שִׁמְעוּ אֶת־הַדָּבָר הַזֶּה אֲשֶׁר אָנֹכִי נֹשֵׂא עֲלֵיכֶם קִינָה בֵּית יִשְׂרָאֵל:

2] The virgin of Israel is fallen,
She shall no more rise;
She is cast down upon her land,
There is none to raise her up.

2] נָפְלָה לֹא־תוֹסִיף קוּם
בְּתוּלַת יִשְׂרָאֵל
נִטְּשָׁה עַל־אַדְמָתָהּ
אֵין מְקִימָהּ:

3] For thus saith the Lord GOD: The city that went forth a thousand shall have a hundred left, and that which went forth a hundred shall have ten left, of the house of Israel.

3] כִּי כֹה אָמַר אֲדֹנָי יְהוָה הָעִיר הַיֹּצֵאת אֶלֶף תַּשְׁאִיר מֵאָה וְהַיּוֹצֵאת מֵאָה תַּשְׁאִיר עֲשָׂרָה לְבֵית יִשְׂרָאֵל:

4] For thus saith the LORD unto the house of Israel:
Seek ye Me, and live;

4] כִּי כֹה אָמַר יְהוָה לְבֵית יִשְׂרָאֵל
דִּרְשׁוּנִי וִחְיוּ:

5] But seek not Beth-el,
Nor enter into Gilgal,

5] וְאַל־תִּדְרְשׁוּ בֵּית־אֵל
וְהַגִּלְגָּל לֹא תָבֹאוּ

And pass not to Beer-sheba;
For Gilgal shall surely go into captivity,
And Beth-el shall come to nought,

וּבְאֵר שֶׁבַע לֹא תַעֲבֹרוּ
כִּי הַגִּלְגָּל גָּלֹה יִגְלֶה
וּבֵית אֵל יִהְיֶה לְאָוֶן׃

6] Seek the LORD, and live—
Lest He break out like fire in the house of Joseph,
And it devour, and there be none to quench it in
    Beth-el—

6] דִּרְשׁוּ אֶת־יְהוָה וִחְיוּ
פֶּן־יִצְלַח כָּאֵשׁ בֵּית יוֹסֵף
וְאָכְלָה וְאֵין־מְכַבֶּה לְבֵית־אֵל׃

7] Ye who turn justice to wormwood,
And cast righteousness to the ground;

7] הַהֹפְכִים לְלַעֲנָה מִשְׁפָּט
וּצְדָקָה לָאָרֶץ הִנִּיחוּ׃

8] Him that maketh the Pleiades and Orion,
And bringeth on the shadow of death in the
    morning,
And darkeneth the day into night;
That calleth for the waters of the sea,
And poureth them out upon the face of the earth;
The LORD is His name;

8] עֹשֵׂה כִימָה וּכְסִיל
וְהֹפֵךְ לַבֹּקֶר צַלְמָוֶת
וְיוֹם לַיְלָה הֶחְשִׁיךְ
הַקּוֹרֵא לְמֵי־הַיָּם
וַיִּשְׁפְּכֵם עַל־פְּנֵי הָאָרֶץ
יְהוָה שְׁמוֹ׃

9] That causeth destruction to flash upon the
    strong,
So that destruction cometh upon the fortress.

9] הַמַּבְלִיג שֹׁד עַל־עָז
וְשֹׁד עַל־מִבְצָר יָבוֹא׃

THIRD SELECTION

Psalms

99 : 1-9

Psalm 99

צט

1] ᵃ-The LORD, enthroned on cherubim, is king,
peoples tremble, the earth quakes.⁻ᵃ

1] יְהוָה מָלָךְ יִרְגְּזוּ עַמִּים
יֹשֵׁב כְּרוּבִים תָּנוּט הָאָרֶץ׃

2] The LORD is great in Zion,
and exalted above all peoples.

2] יְהוָה בְּצִיּוֹן גָּדוֹל
וְרָם הוּא עַל־כָּל־הָעַמִּים׃

3] They praise Your name as great and awesome:
He is holy!

3] יוֹדוּ שִׁמְךָ גָּדוֹל וְנוֹרָא
קָדוֹשׁ הוּא׃

ᵃ⁻ᵃ *Clauses transposed for clarity*

582

4] *b*-Mighty king-*b* who loves justice,
it was You who established equity,
You who worked righteous judgment in Jacob.

אֵעֹז מֶלֶךְ מִשְׁפָּט אָהֵב
אַתָּה כּוֹנַנְתָּ מֵישָׁרִים
מִשְׁפָּט וּצְדָקָה בְּיַעֲקֹב ׀
אַתָּה עָשִׂיתָ׃

5] Exalt the LORD our God
and bow down to His footstool:
He is holy!

רוֹמְמוּ יְהֹוָה אֱלֹהֵינוּ
וְהִשְׁתַּחֲווּ לַהֲדֹם רַגְלָיו
קָדוֹשׁ הוּא׃

6] Moses and Aaron were among His priests,
Samuel, among those who call on His name;
when they called to the LORD,
He answered them.

מֹשֶׁה וְאַהֲרֹן ׀ בְּכֹהֲנָיו
וּשְׁמוּאֵל בְּקֹרְאֵי שְׁמוֹ
קֹרִאים אֶל־יְהֹוָה וְהוּא יַעֲנֵם׃

7] He spoke to them in a pillar of cloud;
they obeyed His decrees,
the law He gave them.

בְּעַמּוּד עָנָן יְדַבֵּר אֲלֵיהֶם
שָׁמְרוּ עֵדֹתָיו וְחֹק נָתַן־לָמוֹ׃

8] O LORD our God, You answered them;
You were a sustaining*c* God for them,
avenging their injuries.

יְהֹוָה אֱלֹהֵינוּ אַתָּה עֲנִיתָם
אֵל נֹשֵׂא הָיִיתָ לָהֶם
וְנֹקֵם עַל־עֲלִילוֹתָם׃

9] Exalt the LORD our God,
and bow toward His holy hill,
for the LORD our God is holy.

רוֹמְמוּ יְהֹוָה אֱלֹהֵינוּ
וְהִשְׁתַּחֲווּ לְהַר קָדְשׁוֹ
כִּי־קָדוֹשׁ יְהֹוָה אֱלֹהֵינוּ׃

b-b Meaning of Heb. uncertain   *c Or "forgiving"*

583

Haftarah Blessings

Before reading the Haftarah

Praised be the Lord our God, for the law of truth and righteousness which He has revealed unto Israel, for the words of the prophets filled with His spirit and for the teachings of the sages whom He raised up aforetime and in these days.

בָּרוּךְ אַתָּה יְיָ אֱלֹהֵינוּ מֶלֶךְ הָעוֹלָם אֲשֶׁר בָּחַר
בִּנְבִיאִים טוֹבִים וְרָצָה בְדִבְרֵיהֶם הַנֶּאֱמָרִים בֶּאֱמֶת,
בָּרוּךְ אַתָּה יְיָ הַבּוֹחֵר בַּתּוֹרָה וּבְמֹשֶׁה עַבְדּוֹ
וּבְיִשְׂרָאֵל עַמּוֹ וּבִנְבִיאֵי הָאֱמֶת וָצֶדֶק:

After reading the Haftarah

For the Torah, for the privilege of worship, for the prophets, and for this Sabbath day, given us for sanctification and rest, for honor and for glory, let us thank and bless the Lord our God.

בָּרוּךְ אַתָּה יְיָ אֱלֹהֵינוּ מֶלֶךְ הָעוֹלָם צוּר כָּל־
הָעוֹלָמִים צַדִּיק בְּכָל־הַדּוֹרוֹת הָאֵל הַנֶּאֱמָן הָאוֹמֵר
וְעוֹשֶׂה הַמְדַבֵּר וּמְקַיֵּם שֶׁכָּל־דְּבָרָיו אֱמֶת וָצֶדֶק:

* נֶאֱמָן אַתָּה הוּא יְיָ אֱלֹהֵינוּ וְנֶאֱמָנִים דְּבָרֶיךָ וְדָבָר
אֶחָד מִדְּבָרֶיךָ אָחוֹר לֹא־יָשׁוּב רֵיקָם. כִּי אֵל מֶלֶךְ
נֶאֱמָן וְרַחֲמָן אָתָּה. בָּרוּךְ אַתָּה יְיָ. הָאֵל הַנֶּאֱמָן בְּכָל־
דְּבָרָיו:

* רַחֵם עַל־צִיּוֹן כִּי הִיא בֵּית חַיֵּינוּ וְלַעֲלוּבַת נֶפֶשׁ
תּוֹשִׁיעַ בִּמְהֵרָה בְיָמֵינוּ: בָּרוּךְ אַתָּה יְיָ. מְשַׂמֵּחַ צִיּוֹן
בְּבָנֶיהָ:

* These paragraphs are omitted from many Reform services.

שַׂמְּחֵנוּ יְיָ אֱלֹהֵינוּ בְּאֵלִיָּהוּ הַנָּבִיא עַבְדֶּךָ וּבְמַלְכוּת בֵּית דָּוִד מְשִׁיחֶךָ. בִּמְהֵרָה יָבֹא וְיָגֵל לִבֵּנוּ. עַל־כִּסְאוֹ לֹא־יֵשֵׁב זָר וְלֹא יִנְחֲלוּ עוֹד אֲחֵרִים אֶת־כְּבוֹדוֹ: כִּי בְשֵׁם קָדְשְׁךָ נִשְׁבַּעְתָּ לּוֹ שֶׁלֹּא יִכְבֶּה נֵרוֹ לְעוֹלָם וָעֶד. בָּרוּךְ אַתָּה יְיָ. מָגֵן דָּוִד:

עַל־הַתּוֹרָה וְעַל־הָעֲבוֹדָה וְעַל־הַנְּבִיאִים וְעַל יוֹם הַשַּׁבָּת הַזֶּה שֶׁנָּתַתָּ לָּנוּ יְיָ אֱלֹהֵינוּ אֲנַחְנוּ מוֹדִים לָךְ וּמְבָרְכִים אוֹתָךְ. יִתְבָּרַךְ שִׁמְךָ בְּפִי כָּל־חַי תָּמִיד לְעוֹלָם וָעֶד. בָּרוּךְ אַתָּה יְיָ מְקַדֵּשׁ הַשַּׁבָּת:

Travels in CANAAN
*Routes of Abraham and Isaac,
Jacob and Esau*
(Modern names and places)

The Great Sea

(Mediterranean Sea)

Damascus

Abraham's Route from Haran

Jacob's Route from Haran

LAKE
KINNERET

BASHAN

(Haifa)

(Tiberias)

YARMUK R.

Edrei

Ramoth-gilead

GILEAD

Tirzah

Shechem

Succoth

Penuel

Mahanaim

JABBOK R.

(Amman)

(Tel Aviv-Jaffa)

JORDAN R.

AMMON

Beth-el

Salem (JERUSALEM)

Ephrath
(BETHLEHEM)

Hebron
(KIRIATH-ARBA)

Salt (Dead) Sea

ARNON

Esau's Route

Hormah

Arad

Beer-sheba

MOAB

Gerar

Sodom & Gomorrah

Zoar

BERED R.

WAY TO EGYPT

Isaac's Route

EDOM

Beer-lahai-roi

Kadesh-barnea

0   10   20   30 MILES